Africa Society of Evangelical Theology Series

We live with the reality that in these days that the center of Christianity has moved to the Global South and Africa is a key player in that movement. This makes the study of African Christianity and African realities important – even more so when it is being done by Africans themselves and in their own context. The Africa Society of Evangelical Theology (ASET) was created to encourage research and sustained theological reflection on key issues facing Africa by and for African Christians and those working within African contexts. The volumes in this series constitute the best papers presented at the annual conferences of ASET and together they seek to fill this important gap in the literature of Christianity.

TITLES IN THIS SERIES

Christianity and Suffering: African Perspectives
2017 | 9781783683604

African Contextual Realities
2018 | 9781783684731

Governance and Christian Higher Education in the African Context
2019 | 9781783685455

God and Creation
2019 | 9781783687565

Forgiveness, Peacemaking, and Reconciliation
2020 | 9781839730535

Who Do You Say I Am? Christology in Africa
2021 | 9781839735325

The Holy Spirit in African Christianity
2022 | 9781839736469

Salvation in African Christianity
2023 | 78-1-83973-918-7

For more information about the Africa Society of Evangelical Theology,
see the Society's Facebook page at:
facebook.com/AfricaSocietyOfEvangelicalTheology
or contact ASET at: asetsecretary@gmail.com

ASET
SERIES

Ecclesiology in Africa

Ecclesiology in Africa

General Editors

David K. Ngaruiya
and
Rodney L. Reed

GLOBAL LIBRARY

© 2024 Africa Society of Evangelical Theology (ASET)

Published 2024 by Langham Global Library
An imprint of Langham Publishing
www.langhampublishing.org

Langham Publishing and its imprints are a ministry of Langham Partnership

Langham Partnership
PO Box 296, Carlisle, Cumbria, CA3 9WZ, UK
www.langham.org

ISBNs:
978-1-78641-024-5 Print
978-1-78641-086-3 ePub
978-1-78641-087-0 PDF

David K. Ngaruiya and Rodney L. Reed hereby assert their moral right to be identified as the Author of the General Editor's part in the Work in accordance with sections 77 and 78 of the Copyright, Designs and Patents Act 1988.

All rights reserved. No part of this publication may be reproduced, stored in a retrieval system or transmitted, in any form or by any means, electronic, mechanical, photocopying, recording or otherwise, without the prior written permission of the publisher or the Copyright Licensing Agency.

Requests to reuse content from Langham Publishing are processed through PLSclear. Please visit www.plsclear.com to complete your request.

Scripture quotations marked (NIV) are taken from the Holy Bible, New International Version®, NIV®. Copyright © 1973, 1978, 1984, 2011 by Biblica, Inc.™ Used by permission of Zondervan.

Scripture quotations marked (RSV) are from Revised Standard Version of the Bible, copyright © 1946, 1952, and 1971 National Council of the Churches of Christ in the United States of America. Used by permission. All rights reserved.

Scripture quotations marked (ESV) are from The Holy Bible, English Standard Version® (ESV®), copyright © 2001 by Crossway, a publishing ministry of Good News Publishers. Used by permission. All rights reserved.

Scripture quotations marked (NKJV) are from New King James Version (NKJV). Copyright © 1982 by Thomas Nelson, Inc. Used by permission. All rights reserved.

Scripture quotations marked (NRSV) are from the New Revised Standard Version Bible, copyright © 1989 National Council of the Churches of Christ in the United States of America. Used by permission. All rights reserved.

British Library Cataloguing-in-Publication Data
A catalogue record for this book is available from the British Library

ISBN: 978-1-78641-024-5

Cover & Book Design: projectluz.com

Langham Partnership actively supports theological dialogue and an author's right to publish but does not necessarily endorse the views and opinions set forth here or in works referenced within this publication, nor can we guarantee technical and grammatical correctness. Langham Partnership does not accept any responsibility or liability to persons or property as a consequence of the reading, use or interpretation of its published content.

Contents

Preface xiii

Acknowledgments xv

1 The Priesthood of All Believers and the Celebration of
  Communion in an African Church 1
  A Case Study of the Evangelical Congregational Church of
  Angola (IECA) During the Emergencies of the Civil War and the
  COVID-19 Pandemic
  Alberto Cotelo Gomes and Rowland D. Van Es, Jr

2 False Prosperity Pronouncements in 1 Kings 22:1–28 and
  Reflections for the Church 23
  Florah M. Kidula

3 A Clash of Cultures 43
  A Social-scientific Exegetical Comparative Examination of the Effects
  of Contextual Background on the Encounter between Christian
  Beliefs and Related Cultural Beliefs, in the Johannine Community
  New Testament Church and the African Church
  Catherine W. Chege

4 Church Architecture in the African Vernacular 61
  Robert Falconer

5 Untethered Agents of Eternal Life 89
  The Ministry of "Single" Women in the Gospel of John and Its
  Implications for the Church in Africa
  Cornelia van Deventer and Jesse Fungwa Kipimo

6 In Pursuit of Contextual Christian Ministry in an African Church . 107
  Exploring the Story of Rev. E. N. Anim, a Twentieth-Century Ghanaian
  Presbyterian Revivalist
  Edwin Buertey and Abraham Nana Opare Kwakye

7 The Church as a Household of God in African Theology. 131
  Reflecting the Values of African Households
  Isaac Ampong

8   The Case for the Ecclesiastical Title "Apostle" and the Gift of
    "Apostle"... 153
        Ephesians 4:11
        Dieudonne Komla Nuekpe

9   Re-imagining Cross-cultural Missional Ecclesiology in an African
    Context... 171
        "I Will Build My *Ekklēsian*" Not "I Will Build My Temple/Synagogue"
        Judy Wanjiru Wang'ombe

10 Communal *Theosis*.. 193
        Considering the Corporate Dimensions of the Doctrine of Deification
        in the Ethiopian Orthodox *Täwaḥədo* Church
        Calum Samuelson

11 Spiritual Parenthood as an Aspect of Emerging Kinship and
    Ecclesiological Structures in Urban African Pentecostalism......... 217
        E. Okelloh Ogera

12 Ecclesiology in Contemporary Africa................................ 233
        Operating in Post-COVID-19 Pandemic and Insecurity Situations
        Benjamin Akano

13 The Church as the Family Writ Large................................ 267
        The Practice and Expression of Kinship at CITAM Valley Road
        Paul N. Mwangi

14 Paucity of Meditation in Christian Worship......................... 283
        Implications for African Evangelicals
        Kelechi Bartram

15 Cash, Cleaning and Cooking... 303
        The Contribution of the Women's Fellowship in the RCZ
        Marike Blok-Sijtsma

16 The Necessity of Balanced Church Growth Strategies in Africa...... 325
        A Biblical Perspective
        Victor Umaru

17 "A Woman Teaches with Heart"....................................... 347
        The Mama Voice in Tanzanian Women's Preaching
        Tamie Davis

18 The Camel Has Four Legs 365
    A Contextual African Practical Ecclesiology
    Joshua Robert Barron

Contributors 401

Subject Index... 405

Scripture Index 409

Preface

Right from its founding, the church stands out as a sustainable institution. With its polycentric nature, the church in its history has flourished in diverse parts of the world including the Middle East, Europe, United States and notably in the African continent of our day. This has led some scholars like Andrew Walls to argue that the church has no native country. Indeed, current data indicates that there are now over two billion Christians scattered across almost every country of the world. It is no wonder then Jesus asserted that "And I tell you that you are Peter, and on this rock I will build my church, and the gates of Hades will not overcome it" (Matt 16:18). Although not immune to suffering, nor alien to opposition by evil forces from multiple sources whether natural or supernatural, the church of Jesus Christ continues to grow. This is a growth that ought to be holistic taking into account Tite Tienou's assertion, "We want Christianity to be in the hearts, minds and deeds of our church members,"[1] in his work *Issues in the Theological Task in Africa Today*.

Currently, Africa is said to be a Christian continent even though Africa has many diverse religions, not least among them Africa Traditional Religion and Islam. Like any other part of the world where Christianity has been an indomitable force, African Christians have their fair share of dealing with matters such as syncretism and pluralism, but these have not lessened the fact that Christianity continues to grow on the African continent. The church in Africa has flourished such that one out of every four Christians on the globe is African and current estimates indicate that there are about 718,096,000 African Christians. Over the years, Africa's Christian population has increased as follows: in 1970 it was 137,866,000; in 2000 it was 384,290,000; and mid-2023 it was 718,096,000.[2]

The chapters in this volume address the important matter of how African Christians understand the church. As an interdisciplinary work, this volume presents ecclesiology in Africa in four parts. The first part is a scriptural examination of some of the realties that the church in Africa cannot ignore.

---

1. Tite Tienou, "Issues in the Theological Task in Africa Today," *Africa Journal of Theology of Evangelical Theology* (1982): 10.
2. Gina A. Zurlo, Todd M. Johnson and Peter F. Crossing, "World Christianity 2023: A Gendered Approach" in *International Bulletin of Mission Research* 47, no. 1 (2023): 19.

This section biblically addresses: the priesthood of all believers and the question of marginalizing laity in the administering of Holy Communion during Angola's civil war and COVID-19 pandemic; proclamation of false prosperity based on 1 Kings 22:1–28; and an exegetical social-scientific analysis of Johannine community church and its subsequent implications for the church in Africa. Included in this section is also an exploration of African-language "architectonic theology" in African churches as well as making a case for inclusion of single women in church ministry based on the Gospel of John.

The second part is a historical theology chapter on Rev. E. N. Anim, a Presbyterian Revivalist from Ghana who sought to transform Western spirituality to have a bearing in mainstream African church ministry. The third part encompasses a systematic examination of "the church as the household of God" that resonates well with African understanding of community being multi-generational. It also makes a case for use of the term "apostle" in today's church.

The fourth part focuses on practical theology and features varied but related understandings of the church in Africa. It is the largest part of the book and addresses a diverse set of issues such as re-imagining the church in Africa, the use of various models and images for the church and its work (e.g. spiritual parenthood and the family writ large), how the church functions and ministers in the society (e.g. post-COVID, situations of insecurity, funerals), the nature of Christian worship, the role of women in the church, and church growth strategies for Africa. This volume provides a contemporary understanding of the burgeoning church in Africa through African voices.

David K. Ngaruiya
Chair, ASET Editorial Committee

Acknowledgments

The papers in the following chapters are selected highlights of the thirteenth annual conference of the Africa Society of Evangelical Theology (ASET), which was held 3–4 March 2023, at Saint Paul's University (SPU) in Nairobi, Kenya. With contributions from academics in several African nations as well as other countries, this volume has a very diverse international input.

Saint Paul's University, which hosted the meeting where these papers were presented, is gratefully acknowledged by the ASET Editorial Committee. We express our gratitude to the authors of these publications and patiently underwent multiple revisions in collaboration with the Editorial Committee. We recognize the critical role that our reviewers played in assessing the conference proposals as well as the post-conference papers. Their efforts played a crucial role in identifying the most scholarly and relevant articles that richly enhanced this volume. We also owe a great deal to the employees of Langham Publishing. Langham has now followed this route to its ninth volume with ASET. Finally, I want to thank my colleagues in the ASET Editorial Committee: Prof. Rodney Reed, Prof. Elizabeth Mburu and Prof. David Ngaruiya the Editorial Committee Chair for their labour to see this volume become an available resource to others. As it states in 1 Corinthians 15:58, "Your labour in the Lord is not in vain."

Professor Nathan Chiroma
Member of ASET Editorial Committee

1

The Priesthood of All Believers and the Celebration of Communion in an African Church

A Case Study of the Evangelical Congregational Church of Angola (IECA) During the Emergencies of the Civil War and the COVID-19 Pandemic

Alberto Cotelo Gomes
Evangelical Congregational Church, Angola (IECA)

and

Rowland D. Van Es, Jr
St. Paul's University, Limuru, Kenya

Abstract

Most Protestant churches acknowledge the doctrine of the priesthood of all believers based on 1 Peter 2:4–5 while still maintaining a clear distinction between the roles of clergy and laity, especially with regard to handling the sacraments and presiding over other church functions like marriage, baptism and funerals. While some tasks may be delegated to elders or deacons and even to evangelists, usually Communion is still reserved for the ordained clergy. This distinction came under pressure in Angola during the civil war (1975–2002) and more recently during the 2020–21 COVID-19 pandemic when the clergy could not physically preside over Communion. This raises the question of when, if ever, the celebration of Communion can be delegated to other members of the church, and if so, which ones could do so, or not, and why. This chapter will compare the existing practice among various churches to see if there are any historical or practical exceptions during extreme circumstances like war or a pandemic such as COVID-19. A case study of the Evangelical Congregational Church of Angola (IECA) will be presented as an example where lay leaders were not allowed to preside over Communion and this caused problems both during the civil war and during COVID-19. Using theological reflection, this research paper will first investigate the various biblical arguments for the priesthood of all believers. Next it will look at the reasons given why Communion can only be presided by an ordained clergy and the arguments by the Anglican Diocese of Sydney against such a continued prohibition. Finally, it will engage the IECA to discuss the celebration of Communion in the context of war and/or a pandemic to see when if ever, exceptions can be made to their existing policy when people cannot get to church to receive Communion or when the ordained clergy cannot get to the people to lead the Holy Communion service. We conclude with recommendations for the IECA and other churches studying this issue.

Key words: clergy, laity, communion, eucharistic theology, priesthood of all believers, 1 Peter 2:4–9, ecclesiology, Evangelical Congregational Church of Angola (IECA)

Introduction

The priesthood of all believers was first introduced in the Old Testament (see Exod 19:6; Isa 61:6) and then reiterated in the New Testament (1 Pet 2:4–9) and also emphasized by the Reformers. But this concept is still misunderstood in many churches. While the priesthood of all believers is not the only theological basis for lay people presiding over Communion, it remains a vital biblical argument for many Christians. Protestants believe that Communion is not a sacrifice, but a memorial. As such it does not need a priest. In any case, ordained Protestants are not technically priests but elders (the English translation of *'presbuteros'*). Still the question remains, what is it about church order (and the nature of ordination) that most churches still require an ordained person (pastor or elder) to preside over communion rather than an ordinary lay member reading from the liturgy who is not ordained?

If all believers are considered as priests, then it does raise a debate over the issue of who can preside over a celebration of Communion or the Eucharist. The issue becomes very crucial in the context of a war or pandemic when ordained clergy (priest or pastor or even an elder) may not be available. Several questions are then raised: Why can't a lay believer celebrate Communion or preside over the Eucharist? Why isn't it valid if celebrated or presided over by a lay leader in such an emergency context? Why does it lose meaning if presided over by a lay leader reading the approved liturgy and Scripture instead of an ordained clergy (or elder) if we are all priests? If Christ is the host and we are all his guests, then why make distinctions between the members present? If lay leaders can preach and teach, then why can't they celebrate Communion as well?

In Protestant Churches like the Evangelical Congregational Church of Angola (IECA) and others, every member is theoretically equal under Christ because they acknowledge the priesthood of all believers. No place in Scripture says that only clergy can celebrate Communion. It does say it must be done correctly and taken in a worthy manner (1 Cor 11:17–34), but precisely who is to preside is never specified. In the Jewish Passover meal, the head of the house led the liturgy. When the early church met in each other's private homes, the laity hosted the agape meal. In the debate about lay participation, scripture plays a key part of any resolution of this issue.

This article engages the IECA on the question of proper celebration of Communion in the context of war or pandemic where there is no ordained clergy available. It provides a space for the IECA and others who now require clergy for Communion to rethink and critically analyze their understanding of the theology of the priesthood of all believers (and ordination) in their current contexts, and going forward into the future, when more and more laity are literate and well educated.

The research investigates biblical arguments for the priesthood of all believers, statements of the Reformers and others. It also examines reasons for and against Communion being presided over only by ordained clergy. It is from this perspective that the researchers then invite the IECA to hold discussions on the celebration of Communion during an emergency situation and whenever ordained clergy (or elders) must always preside or if trained laity can also do so.

Biblical Arguments for the Priesthood of all Believers
Priesthood introduced and transformed in the Old Testament

Before the fall, Cain and his brother Abel each brought to the Lord an offering (Genesis 4). This reminds us that offering a sacrifice to God, which later became one of the activities carried out by a priest, was originally done by all. Also, before the period of the patriarchs, we see in Genesis 8:20 that after the flood Noah built an altar and offered a sacrifice to the Lord. Furthermore, the patriarchs Abraham, Isaac and Jacob all offered sacrifices to the Lord.[1] This early practice of offering sacrifices directly to God only later became an activity usually performed by the Levitical priests in the tabernacle or temple in the Old Testament.

Before Moses and Aaron, offering sacrifices to God was the responsibility of the head of the family (Genesis 8, etc.). Again, it is important that in the Old Testament the very first time the Bible talks about priests is Genesis 14:18, where Melchizedek is called a priest, specifically "a priest of God Most High." The second time the Bible mentions a priest is Exodus 18:1, where Jethro is identified as "the priest of Midian." Neither were Jews.

However, when the Israelites were in the wilderness, we see in Exodus 28 that Aaron and his sons were chosen from among the Israelites to become priests. This new priestly office had many activities such as: offering sacrifices to God on behalf of people, interceding, teaching the law of God, and taking care of the temple and its furnishings. For the Levites and the priests, there was clear division of their responsibilities (see Num 18:1–7).

From this time forward, priests were to come only from the Levites even though not all Levites were priests.[2] But the Passover meal and some other feasts were still celebrated by families in their own homes, as was the weekly family or clan Sabbath celebration.

We see that the Israelite priesthood was reorganized as time went by. What began as the simple act of offering sacrifices to God as a form of thanksgiving, became a priestly activity as an office in which some were chosen as priests, specifically from the tribe of Levi, and they had to be anointed for that task. From Mt. Sinai, up to the United Kingdom and afterwards, priestly activity became an office and priests had to be anointed to perform their activities

---

1. Gerald O'Collins and Michael Keenan Jones, *Jesus Our Priest: A Christian Approach to the Priesthood of Christ* (Oxford University Press: New York, 2010), 1–7.

2. E. Okelloh Ogera, "Jesus Christ as Ker: Toward an African High Priest Christianity," in *Who Do You Say That I Am? Christology in Africa*, eds. Rodney L. Reed and David K. Ngaruiya, (Carlisle: Langham Global Library, 2021), 243–44.

(although Solomon offered the sacrifices in 1 Kings 8:62–66). Later the high priest had the function of a mediator between God and the people of God (Lev 4:3–21; 9:1–24; 21:6–8; 2 Chr 19:11; Num 27:21).

The idea of the priesthood of all believers in the Old Testament was re-introduced by the prophet Isaiah in chapters 56, 61:6 and 66. In Isaiah 56 he said that foreigners joined to the Lord and eunuchs who keep the Sabbath were acceptable within the temple (v. 5) and foreigners were allowed to "minister" to God as "servants" (v. 6). And Isaiah 66:18–21, says God will select some people from among other nations and allow them to serve "as priests and Levites" along with the Israelite priests.[3] Isaiah is opening up priesthood to non-Levites and non-Jews!

Priesthood totally transformed in the New Testament

With the advent of Christianity, Jesus Christ was seen as the great high priest who expiated the sins of all humanity. Jesus offered himself as "a sacrifice once for all," and he was both priest and victim (see Heb 9:25–28; 10:18).[4] The early church had no hereditary priesthood, instead they chose bishops or elders, deacons and deaconesses (see 1 Tim 3:1–12 and Titus 1:5–9). Ephesians 4:11–12a says Christ's gifts were that "some should be apostles, some prophets, some evangelists, some pastors and teachers, to equip the saints for the work of ministry" (RSV).

The concept of the priesthood of all believers in the New Testament is clearly introduced in 1 Peter 2:5 and 9 where we understand that the proclamation of the gospel or the ministry of teaching is being pointed out as one of the tasks that all believers should do. The understanding is that Peter connected the role of a priest or the priestly activity to the missiological task of the church. Christ's priesthood is excellent and superior compared to the Aaronic priesthood; he is the mediator interceding on behalf of everyone without any animal sacrifice.[5] In Hebrews 7, Jesus is a priest in the order of Melchizedek (Gen 14:18), not of Aaron or Levi.

The concept of the priesthood of all believers prophesied in Isaiah 55, 56 and 61 begins already in the New Testament through Jesus Christ as the perfect high priest, and now all of us have the privilege of being priests to and for each other. Through Christ we are all called and given the mission to preach

---

3. O'Collins and Jones, *Jesus Our Priest*, 1–7.
4. O'Collins and Jones, *Jesus Our Priest*, 46–47.
5. Ogera, "Jesus Christ as Ker," 243–44.

the gospel, praise God and intercede for one another (Matt 28:18–19; Jas 5:16; 1 Pet 2:9). We are all now part of Christ's "more excellent ministry" (Heb 8:6).

In the same line of thought, we should all have the privilege to celebrate Communion, especially taking into account the context in which this research is based, which is in the context of war or pandemic such as COVID-19. Passover was celebrated in the homes of the Hebrews (Exod 12:1–11), and the same is true in the New Testament; Jesus Christ and his disciples celebrated the first Lord's Supper in an upper room of a house and not in the temple (Luke 22:7–14). Jesus did the same by breaking bread with the two of them at Emmaus in Luke 24:35.

In the ministry of Paul also, most churches met in private homes, usually twenty to fifty people, and these gatherings were informal and participatory (see 1 Cor 14:26). The host was the head of the household, usually male, but not always. Phoebe (Rom 16:1–2), Lydia (Acts 16:13–15), Nympha (Col 4:15), Chloe (1 Cor 1:11) and other women like Prisca (with her husband Aquila) hosted churches in their homes (Acts 16:3–5) and acted as the hosts of the communal meals that were usually part of these gatherings. This remained the pattern for the first two hundred years.[6]

Exegesis of 1 Peter 2:4–5

The first pericope of 1 Peter 2 goes from verses 1–12 where Christians are being addressed as new-born babies or infants, living stones, a spiritual house, a holy or royal priesthood and a chosen people.[7] Our exegesis here will be focused on verses 4–5.

Cranfield says it is important to note that as newborn infants, as mentioned in verse 2, Christians are advised to long for spiritual milk, which perhaps refers to the word of God. The word of God therefore is a meal that nourishes spiritual life and help Christians to mature and to become adults who can obtain redemption.[8]

Verse 4: Πρὸς ὃν προσερχόμενοι, λίθον ζῶντα, ὑπὸ ἀνθρώπων μὲν ἀποδεδοκιμασμένον παρὰ δὲ θεῷ ἐκλεκτὸν ἔντιμον or "Come to him, to that living stone, rejected by men but in God's sight chosen and precious" (RSV).

---

6. Kevin Giles, "House Churches," CBE International (10 April 2010), https://www.cbeinternational.org/resource/house-churches/.

7. J. N. D. Kelly, *Epistles of Peter and Jude* (London: Bloomsbury Publishing, 2001), 82.

8. C. E. B. Cranfield, *I and II Peter and Jude: Introduction and Commentary* (London: SCM, 1960), 61.

Πρὸς ὃν προσερχόμενοι or "coming unto him." In this sentence Peter used the present tense because the stones continue coming one after the other, it can also refer to a continuing drawing to the redeemer, as a result of conversion.[9]

Προσερχόμενοι is a verb, plural, passive voice, present tense. It means "to come up to, come near to, to proceed." It implies that it is urgent for Christians to come or to convert to Christ for their salvation.[10]

λίθον ζῶντα, "a living stone." The phrase "living stone" has a deeper meaning in Peter's interpretation, which is spiritual. Peter uses the metaphor of stone to reaffirm the importance of purity or holiness.[11] The image "living stone" and "living stones" dominates 1 Peter 2:4–10.[12] Also, the statement "living stone" integrates Old Testament texts which were given christological meaning by the author and his audience (Ps 118:22). In the letter of 1 Peter the stone refers to Christ who was also rejected, and explicitly it was also referring to Christians in Asia Minor who were undergoing suffering. The word "living" is added in order to indicate that Christ rose from the dead, and is able to give life to everyone who suffers because of him.[13] Living also means by implication that Christ is the foundation and provider of life, as it is written in John 1:4.[14]

ἐκλεκτὸν ἔντιμον, "Chosen and precious" means that Christians, even though they were suffering, were being built up by God into a spiritual house. It is possible that the verb is imperative which by implication should be translated as "allow yourselves to be built up."[15]

ἔντιμον, "precious" means that Christians have value before God the Father as the Father values Christ (1 Pet 2:4). Christians are the stones of God's temple, just as Christ is the cornerstone of the temple. Christ is the living stone, and because of his resurrection (1 Pet 1:3), Christians were also made living stones (1 Pet 2:5). Because of Christ's activity as priest it is possible for Christians to give/offer to God acceptable spiritual sacrifices. In addition, the church is a holy temple and priesthood that experiences God's presence (1 Cor 3:16–17).

---

9. Charles Bigg, *A Critical and Exegetical Commentary of the Epistles of St Peter and St Jude* (Edinburgh: T&T Clark, 1902), 128.

10. William F. Arndt and F. Wilbur Gingrich, *A Greek-English Lexicon of the New Testament and Other Early Christian Literature* (Chicago: The University of Chicago Press, 1957), 712.

11. Bigg, *A Critical and Exegetical Commentary*, 128.

12. Craddock, 1995, *First and Second Peter and Jude*, 37.

13. Kelly, *Epistles of Peter and Jude*, 87–88.

14. R. C. Sproul, *The Reformation Study Bible*, English Standard Version (Orlando: Reformation Trust Publishing, 2015), 2244.

15. Kelly, *Epistles of Peter and Jude*, 89.

Because of his love God has chosen his people and lives among them.[16] Also "precious" is an adjective, which means honoured, respected, valuable. It has also the implication of something more honourable in reputation.[17]

ἐκλεκτὸν, "chosen" – it is an adjective meaning chosen out, or elect. By implication it means those chosen out by God and drawn to God. Just like in the OT when the Israelites were chosen by God, in the NT Christians are also chosen by God in order to render special service to God (1 Chr 16:13; Pss 88:4; 89:3; 104:6; Isa 65:9, 15, 23).[18]

Verse 5: "καὶ αὐτοὶ ὡς λίθοι ζῶντες οἰκοδομεῖσθε οἶκος πνευματικὸς εἰς ἱεράτευμα ἅγιον, ἀνενέγκαι πνευματικὰς θυσίας εὐπροσδέκτους θεῷ διὰ Ἰησοῦ Χριστοῦ." Or "And like living stones be yourselves built into a spiritual house, to be a holy priesthood, to offer spiritual sacrifices acceptable to God through Jesus Christ" (RSV).

καὶ αὐτοὶ ὡς λίθοι ζῶντες οἰκοδομεῖσθε οἶκος πνευματικὸς is "and like living stones be yourselves built into a spiritual house." By taking οἰκοδομεῖσθε as indicative, it can be translated as "are being built up." Peter maintains a clear focus on the communal aspect of the Christian life in this passage; the temple is the community as in Ephesians 2:21–22, not the individual person as in 1 Corinthians 3:16–4:19.[19]

οἶκος πνευματικὸς, "a spiritual house" means that the church is the temple of God, inhabited by the Holy Spirit (2 Cor 6:16, Eph 2:19–22). Christ is the cornerstone of the Church, so Christians are recognized as the real temple when they are united with Christ.[20] Remember that most early churches met in private houses or homes.

εἰς ἱεράτευμα ἅγιον, " to be a holy priesthood." Peter quotes Exodus 19:5–6 which implies that the living stones as priests must be holy when they are incorporated into the structure to serve in the temple.[21] "Holy priesthood" also means that all Christians are considered to be priests since we all have the same and direct access to God, and serve God individually.[22] Below is Calvin's commentary on this phrase, "a holy priesthood":

---

16. Edmund Clowney, *The Message of 1 Peter* (London: Inter-Varsity Press, 1988), 87–91.
17. Bigg, *A Critical and Exegetical Commentary*, 268.
18. Arndt and Gingrich, *A Greek-English Lexicon of the New Testament*, 242.
19. Bigg, *A Critical and Exegetical Commentary*, 128.
20. Sproul, *The Reformation Study Bible*, 2244.
21. Bigg, *A Critical and Exegetical Commentary*, 129.
22. Sproul, *The Reformation Study Bible*, 2244.

It is a singular honor, that God should not only consecrate us as a temple to himself, in which he dwells and is worshipped, but that he should also make us priests. But Peter mentions this double honor, in order to stimulate us more effectually to serve and worship God. Of the spiritual sacrifices, the first is the offering of ourselves, of which Paul speaks in Romans 12:1; for we can offer nothing, until we offer to him ourselves as a sacrifice; which is done by denying ourselves. Then, afterwards follow prayers, thanksgiving, almsdeeds, and all the duties of religion.[23]

ἀνενέγκαι πνευματικὰς θυσίας εὐπροσδέκτους θεῷ διὰ Ἰησοῦ Χριστοῦ, or "to offer up spiritual sacrifices acceptable to God through Christ." Peter says that the sacrifices are spiritual. Peter uses the word πνευματικὰς to separate the offering of the law from the spiritual offering, because self-dedication, adoration, faith and prayers are also referred to as sacrifices (Rom 12:1; Phil 2:17; Eph 5:1–2).[24] No separate order of priests here.

"Spiritual sacrifices" also means that through Christ's atonement the Old Testament ritual sacrifice was made unnecessary (see Heb 8:13; 13:9), because the required sacrifice for sin was made by Christ himself. Christians demonstrate spiritual sacrifice in their worship and in their way of life. Since today Christians are members of the church, it is appropriate for them to do the same duties as the priests did in the Old Testament, which was the offering of sacrifices.[25] In the New Testament there is no longer a need for a separate order of priests for offering sacrifices, as we are all priests to and for each other, each sanctified by Christ. We are all called to be mediators and intercessors and we all offer spiritual sacrifices directly now, by praising God with our lips and our lives (Heb 13:15–16).

εὐπροσδέκτους θεῷ διὰ Ἰησοῦ Χριστοῦ, or "acceptable to God through Christ." Here commentators differ in their opinions in regard to how the word "διὰ" (through) relates to the rest of the sentence. Is it to be taken with ἀνενέγκαι (to offer) or with εὐπροσδέκτους (acceptable)? But the order of words in Hebrews 13:15 favours this last interpretation over the first. The perceptions are different from one another. In 1 Peter 2:5 we offer spiritual sacrifices through Christ that are acceptable because they are spiritual. In Hebrews 13:15

---

23. John Calvin, *Commentary on First Peter*, www.biblehub.com/commentaries/calvin/1_peter/2.htm.
24. Bigg, *A Critical and Exegetical Commentary*, 129.
25. Sproul, *The Reformation Study Bible*, 2244.

we offer spiritual sacrifices that are acceptable as they are offered through him and derive their entire value from who presents them to God.[26]

1 Peter 2:4–5 is a key text for the doctrine of the priesthood of all believers. Verse 4 shows Christians can offer acceptable sacrifices (as priests did). Verse 5 shows Christians are a new temple of God, united with Christ. We are now a holy priesthood, all serving God together.

Views during the Reformation on the Priesthood of all Believers and Communion

In this section we discuss briefly Luther and Calvin's views as they defended the church tradition concerning the administration of Eucharist even if they also believed that all Christians are priests. Martin Luther starts his ideas on the priesthood of all believers basing his arguments on Galatians 6:2, "Carry each other's burdens, and in this way you will fulfil the law of Christ." He constructs his view of the priesthood of all believers by seeing baptism as the gateway to the universal priesthood.

Luther says that the priesthood of all believers has three functions; to preach, to come before God with intercessions for one another, and to sacrifice ourselves to God. His emphasis on the priesthood of all believers is that all Christians have the right and duty to teach and spread the word of God and this is the *highest* priestly office. Priests were ordained simply to offer Communion and not to serve the pastoral needs of the faithful.[27] Luther makes a separation when it comes to the role of priests, especially in regard to celebrating Communion. He delegates the task of celebrating it to those who are ordained priests, although ordinary lay believers can still preach, pray and sacrifice themselves to God.

For John Calvin, the office of Christ's priesthood involves the ministry of teaching. Calvin states that the Eucharist is a confirmation and symbol of Christ's once for all sacrifice. He differentiates the priesthood of all believers in terms of functions that are supposed to be done by the ordained person and a non-ordained person. He presents three roles that are supposed to be done by the ordained priest; preaching the gospel, feeding the flock and governing the community.[28]

---

26. Bigg, *A Critical and Exegetical Commentary*, 129.
27. O'Collins and Jones, *Jesus Our Priest*, 129–37.
28. O'Collins and Jones, *Jesus Our Priest*, 150–61.

Although Calvin admits that all Christians are priests, he too makes a distinction in terms of their functions, concretely by saying that the ordained priest has the responsibility to administer the sacraments. At no point does Calvin mention that in an emergency any lay Christian can celebrate the Eucharist. For instance, "he experienced the outbreak of Black Plague in Geneva in his lifetime in 1543, and in his response to that in the year 1545 he has not mentioned anything concerning the administration of the Eucharist by the lay leader."[29] As opposed to Luther, only clergy can preach, teach, or govern the church in Calvin's view.

As to the question of what really happens to Jesus Christ in the Lord's Supper, Keith Dalby says while Luther leans to the objective end of the spectrum (insisting Christ is really present in the elements) and Zwingli leans to the subjective end of the spectrum (insisting that it is an intellectual, not an objective event), Calvin is more in the middle (saying Jesus is the substance of the sacrament and the source of the efficacy).[30] Cranmer insisted that Christ is in heaven and the faithful feed on him spiritually but something happens between the recipient and God. The 1662 Prayer Book was a compromise as some elements are subjective ("take it in remembrance"), while others are objective ("the body of our Lord").[31] It is not just a memorial, because Christ participates with us in it. Protestant views on Communion were thus quite divided. But for both Luther and Calvin and others, laity can preach and teach.

Another useful summary of the debate in the sixteenth century is provided by Robert Doyle. He notes the distinction between a sacramental ontology where God works downward through creation and a word ontology where God works directly through God's word.[32] While Catholics stressed the sacramental view along with a clerical hierarchy, the Reformers stressed God's word which gave more license to the laity. He cites Luther and then Calvin, where (Christ) "alone rules and reigns in church, as well as have authority or pre-eminence in it and this authority should be exercised and administered by his Word

---

29. George Homan, "The Plague in the Sixteenth Century and Now," *JAMA*, 63.2 (1914): 183.

30. Keith Dalby, "Is Lay Administration of the Lord's Supper Consistent with Anglican Identity?" An Occasional Paper for St John the Evangelist Church, Gordon" (2015), 6, citing Calvin's *Short Treatise on the Holy Supper of our Lord Jesus* (see page 9). http://stjohnsgordon.org.au/wp-content/uploads/2015/12/Is-Lay-Administration-of-the-Lords-Supper-Consistent-with-an-Anglican-Identity.pdf.

31. Dalby, "Is Lay Administration," 10, citing the words from the Service of Holy Communion, *Book of Common Prayer*, 1662.

32. R. Doyle, "Lay Administration and the 16th Century: The Move from Sacramental to Word Ontology," *Churchman* 113.4 (1999): 319–30, 320.

alone."³³ His conclusion was that lay leaders can administer the sacrament if they just use the right words.

A Post-Reformation Theology of the Universal Priesthood and Communion

According to the New Testament, the priesthood of ordained priests is ecclesiological.³⁴ But the basis of the theology of ministerial priesthood is christological.³⁵ Furthermore, anyone who presides over the Eucharist *is* a priest, and this is a role of the ministerial priesthood.³⁶ What we want to say here, is that ordained clergy exercise their ministries within the church under Christ, the one and only head of the church. And where two or three are, there Christ is.

In 1990, Greg Ogden wrote *The New Reformation: Returning the Ministry to the People of God* in which he argues for one people/one ministry instead of the current two peoples/two ministries model of the church which divides the church into clergy and laity. Ogden argues that not only are we all ministers directly before God, but we are also priests to each other.³⁷ Ogden also states that we are a "sacramental people"³⁸ and only Jesus is the head of the church.³⁹ He writes against modern clericalism, then argues for his one people/one ministry model.⁴⁰ This goes against the current two peoples/two ministries model (of laity vs. clergy).

Ogden then traces out the implications of his new model in Chapter 4 and in discussing Communion in particular, he emphasizes that it is a common meal, *not* a clergy meal.⁴¹ His contention is that, "the single greatest reinforcer

---

33. Doyle, "Lay Administration," 323, citing Calvin's *Institutes* 4.3.1.

34. David Coffey, "The Common and the Ordained Priesthood," *Theological Studies* 58.2 (1997): 209–36.

35. Leo Andoh Korsah and Francis Appiah-Kubi, "Towards an Understanding of Ministerial Priesthood in the Light of Priesthood of the Baptized," *Asian Horizons* 9, no. 2 (June 2015): 310–23.

36. Leo Andoh Korsah, "Towards an Understanding of Priesthood in the Realistic Sense from the Perspective of New Testament Theology," *Journal of Religion and Theology* 4, no. 2 (June 2020): 6–9.

37. Greg Ogden, *The New Reformation: Returning the Ministry to the People of God* (Grand Rapids: Zondervan Publishing House, 1990), 11–12.

38. Ogden, *The New Reformation*, 31.

39. Ogden, *The New Reformation*, 33, citing Ephesians 4:15–16 and John 15:1–11.

40. Ogden, *The New Reformation*, 56–69.

41. Ogden, *The New Reformation*, 79–82.

of the pastor as priest is the exclusive right of the ordained to preside over the distribution of elements of Communion."[42]

Citing John Stott, he says that "there is nothing inherent in the call of pastors that gives them exclusive right to serve Communion. Giving pastors that right is a matter of expediency, not call."[43] He also reminds us that "nowhere in the New Testament is a special group set apart to protect and administer the sacraments. Leadership does not have an exclusive role in liturgy or worship."[44] He concludes his argument by quoting John Dunn, "If we accept that presiding at the Eucharist in not a charism (gift) distinct from the rest . . . then we should insist . . . that the conduct of Holy Communion must not be confined to a particular group within the diverse ministries of the community of faith"[45] The Eucharist is *for* all and can be done *by* all too.

The debate over who can celebrate Communion also recently went on in the Anglican Church of Australia, led by the Diocese of Sydney, and some of their arguments can guide the ICEA and other churches. The conclusion of Sydney's Doctrine Committee in 1993 was that lay administration of the Lord's Supper was "doctrinally acceptable" and the continued prohibition against lay presidency was "not justified theologically."[46] In 2004 a declaration was passed discouraging disciplinary action against any lay person or deacon who presided at a Eucharist.[47] Both reports are interesting reading as is Chapter 18 of Brian Douglas.

John Woodhouse argues that prohibiting laity from presiding over the Lord's Supper "has no basis in scripture"[48] and while in the past there may have been good reasons for it (illiteracy, etc.), restricting it to clergy today no longer serves its function. Today, we have many gifted and highly educated

---

42. Ogden, *The New Reformation*, 79.

43. Ogden, *The New Reformation*, 80–81, citing *One People*, by John Stott (Downers Grove: Inter-Varsity Press, 1968), 42.

44. Ogden, *The New Reformation*, 81.

45. Ogden, *The New Reformation*, 81, citing an unpublished paper, "Ministry and the Ministry," 26.

46. Brian Douglas, *The Anglican Eucharist in Australia* (Leiden: Brill, 2022), 284–85, citing the Doctrine Committee of the Anglican Diocese of Sydney, "Lay Presidency at the Lord's Supper" (1993), http://enit-syd.sds.asn.au/assets/Documents/synod/Synod1993/laypresidency1993.pdf.

47. Douglas, *The Anglican Eucharist*, 285, citing the Standing Committee of the Anglican Diocese of Sydney, "Lay & Diaconal Administration of Holy Communion" (2004) http://www.sds.asn.au/sites/default/files/synod/lay_and_diaconal_administration.pdf?doc_id=NTMxNA.

48. J. Woodhouse, "Lay Administration of the Lord's Supper: A Change to Stay the Same," *Churchman* 113, no. 4 (1999): 307–18, 307.

lay members who *are* theologically qualified. Since laity can now preach and teach, then they should so also be allowed to preside over and celebrate Communion. He cites Luther saying preaching is the *highest* office, then baptism and Communion. In Communion, he says, "the focus is not on the minster . . . but on the corporate act of remembering by all the believers."[49] The lay prohibition is thus a "vanity and superstition" that now must be removed for the sake of the gospel.[50]

The IECA and others should study the reports of the Diocese of Sydney of the Anglican Church of Australia 1993–2004 and then do a theological reflection of their own practice.

Practice of Administration of the Eucharist in the Evangelical Congregational Church of Angola (IECA)

In the IECA the theology of the administration of Eucharist is Calvinistic. The argument is based on what John Calvin argues, that what makes sacraments special is the using of the right words, stating: "the efficacy of the sacrament requires both word and external sign."[51] According to what Calvin says about the use of the right words, the questions to be raised are: Why isn't a lay leader qualified to read the right words from the liturgy or to quote them from Scripture or be taught how to perform the correct external signs? Why only the ordained clergy? On what biblical basis are other Christians excluded? If it is a liturgical or constitutional matter, can it be changed after deeper reflection on all this?

Communion during the Angolan Civil War

The socio-political context of Angola during the Portuguese colonization had divided the country into three main zones of influence. The IECA was located in the south-central region before the civil war. However, during the civil war there was an exodus of the population to different parts of the country, which caused the IECA to begin to be spread out to places where it had not been before. Many of those who founded the church in these new regions were not clergy at all; and in some areas, they only had lay leaders and not an

---

49. Woodhouse, "Lay Administration," 313.
50. Woodhouse, "Lay Administration," 317.
51. Melvin Tinker, "Language, Symbols and Sacraments: Was Calvin's View of the Lord's Supper Right?" *Churchman* 112, no. 2 (1998): 131–49.

ordained pastor, so the question of administration of Communion became a great challenge. No one could celebrate Holy Communion because church documents stated that only ordained pastors could do so. "The pastor of the pastorate is a minister of the gospel, to dedicate himself specially to preaching the word of God, administering the sacraments."[52] That is why during the period of civil war, it was "legally impossible" to celebrate Holy Communion where there were no ordained pastors.

The eagerness to participate in Communion dominated the faithful, but they could not do so in compliance with the church's guiding documents. The priority was the preaching of the word. During the civil war period there was a standstill as people were dispersed and the mission stations were destroyed, yet it was also at this stage that the church began to increase in number in the cities. However, if one was not ordained, they could not administer Communion in the IECA, regardless of whether it was an emergency context of war or not.

Communion during the COVID-19 Pandemic

Again, the theology of ordination for the IECA, when it comes to the administration of the Eucharist, relies on what Luther has said: that in the context of an emergency or in a situation whereby the ordained priest is not available, any lay believer can assume the responsibility of teaching the word. Luther goes further, stating that any believer must be ready in an emergency situation to perform baptism or grant a deathbed absolution. But a lay leader may not preside over the administration of the Eucharist. The reasons why Luther says this is that the Eucharist should be only presided by an ordained priest because he sees the Eucharist as a public act of the church.[53]

During the time of the COVID-19 pandemic, when the churches were closed, what the IECA did was to adapt to the context, that is, holding online services, sending sermons and Bible studies to their members. But Holy Communion was not celebrated. Although the church recognizes and believes in the universal priesthood, as in 1 Peter 2:4–5, still only ordained pastors were allowed to celebrate Holy Communion. The reasoning was not well explained. Why are lay leaders allowed to baptize in private, but not to celebrate Communion in public?

---

52. Estatuto da Igreja Evangélica Congregacional em Angola. III série- n 181, Quinta-feira, 21 de Setembro de 2017. Diário da República, Órgão Oficial da República de Angola, 22.

53. B. A. Gerrish, "Priesthood and Ministry in the Theology of Luther," *Church History* 34, no. 4 (1965): 404–22, https://www.jstor.org/stable/3163119.

The way forward

From the brief exegesis of 1 Peter 2:4–5 above, it is possible to understand that Peter supports the view that all Christians are priests through Christ who offered himself once for all. During a time of war or pandemic, that for us today has the implication of suffering, Christians might also build up their faith by staying always united to Christ, and they are also called to serve God by offering sacrifices even in difficult circumstances. Because we all have direct access to God, we think that it is not wrong for us to have communion with God through lay celebration of Communion during difficult moments as other Christians did in the apostolic Church, and as Pentecostal and Evangelical churches today do, based on the priesthood of all believers who are sanctified by Christ alone.

For this reason, what the IECA should do today in times like these is to train their believers and allow them to celebrate Communion. Even under more normal circumstances, the ordained priest can preside in one congregation and delegate to the trained laity in others. In the Old Testament, Jews celebrated the Passover in their houses (Exod 12:1–11), which today corresponds to Holy Communion in our houses during COVID-19. Just as the leader of the family or house was responsible for that, so in hardship the same instructions should follow if the believers feel the need to celebrate and they can do so properly using the right words and the right symbols that the church prescribes. The liturgy could be sent out via phone or email!

The IECA has one example whereby the first missionaries celebrated Holy Communion in a house. We can read in the letter written by Dr Nicholas that after their arrival in Benguela Province on October 15th 1881, five of them celebrated the Lord's Supper – but it was not in the church, because at that time they had no churches. Their circumstances and their context led them to have Communion with God in the place where they were. It was not even in their permanent house, because they were going on to Bailundo, in Huambo Province, where the first three missionaries had opened the first missionary station.[54]

Therefore, the way forward today for the church should be to start undertaking serious theological reflection in order to discuss how the church should behave during times of hardship. The church should also train lay leaders on how to preside over Holy Communion in such a context, as long

---

54. The Mission of the American Mission Board to West Central Africa: Pioneer Work, 1881 (Boston: American Board of Commissioners for Foreign Mission, 1882), https://archive.org/details/MN41621ucmf_2/page/n5/mode/2up?view=theater.

as it is allowed by the church according to their new understanding of the priesthood of all believers.

Congregationalists do not now allow lay leaders to preside over Holy Communion, because it is seen as a very important ordinance which is supposed to be done only by an ordained pastor.[55] But, if we consider the Eucharist as a means of grace that helps Christians to connect because it carries Christ's presence,[56] even during a war or a pandemic, then they should try as much as possible to have Communion with God. Why deny them that privilege? If the early church *agape* meal was celebrated informally in people's homes, then why not today, especially if people are suffering and clergy are not available but trained laity are?

The reality of human life can lead people to ask questions that the Bible is supposed to answer.[57] In this case Christians should ask why they cannot celebrate Holy Communion in times of war or pandemics just because they don't have any ordained pastors around. Often people create laws, rules, norms and regulations that are not permanent because they are only applicable within a particular context to deal with certain situations of the moment. We have as a recent example the use of face masks, hand washing and checking of body temperature, and keeping social distance between people, as new rules imposed worldwide due to the COVID-19 pandemic. A new philosophy of life and new rules were imposed to deal with the new reality.

This new experience of life has led people, especially Christians, to revisit their theology regarding the different ways God uses in order to reveal himself or manifest his presence to humanity today. Different situations can lead people to perceive God very differently. God has always revealed himself to people at different times and places in different ways to guide them in what should be done as a way of answering their questions. For instance, during the one to two years that COVID-19 forced people to stay at home, God would still have wanted people to have fellowship by celebrating Communion, just as

---

55. Y. Chung, "Congregational Membership, Church Purity, and Presbyterian and Congregationalist Polemics during the Puritan Revolution," *Tyndale Bulletin* 70.1 (2019): 117–43, https://tyndalebulletin.org, 17–18.

56. Ogden, *The New Reformation*, 31.

57. "Existential Method" refers to human experience and God's presence. Everyday life situations can help people to find God. Moments of pain, as well as of joy, suffering, triumphs, and anxiety can reveal God's activity. Theology interprets and responds to human experience. J. J. Muller, *What Are They Saying about Theological Method?* (New York: Paulist Press, 1984), 22–31.

the Hebrews had their Passover in their houses in the time before there was a temple or an ordained priesthood.

During our study of 1 Peter 2:4–5 we have seen that we offer sacrifices that are acceptable to God through Jesus Christ, so Holy Communion does not lose any meaning when it is offered by a lay leader, because Christ is present and it is done in his name and through him, we can have direct Communion and fellowship with God the Father and the Holy Spirit as well.

Summary and Conclusion

We must look at Scripture, tradition, reason *and* experience in our discussion as we conclude about laity celebrating Communion. To begin with, there is no place in Scripture that says only ordained clergy can preside over Communion. In fact, the Passover meal that Jesus turned into the Lord's Supper, was usually led by the members of the family during a meal, with no ordained priest or Rabbi needed. 1 Corinthians 5:7 calls Christ "our paschal lamb."

While many churches have by their tradition, and restricted the celebration of Communion to the ordained clergy, this was never universal. For the first two hundred years, most churches were house churches and gatherings were informal and participatory.[58] Other traditions have done Communion differently as there is no scriptural mandate for a separate group to preside over it. As Woodhouse argued,[59] maybe tradition must change to allow lay leaders to preside to maintain the gospel we preach. It seems reasonable to us to allow lay members to celebrate, especially during an emergency, but even in other circumstances, as long as they are trained.

The Lord's Table provides spiritual food and drink that can be taken by sinners and is always presided over by a sinner, whether ordained or not. As long as the right words are used and the correct Scripture is read for the words of institution, why does the person reading it matter? As in the Donatist controversy, it is not the holiness of the priest that matters, but the words that are used. With minimal training, anyone can lead a Communion service correctly. The elements are consecrated by Christ, who is present with us, not by the person leading.

What about Christian experience during previous wars and pandemics? If lay people could be trusted by Luther with baptism, confession and even administering the last rites, then why not also Communion? There is no

---

58. Giles, "House Churches."
59. Woodhouse, "Lay Administration."

theological basis for separating Communion as a special class from baptism. There are only two sacraments, and if laity can be allowed to do one, then why not the other? If we now allow lay leaders to preach (the highest office for Luther) then why not allow them to lead Communion as well? Experience has taught us that they can and we all benefit.

In Angola, during the civil war, many Christians could not celebrate Communion for many years, simply because an ordained clergyperson was not readily available. People went for years without receiving the spiritual food and drink they needed to "taste and see that God is good." This was unfortunate and unnecessary if we take the priesthood of all believers seriously.

Again, during the COVID-19 pandemic that suspended many church services in 2020–21, Christians were denied Communion simply because a clergyperson was not always available. What was decreed by the IECA during the civil war was taken as binding on the church during the COVID pandemic, but two wrongs do not make a right. They could have made a new ruling.

Why not offer Communion virtually? If there is a concern about doing it correctly, clergy can read the words with laity serving each other at home as in the Jewish Passover meal and in early house churches. One of the authors did this for his fellowship during COVID-19 and many were blessed by it. Even before and after COVID-19, lay leaders have celebrated Communion. They are also allowed to preach from the pulpit in many churches. If Luther allowed laity to hear confession and even baptize in an emergency, then by what logic were lay people in the IECA forbidden to celebrate Communion during COVID-19 when they had Bibles and could read an approved Communion liturgy with the correct words of institution from 1 Corinthians 11?

It is time to admit we are all priests to each other, and we can all read Scripture and preach, and celebrate the sacraments, with proper training. The IECA and indeed most other churches in Africa and Asia, and anywhere that has a shortage of ordained clergy, should reconsider their policies about who can celebrate Communion and how it needs to be done to be approved by Christ. After all, 1 Corinthians 11:25 just says, "do this, as often as you drink it, in remembrance of me." As long as we partake of it in a worthy manner, there is no biblical stipulation about who can or can't celebrate Communion. All believers are welcome in front of or behind the Lord's table.

Bibliography

Adeyemo, T., ed. *Africa Bible Commentary*. Nairobi: Word Alive, 2006.

Arndt, W. F. and F. W. Gingrich. *A Greek-English Lexicon of the New Testament and Other Early Christian Literature*. Chicago: The University of Chicago Press, 1957.

Bigg, Charles. *The International Critical Commentary: A Critical and Exegetical Commentary of the Epistles of St Peter and St Jude*. Edinburgh: T&T Clark, 1902.

Calvin, J. *Commentary on 1 Peter*. https://biblehub.com/commentaries/calvin/1_peter/2.htm.

———. *Institutes of Christian Religion* (translated by Henry Beveridge). Grand Rapids: Eerdmans, 1989.

———. *Short Treatise on the Lord's Supper*. Monergism, Books. Accessed online at: https://www.monergism.com/thethreshhold/sdg/calvin/Short_Treatise_on_the_Lords_Su_John_Calvin.pdf.

Chung, Y. "Congregational Membership, Church Purity, and Presbyterian and Congregationalist Polemics during the Puritan Revolution." *Tyndale Bulletin* 70, no. 1 (2019): 117–43. https://tyndalebulletin.org.

Clowney, E. *The Message of 1 Peter*. Leicester: Inter-Varsity Press, 1988.

Coffey, D. "The Common and the Ordained Priesthood." *Theological Studies* 58, no. 2 (1997): 209–36. https://theologicalstudies.net/articles/the-common-and-the-ordained-priesthood/.

Craddock, F. *First and Second Peter and Jude*. Louisville: Westminster John Knox Press, 1995.

Cranfield, C. E. B. *I and II Peter and Jude: Introduction and Commentary*. TBC. London: SCM, 1960.

Dalby, Keith. "Is Lay Administration of the Lord's Supper Consistent with Anglican Identity?" An Occasional Paper for St John the Evangelist Church, Gordon (2015). http://stjohnsgordon.org.au/wp-content/uploads/2015/12/Is-Lay-Administration-of-the-Lords-Supper-Consistent-with-an-Anglican-Identity.pdf.

Doctrine Committee of the Anglican Diocese of Sydney. "Lay Presidency at the Lord's Supper." (1993). http://enit-syd.sds.asn.au/assets/Documents/synod/Synod1993/laypresidency1993.pdf.

Douglas, Brian. *The Anglican Eucharist in Australia*. Anglican-Episcopal Theology and History, Volume 8. Leiden: Brill, 2022.

Doyle, R. "Lay Administration and the 16th Century: The Move from Sacramental to Word Ontology." *Churchman* 113, no. 4, 319–30.

Estatuto da Igreja Evangélica Congregacional em Angola. III série- n 181, Quinta-feira, 21 de Setembro de 2017. Diário da República, Órgão Oficial da República de Angola.

Forster, D. A. "Ordained deacons and the Sacraments in the Methodist Church of Southern Africa? Revisiting our doctrine and polity." Pages 181–200 in *Broken Bodies and Redemptive Tables: The Lord's Supper and its Theological, Historical and Socio-political Dimensions*. Edited by Robert Vosloo, Sipho Mahokoto and Mathinus J. Hven. Wellington: Bybel-Media, 2021. https://www.researchgate.net/publication/349398828.

George, P. A. *View of Congregationalism its Principle and Doctrines: The Testimony of Ecclesiastical History in its Favour, its Practice and its Advantages.* Boston: Congregational Board of Publication, 1880.

Gerrish, B. A. "Priesthood and Ministry in the Theology of Luther." *Church History* 34, no. 4 (1965): 404–22. https://www.jstor.org/stable/3163119.

Giles, Kevin. "House Churches." CBE International (30th April 2010). https://www.cbeinternational.org/resource/house-churches/.

Gittens, L. W. "A Journey Through the Traditional and Biblical Church Leadership Practices: With Special Consideration to Administering the Church Ordinances." D. Min Dissertation, George Fox University, 2019. https://digitalcommons.georgefox.edu/dmin/318.

Henderson, L.W. (1990) A Igreja em Angola: Um Rio com Varias Correntes. Editora Alem Mar. Luanda-Angola.

Homan, G. "The Plague in the Sixteenth Century and Now." *JAMA* 63, vol. 2 (1914): 183.

Kelly, J. N. D. *Epistles of Peter and Jude.* London: Bloomsbury Publishing, 2001.

Korsah, L. A. "Towards an Understanding of Priesthood in the Realistic Sense from the Perspective of New Testament Theology." *Journal of Religion and Theology* 4 no. 2 (2020): 6–9. https://www.researchgate.net/publication/342530963.

Korsah, L. A. and F. Appiah-Kubi. "Towards an Understanding of Ministerial Priesthood in the Light of Priesthood of the Baptized." *Asian Horizons* 9, no. 2 (2015): 310–23. https://www.researchgate.net/publication/342134711.

Methodist Church of South Africa. *The Methodist Book of Order: The Laws and Discipline of the Methodist Church of Southern Africa.* 12th Edition. Methodist Publishing House, 2016. https://methodist.org.za/index.php/resources/book-of-order/.

The Mission of the American Mission Board to West Central Africa: Pioneer Work, 1881. Boston: American Board of Commissioners for Foreign Mission, 1882. https://archive.org/details/MN41621ucmf_2/page/n5/mode/2up?view=theater.

Muller, J. J. *What Are They Saying about Theological Method?* New York: Paulist Press, 1984.

O'Collins, G. and Michael Keenan Jones. *Jesus Our Priest: A Christian Approach to the Priesthood of Christ.* New York: Oxford University Press, 2010.

Ogden, Greg. *The New Reformation: Returning the Ministry to the People of God.* Grand Rapids: Zondervan Publishing House, 1990.

Ogera, E. Okelloh. "Jesus Christ as Ker: Toward an Africa High Priest Christianity." Pages 239–55 in *Who Do You Say That I Am? Christology in Africa.* Edited by Rodney L. Reed and David K. Ngaruiya. Carlisle: Langham Global Library, 2021.

Paul, F. J. *Roman and Evangelical Christianity: A study of Origins and Development.* Fisherwick Place, Belfast: Church House, 1940.

Pogorelc, A. J. "Social Construction of the Sacrament of Orders." *Religions* 12, no. 5 (2021): 290. https://www.mdpi.com/journal/religions.

Price, J. E. A. *Handbook of Congregationalism*. England: Quinta Press, 2012.
Sproul, R. C. *The Reformation Study Bible*. English Standard Version. Reformation Trust Publishing, 2015.
Standing Committee of the Anglican Diocese of Sydney. "Lay & Diaconal Administration of Holy Communion." (2004) http://www.sds.asn.au/sites/default/files/synod/lay_and_diaconal_administration.pdf?doc_id=NTMxNA.
Stott, J. *One People*. Downers Grove: InterVarsity Press, 1968.
Tinker, M. "Language, Symbols and Sacraments: Was Calvin's View of the Lord's Supper Right?" *Churchman* 112, no. 2 (1998): 131–49. https://www.academia.edu/download/382804699.
Woodhouse, J. "Lay Administration of the Lord's Supper: A Change to Stay the Same." *Churchman*, 113, no. 4 (1999): 307–18.

2

False Prosperity Pronouncements in 1 Kings 22:1–28 and Reflections for the Church

Florah M. Kidula
Africa International University, Kenya

Abstract

This chapter employs a historical grammatical approach to examine the proclamation of false prosperity in 1 Kings 22:1–28 and thereafter reflects on how this event sheds light on the phenomena today. 1 Kings 22:1–28 records a pre-battle consultation between two kings of Israel and several prophets on whether Israel should go to battle to reclaim Ramoth-Gilead from Syria. About four hundred prophets foresee prosperity and advise pursuit. Micaiah, on the other hand, boldly proclaims doom, thereby sparking a prophetic conflict. This text yields important insights that shed light on the contemporary practice of false prosperity theology (which the study defines as unfaithful representation of God or misuse of his word towards mere self-gratification). The insights are derived from (1) the prophets' devotion, (2) the motivation of prophecy, (3) their reaction to a contrary prophecy from a true prophet, (4) the supernatural influence of their prophecy, (5) the Deuteronomic criteria of discerning false prophecy and, (6) the demonstration of true prophecy through Micaiah. After exploring these insights, the study carries out a theological reflection on how they relate to false prosperity theology in the church today. 1 Kings 22:1–28 is a benchmark of false prosperity proclamations, which the church can learn from, for its edification and to safeguard the truth of God's word.

Key words: false prosperity, falsehood, false prophecy, prosperity theology, prophetic conflict, Micaiah, Ahab, 1 Kings 22

Introduction
Background and context

Authorship of the book of Kings is attributed to either Jeremiah[1] or a composer who lived twenty years later in the Babylonian exile.[2] Historical-critical views of twentieth-century scholars such as Martin Noth, Frank Moore Cross and Gerhard von Rad contend for either single or multiple authorship.[3] This study focuses on the final form, while adopting the canonical approach followed by evangelical scholars such as Paul House and Richard Nelson, who consider the book a unified work by a single author.[4]

The book originated during the period of Israel's defeat and hopelessness as the people tried to make sense of the exile, due to their failure to keep Yahweh's commandments.[5] It was designed to define Israel's identity and to provide guidance for them in the crisis.[6]

The text of 1 Kings 22:1–28 records a pre-battle consultation between two kings of Israel and several prophets, whereby some of the prophets pronounce a false prophecy of prosperity for battle and one proclaims the true prophecy. The subsequent verses (29 to 40) recount the battlefield events, whereby Ahab dies in battle.

The events in this text take place in Samaria, towards the end of Ahab's reign in 853 BC.[7] Before this battle in chapter 22, Ahab led two war campaigns

---

1. Donald J. Wiseman, *1 and 2 Kings: An Introduction and Commentary*, Tyndale Old Testament Commentary (Downers Grove: IVP Academic, 2008), 53. They held that Jeremiah (or one of his companions) compiled the books from around 580 BC at Mizpah, before he went down to Egypt.

2. Wiseman, *1 and 2 Kings*, 53.

3. Mordechai Cogan, ed., *1 Kings: A New Translation with Introduction and Commentary*, 1st ed, The Anchor Bible, vol. 10 (New York: Doubleday, 2001), 96–100.

4. Paul R. House, *1, 2 Kings*, New American Commentary (Nashville: Broadman & Holman, 1995), 38; Richard D. Nelson, *First and Second Kings, Interpretation, a Bible Commentary for Teaching and Preaching* (Atlanta: John Knox Press, 1987), 4.

5. McConville, "Kings, Book of," in *Dictionary of the Old Testament Historical Books* (Downers Grove: InterVarsity Press, 2005), 624.

6. McConville, "Kings, Book of," 632.

7. House, *1, 2 Kings*, 40.

against Syria (1 Kgs 20) and was victorious in both. The interactions of Israel and Syria continue in 2 Kings 1–10; 13. Syria (אֲרָם) lay to the east of Israel. It posed a threat to Israel, mainly during the reigns of Ben-Hadad (880–840) and Hazael (840–805). The contested region, Ramoth-Gilead, lay strategically at the border of Syria and Israel, at the east of River Jordan.

The text is a historical narrative, blended with the sub-genres of predictive prophecy (vv. 6d, 11–12 and 15b) and two vision accounts (vv. 17; 19–22). It can be more specifically classified as a "battle report" (cf. Num 21:21–24; Judg 3:26–30). All the verses report direct speech, except vv. 1 and 2. Therefore, the text is largely also a dialogue report. A parallel narration of 1 Kings 22:1–28 is found in 2 Chronicles 18:1–27.

This narrative adds to the overall picture of sin, false prophecy and divine judgment in 1 Kings and in the Old Testament. 1 Kings begins with the demise of David and the enthronement of Solomon, who enjoys prosperity but entertains foreign wives who mislead him into idolatry, hence the split of Israel into the Southern and Northern kingdoms. The book then narrates the character of kings in both kingdoms, where the failure of the nation in its covenant commitment leads to exile by Assyria and Babylon later on in 2 Kings. The study text provides a conclusion to the Ahab narratives that began in 1 Kings 16:29. Ahab, one of the kings in the Northern kingdom, was known to be a wicked and ungodly king (16:32; 20:32–34; 21), and the narrator's selection of events from 16:29 to 21:29 prepares the readers for his judgment. The purpose of 1 Kings 22:1–40 as a whole is to recount Yahweh's inevitable final judgment of Ahab.[8] 1 Kings 22:1–28 functions literarily as the staging of this judgment which then materializes in vv. 29–40. This staging takes the form of a pre-battle consultation between Ahab and the prophets.

Structure

>Setting: (vv. 1–2)
>Mission: Reclaiming Ramoth-Gilead (v. 2)
>>Problem A: Need for alliance with Jehoshaphat (v. 4a)
>>Resolution A1: Alliance accepted (v. 4b)
>>Problem B: Whether it is Yahweh's will to go to battle (v. 5)
>>Trial Resolution B1: Prophecies of prosperity (vv. 6–14)

---

8. Daewook Kim, "Ahab and Saul (1 Kgs 22.1–38)," *Journal for the Study of the Old Testament* 43, no. 4 (June 2019): 525–38, 534, https://doi.org/10.1177/0309089217743161.

- The 400 prophets say yes (v. 6)
    - Problem(s) B1: The need to consult another prophet (v. 7), Micaiah, but this prophet will probably prophesy doom (8–9).
- Zedekiah and the 400 prophesy victory (vv. 10–12)
    - Trial Resolution to Problem B1: Messenger tries to influence Micaiah's prophecy (vv. 13–14)

Trial Resolution B2: Prophecies of doom (vv. 15–27)
- Micaiah prophesies amiss (vv. 15–16)
- Vision 1: Israel scattered as sheep without a shepherd (v. 17)
    - Problem to Vision 1: Ahab grumbles (v. 18)
- Vision 2: A spirit from Yahweh to deceive Ahab's prophets (v. 19–23)
- Resolution to the Micaiah problem (vv. 24–27)
    - Zedekiah insults Micaiah (vv. 24–25) and Micaiah detained (vv. 26–27)

Trial Resolution B3: Battle outcome to prove true prophecy (v. 28)

The interest of our study lies in Problem B, which is to inquire concerning Yahweh's will for battle. The problem receives three responses: a prediction of victory (B1), a prediction of doom (B2) and a pending of Yahweh's will to the battle outcome (B3).

Study of Key Sections
Problem A: Need for alliance with Jehoshaphat (vv. 1–4)

This section sets the agenda for the events that run up to 22:40. Ahab rhetorically asks his servants why Israel has not regained Ramoth-Gilead. This he does rhetorically in the presence of Jehoshaphat.[9] The question indicates a decisiveness in Ahab's mind and indignation in his heart.[10] It is also aimed at "arousing shame and resentment" among his servants.[11] Upon Ahab's request,

---

9. Jehoshaphat had five army commanders, overseeing an average of 232,000 soldiers each, besides those soldiers stationed in fortified cities all over Judah (2 Chron 17).

10. R. W. L. Moberly, "Does God Lie to His Prophets?: The Story of Micaiah Ben Imlah as a Test Case," *Harvard Theological Review* 96, no. 1 (January 2003): 1–23, 4; Patricia J Berlyn, "Checkmate: The King Is Dead," *Jewish Bible Quarterly* 22, no. 3 (July 1994): 151–62, 156.

11. Simon John De Vries et al., *1 Kings*, Word Biblical Commentary, Vol. 12 (Waco: Word Books, 1985), 266.

Jehoshaphat, a pious king (2 Chr 17:3–4), accepts to support Ahab in battle, despite Ahab's bad reputation. The Chronicler suggests that Jehoshaphat was induced (תוס) by Ahab to support the cause after a splendid welcome party (2 Chr 18:2).

Problem B: Whether it is Yahweh's will to go to battle (vv. 5–28)

Kings in the Ancient Near East oftentimes sought the will of the gods before going to battle.[12] The verb דָּרַשׁ carries a sense of inquiring or investigating a matter.[13] Here in verse 5, it is used in a theological sense where Yahweh is the object of the inquiry. When used in connection with the phrase יְהוָה דְּבַר "word of Yahweh," it refers to "an immediately expected oracle (of Yahweh) which, is hoped, will give direction and help in acute emergency."[14] The intention of Jehoshaphat, therefore, was that they seek Yahweh's instructive word for the battle against Ramoth-Gilead, and that they do so through recognized prophets.

Trial resolution B1 (vv. 5–14): The prophecy of the four hundred and its problems

Ahab's four hundred prophets (הַנְּבִיאִים כְּאַרְבַּע מֵאוֹת) encourage him to go to battle. Prophetic consultations for battle were a norm in Israel, even during the priestly times (c.f. Judg 20:27–28; 1 Sam 23:9; 30:7).[15] This, though, is the first recorded instance where kings of Israel consult prophets before battle. The previously recorded cases involve priests (cf. Num 27:21; 1 Sam 30:7–8).

The four hundred prophets are neither identified as avowed prophets of Baal nor prophets of Yahweh. Ahab simply calls them "prophets." The word נָבִיא is a general term (cf. 1 Kgs 13; 18) for those who would inquire from a deity. Here specifically, Yahweh is the intended object of inquiry (vv. 5, 7, 8, 16). However, the relationship of the four hundred prophets with Yahweh is suspect, considering the convener of the assembly – Ahab – in whose kingdom Yahweh's prophets experienced hostility (1 Kgs 19:14).

---

12. Catherine Quine, "Reading Micaiah's Heavenly Vision (1 Kgs 22:19–23) and 1 Kings 22 as Interpretive Keys," *Zeitschrift Für Die Alttestamentliche Wissenschaft* 130, no. 2 (2018): 204–16, 207, https://doi.org/10.1515/zaw-2018-2006.

13. Ludwig Köhler et al., *The Hebrew and Aramaic Lexicon of the Old Testament*, Study ed. (Leiden; Boston: Brill, 2001), 233.

14. Leipzig Wagner, "דָּרַשׁ," in *Theological Dictionary of the Old Testament. Volume III: Gillûlîm – Haras*, ed. Gerhard Johannes Botterweck and Elmer Ringgren, rev. ed. (Grand Rapids: Eerdmans, 1997), 293–307, 299.

15. Cogan, *1 Kings*, 497.

Two suggestive details on the authenticity of the prophets are found in verse 6, in their reply to the king. Firstly, it is possible that they only wished for the victory instead of explicitly predicting it. Although all English translations render the verb "give" (וְיִתֵּן) as an imperfect, it varies from the conjugation in verse 12 (וְנָתַן) which is translated the same way. It is possible that here (v. 6), it is a jussive, hence the translation "May the Lord give it." Such a case would mean that the prophets did not answer Ahab's question directly, but only wished for Yahweh's victory. Secondly, the prophets use the title אֲדֹנָי for God (which etymologically refers to the supreme being of any religion),[16] and not the Tetragrammaton (יהוה), which is the distinctive personal name of God in the OT.[17] which revealed his character to the covenant community, and was most precious and sacred to the Jews.[18] More than twenty Hebrew manuscripts as well as the Cairo Geniza read יהוה in this verse in place of אֲדֹנָי. Cogan argues that these prophets spoke in the name of יהוה but the title is emended to אֲדֹנָי as a *tiqqune sopherim* in the MT in order not to categorize false prophets with true prophets.[19] This view is disputable, because the same prophets use the covenant name of God later on in their prophecy (vv. 11–12). An emendation on such grounds would have altered all the occurrences of יהוה spoken by these prophets. It is also more likely that אֲדֹנָי would be changed to יהוה for clarity and conformity, rather than the opposite. The covenant name יהוה is the preferred title for God in the book of 1–2 Kings (occurring five hundred times). The title אֲדֹנָי (occurring forty-three times total) is used for kings and masters (thirty-seven times), in combination with יהוה (two times) and alone to refer to Yahweh (four times inclusive of 1 Kgs 22:6).[20] Based on these arguments, the use of the substitute אֲדֹנָי for the divine name is the preferable reading here. By not naming Yahweh Yahweh, their allegiance to Yahweh is suspect.[21]

---

16. "1 Kings 22 Ellicott's Commentary for English Readers," https://biblehub.com/commentaries/ellicott/1_kings/22.htm.

17. Lynn Lundquist, *The Tetragrammaton and the Christian Greek Scriptures: A Comprehensive Study of the Divine Name (YHWH) in the Original Writings of the Christian Greek Scriptures*, 2nd ed. (Portland: Word Resources, 1998), 5.

18. Herbert F. Stevenson, *Titles of the Triune God: Studies in Divine Self-Revelation*, Text (Westwood: Fleming H. Revell Co, 1956), 20.

19. Cogan, *1 Kings*, 490. Cogan notes that the Targum also uses the Tetragrammaton.

20. The other three occurrences are in 1 Kings 3:10, 3:15 and 2 Kings 19:23. 1 Kings 3:10 (of the Lord being pleased with Solomon's request); 3:15 (Solomon before the ark of the Lord), and 2 Kings 19:23 (which quotes Isaiah's oracle against Assyria).

21. Jerome T. Walsh, *1 Kings: Studies in Hebrew Narrative & Poetry*, Berit Olam (Collegeville: Liturgical Press, 1996), 345.

Jehoshaphat proposes further inquiry about God's will (v. 7). Although it was common practice to test omens against each other in the Ancient Near East,[22] confirming prophecy through another prophet is not witnessed in the Bible.[23] The prepositional phrase that Jehoshaphat employs, "a prophet of the LORD" (נָבִיא לַיהוָה) explicitly specifies the identity of who is to seek Yahweh (unlike the generic "prophets" that Ahab employed; v. 6).[24] The mere need for further inquiry, and Jehoshaphat's specification raises doubt about the four hundred.

Micaiah is introduced in verse 8. His identity is not revealed anywhere else in the OT. His relationship with Ahab was unfriendly. The perfect שְׂנֵאתִיו (v. 8) denotes experience, which requires the translation "I hate him."[25] The causal clause כִּי לֹא־יִתְנַבֵּא עָלַי טוֹב כִּי אִם־רָע (v. 8) provides grounds for Ahab's present hatred. The imperfect יִתְנַבֵּא in this clause functions not as a prediction of the future (that Micaiah will prophecy evil) but as an expression of the regular occurrence, hence a customary use of the imperfect יִתְנַבֵּא, best translated, "he never prophesies good upon me."[26] Ahab's attitude towards Micaiah indirectly characterizes the four hundred prophets as those whom Ahab loves because they prophesy favorably to him.

In verses 10–12, the four hundred reinforce their previously stated prophecy (vv. 5–6), perhaps incited by Jehoshaphat's doubt[27] as the assembly awaits the arrival of Micaiah.

Zedekiah enacts his prophecy[28] using iron horns. He was either the leader of the crew, or he may have been simply speaking on their behalf.[29] The use of enactment is similar to the prophetic traditions of Jeremiah and Ezekiel.[30]

---

22. Lester L. Grabbe, *Priests, Prophets, Diviners, Sages: A Socio-Historical Study of Religious Specialists in Ancient Israel* (Valley Forge: Trinity Press International, 1995), 72.

23. Michael J. Biggerstaff, "Unfulfilled Predictions in Kings," *Conversations with the Biblical World* 39 (2019): 43–63, 48.

24. Iain W. Provan, *1 and 2 Kings* (Grand Rapids: Baker Books, 2012), 162; Bill T. Arnold and John H. Choi, *A Guide to Biblical Hebrew Syntax* (New York: Cambridge University Press, 2003), 9.

25. Arnold and Choi, *A Guide to Biblical Hebrew Syntax*, 55.

26. Arnold and Choi, 58.

27. Gene Rice, *Nations under God: A Commentary on the Book of 1 Kings*, International Theological Commentary (Grand Rapids: Eerdmans, 1990), 184.

28. Gordon D. Fee and Douglas K. Stuart, *How to Read the Bible for All Its Worth*, 4th ed. (Grand Rapids: Zondervan, 2014), 202.

29. House, *1, 2 Kings*, 236.

30. Johannes Lindblom, *Prophecy in Ancient Israel*, 9th reprint (Philadelphia: Fortress Press, 1980), 165; Robert R. Wilson, "Prophecy and Society in Ancient Israel," in *The Bible and Liberation: Political and Social Hermeneutics*, ed. Norman K. Gottwald (Maryknoll: Orbis Books,

Enactment symbols would arouse emotions in the audience such as fear, hope or urgency and these would strengthen the spoken oracle.[31] The noun (קֶרֶן) "horn" metaphorically means "strength" (cf. Deut 33:17; Zech 2:1; Jer 48:25).[32] Zedekiah inspired strength and power by conceptualizing Israel overpowering Syria in battle. He also claims that his prophecy is the very oracle of Yahweh by using the messenger speech כֹּה־אָמַר יְהוָה ("Thus says the Lord"), which presented "a self-confirmation of the messenger and his legitimation before the person(s) addressed" (2 Kgs 9:1–3, 4–10, 11–13).[33]

There are some differences between the words of the four hundred in verse 12, and earlier in verse 6. The covenant name of God "Yahweh" is present in verse 12 whereas אֲדֹנָי "Lord" is employed in verse 6 in an attempt of validation and associating closely with Yahweh. There is an addition of the verb צָלַח "prosper" and the object רָמֹת גִּלְעָד "Ramoth Gilead" to the statement which makes the prophecy less ambiguous. The verb נתן "give" now appears as a *waw* consecutive perfect (whereas it is a jussive in v. 6) which shows that they are giving a definite prediction of future victory. These tactics of Zedekiah and his company are only attempts at false legitimizing of their prophesies. These attempts only add suspicion to their authenticity.

In verses 13–14, the narrator leaves the grand scene and shifts to Micaiah's location, in order to give us an idea of what transpired behind the scenes. The messenger tells Micaiah that the four hundred prophets' words are of "one mouth" (פֶּה־אֶחָד) and "good towards the king" (טוֹב אֶל־הַמֶּלֶךְ) (cf. Josh 9:2). The cognate of "one mouth" in Akkadian denotes "action in unison and common cause."[34] The messenger establishes that the words of the four hundred prophets pleased King Ahab and that those prophets had a common goal to speak favorably to the king.

The messenger then asks Micaiah to speak good or favorably (וְדִבַּרְתָּ טּוֹב), that is, words that are "pleasant," "desirable" and "friendly"[35] (cf. Num 10:29; Esth 7:9 and Ps 45:2) and to be in one accord in his words with the four hundred (כִּדְבַר אַחַד מֵהֶם). He wants Micaiah to please the king just as the four

---

1983), 201–34, 210.

31. Lindblom, *Prophecy in Ancient Israel*, 172.

32. Köhler et al., *The Hebrew and Aramaic Lexicon of the Old Testament*, 1144–45.

33. Siegfried Leipzig Wagner, "אמר," in *Theological Dictionary of the Old Testament*, ed. G. Johannes Botterweck and Helmer Ringgren, trans. John Willis, vol. I (Grand Rapids: Eerdmans, 2011), 328–45, 339.

34. Cogan, *1 Kings*, 491.

35. Ludwig Köhler et al., *The Hebrew and Aramaic Lexicon of the Old Testament* א – ע, Study ed. (Leiden; Boston: Brill, 2001), 370–71.

hundred are doing but Micaiah takes an oath in Yahweh's name (חַי־יְהוָֹה) that he will only speak that which Yahweh speaks (v. 14; cf. Deut 13:1–11; 18:14–22).

The narrator's inclusion of the messenger's move to arm-twist Micaiah's prophecy points to the pliable nature of prophets who came before Ahab. It reveals that prophets could be talked into prophesying to please the king. The four hundred knew Ahab's desire and they prophesied to please him.[36]

Trial resolution B2 (vv. 15–27): Micaiah's prophecy and its problems
In this section, Micaiah arrives at the threshing floor and he at first gives a favorable prophecy, which Ahab disputes. He then prophecies doom in two prophetic visions accounts, which earn him mockery from Zedekiah and detainment by Ahab.

In verses 15–16, Ahab questions him as he had done the four hundred, though there is a difference in his question. While he asked the four hundred in the singular, he now asks Micaiah in the plural (הַאֵלֵךְ and אֶחְדָּל versus הֲנֵלֵךְ and נֶחְדָּל).[37] One view sees the inclusion of the multitude as a means that Ahab uses to intimidate Micaiah by setting up the crowd against him.[38] A different view argues that Ahab might have recognized the ambiguity of the four hundred in their prophecy, which did not specify which king the Lord would give victory to (וְיִתֵּן אֲדֹנָי בְּיַד הַמֶּלֶךְ; v. 6) therefore he spoke in the plural for his own inclusion and to get a definite reply.[39] Ahab could also have done so in the hope that Micaiah would easily favor Jehoshaphat, who is a godly king.[40] Either way, his tactic is an attempt to manipulate prophecy towards his desired end.

Micaiah first responds as the messenger had asked him to speak – his words are "good" toward the king just like those of the four hundred. He also addresses Ahab directly in the singular despite having been questioned in the plural, and so he beats the plurality trick of Ahab. His words echo the prophecy of the four hundred just before Micaiah arrived (v. 12), including the covenant name of God.

---

36. Leon James Wood, *The Prophets of Israel* (Grand Rapids: Baker Book House, 1979), 107.
37. Jesse Rainbow, "Micaiah Ben Imlah (1 Kings 22) and the Grammar of the Biblical War Oracle," *Journal of Biblical Literature* 138.3 (2019): 537–57, 551, https://doi.org/10.15699/jbl.1383.2019.727879.
38. Gina Hens-Piazza, *1–2 Kings*, Abingdon Old Testament Commentaries (Nashville: Abingdon Press, 2006), 216.
39. Rainbow, "Micaiah Ben Imlah," 554.
40. Walsh, *1 Kings*, 348.

The plot in verses 17–23 reveals that this was not Micaiah's intended prophecy. One view suggests that there was sarcasm in the form of irony in Micaiah's response, which is unheard by the reader and not clearly evident in the text.[41] This is the preferred view in this study, which also explains Ahab's reply (v. 16). Micaiah repeats the words of Ahab's prophets sarcastically in order to ridicule them (and thereby communicate that they are giving a false prophecy), and to taunt Ahab for being pleased by their false words.[42] The sarcasm prepares for and adds force to his true prophecy which comes next (vv. 17–23). It also heightens the contrast between Yahweh's true word and false prophecy.[43] Finally, it also acts to test Ahab on whether he was being sincere[44] and challenges him to demand the truth,[45] which is what he does next.

In verses 17–23, Micaiah gives two vision accounts, which are his true prophecy. In the first vision (vv. 17–18), Israel is scattered up the mountains like sheep without a shepherd. It is then confirmed that they have no master, and so they should retreat back to their homeland. The vision is reminiscent of Ezekiel 34:5–6, which speaks of Israel being forsaken by its kings. The term רֹעֶה is associated with rulers (Ezek 34:4) and with David (v. 23) and therefore is a metaphor for a king here (cf. Jer 25:34; Zech 13:7; 2 Sam 5:2).[46] The verb פוץ "scatter" (Ezek 34:5, 6; 1 Kgs 22:17) conveys defeat (cf. Num 10:35; 1 Sam 11:11; Ps 68:2). Micaiah's vision metaphorically describes Israel defeated on the battlefield and being without its king[47] who is Ahab.

The second (vv. 19–23) recounts a heavenly scene, resembling the setting at the threshing floor to some extent (vv. 10–12). Micaiah starts with a form of the messenger formula "Therefore hear the word of the Lord" (לָכֵן שְׁמַע דְּבַר־יְהוָה; v. 19) to validate his words as Yahweh's oracle.[48] Yahweh poses a question to the heavenly host, asking who will entice (פתה) Ahab to go into battle at Ramoth-Gilead (v. 20). The heavenly hosts engage in an interchange,

---

41. House, *1, 2 Kings*, 236; Wiseman, *1 and 2 Kings*, 186.

42. Benjamin Uffenheimer, *Early Prophecy in Israel*, Publications of the Perry Foundation for Biblical Research in the Hebrew University of Jerusalem (Jerusalem: Magnes Press, Hebrew University, 1999), 325; Moberly, "Does God Lie to His Prophets?," 7.

43. Provan, *1 and 2 Kings*, 366.

44. Provan, 186.

45. Uffenheimer, *Early Prophecy in Israel*, 325.

46. Nelson, *First and Second Kings*, 148.

47. Gwilym H. Jones, *1 and 2 Kings: Based on the Revised Standard Version*, New Century Bible Commentary (Grand Rapids: London: Eerdmans; Marshall, Morgan & Scott, 1984), 366.

48. True prophets such as Jeremiah, Isaiah and Ezekiel also use the phrase (cf. Isa 39:5; Jer 22:2; Ezek 21:3).

but one spirit comes before Yahweh and volunteers to entice Ahab, through the means of falsehood (שֶׁקֶר; v. 22).

The verb פתה occurs three times in this section (vv. 20, 21 and 22). All the instances of its occurrence in the OT denote susceptibility to an external influence.[49] In its *piel* occurrences, it denotes seduction or enticement (allurement). In 1 Kings 22, the nuance of enticement is most appropriate. The instances that involve man as the subject of enticement are motivated by sin (Prov 1:10; 16:29) or trickery for selfish gain (Judg 14:5; 16:5). Yahweh is the subject of פתה in Ezek 14:9 and Hos 2:16, so these are the closest parallels to our text. In Hosea 2:16, he says that he will entice Israel to the desert (exile) where he will speak tenderly to her (לָכֵן הִנֵּה אָנֹכִי מְפַתֶּיהָ וְהֹלַכְתִּיהָ הַמִּדְבָּר וְדִבַּרְתִּי עַל לִבָּהּ). The purpose of the enticement here is restoration. In Ezekiel 14:9, Yahweh prevailed upon the false prophets to continue in their falsity because they were set on doing evil anyway. The purpose of the enticement here was judgment. Therefore, in the OT, Yahweh is the subject of enticement when the end is restoration or judgment. Here in 1 Kings 22, Yahweh is not the direct subject of פתה though he is closely related to it because he intends for it to be carried out, and he commissions the subject (the spirit). The purpose of פתה in 1 Kings 22 is similar to that in Ezekiel 14:9, which is judgment. Yahweh intends for the spirit to entice Ahab, and make him susceptible to what is necessary for his judgment.[50]

The spirit cites its means of enticement as falsehood (שֶׁקֶר; v. 22). The occurrences of the noun שֶׁקֶר denote "an objective determination of deception and falsity."[51] In the book of Jeremiah, which has 31 percent of its occurrences, it denotes a lack of integrity displayed by the words of those who do not represent Yahweh.[52] Yahweh is never the source or implementor of deception or falsehood (שֶׁקֶר) in the OT.[53] In fact he is strongly dissociated with it (1 Sam 15:29;

---

49. Chou-Wee Pan, "פתה," in *New International Dictionary of Old Testament Theology and Exegesis* נ-שׁ, ed. Willem A. VanGemeren, vol. 3 (Grand Rapids: Zondervan, 1997), 714–16, 715.

50. Mainz R. Mosis, "פתה," in *Theological Dictionary of the Old Testament*, ed. G. Johannes Botterweck, Helmer Ringgren, and Heinz-Josef Fabry, vol. XII (Grand Rapids: Eerdmans, 2003), 162–72, 170.

51. Ladbergen H. Seebass, Oldenburg S. Beyerle, and Selsingen Grunwaldt, "שֶׁקֶר," in *Theological Dictionary of the Old Testament*, ed. G. Johannes Botterweck, Helmer Ringgren, and Heinz-Josef Fabry, vol. XV (Grand Rapids: Eerdmans, 1974), 470–77, 472.

52. Moberly, "Does God Lie to His Prophets?," 10.

53. In Jeremiah 20:7, Jeremiah accuses Yahweh of deceiving him (פִּתִּיתַנִי יְהוָה). This is a use of פתה that denotes deception. One must, however, also note that this was a lament of the prophet as he expressed his frustrations, and not a factual statement of what Yahweh had done, therefore it cannot be regarded as an instance where Yahweh used deception.

Num 23:19).⁵⁴ The closest instance of an association of Yahweh with שֶׁקֶר is here in 1 Kings 22:23 where Micaiah says that a spirit of falsehood has been given to Ahab's prophets (הִנֵּה נָתַן יְהוָה רוּחַ שֶׁקֶר בְּפִי כָּל־נְבִיאֶיךָ). This, however, does not mean that Yahweh lied, since we see earlier that he accomplishes his purpose through the means of a spirit. Furthermore, Yahweh reveals the truth to Ahab through Micaiah hence providing Ahab an opportunity to heed to the truth.⁵⁵

The nature and identity of this spirit (רוּחַ) that volunteered for the task is a matter of debate.⁵⁶ According to the text, the spirit was among the host of heaven (צְבָא הַשָּׁמַיִם; v. 19)⁵⁷ which include the heavenly beings or angels that serve God and do his bidding (cf. Ps 103:21; Luke 2:13). This spirit offered to "become a lying spirit" (וְהָיִיתִי רוּחַ שֶׁקֶר) – implying that it was not originally a lying spirit. It seems to be inherently divine, but takes a form that is related to the function it is to carry out.⁵⁸ Yahweh cannot be assumed to be the source of its falsehood.⁵⁹ Moreover, this act, being God's wise judgment as the recipient deserved, cannot be counted as an immoral or questionable act⁶⁰ on God's part.

In this heavenly scene, the four hundred prophets are referred to as Ahab's prophets. The genitives of relationship "your prophets" and "his prophets" (נְבִיאָיו and נְבִיאֶיךָ; vv. 22, 23) – the pronouns referring to Ahab – explicitly associate the four hundred with Ahab. This is notable especially in contrast

---

54. Eugene Carpenter and Michael A. Grisanti, "שֶׁקֶר," in *New International Dictionary of Old Testament Theology and Exegesis* ת-ש, ed. Willem A. VanGemeren, vol. 4 (Grand Rapids: Zondervan, 1997), 247–49, 247.

55. Geoffrey David Miller, "The Wiles of the Lord: Divine Deception, Subtlety, and Mercy in I Reg 22," *Zeitschrift Für Die Alttestamentliche Wissenschaft* 126, no. 1 (2014): 45–58, 48, https://doi.org/10.1515/zaw-2014-0004.

56. Wiseman, *1 and 2 Kings*, 187; De Vries et al., *1 Kings*, 268; Marco Conti, Gianluca Pilara, and Thomas C. Oden, eds., *1–2 Kings, 1–2 Chronicles, Ezra, Nehemiah, Esther*, Ancient Christian Commentary on Scripture (Downers Grove: InterVarsity Press, 2008), 135; Edward J. Young, *My Servants the Prophets* (Grand Rapids: Eerdmans, 1952), 141; Esther J. Hamori, "The Spirit of Falsehood," *The Catholic Biblical Quarterly* 72, no. 1 (January 2010): 15–30, 18.

57. Cogan, *1 Kings*, 492.

58. Hamori, "The Spirit of Falsehood," 29.

59. Hamori, "The Spirit of Falsehood," 20.

60. W. Roth, "The Story of the Prophet Micaiah (1 Kings 22) in Historical Critical Interpretation 1876–1976," in *The Biblical Mosaic Changing Perspectives*, ed. R. M. Polzin and E. Rothman (Philadelphia: Fortress, 1982), 106–10, 117–21, 131; J. A. Montgomery and H. S. Gehman, *A Critical and Exegetical Commentary on the Book of Kings* (Edinburgh: T&T Clark, 1951); Pierce M. Matheney and Roy Lee Honeycutt, "1–2 Kings," in *The Broadman Bible Commentary. Vol. 3: 1 Samuel, Nehemiah*, ed. Clifton J. Allen, rev. ed. (Nashville: Broadman Press, 1970), 146–296, 223. Early writers such as Kittel (1900), Montgomery (1951) and Gressman (1921), quoted by Roth, argued that this narrative reflects a primitive understanding in early Israel that God had to do questionable acts in order to keep the universe in order.

with Jehoshaphat's request for "a prophet of Yahweh" (נָבִיא לַיהוָה; v. 6). One can easily conclude that these four hundred prophets served the interests of Ahab.⁶¹ Wisemen sees them as "nationalistic prophets . . . uncritically loyal to Ahab . . . since they aimed to please him rather than proclaim the truth."⁶²

It is finally revealed that the four hundred's prophecy was actually a product of the spirit of falsehood. Zedekiah mocks Micaiah's visions as he strikes him (to humiliate him: cf. Lam 3:10; Mic 4:14; Job 16:10; Ps 3:8).⁶³ The prophecy was an insult to the king whom he was bent on pleasing and it implied that he, Zedekiah, was a false prophet who deserved death (Deut 18:18–20) – "an accusation of capital crime."⁶⁴ By his sarcastic question (v. 24), Zedekiah claims that he is the one speaking Yahweh's truth, and he indirectly refutes that the Spirit of God spoke to Micaiah as well.⁶⁵ His aim is to discredit Micaiah's prophecy. Micaiah's response implies that Zedekiah will be a victim of the outcome of the true prophecy.⁶⁶ King Ahab then commands that Micaiah be detained (v. 26) with minimal provision of food and water (in prison rations, cf. Isa 30:20).⁶⁷ This act of Micaiah's detainment betrays Ahab's sincerity concerning inquiring from Yahweh.⁶⁸

Trial resolution B3 (v. 28): Micaiah's final word

Micaiah answers Ahab by referencing the Deuteronomic procedure of discerning true and false prophecy (Deut 18:21–22). According to this criterion, true prophecy is proved by whether or not it comes to pass. Micaiah says that if Ahab returns in safety,⁶⁹ against what he prophesied, then his prophecy shall prove to be false. Micaiah appends his last statement with the words "Hear all you people!" which further call the assembly to look for the actualization of his prophecy.

---

61. Rice, *Nations under God*, 183.
62. Wiseman, *1 and 2 Kings*, 185–86.
63. Cogan, *1 Kings*, 492.
64. Robert R. Wilson, *Prophecy and Society in Ancient Israel* (Philadelphia: Fortress Press, 1980), 211.
65. BHS suggests a probable conjecture in verse 24, which altered the form of the question that Zedekiah asked.
66. De Vries et al., *1 Kings*, 268.
67. Wiseman, *1 and 2 Kings*, 187.
68. Uffenheimer, *Early Prophecy in Israel*, 325; Grabbe, *Priests, Prophets, Diviners, Sages*, 72.
69. Jones, *1 and 2 Kings*, 369.

A Theological Reflection of False Prosperity Prophecies in the Church

In this theological reflection, the exegetical findings are pointed out in light of the church practices and experiences that concern false prosperity theology.

Simply stated, prosperity theology, as it is understood today, advances metaphysical ideologies through the medium of faith. The teachings encourage believers that their relationship with God guarantees the provision of their earthly needs upon either their positive confession, giving in church, or a number of actions proposed by the proponents of the theology. The accused preachers oftentimes only speak affirming messages, yet with a motive of exploitation or greed.

Phiri and Maxwell write, "[the prosperity gospel] is the most sweeping movement within the Continent of Africa."[70] According to the 2006 Pew Forum on Religion and Public Life study, more than 80 percent of believers in Kenya, Nigeria and South Africa[71] who took an interview about their convictions regarding prosperity theology teachings indicated that they firmly upheld some prosperity theology beliefs. For instance, most participants believed that God's blessing to them is proportional to their confession of faith.[72] The influence of prosperity theology has infiltrated many other denominations beyond Pentecostalism. Currently, the presence of prosperity theology churches is most noticeable through Independent mega-churches, especially those that commenced in the mid-1970s, though many more have emerged ever since.[73] These realities of the spread of prosperity theology call for a serious introspection by the church about its beliefs and teachings. The influence of prosperity theology cannot be ignored in ecclesial and theological conversations of our century.

This study has examined a case of prosperity theology within the nation of Israel. The study concludes that the four hundred prophets who prophesied

---

70. Joe Maxwell and Isaac Phiri, "Gospel Riches: Africa's Rapid Embrace of Prosperity Pentecostalism Provokes Concern – and Hope," *Christianity Today* 51 no. 7 (July 2007): 22–29, 26.

71. The movement of Renewalists (Pentecostals and Charismatics) is growing faster than religions like Islam. The 2006 Pew Forum on Religion and Public Life study reported that 147 million out of the 890 million population in Africa are Pentecostals and Charismatics. Within the 147 million are over a quarter of Nigerians, a third of South Africans and more than fifty percent of Kenyans.

72. Maxwell and Phiri, 24.

73. Babatunde A. Adedibu and Benson O. Igboin, "Eschato-Praxis and Accountability: A Study of Neo-African Pentecostal Movement in the Light of Prosperity Gospel," *Verbum et Ecclesia* 40, no. 1 (October 31, 2019): 1–8, 5, https://doi.org/10.4102/ve.v40i1.1987.

victory for Ahab in 1 Kings 22 were false prophets while Micaiah was a true prophet. The following theological reflections are drawn from the study.

i. The devotion of the four hundred to Yahweh is questionable since they did not make use of his personal title for such an important task (v. 6). Whereas false prosperity prophets may not be identified in the contemporary church by their use of certain names of God, the indirect implication of their devotion to Yahweh is crucial. Yahweh's true devotees will represent him faithfully.

This is corroborated by the fact that, Jehoshaphat, a pious King, casts doubt on the prophecy of the four hundred, and requests to hear from another prophet of Yahweh (v. 7). His piety likely opposed the ongoing prophecy, and the alliance he was making with Ahab, a wicked king. When believers are committed to their personal relationship with God, it is easier for them to discern truth and falsity.

ii. The prophecy of the four hundred is at first ambiguous and unclear, and may be only a wish (v. 6). It only becomes clear when opposition is presented. Individual church leaders may have their personal opinions or desires about issues, but faithfulness to accurately represent God against personal preferences should prevail.

iii. The four hundred sought to validate their prophecy when it was challenged. When Micaiah is summoned, they make their prophecy clearer, use the personal title of God, use the messenger formula, and their leader adds symbolism to their act (vv. 11–12). Their increased zeal reveals that they were trying to prove themselves right and be on top of their competition. Such competition for validation is not necessary for a servant of Christ, who relies upon God, and not himself, to fulfill the truth.

iv. The four hundred had a common purpose of speaking favorably to the king rather than being faithful to Yahweh (v. 13). The four hundred are also referred to as "prophets of Ahab" rather than "prophets of Yahweh" (vv. 22–23). When a servant of Christ seeks to please his audience, then faithfulness to Yahweh is easily compromised. The preacher becomes a servant of the people. As Paul clarified, he was not seeking for man's approval, for then he would not be God's servant (Gal 1:10).

v. Ahab, a wicked king with a history of disobedience to Yahweh, easily entertains the four hundred (unlike with Micaiah). The preferred company of Christian leaders easily reveals their convictions. When avowed sinners find a welcoming environment around preachers and not a conviction regarding their deeds, then the preachers should question their allegiance.

vi. Yahweh sent a lying spirit to influence the words of the four hundred (1 Kgs 22:20–23). It is theologically unthinkable that Yahweh would allow a lying spirit to deceive his true prophets. Usually, it is said that false prophets prophesy from their hearts and minds (Isa 9:14f; Ezek 13:7, 9), but in this case, we see a supernatural influence.[74] 1 Kings 16–22 shows that Ahab's heart was set on idolatry and disobedience to Yahweh. Similarly, the conduct of the prophets identifies them as people opposed to Yahweh's will. A similar incident in Ezekiel 14:6–11 illustrates that Yahweh would lead prophets into false prophesy if their hearts and those of their hearers were already set on disobedience and so the false prophecies would in turn be an instrument for their judgment. The New Testament also indicates that divine delusion will be an agent of God's judgment in the end times (2 Thess 2:3–11). The "man of lawlessness" who will have a great following will offer a lie to the masses, who will be thrown into delusion by God such that they will not be able to receive the truth. The reason for the deception is so that "they all may be judged who did not believe the truth, but took pleasure in wickedness."[75] These texts lead to the conclusion that false prophecy is at times an instrument of judgment sent by God on people whose hearts are already set on disobedience.

vii. Zedekiah resorts to violent means of challenging the prophecy of Micaiah, who we know to be a true prophet. He strikes Micaiah and mocks his prophecy (v. 24). His actions were not comely for a prophet of Yahweh, and this speaks to his moral conduct. The moral conduct of a preacher reveals his true identity. A tree is known by its fruit (Luke 6:43–45).

viii. The prophecy of the four hundred proves to be false according to the Deuteronomic criteria of determining true prophecy (Deut 18:21–22) since Israel was defeated and Ahab killed in battle at Ramoth-Gilead (vv. 33–36). God's word always proves its truthfulness and effects its purpose.

ix. The four hundred associated themselves with Yahweh in a manner similar to that of a true prophet. It is possible for false prophets to associate themselves with Yahweh and even exhibit zeal, charisma and confidence in their claims, yet their words are false. This reality recalls the words of Jesus, who said that not all who call him "Lord! Lord!" will enter the kingdom of heaven, and neither will those who spoke in his name and performed mighty acts in his name, yet are not known by him (Matt 7:21–23).

x. Recipients of prophecy may have a role to play in false prosperity prophecy. First, although Jehoshaphat acted piously by raising alarm about the authenticity of the four hundred (v. 7), he remains silent about the matter

---

74. Wood, *The Prophets of Israel*, 107.
75. Gregory H. Harris, "Does God Deceive?: The 'Deluding Influence' of Second Thessalonians 2:11," *The Master's Seminary Journal* 16, no. 1 (2005): 73–93, 73–75.

in the heat of the prophetic conflict, and later joins Ahab in war (a move that was later rebuked by Jehu in 2 Chr 19:2). His silence and diplomatic attitude indirectly give permission for the perpetuation of false prophecy. Secondly, Ahab contributes to the falsity in the manner of his cordial relationship with the prophets. He even supports Zedekiah's insult of Micaiah by detaining him. Ahab had already purposed to go to Ramoth-Gilead (v. 3), and he only sought a religious permit from the prophets[76] and even so only when requested by Jehoshaphat. Indeed, he, in essence, did not need to choose between the two sets of prophets but between his self-satisfying desires and Yahweh's will.[77] It is possible that the audiences' self-seeking desires motivate false prophets to prophesy false prosperity, especially when people's hearts have strayed away from God as Ahab's had. Paul speaks of such a state when people no longer endure sound doctrine, but gather for themselves teachers to satisfy their own desires and support their positions (2 Tim 4:3). The absence of sound doctrine that shuns false prophecy, and the appetite to gratify fleshly desires create a suitable context for the flourishing of false prosperity prophecy. Similarly, there should be rebuke on false doctrine, since silence about it indirectly gives it consent.

Conclusion

The study and reflection of 1 Kings 22:1–28 reveals that a false prophet attends to people's rather than God's interests, is lacking in his moral conduct, may feel the need to validate himself to his audience using various means, associates and takes council with the wicked, prophesies his wishes rather than God's word, and is not devoted to his relationship with God, or even lacks a relationship with God. They also reveal that God may allow false prosperity as an agency of judgment for people who have neglected his ways and are determined to follow their hearts against God's will. Finally, they show that the audience, sometimes play a role in motivating the pronouncements of false prosperity. In an age where false prosperity preaching is rampant, it is crucial for the church to consider these pointers as it strives to safeguard the truth of scripture.

---

76. Harris, "Does God Deceive?," 80–81.
77. Moberly, "Does God Lie to His Prophets?," 15; Robert B. Chisholm Jr., "Does God Deceive," *Bibliotheca Sacra* 155, no. 617 (January 1998): 11–28, 16.

Bibliography

"1 Kings 22 Ellicott's Commentary for English Readers." https://biblehub.com/commentaries/ellicott/1_kings/22.htm.

Adedibu, Babatunde A., and Benson O. Igboin. "Eschato-Praxis and Accountability: A Study of Neo-African Pentecostal Movement in the Light of Prosperity Gospel." *Verbum et Ecclesia* 40, no. 1 (October 31, 2019): 1–8. https://doi.org/10.4102/ve.v40i1.1987.

Arnold, Bill T., and John H. Choi. *A Guide to Biblical Hebrew Syntax*. New York: Cambridge University Press, 2003.

Berlyn, Patricia J. "Checkmate: The King Is Dead." *Jewish Bible Quarterly* 22.3 (July 1994): 151–62.

Biggerstaff, Michael J. "Unfulfilled Predictions in Kings." *Conversations with the Biblical World* 39 (2019): 43–63.

Carpenter, Eugene, and Michael A. Grisanti. "שָׁקַר." Pages 247–49 in *New International Dictionary of Old Testament Theology and Exegesis* שׁ-ת, Volume 4. Edited by Willem A. VanGemeren. Grand Rapids: Zondervan, 1997.

Chisholm, Robert B. Jr. "Does God Deceive." *Bibliotheca Sacra* 155, no. 617 (January 1998): 11–28.

Cogan, Mordechai, ed. *1 Kings: A New Translation with Introduction and Commentary*. 1st ed. The Anchor Bible, Volume 10. New York: Doubleday, 2001.

Conti, Marco, Gianluca Pilara, and Thomas C. Oden, eds. *1–2 Kings, 1–2 Chronicles, Ezra, Nehemiah, Esther*. Ancient Christian Commentary on Scripture. Downers Grove: InterVarsity Press, 2008.

De Vries, Simon John, David A. Hubbard, Glenn W. Barker, Bruce M. Metzger, and Simon John DeVries. *1 Kings*. Word Biblical Commentary 12. Waco: Word Books, 1985.

Fee, Gordon. *Gospel and Spirit: Issues in New Testament Hermeneutics*. Grand Rapids: Baker Books, 1991.

Fee, Gordon D., and Douglas K. Stuart. *How to Read the Bible for All Its Worth*. 4th edition. Grand Rapids: Zondervan, 2014.

Grabbe, Lester L. *Priests, Prophets, Diviners, Sages: A Socio-Historical Study of Religious Specialists in Ancient Israel*. Valley Forge: Trinity Press International, 1995.

Hamori, Esther J. "The Spirit of Falsehood." *The Catholic Biblical Quarterly* 72, no. 1 (January 2010): 15–30.

Harris, Gregory H. "Does God Deceive?: The 'Deluding Influence' of Second Thessalonians 2:11." *The Master's Seminary Journal* 16, no. 1 (2005): 73–93.

Hens-Piazza, Gina. *1–2 Kings*. Abingdon Old Testament Commentaries. Nashville: Abingdon Press, 2006.

House, Paul R. *1, 2 Kings*. New American Commentary. Nashville: Broadman & Holman, 1995.

Jones, Gwilym H. *1 and 2 Kings: Based on the Revised Standard Version*. New Century Bible Commentary. Grand Rapids: London: Eerdmans; Marshall, Morgan & Scott, 1984.

Kim, Daewook. "Ahab and Saul (1 Kgs 22.1–38)." *Journal for the Study of the Old Testament* 43, no. 4 (June 2019): 525–38. https://doi.org/10.1177/0309089217743161.

Köhler, Ludwig, Walter Baumgartner, M. E. J. Richardson, Johann Jakob Stamm, and Benedikt Hartmann.. *The Hebrew and Aramaic Lexicon of the Old Testament* ע - א. Study ed. Leiden; Boston: Brill, 2001.

Lindblom, Johannes. *Prophecy in Ancient Israel*. 9th reprint. Philadelphia: Fortress Press, 1980.

Lundquist, Lynn. *The Tetragrammaton and the Christian Greek Scriptures: A Comprehensive Study of the Divine Name (YHWH) in the Original Writings of the Christian Greek Scriptures*. 2nd edition. Portland: Word Resources, 1998.

Matheney, Pierce M., and Roy Lee Honeycutt. "1–2 Kings." In *The Broadman Bible Commentary, Volume 3: 1 Samuel, Nehemiah*, 146–296. Edited by Clifton J. Allen. Revised edition. Nashville: Broadman Press, 1970.

Maxwell, Joe, and Isaac Phiri. "Gospel Riches: Africa's Rapid Embrace of Prosperity Pentecostalism Provokes Concern – and Hope." *Christianity Today* 51, no. 7 (July 2007): 22–29.

McConville. "Kings, Book of." In *Dictionary of the Old Testament Historical Books*, 623–34. Downers Grove: InterVarsity Press, 2005.

Miller, Geoffrey David. "The Wiles of the Lord: Divine Deception, Subtlety, and Mercy in I Reg 22." *Zeitschrift Für Die Alttestamentliche Wissenschaft* 126, no. 1 (2014): 45–58. https://doi.org/10.1515/zaw-2014-0004.

Moberly, R. W. L. "Does God Lie to His Prophets?: The Story of Micaiah Ben Imlah as a Test Case." *Harvard Theological Review* 96, no. 1 (January 2003): 1–23.

Montgomery, J. A., and H. S. Gehman. *A Critical and Exegetical Commentary on the Book of Kings*. Edinburgh: T&T Clark, 1951.

Mosis, Mainz R. "פתה." Pages 162–72 in *Theological Dictionary of the Old Testament*, XII. Edited by G. Johannes Botterweck, Helmer Ringgren, and Heinz-Josef Fabry. Grand Rapids: Eerdmans, 2003.

Nelson, Richard D. *First and Second Kings. Interpretation, a Bible Commentary for Teaching and Preaching*. Atlanta: John Knox Press, 1987.

Pan, Chou-Wee. "פתה." Pages 714–16 in *New International Dictionary of Old Testament Theology and Exegesis* ש-נ, Volume 3. Edited by Willem A. VanGemeren. Grand Rapids: Zondervan, 1997.

Provan, Iain W. *1 and 2 Kings*. Grand Rapids: Baker Books, 2012.

Quine, Catherine. "Reading Micaiah's Heavenly Vision (1 Kgs 22:19–23) and 1 Kings 22 as Interpretive Keys." *Zeitschrift Für Die Alttestamentliche Wissenschaft* 130, no. 2 (2018): 204–16. https://doi.org/10.1515/zaw-2018-2006.

Rainbow, Jesse. "Micaiah Ben Imlah (1 Kings 22) and the Grammar of the Biblical War Oracle." *Journal of Biblical Literature* 138, no. 3 (2019): 537–57. https://doi.org/10.15699/jbl.1383.2019.727879.

Rice, Gene. *Nations under God: A Commentary on the Book of 1 Kings*. International Theological Commentary. Grand Rapids: Eerdmans, 1990.

Roth, W. "The Story of the Prophet Micaiah (1 Kings 22) in Historical Critical Interpretation 1876–1976." Pages 105–37 in *The Biblical Mosaic Changing Perspectives*. Edited by R. M. Polzin and E. Rothman. Philadelphia: Fortress, 1982.

Seebass, Ladbergen H., Oldenburg S. Beyerle, and Selsingen Grunwaldt. "שֶׁקֶר." Pages 470–77 in *Theological Dictionary of the Old Testament*, XV. Edited by G. Johannes Botterweck, Helmer Ringgren, and Heinz-Josef Fabry. Grand Rapids: Eerdmans, 1974.

Stevenson, Herbert F. *Titles of the Triune God: Studies in Divine Self-Revelation*. Text. Westwood: Fleming H. Revell Co, 1956.

Uffenheimer, Benjamin. *Early Prophecy in Israel*. Publications of the Perry Foundation for Biblical Research in the Hebrew University of Jerusalem. Jerusalem: Magnes Press, Hebrew University, 1999.

Wagner, Leipzig. "דָּרַשׁ." Pages 293–307 in *Theological Dictionary of the Old Testament*. Volume III: Gillûlîm–Haras. Edited by Gerhard Johannes Botterweck and Elmer Ringgren, Revised edition. Grand Rapids: Eerdmans, 1997.

———. "אמר." Pages 328–45 in *Theological Dictionary of the Old Testament*, Volume I. Edited by G. Johannes Botterweck and Helmer Ringgren, translated by John T. Willis. Grand Rapids: Eerdmans, 2011.

Walsh, Jerome T. *1 Kings: Studies in Hebrew Narrative & Poetry*. Berit Olam. Collegeville: Liturgical Press, 1996.

Wilson, Robert R. *Prophecy and Society in Ancient Israel*. Philadelphia: Fortress Press, 1980.

———. "Prophecy and Society in Ancient Israel." Pages 201–34 in *The Bible and Liberation: Political and Social Hermeneutics*. Edited by Norman K. Gottwald. Maryknoll: Orbis Books, 1983.

Wiseman, Donald J. *1 and 2 Kings: An Introduction and Commentary*. Tyndale Old Testament Commentary. Downers Grove: IVP Academic, 2008.

Wood, Leon James. *The Prophets of Israel*. Grand Rapids: Baker Book House, 1979.

Young, Edward J. *My Servants the Prophets*. Grand Rapids: Eerdmans, 1952.

3

A Clash of Cultures

A Social-Scientific Exegetical Comparative Examination of the Effects of Contextual Background on the Encounter between Christian Beliefs and Related Cultural Beliefs, in the Johanine Community New Testament Church and the African Church

Catherine W. Chege
Pan Africa Christian University, Kenya

Abstract

The assembly of the people of God, the *ekklesia*, from the Old Testament times under the old covenant to the New Testament times under the new covenant, has had to engage the religious beliefs of their cultural contexts. The church, *ekklesia*, does not exist in a vacuum. This chapter has done a social-scientific exegetical analysis of the Johannine community New Testament church and how it engaged dissenting beliefs coming from within its cultural and religious context. The converts to Christianity had encountered some religious beliefs and practices which were clashing with their previously held Hellenistic religious beliefs and practices. During the time of writing of the Epistle of 1

John, the church had reached the stage whereby some believers were trying to articulate their ecclesiological self-understanding from their Hellenistic cultural and religious context. This had resulted in dissensions from some believers who wanted to keep their previously held religious beliefs which were anti-Christian. Similarly, the African church has come of age. Just like in the first century church, there has been a resurgence of interest in incorporating traditional African religious beliefs into Christianity. This chapter has drawn lessons from the Johannine community church and its context, which can be applied to the African church in its own cultural and religious context.

Key words: ecclesiology; African church; Johannine community; culture; syncretism; 1 John 2:18–25; 1 John 4:1–6; African Traditional Religion (ATR)

Introduction
Background of the study
Since the beginning of the New Testament *ekklesia*, the gospel has always been preached to people who already had an existing cultural social-context and belief system. The Johannine early Christian community was no exception. The Christian beliefs and culture had met with previously held beliefs and culture of the ancient Greco-Roman world and some clashing had started happening at the time of writing of the epistle of 1 John. The epistle was written between 85–95 AD[1] to refute false teachings that were creeping into the church regarding some fundamental Christian doctrines.

The New Testament *ekklēsia* of the first century was established within the social, cultural and religious context of the ancient Greco-Roman world. The first cultural and religious problem the church encountered[2] was that of Judaizers who wanted to impose Jewish customs on fellow Gentile Christians. Paul had to refute them in order to establish a church that would accommodate Gentiles. After the door finally opened and the gospel was being freely preached to the Gentiles, another contextual problem arose from the believers' Hellenistic religious background. In the selected biblical texts, some members of the church are reported to have left the church because of the syncretistic religious beliefs they held about Jesus.

---

1. Clinton J. Armstrong, *Reformation Heritage Bible Commentary: General Epistles* (St. Louis: Concordia Publishing House, 2014), 334.
2. Acts 15; Galatians 2:11ff.

The Christian religious beliefs and practices and the pre-existing Greco-Roman religious beliefs and practices were clashing in some respects. Some Johannine community church believers had started trying to articulate their ecclesiological self-understanding and identity from the perspective of their Hellenistic background. Secessions by some members had already started happening. The author is therefore addressing these challenges and laying down, once again, the principal doctrines of Christianity.

Similarly, the African recipients of the gospel were not found in a vacuum. They were already preoccupied with their own traditional religious thought system. Several African scholars have produced studies detailing the traditional cultural and belief systems of a few African people groups.[3] Like the Johannine community *ekklēsia* of the first century, the present-day African church has reached the stage whereby believers are articulating their ecclesiological self-understanding from their African cultural context. In the attempt to define itself in its context, the African church has found itself caught between two extreme viewpoints. On one extreme there are those who advocate for fully preserving African identity and culture[4] as they practice Christianity thus embracing syncretism, for example, the African Initiated Churches (AICs). This is what happened with the secessionists of the Johannine community church. On the other extreme end are those who consider African traditional cultural practices as "primitive and to be feared and spurned."[5] There is need, however, for African Christians to be able to express themselves and live out their Christian life within their African context but without syncretizing the gospel. This chapter seeks to discover ways in which this can be realized.

Between the two extremes, this chapter has identified Mburu[6] and Turaki[7] as among African scholars who have offered practical solutions to the problems encountered when the Christian beliefs and African beliefs clash. They have

---

3. John S. Mbiti, *African Religions & Philosophy*, 2nd rev. and enl. ed. (Portsmouth: Heinemann, 1990); Adebisi G. M. Adedeji, "African Concept of God, Evil and Salvation in African Traditional Religion (Atr): Critique from Cultural View Point," *Journal of Global Intelligence & Policy* 5.9 (Winter 2012): 45–55; Molefi Kete Asante and Ama Mazama, eds., *Encyclopedia of African Religion* (Thousand Oaks: SAGE, 2009) among others.

4. Jele S. Mangany and Johan Buitendag, "A Critical Analysis on African Traditional Religion and the Trinity," *HTS Theological Studies* 69, no. 1 (January 2013): 1–13, 1.

5. Cuthbeth Tagwirei, "The 'Horror' of African Spirituality," *Research in African Literatures* 48, no. 2 (2017): 22–36, 23, https://doi.org/10.2979/reseafrilite.48.2.03.

6. Tavis Bohlinger, "African Hermeneutics: Extensive Interview with Elizabeth Mburu," *Logos* (25 February 2021), https://www.logos.com/grow/african-hermeneutics-extensive-interview-with-elizabeth-mburu/.

7. Yusufu Turaki, *Engaging Religions and Worldviews in Africa: A Christian Theological Method* (Carlisle: HippoBooks, 2020).

suggested ways of engaging with and incorporating African traditional culture in the interpretation of Scripture and in Christian practice, while avoiding the danger of syncretism and remaining true to the gospel of Jesus Christ. Turaki applauds the contribution made by African theologians Mbiti and Idowu, among others, to detail the traditional African beliefs and practices. However, he argues that the works of most of these scholars have mainly used descriptive and comparative methods. They are, therefore, only beneficial in providing knowledge and understanding of the traditional religion. They fall short of providing practical solutions as they do not help the African Christian to relate their Christian faith meaningfully to their past cultural heritage.[8]

The main objective of this chapter is to demonstrate how the African church can articulate its ecclesiological self-understanding without losing its African cultural heritage and without syncretizing the message of the gospel. This has been achieved by drawing lessons from the events of the Johannine community church dispute, and insights by authors regarding incorporation of the African cultural heritage without syncretizing the gospel. Social scientific criticism has been used in order to help delve into the contextual backgrounds that inform beliefs and practices of both the Johannine early church community and the African church.

This chapter limits itself to the events described in the selected biblical texts of 1 John 2:18–25 and 4:1–6. It focuses on the dissensions in the Johannine church relating to clashing of cultures between the believers' Christian and Hellenistic context. One example of an African attempt to contextualize the gospel has been cited and analyzed to demonstrate how the lessons learnt can be applied to culture.

This study has been motivated by my personal encounter in instances whereby traditional African beliefs and practices, especially in wedding negotiations, came into a clash with Christian beliefs and practices. The parties involved in the negotiations had to find a compromise based on personal conviction only. No deliberate engagement with the cultural beliefs and practices was employed. This would sometimes result in heated arguments and a standoff between the parties. The findings of this chapter will provide suggestions of proper methods of engagement with the African traditional context and help make such encounters amicable.

---

8. Turaki, xxvii.

An Overview of the First Century Social-Cultural and Religious Context of 1 John 1:18–25 and 4:1–6

John's audience understood the message of the epistle of 1 John within their context. To assist the modern-day reader to understand this message as the first-century believers did, this chapter offers a social-scientific exegetical analysis of 1 John 2:18–25 and 4:1–6. Social scientific criticism is the branch of biblical criticism "interested in ancient social and cultural systems implicit in the writings of the New Testament."[9] Social-scientific criticism of the Bible allows the author to analyze the social and cultural dimensions of the text and of its environmental context.[10] It goes beyond historical context analysis which traditionally asks questions concerning dating, authorship, language, genre, historical background and specific historical events that shape the text. It asks questions to do with the social patterns and cultural conditions which most likely characterized the ancient New Testament world.

The ancient Greco-Roman world, which was the context of the first-century New Testament church, was built on the foundational social and cultural values of honour and shame.[11] Honour "is the value of a person in his or her own eyes," that is, one's claim to worth, "plus that person's value in the eyes of his or her social group."[12] Individual people, were never known or valued because of their own uniqueness, but in terms of their dyad, that is, other people and things within their social context.[13]

Two elements of the honour and shame model,[14] dyadism[15] and challenge-reposte,[16] have been applied to the guiding texts of 1 John 1:18–25 and 4:1–6 to identify the underlying social and cultural factors that informed the actions of the members of the Johannine community church. The dissenters in John's

---

9. Craig L. Blomberg and Jennifer Foutz Markley, *A Handbook of New Testament Exegesis* (Grand Rapids: Baker Academic, 2010), 85.

10. John Hall Elliott, *What Is Social-Scientific Criticism?*, New Testament Series (Minneapolis: Fortress Press, 1993), 15.

11. Bruce J. Malina, *The New Testament World: Insights from Cultural Anthropology*, rev. ed (Louisville: Westminster/John Knox Press, 1993), 28.

12. Malina, *The New Testament World*, 31.

13. Jerome H. Neyrey, "Group Orientation," in *Biblical Social Values and Their Meaning: A Handbook*, ed. John J. Pilch and Bruce J. Malina (Peabody: Hendrickson Publishers, 1993), 88–91, 88.

14. David Arthur DeSilva, *Honor, Patronage, Kinship & Purity: Unlocking New Testament Culture* (Downers Grove: InterVarsity Press, 2000), 23.

15. Malina, *The New Testament World*, 67.; Jerome H. Neyrey, "Dyadism," in *Biblical Social Values and Their Meaning: A Handbook*, ed. John J. Pilch and Bruce J. Malina (Peabody: Hendrickson Publishers, 1993), 49–52.

16. DeSilva, *Honor, Patronage, Kinship & Purity*, 21.

community church were posing a challenge through their false teachings which needed to be responded to by the apostle John.

Dyadism

Dyadism means that individuals basically depend on their social context for their sense of identity, their self-understanding in relation to their role and status in society, their pattern of behaviour and belief system.[17] A dyadic person is therefore group-embedded and group oriented or collectivity-oriented. This is in contrast to individualism whereby a person's behaviour and decisions in life are not based on the opinion of others, they are distinct and unique to the individual.

In a dyadic community, a comprehensively ordered system of beliefs and practices governs the life of the members. This means that the implication of belonging to a social group with certain beliefs and practices may have had an impact on some of the Christians' doctrinal stand. Firstly, religion was not a private matter, it was a communal affair. Christians of the Johannine community church were under communal pressure from their contextual background to either hold onto their Christian beliefs or to align with their traditional religious system. The secessionists chose the latter and started putting pressure on the others to follow them through teaching a syncretistic gospel.

Challenge-response

Challenge-riposte is an attempt by a person to gain honour at someone else's expense by posing a challenge.[18] The honourable person may be subjected to insult or some other challenge. He is then culturally expected to respond, or offer a riposte, and counter the challenge in order to retain his honour. The New Testament world was characterized by many instances of challenge-riposte social contests of honour whereby a person or group of people challenges another with the intent of dishonouring them and acquiring the other person's honour. The person challenged was always expected to respond. The challenge-response element of society made the ancient New Testament world agonistic in nature.[19] The society looked upon all social interactions outside the family or substitute family (circle of friends, ingroup) as a contest for honour.

---

17. Malina, *The New Testament World*, 67.
18. DeSilva, *Honor, Patronage, Kinship & Purity*, 21.
19. Malina, *The New Testament World*, 37.

The apostle John found himself in this kind of challenge when false teachers arose in his churches. The new Christian doctrines were clashing with the Greco-Roman religious beliefs and practices. This provided the occasion for challenge by some dissenters in the church. This combative behaviour was a common cultural phenomenon, and may explain the aggression of the false teachers against John's teachings and the equally strong response from John. The secessionists not only left the church but tried to get others to leave also. This would essentially bring dishonour to John, the apostle of the church. Cerinthus was one of the leading false teachers who were opposing him.[20]

Greco-Roman religion

In the Greco-Roman context, there was no separation between the spiritual and the secular life.[21] Religion was intertwined with social and political life and was controlled by the state. Religion was part of the fabric of life and was practiced both publicly and privately at home. The idea of religion as a separate body of beliefs and practices about the supernatural did not exist. There was therefore no notion of secularism or religion. The term religion only gradually came into existence in relation to Christianity as a way of differentiating Christianity from cultural religious beliefs and practices. It was much later in the sixteenth and seventeenth centuries that the West created the idea of existence of different religions based on the different belief systems and cultures. This idea was then exported to other parts of the world by the colonizers and names assigned to the different belief systems, for example, Hinduism, among others.

One of the major instruments of Hellenization in the first century Greco-Roman world was religious syncretism.[22] There was apparently an effort to universalize local religions by cross-matching the names of deities from different cultures. Local deities of the conquered lands after Greek conquest were given names of Greek gods. This continued with the Roman conquest, the local deities were given additional names of Roman gods. The Samaritans, for example, identified YHWH with the Greek god Zeus and the Roman equivalent god Jupiter. This resulted in a proliferation of deities while at the same time creating a kind of monotheism by assimilating the various supposed equivalent

---

20. Irenaeus, *Irenaeus: Against Heresies* – Book 3 (3.3.4; 3.11.1), edited by Alexander Roberts. Accessed 12 April 2023, http://gnosis.org/library/advh3.htm.

21. N. T. Wright and Michael Bird, *The New Testament in Its World: An Introduction to the History, Literature and Theology of the First Christians* (London: SPCK, 2019), 240.

22. Wright and Bird, *The New Testament in Its World*, 229.

divine beings from different cultures into one. Hellenization did not displace all aspects of the previous culture but mainly gave old beliefs and practices new expression. The old cultures blended with the Greek culture to create hybrid cultural expressions. Acceptance of this kind of syncretism made Hellenization become very powerful.

The first century Johannine Christian community were confronted with a dilemma after becoming Christians. They realized that the doctrine of Christ as taught in the church and the doctrine of Christ as derived from the viewpoint of the Greco-Roman religion were not compatible. They were torn between being faithful to the doctrines of their new-found Christian faith or their Greco-Roman religious traditions. This resulted in an ecclesiastical upheaval. There are those who decided to hold on to the doctrines that were incompatible with the Christian faith and left the church. They decided to incorporate the clashing traditional religious beliefs into their Christian faith and teach others to do the same. This was an attempt to apply Hellenistic thinking in the interpretation of Christian doctrine and create a syncretistic teaching of the humanity and deity of Christ.

The Greco-Roman religion beliefs that were contrary to Christian beliefs included Gnosticism and Docetism, among others. Gnosticism[23] and Docetism[24] taught that a truly divine being could neither become genuinely human nor suffer in a physical body. From this perspective, Jesus's humanity and divinity were brought into question. Gnosticism is derived from the Greek word *gnosis* meaning knowledge. Gnosticism came about in the first two centuries AD either as a mutation of Christianity or Judaism or as an independent religion that rapidly became intertwined with Christianity.[25] Gnosticism held the belief that the spiritual world was good, and the physical world was evil. The real motivation behind Gnosticism is theodicy. It held that a good God could not have made a world filled with evil, suffering and death.[26] Docetism, a form of Gnosticism, is derived from the Greek word *doke*, which means "to seem," "to appear." The Docetists taught that Jesus only "seemed" or "appeared" to be human but in reality, he was purely a spirit projecting an outward appearance.

---

23. D. M. Scholer, "Gnosticism," in Ralph P. Martin and Peter H. Davids, eds., *Dictionary of the Later New Testament & Its Developments* (Downers Grove: InterVarsity Press, 1997), 990–1013.

24. Wright and Bird, *The New Testament in Its World*, 1352.

25. David Brakke, *The Gnostics: Myth, Ritual, and Diversity in Early Christianity* (Cambridge: Harvard University Press, 2010), ix.

26. Wright and Bird, *The New Testament in Its World*, 253.

According to Irenaeus, Cerinthus was one of the most prominent teachers of Gnosticism and an opponent of the apostle John.[27] Irenaeus cited the gospel of John in his writings. The gospel and the epistle of 1 John, cited in this chapter, originated within the same context of the early Christian Gentile mission, the emergence of early gnostic thought, and the destruction of the temple which occurred in AD 70. [28] The epistle also addresses the same issues of dissension and gnostic teaching.

Cerinthus taught that Jesus was not born of a virgin but was the son of Mary and Joseph.[29] In addition, he said that the divine Christ descended on this human Jesus during baptism and then departed from Jesus during his death with Christ remaining impassible. The apostle John is said to have been so upset by his teachings that he could not agree to even be in the same public bathhouse with Cerinthus.

From the foregoing, it can be observed that there are elements of the carrying culture that can be detrimental and others instrumental for the preaching of the gospel and the welfare of the church. The detrimental ones need to be identified and filtered out. According to Turaki[30] a Christian and biblical approach is necessary when dealing with the realities of traditional culture, whether the Greco-Roman culture and religion of the first century or the African Traditional religion in modern Africa.

The African Church Religious, Social and Cultural Context

In the African traditional culture, just as in the first century Greco-Roman world, there is no distinction between spiritual and secular life. Mbiti[31] describes the African as being "notoriously religious." Religion permeates every aspect of life so fully that it is not easy or possible to isolate it. According to Mbiti,[32] African religion is communal, and it covers all aspects of life from birth to

---

27. Irenaeus, *Irenaeus: Against Heresies* - Book 3 (3.3.4; 3.11.1), edited by Alexander Roberts. Accessed 12 April 2023. http://gnosis.org/library/advh3.htm,); Wright and Bird, *The New Testament in Its World*, 1352.

28. Andreas J. Köstenberger, *John*, 4, Baker Exegetical Commentary on the New Testament (Grand Rapids: Baker Academic, 2009), 6.

29. Irenaeus, *Irenaeus: Against Heresies* - Book 3 (3.3.4; 3.11.1), edited by Alexander Roberts. Accessed 12 April 2023. http://gnosis.org/library/advh3.htm); Wright and Bird, *The New Testament in Its World*, 1352.

30. Turaki, *Engaging Religions and Worldviews in Africa*, xxviii.

31. Mbiti, *African Religions & Philosophy*, 1.

32. John S. Mbiti, *Introduction to African Religion*, 2nd ed.; reissued by Waveland Press, Inc (Long Grove: Waveland Press, Inc, 2015), 15.

long after a person has died. It is handed over from generation to generation informally through conversation, proverbs, myths and through practice. Since it is communal, it is also learned through participating in religious activities, for example ceremonies, festivals, rituals among others. This compares closely to the Greco-Roman religion which was also communal and covered all aspects of life.

In addition, Mbiti[33] observes that the African religion gives its followers a sense of security in life. It helps them deal with most of the issues of life. However, he notes that African religion has its flaws. Despite its flaws, many people after conversion to Christianity and other religions are not willing to abandon their traditional religion quickly. This, he argues, would make them feel insecure unless an alternative which gives them an additional or greater sense of security is provided. Therefore, when they become Christians, they tend to mix their traditional religion with Christianity resulting in syncretistic Christianity. That way they feel like they're not losing something valuable but gaining from both religious systems. This compares to the syncretism of Hellenization. The Greeks and Romans introduced their deities and religion in the lands they conquered. The people would cross-match names of the additional deities from other cultures with names of equivalent deities from their own culture ending up with a syncretistic religion.

This is what Mburu[34] refers to as the challenge of living dichotomized lives, whereby traditional practices such as witchcraft, ancestor worship and polygamy are still not uncommon amongst African Christians. The African Christian seems unable to see Christianity in the same way they see ATR[35] – as affecting every aspect of their lives. They are Christians when in church but when faced with life issues, they respond as the worldly people would do.

Currently, there has been a resurgence of interest in the traditional African beliefs and practices.[36] According to Lowery African ecclesiologies have grappled with the question of "how to prioritize the Christian identity without losing other identities."[37] She reports significant agreement amongst African authors that the communal "God's people" identity should be a

---

33. Mbiti, *Introduction to African Religion*, 15.
34. Elizabeth Mburu, *African Hermeneutics* (Carlisle: HippoBooks, 2019), 3.
35. ATR – African Traditional Religion.
36. Turaki, *Engaging Religions and Worldviews in Africa*, 43.
37. Stephanie A. Lowery, *Identity and Ecclesiology: Their Relationship among Select African Theologians* (Eugene: Wipf & Stock Publishers, 2017), 202.

person's principal identity.[38] However, the argument is that this "in Christ" identity should not destroy other social identities – "it should not require relinquishing other communal identities, rather it should incorporate diversity and individuality within itself." For example, Mbiti[39] argues that an African who gets converted and rejects the whole of his people's religion cuts himself off from the total life of his people. This he argues should not be the case. He recommends that where there is no real conflict between African religion and Christianity the convert should retain much of his cultural and religious background. However, in the absence of a "contextualized hermeneutic"[40] this recommendation may lead to syncretism. Both the African and biblical culture and worldviews need to be taken into consideration, but due diligence should be applied to avoid syncretizing of biblical truth.

As a solution, Mburu[41] proposes an African hermeneutic model that incorporates an extra leg which she refers to as "parallels to the African context." This is in addition to the commonly used three hermeneutical legs of: theological context, literary context, and historical and cultural context. The extra leg of "parallels to the African context" allows the reader to apply the African worldview to aid in the understanding of biblical text. This is done through identifying the points of contact between the African context and the biblical context. At the same time, it provides for a way to avoid syncretism by helping identify the wrong assumptions of the African culture and avoiding them.

The resurgence of interest in traditional African culture has been a result of what is viewed as skewed missionary Christianity. The missionaries who brought the gospel carried along their own Western culture and worldview.[42] They brought to Africa a mixture of biblical values, cultural Christianity and Western culture and its worldviews. As a result, many traditional institutions and structures which reinforced traditional beliefs have become eroded over time. Scholars have faulted missionary Christianity for having thrown away the good aspects of African culture, religion and institutions which could have been adopted and modified to become key pillars for social and communal Christianity in Africa.

---

38. Lowery, *Identity and Ecclesiology*, 189.
39. Mbiti, *African Religions & Philosophy*, 15.
40. Mburu, *African Hermeneutics*, 5.
41. Mburu, *African Hermeneutics*, 65.
42. Turaki, *Engaging Religions and Worldviews in Africa*, 6.

Unfortunately, Turaki[43] has observed that African scholarship seems to be simply replacing the era of the missionary presentation of the gospel of Jesus Christ. They are replacing the "missionaries' ideological interpretation of Africa" with the "African ideological interpretations of the gospel and the Bible,"[44] thus replacing one extreme with the other. As a result, the gospel and the Bible is not given the opportunity to confront Africa, rather, it is Africa that confronts the gospel and the Bible through her religious scholars. This leads to syncretism. To avoid such eventuality, Turaki proposes a methodology which begins with an in-depth analysis of the concerned major components of the African traditional religious worldview. He states that the purpose of this analysis is "not to understand Christianity from the perspective of African traditional culture and religion, but to understand African traditional culture and religion from the perspective of a Christian and biblical worldview."[45] This approach allows the gospel and the Bible to confront culture and therefore avoid syncretism.

A Case of the Traditional African Heritage of the Itsekiri People of Nigeria

In a 2021 video,[46] a young modern monarch who is also a professing Christian was coronated in the traditional African Itsekiri style to become the new monarch – Olu of Warri. The Olus of Warri and the Itsekiri people have maintained their traditional African culture while at the same time professing Christianity. For example, the coronation of the Olu of Warri is a complex ritual that involves both Christian and traditional elements, including the use of sacred symbols and the participation of traditional religious leaders. The way in which the new Olu of Warri presented himself during the coronation is an example of an attempt to contextualize their Christianity.

Despite the coronation being a traditional ceremony, the newly coronated Olu of Warri used the platform to worship Jesus during his coronation. Before giving his speech, he led the congregation in a Christian worship song exalting Jesus as the "king of Warri." Through the words of the song the Olu was able to refocus attention from himself toward Jesus before he made his acceptance speech.

---

43. Turaki, *Engaging Religions and Worldviews in Africa*, xxvii.
44. Ibid, xxviii.
45. Ibid, xxix.
46. Channels Television, "Full Video: Coronation Ceremony Of 21st Olu Of Warri 21/08/2021," https://www.youtube.com/watch?v=6242wDWyPSo.

The coronation of the Olu of Warri in 2021 is a good example of African traditional culture that has managed to survive and has been used as a platform for preaching the gospel. The newly coronated Olu of Warri, a staunch Christian, chooses not to reject the leadership opportunity that comes with his cultural heritage. He embraces it and uses the platform to preach the gospel. The traditional culture of the Itsekiri people, however, may still have cultural elements which need to be confronted by the gospel and the Bible. A more in-depth study may be necessary to investigate each of the cultural elements and how the Olu handled each to eliminate any possibility of syncretism.

Exegetical Analysis of the Biblical Text of 1 John 2:18–25; 4:1–6

The following is an exegetical analysis of the selected biblical texts against a backdrop of the ancient Greco-Roman context. In the selected biblical texts, a group of people had seceded from the Johannine community church because they held different views concerning, among others, some fundamental Christian doctrines related to the identity of Christ. The secessionists not only left the church, but they also tried to influence others through their false teaching. They were in essence also challenging John's authority as the apostle of the church in the typical challenge-riposte element of the ancient Greco-Roman culture. This necessitated a response from the apostle John. The epistle of 1 John was addressed to a mainly Gentile Johannine community as a way of addressing this crisis.[47]

1 John 2:18 – ἐσχάτη ὥρα ἐστίν (It is the last hour)

In verse 18, the author, the apostle John,[48] makes an important announcement to draw attention to the events that were happening at the time of writing of the epistle of 1 John. He addresses the believers using the vocative παιδία (children). This is an indicator of emotion and emphasis.[49] This implies that the subject matter John is about to address is very concerning. He follows it by sounding the alarm – ἐσχάτη ὥρα ἐστίν (it is the last hour). The predicate nominative (ἐσχάτη) ὥρα (the last hour) is used here to apply rhetorical force

---

47. David Edward Aune, ed., *The Blackwell Companion to the New Testament*, Blackwell Companions to Religion (Chichester; Malden: Wiley-Blackwell, 2010), 348. Since the time of Ireneaus, tradition has ascribed authorship of 1 John to the apostle John.

48. Aune, *The Blackwell Companion to the New Testament*, 344.

49. Daniel B. Wallace, *Greek Grammar beyond the Basics: An Exegetical Syntax of the New Testament*, 9th reprint (Grand Rapids: Zondervan, 2001), 68.

to the urgency of the hour – "it is the last hour." He goes on to link the events with the imminent return of Christ at the end of time. He gives the reason for his conclusion using the conjunction ὅθεν (whereby, on account of which). The reason why the dissenters have arisen is because it is the last hour. He labels the dissenters ἀντίχριστος (antichrists). The presence of the antichrists is, therefore, confirmation – γινώσκομεν (we know) – that it is the last hour. By referring to the time of writing this epistle as the ἐσχάτη ὥρα (last hour), this could be an indicator that the church had been around for long enough for them to believe they had now come close to Christ's return – the last hour.

In agreement Culy argues that those who interpret John's use of the phrase ἐσχάτη ὥρα as referring to the entire period between Christ's ascension and his second coming distract attention from the rhetorical force of the expression.[50] This is not an announcement of an event way off in the future in John's thinking – it is said with urgency. Beale also, in line with this conclusion, interprets ἐσχάτη ὥρα as an allusion to Daniel's prophesied eschatological hour (Dan 11:36).[51]

1 John 2:19 – ἐξ ἡμῶν ἐξῆλθαν (They went out from among us)

John confirms that the dissenters have already left the church. ἐξῆλθαν (they went out) can be classified as a consummative[52] aorist which indicates that the action of leaving has reached a conclusion. They were therefore infiltrating the church with their teachings from the outside. He argues that they left because from the beginning they did not really belong to their community – οὐκ ἦσαν (they were not) of them. By using the imperfect ἦσαν, identified as a progressive imperfect[53] in this case, he implies that their actions in the past showed that they had never belonged to the community. He follows this with the pluperfect[54] μεμενήκεισαν (they would have remained) as further proof of why in his opinion they left – they never belonged from the beginning.

---

50. Martin M. Culy, *1, 2, 3 John: A Handbook on the Greek Text* (Waco: Baylor University Press, 2004), 47.

51. G. K. Beale, "The Old Testament Background of the 'Last Hour' in 1 John 2,18," *Biblica* 92, no. 2 (2011): 231–54, 237.

52. Wallace, *Greek Grammar Beyond the Basics*, 559.

53. Wallace, *Greek Grammar Beyond the Basics*, 543.

54. Constantine R. Campbell, *Basics of Verbal Aspect in Biblical Greek* (Grand Rapids: Zondervan, 2008), 52. The pluperfect provides supplemental information, beyond the imperfect, that describes, explains, and gives background.

According to John, the dissenters may have never really embraced the doctrines of the Christian faith. They had just joined the church without commitment to the doctrines and had essentially never really become Christians. Initially, the dissenters may not have found any problem in becoming Christians because their Hellenistic background allowed for additional deities.[55] The new deities and religious beliefs could be blended with their previous deities and cultural beliefs to produce hybrid cultural expressions. With time though, they reached a point whereby they started bringing up arguments against the Christian doctrines which were clashing with their previous Greco-Roman religious beliefs.

Another reason for leaving the Christian community may be deduced to be pressure from the two opposing religious, social and cultural contexts – Christian and the Hellenistic contexts. Having come from a dyadic background, whereby individuals' allegiance to group beliefs and practices prevailed and was expected over individual choices, they had succumbed to the pressure. The dissenters had decided to go back to the group norms and beliefs of their former Greco-Roman beliefs and syncretize the Christian beliefs which John and the other apostles had taught them.

1 John 2:22–23 and 1 John 4:2–3 – ἀντίχριστος (The antichrists)

John goes on to define who the dissenters were, based on Christian doctrine. He labels them as ἀντίχριστος (antichrist) (2:18) and says these are those who (1) 2:22a – deny that Jesus is the Messiah – ὁ ἀρνούμενος ὅτι Ἰησοῦς οὐκ ἔστιν ὁ Χριστός (the one denying that Jesus is the Christ); (2) 2:22b – deny the divinity of Jesus – ὁ ἀρνούμενος τὸν Πατέρα καὶ τὸν Υἱόν (the one denying the Father and the Son); and (3) 4:2 – deny that Jesus came in the flesh – Ἰησοῦν Χριστὸν ἐν σαρκὶ ἐληλυθότα.

These three definitions of the antichrist indicate that the dissenters were influenced by the Greco-Roman religious beliefs of Gnosticism[56] and Docetism.[57] Ireneaus[58] refutes this basing his argument on Matthew 3:16–17 and says that the Christ did not descend into Jesus during baptism, nor was one the Christ, and the other Jesus. This explains why the dissenters brought Jesus's

---

55. Wright and Bird, *The New Testament in Its World*, 240.
56. D. M. Scholer, "Gnosticism," in Ralph P. Martin and Peter H. Davids, eds., *Dictionary of the Later New Testament & Its Developments* (Downers Grove: InterVarsity Press, 1997), 993.
57. Wright and Bird, *The New Testament in Its World*, 1352.
58. Irenaeus, *Irenaeus: Against Heresies*, Book 3.

humanity and divinity into question. They were using their previous traditional reasoning which was clashing with the biblical truth John was teaching.

Conclusion

From the foregoing, it is evident that the kind of challenge that the Johannine community church was facing from its Greco-Roman religious background can be compared to the challenges the African church is facing from its ATR background. These two communities, the ancient New Testament church and the modern African church, are grappling with a clash of beliefs from their religious and cultural backgrounds and the Christian context. The selected biblical texts show how John addressed the concerned issues of the ancient New Testament church. In the modern African context, the issues concerned are being wrestled with by the concerned African people themselves as they live life, and by scholars who range from one extreme worldview to the other.

There are lessons that the African church can learn from the way John handled the problem in the Johannine community church. The format John uses includes (1) Identifying and defining the issues concerned (2:22–23; 4:2). By asserting that Jesus is the Messiah (2:22a), he is divine – he is the Son of God (2:22b), and that he came in the flesh (4:2), John is identifying where the problem is. These three cardinal beliefs of the Christian faith were being challenged by the dissenters. If any one of them is denied, then the Christianity being professed becomes syncretistic, and it stops being Christianity. (2) John labels those propagating the clashing traditional beliefs as antichrist. He is essentially showing that the concerned traditional beliefs do not pass the scriptural test and so its proponents are antichrist. John's argument therefore rendered the traditional Docetic and Gnostistic interpretation of the identity of Christ as false and incompatible with Christian belief. (3) John was not negating the whole of the Greco-Roman social-cultural background; he is addressing particular issues and analyzing them based on Scriptures. He is setting an example of how any tradition, ancient or modern, should be addressed. His approach agrees with that of the scholars who propose a balanced approach like Turaki and Mburu, among others.

In the modern African context, the cited example of the coronation of the monarch or Olu of Warri and the Itsekiri people[59] can be seen as an attempt by African Christians to contextualize the gospel as they live life in their context. Applying John's approach and Turaki's methodology which involves an in-depth

---

59. Channels Television, "Full Video."

study of all the concerned major components of the African traditional elements of this ceremony would indicate whether syncretism happened. This allows the gospel and the Bible to confront culture and therefore avoid syncretism. This example implies that incorporating Christian belief and practice into the African context, however noble the effort may be, is not enough by itself. It is imperative that every African cultural element be scrutinized under the lens of Scripture. Where there is a clash between the Scriptures and the traditional African cultural elements, then the Scriptures should be upheld just as John did in the dissention involving the New Testament church.

Bibliography

Adedeji, Adebisi G. M. "African Concept of God, Evil and Salvation in African Traditional Religion (Atr): Critique from Cultural View Point." *Journal of Global Intelligence & Policy* 5, no. 9 (Winter 2012): 45–55.

Armstrong, Clinton J. *Reformation Heritage Bible Commentary: General Epistles*. St. Louis: Concordia Publishing House, 2014.

Asante, Molefi Kete, and Ama Mazama, eds. *Encyclopedia of African Religion*. Thousand Oaks: SAGE, 2009.

Aune, David Edward, ed. *The Blackwell Companion to the New Testament*. Chichester; Malden: Wiley-Blackwell, 2010.

Beale, G. K. "The Old Testament Background of the 'Last Hour' in 1 John 2,18." *Biblica* 92, no. 2 (2011): 231–54.

Blomberg, Craig L., and Jennifer Foutz Markley. *A Handbook of New Testament Exegesis*. Grand Rapids: Baker Academic, 2010.

Bohlinger, Tavis. "African Hermeneutics: Extensive Interview with Elizabeth Mburu." *Logos* (25 February 2021). https://www.logos.com/grow/african-hermeneutics-extensive-interview-with-elizabeth-mburu/.

Brakke, David. *The Gnostics: Myth, Ritual, and Diversity in Early Christianity*. Cambridge: Harvard University Press, 2010.

Campbell, Constantine R. *Basics of Verbal Aspect in Biblical Greek*. Grand Rapids: Zondervan, 2008.

Channels Television. "Full Video: Coronation Ceremony Of 21st Olu Of Warri 21/08/2021." https://www.youtube.com/watch?v=6242wDWyPSo.

Culy, Martin M. *1, 2, 3 John: A Handbook on the Greek Text*. Waco: Baylor University Press, 2004.

DeSilva, David Arthur. *Honor, Patronage, Kinship & Purity: Unlocking New Testament Culture*. Downers Grove: InterVarsity Press, 2000.

Irenaeus. *Irenaeus: Against Heresies* Book 1. Edited by Alexander Roberts. http://gnosis.org/library/advh1.htm.

———. *Irenaeus: Against Heresies* Book 3. Edited by Alexander Roberts. http://gnosis.org/library/advh3.htm.

Lowery, Stephanie A. *Identity and Ecclesiology: Their Relationship among Select African Theologians.* Eugene: Wipf & Stock Publishers, 2017.

Malina, Bruce J. *The New Testament World: Insights from Cultural Anthropology.* Rev. ed. Louisville: Westminster/John Knox Press, 1993.

Mangany, Jele S., and Johan Buitendag. "A Critical Analysis on African Traditional Religion and the Trinity." *HTS Theological Studies* 69, no. 1 (January 2013): 1–13.

Marshall, I. Howard. "New Wine in Old Wineskins: V. The Biblical Use of the Word 'Ekklesia.'" *The Expository Times* 84, no. 12 (1 September 1973): 359–64. https://doi.org/10.1177/001452467308401203.

Mbiti, John S. *African Religions & Philosophy.* 2nd revised and enlarged edition. Portsmouth: Heinemann, 1990.

———. *Introduction to African Religion.* 2nd edition; reissued by Waveland Press, Inc. Long Grove: Waveland Press, Inc, 2015.

Mburu, Elizabeth. *African Hermeneutics.* Carlisle: HippoBooks, 2019.

Neyrey, Jerome H. "Dyadism." In *Biblical Social Values and Their Meaning: A Handbook.* Edited by John J. Pilch and Bruce J. Malina. Peabody: Hendrickson Publishers, 1993, 49–52.

———. "Group Orientation." Pages 88–91 in *Biblical Social Values and Their Meaning: A Handbook.* Edited by John J. Pilch and Bruce J. Malina. Peabody: Hendrickson Publishers, 1993.

Tagwirei, Cuthbeth. "The 'Horror' of African Spirituality." *Research in African Literatures* 48.2 (2017): 22–36. https://doi.org/10.2979/reseafrilite.48.2.03.

Trebilco, Paul. *Self-Designations and Group Identity in the New Testament.* Cambridge: Cambridge University Press, 2011. https://doi.org/10.1017/CBO9781139003438.006.

Turaki, Yusufu. *Engaging Religions and Worldviews in Africa: A Christian Theological Method.* Carlisle: HippoBooks, 2020.

Wallace, Daniel B. *Greek Grammar Beyond the Basics: An Exegetical Syntax of the New Testament.* 9th reprint. Grand Rapids: Zondervan, 2001.

Wright, N. T., and Michael Bird. *The New Testament in Its World: An Introduction to the History, Literature and Theology of the First Christians.* London: SPCK, 2019.

4

Church Architecture in the African Vernacular

Robert Falconer
South African Theological Seminary

Abstract

Most contemporary church buildings in Africa don't have a distinctly "Christian aesthetic" and neither do many have a meaningful African expression. There is no shortage of African church architecture by way of simple wattle and daub/concrete churches, shack churches, traditional churches from the colonial era, marquee tent churches, shopfront churches and megachurches. Traditionally, church architecture has been employed as a visual expression of a church's theology and cultural heritage. Similarly, ecclesiology may articulate into architecture. This chapter explores African vernacular in the built environment for African church architecture that provides a tactile expression of ecclesiology and theology. The methodology employed for this research project is *Architectonic Theology*, designed by me, an architect and theologian, for systematic theology. The chapter begins by exploring current contemporary architecture in Africa, namely the work of the celebrated African architect, Diébédo Francis Kéré, followed by a study on African vernacular architecture and the various church building typologies on the continent. Any theological study needs to be grounded in the biblical text, constructing a foundation for further study, and so here biblical-design principles are extrapolated from the construction motifs of Solomon's temple in 1 Kings 5–8. This provides motifs relevant to church architecture in Africa offering a hybrid solution for the following discussion that develops a synthesis between African vernacular and church architecture. Finally, I explore "form and aesthetics" for contemporary African vernacular church architecture, and offer helpful design principles, providing tactile expression for the praxis and theology of the African church.

Key words: African vernacular architecture; church architecture; hybrid architecture; sustainable architecture; local architecture; indigenous architecture; African vernacular

Introduction

There are numerous journal articles and scholarly volumes on European church architecture, including beautiful coffee table books. These are primarily historical literary works.[1] However, there is little on African vernacular church architecture. I define African vernacular architecture as those buildings on the continent that, (1) employ indigenous building technology from their specific region, (2) employ available natural resources and local labour, (3) respond meaningfully to its specific landscape, vegetation, climate and other economic factors and (4) is traditional and cultural.[2]

Furthermore, one may define architecture as the design of the structure of a building to create an envelope for shelter from the natural elements. In addition, architecture is also about the design and organization of space, and as White and White put it, "church architecture is the organization of space for worship."[3] Hildebrand argues that architecture has two themes, the first is practical, the creation of space, for private and public life, and divine worship. The second theme is artistic beauty.[4] Similarly, Ching describes architecture as follows:

> As an art, architecture is more than satisfying the purely functional requirement of a building program fundamentally, the physical manifestations of architecture accommodate human activity. However, the arrangement and ordering of forms and spaces

---

1. James F. White and Susan J. White, *Church Architecture: Building and Renovating for Christian Worship* (Claremont: OSL Publications, 1998), Preface.
2. Janet B. Hess, "African Architecture: Characteristics, History, Styles, Types, & Facts," *Encyclopedia Britannica*, 2022, https://www.britannica.com/art/African-architecture; Colleen Avice Steenkamp, "Revalidating Vernacular Techniques for a Sustainable Built Environment by Way of Selected Examples in the Eastern Cape" (Master's of Architecture dissertation, University of the Free State, 2012), x–xi.
3. White and White, *Church Architecture*, 1.
4. Dietrich von Hildebrand, *Aesthetics*, vol. 2 (Steubenville: Hildebrand Project, 2019), 47.

also determine how architecture might promote endeavors, the listed responses, and communicate meaning... Form and space presented not as ends in themselves but as a means to solve a problem in response to conditions or function, purpose, and context.[5]

Needless to say, the church building is not the church; the people are the church. However, church buildings do have a special place in the built environment, they help us "explore, discover, and articulate the Christian faith."[6] As I like to put it, church architecture is a tactile expression of our theology. Hildebrand explains, "If a building serves spiritual purposes, there exists a deep connection between its real theme and its artistic beauty." He continues, "A church should have a specifically sacred character."[7] In other words, it needs to communicate something about who God is, who we are as a church, and what we believe.

The question is, how do we incorporate church architecture with the African vernacular? This is the primary objective of this chapter. But first, we will need to explore African vernacular architecture, beginning with the award-winning African architect, Diébédo Francis Kéré. I will then turn to Scripture and highlight the construction motifs from Solomon's temple. These will provide a starting point for developing a synthesis of church architecture with the African vernacular. Finally, I highlight design considerations and offer principles for contemporary African vernacular church architecture.

African Vernacular Architecture
Diébédo Francis Kéré

The year 2022 was a significant year for architecture in Africa. Diébédo Francis Kéré was the first African laureate to win the Pritzker Architecture Prize. The annual Pritzker Architecture Prize is the world's premier architecture award of the highest honour.[8] It celebrates the achievement of a living architect or architects who have demonstrated remarkable "talent, vision, and commitment,

---

5. Francis D. K. Ching, *Architecture: Form, Space, and Order*, 2nd ed. (New York: Wiley, 1996), ix.

6. Murray A. Rae, *Architecture and Theology: The Art of Place* (Waco: Baylor University Press, 2017), 15.

7. Hildebrand, *Aesthetics*, 56.

8. The Pritzker Architecture prize is something like the Nobel Prize of architecture. It was established in 1979 by the Pritzker family of Chicago through their Hyatt Foundation.

which has produced consistent and significant contributions to humanity and the built environment through the art of architecture."⁹

Diébédo Francis Kéré has become a national hero in his country, Burkina Faso. Among others, his buildings include (1) Gando Primary School, (2) Lycée Schorge Secondary School, (3) the Serpentine Pavilion, (4) the Burkina Institute of Technology (BIT) and (5) National Park of Mali.¹⁰

According to *See Africa Today*, Kéré is respected throughout the architectural community for his "forward-thinking, and environmentally conscious designs." His buildings make use of local materials, local labour resources and participatory design methodologies, combining innovative design and social commitment. Kéré designs modern buildings that inspire an afro-futurist vision and yet are grounded in the African tradition. These innovative buildings are pragmatic and respond effectively to the African climate and context.¹¹ He has demonstrated "that traditional building methods and materials can be combined with high-tech engineering."¹² The African 2022 Pritzker laureate has also said, "No one should ever give up on attempting to develop quality simply because of their financial situation."¹³

African vernacular architecture

Indicative of Diébédo Francis Kéré's vernacular architecture, Righini tells us that there has been renewed interest in contextualism, and a re-evaluation of what appropriate technology is for design and construction in light of the vernacular traditions. Even contemporary architecture in Africa has begun to focus on local problems and employ local materials and labour, not to mention developing local stylistic motifs. These give expression to the local culture and context.¹⁴

---

9. The Hyatt Foundation, "About the Pritzker Architecture Prize," The Pritzker Architecture Prize, 2023, https://www.pritzkerprize.com/about.

10. Diébédo Francis Kéré, "Kéré: Work," Kéré Architecture (2023), https://www.kerearchitecture.com/work.

11. See Africa Today, "Meet Africa's Top Architect Diébédo Francis Kéré," *Further Africa* (blog), 2022, https://furtherafrica.com/2022/07/09/meet-africas-top-architect-diebedo-francis-kere/.

12. Amy Frearson, "10 African Architects and Designers Championing Afrofuturism," *Dezeen* (2018), https://www.dezeen.com/2018/04/06/african-architects-designers-championing-afrofuturism/.

13. See Africa Today, "Meet Africa's Top Architect Diébédo Francis Kéré."

14. Paul Righini, *Thinking Architecturally: An Introduction to the Creation of Form and Place* (Cape Town: University of Cape Town Press, 1999), 44.

Maio et al. proclaim that the tradition of vernacular architecture is vital for preserving African cultural communities and their connection to their land. While this certainly includes the built environment, it also involves "construction techniques, lifestyles, and territorial connections, which are intrinsically connected to communities."[15] The heritage of vernacular architecture has become vulnerable due to globalization, and yet "the preservation of vernacular architecture in a holistic approach is believed to revive people's faith in their own culture."[16]

Although Maio et al. write concerning a specific region in Namibia, the same is true in other African countries, where deforestation, veld fires and the scarcity of building materials have pushed local African communities to look for new construction techniques and new materials. This has resulted in substituting or even abandoning their traditional architecture, building materials and construction technology.[17] Added to this, many of these traditional buildings have either not survived the passage of time or have deteriorated making them somewhat rare, according to Opoko, Adeokun and Oluwatayo. Contrary to Righini, they believe that Africa's "rich creative tradition and cultural heritage are at the brink of extinction as the African identity is seriously threatened."[18]

Further, there is a trend in the African built environment that suppresses traditional vernacular construction technology and design in favour of non-African architecture; not dissimilar to the way they adopted "European languages, governing systems, and aspects of European culture during colonization."[19] Contemporary Africans tend to favour so-called "modern" building materials like concrete masonry blocks. Rather than appreciating their vernacular building technology and materials as "effective in their environment" and contextual to their specific "physical and cultural surroundings," many

---

15. Rui Maio et al., "Namibia's Vernacular Architecture: Insights towards the Sustainable Development of Local Communities," *Ge-Conservación*, 11 (2017): 63–70, 63.

16. Maio et al., "Namibia's Vernacular Architecture," 63.

17. Maio et al., "Namibia's Vernacular Architecture," 66.

18. Akunnaya Pearl Opoko, Cynthia Adeokun, and Adedapo Oluwatayo, "Art in Traditional African Domestic Architecture: Its Place in Modern Housing and Implications for the Training of Architects," *Global Journal on Humanites & Social Sciences*, 3 (2016): 675–78, 676.

19. Aimee Buccellato and Megan Reineccius, "Exploring Vernacular East African Architecture: Lessons for the Modern World," in *Vernacular Traditions* (Subtropical Cities 2013, Braving A New World: Design Interventions for Changing Climates, ASCA, 2013), 56, https://www.acsa-arch.org/chapter/exploring-vernacular-east-african-architecture-lessons-for-the-modern-world/.

Africans view this as archaic or old-fashioned.[20] Western architecture, on the other hand, is considered monumental, and therefore, "a sign of prosperity, modernity and technological advancement."[21]

Consequently, we need to promote African vernacular architecture because, as Story says, it "could be the last remaining ecological architecture on earth that has existed since the historical period and still favourably used until today. Each region has its own characteristics and techniques, all rooted in organic architecture that preserves their land and links to their culture."[22] There is a legitimate concern that African vernacular architecture will, in the not-too-distant future, be lost because many Africans think vernacular is obsolete and inefficient, and if they don't take up the challenge to take their vernacular architecture seriously, foreigners will.[23] Already, contemporary architects, irrespective of their ethnicity, are incorporating vernacular elements usually in their resort, tourist and even public design projects.[24]

Maina, Muhammad-Oumar and Saad explain that for us to acquire a holistic expression of traditional vernacular architecture that is truly sustainable, and that "can be applied in the modern context to address contemporary problems," it needs to take cognizance of (1) "the socio-cultural, spatial and economical issues or the technical" aspects, and (2) the "environmental aspects of vernacular and traditional architecture." These go hand in hand.[25]

African church architecture

We have seen that vernacular African architecture is dwindling due to globalization[26] and the perceived notion "that great architecture and architectural innovation originates in the developed world."[27] There is, nevertheless, an online database of African vernacular architecture compiled

---

20. Buccellato and Reineccius, "Exploring Vernacular East African Architecture," 57.
21. J. J. Maina, A. A. Muhammad-Oumar, and H. T. Saad, "Harnessing African Architectural Traditions for Environmental Sustainability" (Centre for Black and African Arts and Civilisation, The Assembly Hall, Ahmadu Bello University, Zaria Nigeria, 2018), 4.
22. The Design Story, "News: 7 Types of African Vernacular Architecture You Should Know About!," *The Design Story* (2022), https://www.thedesignstory.com/blog/news/news-7-types-of-african-vernacular-architecture-you-should-know-about.
23. Maina, Muhammad-Oumar, and Saad, "Harnessing African Architectural Traditions," 11.
24. Maina, Muhammad-Oumar, and Saad, 4, 7.
25. Maina, Muhammad-Oumar, and Saad, 1.
26. Maina, Muhammad-Oumar, and Saad, 3.
27. Buccellato and Reineccius, "Exploring Vernacular East African Architecture," 55.

by the American architect, Jon Sojkowski.[28] Maina, Muhammad-Oumar and Saad[29] point out that foreigners are the ones who collect information and create databases on traditional vernacular architecture, not Africans themselves. Yet, vernacular church architecture in contemporary Africa is scarce. Instead, we find the following common typologies:

1. A simple rectangular church building with walls constructed from wattle and daub or concrete block with a grass or tin roof. Except for a cross above the entrance, nothing else marks the building out to be a church. Other than wattle and daub, there is usually nothing vernacular about the church building.

2. A shack clad with iron sheeting, typical of architecture found in shanty towns or informal settlements. These are typically larger than domestic dwellings to accommodate the congregation. This too may have a cross above the entrance. Other than conforming to its environment, that is, the streetscape context, this typology does not express African vernacular either.

3. A traditional masonry church building typical of a denominational church like an Anglican, Methodist or Presbyterian church. These are furnished with typical English church arched windows, stepped buttresses and a small bell tower or bellcote.[30] Rather than celebrating the African vernacular, people are reminded of their colonial past.

4. A shopfront church that, like a hermit crab, finds a home in a disused space, in this case, a store. The entrance of these shopfront churches is eye-catching with unusual, and sometimes amusing names on signage above the entrance, like *Healing Tsunami Ministries*; *Run for Your Life Ministry*; *Open Heaven Ministries*; *The Resurrection Temple of God*; *Triumphant Church Inc.*, and so on. Although one might argue that these churches are contextual, they are not vernacular. Buccellato and Reineccius explain that "rapid urbanization as a result of globalization has created a host of new development challenges

---

28. Jon Sojkowski, "African Vernacular Architecture," *African Vernacular Architecture: Documentation for Preservation* (2017), https://www.africanvernaculararchitecture.com.

29. Maina, Muhammad-Oumar, and Saad, "Harnessing African Architectural Traditions," 11.

30. You can find beautifully illustrated examples of such Anglican churches in Martin's book, *The Bishop's Churches: The Churches of Anglican Bishop Robert Gray* (Cape Town: Struik, 2005).

for Africans . . . and a shortage of both time and adequate building materials to construct new housing and services. The result of this trend has been seen in other major African cities in the *adaptive re-use of many existing structures*."[31] (emphasis mine). This may well contribute to the proliferation of shopfront churches.

5. A tensile structure, a large marquee peg and pole tent often used for weddings and conferences.[32] Marquee tents usually have large arched paned windows made of translucent material like PVC or polyethylene which poorly imitates the windows found in traditional European churches. This kind of church structure is quick to put up and can be moved easily. It's a practical and convenient option.

6. A sixth typology in African church architecture is the megachurch. This is a "global religious phenomenon exerting significant social influence in urban contexts around the world."[33] Africa has some of the largest megachurches, noticeably in Nigeria, but such megachurches also exist in Kenya, Tanzania, South Africa, Ghana, Uganda and other African countries, which is indicative of Christianity's shift to the global south.[34] Ukah explains that some scholars see these megachurches "in the forefront of socio-religious change through their practices, rituals, social engagement and political activism."[35] Many of the pastors who lead these megachurches look to America for examples of contemporary culture and the Christian life, which includes imitating megachurch architecture.[36] Megachurch Christianity, according to Ukah, also has a sense of "Ecclesiastical plasticity (which) allows church founders to morph into religious entrepreneurs and innovators, to translate and transform religious and cultural ideas and habitus and imbue them

---

31. Buccellato and Reineccius, "Exploring Vernacular East African Architecture," 56.

32. Having been a missionary to Kenya, I have participated in church services from all these church building typologies.

33. Richard Burgess, "Megachurches and 'Reverse Mission,'" in *Handbook of Megachurches*, ed. Stephen Hunt, Brill Handbooks on Contemporary Religion 19 (Leiden: Brill, 2020), 243–68, 243.

34. Burgess, "Megachurches and 'Reverse Mission,'" 243–44; Asonzeh Ukah, "Sacred Surplus and Pentecostal Too-Muchness: The Salvation Economy of African Megachurches," in *Handbook of Megachurches*, ed. Stephen Hunt, Brill Handbooks on Contemporary Religion 19 (Leiden: Brill, 2020), 323–44, 325.

35. Ukah, "Sacred Surplus," 325.

36. Ukah, "Sacred Surplus," 326.

with the aura of the sacred."³⁷ African megachurch architecture, as in most other countries around the world, is designed with a shopping centre, conference centre, or hotel typology – a far cry from the African vernacular.³⁸

Vernacular church architecture in Africa is almost non-existent, except for the eleven ancient, yet impressive monolithic rock-hewn churches carved out of the red tufa in the Western Ethiopian Highlands near Lalibela. Here the church of St. George was excavated out of rock in cruciform, and the churches of St. Mary and St. Mercurius were painted with biblical murals.³⁹ These churches are still in use today. In addition, there are the African Instituted Churches (AIC), which Oduro says take their architectural cue from the Old Testament tabernacle where God instructed the ancient Israelites to use their own materials for construction. This has facilitated church building design that is patterned after their local architecture and therefore is relevant to their communities. According to Oduro, little is known about AIC vernacular architecture, and its significance is not generally known either.⁴⁰ There certainly are no easily accessible examples for further investigation other than building typologies discussed in (1) and (2) above. Be that as it may, their desire to imitate the obedience of the ancient Israelites as they built the Old Testament tabernacle is noble and praiseworthy. So, taking their lead, the following discussion will analyse the construction motifs from Solomon's Temple in 1 Kings 5–8. This will be relevant in a later discussion on African vernacular and church architecture.

Construction Motifs from Solomon's Temple

Paul House explains that the biblical author's purpose in describing the temple construction in 1 Kings 5–8 was not to give a blueprint layout of the original, rather, it was written to "overawe the reader with the grandeur and glory of the

---

37. Ukah, "Sacred Surplus," 328.
38. For a detailed discussion on Megachurch Christianity, see Wanjiru M. Gitau's book, *Megachurch Christianity Reconsidered: Millennials and Social Change in African Perspective* (Downers Grove: IVP Academic, 2018). It won the *Christianity Today 2019 Book of the Year Award* for the category of Missions and the Global church. In her book she explores the rise and the growth of megachurches in our contemporary world, especially in Africa, and notably Nairobi Chapel and its "daughter" church, Mavuno Church.
39. Hess, "African Architecture."
40. Thomas Oduro, "African Christian Theology: The Contributions of African Instituted Churches," *Ogbomoso Journal of Theology* 13, no. 1 (2008): 58–74, 66.

building."[41] We also need to keep in mind that the Old Testament's tabernacle, Solomon's Temple and the Second Temple are different building typologies to Christian church architecture, not to mention that their function was also different. The New Testament synagogue, however, has more in common with a church building. Nonetheless, the construction of Solomon's Temple presents the following helpful motifs for vernacular church architecture in Africa.

The temple was built for the praise of God's name

The newly enthroned King Solomon sent word to Hiram, the king of Tyre, and told him that he intended to build a temple for the Lord, as the Lord had told King David that his son would build a house for his name. The temple building project had a purpose, it was to be for the name of the Lord and to fulfill what God had promised Solomon's father, King David (1 Kgs 5:3, 5).[42]

Hybrid use of local and outsourced skilled labour

One might expect Solomon to make use of skilled local labour only; however, he proposed a hybrid of local and outsourced labour which may have been driven by a need to compensate for the lavish project, according to Alter.[43] He also knew that the Hebrews were not skilled lumberjacks, as were the Sidonians. The Sidonians, sometimes called Phoenicians, lived where there was abundant "timber, which they used to build ships"[44] (1 Kgs 5:6–9). Yet Solomon drafted thirty thousand men and sent them to Lebanon to help with the cedar and cypress timber – they were to do this in shifts. He had seventy thousand burden-bearers, eighty thousand stonecutters who worked in the hill country and three thousand, three hundred men who supervised the building project. Solomon's men quarried out expensive stones and dressed them in preparation for the laying of the temple foundation. Everyone was involved; the local Hebrews, Hiram's skilled workers, and even men from

---

41. Richard D. Nelson, *First and Second Kings: Interpretation: A Bible Commentary for Teaching and Preaching* (Louisville: Westminster John Knox Press, 1987), 43–44.

42. The location of verses in 1 Kings 5 are different in the Hebrew Bible compared to the English translations.

43. Robert Alter, *The Hebrew Bible: A Translation with Commentary*, Prophets (New York: W. W. Norton & Company, 2018), 455.

44. Alter, *The Hebrew Bible*, 455–56.

Gebal[45] (1 Kgs 5:13–18). Solomon employed all the means he had, and then where this was a need he outsourced additional skilled men.

Hybrid use of local and outsourced materials

Solomon also used local *and* foreign building materials. Again, he took a hybrid approach. The cedar and cypress timber was only available from the Lebanon mountain range. These were large trees of strong and durable timber which were not only excellent for large building construction, like temples, but were also considered a luxury. Cedar was used for cross beams and lining interior walls.[46] On the other hand, they likely cut stones locally, from quarries near Jerusalem[47] (1 Kgs 5:15–18; 6:7). Olivewood was also a local material (1 Kgs 6:23, 31–33). Other construction materials probably also came from the vicinity of Jerusalem. Solomon was wise and pragmatic, he sourced any materials that he could locally, and then outsourced those materials that he needed for construction from elsewhere if they were unavailable to him.

The temple design was beautiful and sacred

Although Solomon's temple was functional, it was also beautiful and sacred – it had character. 1 Kings 6:15–18 describes the beauty of the temple, how the internal walls of the house were lined with cedar timber boards, and the floor was covered with cypress wood. The cedar wood in the house was "carved in the form of gourds and open flowers."[48] The space of the inner sanctuary, lined with wood, was a cube, roughly ten metres on all sides and in volume.[49] This space was overlaid with pure gold, together with the cedar altar. The entire interior of the house was overlaid with gold, with golden chains across in front of the inner sanctuary. Two cherubim were made from olivewood and overlaid with gold. They stood about five meters high with wings spanning about two and a half meters (1 Kgs 6:20–28). Monson explains that the cherubim were

---

45. Gebal is an ancient coastal city in Lebanon, also known as Jebeil or Byblos.

46. John Monson, *Zondervan Illustrated Bible Backgrounds Commentary Set: Old Testament*, ed. John H. Walton, *Vol. 3: 1 and 2 Kings, 1 and 2 Chronicles, Ezra, Nehemiah, Esther* (Grand Rapids: Zondervan, 2009), 26.

47. Volkmar Fritz, *1 & 2 Kings*, trans. Anselm Hagedorn, Continental Commentary Series (Minneapolis: Fortress Press, 2003), 64.

48. All biblical quotations and references are taken from the English Standard Version (ESV) Bible translation, unless otherwise indicated.

49. Fritz, *1 & 2 Kings*, 73.

"winged sphinxes or cherub figures from religious and royal iconography in Egypt, (and) Mesopotamia." Solomon may have employed religious images "from surrounding cultures and put them in service of Yahweh," says Monson.[50] Regardless, the iconography and artistry were familiar to the Hebrews at the time which would have made the imagery appropriate.[51] The temple interior was specially designed to communicate beauty and sacredness.

The temple incorporated decorative symbols

Contributing to the temple's aesthetic beauty were the decorative symbols. Some symbols were local, and others were common along the Mediterranean region. Figures of "cherubim and palm trees and open flowers" were engraved on the walls of the inner and outer rooms (1 Kgs 6:29). According to Fritz, "Palm tress [sic] occur quite frequently in ancient Near Eastern art, since they represent the tree of life."[52] The doors to the entrance of the sanctuary were also covered with these same carvings, and then overlaid with gold (1 Kgs 6:32). King Hiram[53] was a skilled coppersmith who did much of the decorative work. He made:

> lattices of checker work with wreaths of chain work for the capitals on the tops of the pillars, a lattice for the one capital and a lattice for the other capital. Likewise, he made pomegranates in two rows around the one latticework to cover the capital that was on the top of the pillar, and he did the same with the other capital. (1 Kgs 7:17–18)

Hiram also crafted lily-work on the capitals of the pillars of the vestibule. The capitals were on the two pillars and above the rounded projection which was beside the latticework. There were two hundred pomegranates in two rows all around, and so with the other capital (1 Kgs 7:19–20). The craftsmanship of the temple's decorative symbols was magnificent and meticulous.

---

50. Monson, *Zondervan Illustrated Bible Backgrounds*, 27.
51. Monson, *Zondervan Illustrated Bible Backgrounds*, 27.
52. Fritz, *1 & 2 Kings*, 74.
53. Alter believes that "it is highly unlikely that the Phoenician king himself would come to Jerusalem to perform or even supervise the building work. What this refers to is that Hiram may have sent master artisans from Tyre to participate in the project." Alter, "The Hebrew Bible," 462.

The temple celebrated creativity and artistry

The decorative artistry in the "carved cherubim and palm trees and open flowers" overlaid with gold (1 Kgs 6:35), along with all the other creative craftsmanship and architectural design features of Solomon's temple demonstrates a celebration of creativity and artistry.

The temple employed technology

One might be forgiven for the oversight of technology employed in the temple. 1 Kings 6:34 tells us that there were two cypress wood doors, each with two leaves that folded. The Hebrew word is, גְּלִילִים and is translated in the ESV as "folding," and in the NASB as "turned on pivots." HALOT renders גְּלִילִים as a revolving door, but may also be a door with a spigot hinge, or a door with some sort of cylinder mechanism.[54] Be that as it may, this technology employed in the temple's ironmongery was likely more advanced than what was used in domestic dwellings.

The temple had good foundations

King Solomon commanded his labour force to quarry "out great, costly stones in order to lay the foundation of the house with dressed stones" (1 Kgs 5:17). And then we are told that in the fourth year, in the month of Ziv, the foundation of the temple was laid (1 Kgs 6:37). Without a good foundation, Solomon's Temple – or any building for that matter – would not stand very long. A building with poor foundation footing would develop structural cracks.

The temple entrance was celebrated

An entrance defines the transition from one space into the next, and in the case of the temple, from the secular everyday space into the sacred. For this reason, the entrance into the inner sanctuary is celebrated with magnificent doors crafted from olivewood and decorated with symbols, together with a lintel and five-sided door posts. The entrance to the nave was also beautifully designed with the folding doors I mentioned earlier, and these too were ornate with carved images of cherubim, palm trees and open flowers, overlaid with gold (1 Kgs 6:31–35). The pillars and their capitals to the vestibule (בָּאוּלָם) were also

---

54. Ludwig Koehler et al., *The Hebrew and Aramaic Lexicon of the Old Testament* (Leiden: Brill, 1999), 193.

beautifully decorated with latticework, pomegranates carvings and lily work (1 Kgs 7:15–22). The ESV renders בָּאוּלָם as a vestibule, and the NASB, KJV, and NET translate it as porch, as per HALOT.[55] According to Manson, the porch was set "atop a broad staircase" and was "a type of transitional passageway linking the courtyard to the temple's main room."[56] In the temple, this was one of several entrances.

The temple facilities and furniture were meticulously built

The temple project also included the design and craftsmanship of facilities and temple furniture. In 1 Kings 7:23–26 we have what is described as a molten sea which was a cast metal "round basin with an outwardly bent and decorated rim."[57] Beneath this brim were two rows of crafted gourds. The sea was filled with water and used for ceremonial cleansing, and "stood on twelve oxen, facing in all four directions," and the "brim was made like the brim of a cup, like the flower of a lily" (1 Kgs 7:25–26). There were also ten stands of bronze. These stands:

> had panels, and the panels were set in the frames, and on the panels that were set in the frames were lions, oxen, and cherubim. On the frames, both above and below the lions and oxen, there were wreaths of beveled work. Moreover, each stand had four bronze wheels and axles of bronze, and at the four corners were supports for a basin. The supports were cast with wreaths at the side of each. (1 Kgs 7:28–30)

There were four wheels "underneath the panels. The axles of the wheels were of one piece with the stands, and the height of a wheel was a cubit and a half. The wheels were made like a chariot wheel; their axles, their rims, their spokes, and their hubs were all cast" (1 Kgs 7:32–33). On the panels, there were carvings of "cherubim, lions, and palm trees, according to the space of each, with wreaths all around" (1 Kgs 7:36). House says it well when he writes, "Even these utterly functional objects were given elegance, style, and beauty. Holy objects in this temple were useful and attractive, a combination rare in the history of ritual

---

55. Koehler et al., *The Hebrew and Aramaic Lexicon*, 41.
56. Monson, *Zondervan Illustrated Bible Backgrounds*, 27.
57. Fritz, *1 & 2 Kings*, 84.

and worship."⁵⁸ There were also ten bronze basins, pots, shovels and other (presumably smaller) basins (1 Kgs 7:38–40). In addition, there were:

> the golden altar, the golden table for the bread of the Presence, the lampstands of pure gold, five on the south side and five on the north, before the inner sanctuary; the flowers, the lamps, and the tongs, of gold; the cups, snuffers, basins, dishes for incense, and fire pans, of pure gold. (1 Kgs 7:48b–50a)

All the temple facilities and furniture were meticulously designed, crafted and built, in addition to the overall temple architecture.

The temple was worthy of God

Solomon's Temple was built for the name of the Lord, that his presence may reside in the holy of holies in the temple. The temple had to be built in such a way that it would be worthy of God's presence. This tells us something about who God is, he is holy, he is blessed, he is the God of Israel and he is faithful in fulfilling his promises (1 Kgs 8:15–16). It was also a reminder of the Mosaic and Davidic covenants, and the "nature of Israel's place in history."⁵⁹ The temple was a place for God's people to worship him.

The temple had a construction timeline

Like any good building project, it appears that the temple also had a construction timeline. The first four years were taken up with the design, preparation and sourcing of materials. The foundation was built in the fourth year, and by the eleventh year, the entire construction, together with all its furniture and parts were complete. The actual construction phase took seven years (1 Kgs 6:37–38).

The African Vernacular and Church Architecture

Before we consider some practical guidelines on form and aesthetics for African vernacular church architecture, I will want to highlight those elements that help create a synthesis of church architecture and the African vernacular.

---

58. Paul R. House, *1, 2 Kings: An Exegetical and Theological Exposition of Holy Scripture*, ed. E. Ray Clendenen, New American Commentary 8 (Nashville: Broadman & Holman Publishers, 1995), 134.

59. House, *1, 2 Kings*, 128.

Learning from construction motifs gleaned from Solomon's temple in 1 Kings 5–8, we need to make sure that our church building is intentional. What is the purpose of our church building? All churches have a spiritual purpose, but what is its unique spiritual purpose? Churches also serve a practical purpose, and we need to ensure we know what that is before we begin designing.[60]

Church buildings are more than just a place to meet, they ought to tell a story about who we are and what we believe, and most importantly who God is. After all, our church architecture should be built for the praise of God's name. We also need to consider the use of skilled labour and materials. The first prize is to employ all local labour and material, but this is not always practical. One should use everything at one's disposal and only if there is a need, then look elsewhere for resources,[61] as Solomon in his wisdom did. So, consider a hybrid use of local and outsourced skilled labour and materials if there is a need to do so. However, keep in mind, as Ejiga, Paul and Cordelia explain, "African traditional architecture is essentially sustainable and had evolved culturally to suit the people. Usually, earth, timber, straw, stone/rock and thatch were constructed together with the simplest of tools and methods to build simple, liveable dwellings."[62] The reality is, however, that the influx of new people, new materials, and new construction technology puts pressure on indigenous architecture. And so, without denouncing either vernacular or modern building methods and materials, communities ought to compare them and employ those elements that are most sustainable,[63] and that best fulfill the purpose of the building without forsaking the cultural and environmental context.

Hybrid technology is an excellent approach. Employ and celebrate modern technology where there is a need in building construction and integrate it with traditional building technology. Maina, Muhammad-Oumar and Saad explain that

> . . . indigenous knowledge consists of a system of methods, customs and traditions which have evolved and been developed over many generations by local people . . . Over time, these methods may

---

60. Hildebrand, *Aesthetics*, 50–51.

61. Johan van Lengen, *The Barefoot Architect: A Handbook for Green Building* (Bolinas: Shelter Publications, 2008), 42.

62. Opaluwa Ejiga, Obi Paul, and Osasona O. Cordelia, "Sustainability in Traditional African Architecture: A Springboard for Sustainable Urban Cities," in *Sustainable Futures: Architecture and Urbanism in the Global South* (Faculty of the Built Environment, Uganda Martyrs University: Kampala, 2012), 97–105, 98–99.

63. Buccellato and Reineccius, "Exploring Vernacular East African Architecture," 63.

evolve into practices as vernacular architecture, which may or may not be in tune with contemporary needs, giving rise to the so-called vernacular tradition of building.[64]

It may help to begin the building design with traditional vernacular architecture and only when one discovers that certain elements of it "may not be in tune with contemporary needs"[65] does one explore the use of modern technology. This way one creates a hybrid of vernacular and modern architecture. We see this beautifully displayed in the work of Diébédo Francis Kéré. It's a "both-and" approach. Ejiga, Paul and Cordelia[66] highlight and articulate this method of fusing traditional African architecture with modern technology:

> To gain knowledge on how traditional building materials have been re-devised in today's architectural customs, two different scopes need to be considered. First, there are those ethnic communities that continue to employ these age-old traditional building practices together with modern techniques that have reached the rural settlement. This practice has been reinvented majorly because of its economic benefits. Secondly, there are contemporary architects and clients that individually or collectively promote and use these materials in innovative ways motivated either by ideology or by individual interest.

Furthermore, considering poverty, and fewer available "modern" resources due to economic problems, churches should be encouraged to employ creativity and innovation in using vernacular materials and technologies, like straw bales, wattle and daub, stone, earth, compressed earth blocks, grass (thatch) and so on. These materials also offer cooler interiors for hot African climates and can be effectively employed for up to two storeys high.[67]

Using the model of Solomon's Temple, if we are going to be serious about synthesizing church architecture with the African vernacular, then we need to create beautiful designs that are sacred – architects sometimes call this "Sacred Space." We need to celebrate African creativity and artistry by incorporating vernacular decorative styles, symbols and patterns. These should include biblical themes. We should design and craft church furniture, like

---

64. Maina, Muhammad-Oumar, and Saad, "Harnessing African Architectural Traditions," 2.
65. Maina, Muhammad-Oumar, and Saad, "Harnessing African Architectural Traditions," 2.
66. Ejiga, Paul, and Cordelia, "Sustainability in Traditional African Architecture," 101.
67. Ejiga, Paul, and Cordelia, "Sustainability in Traditional African Architecture," 103.

seating (pews), pulpit or lectern, clergy seating, the Lord's table, communion rails, baptismal font or pool, collection baskets and so on.[68] The architect and theologian Murry Rea explains sacred space well when he says,

> The arts involved in the shaping of our built environment are adept at negotiating the dialectic between presence and absence. Especially in buildings designed for worship, they have been called upon to give expression to the mystery of the God who is both immanent and yet also transcendent. There are, of course, inept ways to speak through the spatial arts of the presence of God.[69]

Then there is the entrance, the threshold between our everyday lives, and fellowship with one another and with God. The entrance should be a transitional experience as we prepare to meet with him. It is my view that an entrance to an African church needs to be recognizably African. We do African Christianity a disservice if the entrance is bland and uninviting or implies European church architecture – a needless throwback to colonialism.

When synthesizing African vernacular with church architecture, one needs to keep in mind, that successful indigenous buildings are different from one another, coming in a variety of forms and layouts as each responds to its unique conditions, such as landscape, vegetation, climate, and the availability of local labour, traditional construction technology, and local materials, says Lengen.[70] Maina, Muhammad-Oumar and Saad concur when they say that "a plethora of forms, design concepts and strategies have been harnessed and employed by the African people to accommodate various activities and imbue meanings attached to the architectonic forms of different inhabitants on the continent."[71]

Rituals are an important part of African life, both traditional and modern, and Christianity is no stranger to rituals either. Kilde argues that religious space is dynamic, it houses ritual practices, like baptism, the Lord's supper and ordination, but the space also contributes to the meaning of the ritual practices. Church architecture needs to accommodate this by communicating the meaning of worship and ritual activities, as well as the religious, social and cultural context.[72]

---

68. White and White, *Church Architecture*, 4.
69. Rae, *Architecture and Theology*, 287.
70. Lengen, *The Barefoot Architect*, 11.
71. Maina, Muhammad-Oumar, and Saad, "Harnessing African Architectural Traditions," 2.
72. Jeanne Halgren Kilde, *Sacred Power, Sacred Space: An Introduction to Christian Architecture and Worship* (Oxford: Oxford University Press, 2008), 4.

We may also talk of vernacular in terms of nature and landscape. In other words, how does the church building relate and respond to its natural environment or even its urban environment? Hildebrand argues that "the collaboration between architecture and nature is one of the greatest sources of beauty, since all buildings are inserted into the external world that surrounds us, and thereby into nature in the broadest sense."[73] The building needs to maintain a link between itself, the landscape, the cityscape, nature, weather and the climate. One can also use nature to create natural light.[74] Rea says that the transformation of space depends on natural light which has a dramatic effect as it comes and goes. He suggests that natural light offers an analogy of the "Spirit who bears witness to Christ," and opens "vistas to the coming kingdom, and so is about the task of drawing his people into the presence of Christ."[75] Such collaboration, if done thoughtfully with some degree of skill, will promote vernacular beauty.[76] Again, this is why Diébédo Francis Kéré has been such a successful architect in Africa because he knows how to collaborate with nature, the landscape and the climate.

Hildebrand acknowledges that many places have been disfigured by "tasteless buildings, industrialization, or the imposition of a soulless uniformity."[77] And so, the reality is, collaboration with the environment is sometimes limited. And if this is the case, then design a church building that stands out above its disfigured landscape, offering the community a place of hope and sacred beauty.

Form and Aesthetics for African Vernacular Church Architecture

While Europeans built cathedrals that were magnificent monuments to their faith and culture, Africans generally don't build such monuments, except for the ancient Egyptian pyramids; the Great Mosque of Djenné in the Sudano-Sahelian architectural style, in Timbuktu, Mali; and the Great Zimbabwe Ruins. African vernacular churches should make people feel welcome, they should be places where Jesus and his people come to meet, rather than being grand monuments.[78] Church buildings are to be designed to facilitate the participation

---

73. Hildebrand, *Aesthetics*, 47.
74. Hildebrand, *Aesthetics*, 47.
75. Rae, *Architecture and Theology*, 321.
76. Hildebrand, *Aesthetics*, 47.
77. Hildebrand, *Aesthetics*, 47.
78. White and White, *Church Architecture*, 2–3.

of its congregants in communal worship.[79] Like Solomon's temple, the church needs to be functional before we can begin to think about aesthetic beauty, as important as that is.[80]

Now that we have looked at how we might incorporate African vernacular into church architecture, in this discussion, I will focus on form and aesthetics in contemporary African vernacular church architecture. In other words, without being too prescriptive, I will highlight considerations and offer design principles. By "form and aesthetics" I don't mean to treat them as separate elements but rather as that which gives architecture shape and meaning.

Floor layout

Churches have traditionally used a long nave, where the congregation is seated. However, to bring the people closer together in worship, other seating arrangements and layouts have been proposed, while still keeping the liturgical furniture central (like the Lord's table and pulpit).[81] Options might include theatre-style seating, round seating centred around the liturgical furniture, seating in a semi-circle, or having no seating at all, like the Eastern Orthodox. Seating arrangements should enable the movement and participation of the congregants. This is especially important for African churches. It also helps to elevate the focal platform where the primary activity, like preaching, baptism and celebrating the Lord's Supper takes place. This will help provide good sight lines which are vital to the worship space, and also create a "consecrated space."[82]

The concept of a fellowship hall is no longer desirable, according to Cool. He suggests that it is a contrived community setting, and calls it a "multi-useless" space.[83] I think of how Solomon's Temple and even the Second Temple accommodated the community by building colonnades. The vernacular church would need to consider "the vision, mission, values, culture, and story in order to appropriately convey a statement about God,"[84] not only in how they worship him but also in how they come together as a community to fellowship. Each

---

79. White and White, *Church Architecture*, 3.
80. White and White, *Church Architecture*, 7.
81. White and White, *Church Architecture*, 18–19.
82. Ching, *Architecture*, 107; White and White, *Church Architecture*, 23.
83. Tim Cool, *Why Church Buildings Matter: The Story of Your Space*, rev. (independently published, 2017), 150.
84. Cool, *Why Church Buildings Matter*, 22.

church community will probably address this challenge in its own unique way. Keep in mind that exterior space can also be used for fellowship.

Vilakati argues that:

> the Church's theological teaching, denominational and congregational history and liturgical practice . . . amongst others, inform and clarify the decision-making process behind the architectural, artistic, and aesthetic considerations for designing and ordering church space.[85]

It is the ordering of space that gives shape to architectural form.

Architectural form

Firstly, a church needs to look like a church, as the adage goes, "form follows function." In other words, a school does not look like a clinic. Likewise, a church should not be designed with shopping-mall typologies – at best, it is dishonest architecture. The architectural form of a church building should be designed with meaning and purpose and say something about who God is.[86]

According to Vilakati, careful consideration needs to be given to the following: (1) Spatial dynamics, that is, how the design relates to the flow of space and the dynamics of worship. Added to this is the visual focus orientating the congregant's central focus to that which is important in worship. (2) The symbolic resonance – how congregants respond to its meaning. (3) Aesthetic impact, that is, the aesthetic qualities of the building as one's experience of God. (4) The architecture promotes biblical principles of worship and acknowledges and accommodates the church's tradition and rituals, especially if it is a liturgical church. (5) The architectural form of the church building responds appropriately to its context and community. (6) It facilitates holistic worship and communal experience and hospitality.[87]

In other words, as Cool asks, "what are you communicating with your building?"[88] He says that our church building needs to be intentional about telling our story. Does the architecture of our church tell the story of "who we are, who we think we are, what we believe and value, and who we want to

---

85. Vusi Vilakati, "Ordering Our Sacred Space: Considerations for Building and Refurbishing Church Spaces" (Doctrine, Ethics and Worship Committee of the Methodist Church of Southern Africa, 2012), np.
86. Cool, *Why Church Buildings Matter*, 21–22.
87. Vilakati, "Ordering Our Sacred Space."
88. Cool, *Why Church Buildings Matter*, 15.

reach for Christ?"[89] The building and its aesthetics do not need to be opulent, Cool says, but they are important if we want our building to tell a story to our community.[90]

African vernacular church architecture should be a beautiful human space that also articulates, albeit in a limited way, theological truth and celebrates both the community and the divine.[91]

Openings

The thoughtful design of windows and doors, even if they are less stylized than in the church tradition, can contribute to the sacred atmosphere of the church building and promote sublime beauty in its architecture.[92] In addition to beauty, Ching argues that windows and doors may create continuity with adjacent spaces and allow for natural light, ventilation, sound and change in temperature. Further, the view "seen through the openings become part of the spatial experience."[93] Openings also give inquisitive people on the street an opportunity to see what is happening inside[94] and thus initiate the possibility for hospitality and outreach. Openings do not necessarily need to be typical openings, but we need to be innovative in the way they open up onto public spaces creating a connection by exposing the congregation's worship and fellowship activity.[95]

Ventilation and climate control are very important for any building in Africa. Openings can help prevent the church building from becoming too hot – openings higher up in the walls, called clearstories, can also provide an exit for the hot rising air.[96]

Lighting and acoustics

Further, windows provide lighting and sunlight is the best way to brighten the interior of any church. In some instances, small windows may be employed to

---

89. Cool, *Why Church Buildings Matter*, 5.
90. Cool, *Why Church Buildings Matter*, 14.
91. Hildebrand, *Aesthetics*, 48; Rae, *Architecture and Theology*, 288.
92. Hildebrand, *Aesthetics*, 47.
93. Ching, *Architecture*, 24.
94. Christopher Alexander et al., *A Pattern Language: Towns, Buildings, Construction* (New York: Oxford University Press, 1977), 774.
95. Alexander et al., *A Pattern Language*, 774–75.
96. Lengen, *The Barefoot Architect*, 52.

limit unnecessary noise, heat, or excess light.[97] One needs to be creative with small windows: You could have windows in deep recesses (this is easily done with an eco dome or straw bale construction); windows in interesting shapes; cluster small windows together; put them together in a pattern arrangement; use interesting materials like recycled soda bottles, and so on. Whether the windows are small or large, the light from the exterior penetrates the interior – perhaps there is theological meaning here too. One will need artificial light at night, and some thought needs to go into that as well, especially when avoiding Africa's insects.

African vernacular churches require lighting as much as any other church, and good acoustics are just as important.[98] The careful design of ceilings; raised platforms; curved walls to diffuse sound; and the use of sound-absorbing materials in the building will improve the acoustics. Sound amplification systems are common in modern-day churches, and these could be used too in African vernacular churches. However, there is nothing worse than hearing the blaring (and oftentimes crackling) sound system from afar. It is disruptive to the neighborhood and is a poor Christian witness. So, invest in a good system, and keep the sound level reasonable.

Roof and ceilings

I worked for an accomplished architect, Andrew Thomson, who once said the roof is the fifth elevation. In other words, the attention paid to the roof is as important as the façade, so pay attention to it. The roof shelters the church building from the harsh African sun, the wind and rain, but as Ching explains, it "also has a major impact on the overall form of a building and the shape of its spaces." The shape of the roof, he continues, "is determined by the material, geometry and proportions of its structural system and how it transfers its load across space to its supports."[99] Writing for South America, Lengen offers advice that is appropriate for Africa too, he says that "in a hot, dry climate where roofs should be flat, the walls can be moved or the ceiling heights varied to create a more attractive façade . . . in the humid tropics or temperature climates, the roofs are sloped with different pitches or with various types of rooms in all

---

97. Lengen, *The Barefoot Architect*, 54.
98. White and White, *Church Architecture*, 3, 17.
99. Ching, *Architecture*, 115.

climates."[100] Overhanging roofs also offer shade, and even cover paths, creating interesting spaces and protection from the elements.[101]

Then there is the ceiling between the roof and the occupied space. Not all churches need a ceiling, especially if you have trusses that could be aesthetically pleasing, and an open roof volume may help with ventilation and climate control in hot climates. But if you are going to have a ceiling, then consider doing something special with it, as it holds a decisive place in the worship space. One could paint it with cultural and biblical murals, in this case, the ceiling needs to be treated with the utmost care because while it can be a beautiful religious feature, it also could be disastrous if it is poorly painted.[102]

Vernacular artistry

White and White explain that art "can humanize space and make us feel a part of what goes on in it."[103] This is especially true of vernacular art. "Forms, proportions, material, color, and many other factors" help in promoting the artistic beauty in architecture and sacred space, says Hildebrand.[104] One is tempted to think innovation and creativity are more expensive,[105] and they can be. But especially in vernacular African church architecture, if everyone gets involved in vernacular artistry, it may not necessarily be expensive at all.

Exterior space

One of the most neglected spaces in church architecture is the exterior space, yet it is (almost) as important as the interior space. Cool encourages churches to create great outdoor public spaces that people love coming to and that give back to the community.[106] These spaces could be used for reflection, fellowship, meetings, games, and other activities. Exterior spaces also include paths leading to the church building, spaces between buildings, parking areas,

---

100. Lengen, *The Barefoot Architect*, 28–29.
101. Alexander et al., *A Pattern Language*, 775.
102. Hildebrand, *Aesthetics*, 118.
103. White and White, *Church Architecture*, 3.
104. Hildebrand, *Aesthetics*, 47, 54.
105. Cool, *Why Church Buildings Matter*, 87–88.
106. Cool, *Why Church Buildings Matter*, 118.

and the exterior entrance. The use of landscaping may be used to enhance exterior spaces.[107]

Conclusion

This research paper began by discussing the architectural contributions of the African architect and Pritzker prize winner, Diébédo Francis Kéré, who has designed innovative contemporary architecture in the African vernacular. This led to a further discussion on African vernacular architecture in general, its significance and its problems. After this, I turned to African church architecture where I identified six typologies, namely: (1) simple rectangular church buildings with walls constructed from wattle and daub or concrete block with a grass or tin roof, (2) shack churches clad with iron sheeting, typical of architecture found in shanty towns or informal settlements, (3) masonry church buildings, typical of traditional denomination church buildings, (4) shopfront churches, (5) marquee (tent) churches and (6) African megachurches. It was surprising that while there is African vernacular architecture, there are no churches in the African vernacular – at least none that have been studied and documented.

Therefore, this research project argues for a synthesis of church architecture and the African vernacular which was grounded in a study from 1 Kings 5–8 that helped identify the construction motifs from Solomon's Temple, providing some helpful pointers. Together with design considerations and principles from the previous discussion, "Form and Aesthetics for African Vernacular Church Architecture," I provided a way forward for building church architecture in the African vernacular while also accommodating contemporary architectural sensibilities, thus promoting a hybrid approach.

Cool[108] challenges us to innovate and think about how we do church, and how we reach our communities when we design our church buildings. Our future church buildings in Africa should focus on "how vernacular architecture can be adapted to current human needs," *together* with contemporary architectural styles, construction technologies and materials while being sustainable, argues Maio.[109] Ultimately, vernacular African church architecture should express and celebrate the culture, heritage and tradition of the people

---

107. Cool, *Why Church Buildings Matter*, 116; White and White, *Church Architecture*, 10–11.
108. Cool, *Why Church Buildings Matter*, 27.
109. Maio et al., "Namibia's Vernacular Architecture," 68.

who worship there, together with their Christian faith.[110] Although skilled architects are always an invaluable asset in any design project, Frescura is right, "architecture without architects is not only possible but is practiced as an everyday occurrence by ordinary people as part of their ordinary life." My recommendation then is to create awareness of the value and significance of church architecture in the African vernacular and to train local architects, church ministers and laity accordingly.

Bibliography

Alexander, Christopher, Sara Ishikawa, Murray Silverstein, Max Jacobson, Ingrid Fiksdahl-King, and Shlomo Angel. *A Pattern Language: Towns, Buildings, Construction*. New York: Oxford University Press, 1977.

Alter, Robert. *The Hebrew Bible: A Translation with Commentary, Prophets*. New York: W. W. Norton & Company, 2018.

Buccellato, Aimee, and Megan Reineccius. "Exploring Vernacular East African Architecture: Lessons for the Modern World." Pages 55–64 in *Vernacular Traditions*. ASCA, 2013. https://www.acsa-arch.org/chapter/exploring-vernacular-east-african-architecture-lessons-for-the-modern-world/.

Burgess, Richard. "Megachurches and 'Reverse Mission.'" Pages 243–68 in *Handbook of Megachurches*. Edited by Stephen Hunt. Brill Handbooks on Contemporary Religion 19. Leiden: Brill, 2020.

Ching, Francis D. K. *Architecture: Form, Space, and Order*. 2nd edition. New York: Wiley, 1996.

Cool, Tim. *Why Church Buildings Matter: The Story of Your Space*. Revised. Independently published, 2017.

Ejiga, Opaluwa, Obi Paul, and Osasona O. Cordelia. "Sustainability in Traditional African Architecture: A Springboard for Sustainable Urban Cities." Pages 97–105 in *Sustainable Futures: Architecture and Urbanism in the Global South*. Faculty of the Built Environment, Uganda Martyrs University: Kampala, 2012.

Frearson, Amy. "10 African Architects and Designers Championing Afrofuturism." *Dezeen* (2018). https://www.dezeen.com/2018/04/06/african-architects-designers-championing-afrofuturism/.

Fritz, Volkmar. *1 & 2 Kings*. Translated by Anselm Hagedorn. Continental Commentary Series. Minneapolis: Fortress Press, 2003.

Gitau, Wanjiru M. *Megachurch Christianity Reconsidered: Millennials and Social Change in African Perspective*. Missiological Engagements. Downers Grove: IVP Academic, 2018.

---

110. Opoko, Adeokun, and Oluwatayo, "Art in Traditional African Domestic Architecture," 678.

Hildebrand, Dietrich von. *Aesthetics*. Volume 2. Steubenville: Hildebrand Project, 2019.
House, Paul R. *1, 2 Kings: An Exegetical and Theological Exposition of Holy Scripture*. Edited by E. Ray Clendenen. New American Commentary 8. Nashville: Broadman & Holman Publishers, 1995.
Kéré, Diébédo Francis. "Kéré | Work." Kere Architecture (2023). https://www.kerearchitecture.com/work.
Kilde, Jeanne Halgren. *Sacred Power, Sacred Space: An Introduction to Christian Architecture and Worship*. Oxford: Oxford University Press, 2008.
Koehler, Ludwig, Walter Baumgartner, Johann Jakob Stamm, Benedikt Hartmann, Ze'Ev Ben-Hayyim, Eduard Yechezkel Kutscher, Philippe Reymond, and M. E. J. Richardson. *The Hebrew and Aramaic Lexicon of the Old Testament*. Leiden: Brill, 1999.
Lengen, Johan van. *The Barefoot Architect: A Handbook for Green Building*. Bolinas: Shelter Publications, 2008.
Maina, J. J., A. A. Muhammad-Oumar, and H. T. Saad. "Harnessing African Architectural Traditions for Environmental Sustainability," 1–21. Paper delivered at a symposium of the Centre for Black and African Arts and Civilization. The Assembly Hall, Ahmadu Bello University, Zaria Nigeria, 2018.
Maio, Rui, Elao Martin, Jon Sojkowski, and Tiago Miguel Ferreira. "Namibia's Vernacular Architecture: Insights towards the Sustainable Development of Local Communities." *Ge-Conservación* 11 (2017): 63–70.
Martin, Desmond. *The Bishop's Churches: The Churches of Anglican Bishop Robert Gray*. Cape Town: Struik, 2005.
Monson, John. *Zondervan Illustrated Bible Backgrounds Commentary Set: Old Testament*. Edited by John H. Walton. *Volume 3: 1 and 2 Kings, 1 and 2 Chronicles, Ezra, Nehemiah, Esther*. Grand Rapids: Zondervan, 2009.
Nelson, Richard D. *First and Second Kings: Interpretation: A Bible Commentary for Teaching and Preaching*. Louisville: Westminster John Knox Press, 1987.
Oduro, Thomas. "African Christian Theology: The Contributions of African Instituted Churches." *Ogbomoso Journal of Theology* 13, no. 1 (2008): 58–74.
Oliver, Paul, and Janet B. Hess. "African Architecture," *Encyclopedia Britannica* 2024. https://www.britannica.com/art/African-architecture.
Opoko, Akunnaya Pearl, Cynthia Adeokun, and Adedapo Oluwatayo. "Art in Traditional African Domestic Architecture: Its Place in Modern Housing and Implications for the Training of Architects." *Global Journal on Humanites & Social Sciences* no. 3 (2016): 675–78.
Rae, Murray A. *Architecture and Theology: The Art of Place*. Waco: Baylor University Press, 2017.
Righini, Paul. *Thinking Architecturally: An Introduction to the Creation of Form and Place*. Cape Town: University of Cape Town Press, 1999.

See Africa Today. "Meet Africa's Top Architect Diébédo Francis Kéré." *Further Africa* (blog), 2022. https://furtherafrica.com/2022/07/09/meet-africas-top-architect-diebedo-francis-kere/.

Sojkowski, Jon. "African Vernacular Architecture." African Vernacular Architecture: Documentation for Preservation (2017). https://www.africanvernaculararchitecture.com.

Steenkamp, Colleen Avice. "Revalidating Vernacular Techniques for a Sustainable Built Environment by Way of Selected Examples in the Eastern Cape." Master of Architecture Dissertation, University of the Free State, 2012.

The Design Story. "News: 7 Types of African Vernacular Architecture You Should Know About!" *The Design Story* (2022). https://www.thedesignstory.com/blog/news/news-7-types-of-african-vernacular-architecture-you-should-know-about.

The Hyatt Foundation. "About the Pritzker Architecture Prize." *The Pritzker Architecture Prize* (2023). https://www.pritzkerprize.com/about.

Ukah, Asonzeh. "Sacred Surplus and Pentecostal Too-Muchness: The Salvation Economy of African Megachurches." Pages 323–44 in *Handbook of Megachurches*. Edited by Stephen Hunt. Brill Handbooks on Contemporary Religion 19. Leiden: Brill, 2020.

Vilakati, Vusi. "Ordering Our Sacred Space: Considerations for Building and Refurbishing Church Spaces." Doctrine, Ethics and Worship Committee of the Methodist Church of Southern Africa, 2012.

White, James F., and Susan J. White. *Church Architecture: Building and Renovating for Christian Worship*. Claremont: OSL Publications, 1998.

5

Untethered Agents of Eternal Life

The Ministry of "Single" Women in the Gospel of John and Its Implications for the Church in Africa

Cornelia van Deventer and Jesse Fungwa Kipimo
South African Theological Seminary

Abstract

While the function of women remains a contested point in churches over the African continent, the role of single or unmarried women is a particularly thorny issue. From being ignored or discounted, to being antagonized as cursed and labelled potential homewreckers, single women have often felt pressured to marry or have been forced to the margins of the church. However, a reading of the Fourth Gospel reveals a tapestry of women who appear and function in an untethered fashion. Whether they were, in fact, single, or whether their roles in the *missio Dei* were acknowledged outside of their nuptial state, we argue that a survey of these women leaves the church in Africa with a biblical mandate to intentionally include single women in the life and ministry of the church. Through a character study of selected women in the Fourth Gospel, we argue that John's acknowledgement of these untethered female agents, their participation in the gospel narrative, and their roles in fashioning the ideal or implied audience ought to play a transformative role in the way that single women are perceived and received in churches in Africa. With Jesus as her model, the church in Africa ought to be intentional in her dealings with unmarried women, ensuring that they are granted the opportunity to rightfully function as agents in God's mission.

Key words: Gospel of John, single women, unmarried, African church, character study, narrative criticism

Introduction

Singleness in Africa, particularly among women, is becoming increasingly prevalent with direct implications for the participation of these individuals in churches. This chapter engages various African cultural and theological understandings[1] of single women through a survey of five women in the Gospel of John. We begin by discussing African cultural and theological views of single women outside and inside the church. Next, borrowing from narrative analysis, we shall undertake brief character studies of untethered women in the Gospel of John to establish how single women function as key characters within the Gospel narrative, and how they work alongside other characters to weave the ideal audience and thus accomplish the Gospel's aim of creating believers. Finally, we shall highlight the importance for churches in Africa to respond to single women. Without engaging the topic of women's ordination and whilst not approaching the topic and selected texts with a feminist or womanist hermeneutic, this chapter argues that God's generous use of untethered women in the Fourth Gospel necessitates the inclusion of single women in the life and ministry of the church.

Single Women in Africa

Singleness is a term referring to a heterogenous group made up of never married and ever married (divorced, separated, or widowed) women. Single women

---

1. We realize that there is no one African understanding of singleness, nor is there one African church. Moreover, research on this topic is notably sparse, meaning that our analysis will, at best, be a quick glance at various expressions and perceptions of singleness on the African continent. The limited information on this topic perhaps underlines the need for studies like these.

may be living with parents, siblings, friends, or alone[2] and are romantically uninvolved. Danso points out that in "African society, the norm and acceptable expectation are that every adult should get married once. This implies that the African single adults are left to feel like outcasts in their community."[3] Rutoro and Madimbo point out that, in the African worldview, never having married is often regarded as a worse fate than being widowed or divorced.[4] Surveying the Shona culture of Zimbabwe, they explain that singleness for women is traditionally associated with either traditional religious purposes or with a cursed existence.[5] In the case of the former, it is well-accepted that female spirit mediums do not marry, which raises suspicion around the single state of a woman. In the case of the latter, a single woman who has not married at a certain age is often thought to be possessed by a *chinzvi* – a spirit working to repel men from pursuing and marrying her.[6] Agbogli, Kotey, and Adza point to similar perceptions in Ghanaian culture, where single women are often regarded as deviant.[7]

As a woman remains unmarried in the Shona culture, her authority is ever-decreasing as she ages. These perceptions do not simply come from men, but also from fellow women, who perceive single women as a threat to their marriages.[8] Single women are regarded as a bad influence on married women, because they might influence them to rebel against the headship of their husbands. Additionally, a perception around these women is that they are too headstrong, meaning that it will be impossible or hard for a husband to lead them. Finally, perceptions around single women being immoral also often abound in African contexts.[9]

---

2. Rozita Ibrahim and Zahara Hassan, "Understanding Singlehood from the Experience of Never-Married Malay Muslim women in Malaysia: some preliminary findings," *European Journal of Social Sciences* 8 no. 3 (2009): 395–405, 397; Jana M. Bennett, *Water is Thicker than Blood: an Augustinian Theology of Marriage and Singleness* (New York: Oxford University Press, 2008), 84.

3. Michael Danso, *Single or Unmarried?* (Accra: Central Angle, 2022), 69.

4. Ester Rutoro and Maggie Madimbo, "Gender Equality from the Perspective of Single Womanhood," in E. Mouton, G. Kapuma, L. Hansen, and T. Togom (eds.), *Living with Dignity: African Perspectives on Gender Equality* (Stellenbosch: Sun Press), 325–42, 326.

5. Rutoro and Madimbo, "Gender Equality," 327.

6. Rutoro and Madimbo, "Gender Equality," 328.

7. Alice A. Agbogli, Sesi C. Akotey, and Edward K. Adza, "People's Perceptions about Unmarried Women: A Survey in the Kwaebibirem Districts of the Eastern Region, Ghana," *International Journal of African and Asian Studies* 35 (2007): 11–16.

8. Rutoro and Madimbo, "Gender Equality," 332.

9. Rutoro and Madimbo, "Gender Equality," 336.

The above interpretations of singleness are fuelled by the understanding that husband and wife unite to form "a complete human being."[10] This implies that single women are often seen as incomplete by fellow Africans. Such ideas are bolstered by Scriptures like Genesis 2:18 ("It is not good for the man to be alone," NIV). This is aptly illustrated in common language. The Sotho people have an idiom that says *Libetla la mosadi ke bohadi*. This is interpreted as "the grave of a woman is her marriage or in-laws."[11] This idiom implies that every woman is destined for marriage, and she must remain in it even when conditions are no longer bearable. Similarly, the Shona proverb, *Kuzvara hadzi kuzvara ndume* (to beget a woman is to beget a man) implies that a daughter will eventually marry and that a mother who begets a daughter will, therefore, inevitably "beget" a son in law.[12]

Mbiti emphasizes the primacy of marriage in society as follows:

> [M]arriage is a duty, a requirement from corporate society, and a rhythm of life in which everyone must participate. Otherwise, he [sic] who does not participate in it is a curse to the community, he is a rebel and a lawbreaker, he is not only abnormal but 'under-human.' Failure to get married under normal circumstances means that the person concerned has rejected society and society rejects him in return.[13]

Single adulthood for women goes beyond social stigmatization but also holds legal and religious ramifications. In the Congolese context, single women cannot buy property without being represented by a male family member. Moreover, single women face additional challenges, including loneliness, stigma (especially as "husband snatchers," unholy, unsuccessful), low self-esteem, pressure to get married (often from parents or church leaders), sexual harassment, and financial vulnerability. This disregard is worse for women who have been divorced as it is believed that, regardless of the reason for the

---

10. Hertel et al. "She's Single, So What? How are Singles Perceived Compared with People who are Married?" *Zeitschrift für Familienforschung* 19, no. 2 (June 2022): 139–58, 140.

11. Danso, *Single or Unmarried*, 71.

12. Rutoro and Madimbo, "Gender Equality," 330.

13. John S. Mbiti, *African Religions and Philosophy* (Oxford: Heinemann Educational Publishers, 1999), 120.

divorce, if a woman leaves her first marriage she will not be able to remain in any other marriage again.[14]

As a result, some church leaders, as well as members, put undue pressure on adults who are single to marry at all costs. Single women also often resort to marrying any suitable partner – even if it goes against their convictions – to avoid the stigmatisation of singleness as cursed or abnormal.[15] Some African churches even recommend polygamous marriages to remedy the so-called challenge of single women outnumbering single men. Additionally, churches often find it difficult to accommodate single women and, in many cases, devoting themselves to ministry seems like an impossibility. Writing about the church in Nigeria, Rahila reports that the church and culture have collaborated to create and promote structures that are generally discriminatory against women.[16] As alluded to above, Genesis 2:18 has been used to argue that marriage is for everyone and that one is incomplete if unmarried. Very little consideration is given to how single women ought to function in the life and ministry of the church. Madimbo and Rutoro note that, in spite of the fact that the Reformed Church of Zimbabwe holds no official rules against appointing women as deacons, at the time of the publication of their chapter, no single women held the office of deacon in this church; and this in a context where the number of single women and married women who train for ministry are almost equal.[17] In addition, many churches in Africa fail to address the realities and challenges of single men and women from the pulpit.[18]

The presence of single women in African congregations is ever-increasing, especially among the educated women.[19] If the church does not respond beyond encouraging such women to marry, she will not benefit from the gifts and service of our untethered sisters. We hold that the reluctance to celebrate the contributions of single women in the church stems from cultural

---

14. Jakawa L. Rahila, "Pastoral Ministry to Single Women in the Church of Christ in Nigeria, Gigiring Regional Church Council, Jos, Nigeria," (PhD Diss., University of KwaZulu-Natal, 2014), 152, https://researchspace.ukzn.ac.za/handle/10413/10636.

15. Danso, *Single or Unmarried*, 84.

16. Rahila, "Pastoral ministry," 163.

17. Rutoro and Madimbo, "Gender Equality," 333.

18. M. Baloyi, "Pastoral Care and the Agony of Female Singleness in the African Christian Context," *In die Skriflig* 44, no. 3&4 (2010): 723–42, 723.

19. Zoya Gubernskaya, "Changing Attitudes Toward Marriage and Children in Six Countries," *Sociological Perspectives* 53 (2010): 179–200; Lawrence D. E. Ikamari, "The Effect of Education on the Timing of Marriage in Kenya," *Demographic Research* 12, no. 1 (2005): 1–28; Letha D. Scanzoni and John Scanzoni, *Men, Women and Change: a Sociology of Marriage and Family* (New York: McGraw-Hill Book Company, 1981).

perceptions and not thorough biblical enquiry. In order to make this case, what follows will be a character study of selected women in the Fourth Gospel.

Our Untethered Sisters

Lee refers to the Fourth Gospel as "perhaps the most woman friendly of all the New Testament texts," arguing that "its female characters are among the most powerful and encouraging in the New Testament."[20] John's Gospel portrays women as active participants in Jesus's ministry. They are often acknowledged as exemplary disciples (compare, e.g. Nicodemus and the Samaritan woman), yet, they are humanized in a way that makes them relatable (see, e.g. the misunderstandings of the Samaritan woman in John 4). With the exception of Mary of Clopas,[21] no other woman in the Fourth Gospel functions alongside a husband. It would have been customary to introduce a married women in relation to her husband.[22] John, however, introduces several women on their own terms and outlines their participation in God's mission without reference to a male counterpart. This probably indicates that these women were unmarried – whether widowed, divorced, or never married. In the section below, we undertake a brief character study of these single women and their significance in John's Gospel and beyond. The surveyed women include Jesus's mother, the Samaritan woman, Mary and Martha of Bethany, and Mary Magdalene.

The mother of Jesus

Nowhere in John's Gospel is Mary addressed by her name. Rather, she is named the mother of Jesus from her first (ἡ μήτηρ τοῦ Ἰησοῦ; 2:1) to her last (τὴν μητέρα; 19:26) appearance. This is not strange when John's style is considered. It is customary for the Fourth Evangelist to create ideal archetypes by anonymising prominent and noble characters (e.g. the Beloved Disciple).[23]

---

20. Dorothy Lee, *The Ministry of Women in the New Testament* (Grand Rapids: Baker, 2021), 163.

21. See Richard Bauckham, *Gospel Women. Studies of the Named Women in the Gospels* (Grand Rapids: Eerdmans, 2002), 394–96 for a discussion on Mary's potential relationship to Clopas. Bauckham concludes that it is most likely that she was his wife, although he does not completely rule out the possibility that she was his unmarried daughter or even his mother.

22. Bauckham, *Gospel Women*, 393.

23. See Christopher Skinner, "Characterization," in *How John Works*, ed. Douglas Estes and Ruth Sheridan (Atlanta: SBL, 2016), 115–32, 125–27.

Moreover, connecting Mary to her son, Jesus, bestows upon her a great deal of honour[24] and distinguishes her from the many other Marys in the Gospel.[25] What is significant is that she is never identified with her husband, Joseph (cf. Matt 1:19;[26] Luke 2:5[27]). Her lack of wifely association probably indicates that she is widowed at the time of the events that John recounts.

With no birth account in the Fourth Gospel, Jesus's mother makes her entrance at the wedding in Cana (John 2). An apt observation is that John mentions Jesus's mother as the primary attendee of the wedding. He adds, ἐκλήθη δὲ καὶ ὁ Ἰησοῦς καὶ οἱ μαθηταὶ αὐτοῦ ("*Also* invited, were Jesus and his disciples," 2:2; author's translation, emphasis added). Mary is thus at the wedding in her own right. Moreover, as a woman, who would be predominantly in charge of food preparations, Mary might have been privy to information not shared with other guests – in particular, not with men. She shares this information with Jesus in verse 3, which eventually results in his first sign of turning water into wine.[28] This event is a crucial episode in the Johannine narrative for a few reasons. Not only does it mark his first sign and therefore serves as the catalyst for his public ministry,[29] but it also completes Jesus's call of his disciples by being the sign that causes them to believe in him (2:11).

Jesus's mother plays no marginal role in the event. She challenges him to intervene (implied in 2:3) and sets the sign into motion by ordering the servants to do as they are told by Jesus (v. 5). Lee has argued that Jesus's mother here embodies the essence of true discipleship as she displays trust in his word.[30] She notes that Jesus's mother, therefore, serves as an example to the other disciples present and models how to respond to him.[31] Beirne connects Jesus's mother in this scene to the Royal official (4:46–54), as both serve as catalysts for a sign, following a crisis of some sort.[32] It is their faith in Jesus's

---

24. Jo-Ann Brant, *John* (Grand Rapids: Baker Academic, 2011), 56.
25. Keener, *The Gospel of John*, §3a.
26. Matthew links the couple by introducing Joseph as ὁ ἀνὴρ αὐτῆς (her husband).
27. Luke uses the adjectival participle τῇ ἐμνηστευμένη ([Joseph's] betrothed), to introduce Mary.
28. Craig S. Keener, *The Gospel of John: 2 Volumes* (Grand Rapids: Baker, 2003), §3a.
29. Brant, *John*, 55.
30. Lee, *The Ministry of Women*, 143.
31. Lee, *The Ministry of Women*, 137. She singles out Jesus's mother as one of the three Johannine characters portraying exemplary faith (alongside the beloved disciple and John the Baptist).
32. Margaret Beirne, *Women and Men in the Fourth Gospel. A Genuine Discipleship of Equals* (London: Sheffield, 2003), 41, 48.

words, preceding the sign, that sets them apart. While Jesus's response to his mother in 2:4 (τί ἐμοὶ καὶ σοί, γύναι) seems aloof, Beirne makes a compelling argument that it signifies the single-mindedness of Jesus to complete the work that the Father has prepared for him, which, it would seem, included this very first sign.[33] With this in mind, it would be irresponsible to assume that Jesus gives in to Mary because she is his mother. Rather, like all other Johannine characters, it is her belief in him that moves him to act. Beirne affirms that "by having Jesus address her as 'woman' rather than 'mother,' the evangelist is pointing to this reality. Her faith in, and relationship of discipleship to Jesus, is that of a person in her own right."[34]

Jesus's mother's second appearance in the Fourth Gospel is at the crucifixion, making her a participant in two key events in his life: the display of his glory with his first sign and the display of his glory at "his hour" when he is crucified.[35] According to ancient custom, it would be culturally inappropriate for the mother of Jesus to be standing at the scene of his death alone.[36] She is, therefore, surrounded by other females.[37] Additionally before he breathes his last, Jesus tethers her to the Beloved Disciple – a loved one outside of her biological family – who takes her into his home (19:27). She is not tethered to one of her sons or a husband, but is integrated into the faith community of disciples. This adoption initiated by Jesus becomes "the provision of a model of life in Christ, where one cares for members of the community the way one cares for one's own family, especially if they have been robbed of that family through their baptism into the church."[38] The demonstration of these new familial relationships is particularly valuable in the context of brothers and sisters with no or few family members of their own – primary of which is a spouse.

To summarize, in her two appearances in the Fourth Gospel, Jesus's mother appears as an important character in the family of God (see 1:12). As a widow, she functions as a full-fledged disciple of Jesus and shares in his first public sign – not primarily because she was his mother, but because of her belief. She

---

33. Beirne, *Women and Men*, 63.
34. Beirne, *Women and Men*, 64.
35. See Beirne, *Women and Men*, 58.
36. Brant, *John*, 253.
37. Whether there were two or three other women with Mary is up for debate and beyond the scope of this article.
38. Brant, *John*, 257.

also demonstrates a tethering to a new family where she becomes a mother to one who does not share her genes.

The Samaritan woman

In John 4, we meet a Samaritan woman at a well at noon. While there is much speculation on why she finds herself unmarried, the text does not give us much more than the fact that she has had five husbands and that the man she has been residing with at that point was not her legal husband. Whether she was widowed or divorced is simply not disclosed. She thus meets Jesus at the well as a single woman. The setting of a well is not lost on Jesus, nor the Johannine audience. It mimics a typical betrothal scene: a space in which a single woman would have been identified and pursued by a potential suiter (e.g. Gen 24). The potentially romantic undertones are, however, not played into as Jesus chooses to rather engage this woman as theological conversation partner and, eventually, worthy co-labourer. Jesus does not go easy on her either. Similar to Nicodemus (John 3) and the Judeans (6:25–58), he uses symbolic language and effectively illuminates her misunderstanding (see 4:11, 12, 15).

While Jesus orders the woman to bring her "husband" to him, he does so for theological effect, not to shame her. His knowledge of her and her situation at home serves as the basis of her testimony, yet this man is not involved in Jesus's theologizing with the woman, nor in her ministry. Jesus does not interrogate her on *why* she is without a husband, nor does she feel the need to explain, which affirms that, despite much having been made of the woman's moral status, this was not the point of their conversation. Recent scholarship has pushed back significantly against the idea of her as an immoral adulteress.[39] The essence of her encounter with Jesus is the fact that, when the Messiah is revealed, worship of the true God will become available to all. In no uncertain terms, the conversation reaches its climax with Jesus affirming that he, indeed, is the promised Messiah (4:26).

The events that follow are missional and apostolic at heart. She leaves her bucket at the well (implying that she did not first run home) and makes it into town to testify of Jesus (4:28–29). Moreover, the favourable response and conversion of the inhabitants of Sychar is initiated by her words. Her role in the conversion of πολλοί (many) – a group that includes both men and women – is undeniable and she is entrusted with an incredible opportunity:

---

39. See, in particular, Caryn Reeder, *The Samaritan Woman's Story: Reconsidering John 4 After #ChurchToo* (Downers Grove: IVP Academic, 2022).

one that signifies her as one who toils (κοπιάω; see v. 38) – a common term used for ministry. As a single woman, she functions apostolically[40] to lead the town to the living water.[41] Moreover, her testimony serves as the catalyst for the townspeople asking Jesus to stay with them, leading to many more (πολλῷ πλείους) becoming believers (v. 41). Not only does her testimony lead to the initial belief of the inhabitants of the town of Sychar, but her act of testifying leads to one of the most unique confessions in the Johannine Gospel: that Jesus is ὁ σωτὴρ τοῦ κόσμου (the savior of the world; v. 42).

In summary, whether she was divorced or widowed, this woman from Samaria functions as a key Johannine character in many ways: she is invited as a worthy conversation partner to Jesus. Her singleness and the well setting are in no way regarded as a threat to Jesus, who reveals himself to her, resulting in her functioning as a catalyst for life to break out in the town of Sychar.

Mary and Martha

In John 11, we are introduced to the sister pair of Mary and Martha from Bethany. The focus seems to be on Mary in the introduction. This does not imply that she was the better-known sister but is probably due to the importance of her anointing of Jesus's feet – an event that the narrator proleptically mentions here. By introduction, Mary is thus already marked as the protagonist and character of faith.[42] Of significance here is that Martha is introduced as tethered to Mary (Μαρίας . . . τῆς ἀδελφῆς αὐτῆς) and not her brother, Lazarus. Lazarus is also called the brother of this Mary (ἧς ὁ ἀδελφὸς Λάζαρος; v. 2).

Not only are these women introduced on their own terms, but their actions in John 11 are significant for a few reasons. The message that the two sisters send to Jesus, "Lord, behold! The one you love is sick" (11:3; AT) reminds the reader of the indirect request made by Jesus's mother in 2:3.[43] Moreover, the frankness of their interactions with Jesus is indicative of friendship. This is affirmed in verse 5; "Jesus loved Martha and her sister, and Lazarus" (AT). Mary and Martha's relationship with Jesus was, therefore, not brokered by their brother, Lazarus.

Paramount to the events in this pericope is Martha's confession in 11:27, ἐγὼ πεπίστευκα ὅτι σὺ εἶ ὁ χριστὸς ὁ υἱὸς τοῦ θεοῦ ὁ εἰς τὸν κόσμον ἐρχόμενος ("I

---

40. This does not imply that she was an apostle.
41. Lee, *The Ministry of Women*, 147.
42. See Beirne, *Women and Men*, 148.
43. Brant, *John*, 172.

have come to believe that *you* are the Christ, the Son of God, the one coming into the world"; AT). This confession is loaded when one considers the aim of the Fourth Gospel. In 20:31, John asserts that the things in the Gospel have been written down ἵνα πιστεύσητε ὅτι Ἰησοῦς ἐστιν ὁ χριστὸς ὁ υἱὸς τοῦ θεοῦ ("so that you may believe that Jesus is the Christ/Messiah, the Son of God"; AT). This is identical to Martha's confession, making her an exemplary disciple in John's Gospel. Not only does it say something about her, but John as eyewitness, who deemed it necessary to include this grand confession, essentially marked a woman as one to imitate. Martha's confession is also important in light of the controversy around Jesus as Christ (10:24) and the Son of God (10:33) in the preceding chapter.[44] Moreover, she echoes insights from the Johannine prologue – the overture that seeks to weave the implied or ideal audience of the Gospel by making them privy to information from above. The confession that Jesus is the one coming into the world is first uttered by the Johannine narrator in 1:9 (ἐρχόμενον εἰς τὸν κόσμον). This marks Martha as an incredibly insightful character – one that stands apart from most of Jesus's conversation partners and one that shares the point of view of the privileged Johannine audience who has had access to the prologue. Martha's confession characterizes her as one who lives up to the Johannine ideal and invites others (in and beyond the text) to do the same. John does not see the need to add gravitas to her theological affirmations by tethering her to a male counterpart. She stands alone as a "single" woman, uttering that which John wishes his audience to come to believe.

Of further significance is the parallel between Martha's confession and that of Peter in Mark 8:29. Lee, in comparing the confessions and conduct of Peter and Martha, argues that both of them are unaware of the vast implications of their confessions and, after confessing, still exhibit misunderstanding (Peter tries to dissuade Jesus from the path of suffering in Mark 8:32 and Martha tries to prevent Jesus from opening the tomb in John 11:39).[45] This is a remarkable observation as it illustrates the literary and historical parallels in the lives of men and women and how they related to Jesus and his mission. Similar to the Samaritan woman, who functions as robust theological interlocutor alongside Nicodemus and the Jews, Martha and her confession places her alongside her male counterparts without the evangelist qualifying or relegating her to some special form of "female" ministry.

---

44. Lee, *The Ministry of Women*, 155.
45. Lee, *The Ministry of Women*, 155.

Mary, on the other hand, expresses (whether knowingly or unknowingly) her confession through her actions of anointing Jesus's feet, which he interprets as her recognition and preparation for his death and burial (John 12:7–8). Mary's actions connect her to that of Joseph of Arimathea and Nicodemus in 19:38–42. Moreover, her behaviour symbolically exhibits something of the true cost of discipleship. The costliness of the oil she uses functions as a response to the costliness of Jesus's laying down of his life and something of an understanding of it from her side.[46] Her generosity is also contrasted with Judas' greed as he protests her lavishing her Lord with costly oil (12:5).[47] The cost is amplified by the fact that she is portrayed as unmarried, which adds to her financial vulnerability. Yet, this does not impede her willingness to sacrificially and extravagantly give to her Lord. To summarize, Mary and Martha both function as insightful disciples in the Fourth Gospel. They are beloved by Jesus in their own right and function as significant characters for the implied audience to imitate as they share the evangelist's perception "from above" – both in word and deed.

Mary Magdalene

We meet Mary Magdalene at Jesus's cross along with the other women (19:25). Mary is not introduced by the name of a father, brother, or husband, but by her place of origin, Magdala. This implies that she was probably a single woman. In Luke's Gospel, she seems to be portrayed as a woman of means, able to support Jesus financially (Luke 8:2). Important is that Mary is present at key moments of Jesus's life: both at the cross and at the resurrection. She thus stands as a witness to the central confession that Jesus both died and rose again.

Although John has been criticized for overshadowing the female witnesses of the resurrection with that of Peter and the beloved disciple,[48] his retelling of Jesus's appearance to Mary Magdalene in John 20:11–18 exceeds all others. While one has to be careful of treating the first-century context as a monolith, women were rarely eligible to serve as witnesses in Jewish courts since their testimonies were deemed unreliable.[49] While John writes to a mixed audience, his use of Old Testament imagery and emphasis on the festivals indicates that

---

46. Lee, *The Ministry of Women*, 157–58.
47. Beirne, *Women and Men*, 150.
48. Bauckham, *Gospel Women*, 516.
49. Bauckham, *Gospel Women*, 500. However, some exceptions can be found in 2 Maccabees 7:21; Judit 8:29.

a significant portion of the Gospel's audience was Jewish. Moreover, among educated Greco-Roman men, women were often regarded as "gullible in religious matters."⁵⁰

Jesus not only appears to Mary but tasks her with the witness of his resurrection and his immanent ascension (20:17–18). In the interaction between the risen Jesus and Mary, he calls her by her own name (v. 16), setting her apart as one of three Johannine disciples (the others being Lazarus and Simon Peter) that Jesus calls by name.⁵¹ Jesus commissions Mary to "go . . . and tell" (20:17). In a similar fashion to the Samaritan woman, who testified to the mixed πολλοί, Mary takes on a missional and apostolic role – bringing her testimony to a group of men (τοὺς ἀδελφούς). Her witness to the disciples is personal as she uses first-person language in verse 18 ("I have seen the Lord"; author's translation), similar to the language used in the first Johannine epistle.⁵² Moreover, such an encounter with the risen Jesus is something Paul later uses to affirm his apostleship (1 Cor 9:1).

Bauckham argues that John's (and the other Gospel authors) acknowledgement of women as witnesses affirms the high value placed on the testimony of women in the early Christian movement, in spite of the ancient context. John did not need to include the account of the women – he had the account of Peter and the beloved disciple.⁵³ That there was suspicion about the women's account is not doubted. This is clearly seen in the attack launched against Mary Magdalene by the second-century pagan, Celsus, bemoaning that Jesus showed himself to a "half-frantic woman."⁵⁴ In summary, within the Johannine narrative, Mary functions as a credible witness, who affirms the historical death and resurrection of Jesus. Trusting her testimony is essential for anyone who wishes to believe.

Their work continues

While it is significant to analyse these women's mission within the Johannine narrative, their contributions go beyond the pages of the Gospel. A key component to a narrative analysis is to find the implied audience – the ideal

---

50. Bauckham, *Gospel Women*, 500.
51. Lee, *The Ministry of Women*, 152.
52. 1 John 1:1 NIV: "what we have heard, what we have seen with our eyes, what we have looked at, what our hands have touched."
53. Bauckham, *Gospel Women*, 519.
54. See Origen, *Contra Celsum*. 2.55.

audience that the narrator weaves throughout the story and prompts the hearer or reader to become.[55] The Johannine audience is privileged as the narrator spells out the ideal response to the events he recounts. In John 20:31, John clearly states that the aim of the Gospel is to facilitate belief in Jesus as Messiah, Son of God, and, by believing, to have life in his name. When this implied rhetorical effect is considered, the untethered women discussed take on significance beyond the pages of the Gospel. They become agents of belief for those who hear the story of Jesus. Jesus's mother exemplifies something of a persistent trusting and devotion to Jesus – both in moments of glory and agony. Moreover, she models a tethering to the faith community that is a comfort to widowed and divorced women and a call to the faith communities they are immersed in. The Samaritan woman is a worthy catalyst for Jesus's self-revelation,[56] taking the audience on a journey as she peels back the layers of Jesus's true identity, and finds herself moved by the saviour of the world to make disciples of men and women alike. Martha embodies quite precisely what John wants his audience to acknowledge in her statement of faith, becoming the quintessential "spokesperson" for the Johannine confession.[57] Likewise, Mary of Bethany exemplifies an ideal response to Jesus's identity and mission in a non-verbal confession, which is interpreted by Jesus as a faith-filled, prophetic act of preparation (12:7–8) and later demonstrated by Jesus as an ideal response within the family of God (13:1–30). Like the Samaritan woman, Martha and Mary illustrate that single women are not dangerous;[58] they are deserving conversation partners, co-workers, and friends. Finally, Mary Magdalene's witness to the resurrection serves as foundational to the faith of those who "did not see" (20:29).[59] The significance of her testimony to the resurrection has been acknowledged and celebrated for millennia.[60] These five women are

---

55. See Mark A. Powell, "Narrative Criticism," in *Hearing the New Testament: Strategies for Interpretation*, ed. Joel B. Green (Grand Rapids: Eerdmans, 2010), 240–58, 241; Edward Klink III, "Audience," in *How John Works*, ed. Douglas Estes and Ruth Sheridan (Atlanta: SBL, 2016), 241–58, 245–48; Christopher Skinner, "Characterization," 123.

56. See Beirne, *Women and Men*, 80.

57. See Beirne, *Women and Men*, 137.

58. This deserves a caveat. While single women are not dangerous, they are to be protected and honoured in the way that men (married or unmarried) engage them in the public and private sphere.

59. See Bauckham, *Gospel Women*, 519.

60. The early church referred to Mary of Magdala as *apostola apostolorum* – "apostle of the apostles" because of her apostolic role as the first to meet and proclaim the risen Christ (also in Matt 28:1–10; Mark 16:9–11). Lee, *The Ministry of Women*, 153.

thus essential characters in John's weaving of the ideal audience. They function as examples of belief – both for women and men.

Towards the Church's Response to Single Women in Africa

While the above character analyses are only samples of untethered sisters participating in God's mission, they paint a compelling picture of single women functioning as agents of eternal life throughout the life, death, and resurrection of Jesus. It is remarkable that, contrary to the situation in many churches in Africa, single women function as the *most prominent* among Jesus's co-labourers in the Fourth Gospel. Their status allows them to be available in ways that their married sisters were not. As Paul affirms, single women have more capacity than married women (see 1 Cor 7:32–35). Not only are these women named and acknowledged on their own behalf, but their contributions are key. They all line up on the side of the believer – the ideal audience – becoming examples for the Johannine audience to imitate. None of them function *because of* a husband, father, or brother, but they come alongside males to participate in the proclamation of life and light.

Jesus's interaction with these women is also remarkable. Nowhere are they regarded as less than, un-whole, or excluded from the *missio Dei*. It is, therefore, imperative that the church formulate a healthy theology of singleness to empower both single men and women to serve the Lord well. Moreover, single women should become a priority in the strategic planning of African churches. Both marriage and singleness are honoured by God. Churches ought to regard singleness as a valid option or choice for men and women alike and ought to ensure that single women are not overlooked for appropriate[61] leadership roles.[62]

Churches in Africa are thus challenged not only to prepare their daughters for godly marriages, but to prepare them for godly, fulfilled lives in their singleness. As the church prioritizes the participation and value of single women, she will be blessed to benefit from the undivided service of untethered sisters. Like the devoted mother of Jesus, co-labouring Samaritan woman, perceptive sisters from Bethany, and commissioned Mary of Magdala, our

---

61. We use the word "appropriate" to accommodate churches who hold to complementarianism. This chapter does not argue for egalitarianism, but the equal consideration of single and married women for whatever roles the church deems appropriate in their interpretation of Scripture.

62. Baloyi, "Pastoral Care," 725, 737.

single sisters are called for fulfilled lives and fruitful ministry. Without these women, the Johannine audience would be significantly poorer – and so is the church in Africa.

Bibliography

Agbogli, Alice A., Sesi C. Akotey, and Edward K. Adza. "People's Perceptions about Unmarried Women: A Survey in the Kwaebibirem Districts of the Eastern Region, Ghana," *International Journal of African and Asian Studies* 35 (2007): 11–16.

Baloyi, M. E. "Pastoral Care and the Agony of Female Singleness in the African Christian Context." *In die Skriflig* 44, no. 3&4 (2010): 723–42.

Bauckham, Richard. *Gospel Women. Studies of the Named Women in the Gospels*. Grand Rapids: Eerdmans, 2002.

Beirne, Margaret. *Women and Men in the Fourth Gospel. A Genuine Discipleship of Equals*. London: Sheffield, 2003.

Bennett, Jana M. *Water is Thicker than Blood: an Augustinian Theology of Marriage and Singleness*. New York: Oxford University Press, 2008.

Brant, Jo-Ann A. *John*. Paideia. Grand Rapids: Baker, 2011.

Danso, Michael. *Single or Unmarried?* Accra: Central Angle, 2022.

Gubernskaya, Zoya. "Changing Attitudes Toward Marriage and Children in Six Countries." *Sociological Perspectives* 53 (2010): 179–200.

Hertel, Janine, Astrid Schütz, Bella M. DePaulo, Wendy L. Morris, and Tania S. Stucke. "She's Single, So What? How are Singles Perceived Compared with People who are Married?" *Zeitschrift für Familienforschung* 1, no. 2 (June 2022): 139–58.

Ibrahim, Rozita, and Zahara Hassan. "Understanding Singlehood from the Experience of Never-Married Malay Muslim Women in Malaysia: Some Preliminary Findings." *European Journal of Social Sciences* 8, no. 3 (2009): 395–405.

Ikamari, Lawrence D. E. "The Effect of Education on the Timing of Marriage in Kenya," *Demographic Research* 12, no. 1 (2005): 1–28.

Keener, Craig S. *The Gospel of John: 2 Volumes*. Perlego Edition. Grand Rapids: Baker, 2003.

Klink III, Edward W. "Audience." In *How John Works*. Edited by Douglas Estes and Ruth Sheridan, 241–58. Atlanta: SBL, 2016.

Lee, Dorothy. *The Ministry of Women in the New Testament: Reclaiming the Biblical Vision for Church Leadership*. Grand Rapids: Baker, 2021.

Mbiti, John S. *African Religions and Philosophy*. 2nd edition. Oxford: Heinemann Educational Publishers, 1999.

Origen. *Contra Celsum*. Edited and Translated by Henry Chadwick. Cambridge: Cambridge University Press, 1953.

Powell, Mark A. "Narrative Criticism." In *Hearing the New Testament: Strategies for Interpretation*. 2nd edition. Edited by Joel B. Green, 240–58. Grand Rapids: Eerdmans, 2010.

Rahila, L. Jakawa. "Pastoral Ministry to Single Women in the Church of Christ in Nigeria, Gigiring Regional Church Council, Jos, Nigeria." PhD Diss., University of KwaZulu Natal, 2014. https://researchspace.ukzn.ac.za/handle/10413/10636.

Reeder, Caryn A. *The Samaritan Woman's Story: Reconsidering John 4 After #ChurchToo*. Downers Grove: IVP Academic, 2022.

Rutoro, Ester, and Maggie Madimbo. "Gender Equality from the Perspective of Single Womanhood." In *Living with Dignity: African Perspectives on Gender Equality*, edited by Elna Mouton, Gertrude Kapuma, Len Hansen, and Thomas Togom, 325–42. Stellenbosch: Sun Press, 2015.

Scanzoni, Letha D., and John Scanzoni. *Men, Women and Change: a Sociology of Marriage and Family*. New York: McGraw–Hill Book Company, 1981.

Skinner, Christopher W. "Characterization." In *How John Works*, edited by Douglas Estes and Ruth Sheridan, 115–32. Atlanta: SBL, 2016.

6

In Pursuit of Contextual Christian Ministry in an African Church

Exploring the Story of Rev. E. N. Anim, a Twentieth-Century Ghanaian Presbyterian Revivalist

Edwin Buertey
University of Ghana, Legon

and

Abraham Nana Opare Kwakye
University of Ghana, Legon

Abstract

The church in Africa has witnessed a lot of revival movements. Many of these revivals began in the Western mission-founded denominations commonly referred to as mainline churches. Generally, the leaders of such revivals had the aim of making the mainline denominations transform their ministries and become relevant in their context. However, those who initiated such revivals were not accommodated, hence they left the established denominations along with members who shared their aspirations to establish new churches that reflected their ethos and praxis. That notwithstanding, there are instances where the leaders of such revivals persisted in the face of resistance till the reforms were eventually mainstreamed. Such individuals, with their supporters or sympathizers, often operate from the margins until their revival ideas or practices are eventually integrated into the ministries of their denominations. One such case is Ghanaian Presbyterian Minister, Rev. Emmanuel Nyantakyi Anim, who persisted against initial resistance to get the Presbyterian Church of Ghana (PCG) to embrace in its mainstream ministry his revival experiences of prevailing and experiential prayer with expectations of miracles such as healing.

This chapter explores Anim's ministry and its impact on the PCG in the last quarter of the twentieth century. It employs historical and missiological approaches to examine how Anim succeeded in inculturating what he considered to be practical and relevant Christian ministry and experience into the PCG. The study shows that, through the efforts of Rev. E. N. Anim, the PCG shifted from aspects of its Western-inherited spirituality to appropriate practices that respond to the existential realities of its members as Africans, thereby becoming relevant in its context.

Key words: inculturation, *sunsum sore*, indigenous, neo-cultic, *honhom fi*, *tigari, abayifo, sasabonsam*

Introduction

In response to Peter's declaration that "you are the Christ, the Son of the living God" (Matt 16:16 ESV), Jesus remarked that "on this rock I will build my church, and the gates of hell shall not prevail against it" (Matt 16:18 ESV). This statement by Jesus underscores the fact that the church through its witness will take dominion over all realms and bring them to the rulership of Jesus Christ. Thus, the church is expected to address the issues that confront people in their lived experiences so as to be relevant in each context. Failing to do so will amount to not helping those who respond to the gospel and come to faith in Jesus Christ experience the abundant life that Jesus promises (John 10:10). The extent to which the church in Africa has proved itself to be relevant in its context continues to be a subject of discussions.

Whereas Western missionaries have been credited with institutionalizing Christianity in Africa,[1] they have equally been criticized for establishing denominations that were more Western in outlook than African. Hence such

---

1. Kwame Bediako, *Christianity in Africa: The Renewal of A Non-Western Religion*, (Edinburgh: Edinburgh University Press, 1995), 75.

denominations failed to meet the yearning expectations of their contexts. One main reason for such criticism is because such denominations were unable to meet the prevailing existential needs of their members as they took little cognizance of indigenous spirituality and culture. Kwame Bediako analyses the problem as follows:

> If the Christian faith as it was transmitted failed to take serious account of the traditional beliefs held about "gods many and lords many," ancestors, spirits and other spiritual agencies and their impact on human life, then it failed to meet the African in his personally experienced religious need . . ., missionary activity never amounted to genuine encounter and the Christian communities that resulted have never really known how to relate to their traditional culture in terms other than those of denunciation and separateness . . . The Christian tradition as historically received through missionary enterprise has on the whole been unable to sympathize with or relate to spiritual realities in the traditional worldview.[2]

Bediako's view is representative of the several African scholars who find it puzzling that the churches of missionary origin did not meet African expectations. With reference to the Presbyterian Church of Ghana (PCG) specifically, Noel Smith paints the picture as follows:

> the church has failed rather to integrate itself into African society and has not succeeded in coming to terms with the social and religious conditions of its environment but has largely emerged in a marked degree as a bourgeois association largely out of touch with the mass of the people . . . and in constant opposition to the African expression of religion so that no attempt was made to adapt the presentation of the gospel to indigenous Akan (African) life and thought.[3]

Smith's observation, just like that of Bediako, is that of a church detached from its context in that its worship and practices had little or no impact on everyday experiences of its African members. Even though the PCG like all other mission-founded churches officially frowned upon the indigenous culture and spiritual world view as merely superstitious, its members were very

---

2. Bediako, *Christianity in Africa*, 69.
3. Noel Smith, *The Presbyterian Church of Ghana: 1835–1960, A Younger Church in a Changing Society*, (Accra: Ghana Universities Press, 1966), 246.

much alive to it and even had heightened belief in the existence of malevolent spirits, that they believed could interfere in human affairs for good or evil.[4] For this reason, many of the members were attracted to the neo-cultic shrines that emerged in the country in the early twentieth century, a situation that became a cause of much worry for the church.[5] Thus, the PCG for a long time did not overcome the gates of hell so far as the lived experiences of its members was concerned.

Bediako has stated that the ambivalence of missionary Christianity towards the African indigenous world view was "not so much a case of an unwillingness to relate to these realities as not having learnt to do so."[6] For the PCG in particular, there was an admission of spiritual deficiency in its ministry with a desire for "rekindling of spiritual zeal."[7] Hence, as early as the 1920s the PCG put measures in place to revive its spiritual life in order to respond to the yearnings of its members although such efforts did not yield any tangible results.[8]

Although the official arrangements towards providing relevant ministry did not yield many results, some individuals in the church were able to provide what people needed; hence there emerged several prayer groups led by lay persons in the church. Such prayer groups did not have the support of the church, hence they operated on the periphery[9] while others broke away to establish newer churches that are generally referred to as the African Initiated Churches (AICs). In Ghanaian nomenclature the AICs are known as the *sunsum sore* (spiritual churches).[10] The major study on the *sunsum sore* in Ghana is C. G. Baeta's "Prophetism in Ghana." The *sunsum sore* were followed by the Classical Pentecostal denominations and in the last quarter of the twentieth century the neo-Pentecostals also known as the Charismatic Ministries (CMs) came on the scene.[11] The various strands of Pentecostal denominations have been noted

---

4. Cephas Narh Omenyo, *Pentecost outside Pentecostalism: A Study of the Development of Charismatic Renewal in the Mainline Churches in Ghana* (Zoetermeer: Uitgeverij Boekencentrum, 2006), 65.

5. Omenyo, *Pentecost outside Pentecostalism*, 66.

6. Bediako, *Christianity in Africa*, 69.

7. Smith, *The Presbyterian Church*, 245.

8. Omenyo, *Pentecost Outside Pentecostalism*, 128–31.

9. Hans W. Debrunner, *A History of Christianity in Ghana* (Accra: Waterville Publishing House, 1967), 347–48.

10. J. Kwabena Asamoah-Gyadu, *African Charismatics: Current Developments within Independent Indigenous Pentecostalism in Ghana* (Leiden: Brill, 2005), 19–21.

11. Asamoah-Gyadu, *African Charismatics*, 23–27.

to profess spirituality that takes the African worldview more seriously than the mainline churches by way of addressing the existential needs of people. It can be said that for the members of the mainline denominations such as the PCG, the church was not helping them to prevail against the gates of hell which they counted every day. For this reason, several adult members of the mainline churches drifted to the AICs and later the Classical Pentecostal denominations whereas their youth moved into the CMs.[12] The PCG's quest for spiritual renewal and provision of relevant ministry, however, began to yield positive results with the formation of the Bible Study and Prayer Group (BSPG).[13]

Even though the PCG did not generally have an aversion towards the ministries of individual revivalists as stated above, yet one ordained minister with the gift of healing, Rev. Emmanuel Nyantakyi Anim, who is the subject of this chapter, was not only tolerated but welcomed into the mainstream ministry of the church. This became a watershed moment in the church's quest for spiritual renewal particularly with regard to healing. Generally, studies on the renewal movements in the mainline churches in Ghana have either focused on the ministries of those members who had conflicts with their churches, hence seceded to form new denominations, or on the activities of the charismatic groups that operate in such denominations. Individuals who persisted against the odds to be eventually accepted have not been the subject of any academic discussions so far. Herein lies the significance of this chapter as it brings to light the contributions of one such person, Rev. Anim, through the ministry of the PCG.

The discussion on Rev. Anim's ministry in the PCG will begin with a brief background to the commencement of his healing ministry, and will explore his style and mode of ministry. It will then evaluate its impact on the PCG in terms of the extent to which it helped the church to respond to the needs of its context. Data for the chapter was gathered through study and analysis of historical documents on the PCG such as minutes and reports of Synods, the church's newspaper, the *Christian Messenger*, a study of pictures and other materials obtained from Rev. Anim's home in Begoro in the eastern of region of Ghana as well as interviews with people who witnessed Rev. Anim's ministry.

---

12. J. Kwabena Asamoah-Gyadu, "Charismatic Renewal in the Traditional Historic Mission Denominations," in *Christianity in Ghana: A Post-Colonial History*, ed. J. Kwabena Asamoah-Gyadu (Accra: Sub-Saharan Publishers, 2018), 185–97.

13. The BSPG is the PCG's main charismatic renewal group which was formed out of the amalgamation of various individual prayer groups operating in the church and received Synod approval in 1966. See Omenyo, *Pentecost Outside Pentecostalism*, 140–53.

Rev. Emmanuel Nyantakyi Anim's Call to Ministry

Rev. Emmanuel Nyantakyi Anim was commissioned into the ministry of the PCG in 1981 at the age of fifty-three years, having previously been a teacher for many years.[14] He soon established a ministry of healing accompanied by other miracles at his station in Obomeng Kwahu in the Eastern Region through which he gained attention within the PCG and beyond. According to Rev. Anim's own account as reported by G. B. K. Owusu,[15] he received his gift of healing in response to his personal struggle to address the persistent ailments of his wife and children. He recounted that:

> my wife and children suffered from incurable diseases which gave me sleepless nights and worries. I tried various hospitals to find cure to this sickness but in vain. My wife who was suffering from a heart disease would at times fall into coma and I would kneel down and pray to God. As for my children, no doctor was able to diagnose their sickness; it was spiritual so I never stopped praying.[16]

He continued his account that while in training to become a minister at Trinity College, he could not concentrate due to the health conditions of his wife and children. It was during his fasting and prayers that God revealed to him to make a solution of salt and water and give to his wife and children to drink for their healing. He claimed that he heard the voice of God telling him that "I am the same God that asked Elisha to use salt to purify the water of Jericho which was causing deaths and miscarriages, read 2 Kings 2:19–22."[17] Rev. Anim said that he obeyed and proceeded home to administer the salt solution to his family and they were immediately healed. He went on to state that after his commissioning, he was posted to Obomeng-Kwahu in the Eastern Region of Ghana. God again directed him to use salt in healing, which he

---

14. Interview with Mrs. Salome Anim on 3 December, 2022; G. B. K. Owusu, "Rev. Anim Laid to Rest" Christian Messenger, 9 no.3, (March, 1996): 5.

15. G. B. K. Owusu was the editor for the *Christian Messenger*, the monthly newspaper of the PCG for many years. He wrote many of the articles on events or activities that involved the leadership of the PCG and the church as a whole during hie tenure as editor.

16. This narration was in an article with the title "Presbyterian Minister Raises the Dead" written by G. B. K. Owusu and published in the *Christian Messenger* (November/December, 1984): 7.

17. Owusu, "Presbyterian Minister Raises the Dead," *Christian Messenger* (November/December, 1984): 7.

obeyed and the results were that thousands of people received healing.[18] Stories of such disturbing health conditions that defy normal treatment by Western medical practice and indigenous therapy abound in Ghana especially, in the healing stories of founders of some leaders of Pentecostal denominations.[19]

Corroborating Rev. Anim's story, his surviving widow, Mrs. Salome Anim, who is now eighty-five years old and resident in her hometown, Begoro in the Eastern Region of Ghana, said a relative engaged her in a dispute over a house her late father had willed to her. One night, she had a dream in which the said the relative shot her. Three days later, she woke up one night to find blood stains on the floor in their bedroom. Not long after that, she began experiencing pains in her heart for which she sought medical treatment and was diagnosed with hypertension. The doctors advised her not to eat food with salt as part of measures to manage her condition.[20] However, after taking the salt solution prepared by her husband, she never had any trace of hypertension again and has been eating food with salt up to the present. Mrs. Anim further explained that her husband's healing ministry at Obomeng started not long after he had begun pastoral ministry in the town. She mentioned that her husband told her that the voice that told him earlier to administer salt solution to her and their children, and had spoken to him again to use salt to heal people of their sicknesses. They then brought together some members of the church to form a prayer group and through that members who were sick got healed after praying and administering salt solution to them. Through the testimonies of such members more and more people got attracted to their prayer meetings and the ministry boomed from then on.

From Skepticism to Acceptance: PCG's Response to Rev. Anim's Healing Ministry

In the same way as ministries of this nature had been received in the past, the leadership of the PCG initially had some reservations about Rev. Anim's healing ministry. In his case, however, the church chose to test his ministry for its authenticity rather than an outright rejection or ban. Thus, a committee was constituted to investigate Rev. Anim's healing ministry and report on it.

---

18. Owusu, "Presbyterian Minister Raises the Dead," *Christian Messenger* (November/December, 1984): 7.

19. See E. Kingsley Larbi, *Pentecostalism: Eddies of Ghanaian Christianity* (Accra: Centre for Pentecostal and Charismatic Studies, 2001), 97–98, 384–85, 388.

20. Interview with Mrs. Salome Anim on 3 December, 2022.

According to Mrs. Anim, the investigation committee paid an unannounced visit to Obomeng to observe Rev. Anim's healing sessions and to their surprise they witnessed Rev. Anim's miraculous raising of a dead boy to life with other healing encounters. Mrs. Anim stated that the committee was possibly convinced of the authenticity of Rev. Anim's healing ministry as they saw him pray for the dead boy and sprinkled salt solution on him in the full glare of the worshippers. It is obvious that the committee gave a positive report to the church leadership as no one raised objections to his ministry thereafter. Rather, the successive leadership of the PCG openly supported him.

Perhaps what may have convinced the church leadership further was the reported healing of Mrs. Mary Sintim-Misa, the wife of a former Moderator of the PCG, Rev. G. K. Sintim-Misa who reportedly sought the assistance of Rev. Anim to heal his wife who was unwell.[21] Mrs. Sintim-Misa got well after Rev. Anim prayed for her along with administering salt solution to her. This was ample testimony to the leadership of the church to embrace Rev. Anim's ministry as nothing could be more convincing than the news of the former Moderator's wife being healed. Indeed, Mrs. Sintim-Misa was at the prayer session of Rev. Anim on Friday 8 February 1987 where she testified to how she had been healed by Rev. Anim. Her testimony was captured along with several others in the March/April 1987 edition of *Christian Messenger* as follows:

> I was a diabetic patient for many years and doctors asked me not to eat sugar and starchy food. I could hardly walk without crutches but by the grace of God, when I came to Rev. Anim for prayers, I am now completely healed. I can now walk without crutches and I eat any food.[22]

Such a testimony carried in the church's newspaper was obviously enough to let the leadership of the PCG accept Rev. Anim's ministry and give him space to operate.

Open testimonies of this nature were not normal practice in the PCG at the time. It was learned from the Pentecostal denominations just as healing and other practices were. Kwabena Asamoah Gyadu has stated that the "theology of experience" is core to Pentecostal spirituality and it hinges on testimonies

---

21. Interview with Mrs. Salome Anim on 3 December, 2022.

22. Mrs. Mary Sintim-Misah's testimony was captured in an article written by G. B. K. Owusu with the title "The Crippled Walk, The Blind See at Obomeng," *Christian Messenger* (March/April, 1987): 4.

which validate the Pentecostal message.[23] As people testify to what they had experienced, it reinforces the claims of the message and builds faith in others. The practitioners of the Pentecostal type of experiential ministry in the mainline churches, such as Rev. Anim and the Charismatic Renewal Groups, included testimonies in their activities[24] to give concrete evidence of the power of God in their activities. It was from such testimonies that their activities were accepted and brought into the mainstream against initial resistance.

Rev. Anim in the Ministry of the PCG: Evidence of a Validated Ministry

The PCG not only accepted Rev. Anim's ministry but also validated it, as gathered from some reports of the Kwahu Presbytery to successive Synods of the PCG between 1984 and 1988. In 1984, just a few years into Rev. Anim's ministry at Obomeng, the Kwahu Presbytery stated in its report that "having examined the report of Rev. Anim on his healing ministry at Obomeng, a more serious effort must be made by Synod to sustain the idea and practice of divine healing in the church."[25] The Presbytery went further to suggest that pastors and agents of the church should be exposed to the ministry of healing. Rev. Anim's request for an assistant minister to lessen the workload on him, so as to have more time for the healing ministry, was granted by the church. In 1984, only few congregations of the PCG (predominantly in urban settings) had assistant ministers. The granting of Rev. Anim's request for an assistant minister shows that the PCG recognized the uniqueness of his ministry, and that the request was an exceptional one that needed attention.

In 1987, the Kwahu Presbytery again reported that Rev. Anim's healing ministry at Obomeng had progressed and was attracting large numbers of people, which the Presbytery described as commendable.[26] In a surprising turn of events, the PCG seconded Rev. Anim to the Bethel Presbyterian Church in Monrovia, Liberia in 1988.[27] The Kwahu Presbytery did not take such a decision kindly as it reported on the decline in the influx of people to Obomeng for healing. The Presbytery asked the head office of the PCG "if it deliberately did

---

23. J. Kwabena Asamoah-Gyadu, *Contemporary Pentecostal Christianity: Interpretations from an African Context* (Oxford: Regnum, 2013), 92.
24. Omenyo, *Pentecost outside Pentecostalism*, 268–69.
25. PCG, Reports from Presbyteries for 1984, submitted to the 56th Synod (1985): 29.
26. PCG, Reports from Presbyteries for 1987 submitted to the 59th Synod (1988): 33.
27. PCG, Reports from Presbyteries for 1988 submitted to the 60th Synod (1989): 45; G. B. K. Owusu, "Rev. Anim Laid to Rest," *Christian Messenger* 9, no. 3 (March, 1996): 5.

that to collapse the healing ministry at Obomeng."[28] It can be observed that for the Kwahu Presbytery, Rev. Anim's healing ministry was very important for its life and mission, and they expected the head office to have safeguarded this by not transferring him. Rev. Anim returned to Ghana in 1989 due to the outbreak of the Liberian civil war[29] and was posted to pastor the Presbyterian Church in Nsawam where he continued with his healing ministry until he passed on in February 1996.

Besides the favourable reports on Rev. Anim to successive Synods by the Kwahu Presbytery, there were other proofs of his acceptance within the rank and file of the PCG, such as open support declared for him by successive moderators at the time. For instance, in the 1984 edition of the *Christian Messenger* (which has been referred to earlier), the then moderator, Rt. Rev. I. H. Frimpong, was photographed in a handshake with Rev. Anim with the caption "Rt. Rev. I. H. Frimpong, Moderator of the Presbyterian Church of Ghana, congratulates Rev. Nyantakyi Anim on his healing power." Also, the November 1990 edition of the paper had a heading "Presbyterian Church believes in healing – Moderator."[30] In that story, the moderator of the PCG at the time, Rt. Rev. D. A. Koranteng, visited the prayer session of Rev. Anim at Nsawam where he stated that the Presbyterian church, being founded on Christ, believed in divine healing. He cautioned the congregation that Satan also practices healing and so they must be wary and not be led astray. The moderator also encouraged Rev. Anim to be humble and faithful to his call and not "arrogate to himself any inflated ego or dubious powers." This was clear evidence that the moderator was convinced that Rev. Anim's ministry of healing was authentic by the church's standard; hence his support for him.

Further evidence that Rev. Anim's ministry was validated within the PCG is that he did not only carry out his healing ministrations from his stations only. Rather, he went on healing tours to several congregations of the PCG at the invitation of the ministers or leadership of those congregations, including Ghanaian Presbyterian congregations in the diaspora.[31] One of such visits was to the Ghana Presbyterian Church, USA, to mark their tenth anniversary in 1995. The advertisement for the said event read in part as follows, "Spiritual Healing and Revival Crusade led by Rev. E. N. Anim, World Acclaimed

---

28. PCG, Reports from Presbyteries for 1988 submitted to the 60th Synod (1989): 45.

29. Information provided by Mrs. Anim on 3 December, 2022.

30. G. B. K. Owusu, "Presbyterian Church Believes in Healing – Moderator," *Christian Messenger*, November, 1990: 5.

31. Information provided by Mrs. Anim on 3 December, 2022.

Spiritual Healer of the Presbyterian Church of Ghana, Nsawam." From this advertisement, it would be seen that these Ghanaian Presbyterians in the USA, where medical science is advanced, did not lose their sense of spiritual succour for health and healing but rather found in Rev. Anim the means to appropriate their health needs spiritually. The four-day event was held on Friday 24 November, Wednesday 29 November, Thursday 30 November and Friday 1 December, 1995. At the end of the event, the church presented Rev. E. N. Anim with a citation that read, "With Gratitude, Appreciation and Love for Your Enhancing Spiritual Awareness in our Church. You have indeed Showered an Everlasting Spiritual Inspiration on us All." Thus, Rev. Anim's ministry was recognized by Ghanaian Presbyterians both at home and beyond.

Additionally, a number of ministers of the PCG and other denominations visited Rev. Anim at his Nsawam station on a number of occasions. Among the collection of pictures during Rev. Anim's years of ministry at Nsawam were pictures of him with Rev. Prof. Kwame Bediako, an eminent scholar, theologian and an ordained minister of the PCG. In one such picture, Prof. Bediako, together with his wife, were with Rev. Anim and the congregation of the Nsawam Presbyterian Church. It is probable that Prof. Bediako and his family joined the congregation for worship that day. Another picture showed one Rev. Fr. Safo Kantanka, an Anglican priest who was at the prayer session of Rev. Anim at Nsawam where he (Rev. Fr. Safo Kantanka) preached the sermon for the day. There were also pictures of ministers of other denominations with Rev. Anim in the collection. The high-profile visitors Rev. Anim received indicates that such persons recognized and acknowledged the uniqueness of his ministry.

Hail the Healer: Rev. Anim in PCG Headlines

The PCG's validation of Rev. Anim's ministry can also be gleaned from the publicity he received in the church's official newspaper, the *Christian Messenger*, which was published monthly. The headings for these stories were eloquent summaries of how the PCG considered his ministry. The November/December 1984 edition captured the story in the words "Presbyterian Minister Raises the Dead." The actual story went as follows,

> . . . whenever we hear of any miracles being performed in the Christian church, we tend to credit it to the SPIRITUAL CHURCHES.[32] But we forget too that every true and genuine

---

32. In Ghanaian nomenclature, "spiritual churches" refers to the AICs which are called in the Twi language *sunsum sore* meaning "spiritual churches." This is in reference to their

Christian church including the orthodox have the spirit of God behind it . . . the orthodox[33] churches which include the Roman Catholic, Presbyterian, Methodist, and Anglican churches to mention only a few are all spiritual. They have the power to heal and raise the dead in the name of Jesus. If you doubt this, come with me to Obomeng in the Kwahu range where 56 year old Presbyterian minister, the Rev. Emmanuel Nyantakyi Anim is raising the dead and healing the sick.[34]

The story went on to catalogue a number of sicknesses that Rev. Anim had healed including his claim of having raised five people who were dead to life. The Presbyterian church had been under the same charge as other mainline churches for lacking the power to provide authentic Christian ministry especially that which resonates with African realities such as healing. Hence, it is instructive to note that in espousing the healing power of Rev. Anim, the paper found it important to establish that what was happening in the Presbyterian church was capable of occurring in other mainline churches. In effect, members of the mainline churches need not move to the "spiritual churches" but remain in their denominations where they can equally experience the power of God.

Similar headings and narratives were given for other publications of the *Christian Messenger*. For instance, the March/April 1987 edition was titled "The Crippled Walk, the Blind See at Obomeng." The text went on: "the scene at the manse of the Obomeng Presbyterian Church on Friday February, 8 was full of spiritual fireworks. Preaching, testimony, dancing, singing and healing marked the day."[35]

The story described how Rev. Anim took the congregants through teachings followed by singing of "moving Presbyterian hymns and invigorating Pentecostal songs" before the time for healing, which was preceded by testimonies. For the actual healing session, it was stated that:

---

emphasis on spiritual experiences of healing and other encounters. See C. G. Baeta, *Prophetism in Ghana* (London: SCM, 1962), 1 and J. Kwabena Asmoah-Gyadu, *African Charismatics: Current Developments within Independent Indigenous Pentecostalism in Ghana* (Leiden: Brill, 2005), 21.

33. In Ghanaian discourse, orthodox churches refer to the mainline churches such as Presbyterian Church, Methodist Church, Roman Catholic Church, Anglican Church and other similar churches, usually of Western missionary origin. They are called "orthodox" because they have been in the country longer than the Pentecostal denominations.

34. G. B. K. Owusu, "The Crippled Walk, the Blind See a Obomeng," *Christian Messenger* (November/December, 1984): 7.

35. Owusu, "The Crippled Walk, the Blind See at Obomeng," 4.

he took a handful of ordinary salt, mixed it with water and prayed over it reading 2 Kings 2:19–22. A song in twi "Yesu merehwehwe wo" meaning I am looking for you Jesus rocked the place. There were shouts of "Halleluia," "praise God," "he can do it." With a hand raised up, he gave a cupful of saline water to all the sick who have formed a horse shoe. Two songs in twi "Yesu sa me yare" meaning "Lord heal me" and "bre Obonsam ase" meaning "destroy the devil" were sang.[36]

The story went on to catalogue a number of testimonies by people who had been healed, one of them being Mrs. Sintim-Misa who has been referred to earlier.

The mode of ministration described here with nuances of symbolism and ritualism was not common in the PCG at the time. It was rather characteristic of the AICs[37] and the Pentecostal and charismatic churches, though with some variations.[38] In her discussion of healing and deliverance processes in the neo-Pentecostal Churches (NPCs) in Kenya, Philomena Njeri Mwaura stated that such processes, though biblically based, yet are culturally specific, reinforced by traditions in mainline churches and "steeped in ritual and symbolism."[39] Prior to Rev. Anim's emergence, the Bible Study and Prayer Group (BSPG), the charismatic renewal group in the PCG, was promoting a similar spirituality of singing with clapping of hands, intense corporate prayers and fasting with praying in tongues along with healing and deliverance,[40] though with resistance from sections of the leadership and members of the church. For Rev. Anim to employ such methods in his healing ministry at that time shows that he was setting a new paradigm, and suggesting that the church must fully embrace such ministrations. Moreover, for the *Christian Messenger* to report Rev. Anim's ministry with such detail shows that with or without formal approval by the PCG, such a mode of ministry had moved from the periphery to the centre of the church. Indeed, Asamoah-Gyadu says, the mainline churches including the PCG adopted practices of the AICs and later strands of Pentecostalism

---

36. Owusu, "The Crippled Walk, the Blind See at Obomeng," 4.

37. Baeta, *Prophetism in Ghana*, 1, 52.

38. See Paul Gifford, *Ghana's New Christianity: Pentecostalism in a Globalizing Economy* (Bloomington: Indiana University Press, 2004), 27–30, 90–107.

39. Philomena Njeri Mwaura, "Spiritual Warfare and Healing in Kenyan Neo-Pentecostalism," in *Pentecostalism, Catholicism, and the Spirit in the World*, ed. Stan Chu Ilo (Oregon: Cascade Books, 2019), 81–98, 91.

40. See Omenyo, *Pentecost outside Pentecostalism*, 127–53.

to secure their own survival, as it halted the drift of their members to such churches.[41]

There is no doubt that the positive reportage of Rev. Anim in the *Christian Messenger*, including his engagements with Moderators of the church, did much not only to establish his presence but also validate his ministry in the PCG. According to Manuel Castells, power is based on the control of communication and information and that communication power is at the heart of the structure and dynamics of society.[42] In that vein, Asamoah-Gyadu states that by taking advantage of the opportunities offered by the media, Pentecostal-charismatic churches have taken control and exercise the power of religion in the public space. He based this on Castells' position that the "most fundamental form of power lies in the ability to shape the human mind."[43] From that premise, it is obvious that the wide publicity that the *Christian Messenger* granted Rev. Anim went a long way to shape the minds of Presbyterians and certainly non-Presbyterians about his ministry, teaching them that it was authentic by the church's standards. He thus gained influence within the rank and file of the PCG.

Criticism of Rev. Anim's Healing Ministry

Even though at the official level of the PCG Rev. Anim's ministry was validated, yet there were some concerns over his ministration especially from members of the BSPG.[44] The ethos and praxis of the BSPG are more tilted towards practices of the classical Pentecostal denominations in Ghana. For instance, it did not encourage the use of materials to mediate healing[45] as practiced by Rev. Anim in his use of salt. The use of materials in mediating healing and other miracles was very characteristic of the AICs along with other practices which were considered to bear semblance with practices in indigenous religion. For the BSPG, by administering salt or saline solution to almost all problems that came

---

41. Asamoah-Gyadu, *African Charismatics*, 2; *Contemporary Pentecostal Christianity*, 11.

42. Manuel Castells, *Communication Power* (Oxford: Oxford University Press, 2013), 3 cited in J. Kwabena Asamoah-Gyadu, "Taking Territories and Raising Champions: Contemporary Pentecostalism and the Changing Face of Christianity in Africa, 1980–2010," Inaugural Lecture for Promotion to Full Professor (Legon: Trinity Theological Seminary, 2010), 30.

43. Manuel Castells, *Communication Power* (Oxford: Oxford University Press, 2009), 3 cited in Asamoah-Gyadu, *Taking Territories and Raising Champions*, 30.

44. The BSPG had been the main charismatic renewal group of the PCG until recent times.

45. Omenyo, *Pentecost outside Pentecostalism*, 256, 257.

before him, Rev. Anim had routinized his healing ministry which they thought was a departure from accounts of healing in the New Testament.

The use of materials by the AICs, for instance, to mediate healing and other miracles has been criticized by sections of the Christian community which stress unmediated access to God.[46] Furthermore, it has the tendency to establish rituals and shifts attention from God to such items or persons prescribing them.[47] It is in this light that Rev. Anim's use of salt for all ailments or complaints became a cause of concern for members of the BSPG. The BSPG seemed concerned with ensuring biblical sanctity in ministry. It seems, however, that though the PCG longed for renewal or revival, it did not, and still does not have a clear position on what is acceptable or not with regard to issues such as the use of materials in mediating healing.

A guideline on the conduct of prayer centres, healing and deliverance ministries in the PCG prepared in 2000 had a provision that "the use of blessed water, blessed handkerchiefs, blessed cloths . . . water, candles, salt, clay, oil . . . are not permitted except when and where the Holy Spirit directs otherwise."[48] The said document, which has been revised twice (the last time in 2022) instructs in relation to the same subject to "minimize the use of special items such as candles, oil, handkerchiefs, salt, soaps, staff etc. to avoid members idolizing such items."[49] The first as well as the revised provisions on the subject are not clear and seem to suggest that in one breath the church discourages the use of materials but in another breath it permits it under "caution." This gives room for discretionary application as it is almost impossible to verify what someone claims to be under the direction of the Holy Spirit or to measure what is minimal. Such an open-ended situation can be subject to abuse and may also lead to accusations and counter accusations of practices being biblical or not between opposing groups, as happened between the BSPG and Rev. Anim.

---

46. Asamoah-Gyadu, *African Charismatics*, 72.
47. Asamoah-Gyadu, *African Charismatics*, 84.
48. Presbyterian Church of Ghana, *Prayer Centre, Healing/Deliverance Ministry Guidelines*, 2000, section 10.
49. Presbyterian Church of Ghana, *Revised Guidelines for Prayer/Retreat Centres and Deliverance Ministries in and Affiliated to the Church*, 2022, 22.

Overcoming the Gates of Hell: Appraisal of Rev. Anim's Ministry in the Light of Providing Contextual Ministry in an African Church

Having discussed the ministry of Rev. Anim in some detail, and its reception within the PCG, we now turn to appraise it in the light of expectations of its context. At both Obomeng and Nsawam, people flocked to Rev. Anim's prayer sessions with various needs. At Nsawam, Rev. Anim had a register of attendance for people who visited him to seek assistance. They came from diverse religious persuasions, namely Christians of different denominations, Muslims, and adherents of indigenous religion. For instance, there were two visiting Muslims, one from Accra and the other from Tutu Akuapem. One wanted healing for his headache and waist pain while the other sought prayer so that either his brother or his friend who were all abroad would help him by taking him there. He also wanted prayers for a proposed tenant on his land to agree to the terms of the tenancy.[50] Also, there were clients whose faith was stated as "pagans," obviously adherents of African Traditional Religions. The first one wanted success in his trading, the second sought healing for his coughing problem while the third wanted help to stop drinking.[51] The majority of the attendants were Christians with various problems, predominantly health issues. Some reported with stroke, others with waist pains, stomachache, for child birth, marital issues, and some to seek spiritual help in court disputes or for success in exams. The prayer requests of three different women were briefly stated as follows: the first one, frustration, the second was to get a single man to marry and the third one, so that her husband would give her one of his estate houses.[52] The extensive needs presented at Rev. Anim's prayer sessions affirms the proposition of Ghanaian New Testament Scholar John D. K. Ekem, that,

> salvation in traditional Akan (African) thought means the availability of whatever goes into reinforcing life in the here-and-now. This includes good mental and physical health, ability to bear children to perpetuate the family line, abundant food harvest, success in one's daily occupation, and deliverance from the adverse influence of *abayifo*,[53] *sasabonsam*[54] and premature death. The

---

50. Register of Attendance at Rev. Anim's Prayer Sessions at Nsawam, 1990–1993.
51. Register of Attendance at Rev. Anim's Prayer Sessions at Nsawam, 1990–1993.
52. Register of Attendance at Rev. Anim's Prayer Sessions at Nsawam, 1990–1993.
53. *Abayifo* is the Akan word for witches.
54. *Sasabonsam* is the Akan name for an evil spirit monster in the forest which is believed to be the head of all evil spiritual forces. It is believed to terrorize farmers and hunters who go into the forest for their normal activities. According to Kwame Bediako, it has found its way into

latter are typical examples of evils that must be combated and overcome lest they cause damage to groups and individuals.[55]

In effect, African soteriology is comprehensive and holistic, encompassing everything imaginable for life. It was due to the inability of the mainline churches to provide such holistic soteriology that they were described as being deficient and irrelevant in their context. C. G. Baeta wrote of the spiritual churches in Ghana, that petitions presented there covered virtually every area of life from health and healing to economic well-being and protection against malevolent forces. These, he observed, were not different from what were presented at Tigari[56] shrines.[57] This affirms that for the African, religion must invigorate life, and its inability to do so renders it ineffective. This means that a church that does not help people who respond to the gospel message to address these needs is invariably leaving such people to battle with their fears of hell on a daily basis. For such members, the church does not represent what Jesus says it is. The fact that such requests were regular at Rev. Anim's prayer and healing sessions showed that he provided a ministry that was relevant to the people who came to him. Thus, he demonstrated that it was possible for agents and members of the PCG to meet the felt needs of people in pragmatic ways and halt the drift of members from the church. Through him the PCG provided an effective religion for its members and beyond at least within a certain generation.

It is possible for someone unfamiliar with the African worldview to query why issues such as drunkenness, search for a husband or court cases would be presented to a religious functionary for redress. The response for such a query is in Ghanaian philosopher Kwame Gyekye's discussion that a fundamental doctrine in Akan (African) thought is "causality," which is explained as "nothing happens by chance."[58] Thus, there are some occurrences that are considered unexpected and extraordinary, for which supernatural explanations are sought.

Akan Christian vocabulary to designate Satan, the devil. See Bediako, *Jesus in Africa* (Ghana: Regnum Africa; Carlisle: Paternoster, 2000), 10.

55. John D. K. Ekem, *Priesthood in Context: A Study of Priesthood in Some Christian and Primal Communities of Ghana and its Relevance for Mother-Tongue Biblical Interpretation* (Accra: SonLife Press, 2008), 39.

56. Tigare is the name of an indigenous deity that became popular in Ghana from the early parts of the twentieth century. It reportedly gained fame for addressing the existential needs of people such as protection, healing and economic success for those who consulted it.

57. Baeta, *Prophetism in Ghana*, 128–32.

58. Kwame Gyekye, *An Essay on African Philosophical Thought: The Akan Conceptual Scheme* (Cambridge: Cambridge University Press, 1987), 76.

For instance, for a person to persist in drunkenness after all efforts to help him out fails, it implies that the causes lie beyond the physical realm, hence spiritual interpretation and solutions must be sought. Flowing out of the concept of causality is the Akan understanding of the presence of evil that can disrupt human affairs. Max Asimeng, a Ghanaian sociologist, has argued that the key element of religious activities in traditional African society is warding off what the Akan call *honhom fi* (evil spirits) from human affairs.[59] The quest for finding solutions to problems beyond the physical realm is not a matter in indigenous religious or cultural thought only but also active in the Christian conception. Pentecostal prayer, healing and deliverance services are anchored on the faith that there are problems that defy "normal" therapy for which spiritual solutions must be found.[60] Thus, the Pentecostalist conception of power; which is now pervasive in mainline Christianity resonates with indigenous religion.

With reference to health and healing, J. S. Pobee and Gabriel Oshitelu have stated that "in Africa, ministry would be judged as deficient if it does not treat healing as a function of religion."[61] Mercy Amba Oduyoye affirms this position by stating that the search for salvation and liberation in Africa basically has to do with health and wholeness, and the absence of it leads to African Christians moving from church to church or even to the traditional healer to appropriate it.[62] To the extent that Rev. Anim's healing ministry prevented members of the PCG from drifting elsewhere but rather attracted some non-members to receive healing within the precincts of the church, he was useful to the PCG. Indeed, he helped the PCG to be relevant to its context.

Ministering to existential needs such as healing along with applying the Christian faith to cultural elements in African Christianity falls within the purview of inculturation theology in Africa.[63] Indeed, for African Christians, healing is not merely a cultural concern but a reality and an expectation of

---

59. Max Asimeng, *Religion and Social Change in West Africa: An Introduction to the Sociology of Religion* (Accra: Woeli Publishing Services, 2010), 65.

60. Asamoah-Gyadu, *Contemporary Pentecostal Christianity*, 35–38 and Mwaura, "Spiritual Warfare and Healing."

61. John S. Pobee and Gabriel Oshitelu II, *African Initiatives in Christianity: The Growth, Gifts and Diversities of Indigenous African Churches, A Challenge to the Ecumenical Movement* (Geneva: World Council of Churches, 1998), 49.

62. Mercy Amba Oduyoye, *Hearing and Knowing* (Accra: Sam-Wood, 2000), 44.

63. Charles Nyamiti, "African Christologies Today," in *Jesus in African Christianity: Experimentation and Diversity in African Christology*, eds. J. N. K. Mugambi and Laurenti Magesa (Nairobi: Initiatives Publishers, 1989), 17–39.

their Christian experience.⁶⁴ Having come to faith in Jesus Christ, African Christians believe in him as their healer and expect the same. This is based on biblical accounts of Jesus's healing ministry as well as personal experiences. As a result, Jesus as healer is a strong Christological model in the thoughts and experiences of many an African Christian.⁶⁵ It is also curious that Oduyoye describes the meeting of health needs of people as a liberation issue in African Christianity. Thus, she places health on a par with the myriad of social, political and economic deficiencies in Africa which African liberation theologians desire the Christian faith to correct in order to be truly at home in the continent. This idea is shared by Mwaura who says that healing and deliverance set people free from debilitating demonic powers so that people can have the fullness of life promised in Christ.⁶⁶

The theology of deliverance in Ghana, for instance, is hinged on the belief that subsequent to salvation Christians must be freed from militating spiritual forces obstructing their full benefits promised in Scripture.⁶⁷ In effect, healing in the Christian sense is holistic, targeting the entire realm of life. Irrespective of the form it takes, whether from bodily ailments caused by organic or spiritual factors, or psychological, emotional mental issues, or repair of relationships, or the provision of socio-economic or political needs, they are not peculiar to Africa but essentially biblical expectations that accompany appropriation of the Christian faith. Oduyoye and Mwaura therefore share Emmanuel Martey's position that inculturation and liberation are essentially the same issues in African Christianity, and for that matter, African theological discourse.⁶⁸ As far as the church helps people to appropriate these expectations in their lived experiences, it is being relevant, and that is what Rev. Anim helped the PCG to attain based on the preceding discussions.

An appraisal of Rev. Anim's ministry also takes into account a major outcome of his ministry for the PCG. In 1984, Rev. Anim proposed that the PCG should set up a Prayer Centre at Obomeng where he was then the minister in charge. This, he believed would enable him to devote attention

---

64. Diane B. Stinton, *Jesus of Africa: Voices of Contemporary African Christology* (Maryknoll: Orbis Books, 2004), 62–80.

65. Nyamiti, "African Christologies Today" and Stinton, *Jesus of Africa*.

66. Mwaura, "Spiritual Welfare and Healing."

67. Abamfo Ofori Atiemo, "Musuyi and Deliverance" (MPhil Thesis, University of Ghana, Legon, 1994), 89.

68. Emmanuel Martey, *African Theology: Inculturation and Liberation* (Maryknoll: Orbis Books, 1995), 131.

to the sick.⁶⁹ The PCG accepted this idea with a decision to establish the said Prayer Centre at Atibie, also on the Kwahu Ridge.⁷⁰ At the time of taking this decision, the phenomenon of prayer centres had become a major feature in mainline Pentecostalism, especially the Church of Pentecost.⁷¹ Members of the PCG and other mainline denominations were among the major patrons of such prayer centres in search of practical solutions to their problems. The Synod Committee believed that if Rev. Anim was in one place, church members and others who needed assistance in their spiritual issues could easily reach him. The establishment of the centre was rather slow and was only opened in 2003, long after Rev. Anim's death. That notwithstanding, the idea of prayer centres persisted in the PCG and has now become the major avenue of spiritual renewal in the church, supplanting the BSPG which used to spearhead spiritual renewal activities in the PCG.⁷² To show its seriousness about the prayer centres, the PCG usually posts ordained ministers with charismatic gifts to be in charge of the centres the church has directly established⁷³ and has also developed a policy document to regulate their operations. One feature of the prayer centre ministry in the PCG is the twice-yearly pilgrimage to the church's prayer centre on the Abasua Prayer Mountains in the Asante region. The dates for this pilgrimage retreat are fixed on the church's almanac and the Clerk of General Assembly issues letters inviting church members to attend.

The concept of prayer centres where people can access needs such as healing is common in the African cultural and religious setting, in the form of traditional shrines as among the Akans in Ghana.⁷⁴ Priests at the traditional shrines engage in holistic therapy⁷⁵ including treatment for mental

---

69. *Christian Messenger* (November/December, 1984), 7.

70. Edwin Tetteh Buertey, "Prayer Centres as Avenues for Contemporary Spiritual Renewal in the Presbyterian Church of Ghana" (MPhil Thesis, University of Ghana, Legon, 2017), 43.

71. E. Kingsley Larbi, *Pentecostalism*, 87, 371–414; Opoku Onyinah, *Pentecostal Exorcism: Witchcraft and Demonology in Ghana* (Dorset: Deo Publishing, 2012), 187.

72. Buertey, "Prayer Centres as Avenues for Contemporary Spiritual Renewal in the Presbyterian Church of Ghana," 126.

73. By the policy of the PCG, a prayer centre may be established by a court or any level of authority of the church be it the Congregation, District, Presbytery or from the National level by a decision of the General Assembly or the General Assembly Council. Some individual members of the church with charismatic gifts may also establish prayer centres and align themselves to the church provided they are ready to be guided by the policy for operating such centres in the PCG.

74. Ekem, *Priesthood in Context*, 53.

75. Ekem, *Priesthood in Context*, 53.

ailments.⁷⁶ In Ghanaian Christianity, the AICs were the trailblazers of prayer centres followed by the classical Pentecostal denominations at a time when the mainline churches such as PCG derided such centres and mostly discouraged its members from patronizing them. For the PCG to come full circle by accepting prayer centres and bringing them into its mainstream ministry on the back of Rev. Anim's ministry is ample testimony to Rev. Anim's imprint on the church.

Conclusion

The PCG followed its inherited Western mission mode of ministry by preaching the gospel; baptizing members and confirming those baptized in infancy upon reaching teenage years; seeing to the Christian marriage of members; as well as the burial of departed members along with the provision of social services such as education and health care. Yet it failed to meet the needs of its members within their indigenous cultural and religious context, as well as normal expectations of the Christian faith grounded in Scripture. Such lack of practical or experiential ministry meant leaving members to grapple with their daily fears and anxieties, synonymous to hell experiences, which in turn led to the church suffering high attrition of members. However, the ministry of Rev. E. N. Anim brought a turning point in the church's ministry narrative. With his healing ministry, which was initially received with skepticism, Rev. Anim established himself as a revivalist healer who attracted the attention of both clergy and laity, locally and abroad including non-members of the PCG. Indeed, through Rev. Anim, prayer centres, an avenue that was not part of PCG's mode and structure of ministry have become the centre of renewal activities in the church. In stating its official position on the practice of divine healing, the PCG cited Rev. Anim as one of its agents who operated the ministry of divine healing for a long time in the twentieth century.⁷⁷ This means that for the PCG, Rev. Anim's position with regard to helping it to provide relevant ministry in its African context is unquestionable. He helped the PCG to overcome the gates of hell in its context.

The ministry of mainline denominations such as the PCG is mostly collective and does not hover around individuals. However, many of the changes that have occurred in these churches with regard to renewal activities

---

76. Omenyo, *Pentecost outside Pentecostalism*, 259.
77. Nana Opare Kwakye, "The Presbyterian Church of Ghana" in *Christianity in Ghana: Vol. 1 – A Post-Colonial History*, ed. J. Kwabena Asamoah-Gyadu (Accra: Sub-Saharan Publishers, 2018), 30–47.

and provision of practical ministry that resonate with the African context and consistent with biblical witness came through the efforts of individuals such as Rev. Anim. It is therefore important for scholarship on the mainline churches to give some attention to such individuals in order to bring out their contribution to the changing face of the church in Africa. For the PCG, such individuals include Mr. Ebenezer Abboa-Offei of the Grace Deliverance Ministry in Akropong Akuapem and Mr. Daniel Ansu of Jejemireja in the Bono Region. These lay persons have contributed to providing practical ministry that not only resonates with the African reality but is consistent with the biblical witness in the New Testament. Thus, overall, they succeeded in helping the PCG to provide relevant Christian ministry within its African context.

Bibliography

Asamoah-Gyadu, J. Kwabena. *African Charismatics: Current Developments within Independent Indigenous Pentecostalism in Ghana*. Leiden: Brill, 2005.

———. *Contemporary Pentecostal Christianity: Interpretations from an African Context*. Oxford: Regnum, 2013.

———. "Taking Territories and Raising Champions: Contemporary Pentecostalism and the Changing Face of Christianity in Africa, 1980–2010." Inaugural Lecture for Promotion to Full Professor. Legon: Trinity Theological Seminary, 2010.

Asimeng, Max. *Religion and Social Change in West Africa: An Introduction to the Sociology of Religion*. Accra: Woeli Publishing Services, 2010.

Atiemo, Abamfo Ofori. "Musuyi and Deliverance." MPhil Thesis, University of Ghana, Legon, 1994.

Baeta, C. G. *Prophetism in Ghana*. London: SCM, 1962.

Bediako, Kwame. *Christianity in Africa: The Renewal of A Non-Western Religion*. Edinburgh: Edinburgh University Press, 1995.

———. *Jesus in Africa*. Ghana: Regnum Africa; Carlisle: Paternoster, 2000.

Buertey, Edwin Tetteh. "Prayer Centres as Avenues for Contemporary Spiritual Renewal in the Presbyterian Church of Ghana." MPhil Thesis, University of Ghana, Legon, 2017.

Debrunner, A. Hans W. *History of Christianity in Ghana*. Accra: Waterville Publishing House, 1967.

Ekem, John D. K. *Priesthood in Context: A Study of Priesthood in Some Christian and Primal Communities of Ghana and its Relevance for Mother-Tongue Biblical Interpretation*. Accra: SonLife Press, 2008.

Gifford, Paul. *Ghana's New Christianity: Pentecostalism in a Globalizing Economy*. Bloomington: Indiana University Press, 2004.

Gyekye, Kwame. *An Essay on African Philosophical Thought: The Akan Conceptual Scheme*. Cambridge: Cambridge University Press, 1987.

Kwakye, Nana Opare. "The Presbyterian Church of Ghana." In *Christianity in Ghana: Vol. 1 – A Post-Colonial History*, edited by J. Kwabena Asamoah-Gyadu, 30–47. Accra: Sub-Saharan Publishers, 2018.

Larbi, E. Kingsley. *Pentecostalism: Eddies Ghanaian Christianity*. Accra: Centre for Pentecostal and Charismatic Studies, 2001.

Martey, Emmanuel. *African Theology: Inculturation and Liberation*. Maryknoll: Orbis Books, 1995.

Mwaura, Philomena Njeri. "Spiritual Warfare and Healing in Kenyan Neo-Pentecostalism." In *Pentecostalism, Catholicism, and the Spirit in the World*, edited by Stan Chu Ilo, 81–98. Eugene: Cascade Books, 2019.

Nyamiti, Charles. "African Christologies Today." In *Jesus in African Christianity: Experimentation and Diversity in African Christology*, edited by J. N. K. Mugambi and Laurenti Magesa, 17–39. Nairobi: Initiatives Publishers, 1989.

Onyinah, Opoku. *Pentecostal Exorcism: Witchcraft and Demonology in Ghana*. Dorset: Deo Publishing, 2012.

Owusu, G. B. K, "Presbyterian Church Believes in Healing – Moderator," *Christian Messenger*, November, 1990.

———. "Presbyterian Minister Raises the Dead," *Christian Messenger*, March/April, 1987.

———. "Rev. Anim Laid to Rest," *Christian Messenger* 9 no. 3, March, 1996.

———. "The Crippled Walk, the Blind at Obomeng, *Christian Messenger*, November/December, 1984.

PCG, Reports from Presbyteries for 1984, submitted to the 56th Synod, 1985.

PCG, Reports from Presbyteries for 1987 submitted to the 59th Synod, 1988.

PCG, Reports from Presbyteries for 1988 submitted to the 60th Synod, 1989.

Presbyterian Church of Ghana. *Guidelines for Prayer/Retreat Centres and Deliverance Ministries*. Revised edition. 2022.

———. *Prayer Centre, Healing/Deliverance Ministry Guidelines*. 2000.

Stinton, Diane B. *Jesus of Africa: Voices of Contemporary African Christology*. Maryknoll: Orbis Books, 2004.

7

The Church as a Household of God in African Theology

Reflecting the Values of African Households

Isaac Ampong
St. Paul's Anglican Church, Belgium

Abstract

The New Testament presents several images in describing the church, such as people of God, body of Christ, temple of God, household of God, etc. Whereas in many non-African contexts, the "household of God" imagery does not receive significant attention, this image has become the favorite among many African theologians when referring to the church. This is not surprising since the household unit holds an important place in many African societies, perhaps more so than in non-African societies. Furthermore, the "household of God" imagery seems to be a good pushback against some challenges to the church in Africa, such as tribalism. Describing the African church as a household seems to be contextually a good fit for the church in Africa. At the same time, there is a new trend of "youth churches" starting across many African countries in which most, if not all the members (including the leaders), are young men and women. Though they do not explicitly state that older people are not welcome in their worship services, the nature of the worship services is enough to push them away. This new trend clearly runs against the depiction of the church as a household, especially considering the makeup of African households, which are typically multi-generational, consisting of grandparents, parents, and grandchildren. One of the beautiful things in many of these African households is that each age group is not only deemed essential, but also the age groups joyfully support and care for one another. This trend of "youth churches" not only runs against African values, but also deprives the young people of all the mentoring and investment older Christians can invest in their discipleship journey.

Key words: church, household, families, young people, old people, worship, age groups

Introduction

In the Ghanaian university context, most worship and church services are organized and led by the students themselves. In other words, it is students leading other students. Almost everybody, including the leaders, belongs to the same age group. It is therefore a community of peers, mainly made up of young adults between the ages of eighteen and thirty. Since almost everyone in the congregation is a young adult, it is not surprising that these services are vibrant, fun, engaging, energetic, and lively. These church services are typically suspended when the students are on vacation, because many students go back home to their former churches. During my undergraduate studies in Ghana, the typical complaint among the students was that the churches back home were not as vibrant and lively as the ones we had on campus. After experiencing an all-youth service, they did not want to go back to worshipping with older Christians. It was strange to me that a lot of these young people decided to leave their former churches and join churches where the congregation was predominantly made up of young people. Later, I realized this phenomenon was not exclusive to university students but was a growing trend all over the country, as well as in other African countries. In order to prevent their young people from leaving, many churches started creating special services for the young people. These services are tagged as "English Services," but in reality they are just "young people services." Though Scripture indicates that the different age groups should worship together, many churches are deciding to divide them.

This chapter argues that this phenomenon is not just inappropriate theologically but also culturally within the African context. Of all the images used to describe the church in the Holy Scriptures, one that has been preferred by African theologians is the church as a household or family. In many African communities, households are made up of people of different age generations and the interaction of these multi-generational people is one of the things that brings joy to the households. Withdrawing from worshipping with the older generation destroys the bond and unity that exists in African households.

The Church as A Household of God

The New Testament presents several images which illuminate the nature of the church from different angles. Paul Minear in his landmark study *Images of the Church in the New Testament* lists over ninety images used in reference to the church. These include the people of God (2 Cor 6:16), the body of Christ (Eph 4:12; 5:30; Col 1:18 cf. Rom 12:4–5; 1 Cor 10:17; 12:12, 27), the temple of God (1 Cor 3:16–17; Eph 2:22; 1 Pet 2:5), and the household of God (1 Tim 3:14–16).[1]

Some of these images for the church have been overemphasized while other images have been overly neglected. One of the images that has been overly emphasized is the image of the church as "the body of Christ." Louis Berkhof noted that some people in his day regarded the image of the "body of Christ" as "a complete definition of the New Testament church."[2] On the other hand, an image of the church which has not been given much consideration is the image of "the household of God." Malcolm Yarnell has rightly observed that a significant number of systematic theology works that discuss the doctrine of the church, and specifically the images of the church, treat "the household of God" as insignificant by either not mentioning it at all or by just sidelining it.[3] This phenomenon is shocking, since the household image is one of the key images used to describe the church, especially in the Pastoral Epistles. Because a full treatment of the image of the church as a household falls beyond the

---

1. Paul S. Minear, *Images of the Church in the New Testament*, New Testament Library (Louisville: Westminster John Knox Press, 2004). Edmund P. Clowney also discusses some of these images in his essay, "Interpreting the Biblical Models of the Church," in *Biblical Interpretation and the Church: The Problem of Contextualization*, ed. D. A. Carson (Exeter: Paternoster Press, 1985), 64–109.

2. Louis Berkhof, *Systematic Theology* (Grand Rapids: Eerdmans, 1953), 557. Other modern scholars who argue something similar include Michael F. Bird, *Evangelical Theology: A Biblical and Systematic Introduction*, 2nd ed. (Grand Rapids: Zondervan Academic, 2020), 814; Millard J. Erickson, *Christian Theology*, 3rd ed. (Grand Rapids: Baker Academic, 2013), 959; Edmund P. Clowney, "Biblical Theology of the Church," in *The Church in the Bible and the World: An International Study*, ed. D. A. Carson (Grand Rapids: Baker Books, 2002), 13–87, 51.

3. Malcolm B. Yarnell III, "Οἶκος Θεοῦ: A Theologically Neglected but Important Ecclesiological Metaphor," *Midwestern Journal of Theology* 2, no. 1 (Fall 2003): 53–55. Some of the theologians whose works are surveyed by Yarnell include Hans Küng, Leslie Newbigin, Millard Erickson, James Leo Garrett, Stanley Grenz, Wayne Grudem, Augustus Hopkins Strong, etc.

scope of this chapter, this chapter will mainly focus on the Pastoral Epistles where this image is given a lot more prominence.

The "household of God" in the Pastoral Epistles

Even a cursory reading through the Pastoral Epistles would hardly miss the fact that the primary subject is ecclesiology.[4] Raymond Collins has also rightly pointed out that "the 'house' or the 'household' (οἶκος or οἰκία, *oikos* or *oikia*) is the dominant ecclesiological metaphor in the Pastoral Epistles."[5] One of the clues that points to the fact that the household is a significant image for the church in the Pastoral Epistles, can be seen in 1 Tim 3:14–15. These two verses do not only explicitly describe Paul's[6] purpose for writing 1 Timothy,[7] but also portray the church as a household of God. For easy reference, it would be helpful to provide a translation of these two verses:

> Even though I hope to come to you soon, I am writing these things to you so that if I delay, you may know how one ought to conduct himself/herself in the household of God, which is the church of the living God, the pillar and foundation of the truth.[8]

Though the element of most interest to this chapter in these verses is the description of the church as the household of God (οἶκος θεοῦ, *oikos theou*), there are several issues that need to be discussed before we can properly explore the concept of the church as a household of God. One of these issues

---

4. Roger W. Gehring, *House Church and Mission: The Importance of Household Structures in Early Christianity* (Peabody: Hendrickson Publishers, 2004), 260.

5. Raymond F. Collins, *1 & 2 Timothy and Titus: A Commentary*, New Testament Library (Louisville: Westminster John Knox Press, 2002), 102.

6. Many scholars today doubt that the Pastoral Epistles are authentic letters of Apostle Paul, mainly due to stylistic and lexical differences from other Pauline letters. However, Jermo van Nes has very well demonstrated that these differences cannot be used as an argument to deny that Paul wrote the Pastoral Epistles. See Jermo Van Nes, *Pauline Language and the Pastoral Epistles: A Study of Linguistic Variation in the Corpus Paulinum*, Linguistic Biblical Studies 16 (Leiden: Brill, 2018). For response to other arguments raised against Pauline authorship of the Pastoral Epistles, see Robert W. Yarbrough, *The Letters to Timothy and Titus*, The Pillar New Testament Commentary (Grand Rapids: Eerdmans, 2018), 69–90.

7. Thomas C. Oden, *First and Second Timothy and Titus*, Interpretation, a Bible Commentary for Teaching and Preaching (Louisville: John Knox Press, 1989), 43–44. Walter Lock goes further to assert that 1 Timothy 3:15 may serve as a purpose for all of the Pastoral Epistles, which is to "build up a high standard of Christian character and intercourse in the Church as the family of God." See Walter Lock, *A Critical and Exegetical Commentary on the Pastoral Epistles: I & II Timothy and Titus*, International Critical Commentary (Edinburgh: T&T Clark, 1924), xiii.

8. Unless otherwise stated, biblical translations follow the author's own translation.

concerns to what "these things [or instructions]" (ταῦτα, *tauta*) in verse 14 refer. Some scholars argue it refers to chapters 1–3,[9] or even more specifically, 2–3.[10] However, as Samuel Ngewa rightly argues, it is best to take "these things" as referring to the whole epistle.[11] Another issue worth exploring is the referent of "you" (σοι, *soi*). As a singular pronoun, it certainly refers to Timothy who is the primary addressee of this epistle (cf. 1 Tim 1:18). Notwithstanding, 1 Timothy (as well as the other Pastoral Epistles) is not an entirely private letter, since it was expected to be read aloud in the congregation.[12] It therefore hints that the congregation was a secondary addressee to the letter. Another issue concerns whose conduct (ἀναστρέφεσθαι, *anastrephesthai*) is referred to in these verses. Since Timothy is the primary addressee, and also the subject of the main verb, "know" (εἰδῇς, *eidēs*), some commentators argue that it is Timothy's conduct which is referred to in this passage.[13] However, as it has already been argued, 1 Timothy is not a purely private letter but one that is also addressed to the whole congregation. As such and also as reflected in most English translations (such as the NIV, ESV, NASB, CSB, NLT, etc.), Paul is not addressing only Timothy nor describing only official leadership roles, but rather addressing the whole congregation and how they must conduct themselves towards one another.[14]

Having cleared all these issues in 1 Tim 3:14–15, we are ready to explore the meaning of the image "household of God" (οἶκος θεοῦ, *oikos theou*). The term

---

9. Gordon D. Fee, *1 & 2 Timothy, Titus*, Understanding the Bible Commentary (Grand Rapids: Baker Books, 2011), 91.

10. I. Howard Marshall, *A Critical and Exegetical Commentary on the Pastoral Epistles*, International Critical Commentary (London: T&T Clark, 1999), 505; George W. Knight III, *The Pastoral Epistles* (Grand Rapids: Eerdmans, 1992), 178.

11. Samuel Ngewa, *1 & 2 Timothy and Titus*, Africa Bible Commentary Series (Grand Rapids: Zondervan, 2009), 79–80. For a similar view, see J. N. D. Kelly, *A Commentary on the Pastoral Epistles: I Timothy, II Timothy, Titus*, Black's New Testament Commentary (London: A&C Black, 1963), 86.

12. Ngewa, *1 & 2 Timothy and Titus*, 79–80. Contra, Ben Witherington III (*Letters and Homilies for Hellenized Christians: A Socio-Rhetorical Commentary on Titus, 1–2 Timothy and 1–3 John* (Downers Grove: IVP Academic, 2006, 67), who argues that the Pastoral Epistles were purely private letters.

13. Donald Guthrie, *The Pastoral Epistles: An Introduction and Commentary*, rev. ed., Tyndale New Testament Commentaries (Downers Grove: InterVarsity Press, 2009), 102; Marshall, *A Critical and Exegetical Commentary on the Pastoral Epistles*, 507; Collins, *1 & 2 Timothy and Titus*, 101. The KJV (1 Tim 3:15) also adopts this interpretation: "But if I tarry long, that thou mayest know how thou oughtest to behave thyself in the house of God, which is the church of the living God, the pillar and ground of the truth."

14. William D. Mounce, *Pastoral Epistles*, Word Biblical Commentary 46 (Nashville: Thomas Nelson, 2009), 220.

translated as "household" (οἶκος, *oikos*) can also mean "a house," which is the physical structure of a building. The additional descriptions of the church with architectural terms such as pillar (στῦλος, *stylos*) and foundation (ἑδραίωμα, *hedraiōma*) seem to support this translation. The images of house, pillar, and foundation portray the church with the image of a temple of God (cf. 1 Cor 3:16; 1 Pet 2:5). Anthony T. Hanson also perceives several allusions in this passage to Solomon's temple (1 Kgs 8:13 [8:53, LXX]) and the pillar of cloud in the wilderness (Exod 13:21–22; cf. the cloud that filled Solomon's temple at its dedication [1 Kgs 8:10–11]) and thereby concludes that "what this densely packed phrase means is that the Christian church is the true temple of God, the place where his presence is to be found."[15] William Hendricksen also asserts that "'house' is correct here, not 'household' as in verses 4, 5, 12. Believers are God's house or sanctuary."[16]

In spite of the above arguments, we would still argue that the phrase οἶκος θεοῦ, *oikos theou*, in 1 Timothy 3:15 should be translated as the "household of God," with a familial image, instead of "house of God," with a temple image.[17] This is due to the fact that the theme of managing households permeates the epistle. For example, earlier in the chapter Paul required that caretakers of the church of God be good managers of their own households (1 Tim 3:4, 5, 12).

Apart from this, 1 Timothy and the rest of the Pastoral Epistles abound with household language. F. Alan Tomlinson notes that "terms from household management (the primary glossary matrix) find their way into the [Pastoral Epistles] at major seams: letter openings, closings, topic shifts, emphatic charges/exhortations, and formulaic closures."[18]

---

15. Anthony Tyrrell Hanson, *The Pastoral Epistles*, New Century Bible Commentary (Grand Rapids: Eerdmans, 1982), 83. Bertil Gärtner also argues that the phrase οἶκος θεοῦ *oikos theou* portrays the image of God's temple. However, he argues that the allusions point more towards Qumran than the Old Testament texts. See Bertil Gärtner, *The Temple and the Community in Qumran and the New Testament: A Comparative Study in the Temple Symbolism of the Qumran Texts and the New Testament*, Society for New Testament Studies Monograph Series (Cambridge: Cambridge University Press, 1965), 66–71.

16. William Hendriksen, *Exposition of the Pastoral Epistles* (Grand Rapids: Baker Book House, 1957), 136. Other scholars who argue that the phrase should be translated as "house of God" include Peter Weigandt, οἶκος, EDNT 2:501–2; Michel Otto, οἶκος, TDNT 5:126.

17. Arland J. Hultgren, "1–2 Timothy, Titus" in *1–2 Timothy, Titus, II Thessalonians*, Augsburg Commentary on the New Testament (Minneapolis: Augsburg Publishing House, 1984), 76; Daniel C. Arichea and Howard Hatton, *A Handbook on Paul's Letters to Timothy and to Titus*, UBS Handbook Series (New York: United Bible Societies, 1995), 79–80.

18. F. Alan Tomlinson, "The Purpose and Stewardship Theme Within the Pastoral Epistles," in *Entrusted with the Gospel: Paul's Theology in the Pastoral Epistles*, ed. Andreas J. Köstenberger and Terry L. Wilder (Nashville: B&H Academic, 2010), 52–83, 78. Some of these terminologies include οἶκος (*oikos*) (1 Tim 3:4; 2 Tim 4:19: explicitly referring to household),

In 1 Timothy 1:4, Paul introduces the phrase, οἰκονομίαν θεοῦ (*oikonomian theou*), and since οἰκονομία (*oikonomia*) refers to the task of managing a household, the phrase could be describing the household management by God. In Titus 1:7, Paul describes the leaders of the church as οἰκονόμοι (*oikonomoi*), a term which describes someone who manages a household for another person. The picture here describes God as the master who has handed his household to the church leaders to manage for him.[19] Frances Young provides us with a concise summary of this important theological concept in the Pastoral Epistles:

> The theology of the Pastorals unquestionably assumes that God is the apex of a hierarchically ordered society in which obedience is a prime value. The church is God's household, and he is King of the Universe. By God's grace and favor, Christians are members of his household.[20]

All of these highlight the fact that οἶκος θεοῦ (*oikos theou*) in 1 Timothy 3:15 describes the church with a familial image as a household of God. Since this passage in the letter describes the purpose for writing this letter, the familial image here implies "The purpose of the letter is not to outline how to behave when 'in church,' but to describe what is proper conduct for a member of God's family."[21]

The Church as a Household in African Theology

We have briefly noted how the image of the church as the household of God is not given much consideration in many non-African theological works. This phenomenon is flipped on its head when one reviews works produced by Africans or within the African context, for the image of the church as the household of God is a favorite among many African theologians and very

---

οἰκονομία (*oikonomia*) (1 Tim 1:4), οἰκοδεσποτέω (*oikodespoteō*) (1 Tim 5:14), οἰκονόμος (*oikonomos*) (Titus 1:7), οἰκουργός (*oikourgos*) (Tit 2:5).

19. Luke Timothy Johnson persuasively argues that the phrase, οἰκονομίαν θεοῦ (*oikonomian theou*), describes God's ordering of reality, which obviously includes the church but also encompasses all of society. See Luke Timothy Johnson, *The First and Second Letters to Timothy: A New Translation with Introduction and Commentary*, Anchor Yale Bible Commentary 35A (New Haven: Yale University Press, 2008), 147–54. Similarly, Philip H. Towner, *The Letters to Timothy and Titus*, New International Commentary on the New Testament (Grand Rapids: Eerdmans, 2006), 68–70.

20. Frances M. Young, *The Theology of the Pastoral Letters* (Cambridge: Cambridge University Press, 1994), 94.

21. John A. Kitchen, *The Pastoral Epistles for Pastors* (The Woodlands: Kress Christian Publications, 2009), 152.

significant to the expression of ecclesiology in the African context. Joseph Healey rightly observes that "the vision of church as God's family has a natural appeal to African people."[22] As far as my research could ascertain, Bengt Sundkler may be attributed as the first person to truly sense the importance of the image of church as family for the African church. In his work, *The Christian Ministry in Africa*, he stated that

> There is a possibility – that the African Protestant theologian of the future will build on this fact of the family as one of the main pillars of his theology, particularly of his ecclesiology. He may come to regard it as his particular task to see the church in terms of the Great Family.[23]

From that time onwards, several African theologians have explored and preferred the "household" imagery in their ecclesiological formulations.[24] It is therefore not surprising that the image of the household of God was the preferred image adopted to describe the church in Africa during the African synod of bishops in 1994. This is reflected in the Message of the Synod (24), which states:

> To the local churches, the Church-as-Family churches of Africa . . . The Synod has highlighted that *You are the Family of God*. It is for the Church-as-Family that the Father has taken the initiative in the creation of Adam. It is the Church-as-Family which Christ, the New Adam and Heir to the nations, founded by the gift of his body and blood. It is the Church-as-Family which manifests to

---

22. Joseph G. Healey, *Towards an African Narrative Theology* (Maryknoll: Orbis Books, 1996), 145.

23. Bengt Sundkler, *The Christian Ministry in Africa* (London: SCM Press, 1962), 109.

24. A few of these works include John Mary Waliggo, "The African Clan as the True Model of the African Church," in *The Church in African Christianity: Innovative Essays in Ecclesiology*, ed. J. N. K. Mugambi and Laurenti Magesa (Nairobi: Initiatives Publishers, 1990), 111–28; Paul J. Sankey, "The Church as Clan: Critical Reflections on African Ecclesiology," *International Review of Mission* 83.330 (1994): 437–49, https://doi.org/10.1111/j.1758-6631.1994.tb03416.x; Agbonkhianmeghe E. Orobator, *The Church as Family: African Ecclesiology in Its Social Context* (Nairobi: Paulines Publications Africa, 2000); Francis Appiah-Kubi, *Église, Famille de Dieu: Un Chemin pour Les Églises D'afrique* (Paris: Éditions Karthala, 2008); Donatus Oluwa Chukwu, *The Church as the Extended Family of God: Toward a New Direction for African Ecclesiology* (Bloomington: Xlibris Corporation, 2011); Maximian Khisi, *The Church as the Family of God and the Care for Creation* (Mzuzu: Mzuni Press, 2018).

the world the Spirit which the Son sent from the Father so that there should be communion among all.[25]

One of the reasons for the preference of the image of household in describing the church in the African context is the fact that the family or household is among the most cherished African institutions, serving as the bedrock for many African societies.[26] As such, what these African theologians have done is to find a common denominator between African values and the Holy Scriptures, and to emphasize that denominator so that their understanding of the church is both truly African as well as truly scriptural.

At this point, it is important to state that these African theologians are aware that not all elements of the African household can be carried forward into the conceptual understanding of the nature and function of the church. Some of these unwanted aspects within African households include patriarchy, which can be harmful to women and children,[27] as well as the veneration of ancestors.[28]

Practical implications of the church as a household of God in Africa

Recent statistics still portray Africa as the continent with the highest number of Christians.[29] Despite this tremendous growth, the church in Africa is not without challenges. One of the main challenges facing the church in Africa is tribalism and ethnocentrism. As Matthew Michael notes, "The church has become a tribal organization with many tribal churches springing up whose commitment to Christ is often questionable because they often use the church

---

25. Maura Browne, ed., *The African Synod: Documents, Reflections, Perspectives* (Maryknoll Orbis Books, 1996), 76–77. Emphasis original.

26. For a brief discussion on how essential family and household are in African societies, see John S. Mbiti, *African Religions & Philosophy* (New York: Praeger, 1969), 104–9.

27. For a brief but excellent discussion on this, see Benjamin Kiriswa, "African Model of Church as Family: Implications on Ministry & Leadership," *African Ecclesial Review (AFER)* 43.3 (2001): 99–108. For a general overview of some of the positive and negative aspects of adopting this image for the African context, see Aidan G. Msafiri, "The Church as Family Model: Its Strengths and Weaknesses," in *African Theology Today*, ed. Emmanuel M. Katongole (Scranton: University of Scranton Press, 2002), 85–98.

28. Tite Tiénou, "The Church in African Theology: Description and Analysis of Hermeneutical Presuppositions," in *Biblical Interpretation and the Church: The Problem of Contextualization*, ed. D. A. Carson (Exeter: Paternoster Press, 1985), 151–65.

29. Gina A. Zurlo, Todd M. Johnson, and Peter F. Crossing, "World Christianity 2023: A Gendered Approach," *International Bulletin of Mission Research* (January 3, 2023): 11–22, https://doi.org/10.1177/23969393221128253.

as a venue to perpetuate their ethnic agendas."[30] The adage "blood is thicker than water" is unfortunately often quoted as validation for this practice.[31] The emphasis on the church as a family of God in Africa proves effective in pushing against this canker in the African church. For if the church would embrace itself as a family in which every member, irrespective of the tribe they come from, would be accepted in God's unified household, then the problem of tribalism in the church might be dealt with.

Maintaining the age differences in the household of God

Another aspect of the image of the church as a household that could be of significant relevance to the church in Africa is the fact that families, especially African families, tend to accommodate people of different age groups.[32] It is not surprising to see great-grandparents, grandparents, parents, and children (including babies) all residing in a single household. Thus, many African households are made up of three or four generations. The oldest members and the youngest members are not just tolerated or endured, but they are cherished as valuable members of the household. A popular Ghanaian proverb states, "Woe to the one who does not have an elderly person in his household." The elderly people are cherished for their knowledge, wisdom, and experience. It is also the duty of the family system to take care of the elderly members especially in their less productive years.[33] Children, likewise, are seen as blessings from God, and families without children are sometimes perceived as cursed, since the family's lineage will be cut off.[34]

---

30. Matthew Michael, *Christian Theology and African Traditions* (Eugene: Wipf & Stock, 2013), 202.

31. Michael, *Christian Theology and African Traditions*, 202.

32. Molefi Kete Asante, "Family," in *Encyclopedia of African Religion*, ed. Molefi Kete Asante and Ama Mazama (Thousand Oaks: SAGE, 2009), 258–59, 258.

33. Yaw Oheneba-Sakyi and Baffour K. Takyi, "Introduction to the Study of African Families: A Framework for Analysis," in *African Families at the Turn of the 21st Century*, ed. Yaw Oheneba-Sakyi and Baffour K. Takyi (Westport: Praeger, 2006), 1–24, 14.

34. Philistia Onyango and Diane Kayongo-Male state that "a childless marriage is thought of as a troublesome one since marriage seems meaningless without children." See Diane Kayongo-Male and Philistia Onyango, *The Sociology of the African Family* (London: Longman, 1984), 6.

The Presence of Different Age Groups in the Early Church

It seems quite evident that the early Christian gatherings were made up of people of different age groups. The New Testament especially shows that in the gathering of early Christian communities, one could find both the young and the old, and that seemed to have been the norm. We will look at a few of these texts.

Pastoral Epistles

Since we have spent some time in the Pastoral Epistles, we would like to begin from there. In 1 Tim 5:1–2, Paul entreats Timothy not only to recognize the existing age differences of the members of his congregation but to treat them accordingly. Here, Paul instructs Timothy on how to treat older men,[35] younger men, older women, and younger women. Paul instructs him not to sharply rebuke an older man but rather to exhort (παρακάλει, *parakalei*) him as a father. Not only that, but Timothy was also to exhort younger men as brothers, older women as mothers, and younger women as sisters. Children are missing from this list, probably "because they are under the direct responsibility of their parents for both their upbringing and their religious education."[36]

The significance of this passage to our discussion is that not only does Paul recognize that Timothy needs to deal in specific ways with different age groups and genders, but he encourages Timothy more importantly to treat them like family. If Timothy, being the leader, is instructed to treat the older men as fathers, younger men as brothers, older women as mothers, and younger women as sisters, it certainly follows that the other members of the community would also be required to interact with one another as family members.

In Titus 2:1–10, Paul, in a similar style to 1 Timothy 5, instructs Titus not only to acknowledge the age differences in the church but to offer teachings appropriate to different age groups. In other words, Paul wants Titus to differentiate between the older and the younger members of the church and provide age-specific teachings to each of these groups. He wants Titus to give

---

35. The Greek word here is πρεσβυτέρῳ (presbyterō) which could be rightly translated as an ecclesiastical position such as "elder" or "presbyter" (cf. 1 Tim 5:17, 19). Indeed this is how the KJV translates it. However, in light of the parallels with younger men, older women, and younger women, the word here describes someone older than Timothy. On the other hand, it is quite possible that some of these older men were also elders in the community. See Jerome D. Quinn and William C. Wacker, *The First and Second Letters to Timothy: A New Translation with Notes and Commentary*, Eerdmans Critical Commentary (Grand Rapids: Eerdmans, 2000), 410.

36. George T. Montague, *First and Second Timothy, Titus*, Catholic Commentary on Sacred Scripture (Grand Rapids: Baker Academic, 2008), 105–6.

special attention to each of these groups. Another significant aspect of Paul's instruction to Titus is the fact that Paul asserts that the elderly men (v. 2) and women (vv. 3–5) in the church community can make spiritual contributions to the church family. These elderly members can be valuable to the whole church community. Particularly, Paul tells Titus that the older women are to serve as mentors to the younger women by their teaching and training (vv. 3–5). All of these indicate that Paul not only recognizes the reality of multi-generational churches, but sees this aspect of the church as important, and beneficial for all members.

The household codes in Colossians and Ephesians

In the household codes Col 3:18–4:1 and Eph 5:21–6:9, Paul offers instructions about how members of a family are to relate to one another. He offers instructions to wives (Col 3:18; Eph 5:22–24), husbands (Col 3:19; Eph 5:25–28), children (Col 3:20; Eph 6:1–2), fathers (Col 3:21; Eph 6:4), slaves (Col 3:22; Eph 6:5–8), and masters (Col 4:1; Eph 6:9). The significant aspect of this to our discussion is that even though children were not usually addressed directly in Greco-Roman households,[37] Paul speaks to them directly and does not just pass on instructions to the children through the parents. The implication of this, as Margaret MacDonald rightly notes, is that Paul expects the children to "be part of the audience when the letter is read aloud."[38] Benjamin Merkle, also asserts that "This reference to children . . . indicates that Paul expects whole families to be gathered for worship."[39] That Paul addresses children directly in his letter signifies that they were not insignificant members of the community who could be overlooked.[40]

The word translated as "children" (τέκνα, *tekna*) in Ephesians 6:1 does not necessarily imply little children. It is also used to describe adults (cf. Matt 10:21; 21:28; Mark 2:5; Luke 15:31), and also metaphorically describe people

---

37. Benjamin L. Merkle, *Ephesians*, Exegetical Guide to the Greek New Testament (Nashville: B&H Academic, 2016), note on Eph 6:1; S. M. Baugh, *Ephesians*, Evangelical Exegetical Commentary (Bellingham: Lexham Press, 2016), 503.

38. Margaret Y. MacDonald, *Colossians and Ephesians*, Sacra Pagina Series (Collegeville: Liturgical Press, 2008), 332. For the practice of reading Scripture aloud in the early Christian communities, see Valeriy A. Alikin, *The Earliest History of the Christian Gathering: Origin, Development and Content of the Christian Gathering in the First to Third Centuries*, Supplements to Vigiliae Christianae 102 (Leiden: Brill, 2010), 158–78.

39. Merkle, *Ephesians*, note on 6:1.

40. Baugh, *Ephesians*, 504.

without any reference to their ages (Matt 3:9; 23:37; Mark 7:27; Luke 7:35).[41] As such, the word "primarily denotes relationships rather than age."[42] Even though the lexical meaning of τέκνα, *tekna* is broad enough to encompass people of different ages, its contextual usage in Ephesians 6:1, 4 suggests young children are in view.[43] Particularly in verse 4, the τέκνα, *tekna* are described as those who must be brought up (ἐκτρέφετε, *ektrephete*) in the training and instruction of the Lord (ἐν παιδείᾳ καὶ νουθεσίᾳ κυρίου, *en paideia kai nouthesia kyriou*). The imperative verb, ἐκτρέφετε (*ektrephete*), which means "to bring up from childhood,"[44] strongly suggests that the τέκνα (*tekna*) referred to in this section are children. That the τέκνα (*tekna*) here refers to children is affirmed by the usage of παιδείᾳ (*paideia*) and νουθεσίᾳ (*nouthesia*), which describe how the children are to be raised and brought up.[45]

While Ephesians 6:4 shows that the τέκνα (*tekna*) addressed are children, verse 1 shows that they are at the very least not little children. For Paul's address to them not only presumes that they would be able to understand the instruction, but also the reason and basis for the instruction, which involves their relationship with the Lord (ἐν κυρίῳ, *en kyriō*) and the fact that what they have been asked to do is right. All these suggest that, "the children in view here have to be old enough to be conscious of a relationship to their Lord and to be appealed to on the basis of it, but young enough still to be in the process of being brought up (cf. 6:4)."[46] Leslie Mitton on this basis proposes that the τέκνα (*tekna*) would be teenagers.[47] However, this view is too narrow

---

41. Ernest Best, *A Critical and Exegetical Commentary on Ephesians*, ICC (Edinburgh: T&T Clark, 2010), 564–65. See also the discussion by Georg Braumann, τέκνον, NIDNTT, 1:285–87.

42. Andrew T. Lincoln, *Ephesians*, Word Biblical Commentary 42 (Waco: Word Books, 1990), 403.

43. Pace Thorsten Moritz, who asserts that "Eph 6:1, 4 can and should . . . be interpreted as envisaging primarily the religious dimension of the relationship between parents and children irrespective of age." See Thorsten Moritz, *A Profound Mystery: The Use of the Old Testament in Ephesians* (Leiden: Brill, 1996), 170.

44. BDAG, s.v. "ἐκτρέφω."

45. The prepositional phrase, ἐν παιδείᾳ καὶ νουθεσίᾳ κυρίου, most likely conveys how the upbringing should be done. See Merkle, *Ephesians*, note on 6:4; William J. Larkin, *Ephesians: A Handbook on the Greek Text*, Baylor Handbook on the Greek New Testament (Waco: Baylor University Press, 2009), 148.

46. Lincoln, *Ephesians*, 403. Harold W. Hoehner also asserts that "In this context, Paul, no doubt, had in mind children old enough to understand and exercise their free will." See Harold W. Hoehner, *Ephesians: An Exegetical Commentary* (Grand Rapids: Baker Academic, 2002), 786.

47. C. Leslie Mitton, *Ephesians*, New Century Bible Commentary (Grand Rapids: Eerdmans, 1973), 211.

to encompass all the possibilities, for they could be below the teenage years or a little above the teenage years.[48] Though we cannot describe the exact age group of the children, it is certain that there were both older and younger age groups gathering together for worship in the church community. The young children were not insignificant, nor could their membership in the community be regarded as irrelevant. Paul's direct address to them strongly suggests they were regarded as full and valuable members of the community. They would not have only listened to the sections addressed to them, but also listened to the reading of the whole epistle. The children would have heard that God had chosen and predestined them for adoption (Eph 1:4–6) and has marked them with a seal, the promised Holy Spirit (1:13). When Paul prayed that the church in Ephesus would know the hope to which God has called them, and the infinite greatness of his power (1:16–23), he was praying for the young children in the church as well. Again, when Paul prays that Christ may dwell in the hearts of the believers in Ephesus and that they would be able to fully know and comprehend the love of Christ which transcends knowledge (3:14–19), the young children in the church were included in the people he prayed for. Even more importantly, Paul prayed for them alongside the older members of the church. In essence, the church community was made up of people of different age groups, and would be incomplete if one group (whether the older or the younger) left to set up a community of people of similar age.

The Gospels

Though the Gospel accounts do not present a lot of information on the nature of the gatherings of the early church, there are some hints that point towards the fact that they expected people of all ages to worship together. The first clue we find is in Luke 2:46 where Luke tells of the twelve-year-old Jesus sitting among the teachers, listening to them and asking them questions. The narrative suggests that the teachers did not know that the boy Jesus was the Messiah or the Son of God. Yet, the much older teachers welcomed him to sit among them, to ask and respond to questions.

Another instance in the gospel accounts that is suggestive of the fact that Jesus encouraged his followers to be a community of diverse ages is his welcoming and blessing of children whom his disciples tried to turn away (Matt 19:13–15 // Mark 10:13–16 // Luke 18:15–17). Commenting on this passage, Douglas Hare states that

---

48. Best, *A Critical and Exegetical Commentary on Ephesians*, 563.

It seems probable that Jesus's saying was understood by Matthew and his church as authorizing the practice of including children and young people in the corporate life of the church . . . Regarded from a sociological point of view, this may have been one of the reasons why Christianity spread so rapidly in the Roman world. There were popular religions for men (Mithraism) and for women (the religion of the Bona Dea). Christianity offered a family religion in which both sexes and all ages could participate together.[49]

Significance of Keeping the Young with the Old in Churches

Not only does the "youth church" model deviate from the biblical model, but it also poses significant risks for the young members of these churches. Having a church with both young and old members does not just tick the box of following the biblical model, but it also has many benefits for the members of the church community. The young people need the old people in the church, and the old people also need the young people. Since the specific issue this chapter seeks to address is the separation by the younger generation, we will only discuss the benefits they miss by separating themselves from the older generation.

Throughout the Scriptures, young people are often described as strong and energetic, and are encouraged to make use of their strength in their youthful stages, since the strength they possess will dwindle with age (Prov 20:29; Eccl 11:9–12:1; 1 John 2:14). On the other hand, the older generation is characterized with wisdom (cf. Job 12:12). In this sense, when the young people and the older people come together in a Christian community, each group brings along their peculiar gifts and abilities. A church without the older generation lacks the special gifts of wisdom and experience that they bring to the community. Even Solomon, who had been blessed with special wisdom from God, had elders with whom he consulted (cf. 1 Kgs 12:6). His son Rehoboam decided to take a different course when he rejected the counsel of the elders and embraced the counsel of his peers. As the narrative indicates, the results of this decision were devastating for his reign, ultimately leading to a rebellion against him (1 Kgs 12:6–24). By separating themselves from old people, these youth churches are more prone to experience a similar fate,

---

49. Douglas R. A. Hare, *Matthew*, Interpretation, A Bible Commentary for Teaching and Preaching (Louisville: John Knox Press, 1993), 224.

since they do not have the older generation among them to learn from their experience and wisdom.

The first benefit for the young people when they worship with older generations of Christians is that they see what it looks like to grow old in the faith and still be faithful to the Lord Jesus Christ. The Christian journey is certainly not a smooth one. Sometimes, the Christian walk seems easy but at other times, it is quite difficult. Sometimes taking a stand for Christ leads to admiration. At other times, it can result in disdain from others. Sometimes, Christians are not even able to gather the courage to do what they feel is godly. Sometimes they take decisions which they thought were godly but later realized were not. While many young people may not be able to imagine some of these situations, many older people have lived through them and more. They have lived through good times and bad times. They have stories of encountering God's miracles as well as God's silence in dire situations. Throughout their many years of living as Christians, they have seen people who started well but turned their back on the faith. They are the living proofs of God's preservation of the saints and also the endurance of the saints. These old people are significant blessings to the church, for they remind young Christians that no matter how difficult the culture and the temptation to leave the Christian faith can be, it is possible to withstand and persevere. As a young man in my mid-thirties, it is an enormous encouragement to see old Christians who have, and continue to, serve the Lord faithfully and consistently, showing me that this is also possible for me. Few things encourage me more than seeing older people coming to church and dancing with their walking sticks. For many of the old people I know, it takes a lot of effort to walk to church, and yet they hardly miss a church service. They are not just committed in attending services on Sundays, but also during the week. They are also very committed to corporate prayer, for they are almost always present. Their love for the Lord and his work is amazing, their hope is steadfast and firm, and their faith shines brightly so that it is visible to everyone. Such faith in the Lord undoubtedly takes time to grow and mature. The typical response I receive when I tell them that I want my faith in the Lord to be like theirs, is that their faith and confidence in the Lord has been developing over the years, and that I should keep following the Lord and he will use all kinds of circumstances to build up my faith in him.

Another benefit of being in a church community with old people is that they can offer the young people counsel on important life choices such as marriage and career. They can provide support during the struggles and challenges of the early years of marriage and raising children. The old people can also provide support for the young when they experience life challenges such as divorce, illness, job loss, etc. Equally important, the younger generation misses out on the opportunity to help and support the older generation.[50] For in many African societies, helping and supporting the aged is less of a burden and more of an honorable duty.

Conclusion

We have argued that the church as a household is a favorite image among many African theologians, since it emphasizes an essential cultural value cherished by many African communities. This image of the church as a household has been used to fight off some of the pitfalls faced by the African church such as tribalism and ethnocentrism. It must be emphasized that this imagery of the church as a household is not an invention of Africans, who for their love and commitment to family and kinship systems, impose this ideal on the church. On the contrary, this is a biblical image, which is expounded in the Holy Scriptures, taken up by African theologians because it paints a picture which many Africans can identify and connect with. A vital aspect of households in Africa is the fact that they are made up of people of many ages, from the very old, to young adults, teenagers, children, and infants. Yet, there is a new trend of youth churches where the young people want to have their own communities. In other words, they want to create a household of faith (i.e. a church community) which is made up of only young men and women. This trend not only goes against the norm of Scripture and African values, but it also poses significant threats to the faith of these young people.

Bibliography

Alikin, Valeriy A. *The Earliest History of the Christian Gathering: Origin, Development and Content of the Christian Gathering in the First to Third Centuries.* Supplements to Vigiliae Christianae 102. Leiden: Brill, 2010.

Allen, Holly Catterton, and Christine Lawton Ross. *Intergenerational Christian Formation: Bringing the Whole Church Together in Ministry, Community and Worship.* Downers Grove: IVP Academic, 2012.

Appiah-Kubi, Francis. *Église, Famille de Dieu: Un Chemin pour Les Églises D'afrique.* Paris: Éditions Karthala, 2008.

---

50. Holly Catterton Allen and Christine Lawton Ross, *Intergenerational Christian Formation: Bringing the Whole Church Together in Ministry, Community and Worship* (Downers Grove: IVP Academic, 2012), 52–63.

Arichea, Daniel C., and Howard Hatton. *A Handbook on Paul's Letters to Timothy and to Titus*. UBS Handbook Series. New York: United Bible Societies, 1995.

Asante, Molefi Kete. "Family." In *Encyclopedia of African Religion*, edited by Molefi Kete Asante and Ama Mazama, 258–59. Thousand Oaks: SAGE, 2009.

Baugh, S. M. *Ephesians*. Evangelical Exegetical Commentary. Bellingham: Lexham Press, 2016.

Berkhof, Louis. *Systematic Theology*. Grand Rapids: Eerdmans, 1953.

Best, Ernest. *A Critical and Exegetical Commentary on Ephesians*. ICC. Edinburgh: T&T Clark, 2010.

Bird, Michael F. *Evangelical Theology: A Biblical and Systematic Introduction*. 2nd ed. Grand Rapids: Zondervan Academic, 2020.

Browne, Maura, ed. *The African Synod: Documents, Reflections, Perspectives*. Maryknoll: Orbis Books, 1996.

Chukwu, Donatus Oluwa. *The Church as the Extended Family of God: Toward a New Direction for African Ecclesiology*. Bloomington: Xlibris Corporation, 2011.

Clowney, Edmund P. "Biblical Theology of the Church." In *The Church in the Bible and the World: An International Study*, edited by D. A. Carson, 13–87. Grand Rapids: Baker Books, 2002.

———. "Interpreting the Biblical Models of the Church." In *Biblical Interpretation and the Church: The Problem of Contextualization*, edited by D. A. Carson, 64–109. Exeter: Paternoster Press, 1985.

Collins, Raymond F. *1 & 2 Timothy and Titus: A Commentary*. New Testament Library. Louisville: Westminster John Knox Press, 2002.

Erickson, Millard J. *Christian Theology*. 3rd edition. Grand Rapids: Baker Academic, 2013.

Fee, Gordon D. *1 & 2 Timothy, Titus*. Understanding the Bible Commentary. Grand Rapids: Baker Books, 2011.

Gärtner, Bertil. *The Temple and the Community in Qumran and the New Testament: A Comparative Study in the Temple Symbolism of the Qumran Texts and the New Testament*. Society for New Testament Studies Monograph Series. Cambridge: Cambridge University Press, 1965.

Gehring, Roger W. *House Church and Mission: The Importance of Household Structures in Early Christianity*. Peabody: Hendrickson Publishers, 2004.

Guthrie, Donald. *The Pastoral Epistles: An Introduction and Commentary*. Rev. ed. Tyndale New Testament Commentaries. Downers Grove: InterVarsity Press, 2009.

Hanson, Anthony Tyrrell. *The Pastoral Epistles*. New Century Bible Commentary. Grand Rapids: Eerdmans, 1982.

Hare, Douglas R. A. *Matthew*. Interpretation, A Bible Commentary for Teaching and Preaching. Louisville: John Knox Press, 1993.

Healey, Joseph G. *Towards an African Narrative Theology*. Maryknoll: Orbis Books, 1996.

Hendriksen, William. *Exposition of the Pastoral Epistles*. Grand Rapids: Baker Book House, 1957.
Hoehner, Harold W. *Ephesians: An Exegetical Commentary*. Grand Rapids: Baker Academic, 2002.
Hultgren, Arland J. "1–2 Timothy, Titus." In *1–2 Timothy, Titus, II Thessalonians*. Augsburg Commentary on the New Testament. Minneapolis: Augsburg Publishing House, 1984.
Johnson, Luke Timothy. *The First and Second Letters to Timothy: A New Translation with Introduction and Commentary*. Anchor Yale Bible Commentary 35A. New Haven: Yale University Press, 2008.
Kayongo-Male, Diane, and Philistia Onyango. *The Sociology of the African Family*. London: Longman, 1984.
Kelly, J. N. D. *A Commentary on the Pastoral Epistles: I Timothy, II Timothy, Titus*. Black's New Testament Commentary. London: A&C Black, 1963.
Khisi, Maximian. *The Church as the Family of God and the Care for Creation*. Mzuzu: Mzuni Press, 2018.
Kiriswa, Benjamin. "African Model of Church as Family: Implications on Ministry & Leadership." *African Ecclesial Review (AFER)* 43, no. 3 (2001): 99–108.
Kitchen, John A. *The Pastoral Epistles for Pastors*. The Woodlands: Kress Christian Publications, 2009.
Knight, George W., III. *The Pastoral Epistles*. Grand Rapids: Eerdmans, 1992.
Larkin, William J. *Ephesians: A Handbook on the Greek Text*. Baylor Handbook on the Greek New Testament. Waco: Baylor University Press, 2009.
Lincoln, Andrew T. *Ephesians*. Word Biblical Commentary 42. Waco: Word Books, 1990.
Lock, Walter. *A Critical and Exegetical Commentary on the Pastoral Epistles: I & II Timothy and Titus*. International Critical Commentary. Edinburgh: T&T Clark, 1924.
MacDonald, Margaret Y. *Colossians and Ephesians*. Sacra Pagina Series. Collegeville: Liturgical Press, 2008.
Marshall, I. Howard. *A Critical and Exegetical Commentary on the Pastoral Epistles*. International Critical Commentary. London: T&T Clark, 1999.
Mbiti, John S. *African Religions & Philosophy*. New York: Praeger, 1969.
Merkle, Benjamin L. *Ephesians*. Exegetical Guide to the Greek New Testament. Nashville: B&H Academic, 2016.
Michael, Matthew. *Christian Theology and African Traditions*. Eugene: Wipf & Stock, 2013.
Minear, Paul S. *Images of the Church in the New Testament*. New Testament Library. Louisville: Westminster John Knox Press, 2004.
Mitton, C. Leslie. *Ephesians*. New Century Bible Commentary. Grand Rapids: Eerdmans, 1973.

Montague, George T. *First and Second Timothy, Titus*. Catholic Commentary on Sacred Scripture. Grand Rapids: Baker Academic, 2008.

Moritz, Thorsten. *A Profound Mystery: The Use of the Old Testament in Ephesians*. Leiden: Brill, 1996.

Mounce, William D. *Pastoral Epistles*. Word Biblical Commentary 46. Nashville: Thomas Nelson, 2009.

Msafiri, Aidan G. "The Church as Family Model: Its Strengths and Weaknesses." In *African Theology Today*, edited by Emmanuel M. Katongole, 85–98. Scranton: University of Scranton Press, 2002.

Ngewa, Samuel. *1 & 2 Timothy and Titus*. Africa Bible Commentary Series. Grand Rapids: Zondervan, 2009.

Oden, Thomas C. *First and Second Timothy and Titus*. Interpretation, a Bible Commentary for Teaching and Preaching. Louisville: John Knox Press, 1989.

Oheneba-Sakyi, Yaw, and Baffour K. Takyi. "Introduction to the Study of African Families: A Framework for Analysis." In *African Families at the Turn of the 21st Century*, edited by Yaw Oheneba-Sakyi and Baffour K. Takyi, 1–24. Westport: Praeger, 2006.

Orobator, Agbonkhianmeghe E. *The Church as Family: African Ecclesiology in Its Social Context*. Nairobi: Paulines Publications Africa, 2000.

Quinn, Jerome D., and William C. Wacker. *The First and Second Letters to Timothy: A New Translation with Notes and Commentary*. Eerdmans Critical Commentary. Grand Rapids: Eerdmans, 2000.

Sankey, Paul J. "The Church as Clan: Critical Reflections on African Ecclesiology." *International Review of Mission* 83, no. 330 (1994): 437–49. https://doi.org/10.1111/j.1758-6631.1994.tb03416.x.

Sundkler, Bengt. *The Christian Ministry in Africa*. London: SCM Press, 1962.

Tiénou, Tite. "The Church in African Theology: Description and Analysis of Hermeneutical Presuppositions." In *Biblical Interpretation and the Church: The Problem of Contextualization*, edited by D. A. Carson, 151–65. Exeter: Paternoster Press, 1985.

Tomlinson, F. Alan. "The Purpose and Stewardship Theme Within the Pastoral Epistles." In *Entrusted with the Gospel: Paul's Theology in the Pastoral Epistles*, edited by Andreas J. Köstenberger and Terry L. Wilder, 52–83. Nashville: B&H Academic, 2010.

Towner, Philip H. *The Letters to Timothy and Titus*. New International Commentary on the New Testament. Grand Rapids: Eerdmans, 2006.

Van Nes, Jermo. *Pauline Language and the Pastoral Epistles: A Study of Linguistic Variation in the Corpus Paulinum*. Linguistic Biblical Studies 16. Leiden: Brill, 2018.

Waliggo, John Mary. "The African Clan as the True Model of the African Church." In *The Church in African Christianity: Innovative Essays in Ecclesiology*, edited by J. N. K. Mugambi and Laurenti Magesa, 111–28. Nairobi: Initiatives Publishers, 1990.

Witherington, Ben, III. *Letters and Homilies for Hellenized Christians: A Socio-Rhetorical Commentary on Titus, 1–2 Timothy and 1–3 John*. Downers Grove: IVP Academic, 2006.

Yarbrough, Robert W. *The Letters to Timothy and Titus*. The Pillar New Testament Commentary. Grand Rapids: Eerdmans, 2018.

Yarnell, Malcolm B., III. "Οἶκος Θεού: A Theologically Neglected but Important Ecclesiological Metaphor." *Midwestern Journal of Theology* 2, no. 1 (Fall 2003): 53–65.

Young, Frances M. *The Theology of the Pastoral Letters*. Cambridge: Cambridge University Press, 1994.

Zurlo, Gina A., Todd M. Johnson, and Peter F. Crossing. "World Christianity 2023: A Gendered Approach." *International Bulletin of Mission Research* (January 3, 2023): 11–22. https://doi.org/10.1177/23969393221128253.

8

The Case for the Ecclesiastical Title "Apostle" and the Gift of "Apostle"

Ephesians 4:11

Dieudonne Komla Nuekpe

The Church of Pentecost, Ghana, and The Sanneh Institute

Abstract

The fivefold ministry of apostles, prophets, evangelists, pastors and teachers are embraced with different views of continuity or discontinuity by scholars. The preunderstanding of the foundational gifts in Ephesians 2:20 influences the cessationists' view on Ephesians 4:11. Among evangelical Christians, there is an agreement that the Holy Spirit does exist and works in the church today. Nevertheless, there seems to be no agreement on whether the gifts of the Holy Spirit still empower people to function as apostles, prophets and evangelists in the modern-day church. Some cessationists assert that the offices of apostles and prophets in Ephesians 4:11 are an event confined to a distant past when Jesus was alive and appointed men into these offices. They assert that the gifts of apostles and prophets ended with the closure of the New Testament canon of Scripture, and the apostolic era has ended. This view attempts to put the Holy Spirit in a box and limits his work of empowering people for ministry. Pentecostal and charismatic churches believe that God has given miraculous gifts to the church on Pentecost and has enabled them to share in the power of the apostles through the outpouring of the Holy Spirit that empowers them for apostolic ministry. This chapter is an attempt to bring a better understanding of the word "apostle" as used in Ephesians 4:11. It rebuts the view provided by cessationists and offers a further understanding of the use of the word "apostle." The paper frowns upon the abusive use of the title "apostle," which may lead to heresy, autocratic leadership and spiritual pride. However, it concludes that the foundational role played by the twelve apostles does not negate the gift of "apostle" in the modern church. Through literary research methods based on biblical and extrabiblical evidence, it provides proof for the continuous use of the ecclesiastical title and gifts of "apostle" and their implications for twenty-first-century ministry.

Key words: ecclesiastical title, apostle, the gift of apostles, missionary apostles

Introduction

The fivefold ministry of apostles, prophets, evangelists, pastors and teachers is embraced with different views of continuity or discontinuity by scholars. Richard Gaffin represents the cessationists' view on Ephesians 4:11, influenced by the preunderstanding of the foundational gifts in Ephesians 2:20. I am attracted to Gaffin's work because he represents the evangelical, reformed cessationism of most faculty members of the prominent Westminster Seminary.[1] Among evangelical Christians, there is an agreement that the Holy Spirit does exist and works in the church today.[2] However, there seems to be no agreement on whether the gifts of the Holy Spirit still empower people to function as apostles, prophets and evangelists in the modern-day church. Some cessationists assert that the offices of apostles and prophets in Ephesians 4:11 is an event confined to a distant past when Jesus was alive and appointed men into these offices. They assert that the gifts of apostles and prophets ended with the closure of the New Testament canon of Scripture and the apostolic era has ended. Arguably this is to "put the Holy Spirit in a box"[3] and limits his work of empowering people for ministry. The implication is that because the early church did not have a complete Scripture, they needed trustworthy apostles

---

1. Wayne Grudem, "Preface," in *Are Miraculous Gifts for Today?* Edited by Wayne Grudem (Grand Rapids: Zondervan Academic, 1996), 10.
2. Grudem, "Preface," 9.
3. Gaffin Jr., "A Cessationist View," in *Are Miraculous Gifts for Today?* Edited by Wayne Grudem (Grand Rapids: Zondervan Academic, 1996), 25. Gaffin prefers to state this view in terms of "the Spirit has sovereignly chosen to 'box' himself in."

to lay the foundation for standard doctrines. Cessationists believe there is an apostolic function or ministry today but not the office of the apostle. If anyone claims today to be an apostle, he must be seen as a heretic, opening up for false doctrines.[4]

Pentecostal and charismatic churches who trace their ministry to Charles F. Parham and William J. Seymour believe that God has given miraculous gifts to the church on Pentecost and has enabled them to share in the power of the apostles through the outpouring of the Holy Spirit that empowers them for apostolic ministry.[5] This chapter is an attempt to bring a better understanding of the word "apostles" as used in Ephesians 4:11. By means of literary research methods, it rebuts the view provided by Gaffin and offers a further understanding of the use of the word "apostles." Based on biblical and extrabiblical evidence, it provides proof for the continuous use of the ecclesiastical title and gifts of "apostles" and their implications for twenty-first-century ministry.

Apostle in the Hebrew Bible and Septuagint

The term "apostle" or "apostleship" does not exist as such in the Old Testament. However, the root meaning of this term can refer to a person or persons "being sent away," "commissioned" or "appointed" to a specific task. In Hebrew, this is represented by the root verb שָׁלַח *shālaḥ*, which is mostly used to mean "send" or "send away."[6] *Shālaḥ* varies in use, sometimes referring to God as the sending or commissioning agent, and other times it refers to human beings fulfilling this role (Gen 45:5; Exod 3:13–15; Judg 6:14; Gen 41:8; 2 Chr 28:16).[7] The concept of "apostle" is applied to all kinds of representatives, from legal to administrative, such as envoys and ambassadors. In the Septuagint (LXX), the noun occurs only once in 1 Kings 14:6 during an encounter between Jeroboam's wife and the prophet Ahijah. It was used in Judaism to describe a person who led the synagogue congregation in worship, a representative of the Sanhedrin

---

4. Opoku Onyinah, *Apostles & Prophets: The Ministry of Apostles and Prophets throughout the Generations* (Eugene: Wipf & Stock, 2022), 2–3.

5. The General Council of the Assemblies of God, *Apostles and Prophets: Position Papers* (Boonville: Zondervan Publishing House, 2020), 3.

6. Stephen D. Renn, "Apostle, Apostleship," *Expository Dictionary of Bible Words* (Peabody: Hendrickson Publishers Inc., 2005), 1025.

7. Renn, "Apostle, Apostleship," 1025.

sent on official duty, or an outstanding personality like Moses who acted on behalf of God. The term is usually confined to the Jewish community.[8]

The term in Hellenism refers to seafaring, military expeditions – a dispatch of a fleet or army on a military expedition with the sense of sending emissaries.[9] The word *apostolos* is an early Christian title. The basic meaning of the word is "the sending of messengers or envoys." An apostle in this sense can be called *angelos* meaning "messenger," as referenced in Luke 7:24 and 9:52. Apostle also refers to a "herald" as used in 1 Timothy 2:7 and 2 Timothy 1:11. The concept of "apostles" was used in the Hellenistic era as humanly or divinely sent authorities.[10] *Pempō*, "to send," is used interchangeably with *apostello*, which when used, lays emphasis on the purpose of the sending.

The New Testament Apostles

The term "apostle" appears seventy-nine times in the New Testament where the use is biblically confined. It is a transliteration of the Greek *apostolos* derived from *apostellein*, "to send."[11] It lays emphasis on someone who is commissioned, released or dispatched by an authority. When "apostle" is used in the New Testament, it gives the meaning that the one sent had a responsibility towards the sending authority to whom he is also accountable. It is used to represent generally a messenger, whether human or divinely sent by God to proclaim the message of the gospel of Christ (John 13:16; Matt 10:40–42; Gal 4:14). The origin of the apostolic office in the New Testament is traceable in the Gospels to Jesus's calling of the disciples (Mark 3:14–15; 6:30). These were the original apostles who constituted the foundation of the church (Eph 2:20). These apostles were eyewitnesses to all that Christ had accomplished on earth, from the baptism of John to the time of Christ's ascension to heaven (Acts 1:21–22). They initially represented the twelve tribes of Israel (Matt 19:28; Acts 6:2), and the title "the Twelve" was used in the early church designating them (Acts 6:2).[12] The term was also used for Christ as an envoy of God sent

---

8. Everett F. Harrison, "Apostle, Apostleship," *Evangelical Dictionary of Theology*, 2nd ed., ed. Walter A. Elwell (Grand Rapids: Baker Academic, 2001), 85.

9. "*Apostolos*," in *Theological Dictionary of the New Testament*, ed. Gerhard Titel, vol. 1 (Grand Rapids: Eerdmans, 1964), 413.

10. Hans Dieter Betz, "Apostle," *The Anchor Bible Dictionary*, vol. 1 A–C, ed. David Noel Freedman (New York: Bantam Doubleday Dell Publishing Group, Inc., 1992), 309.

11. Harrison, "Apostle, Apostleship," 85.

12. The General Council of the Assemblies of God, *Apostles and Prophets: Position Papers* (Boonville: Zondervan Publishing House, 2020), 3.

by the Father and who represented the Father faithfully (Heb 3:1; Matt 15:24; Luke 4:18, 43). The rabbis of Jesus's time used the word with the Old Testament concept of *shālaḥ* in view. According to the rabbis, "a man's agent is like unto himself"[13] and this concept is very close in meaning to the modern-day power of attorney.

The New Testament apostles were, therefore, selected people expected to share intimate fellowship with Jesus, preach the gospel of the kingdom of God, and participate with Jesus in performing miracles. The purpose of the apostleship was to participate in the mission of God with the authority given by Jesus (Matt 10:5–14; Mark 6:7–11; Luke 9:1–5; Matt 10:6) and later by the Holy Spirit. After Pentecost, the basis of apostleship transformed from tribal (twelve Jews) to personal and spiritual (Acts 14:4, 14; Gal 1:9; 1 Cor 15:5–8; 1 Thess 2:7; Phil 2:25).

Pauline usage

In Pauline thought, apostles were people who were marked or revealed through signs, miracles and wondrous deeds as portrayed in Acts 5:12, 2 Corinthians 12:12 and Romans 15:19. The concept of *apostolos* in the Pauline usage is an administrative designation used for envoys, delegates, or people appointed by the church to represent them; they are the "envoys of the church" (*apostoloi ekklesion*) as revealed in 2 Corinthians 8:23 and Philippians 2:25. Some scholars have thus made a distinction between "apostle of Christ" and "apostle of the church." Paul, in 2 Corinthians 8:23, spoke about certain unnamed brothers as "apostles" of the churches, ἀπόστολοι ἐκκλησιῶν, and an honour to Christ.[14] He spoke of Epaphroditus also as *apostolos* of the church sent to care for him (Phil 2:25). These were delegates or messengers appointed by the churches to represent them. These Scripture verses demonstrate that the term was used for other people in the context of mission outside the twelve apostles.

Todd D. Still notes that Paul identifies himself in his letter to the Colossians as an apostle, not in a way to establish or assert his authority as an apostle but rather in a way to describe his divinely commissioned ministry.[15] The use of

---

13. The General Council of the Assemblies of God, *Apostles and Prophets: Position Papers*, 4.

14. Ralph P. Martin, *2 Corinthians*, Word Biblical Commentary 40, 2nd ed. (Grand Rapids: Zondervan, 2014), 456.

15. Todd D. Still, "Colossians," in *Ephesians–Philemon*, vol. 12, *The Expositor's Bible Commentary Revised Edition*, ed. Tremper Longman III and David E. Garland (Grand Rapids: Zondervan, 2006), 275.

"apostle" in Colossians, therefore, seems to lay emphasis on the concept of divine commission and enablement by Christ and the Holy Spirit to proclaim the good news. The term "apostle" in Colossians does not lay much emphasis on the authority of the apostle as a position of self-glorification but as a position of humble responsibility by God's divine design and enablement towards a specific people (Col 1:1, 24–2:5; 1 Thess 2:4).[16] It refers to a person who is especially sent forth by God to go among men as an ambassador or messenger. Paul presents himself as being, in the fullest sense of the term, an official representative and a spokesman of Christ.[17] The term *apostolos* in Colossians as used by Paul, therefore, reveals that modern-day leaders who are divinely commissioned for specific ministerial duties and are recognized by the church as apostolic in nature, may use the term. Ephesians 4:11 must therefore be read within the context of the entire letter. Paul had already mentioned that the church was built on the foundation of the "apostles" (Eph 2:20). In this instance, he referred to the original twelve who provided a kind of foundational link between the resurrected Jesus and the church. They gave a first-hand interpretation of all Jesus has done for the church by way of edification. However, the foundation must be considered only as a pattern, since the gift of apostleship did not die with the twelve apostles as cessationists believe.

Extrabiblical Support for Non-Cessationism

The use of "apostle" has roots in Old Testament Jewish culture but gained its unique use among early Christians within the context of an ecclesiastical community that recognized God's redemptive mission to all nations as ongoing until Christ's second coming. Etymologically, the words "apostle" and "missionary" were used interchangeably. However, in the modern day, the general use of the word "apostle" emphasizes authority while "missionary" lays emphasis on a task. Originally, both words described someone with both an assignment and the authority to accomplish it. The term "missionary," which is comfortably used by many instead of "apostle," emerged in an era of Christendom and colonization of the world and was viewed through the lens of colonization.[18] The discontinuation of the term "apostle" and the use

---

16. Still, "Colossians," 275.

17. William Hendriksen, *Exposition of Colossians, and Philemon*, Baker New Testament Commentary (Grand Rapids: Baker Academic, 1964), 43.

18. Don Dent, *The Ongoing Role of Apostles in Missions: The Forgotten Foundation*, (Bloomington: WestBow Press, 2019), Kindle Edition, 271.

of "missionary" was the work of Western civilization, which also viewed the apostolic work as fulfilled and discontinued after the New Testament canon was closed. David Bosch rightly points out that the term "mission," from which the adjective "missionary" is derived, is a new word that is historically linked indissolubly with the colonial era, and the missionaries were irrevocably tied to an institution in Europe.[19] Christopher J. H. Wright described the problem of Western missionary stereotypes: the term "missionary" was maintained instead of "apostle" primarily because the West maintained it.[20]

The Didache, the most important first-century document on early Christianity, gave instruction on how Christians should relate to itinerant ministers and especially apostles: "Let every apostle who comes to you be welcomed as if he were the Lord."[21] The allegorical "Shepherd of Hermas," a popular writing from the first century to the fourth century, used the word "apostle" more widely than just for the twelve and affirmed the continuation of the apostolic task of preaching and teaching the word.[22] Origen of Alexandria, commenting on Ephesians 4:11–12, in the third century, stated:

> Grace is given to each of the saints according to the measure of the gift of Christ, so that some are apostles, but some are prophets, and others evangelists, and after them pastors, and above all, teachers . . . It is possible for these to exist continually in the church, perhaps apostles also, to whom it is given to work the signs of an apostle, may be found even now.[23]

Cessationism: A Deficient Understanding of Ephesians 4:11

Gaffin Jr. asserts that some spiritual gifts, including some miracles, are in operation today while others have ceased. The difficulty lies in determining which ones continue today. He categorically questions the continuity of all word gifts, including the Ephesians 4:11 list. He bases his argument on the

---

19. David J. Bosch, *Transforming Mission: Paradigm Shifts in Theology of Mission* (Maryknoll: Orbis Books, 2018), 233.

20. Christopher J. H. Wright, *The Mission of God: Unlocking the Bible's Grand Narrative* (Downers Grove: IVP Academic, 2006), 23–24.

21. William C. Varner, *The Way of the Didache: The First Christian Handbook* (New York: New York University, 2007), 4, in Dent, *The Ongoing Role of Apostles in Missions*, 377.

22. Dent, *The Ongoing Role of Apostles in Missions*, 395.

23. Joseph W. Trigg, "The Charismatic Intellectual: Origen's Understanding of Religious Leadership," *Church History* 50, no. 1 (1981): 5–19, quoted in Dent, *The Ongoing Role of Apostles in Missions*, 411.

"salvation-historical" understanding of the church and its apostolicity indicated in Ephesians 2:20. He considers the apostles as the foundation of the church and argues that the function of "apostles" in Ephesians 4:11, because it references the foundational role, is not repeatable.[24] This deficient understanding of "apostles" in Ephesians 4:11 arises from his preunderstanding of Ephesians 2:20. He asserts that if the builder of a construction knows what he is doing, he lays a foundation once and for all, and the foundation he lays does not need to be laid repeatedly. If the apostles served as a foundation for the church, then he deems that foundation as unrepeatable: the presence of apostles in the design of the divine architect was simply temporary.[25]

This interpretation implies that the apostles and their function were temporary, and thus, remained in the past, unrepeatable. Gaffin further argues from the metaphor of 1 Corinthians 3:11 to express that Christ is the foundation laid by the apostles because of his finished redemptive work (1 Cor 1:18, 23; 2 Tim 2:8). He explained that apostles are the foundation of the church – not in the sense that they supply any lack in Christ's work but in the sense that they bear gospel witness to the work of Christ, since what is left is an adequate witness to the finished work of Christ. In Gaffin's assertion, apostles are authorized witnesses appointed by Christ to bear witness to his resurrection (Acts 1:2, 8; 1 Cor 9:1)[26] and became witnesses because of that inspired revelation of Christ (Eph 3:5). Therefore, the witness of the apostles is once and for all: it has ended with the closure of the New Testament canon. Any view that supports the continuation of apostles, whether as office or function, would then be in direct contradiction with the canonicity of the New Testament (Gal 1:11–12; 1 Thess 2:13), undermining the inspiration and authority of Scripture. Gaffin views the interpretation of the continuation of apostles and their function as an attempt to reopen the canon and render the sufficiency of Scripture and its canonicity incomplete or relative.[27] He argues that even though there is biblical evidence of succession to Paul (Timothy), Paul never called Timothy an apostle by name in spite of Paul's injunction to Timothy to guard the apostolic deposit (Phil 2:20–22; 2 Tim 1:14).[28] In 1 Thessalonians 3:2 he calls him "co-worker of God."

---

24. Gaffin Jr., "A Cessationist View," 42–43.
25. Gaffin Jr., "A Cessationist View," 42.
26. Gaffin Jr., 43.
27. Gaffin Jr., 45.
28. Gaffin Jr., 48.

In contrast, the opposing view supports the continuous use of apostles. 1 Corinthians 13:8–12 reveals that both prophets and apostles will continue until the coming of the Lord, which is expressed as "the perfect." Then "the partial" understanding of apostles and prophets will pass away. Revelatory gifts of prophecy and apostles ended when the canon of Scripture terminated, but the declaratory gifts continue until we appear before the perfect Lord.[29] For this reason, the original apostles and prophets belong to the "already" but not to the "not yet." I agree with Gordon Fee that the function of an apostle is as *charismata*, and thus, the gifts of the Spirit will continue until the final consummation.[30] The *charismata* is inseparable from the office of the apostle because the gifts reveal the office.

The empowering work of the Spirit, who gives the *charismata* to believers, is an ongoing work that includes generations to come (Acts 2:39). The Spirit still works in appointing apostles (Acts 13:1–3). The gifts listed in Ephesians 4:11, 1 Corinthians 12 and Romans 12:3–8 are all linked with the idea of ministry, and all ministries are "concrete ways in which God works his grace among his people."[31] The *charismata* can be defined narrowly and broadly depending on the context of the passage. In Ephesians 4:11, the *charismata* cannot be limited to the apostolic era while the church still lives in the context of Ephesians: "The gifts of the Spirit are the functions of the Spirit that Paul identifies with Christian ministry."[32]

Additionally, Gaffin's use of the foundational argument in Ephesians 2:20 to support Ephesians 4:11 is not appropriate because the subject matter in Ephesians 2:20 is about offices, whereas Ephesians 4:11 is about gifts within the context of the church.[33] While the text in Ephesians 2:20 emphasizes the foundational function of the apostles, it does not mention discontinuation. Jesus is the foundation, and the twelve apostles were only the layers of God's building, the church (1 Cor 3:10). The apostles in Ephesians 2:20 were

---

29. Simon J. Kistemaker, *Exposition of the First Epistle to the Corinthians*, Hendriksen-Kistemaker New Testament Commentary (Grand Rapids: Baker Academic, 1993), 465.

30. Gordon Fee, *Gospel and Spirit: Issues in New Testament Hermeneutics* (Grand Rapids: Baker Books, 1991), quoted in Gaffin Jr., et al., *Are Miraculous Gifts for Today?*, 59.

31. E. Earle Ellis, *Pauline Theology: Ministry and Society* vol. 1 Lanham: University Press of America, 1997), quoted in Kenneth Berding, "Confusing Word and Concept in Spiritual Gifts: Have We Forgotten James Barr's Exhortation?" *JETS* 43.1 (March 2000), 37–51, 47–49.

32. Ellis, *Pauline Theology Ministry and Society*, 47–49.

33. Hendriksen, *Exposition of Ephesians*, Hendriksen-Kistemaker New Testament Commentary, 195.

custodians of special, normative revelation,[34] and the foundation in Ephesians 2:20 can imply a "pattern" to be replicated, not necessarily a once-and-for-all, dead-in-the-past, apostolic office. The foundation represents Jesus Christ himself and the reoccurring "inspired foundational confession" of apostles. Peter's confession, which was deemed as foundational in Matthew 16:16–18, was expected to be a recurring confession for every generation because it was a pattern to be followed.[35] The "apostles" in Ephesians 4:11 are to be considered as representatives and custodians of the original revelation and traditions passed on by the twelve apostles. They are those spiritual leaders expected to keep the norms for the church's existence.[36]

Gaffin states that the reoccurrence of apostolic office undermines the canon of Scripture.[37] However, Scripture clearly reveals that the gift of apostleship was not limited to the twelve apostles alone. Apostleship went beyond a physical link with Jesus to a spiritual link through the Holy Spirit (2 Cor 3:17; 5:16).[38] Just as the anonymous disciples in Ephesus (Acts 19:1–7) prophesied after their encounter with Paul, and the daughters of Philip who prophesied (Acts 21:9) were not a once-and-for-all foundation of the church, so also are modern apostles not part of a once-and-for-all foundation.[39] In Ephesians 4:11, Paul was referring to the gifts, which are open to all, in the same way, he prayed that other believers might be given the Spirit of wisdom and revelation (Eph 1:18–22). That gift has nothing to do with the inspired authoritative canon of Scripture. It is not a new revelation outside the canon but rather a revelation within the canon of Scripture by means of the inspiration of the Holy Spirit. The function of the apostles is likewise submitted to the authority of Scripture.

The claim that there are no apostles today is an attempt to say the gift of the Holy Spirit died with the early apostles. However, when the gifts are discussed, the biblical authors never spoke of cessation.[40] Oss observes that the doctrine of cessationism originated in a lack of miracles in the Christian experience, which makes people attempt to explain this lack with the temporary discontinuity of

---

34. Samuel Storms, "A Third Wave Response," *Are Miraculous Gifts for Today?* (Grand Rapids: Zondervan Academic, 1996), 81.

35. John Ruthven, "The Foundational Gifts of Ephesians 2:20," *JPT* 10.2 (2002): 28.

36. Andrew T. Lincoln, *Ephesians*, Word Biblical Commentary 42 (Grand Rapids: Zondervan, 1990), 252.

37. Gaffin Jr., "A Cessationist View," 45.

38. Ruthven, "The Foundational Gifts of Ephesians 2:20," 41.

39. Storms, "A Third Wave Response," 80.

40. Storms, "A Third Wave Response," 92.

apostolicity.⁴¹ Likewise, the view that Gaffin represents based on Ephesians 2:20 was influenced by the polemics of the Reformers against the papacy. Protestant reformers opposed the papal claims to ultimate religious authority by means of apostolic succession. Their objection to the reoccurrence of the apostolic office was not based on thorough biblical exegesis. Their concern was the papal claim of absolute apostolic authority over the universal church.⁴²

Further discussion on cessationist ideas of apostleship

The cessationist position is partly based on Peter's qualification for Judas' replacement in Acts 1:21–22 and the fact that Paul declared he was the last to see Jesus (1 Cor 15:8).⁴³ F. F. Bruce says, "The apostles, as an order of the ministry of the church, were not perpetuated beyond the apostolic age, but the various functions they discharged did not lapse with their departure but continued to be performed by others – notably the evangelists and pastors and teachers."⁴⁴ If the Holy Spirit is the same source of the gifts given to evangelists and pastors, there is no reason why the first two, apostles and prophets, are no longer functional.

Charles Hodge notes that the apostles are the witnesses of Jesus who also bear witness to his doctrine, miracles, and resurrection. These apostles' teachings were infallible in nature and absolute in inspiration and commission. No other person after them could be termed as "apostles" unless they were immediately appointed by the Lord Jesus Christ, had seen Christ after his resurrection, and received the Gospel by revelation.⁴⁵ Though Hodge is right in pointing out the qualities that constitute the office of an apostle, he fails to indicate that there were other people called "apostles" in the mission of the church who did not necessarily possess the new revelation but functioned as missionaries and church planters. While many evangelicals are uncomfortable in using the word "apostles" for their missionaries,⁴⁶ we cannot rule out completely the use of the ecclesiastical title "apostles" for modern-day church

---

41. Douglas A. Oss, "A Pentecostal/Charismatic View," in *Are Miraculous Gifts for Today?* Edited by Wayne Grudem (Grand Rapids: Zondervan Academic, 1996), 264.
42. Ruthven, "The Foundational Gifts of Ephesians 2:20," 28.
43. Dent, *The Ongoing Role of Apostles in Missions*, 836.
44. R. Kent Hughes, *Ephesians: The Mystery of the Body of Christ, Preaching the Word* (Wheaton: Crossway Books, 1990), 133.
45. Charles Hodge, *A Commentary on the Epistle to the Ephesians* (New York: Robert Carter and Brothers, 1856), 222–23.
46. Dent, *The Ongoing Role of Apostles in Missions*, 243.

planters and proven missionaries recognized by their sending local authorities as possessing the gifts of apostles.

The concept of "apostles" is mainly used by Pentecostals in the majority world, Latin America and some parts of Asia. Alan Johnson notes that early Pentecostals identified themselves and their mission as part of a restoration of apostolic power and practice.[47] J. E. Young, a proponent of "pneumatic apostolicity," states that Christ may have initiated apostleship through the original twelve apostles but continued to call others into apostleship by means of the Holy Spirit for the mission.[48] Vinson Synan, a Pentecostal scholar, asserts that "most people in church history who have claimed to be new apostles have been branded as heretics and excommunicated from the church."[49] However, it must be noted that people who assume the ecclesiastical title "apostles" do not apply it within the context of the original twelve apostles but rather as missionaries endowed with apostolic giftings, as in Ephesians 4:11.

Wayne Grudem observes that since no one can claim to be an eyewitness to the risen Lord, there can be no apostles today. Someone may object that Christ could appear to someone today and appoint that person as an apostle. However, Grudem states that the foundational nature of the office of the apostle (Eph 2:20; Rev 21:14), and the fact that Paul was the last of all the apostles (1 Cor 15:8), points to the fact that no new apostle could exist today. Furthermore, God's history of redemption started but did not continue with the call of apostles (Eph 2:20).[50] Grudem seems to repeat the same idea represented by Gaffin, and this points to some measure of agreement on both sides: though we may use the word apostle today to mean effective church planters or pioneer missionaries, we must be careful not to pride ourselves in claiming these titles. Not even the major Christian leaders in history such as Athanasius, Augustine, Luther, Wesley or Whitefield have taken upon themselves such a title as "apostle."[51] Grudem further states:

> If any in modern times want to take the title "apostle" to themselves, they immediately raise the suspicion that they may be motivated

---

47. Alan Johnson, "Apostolic Function and Mission," *Journal of Pentecostal Theology* 17 (2008): 234–54, 259.

48. J. E. Young, "That Some Should Be Apostles," in Charles J. Conniry, "Identifying Apostolic Christianity: A Synthesis of Viewpoints," Faculty Publications – Portland Seminary (1994), 11.

49. Vinson Synan, "Who Are the Modern Apostles?" *Ministries Today* (March–April, 1992), 45.

50. Wayne Grudem, *Systematic Theology* (Grand Rapids: Zondervan, 2000), 911.

51. Grudem, *Systematic Theology*, 911.

by inappropriate pride and desires for self-exaltation, along with excessive ambition and a desire for much more authority in the church than any one person should rightfully have.[52]

Douglas notes that when people in church history claimed to be new apostles, they may have confused the twelve and were considered heretics.[53] They confused the twelve original apostles with the gifts of apostles. As noted by Peter Wagner, apostleship is a special ability that God gives for leadership and oversight, not limited to particular people but to all who give counsel and preach the gospel, including peacemakers, troubleshooters and problem solvers.[54] Anyone called by God, endowed with the manifestation of the Spirit for counseling, teaching, administration, preaching, counseling or with a specific duty for the salvation of people, is working as an apostle. After examining the New Testament, Dent, and several other scholars concluded that there are four categories of apostles, namely, "the Twelve, other commissioned eyewitnesses, missionary apostles, and apostles of the church."[55]

Historically, Christians who objected to the continuity of apostolic office and gifts were the same people who thought the Great Commission was limited to the twelve apostles in whom it found its fulfilment by the close of the New Testament canon of revelation. William Carey recognized the ongoing nature of apostleship within the context of participation in God's mission, whose task and authority remain inseparable. His argument formed the basis of English-speaking protestants' change and engagement in the Great Commission.[56] In Church history, first-century missionaries like Addai of Edessa (North East of Antioch), Saint Patrick, and many more were recognized and called apostles. The fact that some early Christian workers did not apply the titles does not mean the use of apostles was unbiblical or undermined the canon. Missionaries who did not apply the title even though they possessed the gift were simply being humble and avoiding confusion with the original twelve apostles.

---

52. Grudem, *Systematic Theology*, 911–12.
53. Synan, "Who Are the Modern Apostles?" 42–47.
54. Peter C. Wagner, *Your Spiritual Gift Can Help Your Church Grow*, rev. ed. (Ventura: Regal Books, 1994), 181–82.
55. Dent, *The Ongoing Role of Apostles in Missions*, 1030.
56. Dent, *The Ongoing Role of Apostles in Missions*, 1410.

A Broader View of Apostles

In Ephesians 4:11, "apostle" refers to people with special gifts endowed by the Spirit for the equipping and edification of the church. Paul has a broad view of a category of "apostles" whose messages and character have to be tested by the congregation. They were specially appointed delegates and missionaries from local churches who were not foundational for the universal church. Similarly, Luke spoke of a broader sense of leaders (prophets) in the Antioch church (Acts 13:1–3).[57] Ephesians 4:11, καὶ αὐτὸς ἔδωκεν, "and it was he who gave," indicates it was gifts that Christ gave.[58] Though most translations render ἔδωκεν as "gave," it can also be translated as "appointed" in the sense that "apostles" is both office and gifts. It carries the meaning of appointing someone to a special responsibility.[59] A closer look at the list reveals that Christ gave specific ministries to people after his triumphant ascension for the continuation of his mandate. Apostles are part of the gifts given by the exalted Christ and also occupy an office created by the church. The gifts Christ gave to the church were gifts of people, a particular people who will proclaim his word and lead the church. Contrary to Ephesians 4:7 and 8b, where Christ simply gave grace gifts to people, in Ephesians 4:11 he specifically gives "people to people."[60] As shown in Ephesians 4:7, 8b and 11, Christ gives grace gifts to the church (Rom 12:3–8; 1 Cor 12:1–11), but at the same time, he appoints ministers including "apostles" (1 Cor 12:28–29). The grace gifts are for various ministries or functions, whereas the ministers are the offices. "Apostles" as in Ephesians 4:11 are not simply functions but also offices that the resurrected and exalted Christ has given to the church for its edification.

Historically, the exercise of *charismata* demanded proper evaluation and affirmation by the local congregation during the time of Paul. Some congregations in Paul's time clearly recognized and defined leaders. If the recognition of a local community of specifically ordered leaders makes it an office, then the ministers in Ephesians 4:11 who were active at that time are officers. Offices were constitutive for the life of the church; therefore, the list in Ephesians 4:11 falls within initialized offices.[61]

The duties of apostles include preaching, teaching, administration, and responsibility for the life and welfare of the Christian community. They initially

---

57. Lincoln, *Ephesians*, 153.
58. Lincoln, *Ephesians*, 248.
59. δίδωμι, BDAG (Chicago: Chicago University Press, 2000), 242.
60. Lincoln, *Ephesians*, 249.
61. Lincoln, *Ephesians*, 252.

administered the common fund to which the believers contributed (Acts 4:37) and took lead in worship and discipline (Acts 5:1–11); they imparted the gift of the Holy Spirit to believers (Acts 8:14; 9:32; 8:15–17) and resolved difficult challenges in the church (Acts 15:6). These functions are ongoing because the Holy Spirit is still at work in the church.[62]

Missionary apostles

The term "apostle" is used generally for missionaries and preachers of the gospel (Acts 13:1–3). The task of apostles is centered on the proclamation of the gospel of Jesus and the founding and administering of new churches (Eph 2:20; 4:11). Paul considered his apostleship a demonstration of divine grace and a divine call to sacrificial labour rather than an occasion for self-glorification (1 Cor 15:10). Paul, even though not part of the original twelve disciples, boldly ranked himself alongside Cephas and the Twelve (1 Cor 15:3–10), while facing resistance from churches he did not plant. Paul gave the office of the apostle a new interpretation based on a different theological presupposition: physical eyewitness alone does not make one an apostle.[63]

Paul did not always call himself an apostle (Gal 2:8; Phil 1:1; 2:25; Phlm 1). He first used the term to describe himself in Galatians 1:1 perhaps because of the conflict in Antioch (Gal 2:11–14) and continued the use in 1 Corinthians 2:7 (2 Cor 1:1; Rom 1:1; Col 1:1; Eph 1:1; 1 Tim 1:1; 2 Tim 1:1). Paul disagreed with the idea of being an eyewitness of Christ as a validating prerequisite of being an apostle (2 Cor 5:16). Hans Dieter Betz observes that the message of Christ was only fully understood by his own family and disciples after the resurrection. If witnessing the resurrection was a criterion for apostleship, then Paul had qualified since he had a vision of Christ after the resurrection (Gal 1:16; 1 Cor 9:1–5; 15:1–10). If the criteria is based on the founding of churches, Paul had founded more churches (1 Cor 15:10; Rom 1:5–7, 13–15; 11:13; Gal 1:15–16).[64] In Pauline thought an apostle is one called for a unique role (1 Cor 1:1), *kletos apostolos*, not appointed by human authorities (Gal 1:1, 12) but by divine authority to represent Christ on earth (1 Thess 1:6; Phil 3:17). The appointing authority today is the Holy Spirit. Apostles in Pauline thought are to be representatives of the crucified and resurrected redeemer (Gal 6:14, 17; 2 Cor 2:14–5:21; 6:4–10; 12:7–10; 13:3–4; Phil 3:10) and envoys

---

62. Harrison, "Apostle, Apostleship," 86.
63. Betz, "Apostle."
64. Betz, "Apostle," *The Anchor Bible Dictionary*, 309.

who prepare the church of God in readiness and present the same to Christ unblemished and pure (1 Thess 2:10–12; 5:23; 1 Cor 1:8; 2 Cor 1:14; 11:2; Phil 2:15; Col 1:2; Eph 5:27).[65] John Tiller opines that apostleship is reserved for those appointed for a specific function in the church.[66] As long as the church remains on earth, the gifts of apostles will operate.

Application for the Twenty-First Century Church

Barnabas and Paul were sent by the Antioch church (Acts 14:4, 14), and they gave a report at the end of their mission (Acts 14:27). Even though they were not recognized in Jerusalem as apostles (Acts 9:27), Luke identified Barnabas as such using the word *apostolos*. Prior to their missionary journey, Barnabas had already encountered members of the twelve apostles in Acts 4:36 and Acts 9:27, but in each case, he was not called apostle until he was commissioned by the Holy Spirit (Acts 14:4, 14). The implication is that he was not part of the original twelve apostles. Apostles were a gift of the Spirit to the church (1 Cor 12:28; Eph 4:11), interpreters of the Christian faith. The gifts in Ephesians 4:11 are not only historical but also a contemporary heritage of the modern church.[67]

Conclusion

An apostle is a faithful and humble messenger of Christ commissioned by the Lord and anointed by him to represent Christ on earth. It is not a position to claim with pride of spiritual superiority but a service to God and mankind, a call to suffer for Christ and to be an example of Christ on earth. As observed by Jethani Skye, many people today are still involved in apostolic ministry even though they do not assign the term "apostle" to themselves.[68]

People are gifted to be messengers, disciples and missionaries of Christ, but care must be taken that we do not pride ourselves in the use of "apostle" as a title. It is a divine responsibility towards God and man, with the purpose of making people ready for heaven. Apostleship must be seen as a leadership quality that enables the children of God to sacrificially serve God, be

---

65. Betz, "Apostle," *The Anchor Bible Dictionary*, 310.

66. John Tiller, "Apostle," *The New International Dictionary of the Christian Church*, ed. Douglas James Dixon (Grand Rapids: Zondervan Publishing House, 1978), 58.

67. The General Council of the Assemblies of God, *Apostles and Prophets: Position Papers*, 26.

68. Jethani Skye, "Apostles Today?" *Leadership* 29, no. 2 (Spring 2008): 37–39.

obedient to his calling, and be accountable to God and a human sending authority. To interpret Ephesians 4:11 in support of the cessation of apostles is hermeneutically inappropriate; it is going beyond the text. The foundational role played by the twelve apostles does not negate the gift of apostles in the modern church. The church still needs apostles, and those who are identified as such by their local congregations must be allowed to exercise their gifts with humility and caution that does not lead to heresy and autocratic leadership.

Bibliography

Alpha Omega Ministries Inc. *Galatians–Colossians, The Preacher's Outline and Sermon Bible*. Chattanooga: Leadership Ministries Worldwide, 1996.

Berding, Kenneth. "Confusing Word and Concept in Spiritual Gifts: Have We Forgotten James Barr's Exhortation?" *JETS*, 43 no. 1 (March 2000): 37–51.

Betz, Hans Dieter. "Apostle." In *The Anchor Bible Dictionary*, vol. 1 A-C, edited by David Noel Freedman. New York: Bantam Doubleday Dell Publishing Group, Inc., 1992.

Bosch, David J. *Transforming Mission: Paradigm Shifts in Theology of Mission*. Maryknoll: Orbis Books, 2018.

Danker, Frederick W., Walter Bauer, William F. Arndt, and F. Wilbur Gingrich. *Greek-English Lexicon of the New Testament and Other Early Christian Literature*. 3rd ed. Chicago: University of Chicago Press, 2000 (Danker-Bauer-Arndt-Gingrich).

Dent, Don. *The Ongoing Role of Apostles in Missions: The Forgotten Foundation*. Bloomington: WestBow Press, 2019. Kindle Edition.

Ellis, E. Earle. *Pauline Theology: Ministry and Society*. Volume 1. Lanham: University Press of America, 1997.

Fee, Gordon. *Gospel and Spirit: Issues in the New Testament Hermeneutics*. Grand Rapids: Baker Books, 1991.

Gaffin Jr., Richard B. "A Cessationist View." In *Are Miraculous Gifts for Today?* Edited by Wayne Grudem, 23–70. Grand Rapids: Zondervan Academic, 1996.

Grudem, Wayne. *Systematic Theology*. Grand Rapids: Zondervan, 2000.

Harrison, Everett F. "Apostle, Apostleship." In *Evangelical Dictionary of Theology*. 2nd edition, edited by Walter A. Elwell, 85–87. Grand Rapids: Baker Academic, 2001.

Hendriksen, William. *Exposition of Colossians and Philemon*. Baker New Testament Commentary. Grand Rapids: Baker Academic, 1964.

Hodge, Charles. *A Commentary on the Epistle to the Ephesians*. New York: Robert Carter and Brothers, 1856.

Hughes, R. Kent. *Ephesians: The Mystery of the Body of Christ*. Preaching the Word. Wheaton: Crossway Books, 1990.

Johnson, Alan. "Apostolic Function and Mission." *Journal of Pentecostal Theology* 17 (2008): 234–54.

Kistemaker, Simon J. *Exposition of the First Epistle to the Corinthians.* Hendriksen-Kistemaker New Testament Commentary. Grand Rapids: Baker Academic, 1993.

Lincoln, Andrew T. *Ephesians*, Word Biblical Commentary 42. Grand Rapids: Zondervan, 1990.

Martin, Ralph P. *2 Corinthians*, Word Biblical Commentary 40. 2nd edition. Grand Rapids: Zondervan, 2014.

Onyinah, Opoku. *Apostles & Prophets: The Ministry of Apostles and Prophets Throughout the Generations.* Eugene: Wipf & Stock, 2022.

Oss, Douglas A. "A Pentecostal/Charismatic View." In *Are Miraculous Gifts for Today?* Edited by Wayne Grudem, 239–83. Grand Rapids: Zondervan Academic, 1996.

Renn, Stephen D. "Apostle, Apostleship." *Expository Dictionary of Bible Words.* Peabody: Hendrickson Publishers Inc., 2005.

Ruthven, John. "The Foundational Gifts of Ephesians 2:20." *JPT* 10, no. 2 (2002), 28–43.

Skye, Jethani, "Apostles Today?" *Leadership* 29, no. 2 (Spring 2008), 37–39.

Still, Todd D. "Colossians." In *Ephesians–Philemon. Volume 12. The Expositor's Bible Commentary Revised Edition*, edited by Tremper Longman III and David E. Garland, 265–72. Grand Rapids: Zondervan, 2006.

Storms, Samuel. "A Third Wave Response to Richard B. Gaffin, Jr." In *Are Miraculous Gifts for Today?* Edited by Wayne Grudem, 72–85. Grand Rapids: Zondervan Academic, 1996.

Synan, Vinson. "Who Are the Modern Apostles?" *Ministries Today* (March–April, 1992), 42–47.

The General Council of the Assemblies of God. "Apostles and Prophets: Position Papers." Boonville: Zondervan Publishing House, 2020.

Tiller, John. *The New International Dictionary of the Christian Church.* Revised edition. Edited by Douglas James Dixon. Grand Rapids: Zondervan Publishing House, 1978.

Titel, Gerhard. *Theological Dictionary of the New Testament.* Volume 1. Grand Rapids: Eerdmans, 1964.

Trigg, Joseph W., "The Charismatic Intellectual: Origen's Understanding of Religious Leadership." *Church History* 50, no. 1 (1981): 5–19.

Varner, William C. *The Way of the Didache: The First Christian Handbook.* New York: New York University, 2007.

Wagner, Peter C. *Your Spiritual Gift Can Help Your Church Grow.* Revised edition. Ventura: Regal Books, 1994.

Wright, Christopher J. H. *The Mission of God: Unlocking the Bible's Grand Narrative.* Downers Grove: IVP Academic, 2006.

Young, J. E. "That Some Should Be Apostles." In *Identifying Apostolic Christianity: A Synthesis of Viewpoints*, edited by Charles J. Conniry, 247–61. Portland Seminary: Faculty Publications, 1994.

9

Re-imagining Cross-cultural Missional Ecclesiology in an African Context

"I Will Build My *Ekklēsian*" Not "I Will Build My Temple/Synagogue"

Judy Wanjiru Wang'ombe
Africa International University, Kenya

Abstract

The contemporary shift from the centre of Christianity in the western hemisphere to the Global South elicits excitement and jubilations, yet it also provokes a pertinent question that cannot be disregarded. As the projected number of African Christians increases, will this be commensurate with an increase in the cross-cultural missional outlook of the church in Africa? The African church has joined the twenty-first century mission force and African scholars are increasingly contributing to missiological conversations that aim at grappling with the contextual missional issues. Yet, on the other hand, there seems to be insularity among many African church leaders concerning the mission, which may have been occasioned by past ecclesiological trends. Such trends have created a lacuna in African ecclesiology, which tends to miss a concerted cross-cultural missiological focus. This chapter uses historical, biblical and theological approaches to call for a re-imagining of a cross-cultural, missional ecclesiology within the African context. The historical approach briefly examines the output of pioneer non-African missionaries in (de)motivating local Africans to understand what the mission is. The theological perspective discusses a contextualized missional ecclesiology that is deemed necessary to motivate an African missional outlook. Such a motivation stems from re-imagining a cross-cultural missional theology based on Matthew 16:18 "I will build my *ekklēsia*." Jesus did not say, "I will build my synagogue or temple" because he meant to show his disciples that he was gathering people, including non-Jews, to himself. This chapter delves into the implication of *ekklēsia* as an assembly to understand the concept of cross-cultural missional ecclesiology since it aligns with what Jesus meant when he was building his *ekklēsia*. This chapter undertakes literary research by examining appropriate sources written on cross-cultural missional ecclesiology. The chapter provides recommendations for the African church that are deemed significant to propel a cross-cultural missional outlook with a particular interest in "public missiology."

Key words: missional *ekklēsia*, missionary, ecclesiology, African church, public missiology, contextual

Introduction

This article is occasioned by a clarion call for a more cross-cultural missional outlook of the African church[1] in light of the shifting gravitational centre of Christianity southwards. Philip Jenkins discusses the "Next Christendom" that would be situated in non-Western regions of Asia, Africa, and Latin America if the contemporary trend of Christianity continues.[2] It is further predicted that by 2050 African Christians will double their current numbers, and will be a staggering 1.325 billion Christians, projected to be more than the number of Christians in Latin America and Europe combined at the time.[3] Statistics may not be Scripture-true, yet the trends are evident about the movement of Christianity to the Global South. There is a keen focus on the African continent with projected growth in 2050. This anticipated increase provokes excitement

---

1. The term "African church" in this chapter refers to the Protestant evangelical church in Africa.
2. Philip Jenkins, *The Next Christendom*, 3rd ed. (New York: Oxford University Press, 2011).
3. Yaw Perbi and Sam Ngugi, *Africa to the Rest: From Mission Field to Mission Force (Again)* (Maitland: Xulon Press, 2022), 75.

that is mixed with apprehension and missiological questions. Perbi and Ngugi ask pertinent questions and also offer consequent inferences about the African situation regarding mission and maturity:

> How do African Christians double by 2050 and at least not double in missionary-sending numbers? How come the most Christian continent isn't the most missionary sending? (Italics by the authors) Seriously, either the African missionary projection is wrong, or the kind of African Christianity is wrong! We also know that a church's spiritual maturity can be measured by mission, that is, a truly missional church (or a Great Commission church) is defined by the mission of God on identity, worldview and activities. Therefore, it goes without saying that these statistics indicate a yet-to-mature African Church by 2050.[4]

Anybody reading what Perbi and Ngugi assert in the above quotation will presumably recall the adage concerning African Christianity, which is said to be "a hundred miles wide and a few inches deep."[5] If this is the real representation of the church in Africa, then there is a big problem. Yet, problems are not meant to discourage, but to give motivation to find out what is the cause of such superficiality and then address it appropriately.

Much has been written and will continue to be written by both African and non-African theologians, missiologists, etc., each trying to examine and propose solutions to the bottleneck explained above. The clarion call has been sounded and the time is ripe for concerted efforts. This chapter responds to this call from both historical and theological approaches using missional ecclesiology as a theoretical framework. Literary research was carried out, which entailed examining appropriate sources, and thereafter providing recommendations that are based on the historical and theoretical findings.

The Term *ekklēsia* in Matthew 16:18

Understanding the correct meaning of the Greek term εκκλησία (*ekklēsia*) is important for this chapter that seeks to contribute towards re-imagining a cross-cultural missional ecclesiology in African contexts. The meaning of εκκλησία is a "congregation or assembly," and it occurs about 114 times in the

---

4. Perbi and Ngugi, *Africa to the Rest*, 76.
5. The origin of this popular saying is uncertain, according to Balcomb in "'A Hundred Miles Wide, But Only a Few Inches Deep!'? – Sounding the Depth of Christian Faith in Africa," *Journal of Theology for Southern Africa* 140 (July 2011): 20–33, 20.

New Testament. It has often been mistranslated into English as the *church*, which in classical Greek is *kuriakos*. Jesus told Peter, "I will build my *ekklēsian*" (Matthew 16:18). He did not say, "I will build my synagogue or temple," because he meant to show his disciples that he was gathering people to himself. The Septuagint uses the Greek word *ekklésiazō* to translate the Hebrew word *qāhal*, which means "to summon an assembly" in Deuteronomy 4:10 ("Assemble the people before me," NIV). Biblical scholars have discussed the usage of these two words *ekklēsia* (Greek) and *qāhal* (Hebrew).[6] It is beyond the scope of this chapter to delve into many details of this discussion. Suffice it to note that Jesus referred to the church as a gathering or assembly of people "called out" to follow Christ from beyond the Jewish context. This broad outlook could have been the reason why Jesus did not say, "I will build my temple/synagogue" even though those were the prominent Jewish religious institutions.

The idea of *ekklēsia* was borrowed from the Graeco-Romans who used it to refer to a civic assembly, which Jesus and his disciples already understood in their context. Such an assembly was intended to contribute to the common good of the people. Members of specific assemblies or *ekklēsia* during the Graeco-Roman times were influenced positively to be useful citizens with "transformative potential."[7] Jesus thus adopted this meaning when he said he would build his *ekklēsia*. It was not supposed to be an institutionalized entity with massive buildings with an inward look. Neither was it to be an exclusive religious assembly.[8] It was supposed to be a living organism that would be transformative and exist for the common good of people.

After establishing that Jesus meant the *ekklēsia* as an assembly, it is important to understand the concept of missional ecclesiology since it aligns with what Jesus meant when he was building his *ekklēsia*. The phrase "cross-cultural missional ecclesiology" is coined to emphasize that the ecclesiology is outward-looking. This envisions the church as the *ekklēsia* that is not confined to its backyard but reaches out to people who are not included in its membership and who are culturally different. A germane question that occasions this chapter is whether the African church is engaging in such an outward look. The answer to this question raises a contemporary necessity in light of the phenomenal growth of Christianity in the Global South. It has

---

6. William Tyndale translated the Greek word *ekklēsia* as "congregation" instead of the word "church" when he produced the first English Bible in 1526.

7. Paul Christopher, Pamela Klassen, and Winnifred Fallers Sullivan, *Ekklesia: Three Inquiries in Church and State* (Chicago: University of Chicago Press, 2018), 4.

8. Tara Caudle, "The Ekklesia as an Assembly That Invokes Response," *Liberty University Journal of Statemanship & Public Policy* 1, no. 1 (2020): 1–15, 8.

been mentioned above that the situation in the continent is dire and that the face of ecclesiology in Africa needs to be re-imagined to give a more cross-cultural and missional outlook.[9] To understand why the situation is as it is in the contemporary African context, it is important to briefly discuss the historical background within which the African church was established.

Brief Historical Background to African Ecclesiology

Many African communities were recipients of the Christian message from different overseas missionary organizations like the Scottish Mission, Africa Inland Mission, Church Missionary Society, and others. Such missionary endeavours began to take shape in the 1800s with the coming of renowned missionaries like David Livingstone and others. The historical accounts of these great men and women on the continent are profound, to say the least. They made considerable accomplishments like building hospitals, schools, and other developmental activities that influenced African communities to date. Africans are forever indebted to such efforts that were not without huge sacrificial costs. Yet, we realize that most, if not all, of these pioneer Western missionaries were children of their time. They tended to be influenced by the prevailing Enlightenment age which was very rationalistic and tainted by the social Darwinism of the time.[10] This, I propose, could have made the Western missionaries not give much thought to Africans' ability to propagate the gospel cross-culturally. Furthermore, the missionaries did not seem to have acquired adequate training in cross-cultural engagement. David Sandgren recounts that the pioneer missionaries "fostered great insensitivity to East African culture," which did not auger well with the Africans.[11] Thus, when the disciples tended to have minimal cross-cultural understanding, the disciple could not be enthused to reach out beyond their cultural confines. This, however, does not mean that there were absolutely no cross-cultural endeavours. It should be noted that a few pioneer African Christians reached out cross-culturally. Emma Wild-Wood gives the example of Apolo Kivebulaya (c. 1865–1933), who was considered by the Anglican Church in East Africa as an outstanding churchman and

---

9. The Church in Nigeria has made great strides towards a cross-cultural missional outlook. Yet, this cannot be said of most African countries with a Christian population.

10. Caleb C. Kim, *Cultural Anthropology from a Christian Perspective* (Eldoret: Utafiti Foundation, 2019).

11. David Peter Sandgren, "The Kikuyu, Christianity, and the Africa Inland Mission" (PhD Dissertation, University of Wisconsin-Madison, 1976), 83.

missionary in the late 1800s.[12] Such efforts were germane but not replicated wholesomely in the African church, especially in East Africa.

African ecclesiology, therefore, inherited a missing missiological link, which could justify what authors Andria and Saayman describe as a "defective ecclesiology." These writers agree that the root of the problem goes back to the pioneer mission work. These efforts were well intended but lacked a "real discourse on mission" that failed to place mission as an integral part of ecclesiology.[13] Some churches in Africa attempted to be missional, but their strategy was basically to replicate their churches in other geographical regions. This trend has continued with most evangelical churches in Africa. A few indigenous organizations have taken up the mandate to reach people who have no Christian witness among them. Such efforts have elicited the age-long debate concerning "church" and "para-church" movements as missiologists discuss the sodality-modality missional preferences.

The establishment of the sodality mission agencies (para-churches) that were supposed to operate "alongside" the modality (church) setting, was occasioned by the latter's reluctance to propagate the gospel to regions beyond themselves. This is still the case today. In Kenya, for instance, some people have established indigenous mission organizations that are not affiliated with any denomination or local church. Some attempts have been made to try to integrate such para-churches under the oversight of local churches. The reason for such attempts is because of the criticism that para-churches as entities are not mentioned in the Bible and they cannot therefore form biblical structures per se. However, despite such criticisms, para-church mission organizations have continued to mushroom in Africa because of the laxity of the structured churches in engaging in cross-cultural missions. Thus, should we, the para-churches, be allowed to continue while the modality structure maintains the status quo? This chapter advocates for the contrary and accordingly places a clarion call for the African church to take up its mandate to engage in cross-cultural missions. Learning from the historical misgivings mentioned in this section, the church should encourage an outward missional outlook. Reaching the unreached/least reached and discipling them after they come to the saving knowledge of Christ, should also require that they be encouraged to not

---

12. Emma Wild-Wood, *The Mission of Apolo Kivebulaya: Religious Encounter & Social Change in the Great Lakes c.1865–1935* (Woodbridge: James Currey, 2020).

13. Solomon Andria and Willem Saayman, "Missiology and Ecclesiology: A Perspective from Africa," *Missionalia* 31, no. 3 (November 2003): 503–17, 505–6.

only reach their people, but they can look outward as well and engage other unreached/least reached people groups within their vicinity.

A Call to Re-imagine the Face of African Missional Ecclesiology

The significance of an ecclesiology that is rooted in missiology cannot be underrated at all. Missiologist Chris Wright advocates that any ecclesiology "must be rooted in missiology."[14] Consequently, the face of African ecclesiology must also be rooted in missiology, which needs to integrate the cross-cultural aspect of the mission. Africans are known to be community-based as espoused in the *ubuntu* philosophy of "I am because we are." Indeed, the description of *ekklēsia* as communities where other-centred relationships thrive fits African contexts. Traditionally, a person would look out to see if there is smoke coming from the neighbouring grass-thatched house. The absence of smoke during meal preparation time would be an indicator that there is no food in that homestead. The person who would notice that quickly packed some food and took it to the neighbouring hut to ensure nobody slept hungry.

A similar picture is painted in 2 Kings 7:1–10 about the four lepers who went to the Arameans' camp and found food and other goods. As they took the substances after eating and drinking, they said to each other: "We are not doing right. This is a day of good news and we are keeping it to ourselves" (2 Kgs 7:9 NIV). The ostracized lepers found themselves in a dilemma: would they share their newly found fortunes with those who had kept them away, and who were in dire need, or should they indulge in all of it alone as banished people?

Re-imagining the face of African missional ecclesiology requires a deep reconsideration like the four lepers: "This is a day of good news and we are keeping it to ourselves." The African church has been a recipient of the good news about Jesus's love. Yet not everyone has received this good news. There are still nine hundred and ninety-one unreached people groups (26.8 percent) in Africa, with the majority situated in predominantly Islamic areas, according to the report by the Joshua Project.[15] Such statistics necessitate a germane question: what is the African church doing about this situation? Is it keeping the good news to itself? Is it not bothered about the plight of the unreached/least

---

14. Christopher J. H. Wright, *The Mission of God: Unlocking the Bible's Grand Narrative* (Downers Grove: IVP Academic, 2006).

15. According to the Joshua Project, an Unreached or Least reached people group is an ethnical group of people with no indigenous community of Christian believers with adequate resources to evangelize their own people (https://joshuaproject.net/continents).

reached people? Re-imagining an African missiological ecclesiology requires thoughtful consideration of these questions by both church leaders and lay people. Some churches have considered these questions and also taken steps towards heeding the call to reach the unreached/least reached people groups. Such endeavours have endured both external and internal barriers to effectively fulfil the mandate of taking the gospel to cross-cultural settings where the unreached/least reached people are.

Dilemma of African Missiological Ecclesiology

The historical background of the non-participation of African Christians in pioneer missions has been discussed briefly in the previous section above. It is expedient to highlight some contemporary hindrances that prevent African ecclesiology from displaying a missional outlook as biblically mandated. Having served with an indigenous mission organization, I have come to realize that African missiology must be domiciled within a contextualized ecclesiological context. Such a context differs substantially from the Western situation that pioneered cross-cultural missions during the eighteenth-nineteenth centuries. The inherent dilemma accrued herein is how to engage in contextual mission activities, yet the training materials and resources of training personnel have largely been derived from the western hemisphere. Seminal books on mission theories and praxis have been penned by great missiologists like David Bosch, John Piper, and others. These have served as textbooks in institutions that teach mission courses, especially in the West. Consequently, professors of mission have heeded the call to travel overseas to train non-western Christians about the mission while still referring to these books. It is only recently that African missiologists have begun to write books and articles. Gwinyai Muzorewa's book, *An African Theology of Mission*, published by E. Mellen Press in 1990, was considered the first monograph by an African theologian to explore the issue of mission.[16]

A second dilemma that faces African missiological ecclesiology concerns finances. In the wake of the prevalent prosperity gospel, many African churches have found themselves in a quandary, whether to support pioneer missionary work or contain the finances within the church compound and support internal church programmes including the remuneration of the pastoral teams. Additionally, African ecclesiology is based on meeting the felt needs of people

---

16. John Mbiti, "Review of An African Theology of Mission by Gwinyai Muzorewa," *International Review of Mission* 82 (1992): 418.

as Kalemba Mwambazambi reiterates, "African ecclesiological methods begin with African existential experiences."[17] Mwambazambi considers the wider felt needs that cover a wide spectrum. My focus here is on the economic felt needs of Africans that become a crucial focus of church leaders towards their immediate congregation. This emphasis then becomes more inward and prevents any outward look and thus inhibits a cross-cultural ecclesiology. A germane question is whether the African church is well endowed to fulfil both inward and outward financial obligations in terms of reaching the economic felt needs of the "reached" and unreached/least reached people. Some churches have attempted this.

There are several mega-churches within the main cities of the African countries. Some of these churches have been involved in reaching the unreached/least reached people and they have been able to finance such endeavours. Wanjiru Gitau's award-winning book, *Megachurch Christianity Reconsidered*, is a case study of one such mega-church that has attracted a sizeable number of "millennials" of the urban cities, who are eager to practice their Christianity differently from their "grandma's Church."[18] Such megachurches have ventured into cross-cultural pioneer missions; yet is their number adequate to accomplish the mandate of taking the good news to the remaining unreached/least reached people? The missional mandate is not only for economically endowed churches. It is for the whole church of God where people gather and give their offering every Sunday as they acknowledge that people should not go to God's house empty-handed. Thus, the economic situation of the African church should not be the bottleneck that prevents the furtherance of the gospel to unreached/least reached people groups. The fact that cross-cultural pioneer missions can be an expensive endeavour seems to have made the African church maintain an unhealthy donor-dependency syndrome. John Gatu[19] explains how pioneer African church leaders like him took over leadership of the churches from Western missionaries and still maintained the socio-economic projects. Such projects were already expensive to the African leaders, who kept depending on the West for maintenance

---

17. Kalemba Mwambazambi, "A Missiological Reflection on African Ecclesiology," *Verbum et Ecclesiology* 32, no. 1 (2011): 1–8, 4.

18. Wanjiru M. Gitau, *Megachurch Christianity Reconsidered: Millennials and Social Change in African Perspective* (Downers Grove: IVP Academic, 2018), 33.

19. John Gatu made a historical moratorium call ("missionary go home") in 1973 during the World Council of Churches Commission for World Mission and Evangelization in Bangkok.

money.[20] Not all African churches adopted such expensive structures, but the missionary enterprise has continued to be viewed as a Western thing that must be run with the Western dollar for it to survive on African soil. This has become a major impediment to cross-cultural missions to unreached/least-reached people groups in many parts of Africa.

Post-dilemma Re-imagining of African Missiological Ecclesiology

This chapter is premised on the need to re-imagine an African ecclesiology that is rooted in missiology that also focuses on cross-cultural pioneering work among remaining unreached/least reached people groups in Africa. The immediate previous section highlights the dilemmas of the African churches in accomplishing this remaining mandate. This current section commences a discussion on how Africans can begin to re-imagine a missiology that is not skewed to only "comfortable" and reachable regions, but one that deliberately seeks to reach the unreached/least reached areas. Most of the time, these regions have been known to be geographically far and also have difficult terrains and harsh weather conditions. Yet, concerning the biblical precept that forms the backdrop of this chapter, Jesus did not say, "I will build my temple/synagogue," rather he said, "I will build my *ekklēsian*" (Matt 16:18). Michael J. Berry asserts Jesus uttered these words at Caesarea Philippi to reveal God's mission (*missio Dei*) "when he employed the term εκκλησία," which has unfortunately been mistranslated and misinterpreted.[21] Such misrepresentation has led to the church being a "siloed institution," that has not undertaken its full missional mandate as Jesus required when he employed the word εκκλησία. Thus, as we re-interpret the term, we are also re-imagining the face of African missiological ecclesiology that transcends the dilemmas highlighted in the previous section.

An important starting point for such a re-imagination is the need to contextualize some key missional terms. One such concept is *missio Dei*. According to Paul Bendor-Samuel, the executive director of the Oxford Centre for Mission Studies (OCMS), the term *mission* is "wrapped up in its Latin origins (*missio*, to send)" thus confining mission endeavours to only physical

---

20. John Gatu, "The Rationale for Self-Reliance" (Presentation, Consultation on Self-reliance of the churches in Africa, Limuru, Kenya, 1996), www.wmausa.org/page.aspx?id=83845.

21. Michael J. Berry, "Re-Imagining Ecclesiology: A New Missional Paradigm for Community Transformation" (DMin Dissertation, Portland Seminary, George Fox University, 2021), 21.

sending and going.[22] Bendor-Samuel's assertion raises two germane aspects that are significant for African missiological ecclesiology.

First, there is a need to contextualize the term *missio Dei* so that it can resonate with an African ecclesiology. This proves to be a challenge because Africans are richly diverse in language, and there is no single language that can represent the Sub-Saharan region. However, there is a need to redefine the term *missio Dei* in a way that is embedded in African ecclesiology. To redefine *missio Dei*, there is a need to decolonize the term. The first generations of African Christians associated missions with white people. There arose a popular adage in the Kikuyu language that was propagated to show how the Kenyan Africans perceived the white missionaries: *Gutire muthugu na mubia* ("there is no difference between a European settler and a missionary"). Historian Julius Gathogo explains that the Africans coined this slogan based on some ignorance since there were "commonalities and huge differences among the trio (settler-farmers, missionaries, and colonial administrators)."[23] Nevertheless, it is also expedient to note that such a perception persisted among Africans who associated mission work with the white people, thus an African could not be considered a missionary per se. This demarcation seems to have endured to date where African ecclesiology has tended to relegate mission work to specific people. Thus, re-imagining African ecclesiology that is firmly grounded in a missional outlook, therefore, requires the church to realize that mission work is a mandate for the whole congregation and not only for a few.

Second, re-defining the term *missio Dei* from an African perspective requires African missiologists and missionaries alike to think keenly of a term that would represent the holism of the nature of the missional mandate. Confining mission work to only physical sending does not bring out the essence of what Jesus meant when he said he would build his εκκλησία (Matt 16:18). Stroope cites several missiologists, including Christopher Wright, who consent to the need to move from a "narrow missionary definition of mission to a more holistic expression of salvation. Such an expression includes demonstrations of 'love, peace/reconciliation, justice' as dimensions of the 'missional God'"[24] Such holism, therefore, notes that cross-cultural mission work is not confined to those endowed with evangelistic gifts, but also gives a place for everyone

---

22. Paul Bendor-Samuel, "Covid-19 Trends in Global Mission, and Participation in Faithful Witness," *Transformation* 37, no. 4 (2020): 255–65, 261.

23. Julius Gathogo, "Settler-Missionary Alliance in Colonial Kenya and the Land Question," *Studia Historiae Ecclesiasticae* 46, no. 2 (2020): 4.

24. Michael W. Stroope, *Transcending Mission: The Eclipse of a Modern Tradition* (Downers Grove: InterVarsity Press, 2017), 44.

to use their gifting/calling or profession in various ways. Those imbued with intercessory ministries in the church can pray intently for those who go. People with the gift of hospitality can open their homes to missionaries when they need to be accommodated. And thus, the whole church participates joyfully in mission activities in one way or the other.

Third, re-imagining an African missional ecclesiology also requires an African hermeneutical reading of the Bible. Stroope asserts that the term "missional hermeneutic" is a recent development that continues to evolve accordingly.[25] Indeed, this behooves the African missiologists to join this band and begin a conversation towards developing an African hermeneutics for the mission. George Hunsberger proposes four different streams of thought about missional hermeneutics that can serve as a beginning point for African hermeneutics:[26]

1. The missional direction that retells *missio Dei* as God's story
2. Finding the missional purpose of the canonical narrative
3. Missional locatedness of the scriptural readers
4. Missional engagement with cultures

Each of the four streams offers a significant direction towards developing appropriate missional hermeneutics. I would suggest that the most immediate one towards developing an African missional hermeneutic would be the fourth one that grapples with an engagement with cultures. This call to contextualize the gospel aligns with the 1974 Lausanne Covenant's affirmation of the authority and power of the Bible:

> The message of the Bible is addressed to all men and women . . . Through it [the Bible] the Holy Spirit still speaks today. He illumines the minds of God's people in every culture to perceive its truth freshly through their own eyes, and thus discloses to the whole Church ever more of the many-colored wisdom of God.[27]

This, then, is the beauty of God's word that allows every person to hear God speak in his or her vernacular language.

Elizabeth Mburu's work invites African missiologists to reconsider the place of African hermeneutics within missional circles. She proposes an

---

25. Stroope, *Transcending Mission*, 44.
26. George R. Hunsberger, "Proposals for a Missional Hermeneutic: Mapping a Conversation," *Missiology: An International Review* xxxix, no. 3 (2011): 309–21.
27. John Stott, "The Lausanne Covenant," Lausanne Movement (2009), 27.

African contextualized hermeneutical approach, which she illustrates using the four legs of a stool:[28]

Leg 1: Parallels to the African Contexts

Leg 2: Theological context

Leg 3: Literary context

Leg 4: Historical and cultural context

I appreciate that this hermeneutical model begins with a consideration of the African context as the starting point; in other words, from the known to the unknown. Such a stance resonates well with an African missional hermeneutic that calls for any cross-cultural endeavours to require an initial understanding of the people before commencing to proclaim the evangelistic contents. Mburu explains this first leg as a venture that seeks to identify the "theological and cultural contexts that are the primary contributors to our worldview, as well as any relevant features of our social, political, and geographical contexts."[29] This statement authenticates the need to take time to study and understand the "other." Yet, it is important to realize that the African missional hermeneutic cannot be confined to one monolithic worldview, which Mburu calls the "African worldview" (Chapter 3). There may be common elements in different African contexts like the honour-shame value, the four laws governing morality, etc. Yet, under such surface commonalities, lay great contextual differences that are unique to every cultural group. It is therefore more appropriate to use the term "African worldviews" in missional hermeneutics to recognize the richness of African diversities.

Another germane aspect that should be inculcated in missiological hermeneutics for the African church is the need to read the great commission in the context of the whole biblical text. Often, we have confined the mandate to specific verses like Matthew 28:18–20, John 20:19–23, etc. Yet, as we redefine the term *missio Dei*, we are also considering that the biblical mission mandate is found throughout the whole Bible, from Genesis to Revelation. I first encountered this assertion while listening to a lecture on biblical foundations of mission theology at the Oxford Centre for Mission Studies in 2020. Indeed, confining the missiological mandate to a set of passages in the New Testament tends to miss out on the whole story of God's mission as he engages people

---

28. Elizabeth Mburu, *African Hermeneutics* (Carlisle: HippoBooks, 2019), 66.
29. Mburu, *African Hermeneutics*, 67.

throughout the Scriptures, as Christopher Wright reminds us.[30] I agree with this holistic reading of Scripture because it is expedient for African missional ecclesiology to find a biblical theology for a mission that is appropriate and foundational. Beginning with Genesis is suitable as it shows God at work from the very beginning. African cultures are rife with creation stories that place God as the creator. Kanu and Ndubisi affirm this in their discussion on the topic of creation in African ontology, which was present before the advent of Christianity in Africa. The two authors bring out the fact that the different African creation stories show the diverse religious traditions of Africans. Despite such diversity, one similarity is the idea that these creation stories trace back to God as the supreme creator.[31] The implication of these creation stories, therefore, buttresses the need for the African church to start from the beginning when providing a missional theology.

Re-imagining African Ecclesiology through Public Missiology

The theme of the Edinburgh 2010 conference, "Witnessing to Christ Today," was coined in recognition of the dynamic contemporary world. Dana Robert looks at this seminal conference that witnessed an explosion of deliberations on how to engage in mission in light of the contemporary global complexities. One such deliberation was the need for the church to be a witness for Christ in all sectors of society, for instance, speaking up against racial trends in the United States.[32] Greg Okesson reflects on the years he spent as a missionary and concludes that the African public realm has a "thickness" (complexity) that defies simplistic solutions. Okesson advances the concept of public missiology, recognizing Lesslie Newbegin as the "father of public missiology." Even though it is a relatively new concept, public missiology has different facets and Okesson has chosen to focus on the public missiology of the local *ekklēsia* (congregation). This chapter also follows Okesson's emphasis since it focuses on local missional ecclesiology.

Re-imagining an African ecclesiology that is mission-focused would do well to heed Okesson's recommendation. Okesson highlights the necessity of parishioners being evangelists/missionaries in and through their respective

---

30. Wright, *The Mission of God*.

31. Ikechukwu Anthony Kanu and Ejikemeuwa J. O. Ndubisi, "On the Concept of Creation in African Ontology," *Origisi: A New Journal of African Studies* 17 (2021): 199–212, 210.

32. Dana L. Robert, "One Christ – Many Witnesses: Visions of Mission and Unity, Edinburgh and Beyond," *Transformation* 33, no. 4 (2016): 270–81, 275.

"publics" as they go about their daily life.³³ Heeding Okesson's call, there are three dimensions I perceive in this conversation on public missiology.

First, members of an already existing congregation become faithful witnesses of Christ wherever they are situated, at workplaces, homes, etc. In terms of cross-cultural mission engagement, professionals, business people, etc., who find themselves in a place where there are unreached/least reached people groups, are encouraged to be living witnesses in their daily encounters with the latter.

The second dimension of public missiology is the call for a mission strategy that includes public advocacy that seeks to address the "thick" issues found in the public realm. This is the "integral witness" that is defined as "the task of bringing the whole of life under the lordship of Christ," while affirming that there is "no biblical dichotomy between evangelistic and social responsibility in bringing Christ's peace to the poor and oppressed."³⁴ Ecuadorian theologian Rene Padilla coined the concept of "integral mission" when he stood "against the Evangelical barrier between social action and evangelism in the aftermath of the First Latin American Congress for Evangelization" held in November 1969.³⁵ Integral mission marries social action with evangelism to influence positive change in the society of interest. James Nkansah-Obrempong advises the African church to advocate for a holistic gospel that answers the daunting task of the church in responding to the dire humanitarian needs on the continent. He mentions five ways of mitigation: partnership with non-governmental organizations, educational and social amenities, relief model, advocacy, and engaging in policy formulation.³⁶

The third aspect of public missiology as postulated in this chapter is the need to re-imagine an appropriate "incarnational" model for cross-cultural witness. "Incarnational model/ministry/approach" has been a significant concept in cross-cultural witness for more than two decades. Missionaries are urged to emulate the incarnational approach of Christ as found in verses like Philippians 2:5–8 and John 1:14a. They are to "leave the compound, learn the language, become one with the people in need, just as Christ became

---

33. Greg Okesson, *A Public Missiology: How Local Churches Witness to a Complex World* (Grand Rapids: Baker Academic, 2020), 10.

34. "Integral Mission," Lausanne Movement, https://www.lausanne.org/networks/issues/integral-mission.

35. David C. Kirkpatrick, "C. Rene Padilla and the Origins of Integral Mission in Post-War Latin America," *Journal of Ecclesiastical History* 67, no. 2 (April 2016): 351–71, 354.

36. James Nkansah-Obrempong, "The Mission of the Church and Holistic Redemption," *Evangelical Review of Theology* 42, no. 3 (2018): 196–211, 208–10.

one with a particular human culture."[37] Yet, this incarnational approach to mission has come under negative criticism by writers like Harriet Hill and Todd Billings. The latter, for instance, asserts that incarnational ministry is not possible especially when one asks, "complicated questions that cut to the heart of contemporary mission to the poor."[38] Such questions include:

> How can I become one with the people when I have a different history and cultural background? How can I become one with the poor when I still have a network of family and mission that can bail me out of bad situations? Am I not being dishonest with myself and the poor by simply nudging for change from the ground up rather than using my resources to help meet needs?[39]

These questions are valid, and they need to be thought through by the African church as it re-imagines its missiological engagement. It must re-think the meaning of the term "incarnate/incarnation" to understand its relevance for contemporary missions. Etymologically, the noun "incarnation" is derived from the Latin verb *incarno*, which means, "to make into flesh." Thus, only Jesus became flesh when he became man. "Incarnation" therefore would apply only to the person of Jesus Christ, while the verb "incarnate" applies to what Jesus did when he became human. However, the adjective "incarnational" can apply to any person other than Christ, and thus it qualifies/describes an outlook or approach to life where a Christian seeks to live like Christ.

An appropriate "incarnational" approach to cross-cultural witness should therefore not seek to "become one" with people of different cultures. Although Paul said, "To the Jews, I become like a Jew" he could not become totally like a Jew. There were aspects of Jewishness that Paul had to relinquish even though he was born a Jew. Likewise, a missionary reaching the unreached/least-reached people cannot become like them or identify with them because there are aspects of their culture that the missionary cannot indulge in as a Christian. The recommended "incarnational" approach is that of "walking alongside" the people and helping them move towards the salvific knowledge and experience of Christ. Essentially, this is the model of love for God and his people. The plight of the unreached/least reached people, for instance, motivates missionaries to immerse themselves in the life of the people to understand them better and

---

37. Todd J. Billings, "Incarnational Ministry and Christology: A Reappropriation of the Way of Lowliness," *Missiology: An International Review* 32, no. 2 (2004): 187–201, 188.
38. Billings, "Incarnational Ministry and Christology," 188.
39. Billings, "Incarnational Ministry and Christology," 188.

thus know how to reach them relevantly. Such an approach requires Christlike values like love, humility, self-denial, compassion, etc. These values are appropriated through the power and working of the Holy Spirit. Just as Jesus breathed on his disciples and said, "Receive the Holy Spirit" in John 20:22, the African church needs the Holy Spirit's empowerment to be effective witnesses for Christ in the contemporary world.

Jesus was empowered by the Holy Spirit to fulfil the prophecy of Isaiah 61:1–3, "The Spirit of the Sovereign Lord is on me because the Lord has anointed me to preach good news to the poor. He has sent me to bind up the brokenhearted, to proclaim freedom for the captives and release from darkness for the prisoners . . ." Similarly, when he commissioned his disciples to go forth, he knew they would need similar empowerment as they spread the gospel. The contemporary African church must engage in a relevant "incarnational" model that seeks to understand the respective worldviews of the unreached/least people groups. Most, if not all, of these worldviews have a supernaturalistic orientation that has conspicuous beliefs and practices, which revolve around supernatural powers and beings. Any missional endeavours in Africa must be cognizant of this orientation and thus seek to address it through the power of the Holy Spirit.

Example of a Local Kenyan Church Engaging in Public Missiology

ACC[40] was started as a missional church right from its establishment. Founded in 1996, ACC stipulated that its task was to be a mission-mobilized church and intentionally inspire its members to participate in God's mission in their respective capacities and abilities. ACC has been able to send missionaries to one particular unreached people group along the coastal region of Kenya. For the last two decades of existence, ACC looks back at its missional activities and sees God at work in turbulent times including the COVID-19 pandemic. ACC has recently re-launched a new phase of its mission work, whose ethos is closely aligned with what I have discussed in this chapter on re-imagining an African cross-cultural missional ecclesiology. I particularly want to discuss how ACC aligns with the three aspects of public missiology discussed above:

1. Local Christian community/congregational witness: Discipleship Making Movement

---

40. ACC is a pseudonym of a local community church based in Nairobi, Kenya. Because of the sensitive nature of the mission work the church engages in, usage of the pseudonym is deemed appropriate.

2. Integral mission: Advocating for the rights of the unreached people
3. Re-imagine an appropriate "incarnational" model for cross-cultural witness.

Congregational witness

The mission pastor at ACC began a strategic endeavour of engaging the local Christian community surrounding the particular unreached people group that ACC reaches. He is doing this through the Discipleship Making Movement (DMM), whose goal is to assist Christians live out their love for God and others, and also who make disciples in their everyday life. The DMM disciples are ordinary/lay people who are trained in the DMM principles to be able to reach their families, friends, and communities. The current participants of DMM that the ACC mission pastor has engaged come from different local churches and consist of both men and women. They have tried to reach the unreached people group that ACC has targeted. Unfortunately, frequent terrorist attacks have hampered the consistency of the DMM participants, some of whom have been forced to flee from their homes for fear of attacks by Muslim insurgents. However, the mission pastor at ACC continues to motivate the DMM participants as they pray for peace to be restored in the region.

Integral witness

ACC reaches the unreached group that has suffered marginalization for a long time probably because of their small population. They have suffered injustices from external forces including exploitation, domineering by other larger tribes, and the current transportation project undertaken by the Kenyan government. Anyone who has encountered this particular people group, who have been hunters and gatherers, is obliged to offer a *cri de coeur* (cry from the heart/passionate appeal) on their behalf. Such an appeal is best termed as advocacy where the ACC church seeks to advocate for the rights of the people. Land, for instance, is a pertinent issue that has seen the people group being pushed away from their ancestral land as the government project continues to be implemented. Other advocacies include the rights of children to education, where ACC has been supporting several children. Some of these children who have completed their secondary and tertiary education have earned themselves good government jobs and thus can support their families adequately.

ACC is a relatively small church with a congregation of less than five hundred members. The financial basket is not as endowed as other megachurches, and thus ACC has entered a partnership with an overseas church. This church has contributed to some of the financial requirements for missional activities like medical camps and also educational support.

Appropriate "incarnational" approach

ACC continues to sensitize its congregational members to participate in missions by going, giving, praying, or supporting ministries (e.g., offering accommodation to missionaries on transit). The missionaries who have gone to live among the unreached people group have adapted an "incarnational" approach that is founded on Christ-like values of love, humility, compassion, and self-giving as they look up to the power of the Holy Spirit. Such an attitude helps them to avoid a condescending or patronizing attitude towards the unreached people group, which has earned them acceptance by the people. These missionaries have continued to engage with the people by learning about their culture and participating in different cultural events for a comprehensive understanding.

Conclusion

This chapter ends with the example of the church ACC to show that the call to re-imagine a cross-cultural missional ecclesiology in Africa is plausible. This example further serves as an encouragement to the church that it is possible to have such an ecclesiological outlook that is motivated by the words of Matthew 16:18. Jesus said, "I will build my *ekklēsian*," and not "my temple/synagogue," because he envisioned an outward missional outlook. The brief historical background of African ecclesiology provided in this chapter shows that the missing missional link was occasioned by the kind of discipleship provided during the pioneer mission endeavour. Thus, the call to re-imagine the face of African ecclesiology that intentionally includes a cross-cultural dimension.

This chapter acknowledges the problems involved in this call to re-imagine an African missiological ecclesiology. Yet, these problems are not insurmountable and should not prevent the African church from proceeding with the call. Three aspects of a re-imagining are suggested: the need to contextualize key missional terms like *missio Dei*; the need to re-imagine an African missional hermeneutics that acknowledges the cultural dimension; and also that considers a more holistic biblical mandate.

The final part of this chapter re-imagines African ecclesiology through public missiology. The paper also shows the plausibility of such a proposal by giving a case study of a missional church. Three aspects of public missiology are applied and can be emulated by the African church accordingly. Essentially, the emphasis on public missiology resonates well with the words of Jesus in Matthew 16:18 to build an *ekklēsia* that is outward looking and missional.

Bibliography

Andria, Solomon, and Willem Saayman. "Missiology and Ecclesiology: A Perspective from Africa." *Missionalia* 31, no. 3 (November 2003): 503–17.

Balcomb, A. O. "'A Hundred Miles Wide, But Only a Few Inches Deep!'? – Sounding the Depth of Christian Faith in Africa." *Journal of Theology for Southern Africa*, no. 140 (July 2011): 20–33.

Bendor-Samuel, Paul. "Covid-19 Trends in Global Mission, and Participation in Faithful Witness." *Transformation* 37, no. 4 (2020): 255–65.

Berry, Michael J. "Re-Imagining Ecclesiology: A New Missional Paradigm for Community Transformation." DMin Dissertation, Portland Seminary, George Fox University, 2021.

Billings, Todd J. "Incarnational Ministry and Christology: A Reappropriation of the Way of Lowliness." *Missiology: An International Review* 32, no. 2 (2004): 187–201.

Caudle, Tara. "The Ekklesia as an Assembly That Invokes Response." *Liberty University Journal of Statemanship & Public Policy* 1, no. 1 (2020): 1–15.

Christopher, Paul, Pamela Klassen, and Winnifred Fallers Sullivan. *Ekklesia: Three Inquiries in Church and State*. Chicago: University of Chicago Press, 2018.

Gathogo, Julius. "Settler-Missionary Alliance in Colonial Kenya and the Land Question." *Studia Historiae Ecclesiasticae* 46, no. 2 (2020): 1–20.

Gatu, John. "The Rationale for Self-Reliance." Presentation at the Consultation on Self-Reliance of the Churches in Africa, Limuru, Kenya, 1996.

Gitau, Wanjiru M. *Megachurch Christianity Reconsidered: Millenials and Social Change in African Perspective*. Downers Grove: IVP Academic, 2018.

Hunsberger, George R. "Proposals for a Missional Hermeneutic: Mapping a Conversation." *Missiology: An International Review* xxxix, no. 3 (2011): 309–21.

"Integral Mission," Lausanne Movement, https://www.lausanne.org/networks/issues/integral-mission.

Jenkins, Philip. *The Next Christendom*. 3rd edition. New York: Oxford University Press, 2011.

Kanu, Ikechukwu Anthony, and Ejikemeuwa J. O. Ndubisi. "On the Concept of Creation in African Ontology." *Origisi: A New Journal of African Studies* 17 (2021): 199–212.

Kim, Caleb C. *Cultural Anthropology from a Christian Perspective*. Eldoret: Utafiti Foundation, 2019.

Kirkpatrick, David C. "C. Rene Padilla and the Origins of Integral Mission in Post-War Latin America." *Journal of Ecclesiastical History* 67, no. 2 (April 2016): 351–71.

Mbiti, John. "Review of An African Theology of Mission by Gwinyai Muzorewa." *International Review of Mission* 82 (1992): 418–19.

Mburu, Elizabeth. *African Hermeneutics*. Carlisle: HippoBooks, 2019.

Mwambazambi, Kalemba. "A Missiological Reflection on African Ecclesiology." *Verbum et Ecclesiology* 32, no. 1 (2011): 1–8.

Nkansah-Obrempong, James. "The Mission of the Church and Holistic Redemption." *Evangelical Review of Theology* 42, no. 3 (2018): 196–211.

Okesson, Greg. *A Public Missiology: How Local Churches Witness to a Complex World*. Grand Rapids: Baker Academic, 2020.

Perbi, Yaw, and Sam Ngugi. *Africa to the Rest: From Mission Field to Mission Force (Again)*. Maitland: Xulon Press, 2022.

Robert, Dana L. "One Christ – Many Witnesses: Visions of Mission and Unity, Edinburgh and Beyond." *Transformation* 33, no. 4 (2016): 270–81.

Sandgren, David Peter. "The Kikuyu, Christianity, and the Africa Inland Mission." PhD Dissertation, University of Wisconsin-Madison, 1976.

Stott, John. "The Lausanne Covenant." Lausanne Movement, 2009.

Stroope, Michael W. *Transcending Mission: The Eclipse of a Modern Tradition*. Downers Grove: InterVarsity Press, 2017.

Wild-Wood, Emma. *The Mission of Apolo Kivebulaya: Religious Encounter & Social Change in the Great Lakes c.1865–1935*. Woodbridge: James Currey, 2020.

Wright, Christopher J. H.. *The Mission of God: Unlocking the Bible's Grand Narrative*. Downers Grove: IVP Academic, 2006.

10

Communal *Theosis*

Considering the Corporate Dimensions of the Doctrine of Deification in the Ethiopian Orthodox *Täwaḥədo* Church

Calum Samuelson
Africa Nazarene University, Kenya

Abstract

Spiritual growth and formation are vital aspects of ecclesiology. Many churches within the evangelical tradition (and the Protestant tradition more broadly) have historically struggled to sustain strong emphasis in this area. One major exception to this general rule has been churches that strongly identify with John Wesley's robust programmes for fostering sanctification. Regardless, evangelical churches throughout Africa on the whole have largely inherited the Protestant preoccupation with attainment of "salvation" and continue to struggle to develop deep spiritual maturity within their members, producing what is increasingly recognized as a "discipleship crisis" across the continent.

It is largely for this reason that examination of the Ethiopian Orthodox *Täwaḥədo* Church (EOTC) may be instructive for evangelical churches across Africa. In comparison to other African Christians, the roughly fifty million adherents of the EOTC demonstrate striking devotion, solidarity, and theological coherence (e.g. nation-wide fasting and memorization of litanies). This is significant not only because the EOTC represents a different

Christian perspective from Protestantism but – more importantly – because it represents an ancient expression of an "African" Christianity distinct from the Mediterranean milieu of most early Christianity.

Like other churches in the Orthodox tradition, the EOTC has a stronger focus on the ongoing maturation of Christians than on a precise moment of justification. This process, known alternatively as *theosis* (Greek) or the doctrine of deification (Latin), suggests one of the possible factors contributing to the spiritual vitality of Christians in Ethiopia. A common critique levelled against the notion of *theosis* is that it too easily becomes an individualistic project. Crucially, Ethiopia represents a pronounced "collectivistic" culture quite distinct from many countries where other Orthodox churches flourish and may, therefore, contain valuable insights for other African churches in more "collectivistic" contexts.

Key words: African Christian theology, *theosis*, Ethiopian Orthodox *Täwaḥədo* Church, spiritual formation, Pentecostal-charismatic Christianity, evangelicalism, discipleship

Introduction

Westerners who are aware of Ethiopia's ancient Christianity often associate it with iconic images of solitary monks in remote, arid regions – perhaps holding an aged, Ethiopic goatskin Bible. Such images do reflect some important aspects of Ethiopian Christianity. Indeed, the mountainous terrain of regions like Tigray have been regarded as some of the most extreme and liminal spaces for monastic endeavours ever since the desert fathers began to remark how their followers had turned the desert "into a city."[1] Again, monastics play a pivotal role in Ethiopian Christianity that probably exceeds the importance of the role played by monks in any other Christian tradition. However, despite these important aspects, it is highly problematic to view Ethiopian Christianity as something exotic, extreme, or even obscure – especially for other African Christians. The truth is that the ancient Christianity of Ethiopia is a wonderful example of how the riches of God's glory can be contextualized to meet the quotidian needs of common people. And even though the image of solitary ascetics in Ethiopia is pervasive (both within and without), it would be a

---

1. Athanasius, *Life of Antony*, 14, trans. Robert Gregg, Classics of Western Spirituality (London: Paulist Press, 1980), 42–43; Cf. John Binns, *The T&T Clark History of Monasticism: The Eastern Tradition* (London: T&T Clark, 2021), 2; John Binns, *Ascetics and Ambassadors of Christ: The Monasteries of Palestine, 314–631* (Oxford: Oxford University Press, 1994).

serious mistake to conclude that spiritual progress and maturity is primarily conceptualized in individualistic terms. This chapter will demonstrate just how greatly the goal of communion with God shapes the *collective* Christian consciousness of the Ethiopian Orthodox *Täwaḥədo* Church (EOTC).

Africa now firmly bears the title of "most Christian continent."[2] Amidst the tremendous growth of Christianity, however, the availability of training and resources is being considerably outpaced by the need among fledgling Christian believers and communities. This gap is often acknowledged and is very important but does not explain the entire situation behind the growing nominalism[3] and "cultural Christianity" of Africa. Other factors contributing to the "discipleship crisis"[4] are nuanced and will be discussed below. Even if the description of a "discipleship crisis" seems too drastic for more optimistic Christian leaders, few would deny the extent of the need throughout Africa for its Christians to move on from "milk to meat."[5]

The changes initiated by Vatican II helped to bring a new set of vocabulary to the fore of Western Christianity, and Protestantism has increasingly embraced this vocabulary as well. Thus, many Protestants find the language of "spiritual formation" to be a helpful way to understand the dynamics involved in our maturation as Christians and even a helpful alternative to dimensions of human effort often associated with words like "discipline." Hence, Robert Mulholland's description of a "pilgrimage of deepening responsiveness to God's control of our life and being"[6] has found considerable resonance among evangelicals and Protestants more broadly (along with other definitions emphasizing the more passive dimensions of spiritual growth).[7]

This chapter will favour the phrase "spiritual formation" as a functional approximation for all other expressions of Christian growth, maturation,

---

2. This change occurred when it surpassed Latin America in 2018. See https://www.gordonconwell.edu/blog/who-owns-global-christianity/.

3. The nominalistic faith of a place such as 1960s America or John Wesley's England are, of course, very different from the growing nominalism of sub-Saharan Africa. Nevertheless, it is vital to acknowledge that the missionary heritage of entire villages converting to Christianity still causes many Africans to claim Christianity because of their group rather than because of any personal choice or decision.

4. Just one recent example of this phrase being used in academic discourse is found in Jerry M. Ireland, "A Classical Pentecostal Approach to Discipleship in Missions," *Journal of Pentecostal Theology* 28, no. 2 (2019): 243–66, 244.

5. See 1 Corinthians 3:2; Hebrews 5:12.

6. M. Robert Mulholland and Ruth Haley Barton, *Invitation to a Journey: A Road Map for Spiritual Formation*, rev. and exp. edition (Downers Grove: IVP Books, 2016), 12.

7. Popular works by Henri Nouwen, Dallas Willard, and Richard Foster all demonstrate similar emphases.

discipleship, progress, sanctification, etc. Much – if not all – of what these terms seek to articulate has been classically expressed in the Byzantine tradition by the Greek term *theosis* (θέωσις) – which is sometimes known by its Latin equivalent "deification."[8] Because the EOTC locates itself within the broadly Orthodox/Byzantine tradition,[9] the term *theosis* is probably the most accurate way of expressing what happens as Ethiopian Christians collectively become more like Jesus.

The Orthodox affiliation and orientation of the EOTC is a serious obstacle for many Protestants in Africa – largely due to doctrinal factors such as the veneration of saints and for reasons connected to ecclesiastical polity – and cannot be flippantly overlooked nor disregarded. However, economic, political, and demographic factors strongly suggest that Ethiopia's impact upon global Christianity will only increase in coming decades. Not only is Ethiopia projected to be the single largest Orthodox nation in the world by 2050 (surpassing the Russian Orthodox Church), but it is also quite likely to be the second largest Protestant nation in all of Africa![10] These factors suggest that careful study of Ethiopia and the EOTC is a worthy pursuit in its own right for all Africans. However, the deep solidarity, commitment, and coherency of Ethiopian Orthodox Christians is especially relevant to the dilemma of spiritual formation throughout Sub-Saharan Africa.[11]

To be clear, the intention of this article is not to argue that all of Africa should adopt Ethiopian modes of worship, fellowship, or spiritual formation.[12] Instead, the goal is to demonstrate how the EOTC has developed methods of spiritual formation that are uniquely tailored to the African context, which

---

8. It should be noted that any direct equivalence between *theosis* and Protestant notions of "spiritual formation" is difficult. As the definition from Norman Russell below indicates, *theosis* is probably more expansive and encompassing than the phrase "spiritual formation."

9. Speaking precisely about the doctrinal alignment of the EOTC can be difficult because of the various assumptions associated with different terminology. Cleary, the EOTC is one of the miaphysite churches of the Oriental Orthodox family. For reasons that can't be explored here, both of these terms are viewed as problematic by some. However, this author feels that both are better than the term "non-Chalcedonian," which is fundamentally exclusive in its orientation. For the purposes of this chapter, it may be acceptable to speak of the EOTC as being "Byzantine derived" due to the strong connections to Constantine that are expressed in the ክብረ ነገሥት (Kəbrä Nägäśt), or "Glory of the Kings."

10. Patrick Johnstone, *The Future of the Global Church: History, Trends and Possibilities* (Downers Grove: IVP Books, 2011), 93–118.

11. Ralph Lee and Daniel Seifemichael, "Orthodox," in *Christianity in Sub-Saharan Africa*, ed. Kenneth R. Ross, J. Kwabena Asamoah-Gyadu, and Todd M. Johnson, Edinburgh Companions to Global Christianity (Edinburgh: Edinburgh University Press, 2017), 264–76.

12. This article is primarily concerned with Sub-Saharan Africa. Further clarification is provided when needed.

may be instructive for other African churches that are seeking to address the "discipleship crisis" apparent throughout the continent. Just as Western methods of "discipleship" should not expect to be fully effective if imported wholesale and uncritically into African contexts, one should not expect any insights gleaned from the EOTC to act as a panacea for the rest of Africa. Rather, careful contextual work will inevitably be required if any insights from the EOTC are to be beneficial for the rest of Sub-Saharan Africa.

The Challenge of Spiritual Formation in Africa

Any attempt to speak generally about the African continent is increasingly fraught with difficulty, especially as growing knowledge of African Traditional Religion(s) demonstrates the extent of irreducible diversity found throughout Africa's many cultures. Nevertheless, some generalizations are possible and necessary when it comes to the status and condition of the Christian faith. Although Christianity has now flourished in Sub-Saharan Africa for hundreds of years, many feel that the fruit of this reality has lagged behind expectations and hopes. One of the best assessments of this situation came from Emanuel Katongole, whose incisive critiques still await clear, concerted responses.[13] Christians more aligned with Pentecostal-charismatic Christianity (PCC) tend to reject social and institutional transformation as a legitimate indicator of established Christian faith, choosing to focus mostly on the behaviours of Christians themselves.[14] Although obviously more complex than the mere aggregated behaviour of the individuals involved, the Rwandan genocide still stands as a tragic witness against the actions of a majority population who claimed to be disciples of Christ. It is likely too simplistic to equate the historic Rwandan situation with a "discipleship crisis,"[15] but it is nevertheless clear that Christianity is struggling to take root in the deep way required to transform the culture, institutions, and social behaviours of many Africans.

Much has been said and written about the challenge of spiritual formation in Africa. For the purposes of this chapter, three major dimensions will

---

13. Emmanuel Katongole, *The Sacrifice of Africa: A Political Theology for Africa* (Grand Rapids: Eerdmans, 2010).

14. For an interesting perspective on this issue, see Selina Stone, "Pentecostal Power: Discipleship as Political Engagement," *Journal of the European Pentecostal Theological Association* 38, no. 1 (2018): 24–38.

15. For a more nuanced assessment, see Adriaan Verwijs, "Growing in Christ on African Soil: Thoughts on Enhancing the Contextualization of Discipleship Training in Rwanda," *Cairo Journal of Theology* 2 (2015): 132–51.

be considered because of corresponding examples in the EOTC: *telos*, *individualism*, and *ecclesiology*.

Telos[16]

In Matthew 5:48, Jesus uses the adjectival form of *telos* (τέλειοι) to express the divinely-oriented goal of humans, and the same word is used in the striking passage of Philippians 3:12–21 to express the "stretching forward to the things that lie ahead"[17] (τοῖς δὲ ἔμπροσθεν ἐπεκτεινόμενος). This picture then leads Paul to urge the Christians in Philippi to imitate (συμμιμητής) him even as he imitates Christ – an idea which is also expressed in 1 Corinthians 11:1.

Various images and metaphors have been used throughout church history (with varying levels of effect) to convey the spiritual progress expected of Christians: biological growth, financial return on investment, an "upward" ascent of a ladder or mountain.[18] However, because every human is inescapably bound by the realities of time, the chronological urgency of future-orientation has remained central – even paramount – for Western Christians. This is problematic not just because it subverts other biblical metaphors in favour of the one most relevant to a particular culture, but also because of the implications of time for Africans. Although his sweeping conclusions have rightly been criticized, John Mbiti famously highlighted the effective absence of the future tense within his own Akamba language and demonstrated how distinctly many Africans conceptualize the future in contrast to Western notions.[19] A helpful summary of Mbiti's view is provided by A. Scott Moreau:

> Mbiti's view of the African understanding of time may in one sense be likened to a man standing in a river and facing downstream. The current may be thought of as the flow of time, with the view of the man in the river including primarily that which is peripherally around him and secondarily on that which has already gone past him (downstream) . . . The future is only what can be seen in peripheral vision, and so the "upstream" time holds little

---

16. "Telos" is used here loosely to express the basic trajectory of the human person, rather than being used in its more philosophical dimensions.

17. Author's own translation.

18. One of the most influential works that utilizes this metaphor is the *Ladder of Divine Ascent* by John Climacus. See Saint John Climacus, *Ladder of Divine Ascent*, 4th ed. (Boston: Holy Transfiguration Monastery, 2012).

19. John Mbiti, "Christian Eschatology in Relation to the Evangelization of Tribal Africa" (PhD Dissertation, University of Cambridge, 1963).

importance in the perceptions of the man in the water. It will pass when and how it passes, and then it will become of consequence to him. Only what is currently passing or has already passed is of significance, for it has become part of his concrete reality and is therefore important . . . Since he knows it will reach him eventually, there is no need to focus on it, and he cannot speed its advance (which does not mean the African is fatalistic, only not overtly mindful of the future).[20]

Regardless of the limitations of this view, Mbiti was clearly correct to relate culturally unique perceptions of time to the impact they have on eschatological dimensions of Christianity.[21]

In a slightly dated but perceptive article, Cheryl Bridges Johns critiqued the contemporary dominance of the "developmental paradigm" of spiritual growth and argued instead for models more focused on participation.[22] If it is possible that one impediment to spiritual formation in Africa has historically been an ill-fitting focus upon future spiritual "benchmarks" disconnected from concrete events or relationships, the idea of participation merits serious consideration. Furthermore, it must be acknowledged that the biblical language of *telos* is not primarily chronological in nature but relational. As has been shown, the Christian *telos* is connected to becoming like the Father, or like Paul as he becomes like Christ.

Taking such a relational approach to spiritual formation requires a serious question: Who, in fact, are the spiritual examples that young African Christians seek to emulate? The first unavoidable example is the successful church leader. Whether such leaders claim the title of "pastor," "reverend," "bishop," "apostle," "prophet," or some combination of these, they garner attention because they have somehow led a church to position of prominence. Examples of excess are all too familiar, but even in smaller churches many leaders are often admired as much for the social recognition and status they have achieved as for the spiritual fruit they exhibit. A second example, of course, is the category of political leaders and other people of influence. Sometimes, it can seem that

---

20. A. Scott Moreau, "A Critique of John Mbiti's Understanding of the African Concept of Time," *East Africa Journal of Evangelical Theology* 5, no. 2 (1986): 36–48, 39.

21. Some critics claim that Mbiti's view is too simplistic. For more discussion, see Sunday Fumilola Babalola and Olusegun Ayodeji Alokan, "African Concept of Time, a Socio-Cultural Reality in the Process of Change," *Journal of Education and Practice* 4, no. 7 (2013): 143–47.

22. Cheryl Bridges Johns, "From Strength to Strength: The Neglected Role of Crisis in Wesleyan and Pentecostal Discipleship," *Wesleyan Theological Journal* 39, no. 1 (2004): 137–53.

the only way to live a life of real purpose in Africa is to secure money and influence by whatever means possible.

A third group of people are those who live counter-culturally and incarnationally. Unfortunately, because of the humble lifestyle, these figures are often unknown to the vast majority of Africans who could benefit from their example. Exceptions do exist and are gratefully increasing. But even godly people such as Kwame Bediako – who returned to his home country to share his gifts – still present a somewhat mixed message: Must an African Christian leave Africa in order to receive the training needed to benefit Africa? Additionally, many of those most lauded tend to be missionaries with resources, connections, and the ability to travel and share their examples with more people. The broad recognition and subsequent benefit stemming from (canonized) saints in other traditions is not usually seen in this light, but it is worth considering vis-à-vis the existing gap in Africa that has been highlighted here. Wouldn't it be beneficial to share the stories of African Christians who followed Christ in exemplary ways? We know of accomplished individuals like Desmond Tutu and Nelson Mandela, but what of other African saints whom the marginalized can truly "imitate" in their daily lives?

Individualism

Just as tested Western methods of spiritual formation may be too focused on disembodied, future expectations to be fruitful in African settings, they may also be excessively focused on *individual techniques* at the expense of the group. This insight is not new. Isolated attempts at Scripture memorization or study have long been problematic in African contexts due to traditional preference for communal activities and also because of the obvious twin challenges of literacy and Bible ownership. These are some of the major reasons why resources such as the *Africa Study Bible* have met such a serious need. Moreover, individual moral struggle against temptations and sin is especially problematic in most African cultures where honour and shame are major factors – especially if there is anticipation of confession before a group (as in the methods of John Wesley). Indeed, some scholars have gone so far as to claim that "sin" in the African context is only realized when brought to light before the entire group.[23] Serious as these examples are, the effects of what is here being called "individualism" reach well beyond private endeavours.

---

23. S. E. Freeman and Richard D. Calenberg, "Understanding Honor-Shame Dynamics for Ministry in Sub-Saharan Africa," *Bibliotheca Sacra* 175, no. 700 (2018): 425–59, 432.

It is also well known that growing secularism and globalization throughout Africa are fuelling unprecedented levels of individualistic behaviours.[24] Especially as younger generations abandon village life for the opportunities afforded by large cities, traditional modes of interdependence are increasingly being supplanted by desires to attain a level of security which might then be used to benefit family left behind in the village. With this view, it is hardly surprising that manifestations of the (individualistic) prosperity gospel have found such fertile soil in Africa. Africa has not ceased being "incurably religious,"[25] but the units of beneficiaries have undeniably shifted away from the village and towards the individual.

The impact that this atmosphere has upon church life is palpable. Churches and church traditions that are driven by experiential criteria usually select individuals for advancement based upon the effect of their unique giftings or charisma.[26] Thus, the teenage boy is allowed to preach because he can excite responses within the congregation and the young mother is given a microphone because her singing voice is the most impressive to the listeners. Such prioritization of experience above more biblical criteria such as godliness and character (see 1 Tim 3) create *de facto* environments in which careful, introspective spiritual disciplines prove to be inefficient and ineffective routes to acceptance and recognition by the Christian group.

Thus, it may be said that many African Christians are struggling against simultaneously counter-acting forces of Christian individualism (in Western discipleship methods) and secular individualism (in various media and social propaganda). Stated differently, it can sometimes appear that in order for an African to grow spiritually in the ways approved by Western leaders, they must step into the same individualistic and secular space which is so acutely plaguing Western Christianity! Just as Africans may need more concrete measures for the "forward" trajectory of the spiritual growth, so also may they require opportunities to grow *communally* rather than as isolated spiritual soldiers.

---

24. Willem J. de Wit, "Secularization and Discipleship in Africa: Conclusions and Recommendations," *Cairo Journal of Theology* 2 (2015): 152–60. It is especially interesting to note the question asked at the end (p. 160) about a possible *via media* between Western and African forms of discipleship.

25. Geoffrey Parrinder, *Religion in Africa* (Hammondsworth: Penguin Books, 1969), 235.

26. Chammah J. Kaunda, "Making Critically Conscious Disciples: A Zambian Pentecostal Pneumato-Discipleship Missiology," *International Review of Mission* 106, no. 2 (December 2017): 322–35.

Ecclesiology

The fact that many Sub-Saharan African nations are saturated by Christianity means that one can often find churches on every street and corner. This saturation has a profound effect upon the subconscious ecclesiology of lay people. The fact that many of these churches are independent of denominational accountability and authority structures also seriously affects the default ecclesiology of many African Christians. In places where the constant threat of malevolent spirits and forces is mostly taken for granted, church services and church involvement can sometimes drift towards a sort of spiritual pragmatism: attend the service to keep the evil spirits at bay. Of course, analogous situations exist in most other Christian nations, and it will soon be shown how a similar accusation of "spiritual pragmatism" could be made about the EOTC. However, the pernicious feature connected to this mindset in most of Sub-Saharan Africa is the concern given to effectiveness and accessibility of the spiritual *mechanisms* of local churches.

Much has been written about the nuances and variety of African Independent Churches (AICs), but one outstanding feature is that they tend to orbit around the leadership of a strong, charismatic leader. This tendency is also found in varying degrees among many other African churches as well. Despite the existence of liturgical emphases within a small percentage of AICs, the dominance of an exclusive leadership often necessitates that any type of growth, reception, or spiritual comfort is mediated through approved individuals rather than any consistently accessible services or sacraments from the church itself.[27] Obviously, this means that there is relatively little an individual Christian can truly do on their own to grow in their faith. While the problems of non-relational forms of discipleship have already been mentioned above, the bottleneck of narrow ecclesial leadership may demonstrate an instance of the pendulum swinging to the opposite extreme. Deep relational connections within churches are good, but not if they prohibit individual Christians from encountering God with confidence beyond the four walls of their church building.

Prayer has always been a critical component of the life of the church. Despite the strong communal dynamic in African churches, however, priority is often given to the person who can express the congregation's need with

---

27. Asamoah-Gyadu explores these dynamics and others with great clarity here: J. Kwabena Asamoah-Gyadu, "'Go Near and Join Thyself to This Chariot . . .': African Pneumatic Movements and Transformational Discipleship," *International Review of Mission* 106, no. 2 (December 2017): 336–55.

the most passion rather than priority being given to the group praying as one, united body. This signals the (healthy) need for attendance of the weekly gathering, but may perhaps diminish the sense of Christian community from Monday to Saturday. Such a struggle is found in most other traditions and has been addressed to varying levels of effect (through mid-week prayer services, Bible studies, etc.), but the African church seems caught in a dilemma. How can individual Christians grow in their faith outside of their church while they are being taught (implicitly or explicitly) that all of the means of spiritual maturity are contained within the church building? Churches in the Wesleyan tradition do well to emphasize the various "means of grace" accessible to all Christians, but usually struggle in seeing their members take advantage of these "disciplines" beyond a group setting. "Why should I grow stronger if my brother is left behind?"[28]

Once again, communal prayer is a wonderful exercise for Christians and frequently serves as a corrective to excessive habits of private, individualistic prayer as practiced in the West. But considering the difficulty of midweek gatherings for many Africans (work, travel, appropriate spaces, parenting duties, even lighting and electricity), Sunday morning can functionally become the supreme locus of prayer – which is troubling if prayer is one's primary weapon against malevolent evil spirits (see Mark 9:29). *Lex orandi, lex credendi*.

Ultimately, the lack of de-centralized ecclesial ministries and models may be located as one of the most serious impediments to the maturation of church members individually and, by extension, the maturation of the church family as a whole. If the beauty of African Christianity is expressed by the notion of *ubuntu*, its weakness might be expressed by the notion of "least common denominator" – the group tends to drift towards the conduct of the majority of its members (cf. 1 Cor 12:23). As Mulholland so aptly states: "Left to ourselves in the development of our spiritual practices, we will generally gravitate to those spiritual activities that nurture our preferred pattern of being and doing."[29]

The Example of Ethiopia

Ethiopia is far from a perfect country, as anyone who has spent time there knows well. Moreover, the ancient Christianity of Ethiopia that has been stewarded by the EOTC is also far from perfect. But as already stated in the introduction,

---

28. This was an earnest question asked of the author while leading a Bible study in May, 2014 in the Democratic Republic of the Congo.
29. Mulholland and Barton, *Invitation to a Journey*, 57.

perfection is not prerequisite for the best features of a given Christian tradition to benefit and bless other Christians outside its own reach. What should be prerequisite is a strong measure of orthodox belief and evidence of the Spirit's activity. This is not the place to explore or defend the theology of the EOTC in detail, but several comments are in order.

Traditionally, the same basic obstacles to fellowship with Protestantism that are true of other Orthodox churches are also true of the EOTC, which gained full autocephaly from the Coptic Church in 1959.[30] These include: The veneration of the *Theotokos*, the "canon" of Scripture,[31] the cult of saints, and the emphasis placed on the place of righteous deeds in conjunction with faith in the righteous deeds of Christ. Despite these typical differences, the EOTC has almost always been understood as a faithful part of the Global Body of Christ,[32] acting as a founding member of the World Council of Churches and maintaining full communion with all of the other Oriental Orthodox Churches. Perhaps most important is the deep Christian witness and solidarity that the EOTC has maintained in the midst of turmoil and persecution – especially when one considers that it is surrounded by nations that became dominated by Islam. Against imposing odds, the EOTC was able to maintain its vitality during the communist period of government. In more recent times, the tragic violence which has been radiating from Tigray and beyond has been strongly and consistently opposed by many in the church, including the Patriarch.[33] Finally, at the time of this writing, the unity of the EOTC and the peace of the entire nation has been threatened by three rogue bishops declaring a new Oromia Synod, claiming that the EOTC Synod refused to allow Oromo and other southern nations to worship in their native languages. Remarkably, the vast majority of Ethiopian Christians undertook a period of public mourning by fasting, praying, and wearing black clothing as they pleaded with God to preserve the unity of their Christian faith and witness – despite significant government pressure to prevent public mourning. Whatever one wishes to say

---

30. Ayele' Taklahāymānot, "The Egyptian Metropolitan of the Ethiopian Church: A Study on a Chapter of History of the Ethiopian Church," *Pontificium Institutum Orientalium Studiorum* 54 (1988): 175–222.

31. For an excellent treatment about the dynamics of this issue, see Bruk A. Asale, "The Ethiopian Orthodox Tewahedo Church Canon of the Scriptures: Neither Open nor Closed," *The Bible Translator* 67, no. 2 (August 2016): 202–22; See also Roger W. Cowley, "The Biblical Canon of the Ethiopian Orthodox Church Today," *Ostkirchliche Studien* 23, no. 4 (1974): 318–23.

32. One major historical exception was the opinion of the Jesuits who came to Ethiopia in the sixteenth century.

33. See https://www.aljazeera.com/news/2021/5/8/ethiopias-orthodox-church-patriarch-condemns-tigray-genocide.

at a theological level, it seems supremely unwise to risk blaspheming the Holy Spirit by claiming that God is not actively at work within the EOTC.

As a reminder, this chapter considers dimensions of *theosis* within the EOTC not because it is seen to be somehow superior or more correct than Protestant notions of "spiritual formation," but primarily because that is the terminology classically used in the broad Orthodox tradition within which the EOTC locates herself. It must be stated from the outset that neither the word *theosis* nor "deification" appear in the traditional corpus of the EOTC, nor does there seem to be any directly equivalent term in *Ge'ez* (ግዕዝ) – the language in which the writings of the church are transmitted. Instead, there is a wide variety of words, phrases, metaphors, and descriptions that discuss how humanity grows closer to and experiences increasing communion with God.[34] Although it creates more work for theologians, in some ways the absence of a single term is beneficial because it prevents such a vital Christian goal from being pigeonholed. As Protestant interest in *theosis* has surged in the last several decades,[35] some feel that the idea has been excessively parsed and stripped of mystery. Consequently, this chapter offers a definition from Norman Russell to act as a basic foundation for the ensuing discussion: "Deification, or *theosis*, is a complex term with both anthropological and economic components – that is to say, it concerns our growth as human beings towards ultimate fulfilment in God, while simultaneously encompassing the whole of God's plan of salvation."[36]

In order to explore the corporate dimensions of *theosis* within the EOTC and how such things may be of benefit for other African churches, three topics will be considered: the veneration of the saints, prayer, and corporate worship. While these are far from an exhaustive representation, the hope is that the dynamics at play within these three facets of the EOTC will provide corresponding and corrective insights to the dimensions of African Christianity currently limiting spiritual formation that were assessed above.

---

34. These are conclusions drawn from the present author's own research, which is being published gradually in different articles and book chapters.

35. An unpublished thesis from Bobby Rackley provides the best summary of Protestant interest currently available. See Bobby Lynn Rackley, "Recovery of the Divine Nature: Wesleyan Soteriology and Theosis Calmly Considered" (ThD Dissertation, Duke University, 2020).

36. Norman Russell, *Fellow Workers With God: Orthodox Thinking on Theosis* (Crestwood: St. Vladimir's Seminary Press, 2009), Kindle edition, 13. Sometimes, efforts are made to compare *theosis* with the Wesleyan notion of entire sanctification or Christian perfection. Although several similarities are present, this author would argue that these Wesleyan terms are fundamentally less comprehensive than the traditional Orthodox understanding of *theosis*.

The veneration of the saints

Speaking of "veneration" in Protestant contexts is often a sure-fire way to incite conflict. However, the careful distinction made by the Orthodox between worship and veneration is also one of the most carelessly treated aspects of their theology by Protestants. As with several other subjects mentioned in this chapter, a detailed treatment here is simply impossible. One vital and helpful distinction to make for Protestants about the veneration of saints within the EOTC relates to the use of relics. Unlike the excesses against which Martin Luther reacted in the Roman Catholic Church, the EOTC is relatively unconcerned with relics of their saints.[37] This is also why this section has eschewed the traditional phrase "cult of saints," which primarily refers to the complex of practices which rose to prominence in Late Antiquity.[38]

For this chapter, the main import of the saints in the EOTC relates to the notion of *telos* discussed in the previous section. While millions of African Christians are quite literally searching for godly examples to imitate just as Paul instructed, Ethiopian Christians are quite literally surrounded constantly by striking visual and audible reminders of the godly believers who have gone before them. Part of this is achieved through an abundance of iconographic imagery in churches, monasteries, homes, and places of business. The fact that all of the most popular saints have dark skin, familiar stories, and local origins greatly adds to the sense that following their godly example is both sensible and possible for the common Ethiopian. Furthermore, the fact that inspiring lives of the saints are read from the *Synaxarion* every single day in most churches helps foster an imperative reminder in the life of faith: By grace, you are part of something truly glorious; but by grace you must continue to press on towards the holiness exemplified by the saints that seems so far removed!

Perhaps the most tangible extension of the example of saints are the thousands of active monks and ascetics of Ethiopia who regularly interact with lay people. It is impossible to overstate the importance and impact of monks upon the EOTC. In such men (and women), Ethiopians have a close connection to reminders of the sacrifice, dedication, and singular[39] focus that God expects of all his children. Unlike nearly all other Orthodox countries still

---

37. It should be noted, however, that certain instances are still important. For example, the uncorrupted bodies of various kings are clearly venerated at Degga Estifanos monastery on Lake Tana. It is possible that the possession of the Ark of the Covenant in Axum essentially "trumps" the relics of various saints that might otherwise be venerated.

38. Peter Brown, *The Cult of the Saints: Its Rise and Function in Latin Christianity* (Chicago: University of Chicago Press, 1982).

39. The word "monk" comes from the word for "single" or "solitary."

thriving today, the monks of Ethiopia are deeply intermingled with common life – frequently spotted walking on sidewalks and sitting on benches just like the common folk. Because most priests are selected from the monasteries and because most venerated saints also shared the monastic vocation, monks are rarely viewed as aloof, isolated hermits (even though some of those do exist).[40] Instead, the general perception is that such devoted members of Christ's body play a vital – but not superior – role in helping the entire church move deeper into the goodness and love of God. Monasteries often act as centres for spiritual retreat, renewal, and pilgrimage, while the monks themselves frequently act as mentors and spiritual confessors.[41]

All of these factors contribute to a rich conception of the individual's place in God's divine economy and the church's place in Christian history. Like other places in Africa, Ethiopia's sense of time is markedly different from that dominant in the West. For instance, Messay Kebede argues that the Ethiopian sense of time is also basically "two-dimensional."[42] However, the deep identification with biblical prophecy and unique influence of 1 Enoch in particular creates a powerful sense of eschatological telos among Ethiopian Christians,[43] or what Kebede calls a "teleological occurrence."[44] Ultimately, it may be fitting to draw from biblical language to describe how the unique Ethiopian understanding of salvation history affects practical *theosis* among adherents of the EOTC. All the elements mentioned inculcate a dynamic sense of the "great cloud of witnesses" that participates in the worship and daily activities of God's church – thus extending "backward" to beloved Christian

---

40. Much like prophets of the Old Testament, a vital role of the *baḥtawi* or *täbaḥtawi* (ባሕታዊ; ተባሕታዊ) is occasionally revisiting civilized places in order to deliver vital, prophetic messages from God.

41. Some will likely contend that these activities are simply responses to the growth of Protestantism in Ethiopia. Although these activities have undoubtedly experienced a certain revival in the last thirty years, these practices were common long before Protestantism came to Ethiopia. For a perceptive treatment, see Ralph Lee, "'Modernism' and the Ethiopian Orthodox Sunday School Movement: Indigenous Movements and Their International Connections," *The Journal of Ecclesiastical History* (November 18, 2021): 1–17; Ralph Lee, "Discipleship in Oriental Orthodox and Evangelical Communities," *Religions* 12, no. 5 (2021): 320–32; John Binns, *The Orthodox Church of Ethiopia: A History* (London: I. B. Tauris, 2016).

42. Messay Kebede, "The Ethiopian Conception of Time and Modernity" (2013), Philosophy Faculty Publications, Paper 111, http://ecommons.udayton.edu/phl_fac_pub/111.

43. Ralph Lee, "The Reception and Function of 1 Enoch in the Ethiopian Orthodox Tradition," in *Rediscovering Enoch? The Antediluvian Past from the Fifteenth to Nineteenth Centuries*, ed. Ariel Hessayon, Annette Yoshiko Reed, and Gabriele Boccaccini (Leiden: Brill, 2023), 311–25.

44. Kebede, "The Ethiopian Conception of Time and Modernity."

ancestors and "forward" towards the prize for which they are cheering us onward (Phil 3:14; Heb 12:1).

Prayer

As an ancient church, the EOTC has preserved thousands of manuscripts featuring hundreds of biblical, patristic, monastic, and spiritual texts. Unsurprisingly, many of these texts are prayers and the most popular biblical texts in all of Ethiopia are those in the Psalter.[45] Although these traditional prayers have been originally preserved in *Ge'ez* (ግዕዝ), an abundance of Amharic and other contemporary language materials make them accessible for millions of common Christians. Moreover, even before Amharic translations were widely available, many of these prayers were memorized and repeated with great consistency and regularity. In fact, Ethiopia boasts a remarkable system of traditional church education that is conducted almost entirely by memory and may represent the oldest continual method of education still in existence today.[46] All of this means that even when these prayers are prayed individually at home in the "prayer closet" as Jesus instructed, there is still a deep and profound communal aspect to the prayers.

Adding to this sense of solidarity is the fact that several of the most popular prayers have been arranged to be prayed on specific days of every week and printed in very cheap, accessible, pocket-sized books to be used in the most common of situations. One of the most popular prayer books, *Wədasse Amlak* (ውዳሴ አምላክ; "The Praise of God"), includes prayers that are hundreds of years old and speak powerfully of the ways that God "dwells in each and every

---

45. The Ethiopic Psalters contain: psalms attributed to King David, the biblical canticles, the Song of Songs and usually additional devotional texts, the most common of which are: *Wədasse Maryam* and the *Anqäṣä Bərhan*. The fifteen biblical canticles of the P. are as follows: (1) First Song of Moses (Exod 15:1–19); (2) Second Song of Moses (Deut 32:1–21); (3) Third Song of Moses (Deut 32:22–43); (4) Song of Hannah (1 Kgs [1 Sam] 2:1–10); (5) Prayer of Hezekiah (Isa 38:10–20); (6) Prayer of Manasseh (apocryphal); (7) Song of Jonah (Jonah 2:3–10); (8) First Song of the Three Youths in the Furnace (Dan 3:26–45); (9) Second Song of the Three Youths (Dan 3:52–56); (10) Third Song of the Three Youths (Dan 3:57–88); (11) Song of Habakkuk (Hab 3:1–19); (12) Song of Isaiah (Isa 26:9–20); (13) Song of Our Lady Mary (the Magnificat) (Luke 1:46–55); (14) Song of Zechariah (Luke 1:68–79); (15) Song of Simeon (nunc dimittis) (Luke 2:29–32). See M. E. Heldman "Psalter" in *Encyclopaedia Aethiopica: Vol 4: O–X*, eds. S. Uhlig and A. Bausi et al. (Wiesbaden: Harrassowitz Verlag, 2010), 231–33. For more info, see Thomas C. Oden and Curt Niccum, eds., *The Songs of Africa: The Ethiopian Canticles* (New Haven: ICCS Press, 2017).

46. John Binns, "Theological Education in the Ethiopian Orthodox Church," *Journal of Adult Theological Education* 2, no. 2 (March 17, 2005): 103–13.

believer" and causes them to rejoice in his beauty and radiance.[47] Many in the Wesleyan tradition will be familiar with the Book of Common Prayer so important to the Anglican tradition, but few examples in modern global Christianity match the pervasiveness, popularity, and zeal evidenced in the use of the different prayer books of the EOTC.

Another factor is also at play. Rather than encountering extemporaneous or simultaneous prayer as is typical in much of PCC and AICs, Ethiopian Christians are consistently exposed to the same sets of prayers in the Divine Liturgy and other services. Thus, even as literacy is a limiting factor for many Ethiopian Christians, the ability to hear and participate in familiar prayers is a powerful reminder of belonging. Finally, the ancient and widespread nature of the prayers used in the EOTC unmistakably shift the focus away from any single individual and instead towards the historic community of the faithful. If the African perception of time is largely rooted in the past and cognizant of those who have gone before, perhaps prayers that are passed down through generations are precisely the means by which African Christians can stretch toward the future without abandoning their past? Afterall, the prayer that Jesus taught his disciples to pray is an ancient prayer that simultaneously visualizes current needs (daily bread) and future hopes (the kingdom).

Corporate worship

This final dimension of analysis relates to, but is not identical with, the topic of ecclesiology discussed in the previous section. If *theosis* is truly a collective journey, then surely it must be evident within the most precious and central times of the EOTC's worship. Probably the most important moment of the Divine Liturgy is the Eucharist. The language used in the EOTC – in contrast to much of the common verbiage in Protestantism – is explicitly corporate and plural, and clearly speaks in terms of *theosis*:

> We, who are gathered together to make remembrance of thy sufferings and partake in thy resurrection from the dead, beseech

---

47. *Wǝdasse Amlak*, Thursday, 6. Author's own translation. The full text reads: ወአንተ ሀላው በውስተ ኵሉ ለለ አሐዱ አሐዱ እምኔሆሙ በፍጻሜ እንበለ ጌጋይ፡፡ ወይሬእየከ ወይትፌሥሑ በስንከ ወያነክሩከ ወይዔዝቡ ከመ አንተ ሀላው በውስቴቶሙ ለለ አሐዱ አሐዱ እምኔሆሙ በበሕቲቶሙ ወለለሁ የኣክል ከመ ትጎድር ውስቴቱ ወአንተ ሎቱ ርስቱ ወመዝገብ ሕይወት ለለቡሉሁ መመዝገብ ድፋን ወክቡት ውስቴቱ፡፡ ወአንተሰ ኮላንታክ ሀላው በውስተ ኵሉ ለለ አሐዱ አሐዱ እምኔሆሙ ይሬእየከ በምጽሐተ ልቡናሁ ይሬእየከ ጎቱሙ፡፡ ስብሐት ለከ ኦ ከካብ ዘየዕቆብ ዘዘንቱ ፀዳሉ ዘሥረቀተ ከነ እምአብ ወያስተርእ በልቡና ወይሠርቅ በልዐላውያን ወመትሕታውያን፡፡ ወአንተሂ ትሠርቅ ሎሙ እምውሥጥ ወታስተፌሥሐሙ እምአፍኣ ለከ ስብሐት እግዚአ እምኵሎሙ ፍጡራኒክ ወአኃ አስግድ ለከ በመንፈስ፡፡

thee, Lord our God, as this bread which was scattered among the mountains and the little hills, in the forests and the vales, being gathered together, became one perfect bread, likewise gather us together, through thy divinity, out of all evil thought of sin into thy perfect faith. As with the mixture of this wine with water, the one cannot be separated from the other, *so let thy divinity be united with our humanity, and our humanity with your divinity*, and let thy greatness be united with our humility and our humility with thy greatness. Lord, accept this our offering from us for a memorial of righteousness before thee [emphasis added].[48]

Moreover, the term used to describe the Eucharistic Liturgy in the EOTC, *qəddase* (ቅዳሴ), itself means "sanctification, hallowing." It is significant that the (secular and academic) *Encyclopaedia Aethiopica* describes this ritual as "a process of transformation of a community into the body of Christ through the growing communion brought about by the Holy Spirit."[49] Andualem Dagmawi, in his helpful study on the Ethiopian Liturgy, claims that the "deification of humanity" is a "key theme."[50]

Some would contend that the participation in the liturgy is often only partial or incomplete. In many places, church architecture is such that many Christians must stand outside of the building during the service. This presents a fascinating juxtaposition with the ecclesial understandings explored above. Whereas many African churches effectively restrict their benefits to regulated participation within the building and in proximity with the charismatic authority figure, the EOTC and its adherents recognize that the ancient and sacred acts being performed can benefit anyone who believes that God is extending his grace through such means. Much like the bleeding women who simply touches the hem of Jesus's robe, it is common to see Ethiopian Christians simply touching the doors of a church or crossing themselves at the gate. Spiritual warfare and concern about malevolent spirits are probably just as pervasive in Ethiopia as in the rest of Africa, but the role of the church is perceived somewhat differently. Victory is not sought as something that the church distributes to its faithful members but rather a historical reality that

---

48. Marcos Daoud, ed., *The Liturgy of the Ethiopian Church*, rev. (Kingston: Ethiopian Orthodox Church, 1991), 123.

49. Siegbert Uhlig and Alessandro Bausi et al., eds., *Encyclopaedia Aethiopica: O-X*, vol. 4 (Wiesbaden: Harrassowitz Verlag, 2010), 271.

50. Andualem Dagmawi, "Some Ideas of Deification as Reflected Throughout the Ethiopic Divine Liturgy," *Collectanea Christiana Orientalia* 6 (October 1, 2009): 45–66, 48–49.

has been promised to the church. Although still in progress, there is clear recognition that the only way to be victorious is to remain connected to the body that God has promised to save and deliver at the fulfilment of time. Once again, this understanding is rooted in the literature of 1 Enoch and specifically the Apocalypse of Weeks, which provides a deeply hopeful view of inaugurated eschatology for the entire EOTC – as opposed simply to individual, faithful members.[51]

Finally, a pronounced and inspiring revival has been growing in Ethiopia in the last three decades. It has taken a few different forms, but one of the key features is that "associations" of young people have taken the initiative to organize themselves and meet for regular prayer, worship, service projects, and fellowship outside the normal hours of church. Ralph Lee provides the following description about one of the most prominent of these associations:

> Since the fall of the Communist Dərg regime in May of 1991, the Maḫbärä Qəddusan has taken the lead in Orthodox spiritual activity in all of Ethiopia's higher education institutions, as well as also having a strong role among young professionals. Members pay 2 per cent of their income to the association, make regular pilgrimages for spiritual guidance and offer professional services to the association and to monasteries free of charge.[52]

This movement has changed the landscape of Christianity in Ethiopia and is represented by hundreds of thousands of young people.[53]

Possible Applications

Having now examined some major dimensions of how *theosis* is experienced communally in the EOTC, it is appropriate to share several suggestions about how these ancient (and modern) practices might benefit African Christians in other parts of the continent who are struggling to move deeper into "participation in the divine nature" (2 Pet 1:4). First, when it comes to perception of *telos* and the place of both individual and group in God's divine

---

51. Lee, "The Reception and Function of 1 Enoch in the Ethiopian Orthodox Tradition." The book of 1 Enoch divides "salvation history" into a period of ten "weeks" and locates Christians within that timeline in a very hopeful manner.

52. It should be noted that many Protestants have a very low view of the *Maḫbärä Qəddusan*, which is partly why this author believes this discussion is so vital. Lee, "'Modernism' and the Ethiopian Orthodox Sunday School Movement," 13.

53. Lee, "Discipleship in Oriental Orthodox and Evangelical Communities."

economy, it seems that more effort could be directed towards remembering and honouring deceased African Christians who were known for their godliness and holiness in order to emulate them in the present and future. More generally, African Christians would do well to bear in mind their tendency to stay connected to people in the past and leverage this characteristic to help them move towards the eschatological *telos* of God. To be clear, this does not necessitate the use of icons or any type of "veneration" as practiced within Orthodoxy. This author is simply suggesting that a concerted attempt be made to highlight Christlike African Christians for others to imitate. Ideally, such an endeavour will be animated by the unique and creative impulses of Africans themselves, but it may begin with something as simple as the desire to collect beautiful and inspiring stories of sacrifices made by African Christians – much as Foxe did for England in his *Book of Martyrs* or as the *Synaxarion* has done for the EOTC. Perhaps Protestants throughout Sub-Saharan Africa will be able to bless the rest of Protestantism by generating fresh ways of allowing the "cloud of witnesses" to inform corporate worship – even as they prayerfully consider the traditional dynamics of ancestor veneration within their own contexts.

Concerning the increasing gravitational pull of individualism throughout Africa, it has been shown above how prayers in the EOTC may serve to undermine such forces and strengthen the bond within and among local churches. More generally, Africans should be conscious of their tendency to preserve group stasis and utilize it to catalyze new expectations for Christian communities. Once again, this may simply involve a concerted effort among international African Christians to begin composing and collecting prayers that reflect and articulate the needs of a large cross-section of Africans by using collective and communal language. Over the span of several decades, the most helpful and most popular prayers could be culled to form some type of international African devotional prayer book, much like the *Book of Common Prayer* or the *Wədasse Amlak*. Crucially, this enterprise should be pursued with the challenge of literacy and the power of orality in African cultures both in view. If prayers are rooted in Scripture, composed with simple structures and recurring themes, and even feature shared indigenous African references, their power is more likely to transcend the constraints of printed material and specific languages. Perhaps a new surge of prayers from the Heart of Africa will eventually help to heal Western Christianity from the hobbling effects of individualism to which it continues to succumb?

Finally, several recommendations may be made in relation to the dynamics of ecclesiology and corporate worship. Given the preceding observations, it seems apparent that African Christians must continue to think in terms of the entire local Christian community. Considering the absence of unity among many uncooperative AICs and other churches, African Christians could benefit greatly by joining together around their shared vigilance about spiritual warfare. Generally speaking, it could be said that African Christians are most likely to succeed in their kingdom calling by capitalizing on this widely-held worldview and moving forward as a collective unit (as opposed to Western methods of "survival of the fittest"). Drawing from the example of the EOTC, this could involve large-scale periods of fasting and mourning for millions of people.[54] Because nearly all African Christians believe in the potency of evil spirits and the supremacy of Christ's power over them, international times of prayer connected to this general theme may be more feasible than sometimes acknowledged.[55] Afterall, victory over and freedom from indigenous demonic forces has long been (and continues to be) a significant element in the transformation of communities and societies into Christlikeness.[56] Additionally, shared history and experience of colonialism could serve as a powerful element in fostering solidarity in these efforts. In order for any large-scale ecclesial activities to be effective in Africa, one familiar requirement seems clear: The group dynamic must be leveraged away from seeking the "lowest common denominator" and towards seeking the "prize for which Christ has called us heavenward." Accordingly, the fasts, prayers, and other corporate activities of the EOTC which seem so "extreme" to many others, may in fact be precisely what is needed for effective African spiritual formation and the deep transformation of the Christian nominalism spreading throughout sub-Saharan Africa.[57]

---

54. Again, such activities need not look identical to those in Ethiopia. For instance, the fast could simply involve abstinence from one food group, but not necessarily meat.

55. Note that this suggestion should not be reduced merely to engaging in more "spiritual warfare." Instead, this chapter proposes a broader and more balanced approach – rooted in prayer – that could work towards increased recognition of how demonic forces may be operative within given contexts and how Christians might confront those forces through social and compassionate efforts.

56. This fact is often associated primarily with the Majority World since the advent of the so-called "modern missionary movement." However, this pattern has also been consistent across the West for most of Christian history. An excellent example is found in the hagiography of St Patrick and the origins of Celtic Christianity.

57. Binns, *The Orthodox Church of Ethiopia*, 96–97.

Bibliography

Asale, Bruk A. "The Ethiopian Orthodox Tewahedo Church Canon of the Scriptures: Neither Open nor Closed." *The Bible Translator* 67, no. 2 (August 2016): 202–22.

Asamoah-Gyadu, J. Kwabena. "'Go Near and Join Thyself to This Chariot . . .': African Pneumatic Movements and Transformational Discipleship." *International Review of Mission* 106, no. 2 (December 2017): 336–55.

Athanasius. *Life of Antony*. Translated by Robert Gregg. Classics of Western Spirituality. London: Paulist Press, 1980.

Babalola, Sunday Fumilola, and Olusegun Ayodeji Alokan. "African Concept of Time, a Socio-Cultural Reality in the Process of Change." *Journal of Education and Practice* 4, no. 7 (2013): 143–47.

Binns, John. *Ascetics and Ambassadors of Christ: The Monasteries of Palestine, 314–631*. Oxford: Oxford University Press, 1994.

———. *The Orthodox Church of Ethiopia: A History*. London: I. B. Tauris, 2016.

———. *The T&T Clark History of Monasticism: The Eastern Tradition*. London: T&T Clark, 2021.

———. "Theological Education in the Ethiopian Orthodox Church." *Journal of Adult Theological Education* 2, no. 2 (March 17, 2005): 103–13.

Brown, Peter. *The Cult of the Saints: Its Rise and Function in Latin Christianity*. Chicago: University of Chicago Press, 1982.

Climacus, Saint John. *Ladder of Divine Ascent*. 4th ed. Boston: Holy Transfiguration Monastery, 2012.

Cowley, Roger W. "The Biblical Canon of the Ethiopian Orthodox Church Today." *Ostkirchliche Studien* 23, no. 4 (1974): 318–23.

Dagmawi, Andualem. "Some Ideas of Deification as Reflected throughout the Ethiopic Divine Liturgy." *Collectanea Christiana Orientalia* 6 (October 1, 2009): 45–66.

Daoud, Marcos, ed. *The Liturgy of the Ethiopian Church*. Revised. Kingston: Ethiopian Orthodox Church, 1991.

Freeman, S. E., and Richard D. Calenberg. "Understanding Honor-Shame Dynamics for Ministry in Sub-Saharan Africa." *Bibliotheca Sacra* 175, no. 700 (2018): 425–59.

Ireland, Jerry M. "A Classical Pentecostal Approach to Discipleship in Missions." *Journal of Pentecostal Theology* 28, no. 2 (2019): 243–66.

Johns, Cheryl Bridges. "From Strength to Strength: The Neglected Role of Crisis in Wesleyan and Pentecostal Discipleship." *Wesleyan Theological Journal* 39, no. 1 (2004): 137–53.

Johnstone, Patrick. *The Future of the Global Church: History, Trends and Possibilities*. Downers Grove: IVP Books, 2011.

Katongole, Emmanuel. *The Sacrifice of Africa: A Political Theology for Africa*. Grand Rapids: Eerdmans, 2010.

Kaunda, Chammah J. "Making Critically Conscious Disciples: A Zambian Pentecostal Pneumato-Discipleship Missiology." *International Review of Mission* 106, no. 2 (December 2017): 322–35.

Kebede, Messay. "The Ethiopian Conception of Time and Modernity" (2013). Philosophy Faculty Publications. Paper 111. http://ecommons.udayton.edu/phl_fac_pub/111.

Lee, Ralph. "Discipleship in Oriental Orthodox and Evangelical Communities." *Religions* 12, no. 5 (2021): 320–32.

———. "'Modernism' and the Ethiopian Orthodox Sunday School Movement: Indigenous Movements and Their International Connections." *The Journal of Ecclesiastical History* (November 18, 2021): 1–17.

———. "The Reception and Function of 1 Enoch in the Ethiopian Orthodox Tradition." In *Rediscovering Enoch? The Antediluvian Past from the Fifteenth to Nineteenth Centuries*, edited by Ariel Hessayon, Annette Yoshiko Reed, and Gabriele Boccaccini, 311–25. Leiden: Brill, 2023.

Lee, Ralph, and Daniel Seifemichael. "Orthodox." In *Christianity in Sub-Saharan Africa*, edited by Kenneth R. Ross, J. Kwabena Asamoah-Gyadu, and Todd M. Johnson, 264–76. Edinburgh Companions to Global Christianity. Edinburgh: Edinburgh University Press, 2017.

Mbiti, John. "Christian Eschatology in Relation to the Evangelization of Tribal Africa." PhD Dissertation, University of Cambridge, 1963.

Moreau, A. Scott. "A Critique of John Mbiti's Understanding of the African Concept of Time." *East Africa Journal of Evangelical Theology* 5, no. 2 (1986): 36–48.

Mulholland, M. Robert, and Ruth Haley Barton. *Invitation to a Journey: A Road Map for Spiritual Formation*. Revised and Expanded edition. Downers Grove: IVP Books, 2016.

Oden, Thomas C., and Curt Niccum, eds. *The Songs of Africa: The Ethiopian Canticles*. New Haven: ICCS Press, 2017.

Parrinder, Geoffrey. *Religion in Africa*. Hammondsworth: Penguin Books, 1969.

Rackley, Bobby Lynn. "Recovery of the Divine Nature: Wesleyan Soteriology and Theosis Calmly Considered." ThD Dissertation, Duke University, 2020.

Russell, Norman. *Fellow Workers With God: Orthodox Thinking on Theosis*. Crestwood: St. Vladimir's Seminary Press, 2009.

Stone, Selina. "Pentecostal Power: Discipleship as Political Engagement." *Journal of the European Pentecostal Theological Association* 38, no. 1 (2018): 24–38.

Taklahāymānot, Ayele'. "The Egyptian Metropolitan of the Ethiopian Church: A Study on a Chapter of History of the Ethiopian Church." *Pontificium Institutum Orientalium Studiorum* 54 (1988): 175–222.

Uhlig, Siegbert, Alessandro Bausi, et al., eds. *Encyclopaedia Aethiopica: O–X*. Vol. 4. Wiesbaden: Harrassowitz Verlag, 2010.

Verwijs, Adriaan. "Growing in Christ on African Soil: Thoughts on Enhancing the Contextualization of Discipleship Training in Rwanda." *Cairo Journal of Theology* 2 (2015): 132–51.

Wit, Willem J. de. "Secularization and Discipleship in Africa: Conclusions and Recommendations." *Cairo Journal of Theology* 2 (2015): 152–60.

11

Spiritual Parenthood as an Aspect of Emerging Kinship and Ecclesiological Structures in Urban African Pentecostalism

E. Okelloh Ogera
Great Lakes University of Kisumu, Kenya

Abstract

Whereas spiritual parenthood is as old as Christianity, in contemporary Pentecostalism it has metamorphosed in significance. Currently, many Pentecostal pastors are affectionately referred to as daddy or mommy by their congregants. In Africa, this poses several questions as to the kind of relationships the congregants have with their pastors. For example, what is the essence of an elderly person referring to their pastor as "daddy" or "mommy," yet the pastor is several years their junior? Without romanticizing traditional African kinship structures, this chapter explores the intricacies and nuances of these emerging kinship structures and draws attention to the points of divergences and convergences with the kinship structures of African traditions. Using Jubilee Christian Church, a Neo-Pentecostal church in Nairobi, as a case study, the paper examines the understanding and utilization of spiritual parenthood to develop alternative kinship structures within African ecclesiologies. The paper argues that contemporary Pentecostal churches utilize spiritual parenting aspects such as discipleship, mentorship, communality and appropriation of spiritual genealogies to create alternative forms of kinship. These alternative kinship patterns, while mirroring traditional African patterns, are however very creative in overcoming traditional barriers to kinship and family, such as ethnicity, age, race and gender among others. The chapter concludes that aspects of kinship are still vital for Africans who espouse the *ubuntu* philosophy of communality, hence the innovations in kinship structures.

Key words: spiritual parenthood, kinship structures, *ubuntu*, African Pentecostalism, church

Introduction

This chapter focuses on spiritual parenthood as it is appropriated by African urban Pentecostalism. The paper emanates from a larger Nagel Institute for the Study of Religions funded research project on Engaging African Realities. The research project sought to identify appropriations of kinship structures in urban African Pentecostalism, focusing on three ecclesiastical organizations in Nairobi. These were the Jubilee Christian Church (JCC), Christ is the Answer Ministries (CITAM) and the Kenyatta University Christian Union (KUCU). For this chapter, the focus will be on the practices examined at JCC. Utilizing Grounded Theology methodology, the research adopted participant observations, in-depth interviews and the analysis of literature from the said church over a period of eighteen months. This chapter utilizes aspects of this research to argue that spiritual parenthood has become a key feature of African Christianity, and a significant aspect of African ecclesiology. Aspects of spiritual parenthood such as mentorship and the daddy/mommy phenomenon are utilized to draw conclusions concerning emerging kinship structures with urban African Pentecostalism. The paper also argues that there is a close affinity between the emerging kinship structures in urban Pentecostalism and African indigenous culture and philosophy; specifically the philosophy of *ubuntu*. The paper builds on this aspect to argue that Christianity is supposed to be about a relationship with God and each other, which in turn aids in the fulfilment of the two greatest commandments of Jesus.

Precedents of Spiritual Parenthood

As Christians, Jesus taught us to refer to God as "our Father who is in heaven." The aim was that Christians should be able to identify with God as a loving caring spiritual father. The idea of a spiritual father is not new in the Bible. The Bible provides many examples and characters of men and women who functioned and demonstrated characteristics of a father or mother either to individuals, tribes, or assemblies in some form. The idea of spiritual parenthood and specifically fatherhood emanates from the Old Testament with Abraham, who is regarded as the father of faith. Perhaps Abraham was selected among all the men in the world to be the patriarch of Israel due to him being a good natural and spiritual father. The idea of a "father"[1] figure when it comes to matters of faith is further enhanced with the patriarchal narratives of Abraham, Isaac and Jacob. The other major example in the Old Testament is the relationship between Elijah and Elisha. It can be argued that their relationship was that of a father and son rather than a master and disciple. That's why in 2 Kings 2:12, as Elijah was taken up to heaven, Elisha[2] called him "my father, my father." In the narratives that follow, we see Elisha, having been groomed by Elijah, inheriting the prophetic mantle that had been his predecessors.

An interesting scenario of spiritual parenthood is also seen with Naomi and Ruth. Ruth and Naomi were two women who had a unique relationship like mother and daughter even though Ruth was not the biological daughter of Naomi. Naomi evidently must have had a close relationship with Ruth regarding the cultural ways and religious traditions of her faith, so close that it could be said that Naomi "rubbed off" on Ruth, so much so that she could make the kind of statement that nothing but death could separate her from Naomi.

In the New Testament, Paul manifested the whole concept of fatherhood and sonship in his relationship with people such as Timothy, Silas, Titus, Onesimus, Aquila and Priscilla and many others. This is the reason why in 1 Corinthians 4:15 he writes that "for though you might have ten thousand instructors in Christ, yet you do not have many fathers; for in Christ Jesus I have begotten you through the gospel" (NKJV). Paul carries this spirit and stature of a father in relation to all the saints and all the churches he has begotten in Christ through the gospel. He carries them in his bosom, as a father to his children, and cannot rest until they are as they should be. Hence Paul labours for them continually in prayer, in much affliction and loneliness, in much fasting, laying down his life so that they might live and arrive at the goals God has set for them. This is the work of a spiritual father in a demonstration. Other apostles too manifested spiritual parenthood. John was considered to be an early model for the continuation of fatherhood in Christ. Tradition therefore

---

1. It needs to be noted that the ancient Jewish culture was highly patriarchal, and therefore the very idea of a matriarch would have been repugnant. Even the story of Ruth is not complete without her being attached to a man, Boaz.

2. Elisha himself also had his own "sons" whom he was mentoring to become prophets.

has it that he passed on his apostolic authority through Saint Polycarp and Saint Prochorus as well as others.³

The spiritual parent derives authority from Christ, just as Christ drew authority from (God) the Father. In this way, Christ's authority as the spokesperson and agent of the Father is communicated by extension to those he sends out into the world. "We find this in his prayer to the Father in John: 'As thou didst send (ἀπέστειλας) me into the world, so I have sent (ἀπέστειλα) them into the world' (John 17:18)."⁴ Under this theological paradigm, every believer begins as a disciple when he receives by faith those whom God has sent; after which, having received Christ through them and having been fully taught, some are then chosen by God to become fathers to others and are sent out by Christ as apostles and prophets.

Spiritual Parenthood in Urban African Pentecostalism

It can be argued that the issue of single parenthood may have aided in the rise of spiritual parents within ecclesiastical circles, as people seek appropriate role models to fill the gap of the absentee parent. Single parenthood has gained traction in contemporary times, where contrary to African cultural heritage and communal set-up, children are raised by a single parent and not both parents as would have been expected. In terms of comparisons, single parenting is higher in females compared to males.⁵ In Kenya for example, the evolving face of the family is characterized in the 2019 national census where families headed by single parents rose from 25.1 percent in 2009 to 38.2 percent in 2019.⁶ This puts in sharp focus the significant role that spiritual parents play in the lives of people. It would appear they are filling a void that is being created due to post-modernity, globalization and rapid urbanization as experienced in urban African circles. Spiritual parenthood is manifested in several ways such

---

3. For a historical treatise on spiritual fatherhood in the medieval period, see Martin Mayerhofer, "The Spiritual Fatherhood of the Priest in Patristic and Medieval Pauline Commentaries," *Logos: A Journal of Catholic Thought and Culture* 23, no. 2 (2020): 105–28, https://doi.org/10.1353/log.2020.0014.

4. Christopher Lockwood, "Spiritual Fatherhood after the Model of Christ in the Gospel According to John," *Greek Orthodox Theological Review* 59, no. 1–4 (2014): 81–127, 100.

5. Joshua N. Mbithi, "Single Parenting in Kenya: Issues, Challenges and Solutions," *European Journal of Social Sciences Studies* 4, no. 1 (2009): 84–91.

6. Bashir Mbuthia, "President Kenyatta Sounds Alarm over Increase in Single Parent Families," Citizen Digital (June 1, 2022), https://www.citizen.digital/news/president-kenyatta-sounds-alarm-over-increase-in-single-parent-families-n299280.

as the mommy or daddy phenomenon, mentorship programmes and ecclesial groupings. We will look at each of these in turn.

Mommy / daddy phenomenon

Whereas for some people it is not proper to refer to pastors as daddy or mommy, the phenomenon has gained traction in recent times. Opponents of the idea cite Matthew 23:9 which says "Call no man your father upon the earth." They argue that people have only one spiritual Father in heaven, God; and one biological father on earth. Roman Catholics call their priests fathers yet the priests are neither married nor the biological fathers of the membership of their congregations. In the Jubilee Christian Church (JCC) a Nairobi-based neo-Pentecostal church, the use of the terms daddy and mommy to refer to the pastors is prevalent. The leader of the church, Bishop Allan Kiuna, is affectionately referred to as daddy, and his wife with whom he co-pastors, Rev. Kathy Kiuna, is known as mommy. Together they act as the spiritual parents to the congregation.

The Kiunas see their role as the spiritual parents to their congregants as entailing raising them spiritually. This they see as their God-given mandate. As Allan Kiuna states, "We were raised by a spiritual mother in order to raise sons and daughters who will do exploits for God."[7] What Kiuna is refereeing to is the fact that he was raised spiritually by Rev. Teresa Wairimu, a well-known evangelical Christian leader and founder of the Faith Evangelistic Ministries (FEM). The Kiunas see their task as giving out knowledge, understanding, wisdom, counsel, and blessing to their spiritual children. In other words, for them, their primary goal is to make their spiritual children successful in knowing the Lord and fulfilling the call of God. As daddy and mommy to their congregation, they nurture and protect their "children."

Mentorship programmes

In 2 Timothy 3:10–11, Paul says, "Now you have observed my teaching, my conduct, my aim in life, my faith, my patience, my love, my steadfastness, my persecutions, and my suffering" (NRSV). Too many people are confused about the difference between a spiritual father and a mentor. In many instances both can be the same, yet on lots of occasions they can be different. Different people

---

7. "Raised for Exploits" (Sermon, Men's Breakfast, JCC Parklands Church, April 12, 2021).

can play these roles in your life over a period. Bishop Kiuna of JCC for example runs a mentorship programme for men only, and most of them meet twice a year during the men's breakfast conventions for group empowerment sessions.

Rev. Kathy also mentors a thriving Ladies' Mentorship School which was necessitated by the great impact that the Daughters of Zion[8] ministry has had since its inception in 2003. This was to facilitate a maximum personal impact in the lives of the women. Whereas Rev. Kiuna will have one on one mentorship sessions with several ladies, this notion of mentorship and its efficacy can be challenged. This is because the ladies are expected to pay for the mentorship sessions.

Part of the mentoring initiative of Bishop and Rev. Kiuna is the fact that they have written several inspirational books to help their mentees in various aspects of life. JCC has a college of pastors who are being mentored for ministry. These young pastors are under the tutelage of Bishop Kiuna and Rev. Kathy, and they are being trained to take pastoral ministry roles in the church. So while the Kiunas are spiritual parents to the congregation in a general sense, they are more than just mentors to these "pastors in training." These mentorships give the Kiunas the opportunity to interact on a very personal level with their mentees, thus having a greater impact in the mentees' lives. While there are asynchronous relations of these mentorship programmes with the aspects of daddy and mommy, the levels of engagement are what brings about the difference.

Ecclesial groups and associations

In these church groups and associations, people are trained to minister together. JCC expects members to offer ministry through the different departments in the church. These departments include choir and praise and worship, protocol, catering, media, ushering and sports. The membership of these groups is designed in such a way that they look like family. Members spend a lot of time together, either in practice sessions, prayer sessions, on retreats and so on. All these are meant to foster a sense of belonging and cohesiveness. These groups function basically as the cell groups or the Small Christian Communities (SCCs) associated with the Catholic Church. The difference is that the level of engagement within the group and between group members is more intense

---

8. The Daughters of Zion (DOZ) ministry is an interdenominational women's empowerment and mentorship programme, where women meet once a month for fellowship and mentorship sessions.

because membership is geared towards a particular goal and exercising similar gifts and talents.

Like the SCCs, these groupings provide alternative ecclesial communities to correct the anonymity and impersonality characteristic of membership in megachurches.[9] These groupings are small enough to facilitate close and meaningful relationships and flexible enough to address a variety of issues in the everyday life of Christians. The difference between the cell groups and SCCs associated with mainline churches is that these groups are not formulated on the basis that members live within proximity of each other. The fact that the members would rather travel distances to be part of the group shows a high degree of commitment. It needs to be noted that the majority of members are also young people, mostly in their late teenage and early twenties. It is no wonder that through these groups, members date and find life partners. Within these ecclesial groupings, the emphasis is on lay leadership which makes everyone equal. This implies a greater sense of ownership among congregants and membership, leading to increased participation of the laity. The ecclesial groupings represent a form of ecclesiological devolution that allows lay Christians to assume and exercise leadership roles.[10] For African Christians, it also means that they exhibit *ubuntu*, which is done by prizing communal relationships with other people.

Contemporary spiritual parenthood and African kinship structures

There seems to be an affinity between spiritual parenthood and African indigenous kinship structures. As the African philosopher Kwame Gyekye[11] noted, communality is the essence of being human in Africa. In a context where due to urbanism and post-modernism the indigenous ethos of commonality seems to be dissipating, African people seek to re-imagine what it means to be human in an individualistic society. The notion of communalism or *ubuntu* is central to issues in Africa. *Ubuntu* as a philosophy has been employed in an array of African theological discourses such as peace and reconciliation, African spirituality, ecological theology and on economic justice. Talking

---

9. Agbonkhianmeghe Orobator, "Small Christian Communities as a New Way of Becoming Church: Practice, Progress and Prospects," in *Small Christian Communities: Fresh Stimulus for a Forward-Looking Church*, ed. Kramer Klaus and Vellguth Klaus (Quezon City: Claretian Communications Foundation, 2013), 113–25.

10. Orobator, "Small Christian Communities as a New Way of Becoming Church," 119.

11. "Person and Community in African Thought," in *Philosophy from Africa*, ed. P. H. Coetzee and A. P. J. Roux (Johannesburg: International Thompson Publishing, 1998), 317–36.

of *ubuntu* in relation to ecclesiology, we note Benzet Bujo's assertion that "a process of coming into existence in the reciprocal relatedness of individual and community, where the latter includes not only the deceased but also God."[12] We can conclude here then that *ubuntu* carries connotations of communality, communion and interrelatedness. This chapter is of the opinion that *ubuntu* is a living tradition that is constantly reinvented owing to cultural dynamism.

The ethic of *ubuntu* entails respect for others. A community that is informed by the ethic of *ubuntu* can rightly be spoken of in terms of a moral community in so far as *ubuntu* entails a moral ethic. It is in this regard that spiritual parenthood seeks to raise people who are equally morally upright. Christian and African ethics share some commonalities. African ethics is defined as a set of values central among which are reciprocity, common good, peaceful relations, emphasis on human dignity, and the value of human life as well as consensus, tolerance, and mutual respect.[13] These values are equally prevalent in Christianity as indicated in Galatians 5:22–23: "But the fruit of the Spirit is love, joy, peace, forbearance, kindness, goodness, faithfulness, gentleness and self-control" (NIV). From the perspective of *ubuntu*, spiritual parenthood manifests ideas expressed in maxims such as "a person is a person through other persons" or "I am because we are." These maxims include prescriptive or normative meanings: they instruct one to become a real person or to realize one's true self, and to do so by relating to other people in certain ways.[14]

Aspects of spiritual parenthood such as mentorship, ecclesial groupings, and the mommy/daddy phenomenon are equally attractive to an interdenominational audience, thus enhancing prospects of lived ecumenism. As the South African theologian Teddy Sakupapa argues:

> The notion of *ubuntu* has the potential for developing an ecumenical ethic that underpins both the ecumenical search for unity and the social responsibility of the church. This is derived

---

12. *Foundation of an African Ethic: Beyond the Universal Claims of Western Morality* (Nairobi: Paulines Publications Africa, 2003), 114.

13. Philip Ogochukwu Ujomudike, "Ubuntu Ethics," in *Encyclopedia of Global Bioethics*, ed. Henk ten Have (Cham: Springer International Publishing, 2016), 2869–81, https://doi.org/10.1007/978-3-319-09483-0_428.

14. Thaddeus Metz, "The African Ethic of Ubuntu," *1000-Word Philosophy: An Introductory Anthology* (blog), September 8, 2019, https://1000wordphilosophy.com/2019/09/08/the-african-ethic-of-ubuntu/.

from the integrative capacity of *ubuntu* as a relational concept and as a moral vision.[15]

It is in this regard that proponents of ecclesiological models patterned after the African family find the notion of *ubuntu* attractive for fostering ecumenism, given the stress on solidarity, fraternity, openness and inclusivity which these values elicit.[16] This fact is exemplified by the ecclesial associations found in urban Pentecostalism. The engagement within these associations corresponds to uniquely African values of interdependence, harmony, cooperation and hospitality that are constitutive elements of the human community commonly rendered as *ubuntu*.[17] Within the context of the study, there are no references to the Kiunas as being related to other people on an equal level, say as a brother or sister. However, what is clear is the fact that the church operates from a patriarchal perspective, where even Rev. Kathy has to constantly reference the authority of her husband as the "bishop" and "father" to the entire congregation, affirming that she operates under his "authority."

It needs to be noted however that some of the people who embrace the new kinship structures in urban Pentecostalism are people who have felt excluded and marginalized by mainstream Christianity. There were indications that some of the membership of JCC had moved to the church after having been excluded from their erstwhile churches either through gender, age, or leadership factors. The common thread running through most experiences of marginalization and not feeling included hinges on the principle of subordination of persons, especially women and the youth. There have been claims that women who find themselves as single parents are more often than not viewed with suspicion in many churches, and are subordinated overtly and covertly to their "properly married" counterparts. Among the most stringent injustices against women needing urgent attention are the exclusion of women's voices from decision-making in families, communities and the church. In addition, there are cultural practices in church and society which undermine women's human dignity when they relegate women to secondary positions. We probably need to heed the call of Emmanuel Martey, an African theologian who said, "Today, it is impossible for African theology to emerge and bloom unless both African

---

15. Teddy Sakupapa, "Ecumenical Ecclesiology in the African Context: Towards a View of the Church as Ubuntu," *Scriptura: Journal for Contextual Hermeneutics in Southern Africa* 117, no. 1 (2018): 1–15, 9.

16. See John Mary Waliggo, "The African Clan as the True Model of the African Church," in *The Church in African Christianity: Innovative Essays in Ecclesiology*, ed. J. N. K. Mugambi and L. Magesa (Nairobi: Acton Publishers, 1998), 111–27, 118.

17. Orobator, "Small Christian Communities as a New Way of Becoming Church."

churches and African theology start out from, and develop around the situation of women in Africa."[18]

Emergent African Ecclesiological Structures

In 1994, the Roman Catholic Church Synod on Africa adopted the theme of "Church as the Family of God" as enshrined in the emergent document *Ecclesia in Africa*.[19] The guiding principle of this thinking was that in Africa the need to apply the gospel to concrete life is felt very strongly due to life situations marked by a collective fact of misery resulting from injustices: inequality; a general sense of insecurity and risk of meeting violence; the increasing poverty of many; the blindness of the rich and privileged; tensions and struggle for power without service; as well as ethnic divisions.[20] On the other hand, Africans have positive cultural values which include a sense of solidarity, family and community, respect for life and the gift of children. These positive cultural values are very useful in the understanding of ecclesiology from an African perspective.

The Nigerian theologian Agbonkhianmeghe Orobator had in 1996 rhetorically asked whether there is a systematically elaborated theological conception of the origin, nature, mission and meaning of the African church "in terms which are peculiar to and expressive of the African way of being church."[21] It is in this context that we note that several African inculturation theologians have employed a variety of metaphors to describe the church within the African context. These metaphors include but are not limited to understanding the church as a clan, family, and community.[22] All these metaphors and theologizing seem to premise the understanding of the church from the communal or family perspective. However, with recent developments especially emanating from spiritual parenthood, we may begin to wonder

---

18. Immanuel Martey, *African Theology: Inculturation and Liberation* (Eugene: Wipf & Stock, 2009), 84.

19. A. G. Msafiri, "The Church as a Family Model: Its Strength and Weaknesses," in *African Theology Today*, ed. Emmanuel Katongole (Scranton: University of Scranton Press, 2002), 85–98.

20. Rose Uchem, "The Church as Family of God in Enugu Diocese: Experiences in Small Christian Communities," in *Evangelization and Renewal in the Church in Enugu Diocese in the Third Millenium. Acts and Declarations of the Second Synod of the Catholic Diocese of Enugu* (2002): 193–204.

21. Agbonkhianmeghe Orobator, "Perspectives and Trends in Contemporary African Ecclesiology," *Studia Missionalia* 45 (1996): 267–81, 268.

22. Sakupapa, "Ecumenical Ecclesiology in the African Context."

whether the family is the endgame, and not the starting point: in other words, is the church becoming the domestic family?

Spiritual parenthood as an ecclesiological paradigm aligns with the theologian Kä Mana's ideas when he similarly locates the church as the site where God's people are "mobilized for new activities and new strategies for social change and for building a new society."[23] He accordingly considers the role of theology as "the creation of a visionary, creative and resourceful society for the struggle against all the negative forces that Africa is suffering from" including socio-political and economic powers that are embodied in sterile local and international institutions and social structures.[24] Sakupapa concurs through his assertion that "The Church as the *ubuntu* community is expected to be a community of sharing, interdependence and solidarity. This however requires a reinterpretation and theological enrichment (through Scripture) of negative forms of solidarity such as those based on essentialist notions of identity whether that is in the form of race, ethnicity or even religion."[25]

As has been noted, spiritual parenthood in urban African Pentecostalism is not limited to father figures. Female pastors being referred to as "mommy" has become quite common. The significance of this development is the fact that it implies the ethic of care prevalent within the *ubuntu* philosophy. The "spiritual mommy" highlights aspects of womanhood in general and motherhood in particular. The significance of this is that such ecclesiological reflections have a starting point in the lived experiences of marginalization and oppression to which African women are subjected in both church and society.[26] Hence the spiritual parenthood motif is very much in line with African women theologians who have previously critiqued ecclesiologies which undercut the dignity of women. For example, Isabel Phiri[27] notes the need for just relations between men and women against the background of the marginalization of women in the African church.

From the African religious ethos that underpins *ubuntu*, community transcends the human community of the living to include the living dead and the whole of creation.[28] This aspect indicates a cosmic union of living

---

23. Ka Mana, *Christians and Churches of Africa: Salvation in Christ and Building a New African Society* (Maryknoll: Orbis Books, 2004), 103.

24. Mana, *Christians and Churches of Africa*, 103.

25. Sakupapa, "Ecumenical Ecclesiology in the African Context," 12.

26. Sakupapa, "Ecumenical Ecclesiology in the African Context."

27. Isabel Phiri, "The Church and Women in Africa," in *The Wiley-Blackwell Companion to African Religion*, ed. Elias Kifon Bongmba (Chichester: Blackwell Publishing, 2012), 255–68, 265.

28. See John S. Mbiti, *African Religions and Philosophy* (London: Heinemann, 1970), 175.

Christians with the departed saints. From the perspective of Christian history, there are lessons to be learned from the lives of the early martyrs. These are invaluable lessons for contemporary Christians. All of these point to the fact that indeed, the church becomes the domestic family: a family that seeks to learn from its departed members yet is concerned about the faith and spirituality of the younger generation.

Of course, this also presents several challenges. One of the critiques of spiritual parenthood as practised by contemporary urban Pentecostals is that it tends to emphasize a constriction of individuality by demanding oppressive conformity and loyalty to the "group" or "community." Equally, just like the ecclesiastical models of family and clan, spiritual parenthood also carries potentially damaging associations. The mommy or daddy pastors as matriarch or patriarch espouse a hierarchical structure with little room for others to showcase their leadership qualities. Since most of the power is also concentrated at the top, this could be "an incentive to nepotism, corruption and the advancement of one social group to the detriment of others."[29]

The notions of clan typically reinforce a preoccupation with internal relations amongst members to the detriment of the "world" outside. Further, the view of the church as a family may well entail a narrow conception of the universality of the church. Given the hierarchical and unequal nature of family relations in both contemporary and traditional Africa, Waliggo sees the need for "a vision of an African family where equality is guaranteed, sharing of responsibility is accepted, the clear option for the disadvantaged members is made, and deadly tensions are eliminated."[30] Without this, he contends, the theology of the church as a family is a double-edged sword that may be used profitably but may also lead to benign paternalism.

One of the weaknesses of spiritual parenthood is that some pastors may try to control the thinking and behaviour of their congregants with the concept of "spiritual fatherhood." This will be exhibited by the way they demand the utmost, sometimes blind loyalty. When their relationship with their congregants and spiritual children is examined, one sees that the only benefactor is the pastor. Such pastors are more concerned with their own position of power and prominence than they are with the spiritual well-being of other people. Submitting to a controlling spiritual parent will damage believers. Spiritual fathers should be free, releasing, and empowering. However, parents

---

29. Waliggo, "The African Clan as the True Model of the African Church," 124.
30. Waliggo, "The African Clan as the True Model of the African Church," 118.

who have control issues are deeply wounded themselves and have no business fathering spiritual children.

Ultimately, spiritual parenthood is a useful analogy for African ecclesiology. This is because when people identify with others, it is for people to treat themselves as members of the same group: to conceive of themselves as a "we," to take pride or feel shame in others' activities, and to engage in joint projects, coordinating to achieve shared or at least compatible goals. This kind of solidarity in part involves engaging in helpful behavior and acting in ways that are reasonably expected to benefit others. Solidarity involves attitudes, emotions and motives being positively oriented toward others' good, say, by sympathizing and helping them for their sake.[31]

Conclusion

Pastors of congregations can confuse people when they say they are a "spiritual father" to everyone. In the natural world, how many children can one father effectively? If a pastor is claiming to be a spiritual father to hundreds or thousands, many of those children are going to be overlooked, neglected, and hurt. This is evidenced by the fact that many congregants of churches that adore their pastors as daddies or mommies have never met the pastors for a one-on-one session.

However, this does not mean that there aren't any genuine pastors who are keen on nurturing the next generation of Christians. This genuineness fosters close relations between the pastors and their mentees in such a way that can be referred to as spiritual parenthood. Spiritual parenthood is utilized to create intentional communities. This means that geographical or socio-economic boundaries are not rigid lines of demarcation for determining membership.

It can therefore be argued that spiritual parenthood creates a family in the church or turns the church into a family; it is a significant aspect of understanding African ecclesiology. In other words, spiritual parenthood exhibits *ubuntu* in its conception of the good life which is meant to guide individuals in the choices they make, and it has also influenced societal decision-making in African societies. Spiritual parenthood as practiced through mommy daddy phenomenon; mentoring and church groupings all display aspects of *ubuntu*. Concretely, this means that one finds meaning in their being through communal or harmonious relationships with others. Through this harmonious communal expression of being, one exhibits excellence

---

31. Metz, "The African Ethic of Ubuntu."

insofar as one displays character traits such as politeness, kindness, sympathy, compassion, benevolence, altruism, sacrifice, forgiveness, mercy, and tolerance.

True and proper spiritual parenthood should be able to identify with the spiritual children in such a way that everyone treats themselves as members of the same group. They conceive of themselves as a "we," and take pride or feel shame in others' lives.[32] Ultimately, we cannot hide from the fact that spiritual parenthood represents an emerging way of being *a* church; it isn't a finished product or prefabricated ecclesial reality. In this sense, the process takes precedence over events as key markers of the ecclesiological comprehension of spiritual parenthood.[33]

Bibliography

Bujo, Benezet. *Foundation of an African Ethic: Beyond the Universal Claims of Western Morality*. Nairobi: Paulines Publications Africa, 2003.

Gyekye, Kwame. "Person and Community in African Thought." In *Philosophy from Africa*, edited by P. H. Coetzee and A. P. J. Roux, 317–36. Johannesburg: International Thompson Publishing, 1998.

Kiuna, Allan. "Raised for Exploits." Sermon presented at the Men's Breakfast, JCC Parklands Church, April 12, 2021.

Lockwood, Christopher. "Spiritual Fatherhood after the Model of Christ in the Gospel According to John." *Greek Orthodox Theological Review* 59, no. 1–4 (2014): 81–127.

Mana, Ka. *Christians and Churches of Africa: Salvation in Christ and Building a New African Society*. Maryknoll: Orbis Books, 2004.

Martey, Emmanuel. *African Theology: Inculturation and Liberation*. Eugene: Wipf & Stock, 2009.

Mayerhofer, Martin. "The Spiritual Fatherhood of the Priest in Patristic and Medieval Pauline Commentaries." *Logos: A Journal of Catholic Thought and Culture* 23, no. 2 (2020): 105–28. https://doi.org/10.1353/log.2020.0014.

Mbithi, Joshua N. "Single Parenting in Kenya: Issues, Challenges and Solutions." *European Journal of Social Sciences Studies* 4, no. 1 (2009).

Mbiti, John S. *African Religions and Philosophy*. London: Heinemann, 1970.

Mbuthia, Bashir. "President Kenyatta Sounds Alarm over Increase in Single Parent Families." *Citizen Digital*, June 1, 2022. https://www.citizen.digital/news/president-kenyatta-sounds-alarm-over-increase-in-single-parent-families-n299280.

---

32. Metz, "The African Ethic of Ubuntu."
33. Orobator, "Small Christian Communities as a New Way of Becoming Church."

Metz, Thaddeus. "The African Ethic of Ubuntu." *1000-Word Philosophy: An Introductory Anthology* (blog), September 8, 2019. https://1000wordphilosophy.com/2019/09/08/the-african-ethic-of-ubuntu/.

Msafiri, A. G. "The Church as a Family Model: Its Strength and Weaknesses." In *African Theology Today*, edited by Emmanuel Katongole, 85–98. Scranton: University of Scranton Press, 2002.

Orobator, Agbonkhianmeghe. "Perspectives and Trends in Contemporary African Ecclesiology." *Studia Missionalia* 45 (1996): 267–81.

———. "Small Christian Communities as a New Way of Becoming Church: Practice, Progress and Prospects." In *Small Christian Communities: Fresh Stimulus for a Forward-Looking Church*, edited by Kramer Klaus and Vellguth Klaus, 113–25. Quezon City: Claretian Communications Foundation, 2013.

Phiri, Isabel. "The Church and Women in Africa." In *The Wiley-Blackwell Companion to African Religion*, edited by Elias Bongba, 255–68. Chichester: Blackwell Publishing, 2012.

Sakupapa, Teddy. "Ecumenical Ecclesiology in the African Context: Towards a View of the Church as Ubuntu." *Scriptura: Journal for Contextual Hermeneutics in Southern Africa* 117, no. 1 (2018): 1–15.

Uchem, Rose. "The Church as Family of God in Enugu Diocese: Experiences in Small Christian Communities," in *Evangelization and Renewal in the Church in Enugu Diocese in the Third Millenium. Acts and Declarations of the Second Synod of the Catholic Diocese of Enugu*, 193–204. 2002.

Ujomudike, Philip Ogochukwu. "Ubuntu Ethics." In *Encyclopedia of Global Bioethics*, edited by Henk ten Have, 2869–81. Cham: Springer International Publishing, 2016. https://doi.org/10.1007/978-3-319-09483-0_428.

Waliggo, John Mary. "The African Clan as the True Model of the African Church." In *The Church in African Christianity: Innovative Essays in Ecclesiology*, edited by J. N. K. Mugambi and L. Magesa, 111–27. Nairobi: Acton Publishers, 1998.

12

Ecclesiology in Contemporary Africa

Operating in Post-COVID-19 Pandemic and Insecurity Situations

Benjamin Akano
Nigerian Baptist Theological Seminary, Ogbomoso

Abstract

Of the different contemporary contextual challenges facing Africa, including corruption, political instability, ethno-religious clashes, poverty, endemic diseases, unemployment, and climate change, the effects of the COVID-19 pandemic and insecurity have been intense. Together, they affect the church's self-expression in the world and its attempts at fulfilling the Great Commission mandate to disciple all nations. While insecurity has made some Christians hate the very people they should disciple, insecurity and the pandemic have restricted face-to-face ministry opportunities and the faith of some has become shipwrecked as they turn to syncretic solutions to their fears. Many had to migrate from their ancestral homes for security and economic reasons. This descriptive study examines relevant literature and observable realities, particularly in Nigeria, to prescribe a sustainable ecclesiology for contemporary Africa. The argument is that contemporary Africa needs an ecclesiology that responds adequately to the existential challenges of the pandemic, post-pandemic conditions and insecurity that have affected the faith and ministry of some African Christians. Such an ecclesiology must reveal the church's faithfulness in nature and mission. The writer using Paul's concept of "church" in Ephesians, examines the African context of the pandemic, post-pandemic and insecurity situations and identifies four critical issues for such an ecclesiology. First, its operation must embrace the disciple-making movement model that is built on the household metaphor of the church to overcome the restriction challenges. Second, it must be incorporated into the daily lives of its members through holistic and integral missions since the traditional mission strategy is being hindered by the current situations. Third, it must engage a comprehensive approach to missions, being intentional about centripetal and centrifugal mechanisms simultaneously, because of multi-directional migrations. Finally, such ecclesiology that will keep the church upon the Rock, remaining faithful to its nature and purpose amid various contextual challenges, must emphasize Pentecostal power manifestations so African Christians may find the courage to hold on to authentic biblical faith and power amid their spiritual realities.

Key words: church, COVID-19, ecclesiology, disciple-making movement (DMM), insecurity, pandemic, Pentecostal power, manifestation

Introduction

Africans have lived with many contextual issues threatening their growth and development. These include corruption, economic difficulty, political instability, ethno-religious clashes, poverty, endemic diseases, unemployment, and climate change.[1] However, both the COVID-19 pandemic and insecurity are recent, and significant in their intensity and how they compound the other challenges. These hydra-headed twin problems have critical impacts on the operation of the contemporary church. The church that is to bring *shalom* to the hurting world is also facing the severe challenges of hurt through threats to its nature and missions. Therefore, this study considers it imperative to examine ecclesiology in contemporary Africa – with its changing and challenging contexts. It focuses on the church's effective operations in pandemic, post-pandemic, and insecure situations.

Drawing illustrations primarily from the Nigerian experience, the writer stresses that contemporary Africa needs an ecclesiology that makes

---

1. Sunday B. Agang, H. Jurgens Hendriks, and Dion A. Forster (eds), *African Public Theology* (Carlisle: HippoBooks, 2020).

an adequate response to the existential challenges of the pandemic, and also post-pandemic conditions and subsequent insecurity that affect the faith and ministry of African Christians. Such an ecclesiology will sustain the church's faithfulness in nature and mission. This study considers Paul's concept of "church" in Ephesians, examines the African context of the pandemic, with its post-pandemic and insecurity situations, and identifies four critical issues. First, ecclesiology in Africa must embrace the disciple-making movement model of operations to overcome the restriction challenges due to pandemics and insecurity. Second, the traditional strategy of church operation is becoming ineffective due to restriction challenges occasioned by insecurity and fear of any similar pandemic. Thus, it requires an ecclesiology that incorporates Christian missions into the daily lives of church members through holistic and integral missions. Third, given an increasing need for diaspora missions, such an ecclesiology must engage a comprehensive approach to missions and be intentional about centripetal and centrifugal mechanisms. Fourth, because spiritual power is an essential dynamic in Africa, such an ecclesiology that will keep the church upon the Rock must emphasize Pentecostal power manifestations so that African Christians may find the courage to hold on to authentic biblical faith and transmit the same to the next generation.

Ecclesiology is a theological discipline that deals with the understanding of the church.[2] The understanding and practices of any given church mutually affect each other. Thus, ecclesiology goes beyond the doctrine to include:

> self-understanding of any given ecclesial community and the church as a whole, along with study of same. It also embraces the study of the story and ongoing development of church, the conversations and disagreements within and without the church, and must also include the aspirations of the church, in local and universal context alike.[3]

The implication is that while the contextual realities form an important factor in describing the church, the universal factors are also critical to make the emerging church a "glocal" entity, globalizing the local while localizing the global. Thus, this science of envisioning the church "always involves engagement with Scripture and ongoing Christian tradition(s). Historical consciousness

---

2. C. J. P. Niemandt, "Trends in Missional Ecclesiology," *HTS Theological Studies* 68, no. 1 (2012): 1–9, http://dx.doi.org/10.4102/hts.v68i1.1198.

3. Gerard Manion, *Ecclesiology and Postmodernity: Questions for the Church in Our Times* (Collegeville: Liturgical Press, 2007), xiii.

and hermeneutical principles will always be central to any ecclesiological undertaking."[4] Any authentic ecclesiology has its root in the Scriptures.

Thus, ecclesiology may be understood as a co-discipline with missiology, which is an ongoing reflection on the practice of Christian missions, attempting "to answer questions and wrestle with issues that missions has posed from the front lines of engagement. Without a vibrant [practical] missionary involvement, there are no new questions, and missiology cannot thrive"[5] It brings in theology, history, social sciences, methods, motives, strategies, and other relevant factors for scientific and critical investigation as the churches fulfil their mandate in their particular age and context.[6]

Therefore, ecclesiology will be an ongoing reflection on the nature and practical operation of the church. The reflection is ongoing because of the changing contexts and the emerging questions to which such reflection must respond. The implication is that any good ecclesiology will serve as a tool for contextualising the church to its changing context of existence and operation, making it relevant to the ministry context without violating the faithfulness to biblical truth. Such reflection involves identifying the theological issues involved in church operations; reflecting on similar church history experiences that might shed light on the issues involved; and subjecting the insight to four governing themes – the *missio Dei*, the Trinity, the new creation and the global church.[7]

Church, Church Planting and *Missio Dei*
Nature and mission of the church

Church planting has remained a valid strategy for fulfilling the Great Commission mandate (Matt 28:19–20) across history. Unfortunately, some people have equated church planting with the Great Commission mandate. Furthermore, to compound the problem, while most Christians understand that the church refers to the people, not the building, whenever they mention the word "church," it draws attention to the physical structure where the people meet. Consequently, the thought of church planting, which some wrongly

---

4. Manion, *Ecclesiology and Postmodernity*, xiii.
5. Timothy C. Tennent, *Invitation to World Missions: A Trinitarian Missiology for the Twenty-First Century* (Grand Rapids: Kregel Publications, 2010), 496.
6. Craig Ott, Stephen J. Strauss, and Timothy C. Tennent, *Encountering Theology of Mission: Biblical Foundations, Historical Developments, and Contemporary Issues* (Grand Rapids: Baker Academic, 2010), xx, 265, 282.
7. Tennent, *Invitation to World Missions*, 498–99.

misconstrue as an end rather than means, often envisions a conventional church structure for housing people or, at best, people assembling in a designated structure – a place of worship. A wrong understanding of the meaning and nature will affect the purpose.

The nature or being of an organization is usually associated with its purpose. When manufacturers design a tool, they have its use in mind. A manufacturer foresaw the function before designing the tool with peculiar features. God had a function in mind for the church to be his primary agent of *missio Dei* when he brought the church into being. According to Ephesians 2:10, he re-created believers in Christ with the intention of these good works.[8] Thus, one cannot separate the nature of the church from its mission to be the primary agent of the *missio Dei*.

Ott et al. affirm that "God has called the church into existence for the very purpose of serving his mission."[9] The church and its mission are intimately intertwined so that one cannot discuss one without the other. The implication is that mission is not just a church project; it is its real essence of existence. In addition, while God, in his sovereignty, has different means of fulfilling his purpose on earth, he has chosen the church to be his primary agent, at least for now.[10] One cannot equate the church and its mission "because God often works both beyond and despite the church to accomplish his redemptive plans. Nevertheless, central to a biblical vision of God's mission is that God does, in fact, work in and through his church and that it is central, not ancillary, to his mission."[11] God's mission or *missio Dei* is where the church derives its mission.[12]

Missio Dei, a concept from the Augustinian doctrine of the Trinity, defines mission from a theocentric, rather than an anthropocentric, perspective. It considers mission as essentially the work of the triune God from the beginning to the end, aiming primarily at the coming kingdom of God with God's word, the church, and every believer as its instrument.[13] In *missio Dei*, "God the Father is the only source of all mission, Jesus Christ the only Lord and Saviour

---

8. Yusuf Turaki, "Ephesians," in *Africa Bible Commentary*, ed. Tokunboh Adeyemo (Nairobi: Word Alive, 2006), 1451–64, 1429.

9. Ott et al., *Encountering Theology of Mission*, 137–62.

10. Ott et al., *Encountering Theology of Mission*, 193–95.

11. Tennent, *Invitation to World Missions*, 58–59.

12. Tennent, *Invitation to World Missions*, 56.

13. Tormod Engelsviken, "Missio Dei: The Understanding and Misunderstanding of a Theological Concept in European Churches and Missiology," *International Review of Mission*, XCII.367: 481–97, 481, 482.

and the Holy Spirit the only divine life giver and power."[14] The three Persons of the Godhead work indivisibly as they are indivisible to "create a divine unity of one and the same essence in an indivisible equality, though they are distinguished in person."[15] Thus, the mission of God in which the church participates is trinitarian.

Patrick Franklin also agrees with the Augustinian understanding of *missio Dei*, noting that the redemptive work is the combined activity of Father, Son and Spirit. God's love predicated and set redemption in motion, historical events that culminated in the death and resurrection of Jesus Christ effected it, and the Holy Spirit actualized it in the life of believers (Rom 5:5, 8). He explains further that *missio Dei* is rooted in *caritas Dei* (the love of God). He explains further that understanding mission only from ecclesiological and anthropocentric perspectives may promote a pragmatic and functional approach to church, a form of programme-centred consumer ecclesiology. However, *missio Dei* is ontologically grounded in the nature of God.[16] Thus, the mission of the church may be summarized in Franklin's words as follows:

> Our mission is first and foremost, God's mission, made possible through our union with Christ in the Spirit . . . All that we proclaim to the world and demonstrate with our lives as a living hermeneutic of the gospel comes from God the Father through the priestly and salvific mediation of Christ the Son in and by the new-creation power, illuminating guidance, and personal, fruit-bestowing presence of the Holy Spirit.[17]

Consequently, the nature of the church and the ecclesiology that defines and sustains it must be located within *missio Dei*, and deeply rooted in *caritas Dei*. Such ecclesiology also serves as the operational framework for the church within any context.

---

14. Engelsviken, "Missio Dei: The Understanding and Misunderstanding," 483, 494.

15. Han Byung-Soo, "The Structure of the Trinity in Augustine," *Korean Presbyterian Journal of Theology* 52, no. 4 (2020): 97–125, 99, 101, 106.

16. Patrick S. Franklin, "The God Who Sends Is the God Who Loves: Mission As Participation in the Ecstatic Love of the Triune God," *Didaskalia* 28 (2017–2018): 75–79.

17. Franklin, "The God Who Sends Is the God Who Loves," 94.

Paul's household metaphor of the church

Like general metaphors, church metaphors are significant in helping believers understand and appreciate their relationship, privilege and purpose in Christ.[18] The writer of Ephesians used seven such metaphors – the body of Christ (1:22–23; 4:12; 5:23–24, 28–32); the fullness of Christ (1:23); new humanity (2:15); the household or family of God (2:19); new nation (2:19); the temple (2:20–22); and the bride of Christ (5:22–23). Ephesians is significant because it reveals similar challenges to those confronting the contemporary church – the cultural division between the Jews and the Gentiles (Acts 19:17), the persecution, and a multicultural and multi-religious society where idolatry and magic was a norm, as in Africa.[19] Paul was aware of these and qualified to write about them objectively and intelligently, too, being sensitive to the need of the church to be a good witness in such a context. The purpose of Ephesians is to explain the blessings and riches experienced by believers in Christ (1:1–3:21) and to live in peace and harmony amidst tribal, ethnic and cultural differences (4:1–6:24).[20] This is crucial for the situation of fear associated with insecurity and pandemic to which the contemporary African church needs to respond.

The household metaphor stresses the togetherness and interdependence of the members as everyone plays their roles. James Dunn asserts that, though Paul sees the church as the continuity of "the assembly of Yahweh," his conception is not of something worldwide but one in a particular location. The implication is that the "church-ness" of a community relates primarily with a direct link with Christ through apostolic teachings by which it derives vitality, not its size or being part of some universal entity. His writings, whose focus and greetings were more on house churches, often reflect that a house church is just as much of a church as a community, a city or a national church.[21] He used different metaphorical expressions to reveal various meanings for his readers to understand this church concept. This idea also conveys Paul's interest in forming Christian communities instead of mere conversion of individuals and emphasizes the relationships the people have with God and one another.[22]

---

18. Wayne Grudem, *Systematic Theology: An Introduction to Biblical Doctrine* (Nottingham: Inter-Varsity Press, 2000), 859.

19. Craig S. Keener, *The IVP Bible Background Commentary: New Testament* (Downers Grove: InterVarsity, 1993), 539–40.

20. Turaki, "Ephesians," 1425.

21. James D. G. Dunn, *The Theology of Paul the Apostle* (Grand Rapids: Eerdmans, 1998), 540, 541.

22. D. W. Fowlkes and P. Verster, "Family (*oikos*) Evangelism for Reaching Forward Caste Hindus in India," *Verbum et Ecclesia* 27, no. 1 (2006): 321–38, 328.

David Lim sheds light on the concept of household in the New Testament. It refers to family or kinship, which differs from the Western conception of family. It takes the pattern of the extended family structure of Graeco-Roman households to form networks of house churches.[23] This comprehensive form of the family could reach fifty people depending on their connections.[24] This understanding is significant to the African complex family system, where family collectivity is more critical than individual standing. For instance, *ẹbí* means family or kinship among the Yoruba people in southwest Nigeria.[25] As the appropriate term for the basic unit of the Yoruba society, it may be difficult to subject it to the Western classification of nuclear, stem, linear, extended and compound families because it has both denotative and connotative meanings. Denotatively, it comprises people living together under one household such that the public identifies individuals not with their direct parents but with their residence. In this respect, three or more generations may occupy a large compound called *agbo-ilé* (a conglomerate of houses), each with their apartments.[26]

In the connotative term, *ẹbí* refers to more than what is found within a nuclear or extended family. It also includes the adopted children and those with whom they have marriage affinities.[27] Thus, marriage is not just a relationship that binds two individuals; the two families become *ẹbí*. For them, no further marriage is expected to be contracted between two individuals from these families. The saying, *a kìí bá ẹni tan kí á tún fa' ni ní'tan ya*, meaning sexual activities between relations is a taboo, affirms the point.[28] This is why "Yoruba, family lineage and consanguinity are very important. Thus people have fourth, fifth, sixth, or seventh cousins. They may refer to people from their village or town as brothers or sisters and create associations to perpetuate linkage."[29]

---

23. David S. Lim, "God's Kingdom as *Oikos* Church Networks: A Biblical Theology," *International Journal of Frontier Missiology*, 34, no. 1-4 (2017): 25-35.

24. Fowlkes and Verster, "Family (*oikos*) Evangelism," 328.

25. Olabiyi Babalola Yai, *Yoruba-English English-Yoruba Concise Dictionary* (New York: Hippocrene Books, 1996), 12.

26. Abdul Olanrewaju Shitta-Bey, "The Family as a Basis of Social Order: Insight from the Yoruba Traditional Culture," *International Letters of Social & Humanistic Sciences* 23 (2014): 80-81.

27. Shitta-Bey, "The Family as a Basis of Social Order," 79-89, 81-82.

28. Oyekan Owomoyela, *Yoruba Proverbs* (Lincoln: University of Nebraska Press, 2005), 312.

29. Samuel F. Ogundare, "Change in Family Types and Functions among Yoruba of Southwestern Nigeria since 1960," *Journal of GLBT Family Studies* 6 (2010): 447-57, 448.

Thus, *ẹbí* is a complex system of kinship among the Yoruba people. Other African cultures may relate to this system too.

A further explanation of the church's portrait as a household focuses on the breaking down of the walls of ethnic, racial and other partitions. It is a household or family where Jewish and Gentile believers were members. Unlike the OT understanding, it extends beyond the nation of Israel, with each of the twelve clans and each family of Jews as the basic unit of the society. It covers the non-Jews.[30] This is significant for contemporary multicultural, multi-ethnic, and multi-ideology Africa. Despite this diversity, African Christians must see themselves as belonging to a large family comprising sons and daughters who are brothers and sisters. They are to be characterised by love and fellowship, irrespective of their differences.[31] Moreso, it implies that regardless of their biological roots, including race, ethnicity or clan, they all have equal rights in the family as fellow heirs of the promises of God.[32] Commenting on Ephesians 1–3, MacArthur affirms that all Christians receive rights, privileges, and honours, irrespective of their race, because they belong to the heavenly Father.[33] Considering Ephesians 3:6–7, Mark DeYmaz refers to this coming together of all ethnic people in Christ as a family, a mystery.[34] This mystery is critical for contemporary Africa, where ethnic and cultural affiliation often easily divide people.

The foregoing on the church household metaphor confirms that the water of baptism is thicker than the blood of tribalism. Unfortunately, the contemporary conception of the church may not necessarily promote some of what this metaphor represents. Hence, it is necessary to consider the contemporary concept of the church.

Contemporary church conceptions

There is a generally wrong conception about the universal church, established by Christ when he declared, "I will build my church" (Matt 16:18 ESV), and

---

30. Brent R. Kelly and E. Ray Clendenen, "Family," in *Holman Illustrated Bible Dictionary*, Completely Revised, Updated, and Expanded edition eds. C. Brand, C. Draper and A. England (Nashville: Holman Bible Publishers, 2003), 555–57, 556, 558.

31. Grudem, *Systematic Theology*, 858, 859.

32. Turaki, "Ephesians," 1431, 1432.

33. John MacArthur Jr., *The Body Dynamic: Finding Where You Fit in Today's Church* (Colorado Springs: Chariot Victor, 1996), 61.

34. Mark DeYmaz, "Understanding the Mystery of Christ," *The Christian Post* (September 17, 2013), www.christianpost.com.

the local church like that in Ephesus that Paul called its elders to come to him in Miletus (Acts 20:17). Consequently, some Christians, and even some leaders, consider church planting as the essence of Christian missions, instead of a viable means of achieving the mandate to disciple nations. My casual interaction with some pastors, including those who have been in ministry for about ten years, confirms this reality. Thus, "church," as in gathering believers in a local worship centre, and usually designated by a building where they worship or an organization with a name, becomes an end rather than a means of achieving the Great Commission mandate to make disciples among the nations.

Consequently, programmes of activities have taken over so many contemporary churches in Africa that some have lost the purpose of the church. To some pastors, participation is a mark of spirituality. Aside from special monthly programmes, I know of some churches in southwestern Nigeria where members are in church for five or six days a week. Apart from regular weekly programmes – Sunday worship, prayer meetings, Bible study days, and subgroup meetings, they usually fix monthly and quarterly meetings – there are also church-wide night vigils and retreats, workers' conferences, and subgroup picnics and night vigils. In some churches, these meetings may run during working hours or at night during weekdays, so the participants cannot give their full strength to the work for which they receive their pay.

This programme-centred style of church operation raises some pertinent issues. It raises questions about where and when members would have time to practise whatever they learn in these meetings. Sometimes they cannot relate well at work because they rush out, eager to be in "church." They have no time left to interact with other people in their world. More so, civil servants and other employees become unfaithful or uncommitted to their employers. Business owners cannot grow their businesses as models for others in their worlds. Thus, a local church that fails to engage its society (the local community where its members live, work, interact, and socialise) to bring *shalom* to it, as saints do the work of ministry through various walks of life (Eph 4:13), fails in its noble purpose. In its mission, the church becomes more inward and church-centred (self-centred) than kingdom-centred (others-centred). The church's mission that emerges from *missio Dei* is a kingdom-centred mission with an outward focus.

A strong reason some church pastors introduce different activities and programmes supposedly relates to the African holistic worldview that sees religion as part of everyday life. Thus, they assert that those activities would turn Christianity from a weekly religion to a daily faith. However, it is noteworthy that this religio-centric worldview is not about programmes and activities in designated worship centres. Instead, it concerns its ethical implications on all aspects of life. This means taking religious virtues, values, beliefs, and ideologies into every part of their lives – work, diet, ceremony, family relationships, choice of vocation, dress and friendship, among others. John Mbiti considers the African religious view an ontological phenomenon. A person's whole being and existence, which begin before birth and continues after death, are interpreted religiously because religion is complexly woven into events of the daily life of belief and action.[35] It is more of the person's mindset, and such beliefs are notable in the ethical conduct of some religious sects. It forms part of some religious taboos among some African people.

For example, "in the Yoruba speaking area of Nigeria 'Orisala' worshippers do not eat snails . . . 'Esu' worshippers will not eat fried maize while 'Ogun' worshippers will not eat fried yam."[36] Some African traditional attires are attached to religious identity, ethnicity, and nationality and religious-spiritual meanings, benefits, instrumental values or end goals motivate them toward such identity.[37] Thus, to say Africans are religious is to talk about their self-consciousness of spirits, deities, gods, or ancestors in every aspect of their lives and living to secure their pleasures at every moment. It is not really about daily gatherings at the shrines or worship locations. They have some of these shrines within the family compounds. John Olopade affirms that, while being conscious of the divinities' presence wherever they are and in whatever they do, their corporate worship could be regular and occasional and "where people have the shrines of their ancestors in their dwelling houses, worship takes place regularly every morning."[38] The implication is that corporate worship runs daily at the family and individual levels.

From the foregoing, the African religious worldview is not about having daily religious activities in the worship centres, as some contemporary African pastors conceived. They associate corporate worship with being necessarily done in a "church" (building). Enyinannya affirms that this wrong mindset caused many Christians, including some pastors, to consider the government

---

35. John Mbiti, *African Religions and Philosophy* (Ibadan: Heinemann Educational, 1969), 2–4, 15.

36. Bolanle Wahab, "African Traditional Religions, Environmental Health and Sanitation in Rural Communities," *The Environscope* 1, no. 1 (April 2004): 1–9, 3.

37. Fatou Diop and Dwight Merunka, "African Tradition and Global Consumer Culture: Understanding Attachment to Traditional Dress Style in West Africa," *International Business Research* 6, no. 11 (2013): 1–14, 2, 7, 8, 12. doi: 10.5539/ibr.v6n11p1.

38. John A. Olopade, *Introduction to World Religions* (Osogbo: Oluwatoyin Publishers, 2018), 85.

order for the closure of public meeting places, during the peak of the COVID-19 pandemic, as persecution, anti-Christian policy, or even a manifestation of the Antichrist. He notes that the events surrounding the pandemic have raised the need for the church in Africa to take the definition of church in terms of the people rather than the building more seriously. According to him, while this definition is so simple and unassuming, "we have gotten accustomed to thinking of the church as a place, a building; that we seem to have lost the sight of the truth that the church building is simply a place, the venue where the church meets."[39] He advocated for an ecclesiology that uses the nuclear family and house fellowship principles as its instruments.

Thus, an ecclesiology that suits the current situations in Africa will consider the worldview of worship in African traditional religions. There, worship and allegiance to the gods are holistic; they are not limited to a building at a particular time. It is an issue of mindset and lifestyle that reflect every aspect of a Christian's everyday life. This is *missio integra* and is not about religious activities in a worship centre. It is about expressing private or personal faith in public domains. Worshippers of a god or goddess are not identified only in their shrines – they know them by their lifestyles. Thus, without understanding the church from this perspective, it is difficult for it to operate (its life and mission), expressing its nature in the post-COVID-19 and insecurity situations that have become the norm in some African countries.

Contemporary Africa, Post-COVID-19 and Insecurity Situations

Churches at different periods and locations have responded differently to situations of insecurity and pandemic. The early persecutions and crusades are examples of insecurity. Thorwald Lorenzen affirms that the reality of persecution resulted in martyrdom, and they form the theme of some epistles like 1 Peter, Hebrews and Revelation.[40] On the pandemic issue, Enyinnanya asserts that the crisis condition so created was emotionally reduced by a sense of awareness that there had been a similar experience in history, including the Spanish flu between 1918 and 1919.[41] This section examines some challenges that form the operational context of the contemporary church.

---

39. John O. Enyinannya, "Ecclesiological Talking Points for the Post-Covid-19 Era," in *The Church and the Covid-19 Pandemic*, eds. Emiola Nihinlola and Folashade Oloyede (Ogbomoso: Kingdom Impact Publishing & Media, 2020), 29–38, 30.

40. Thorwald Lorenzen, "Persecution," in *Holman Illustrated Bible Dictionary*. eds. Chad Brand, Charles Draper, and Archie England (Nashville: Holman Bible Publishers, 2003), 1278.

41. Enyinnaya, "Ecclesiological Talking Points for the Post-Covid-19 Era," 29.

Contemporary Africa faces different contextual challenges, including corruption, political instability, ethno-religious clashes, poverty, diseases, unemployment, and climate change. Recently, the COVID-19 pandemic and conditions of insecurity have become so pronounced that their joint effects are intense, affecting every aspect of people's lives. They affect the church's self-expression in the world and its attempts at fulfilling the Great Commission mandate to disciple all nations. These two situations directly impact the church's nature and mission. The COVID-19 pandemic is a form of emergency that "has come with several crumbling effects on individuals, business and religious organizations, educational institutions and the world at large."

Similarly, Michael Ogunewu asserts that it is becoming difficult for the church to operate amid increasing insecurity which often includes Islamic religious terrorism, fundamentalism and militancy, cultism, kidnapping, and an increased crime rate.[42] Although both the pandemic and the insecurity have some historical antecedents that can encourage the contemporary church to remain faithful amid unpleasant situations, there are some inevitable challenges they pose to the church. Some of these emerging challenges are listed here.

Operational hindrances and depleted resources

The two situations have undoubtedly and jointly hindered the church from carrying out its existential functions. This operational impediment has resulted from the restriction of movement and depletion of resources. There is no gainsaying that both have led to losing lives and properties. Some of these lives are potential or active gospel bearers at various levels. In other cases, the situations have sent fear into people who would be involved in the church's mission. For instance, the Nigeria Evangelical Missionary Association (NEMA) laments the negative impact of insecurity on the missionary workforce. According to its survey between 2019 and 2021, insecurity ranks fourth as a leading cause for missionary attrition among fifty-two of the sixty-one member agencies surveyed. During this period, about two hundred and eighty-nine missionaries from twenty-seven member agencies were victims of violent attacks. Of these, there were eight deaths and eighty-four attritions.[43]

---

42. Michael Adeleke Ogunewu, "William Carey's Missions Experience in India as Model for Present-Day Missionaries in Africa," *Nigerian Journal of Church History and Missiological Studies* 1, no. 1 (2019): 167–85, 171.

43. Research & Strategy Department, Nigeria Evangelical Missions Association, Harvest Scope 2.0, December 2021.

The World Health Organization also has statistics on the death toll due to the COVID-19 pandemic. Thus, the pandemic and insecurity have caused movement restrictions for missionary operations in many parts of the world. Such restrictions include those imposed by the authorities to curtail the situation's spread and the associated fears.

In 2010, I travelled by road with a group of volunteers from Nigeria to Chad through the Cameroonian borders without fear of any security threat. Similarly, Birnin-Gwari to Kaduna in Kaduna state of Nigeria was a regular route for my family's missionary endeavours between 2011 and 2015. Today, both routes are challenging because of the increased level of insecurity.

Further, the situations of pandemic and insecurity have affected mission resources negatively. They are associated with the excessive consumption of human and material resources. The International Centre for Investigative Reporting (ICIR) reports that Nigeria's ransom payments between 2011 and 2020 were over $18.34 million.[44] At different times, the assailants have demanded ransom payments before releasing their captives. Such ransom payments drastically reduce the funds the church has for its missions. Observably, churches in Africa have always practised holistic missions involving the holistic needs of people. Unfortunately, insecurity has hindered these central missionary functions of evangelism and service. Apart from situations with direct opposition to Christian religious activities, mission groups and agencies often advise their missionaries to withdraw from the field where their security is not guaranteed. This security threat poses a significant challenge to Christian missions. It is not different from the pandemic situation, where both secular and religious organizations have had to commit resources to fight the spread of the pandemic. Such expenses reduce what they commit to direct fulfilment of the organizational missions.

Stereotypes, hatred, and distorted communication

The pandemic and insecurity have jointly increased the degree of inter-group hatred that leads to reprisal attacks and increased violence among different people groups, tribes, and clans in Africa. This is because the fallout of these challenges creates emotional tension in people. Various news and social media attest to the reality of attacks that reflect grievances and hatred, as people

---

44. Yekeen Akinwale, "In 10 years, $18.34m was paid to kidnappers as ransom in Nigeria" *ICIR* (May 27, 2020), https://www.icirnigeria.org/in-10-years-18-34m-was-paid-to-kidnappers-as-ransom-in-nigeria/.

have probably been "pushed to the wall."⁴⁵ Unfortunately, these attacks are often associated with stereotypes, where people negatively consider every member of a religious or ethnic group as having a particular characteristic that some of them exhibit or as performing the crime that a few or some perform without affirming its authenticity.⁴⁶ Stereotyping often leads to unnecessary mutual suspicion among individuals from different groups of conflicting cultural ideologies or people similar to them. Eventually, they may unleash reprisal attacks on the innocent members of the group. For instance, some people assume that all Fulani are killer herdsmen; they do not even know Fulani Christians exist. Also, some Southerners see all Northerners as potential members of Boko Haram. This target hatred replaces love that should motivate missions.

Inter-group suspicion affects the effectiveness of communication in the mission of its members and the outsiders because humans are "inherently social beings whose lives revolve around communication, relationships and communities and who operate from multiple and shifting identities."⁴⁷ People's identity affects their daily interactions and relationships with people from other groups. Thus, they look at people of other groups from the perspectives of their involvement in the insecurity crisis – as either friends or foes. There have been situations of violence within the church due to inter-ethnic differences. In other cases, it makes Christian missions difficult because the target people do not welcome the tribe of the missionary. Any ecclesiology that will enable the church to be stable in nature and purpose must biblically respond to these complexities of identity, hatred and communication.

Displacement trauma

Many internally displaced persons have migrated from their ancestral homes to relatively safer regions. In Katsina State, Northwest Nigeria, most people living in a village I had served as a missionary no longer sleep in their respective

---

45. Ibrahim Wuyo, "Three herders killed in reprisal attacks in Kaduna community, houses burnt," *Vanguard* (August 22, 2021), https://www.vanguardngr.com; "42 Killed In Attacks, Reprisals In Kaduna," *Daily Trust* (September 28, 2021), https://www.dailytrust.com; Ihuoma Ilo, "8 killed in reprisal attacks in Kaduna community," *HumAngle* (September 28, 2021), https://www.humanglemedia.com.

46. Brooks Peterson, *Cultural Intelligence: A Guide to Working with People from Other Cultures* (Yarmouth: Intercultural Press, Inc., 2004), 26.

47. Michael Hecht, "Communication Theory of Identity," in Stephen W. Littlejohn and Karen A. Foss (eds), *Encyclopedia of Communication Theory* (Los Angeles: SAGE, 2009), 139.

villages. They have migrated to nearby towns for fear of abduction. A young man who attempted to sleep in the village eventually spent eleven days in the hands of the abductors before they released him after his parents paid the demanded ransom.

Similarly, the influx of people from northern parts to southern Nigeria shows that people are moving away from their ancestral homes to more peaceful regions. This has ecclesiological implications on how the church of Nigeria's south will cater for these migrants or internally displaced persons. Stephen Ayankeye considers the COVID-19 pandemic and insecurity as examples of emergencies associated with "crumbling effects on individuals, business and religious organizations, educational institutions and the world at large."[48] Emergencies lead to fear of the unknown, associated with worries and conflict tendencies. In other cases, people face the trauma of displacement. A missional ecclesiology must respond to these needs in the lives of Africans.

Neo-paganism

There is a revival of African traditional religious practices, including charms and amulets. Churches now allegedly employ ethnic vigilante groups who use charms to protect the church parishioners and their properties. In an interaction with the writer, a missionary in Niger State of Nigeria lamented that Christians and Muslims in the village where he was serving agreed that their vulnerability was because they had abandoned their traditional means of dealing with insecurity. Another pastor in the Oke-Ogun area of Oyo state in southwest Nigeria reported that when bandits came to attack them in 2021, some young men, including the purported Christians, went with charms and other ammunition to put their assailants to flight.

Historically, the formation of indigenous Pentecostalism was vital to the growth of Christianity in twentieth-century Africa.[49] Pentecostal power responded adequately to their fears and existential needs for miracles, healings,

---

48. Stephen Oladele Ayankeye, "Handling Emergencies in Life: Covid-19 as Analogy," in *The Church and the Covid-19 Pandemic*, eds. Emiola Nihinlola and Folashade Oloyede, (Ogbomoso: Kingdom Impact Publishing & Media Ltd, 202), 17–27, 17.

49. Ezekiel O. Ajani, "Leadership Dynamics and the Trans-Nationalisation of Nigeria Pentecostal Missions," *Ogbomoso Journal of Theology*, XIII, no. 1, 2008: 154; B. I. Akano, "Mentoring as an Effective Strategy for Leadership Development in Contemporary African Pentecostalism," *Pentecostalism, Charismaticism and Neo-Prophetic Movements Journal (PECANEP)* 3, no. 2 (July, 2022): 21–23.

signs and wonders.[50] Thus, contemporary Africa needs an ecclesiology that emphasises Pentecostal power manifestations to give contemporary Christians and would-be Christians the courage they need to live authentic biblical Christian lives amid the current challenges of Africa. They will not need to seek another power when they are sure of this power. James Plueddemann agrees that churches in Africa require a strong emphasis on spiritual warfare and spiritual gifts for effective missionary endeavour. He holds that the growth of the churches in the majority world is not so much the result of paper plans and strategizing as those of the moves of the Holy Spirit in Bible teaching and discipleship.[51] An ecclesiology that would keep the church stable on its biblical foundation of identity and purpose, despite the existential and emerging challenges in Africa, must emphasise the power of the Holy Spirit.

Effective Church Operation Amid Insecurity and Pandemic

Charles Engen describes the Great Commission as a reflection and follow-up to Jesus's earthly ministry. His disciples are to:

> proclaim the coming of the kingdom of God, to invite all peoples to become Jesus's disciples and responsible members of Christ's church (Matt 28:18–20). This understanding of mission is most basic and should never be lost or eclipsed by subsequent discussions and refinements.[52]

The church must remain faithful to its interwoven identity and mission. Engen states further that a church that will achieve this identity-mission standard must be contextual, intentional, proclaiming, reconciling and healing, sanctifying, unifying, and transforming.

> One of the crucial missiological problems of the second half of the twentieth century has been how to accomplish a successful transition from an easier church-centred theology of mission

---

50. Mbiti, *African Religions and Philosophy*, 232–34.
51. James E. Plueddemann, "Theological Implications of Globalizing Missions," in *Globalizing Theology: Belief and Practice in an Era of World Christianity*, eds. Craig Ott and Harold A. Netland (Grand Rapids: Baker Academics, 2006), 256–58.
52. Charles van Engen, "'Mission' Defined and Described," in *Mission Shift: Global Mission Issues in the Third Millennium*, eds. D. J. Hesselgrave and Ed Stetzer (Nashville: B&H Publishing, 2010), 7–29, 12.

to a kingdom-oriented one without loss of missionary vision or betrayer of biblical content.[53]

Kingdom orientation is central to the Trinitarian *missio Dei*.

The COVID-19 situation, the associated lockdown measures, and the hydra-headed insecurity in some African regions have affected the churches' operations differently. Benjamin Akano asserts that the COVID-19 changed the operational atmosphere of churches from the conventional centralized "church" mode to a decentralized home or cell mode. Their counterparts in the developed world switched over to virtual mode.[54] Contemporary insecurity is similar to the pandemic in shutting people into their locality, taking the form of Islamic religious terrorism, fundamentalism and militancy, cultism, kidnapping, and an increased crime rate. Thus, it is becoming difficult for the church to operate its mission.[55] Though churches in Africa are coming to terms with the technological platforms for operating in its contemporary contexts of post-COVID-19 and insecurity, it requires care and a gradual process to get to that level where churches in the developed world operate.

Three reasons are prominent in Africa's inability to rush into the new normal. First, some Africans still need a level of re-orientation of worldview to the new normal of operating the church online. Africans value real, personal relationships over abstract phenomena. They live in and derive their pride from the sense of community by which they form kinship ties where everyone is related to everyone else in togetherness.[56] For them, the virtual mode of fellowship cannot compare with real physical encounters. I met some adult Christians during the lockdown periods who did not feel they had gone to church after a live zoomed worship. This requires a cognitive change of orientation through more teaching and awareness.

For some Africans who have been re-orientated to accept the technology-based church operation, there is the two-in-one challenge of availability and affordability of appropriate technology. While technology is a global phenomenon that has turned the world into a global village, and though Africans, especially youths, are on various social media platforms, the critical challenge is that maintaining it for church operations is both costly and

---

53. Charles Van Engen, "'Mission' Defined and Described," 25–26.

54. Benjamin I. Akano, "Equipping the Saints in Ephesians 4:12 and Clergy-Laity Lacuna in Post Covid-19 Africa," *Ogbomoso Journal of Theology* 26 no. 1 (2021): 75–91, 75, 90.

55. Ogunewu, "William Carey's Missions Experience," 171.

56. J. A. Ojo, *Christian Anthropology and Ecclesiology* (Ogbomoso: Adebayo Calvary, 2011), 2–3; G. E. Idang, "African Culture and Values," *Phronimon* 16, no. 2 (2015): 97–111, 108.

sometimes challenging due to an erratic power supply. The existential poverty level compounds this due to the uneven distribution of wealth. Only megachurches have the strength and financial wherewithal to keep on with such technology, especially when thinking of synchronous live operations, which Africans prefer when they have accepted technology.[57]

While the three challenges above are being tackled, and when they become fully resolved for the church in Africa, this study proposes four existing dynamics of all time that may be critical for its operation in Africa. These dynamics are rooted both in the cultural milieu of Africa and the nature and purpose of the biblical church. Thus, they are biblically sound and contextually relevant. They include the family metaphor expressed through the disciple-making movement model, the holistic and integral nature of church mission, the comprehensive mechanism of missions, and Pentecostal power manifestations.

Dynamics of family metaphor through disciple-making movement model

The core mandate of the Great Commission remains the discipling of nations and to keep doing it trans-generationally. Then whether it happens in a "church" (church building or institutional church) or a home level, the critical issue is to make disciples biblically. With the contemporary insecurity and pandemic situations, traditional disciple-making in a "church" environment has become difficult. The need to revisit the church's operational model is imperative. The disciple-making movement (DMM) is a proven model for such a difficult situation because its operational emphasis is on the family structure typical of the African context. Thus, there are two critical issues about DMM: the first is its focus on continuous disciple-making, which is the essence and intrinsic nature of the Great Commission, to disciple others who are to disciple others in turn (Matt 28:19; 2 Tim 2:2). The second is the family network that serves as its basis of operation and fits into the contemporary situations of pandemic and insecurity.

Erst Conradie considers the *oikos* (household) metaphor important in the African understanding of the church. Unlike the institutional church, the family of God, kinship, clan, and ancestral communion are similar to the African family network, which serves as a platform for sharing all aspects of

---

57. Benjamin Akano, "Disciple-making Movement: An Effective Operational Model for Churches in Africa amid Covid-19 Pandemic," in *The Church and the Covid-19 Pandemic*, eds. Emiola Nihinlola and Folashade Oloyede (Ogbomoso: Kingdom Impact Publishing & Media, 2020), 137–48, 140, 141.

life and addressing all societal concerns. Such an understanding of the church would incorporate the questions and circumstances of the African context in its nature and mission. It also helps them associate with their faith ancestors as they often did with their biological ancestors in their traditional worldview.[58] The New Testament conception of the church reflects such ancestral links. Church applies to all the believers of all time, referring to the Old and New Testaments. In their usage, the connection between the OT Hebrew *qahal* and the NT Greek *ekklēsia* associates ancestors with the church concept. The ancestors-in-faith are the "cloud of witnesses" in Hebrews 12:1 (Deut 4:10; Acts 7:38; Heb 2:12; Ps 22:22).[59]

Because of the lockdown measures introduced to curtail the spread of the COVID-19 pandemic, conventional institutional church operations were affected. While churches in the West went virtual during the pandemic situation, a platform that may be suitable for insecurity too, their African counterparts found it challenging to shift from face-to-face church operations to a virtual approach for different reasons. Benjamin Akano identifies four challenges African church operations faced during the pandemic. First, the sense of real kinship they treasure in a local assembly fellowship was unavailable in a virtual meeting. Second, the technology needed for virtual church operations was not available in most African communities, and where it was available, the cost was high. Third, the pandemic, as does insecurity, inflicted untold hardship on church members and, by extension, the church's economy. Fourth, a psycho-spiritual dimension is associated with such situations of pandemic and insecurity because of how Africans explain their existential challenges.[60] A common solution for Africans in different places was the *oikos* model church or any similar small group.

Therefore, Africa requires a familial ecclesiology rooted in the family system. However, such ecclesiology must respond to the negative tendencies of the African family system, including the patriarchal principle that sometimes leads to the oppression of women and children. It must be based on equity and mutuality as they relate to the family. This is critical when women are naturally dominant in most African churches because of their emotional love for religious feelings and compounded by insecurity that creates more

---

58. Erst Conradie, "The Whole Household of God (Oikos): Some Ecclesiological Perspectives," in *Ecclesiological Investigations (Volume 4): Church and Religious "Other,"* ed. Gerard Mannion (London: T&T Clark, 2008), 41–56, 48–51.

59. Grudem, *Systematic Theology*, 853, 854.

60. Akano, "Disciple-making Movement," 140, 141.

widows. Some African institutional churches, including indigenous churches like the Nigerian Christ Apostolic Church, subordinate women in leadership operations.[61] Conversely, though African cultures are predominantly patriarchal, they still have high regard for women, particularly in religion. Thus, such "household-based" ecclesiology must reflect all these characteristics. The disciple-making movement (DMM) is a good vehicle for such ecclesiology.

DMM is biblically rooted in Matthew 28:19 and 2 Timothy 2:2. In Matthew 28:19, the Greek word *matheteuo*, translated "make disciples" by most modern translations, including American Standard Version, English Standard Version, New International Version, and New Living Translation, present an expression of a movement or network of disciples resulting from a multiplication or replication effect of disciple-making. However, unlike a typical rabbi, the disciples are not to be made after themselves but after Christ.[62] This means everyone – the first disciple, the disciple of this first disciple, and each resulting from these – has an equal relationship with the Father. They also have the same commission and authority to repeat the process unendingly. This replicative understanding is evident in Paul's strategy of church planting in Ephesus and his instruction to his son in 2 Timothy 2:2.[63] He expected the disciples to, in turn, make disciples who would keep the cycle of disciple-making unbroken. Therefore, to be a disciple is to live a kingdom life and bear verbal testimony to the kingdom. Hence, there are no second-generation disciples in the technical sense of his intention. One of the methods for carrying out DMM is Discovery Bible Study (DBS).

DBS is a disciple-making method developed by David L. Watson to aid individuals in understanding the response of the Bible to big questions of life without any external assistance.[64] It is an inductive process of participatory group Bible study focusing on discovering biblical truth, obedience, accountability and sharing the same truth within one's relationship circle.[65] DBS possesses two important dynamics for sustaining the nature and mission of the church – obedience-based and sharing-enhanced. The obedience section leads to holistic transformation in line with the nature of the church

---

61. Conradie, "The Whole Household of God (Oikos)," 48, 51.

62. Geoffrey W. Bromiley, *Theological Dictionary of the New Testament* (Grand Rapids: Eerdmans, 1985), 562.

63. Ott et al., *Encountering Theology of Mission*, 28.

64. D. Watson, *Obedience Based Discipleship: Field Testing Guide Version 1.5* (2008), https://www.internationalproject.org.

65. S. Smith and S. Parks, "T4T OR DMM (DBS)? Only God Can Start a Church-Planting Movement (Part 2 of 2)," *Mission Frontiers* (January/February 2015): 36–38.

to be the salt and light. The sharing aspect works through the network of relationships and ensures the sustenance of the church's mission, leading to a disciple-making movement. This is critical because the institutional church often requires space and structure, which may not be allowed in situations of pandemic and insecurity.

Dynamics of a holistic and integral missions

Hospitality and mutual caring are central to the African sense of family.[66] The pandemic and insecurity create critical cases for a sense of hospitality. Fortunately, the nature of missions is holistic, comprising the inseparable tasks of witness (*martyria*) and service (*diakonia*). They must live and love, witness and serve, suffer and die for Christ.[67] It is also referred to as the two inseparable mandates of creation (cultural or social) with an ethical obligation on all people, and the gospel (also spiritual, new creation, or redemptive) mandate, which deals with the broken relationship of God. They are inseparable because they belong together, and while dichotomizing leads to imbalance, the distinction between them helps keep each in focus.[68] Through holistic missions, the church brings *shalom* (spiritual, physical, psychological and social peace) to the world. *Shalom* is a three-phase mediatorial priestly role: bearing witness to call people to salvation, nurturing the believers, and bringing healing of hearts, souls, bodies, and societies.[69] The joint effects of insecurity and pandemic demand that a local church (zonal, regional, or national) expresses its *diakonia* function more generously than before.

During the COVID-19 pandemic, some people lost their means of livelihood, either directly or indirectly. As daily reports monitored by national and other news media confirm, some Africans defied measures put in place by their government to combat hunger, mainly for a lack of appropriate mechanisms for appropriate sharing. I know organizations that paid no salary or reduced salaries during the period. The May 6, 2020 *Vanguard* newspaper reports that the American University of Nigeria, Yola sacked over four

---

66. Conradie, "The Whole Household of God (Oikos)," 51.

67. John Stott, *Issues Facing Christians Today*, 4th ed. (Grand Rapids: Zondervan, 2006), 44–45.

68. Ott et al., *Encountering Theology of Mission*, 137–62.

69. A. Scott Moreau, G. Corwin, and G. McGee, *Introducing World Missions: A Biblical, Historical, and Practical Survey* (Grand Rapids: Baker Academic, 2004), 86–87.

hundred of its workforce.⁷⁰ Other organizations even folded up. Some affected people depended on palliative measures established by religious bodies, non-governmental organizations (NGOs), and some philanthropists. Two recent ransom payments directly related to the Church in Nigeria include the one paid for the release of the students of Bethel Baptist School in Kaduna and the other for the prelate of the Methodist Church, Nigeria, kidnapped with two other persons.⁷¹ This is in addition to lives and properties being destroyed and subjected to unprepared expenses. Unfortunately, such is a constant experience of some people subjected to continuous attacks from their assailants against the prevailing existential poverty. It has forced others to relocate to seek greener pastures elsewhere.

Therefore, an ecclesiology for the contemporary context of insecurity and post-pandemic must be generous in its *diakonia* functions. This need is critical in Africa because of the existential backwardness. Because of corruption and bad leadership, average African societies lack existing systems to cushion the effects of these challenges. The key thesis of *African Public Theology*, written by thirty authors from different parts of Africa, is that the church remains a key solution for the dream Africans want.⁷² However, it is noteworthy that such acts of service are not to serve as bait to lure people into the "trap of salvation" in Christ. They are essentially part of the good works to which the church has been called (Eph 2:10). While the salvation of souls is the primary focus, the secondary aspects of societal and physiological well-being are an essential part that Christian missions should not neglect. An empty stomach has no ear to listen to the gospel message.

However, there are two cautions with ecclesiology that emphasize the church's *diakonia* function. The first is the danger of reductionism, which reduces Christian missions to social services and meeting people's physiological and psychological needs. Though these good deeds are parts of Christian life and complement the gospel message, the mission is incomplete without written or oral sharing.⁷³ The second concern is the danger of creating dependency

---

70. Umar Yusuf, "Atiku Abubakar varsity sacks 400 staff," *Vanguard* (May 6, 2020), https://www.vanguardngr.com/2020/05/atiku-abubakar-varsity-sacks-400-staff/.

71. Ibrahim Wuyo, "Kidnappers of Bethel students renege on promise, demand fresh N50m Ransom," *Vanguard* (July 31, 2021), https://www.vanguardngr.com/2021/07/kidnappers-of-bethel-students-renege-promise-demand-fresh-n50m-ransom/; EbunOluwa Olafusi, "Lagos CAN chairman: We paid N100m ransom for Methodist prelate," *The Cable* (May 31, 2022), https://www.thecable.ng/lagos-can-chairman-we-paid-n100m-ransom-for-methodist-prelate.

72. Agang, Hendriks, and Forster (eds), *African Public Theology*.

73. Mark Dever, *The Gospel and Personal Evangelism* (Wheaton: Crossway Books, 2007), 74–76.

syndrome, where people continue to depend on the church for their physical needs. This may lead to a situation where the highest bidder gets their attention. A simple way out of these twin dilemmas is an understanding and application of the integral nature of Christian missions.

Integral mission, *missio integra*, emphasizes the inter-relatedness of the Christian proclamation and demonstration. It is more than having evangelism and social involvement alongside each other; the whole of a believer's life comes under the lordship of Jesus Christ. This implies that every Christian, clergy or laity, has specific responsibility in the mission of the church in partnering with the triune God in *missio Dei*. Therefore, since every disciple of Christ has this role, their diverse networks and circles of influence, including family, workplace, and other social platforms, become platforms for being his witnesses. It is about "being witnesses" in public places as they demonstrate the kingdom lifestyle.[74] This requires a mindset and worldview of the kingdom centred around *missio Dei*. This is the African way of thinking about life – religion permeating every facet of life.

Instrumentally, the nature of religion in Africa is holistic and integrative. Religion is a full-time affair – twenty-four hours each day. John Mbiti's assertion that Africans are notoriously religious is still valid. Contemporary Africans still demonstrate their religious passion in all they do. In the southwestern part of Nigeria, where I came from, religious acts (as ministries) are usually spontaneous. For instance, ministry of help may not necessarily be weekly affairs done through giving designated offerings, but daily as occasions demand, since such activities are natural parts of their communal living. Spiritually, they also engage in spontaneous incantation and invocation of the gods or ancestors. While there may be fixed periods of festivals and celebrations, they do not have to wait till a specific time in a particular place of worship before "being spiritual." Therefore, since authentic spirituality and religion among Africans relates to their day-to-day activities in all aspects of life rather than what they perform in designated places of worship, ecclesiology that would triumph amid such situations of pandemic and insecurity must take the "church" to these places of daily activities.

Consequently, theological education for all members, rather than just the clergy, becomes imperative. Walls asserts that theological education is teaching

---

74. Lausanne Movement, "Integral Mission," https://lausanne.org/networks/issues/integral-mission; Rebecca Waweru, "Integral Mission: An Overview of Four Models and Its Role in Development," *International Journal of Novel Research in Humanity and Social Sciences* 2, no. 1 (Jan–Feb 2015): 13–18.

for the church as a whole. The teaching ministry is given to the church to equip all its members. He captures it as follows:

> It is one of the special gifts the Holy Spirit bestows on some for the benefit of all. Such concentrated and extensive bodies of teaching as the Epistles to the Romans and to the Hebrews were not given as lectures to Divinity students; they were written to be read in churches. Our concern, therefore, is theological education, not simply education for the ministry. We are interested in how the whole church receives the divine *paideia* [instrument of education], not just how some of its practioners are trained.[75]

This agrees with Akano's advocacy for bridging the clergy-laity lacuna in current ecclesiology practice. According to Ephesians 4:12, the purpose of the leadership or ministry gifts in the church is not to saddle the leaders alone with the ministry responsibilities. They are to equip the members for the work of ministry in their various circles of influence.[76] Thus, contemporary Africa needs an ecclesiology that enhances marketplace witness so believers can transmit their faith naturally wherever they are.

Dynamics of comprehensive mechanism of missions

The Masters' commission is for the disciples to be witnesses in all domains – both in Jerusalem and all Judea, and in Samaria, and to the ends of the earth. Missional churches have considered this commission a command to leave their comfort zones and search for the heathen nations inhabiting the ends of the earth. While this is commendable, there is a tendency to aim at the ends of the earth geographically when the targeted heathens have already relocated to the "Jerusalem" of the church. Today, there are many migrations for economic, security and other reasons. Acts 1:8 shows that the monocultural young Jewish church was to reach three categories of people – the Jews, the Samaritans and the Gentile nations. To reach the non-Jews (Samaritans and Gentiles), the church had to leave its comfort zone (Judea region), and its ideological and cultural milieu. However, this did not mean they would not reach out to Jews and non-Jews within the Judea region. It made it a little easier for them.

---

75. Andrew Walls, "Theological education from its earliest Jewish and African Christian beginnings – Some currents in the wider history of Christianity," in *Handbook of Theological Education in Africa*, eds., I. A. Phiri and D. Werner (Oxford: Regnum Books International, 2013), 3–12, 3.

76. Benjamin Isola Akano, "Equipping the Saints in Ephesians 4:12," 76, 88.

In Nigeria's case, the current situation, especially insecurity, has caused serious relocations from North to South. Thus, there is a tendency for the church to look for the people of the unreached nations in the north when in reality, a good number have had to relocate to the "Judean" region where the church can easily reach out to them. Thus rather than looking for the nations at the far ends of the earth, there are two groups of nations – some within the Judean region of the church and others at the ends of the earth. The ecclesiology for continued service must incorporate mission strategies for both.

Akano contends that while the church is responsible for leaving its comfort zone to go after and bring the lost to Christ, it must not forget that "going" is only a means of getting to locate these lost and give them the gospel message. Thus, when the lost have decided, or have been forced, to come to where the church is, it must make an intentional effort and design strategies to respond to them. Incorporating the strategies that involve either the going or the intentional response to the already attracted is a comprehensive missionary mechanism and refers to both centrifugal and centripetal structures.[77] Globally, there is a shift in the centre of Christian gravity from the West towards the Majority World in the South due to different factors. This is what Timothy Tennent calls the collapse of the "West-Reaches-the-Rest" paradigm of Christian missions. Christian identity is no longer a matter of geography or race; missional engagement must move alongside the people.[78] There is also a local version of this phenomenon in different countries.

For instance, while northern Nigeria still has more unreached people groups than the southern part, the insecurity and pandemic situations have forced some northerners to migrate southwards where the impact of this menace is low. More northerners have relocated in the last five years than in previous years. Thus, an ecclesiology that will help the church fulfil its purpose, which is integral to its nature, must embrace a comprehensive mission mechanism. This is critical because, as earlier established, the church exists on earth for *missio Dei*.

---

77. Benjamin Isola Akano, "Missionary Motif and Mechanisms in the Book of Ezra: Seven Lessons for Contemporary Church in Nigeria," in *Crying for Spiritual Awakening*, eds. Emiola Nihinlola and Folashade Oloyede (Ogbomoso: Kingdom Impact Publishing & Media Ltd), 191–202, 195, 198.

78. Tennent, *Invitation to World Missions*, 18, 31, 33.

Dynamics of Pentecostal power manifestation

Another essential dynamic in *oikos* church metaphor is what Conradie calls recognizing centrifugal pneumatology. The metaphor emphasizes the "presence and activities of the Spirit of Christ in every sphere of the household."[79] The implication is that power does not reside only with the leader of the household: kingdom power manifestation is mutual among the members of the household. In most African settings, every family member is fortified by the power of the family god or goddess. Mbiti affirms that power is fundamental to human living in Africa because they fear enemies may use evil magic on them. Thus, they want to fortify every family member through general rituals in the family compound or as amulets tied by each family member. Other times, each member has learned to chant incantations against enemy forces by invoking some ancestral spirits to fight on their behalf.[80] In Nigeria, some indigenous church traditions have "prayer amulets" they tie on their children to avoid the attacks of evil magic. However, though debatable, some evangelical Christians believe that some of these "prayer amulets" are rather syncretic. The centrifugal pneumatology of the *oikos* church must respond to the African need to confront their existential fears.

Olopade is unequivocal about the fact that insecurity and pandemics are part of the dangers for which Africans seek supernatural protection.[81] A private survey I carried out in January and February 2021 confirms this assertion. I randomly sampled the opinions of some Christians from different parts of Nigeria on their expectations from the church during the COVID-19 pandemic using a Google form. Apart from the open-ended questions in the questionnaire, I also administered unstructured interviews in the streets of Ogbomoso in Nigeria's southwest for a qualitative analysis. The outcome shows that over 72 percent associated their expectations of the churches with one form of religious activity or another in their short answers. These include prayer, gospel ministry, faith and the manifestation of the gifts of healing.

Similarly, individuals and groups, including Christians, have sought spiritual solutions to the insecurity challenges. Ironically, in seeking protection for their members and properties, some churches prefer to engage the services of the local militia rather than the regular security outfits like the police because they know these militias have some "spiritual" weapons in addition to the regular weapons. In February 2020, a missionary pastor working in a border

---

79. Conradie, "The Whole Household of God (Oikos)," 53.
80. Mbiti, *African Religions and Philosophy*, 197–201.
81. Olopade, *Introduction to World Religions*, 88, 89.

village between Kaduna and Niger states of Nigeria's northwest reported at a training session that the Muslims and Christians in his town met and agreed to seek a traditional solution to the banditry problem that had bedevilled them. Sometimes they make such a choice because of the cheaper cost of employing the local militia than the regular security outfit. Banditry, herders' attacks, Islamist terror, and kidnapping can only be imagined by those who have not experienced them. They force people to look for any available solutions, and Africans believe more in spiritual solutions.

The quest for a spiritual solution to the challenges of insecurity and pandemic is a root cause of neo-paganism in Africa. Anthony Ezeogamba and Pascal Umeoduagu assert that neo-paganism is common among believers and unbelievers in Nigeria. They seek to revive ancient polytheistic religions like African Traditional Religion (ATR).[82] In the process of this writing, I monitored some programmes sponsored by adherents of the ATR on the local radio. They introduced some Christian liturgy elements to attract non-adherents and modern minds. For instance, they introduced preaching sections, quoting from the oral traditions of their deities. Also, contemporary divination is no longer associated with the dirty environment that used to be the case. The diviners and witch doctors now drive cars and use computers for consultations. Contemporary ecclesiology that would thrive and keep the church on the Rock, being what it should be to do what it should do, must respond to this kind of context that Africa finds itself. It must be an ecclesiology with Pentecostal power manifestation.

Historically, the formation of indigenous Pentecostalism was critical to the growth of Christianity in twentieth-century Africa.[83] It responded to their fears, and Christianity became meaningful to them, and its God is dependable to overcome all challenges and battles of life. Thus, the ecclesiology that would be meaningful to the contemporary pandemic and insecurity must emphasize Pentecostal power manifestation. James Plueddemann asserts that "the growth of the emerging church is not so much the result of goal setting with logarithmic graph paper but instead comes from Bible teaching, discipleship, and the movement of the Holy Spirit."[84] The ecclesiology for the African context must reflect this critical factor. An important caveat here is

---

82. Anthony Ezeogamba and Pascal C. Umeoduagu, "The Church is in the World but Not of the World (John 17:16–26): Church in Nigeria and Scandal," *Tansian University Journal of Arts, Management & Social Science*, 7.1 (April 2020): 113–28, 114.

83. Ezekiel O. Ajani, "Leadership Dynamics," 154; Benjamin I. Akano, "Mentoring as an Effective Strategy," 23.

84. Plueddemann, "Theological Implications of Globalizing Missions," 256.

that such manifestations must agree with the evangelical teaching on courage in the face of suffering, persecution, and martyrdom, according to *Bad Urach Statement*, to avoid creating a kind of new Christian magic.[85]

Conclusion

For the church in Africa to triumph, thrive and sustain its authentic biblical nature and mission, it must develop a viable ecclesiology that is both biblically sound and contextually relevant. Such ecclesiology must be ongoing, responding to various changes associated with the contextual African realities. This will enable the church to remain solidly on the Rock of its foundation, serving the purpose of God as his primary agent on earth. This requires a mindset that is centred on *missio Dei*. To this end four issues have been identified as imperatives.

First, ecclesiology in Africa must focus on the core mandate of the Great Commission that the Lord gave to the church. Since the difficulty posed by the pandemic and situations of insecurity may not allow traditional structures and strategies, it should allow flexibility by engaging the intersection of the biblical family metaphor of the church and the African cultural family milieu. Since the mandate is trans-generational, it must embrace the disciple-making movement model of operations to overcome the restriction challenges due to pandemics and insecurity. The core mandate of the church on Earth is to disciple all nations. Second, such ecclesiology must reflect the holistic nature of missions with inseparable functions of witness (*martyria*) and service (*diakonia*). While soul-winning is central to the mandate, it must not overlook the economic challenges and physical needs caused by the pandemic and insecurity. In addition, the mission of such a church should not only be holistic, it must be integral, entrenching the kingdom values and ideology in the worldview of the believers and reflecting the same in all areas of life. Third, because of the increasing need for diaspora missions, any ecclesiology that will remain stable in its nature and mission must engage a comprehensive approach to missions and be intentional about centripetal and centrifugal mechanisms. Finally, since spiritual power is an essential dynamic in Africa, an ecclesiology that will help the church to remain what it should be and do what it should do must emphasize Pentecostal power manifestations so that African Christians

---

85. Christof Sauer and Richard Howell, "Introduction," in *Suffering, Persecution, and Matyrdom: Theological Reflections*, eds. Christof Sauer and Richard Howell (Johannesburg/Bonn: AcadSA Publishing/Culture & Science Publ., 2010), 1–2.

may find the courage to hold on to authentic biblical faith and transmit the same to the next generation without reverting to unbiblical powers from their African religious background.

Bibliography

Agang, Sunday B., H. Jurgens Hendriks, H. Jurgens & Forster (eds). *African Public Theology*. Carlisle: HippoBooks, 2020.

Ajani, Ezekiel O. "Leadership Dynamics and the Trans-Nationalisation of Nigeria Pentecostal Missions." *Ogbomoso Journal of Theology* XIII, no. 1, 2008: 152–66.

Akano, Benjamin I. "Disciple-making Movement: An Effective Operational Model for Churches in Africa amid Covid-19 Pandemic." In *The Church and the Covid-19 Pandemic*, edited by Emiola Nihinlola and Folashade Oloyede, 137–48. Ogbomoso: Kingdom Impact Publishing & Media, 2020.

———. "Equipping the Saints in Ephesians 4:12 and Clergy-Laity Lacuna in Post-covid-19 Africa." *Ogbomoso Journal of Theology* 26, no. 1 (2021): 75–91.

———. "Mentoring as an Effective Strategy for Leadership Development in Contemporary African Pentecostalism." *Pentecostalism, Charismaticism and Neo-Prophetic Movements Journal (PECANEP)* 3, no. 2 (July, 2022): 21–23.

———. "Missionary Motif and Mechanisms in the Book of Ezra: Seven Lessons for Contemporary Church in Nigeria." In *Crying for Spiritual Awakening*, edited by Emiola Nihinlola and Folashade Oloyede, 191–202. Ogbomoso: Kingdom Impact Publishing & Media Ltd.

Akinwale, Yekeen. "In 10 years, $18.34m was paid to kidnappers as ransom in Nigeria." *ICIR* (May 27, 2020). https://www.icirnigeria.org/in-10-years-18-34m-was-paid-to-kidnappers-as-ransom-in-nigeria/.

Ayankeye, Stephen Oladele. "Handling Emergencies in Life: Covid-19 as Analogy." In *The Church and the Covid-19 Pandemic*, edited by Emiola Nihinlola and Folashade Oloyede, 17–27. Ogbomoso: Kingdom Impact Publishing & Media Ltd, 2020.

Bromiley, Geoffrey W. *Theological Dictionary of the New Testament*. Grand Rapids: Eerdmans, 1985.

Byung-Soo, Han. "The Structure of the Trinity in Augustine." *Korean Presbyterian Journal of Theology* 52 no. 4 (2020): 97–125.

Conradie, Erst. "The Whole Household of God (*Oikos*): Some Ecclesiological Perspectives." In *Ecclesiological Investigations (Volume 4): Church and Religious "Other,"* edited by Gerard Mannion, 41–56. London: T&T Clark, 2008.

Dever, Mark. *The Gospel and Personal Evangelism*. Wheaton: Crossway Books, 2007.

DeYmaz, Mark. "Understanding the Mystery of Christ." *The Christian Post* (September 17, 2013). www.christianpost.com.

Diop, Fatou, and Dwight Merunka. "African Tradition and Global Consumer Culture: Understanding Attachment to Traditional Dress Style in West Africa." *International Business Research* 6, no. 11 (2013): 1–14. doi: 10.5539/ibr.v6n11p1.

Dunn, James D.G . *The Theology of Paul the Apostle*. Grand Rapids: Eerdmans, 1998.

Engelsviken, Tormod. "*Missio Dei*: The Understanding and Misunderstanding of a Theological Concept in European Churches and Missiology." *International Review of Mission* XCII, no. 367: 481–97.

Engen, Charles Van. "Mission Defined and Described." In *Mission Shift: Global Mission Issues in the Third Millennium*, edited by David J. Hesselgrave and Ed Stetzer, 7–29. Nashville: B&H Publishing, 2010.

Enyinannya, John O. "Ecclesiological Talking Points for the Post-Covid-19 Era." In *The Church and the Covid-19 Pandemic*, edited by Emiola Nihinlola and Folashade Oloyede, 29–38. Ogbomoso: Kingdom Impact Publishing & Media, 2020.

Ezeogamba, Anthony, and Pascal C. Umeoduagu. "The Church is in the World but Not of the World (John 17:16–26): Church in Nigeria and Scandal." *Tansian University Journal of Arts, Management & Social Science* 7, no. 1 (April 2020): 113–28.

Fowlkes, D. W., and P. Verster "Family (*oikos*) Evangelism for Reaching Forward Caste Hindus in India." *Verbum et Ecclesia* 27, no. 1 (2006): 321–38.

Franklin, Patrick S. "The God Who Sends Is the God Who Loves: Mission As Participation in the Ecstatic Love of the Triune God." *Didaskalia* 28 (2017–2018): 75–95.

Grudem, Wayne. *Systematic Theology: An Introduction to Biblical Doctrine*. Nottingham: Inter-Varsity Press, 2000.

Hecht, Michael L. "Communication Theory of Identity." In *Encyclopedia of Communication Theory*. Edited by Stephen W. Littlejohn and Karen A. Foss, 139–41. Los Angeles: SAGE, 2009.

Idang, G. E. "African Culture and Values." *Phronimon* 16, no. 2 (2015): 97–111.

Ilo, Ihuoma. "8 killed in reprisal attacks in Kaduna community." *HumAngle* (September 28, 2021). https://www.humanglemedia.com.

Keener, Craig S. *The IVP Bible Background Commentary: New Testament*. Downers Grove: InterVarsity, 1993.

Kelly, Brent R., and E. Ray Clendenen. "Family." In *Holman Illustrated Bible Dictionary*, edited by Chad Brand, Charles Draper, and Archie England, 556–58. Nashville: Holman Bible Publishers, 2003.

Kosse, Kuzuli. "Unity of Believers." In *Africa Bible Commentary*. Edited by Tokunboh Adeyemo, 1288. Nairobi: WordAlive, 2006.

Lausanne Movement, "Integral Mission." https://lausanne.org/networks/issues/integral-mission.

Lim, David S. "God's Kingdom as *Oikos* Church Networks: A Biblical Theology." *International Journal of Frontier Missiology* 34, no. 1–4 (2017): 25–35.

Lorenzen, Thorwald. "Persecution." In *Holman Illustrated Bible Dictionary*, Completely Revised, Updated, and Expanded edition, edited by Chad Brand, Charles Draper, and Archie England, 1277–78. Nashville: Holman Bible Publishers, 2003.

MacArthur Jr., John. *The Body Dynamic: Finding Where You Fit in Today's Church*. Colorado Springs: Chariot Victor, 1996.

Makumba, M. Mwaura. *Introduction to African Philosophy: Past and Present*. Nairobi: Pauline Publication Africa, 2007.

Manion, Gerard. *Ecclesiology and Postmodernity: Questions for the Church in Our Times*. Collegeville: Liturgical Press, 2007.

Manus, Ukachukwu Chris. *Intercultural Hermeneutics in Africa: Methods and Approaches*. Nairobi: Acton, 2003.

Mbiti, John S. *African Religions and Philosophy*. Ibadan: Heinemann Educational, 1969.

Moreau, A. Scott, G. Corwin, and G. McGee. *Introducing World Missions: A Biblical, Historical and Practical Survey*. Grand Rapids: Baker Academic, 2004.

Niemandt, C. J. P. "Trends in Missional Ecclesiology." *HTS Theological Studies* 68, no. 1 (2012): 1–9. http://dx.doi.org/10.4102/ hts.v68i1.1198.

Ogundare, Samuel F. "Change in Family Types and Functions among Yoruba of Southwestern Nigeria since 1960." *Journal of GLBT Family Studies* 6 (2010): 447–57.

Ogunewu, Michael Adeleke. "William Carey's Missions Experience in India as Model for Present-Day Missionaries in Africa." *Nigerian Journal of Church History and Missiological Studies* 1, no. 1 (2019): 167–85.

Ojo, J. A. *Christian Anthropology and Ecclesiology*. Ogbomoso: Adebayo Calvary, 2011.

Olafusi, EbunOluwa. "Lagos CAN chairman: We paid N100m ransom for Methodist Prelate." *The Cable*. May 31, 2022. https://www.thecable.ng/lagos-can-chairman-we-paid-n100m-ransom-for-methodist-prelate.

Olopade, John A. *Introduction to World Religions*. Osogbo: Oluwatoyin Publishers, 2018.

Ott, Craig, Stephen J. Strauss, and Timothy C. Tennent. *Encountering Theology of Mission: Biblical Foundations, Historical Developments, and Contemporary Issues*. Grand Rapids: Baker Academic, 2010.

Owomoyela, Oyekan. *Yoruba Proverbs*. : University of Nebraska Press, 2005.

Peterson, Brooks. *Cultural Intelligence: A Guide to Working with People from Other Cultures*. Yarmouth: Intercultural Press, Inc., 2004.

Plueddemann, James E. "Theological Implications of Globalizing Missions. In *Globalizing Theology: Belief and Practice in an Era of World Christianity*, edited by Craig Ott and Harold A. Netland, 256–66. Grand Rapids: Baker Academics, 2006.

Research and Strategy Department, Nigeria Evangelical Missions Association. *Harvest Scope* 2.0. December 2021.

Sauer, Christof and Richard Howell. "Introduction." In *Suffering, Persecution, and Martyrdom: Theological Reflections*. Edited by Christof Sauer and Richard Howell, 12–17. Johannesburg/Bonn: AcadSA Publishing/Culture & Science Publ., 2010.

Shitta-Bey, Abdul Olanrewaju. "The Family as a Basis of Social Order: Insight from the Yoruba Traditional Culture." *International Letters of Social & Humanistic Sciences* 23 (2014): 79–89.

Smith, S., and S. Parks. "T4T OR DMM (DBS)? Only God Can Start a Church-Planting Movement (Part 2 of 2)." *Mission Frontiers* (January/February 2015): 30–38.

Stott, John. *Issues Facing Christians Today*. 4th edition. Grand Rapids: Zondervan, 2006.

Tennent, Timothy C. *Invitation to World Missions: A Trinitarian Missiology for the Twenty-first Century*. Grand Rapids: Kregel Publications, 2010.

Turaki, Yusufu. "Ephesians." In *Africa Bible Commentary*, edited by Tokunboh Adeyemo, 1425–38. Nairobi: WordAlive, 2006.

Wahab, Bolanle. "African Traditional Religions, Environmental Health and Sanitation in Rural Communities." *The Environscope* 1, no. 1 (April 2004): 1–9.

Walls, A. "Theological education from its earliest Jewish and African Christian beginnings – Some currents in the wider history of Christianity." In *Handbook of Theological Education in Africa*, edited by I. A. Phiri and D. Werner, 3–12. Oxford: Regnum Books International.

Watson, D., 2008. *Obedience Based Discipleship: Field Testing Guide Version 1.5*. https://www.internationalproject.org.

Waweru, Rebecca. "Integral Mission: An Overview of Four Models and Its Role in Development." *International Journal of Novel Research in Humanity and Social Sciences* 2, no. 1 (Jan–Feb 2015): 13–18.

Wuyo, Ibrahim. "Kidnappers of Bethel students renege on promise, demand fresh N50m Ransom." *Vanguard* (July 31, 2021). https://www.vanguardngr.com/2021/07/kidnappers-of-bethel-students-renege-promise-demand-fresh-n50m-ransom/.

Yai, Olabiyi Babalola. *Yoruba-English English-Yoruba Concise Dictionary*. New York: Hippocrene Books, 1996.

Yusuf, Umar. "Atiku Abubakar varsity sacks 400 staff." *Vanguard* (May 6, 2020). https://www.vanguardngr.com/2020/05/atiku-abubakar-varsity-sacks-400-staff/.

13

The Church as the Family Writ Large

The Practice and Expression of Kinship at CITAM Valley Road

Paul N. Mwangi
South Eastern Kenya University

Abstract

The social dimension of the church borrows heavily from the family in the propagation, regulation and maintenance of social relationships within the church. Christ is the Answer Ministries (CITAM) Valley Road is an intentional urban ministry where people gather for worship and fellowship. The current study is an attempt to evaluate how individuals and families that worship and fellowship at CITAM Valley Road can cultivate social relationships and maintain one of the most successful urban Pentecostal churches in Kenya. Through unstructured observation, participant observation and qualitative interviews the study has used qualitative data about the practice and expression of kinship at CITAM Valley Road. Jesus Christ founded the church as an institution and as a relationship between human beings and God, and relationships among human beings themselves with a promise of victory and posterity. The church therefore thrives when it adapts family characteristics and patterns that are founded on identity, belonging and purpose.

The current paper demonstrates how adopting family characteristics and patterns has helped CITAM Valley Road to overcome and thrive in an urban context. In the church, like in the family, a sense of identity, belonging and purpose helps in propagating, regulating and maintaining social bonds in perpetuity. The paper points out that when Christians as individuals and as the body corporate appreciate and embrace the role of the Holy Spirit in their identity, belonging and purpose in Christ and to each other, then the victorious church becomes evident. The church appears to be a magnification (writ large) of the family.

Key words: belonging, church, family, institutions, kinship, perpetuity, urbanization, Safari Group, transformation

Introduction

Social change is a concept many people take for granted or do not even understand. However, no society has ever remained the same. Change is always happening to human beings, society and institutions. For the sake of survival, human beings accept change as inevitable. Sociologists define social change as changes in human interactions and relationships that transform cultural and social institutions.[1] These changes occur over time and often have profound and long-term consequences for society, and are notable in social institutions. When social change is evident in the social arena of life and the attendant social institutions then there is social transformation. Social transformation refers to the process of change in institutionalized relationships, norms, values, and hierarchies over time, but mainly associated with industrialization and the formation of nation-states.[2] It is how society changes due to economic growth, science, technological innovations, and war or political upheavals. Social transformation affects people's interactions and lifestyles at all levels.

The family and religion are two basic institutions that are instrumental in social change and social transformation. From a sociological point of view, religion is defined as a system of roles and norms organised around the sacred realm that binds people together in social groups, the definition links religion

---

1. Paul N. Mwangi, "Religion and Kinship in Social Transformation: Challenges and Opportunities," in *2022 International Research Conference*, Global Research Dynamics and Innovative Solutions for Societal Transformation (PAC University: PAC University, 2022).

2. Stephen Castles, "Studying Social Transformation," *International Political Science Review* 22, no. 1 (January 2001): 13–32.

with the family as the basic unit in a society.³ The family is a group of people who are related by marriage, blood or adoption and who live together and share economic resources. Kinship refers to a network of people who are related by marriage, birth or adoption.⁴

Urbanization refers to the population shift from rural to urban areas, the corresponding decrease in the proportion of people living in rural areas, and how societies adapt to this change.⁵ It is predominantly the process by which towns and cities are formed and become larger as more people begin living and working in central areas. As people move from rural areas to urban areas and cities, their basic guarantors of identity, the family and religion, are disrupted. In the rural areas, kinship and family ties are stronger compared to those in the urban centres. Anonymity in the urban centre and the city is a common feature. In this anonymity, neighbours may see each other for years but they do not know each other. Life in the city leaves little time or energy to worry about anyone beyond my immediate family.⁶ It is a man-eat-man society. Christians in the city are therefore expected to make choices of either resigning to being part of a dog-eat-dog society or subscribing to the law of the jungle (every man for himself and the devil take the hindmost), or to seek the peace and prosperity of the city.⁷

In the family, identity is protected by protecting the other and affirming the other. The attitude in a good functioning family and in this case a Christian family is that we are not well unless all of us are well. In so doing we give expectations to the other. In rural areas, the expectation that I can depend on you and you can depend on me is common. We need each other for our wellbeing. With increased populations and in some cases the presence of slums, urban centres and cities can be hostile places with types and levels of crime being high compared to the same in rural areas. To survive in a hostile environment like an urban centre, people need to increase friends and minimize competition and conflicts. The challenge for CITAM is to rise above the character of the city and instead be a *shalom* community, revealing the dynamics of God's kingdom within the present.⁸

---

3. W. LaVerne Thomas, *Sociology: The Study of Human Relationships*, 5th ed. (New York: Harcourt Brace & Company, 1995), 361.
4. A. Reginald Radcliffe-Brown and Forde C. Daryll, *Africa Systems of Kinship and Marriage* (London: Oxford University Press, 1950), 40.
5. Thomas, *Sociology*.
6. Linda Ochola Adolwa, *Engaging the City* (Nairobi: Fearless Influencers, 2010), 12.
7. Adolwa, *Engaging the City*, 12.
8. Adolwa, *Engaging the City*, 15.

Human beings are social beings and as such their identity is tied to belonging. In seeking to belong human beings express their craving for identity. In urban centres and cities, both identity and belonging are fluid and in jeopardy. Urban life demonstrates inequality in almost everything. Yet CITAM has set itself mainly as an English urban ministry, therefore putting effort into the peace and prosperity of the urban areas and cities where there are CITAM assemblies. This is notable by the language and practice of hospitality, hybridity, ecumenicity and reconciliation in the context of different tribes that have been set against each other by politicians. The current research demonstrates how CITAM has initiated urban ministries in urban centres in Kenya to be able to care for people who feel vulnerable, yet want to genuinely express their Christian faith. The research identifies the pull and push factors that have made CITAM one of the successful church stories of our time.

The family in any society moves through a cycle of development.[9] In most societies, especially industrial societies, a new family is begun with each marriage based on ways in which family structure should be organized.[10] The family expands as children are born into the union. With the maturation of the children, a dispersion process to urban centres and other productive areas in society occurs. In the process of dispersion, sons and daughters acquire professional and technical competence and marry. The young adults enter into contractual arrangements with agents of socialization, which may take or send them to different parts of the country or even the world. Urban life and life away from the family of orientation means that parents are often isolated, and children born in new marriages are commonly raised with little or no contact with the network of people who are related to them by marriage, birth or adoption. It is easy for this lot to seek family ties in the church where they become members. The challenge here is for the church to make people who feel alienated feel that they belong. Without that, the end product may be a lack of a sense of community for a majority of members. Observations made at different church meetings and programmes indicate that a majority of people at CITAM have little or no personal or social involvement in the organization (Table 1). Apart from the Sunday worship services, other church programmes do not attract even half the attendance that is observable on Sundays. However, those who are in the same department exhibit kin group characteristics but it tends to be contractual. For instance, there is a monthly contribution for

---

9. Mwangi, "Religion and Kinship in Social Transformation," 7.
10. Thomas, *Sociology: The Study of Human Relationships*, 296.

membership welfare among many ministry teams and in the home fellowships also called Safari Groups.[11]

The impersonal circumstances in the urban centres necessitate that each build for oneself one's social universe, and the great mobility of the population may require that this be done numerous times during one's lifetime.[12] Blood and marriage-based kinship, on the other hand, is forever. Social ties based on kinship remain intact and provide a large measure of security to the individual. However, social ties based on contractual relations are often temporary and provisional. As individuals seek to fulfil their needs and wants in social ties, contractual relations foster insecurity. The church in this case has the challenge of dealing with the impersonality and fragmentation of relationships that comes with urbanization. Malachi may have thought of insecurity when he said that, unless the heart of the fathers is turned to the children and the heart of the children to the fathers, the earth should be smitten with a curse (Mal 4:5–6).

Purpose

The purpose of this study is to investigate and analyse how the language and the theme of the family are critical among the people of God. The family is one of the enduring social institutions despite the changes and chances in the world. As such, any social institution that seeks posterity needs to look at the family. The current study takes CITAM Valley Road as a case study to find out how an urban Pentecostal church has grown from one single congregation to almost forty congregations in major urban and sub-urban areas in Kenya. The growth has taken less than sixty-five years and more growth is still being registered. Today CITAM qualifies for the title of megachurch that stands out as a franchise.[13]

Church growth entails a healthy Christian community in the implementation of the Great Commission to make disciples of all nations. The process combines the eternal principles found in the Bible with the best insights of social and behavioural sciences employing the corporate world as its frame of reference. The research demonstrates how the corporate image of CITAM has embraced family values and used the ministry to the family as a pillar in

---

11. The researcher had been a member of the Safari Group since 2022 and witnessed the contributions being done, recorded and used for cases agreeable to the group.

12. Jules Henry, *Culture Against Man* (New York: Random House, n.d.), 147.

13. Wanjiru M. Gitau, *Megachurch Christianity Reconsidered: Millennials and Social Change in African Perspective* (Downers Grove: InterVarsity Press, 2018).

intentional discipleship. As such CITAM comes out as one big family and is committed to ministry to the family as the foundational unit in any society.[14]

The ministry to the family takes place along the life cycle of an individual in the family and the community. The major stages of the human lifecycle include conception, infancy, toddler years, childhood, puberty, older adolescence, adulthood, middle age, and the senior years.[15] This growth and development take place naturally in the family. The current research seeks to find out how CITAM ministers to the individual and the family to enhance and sustain church growth. The study uses ethnographic research to achieve this purpose. Ethnography involves the researcher immersing himself in the life of the community during the collection and then allowing the data to speak during the analysis of data. In the collection of data and the analysis of the data, the concept of the family and the life cycle in intentional discipleship marries with the theme for the ASET 2024 conference theme "I will plant my church and the gates of hell shall not overcome it." The family has withstood the test of time as a social institution. It is no wonder then that the church and, in this case, CITAM uses family language and seeks to minister to the individual in the family, not outside the family. The family is also the target in intentional discipleship for sustained church growth for victory: the gates of hell shall not prevail against it.

Methodology

Ethnographic research has different stages or steps. The steps are: preparation, data collection, data analysis, and finally, report writing. The current research is part of a major research project and as such, the current study is part of data analysis and report writing. The research focuses on emerging concepts and their relationships and integrates what secondary data sources or literature say about the emerging concept. In data collection, various methods have been used. The methods include unstructured observation and participant observation. The following are some of the unstructured observation sessions in which I have been involved:

a) Attending Sunday worship services

b) Attending Tuesday evening prayers

---

14. CITAM, "The Revised Constitution of Christ Is the Answer Ministries 2019," 2019, 6.
15. Paul D. Meier, Frank B. Minirth, and Frank B. Wichern, eds., *Introduction to Psychology and Counseling* (Grand Rapids: Baker Book House, 1982), 91.

c) Attending a wedding service and wedding reception
d) Attending two Solemn Assemblies
e) Attending online prayers with different themes
f) Joint Men's and Women's Fellowship meeting
g) Attending the online Springboard Conference

Table 1: Unstructured Observed Sessions against Time between September 2021 and 10 February 2023

S/No	Event Activity	Hours Per Session	Number of Sessions	Total Hours
1.	Sunday Worship Service	3hrs	41	123
2.	Tuesday evening prayers	2hrs	6	12
3.	Wedding Ceremony	3hrs	1	3
4.	Wedding reception	5hrs	1	5
5.	Solemn Assembly	4hrs	2	8
6.	Online prayers	1hr	15	15
7.	Spiritual Emphasis	1hr	7	7
8.	Online Springboard Conference 20–24 Sept 2022	5hrs	3	15
9.	Healing and restoration	1hr 30mins	3	4hrs 30min
10.	Revival online prayers	1hr	3	3
11.	Joint Men's and Women's Fellowship meeting	4hrs 30mins	1	4hrs 30mins
12.	Attended cross-over prayers	8hrs	1	8
13.	Participated in the new year 21 Days of Prayer and Fasting (12 online sessions)	1hr	12	12
	Total hours			220

After attending the above CITAM Valley Road activities, it became apparent that despite the huge congregation, CITAM Valley Road has different small ministry groups such as the Hospitality Team, Praise and Worship Team, the CITAM Choir, Men's Fellowship, Protocol Team, Christian Education Department, Women's Fellowship, Sunday School, Youth Church, Teens Church, and Safari Groups. The assumption is that in the small ministry groups one will find more kinship structures, practices and language compared to the huge congregation. Even with unstructured observation going on, it became apparent that it would be significant to gain access and become a participant observer in a few of the small ministry groups. When I thought about the different ministry groups and the best one to join, I picked Safari Groups, Membership Classes 101 and 203, and the Christian Education Department because they are ministry groups that are open to everyone. I was a participant observer in a Safari Group and the Men's Fellowship. The other ministry groups have some natural restrictions of some kind, mainly on age and gender.

The table below indicates the various sessions where I was a participant observer. In total, by 10 February 2023, I had one hundred and ten hours of participant observation of CITAM Valley Road Safari Group and Men's Fellowship.

Table 2: Participant Observer Events Activities from September 2021 to 10 February 2023

S/No	Activity	Hours per session	No. of sessions	Total
1.	Safari Grp Online Bible Study	1	34	34
2.	Safari Grp in-person Bible Study	2	5	10
3.	Safari Grp in-person visits	2	2	4
4.	Men's Fellowship Evening Meetings	2	4	8
5.	Attended CITAM Membership Class 101	3	1	3
6.	Attended CITAM Membership Class 201	3	1	3
7.	Attended CITAM Impartation meeting	4	1	4
8.	Attended CITAM membership interview	1	1	1
9.	Attended CITAM Valley Road CED briefing meeting	1	1	1
10.	Participated in Men at Work Jamuhuri Prison Visit	5	1	5
11.	Participated in Men at Work men's hymns worship night preparation	2	3	6
12.	Participated in the Commissioning Service for new members	3	1	3
13.	Participated in the Consistent Bible Orientation	1	2	2
14.	A member of the Consistent Bible Reading Cohort 4 WhatsApp Group	1	26	26
	Total hours			110

Access to a Safari Group, Men's Fellowship and the Membership Class 101 as a participant observer has continued to yield data that is significant for the research questions, objectives and purpose. The application of grounded theory in ethnographical research means that one has deep access to the community or group under investigation. Being a participant observer has helped in immersing myself in the community without the erosion of my identity as a researcher. In the words of Jeff Astley, the participant observer may be portrayed as being involved in a dialogue and in a dance where the group under investigation (Safari Group, Membership Classes, Men's Fellowship, or Christian Education Department) is at the centre. As a participant observer, I took note of the conversations that took place during the meetings. The conversation and dance are a strong metaphor in participant observation that the researcher becomes a participant:

> The conversation they engage in, as they go backwards and forwards, circles around some concern or another, but always returns to the point from which the dance began. It is real conversation, for the partners speak during the dance; and as with all authentic conversation, critical freedom and receptivity are equally important in allowing the subject matter to take over in the back-and-forth movements between text and interpreter.[16]

However, both the unstructured observation and participant observation methods yielded different data types and data forms. For better results, the application of grounded theory requires constant honing of the research senses so that one is not carried away by the dance or the conversation and forgets the purpose for which one is so involved. Being in a research team, I continued to have fortnightly meetings even as I proceeded with the research project. During the meetings, the team members share their experiences and ask each other questions based on the purpose and objective of the study. The sessions assist in clarifying our research questions as we continue with the research and help in refocusing our attention on the data that is related to the research questions and research objectives. The current presentation is part of the process of honing the researcher's senses and refocusing the research lenses.

---

16. Jeff Astley, *Ordinary Theology: Looking, Listening and Learning Theology*, Explorations in Practical, Pastoral and Empirical Theology (London: Routledge, 2017), 3.

Type and Form of Data Collected

In the words of Jeff Astley, the researcher is involved in looking, listening and learning in theology as it is expressed from the ground:[17] in other words, looking at structures at CITAM Valley Road which enable persons to live together and cooperate with one another in an orderly social life similar to African kinship.[18] As of 10 February 2023, I had done 220 hours of unstructured observation and 110 hours being a participant observer. The total is three hundred and seven hours. The hours have made it possible for me to collect data in different types and forms. From unstructured observation and participant observation, I continued to collect data that was of different types: mainly words, images, or objects. I also obtained different published materials used for Bible Study guides for the membership classes and a guide into different CITAM ministries. The materials help in identifying how CITAM links persons together by convergence of interest and sentiment and how it controls and limits conflicts that are always possible as a result of divergence of sentiment and interest.[19]

The forms of qualitative data collected include participant observation notes, field notes, photos, videos and reflections on various activities observed. The data point to how social links, and social capital at CITAM Valley Road are nurtured and maintained. Of interest is the individual and the family in the ministry at CITAM. The data point to how the web of deep-seated longings of fluctuating variability are fulfilled for the individual, family, group and congregation. More research will bring more data and sufficient data will lead to better interpretation that leads to better understanding.

Theorizing on the Family and the Ministry to the Family

Individuals will always be part of a family and as members of a family, each individual goes through the life cycle of a human being.[20] Observable at CITAM Valley Road is a focus on the individual and the family through the various church programmes and even the built environment. The built environment and the church programmes capture the needs and the ages of various members of the family. For instance, in the main sanctuary, there are spaces for mothers and their children to follow the service as it goes on. For the children that are

---

17. Astley, *Ordinary Theology: Looking, Listening and Learning Theology*.
18. Reginald and Daryll, *Africa Systems of Kinship and Marriage*, 3.
19. Reginald and Daryll, *Africa Systems of Kinship and Marriage*, 3.
20. Paul D. Meier, Frank B. Minirth, and Frank B. Wichern, *Introduction to Psychology and Counseling: Christian Perspectives and Applications* (Grand Rapids: Baker Book House, 1982).

old enough to attend Sunday School classes, there are teachers, programmes and spaces set aside for them in an adjacent building called the Jubilee Ministry Centre (JMC). The spaces within the main sanctuary are shared according to the age of the children. The walls and the floors are designed to give the keen eyes of children something to look at and enjoy. The building is also accessible to any family member who has a disability. The JMC building has a ramp from the ground floor to the top floor. The main sanctuary has a ramp into it. As such the structure of the building is set to accommodate individuals even when they are at a vulnerable stage of growth and development.

In the JMC building, there is a famous boardroom where departmental meetings are held.[21] The notable aspect of the boardroom is the portraits of those who have served as senior pastors at CITAM Valley Road. After the ministry of Dennis White and his wife as Senior Pastor, the ministry took a new dimension in leadership and growth. In terms of growth, Nairobi Pentecostal Church Valley Road became Christ is the Answer Ministries and the one assembly led by Dennis White and others before him, has become an urban ministry in Kenya with almost forty other local assemblies across the country. With this growth and expansion, the senior clergyperson for the ministry is now called the CITAM presiding bishop. The current presiding bishop is the third one. The portraits of the presiding bishops who have retired are also on display. The boardroom has been intentionally named the Founders Boardroom. Interestingly from an African perspective one of the officials from the Men's Fellowship while in a meeting called them the ancestors.[22] Ancestors are a major component of the African family. They are respected and their lives are to be emulated for their blessings to flow to the living.[23]

In addition to the accessibility of JCC, the entrance main sanctuary has ramps. There are also accessible parking slots always reserved for People with Disabilities (PWDs). Accessibility is also addressed when it comes to the seating spaces. The researcher has observed wheelchair users being able to get to the ground floor of the sanctuary and even access the altar and preach. Observable is the fact that in almost every service there is a sign language interpreter. The announcements are also in print and audio mode. Both models are projected onto the huge screens that are in the sanctuary. To crown this concern for

---

21. I had the privilege of attending two meetings in the Founders Boardroom.
22. On 9 February 2023 in a meeting between the leaders of Men at Work officials, some members and the Voices of Hope Africa, one of the officials indicated that the portraits are for the ancestors and they hear what is discussed in meetings.
23. Samuel Waje Kunhiyop, *African Christian Ethics* (Carlisle: HippoBooks, 2008), 68.

members of the congregation who are PWDs, there is a Christian Education Department (CED) group for them. The group is called the Challengers. Their matron is an elder who is a wheelchair user after she had an accident and lost the ability to walk. The care for PWDs demonstrates family values where each member (and more so in a church) are to be given their space to grow in faith and practice their faith and minister to others.

Observable every first Sunday of the month is the presence of children, youth and teens in the main service. The service is also a holy communion service so the whole family is ministered to from the same pulpit and by the same people. Such family services should be more frequent if not being made to be the norm.[24] The intention is an intergenerational handing over of the faith. If intergenerational handover does not take place, old members leave the scene and the CITAM culture and tradition has no one to pick and take it forward. The senior Pastor Justus Mugambi keeps reminding the congregants to be comfortable with the children in the service. He also encourages the parents to make the children comfortable so that they enjoy the service. Observable in the same service is the inclusion of the youth into the praise and worship team leading the service. The family service targets the individual in the family and the family unit as well. During such services, the four-thousand-seater sanctuary is full and spilling over for both services.

Notable also every third Sunday of the month is the dedication of children. The event has been hailed as a sign of biological evangelism. The children thus dedicated are expected to grow and join the various CED groups and eventually become CITAM members. The parents of the children are taken through training on how to raise their children in a Christian way. The parents are to endeavour to raise their children to be disciples of Christ so that when they are eighteen years and above, they can consent to be CITAM members and abide by the teachings that uphold CITAM. The training of parents is made possible through an equipped counselling centre aimed at helping people with life challenges to find their bearing in God. It was reported during the fourth Northern Region Annual General Meeting that the counselling centre not only ministers to members of CITAM Valley Road but even those who are not CITAM members. The counselling is geared toward holistic human development. Age-related physical, intellectual, and social changes occur

---

24. John Nganga, Sermon on Responding to Emerging Trends: The Safari (23 October 2022).

throughout life and therefore ministry to the whole person needs to be centred on the human development cycle.[25]

When caring for the family, food is an important component. Food brings a family together. At CITAM Valley Road there is the Tulivu Cafeteria that serves food, cold drinks and snacks from 6:30 am to 8:30 pm, even on Sundays and even when the worship services are going on. When Jesus was ministering to multitudes, all members of the family were seen to be present and food was shared. At one point, when the children wanted to get to Jesus, the apostles pushed them away; but Jesus reprimanded them and told them to allow the children to come to him. He told them that they must receive the kingdom of God with the innocence of children. Another demonstration of the family members in Jesus's meetings is when he fed the multitude. It is reported that there were men, women and children. The disciples wanted the people to be dismissed so that they go and feed. However, Jesus asked them what they had so that the multitude would be fed. With two fish and five loaves of bread the multitude of five thousand men was fed and twelve baskets remained. Food is essential in nurturing memories and constructing identities.[26] The online celebration of the Holy Communion during the COVID-19 lockdown maintained CITAM's identity in a time of crisis. It also helps to bring more people to the CITAM family.

The Tulivu Café also prepares meals for the pastors and the elders every Sunday and any time there are meetings. This means that one cannot give an excuse of hunger when one fails to offer excellent service to the waiting congregations. On the other hand, it saves time since one does not need to go outside of the church compound to look for a meal or a snack.[27] The Tulivu Café is a copy of the CITAM Kadolta Resort that offers meals, and conference facilities for board meetings and for groups that go for team building activities. The Resort is advertised most of the time during the holiday season. When I visited the Resort, I met an elderly couple who said they were on holiday. The man was holding a Bible on one side and they seemed to be enjoying their stay. Although it is an income-generating project, the Resort has been hailed as a means of saving money for the ministry since CITAM does not need to hire facilities for conferences and team building.[28] During a visit to the

---

25. James S. Nairne, *Psychology*, 4th ed. (London: Vicki Knight, 2006), 99.

26. Monica Janowski and Fiona Kerlogue, eds., *Kinship and Food in South East Asia* (Copenhagen: Nordic Institute of Asian Studies, 2007).

27. *60 Years Anniversary: CITAM @60 Torch* (CITAM Eldoret: CITAM Eldoret TV, 2019).

28. *Celebrating Milestones: CITAM @ 60* (CITAM Online: CITAM Church Online, 2019).

Resort, various CITAM groups were having different sessions at the Kadolta Resort. Tulivu Café and Kadolta Resort are examples of Christian businesses in a secular context.

During Cantata,[29] the CITAM children's ministry teams up with the other ministries to minister to the congregation about the birth of Jesus.[30] The other ministries involved in the Cantata service are the drama ministry, the youths, the choir, the praise and worship and the teenagers. The combination of the various groups demonstrates a family setup both for the team ministering and the content that is presented. The audience coming from families will be entertained and blessed and learn more about the Christian faith in a family setup. One would imagine the amount of time and effort that is put into the preparation for a Cantata service that touches the lives of all members of the family, and the presenters are representatives of the members of the family. The theme of the relevance of the family in intentional discipleship runs through a majority of the programmes if not all the programmes at CITAM Valley Road. The CITAM Valley Road Education Department (CED) coordinates all the programmes and the various ministries by resourcing them and training those who are responsible for the various CED groups. A recurrent theme in the CED literature for different groups and different trainings is intentional discipleship.[31]

The language of the family about the people of God or church is well grounded in the Bible. In the Old Testament, Israel is seen as the children of God. In the New Testament Christians have been birthed into the family of God through the sacrifice of Christ at the cross. As children of God, Christians are therefore members of one big family, hence the Pentecostal reference of brother and sister. The names express a relationship that members have with each other and with the one who has called them. The relationship is that of a covenant and not a contract which is an exchange of goods.[32] The apostle Paul goes further to talk about the spirit of sonship and how Christians are right in calling God "Abba Father." Therefore, truthfulness to Scripture and truthfulness to the African culture endear the language of the family to CITAM members.

---

29. Cantanta is a concert in celebration of Christmas some days before Christmas.

30. The researcher observed two Cantata services: one in 2021 and another in 2022. The 2022 was a great improvement from the 2021 one.

31. Christ is The Answer Ministries (CITAM) Valley Road, *Transforming God's People to Transform the World: Ministry Booklet* (Nairobi: CITAM Valley Road, n.d.), 2.

32. Silvano Borruso, *The Art of Total Living* (Nairobi: Paulines, 2008), 103.

In an urban Pentecostal church in Africa, the need for belonging and identity are serious needs. In facing this challenge CITAM has identified Safari Groups, what is called in other quarters Small Christian Communities, as the basic unit of the church next to the various CED groups in the church.[33] It is in the Safari Groups (SG) that individual members of CITAM have a chance for structured fellowship that can be hard if not impossible in the megachurch. Individual believers are expected to attend the SG meetings with their families. In an urban context, however, getting the entire family into an SG meeting is next to impossible. The city dynamics compromise the availability of members. This challenge has been compounded by the COVID-19 pandemic. However, the intention to have the family in the SG on the part of CITAM leadership is noble. This intention is backed by thematic Bible study materials that help the individual members to grow in faith in the context of the family and express their life in their daily living. Scripture therefore plays a normative role in guiding the expression of community.[34]

Summary and Conclusion

The city is a space and that space is not neutral.[35] People from different backgrounds come to the city with their different beliefs and practices. In Nairobi for instance, one can notice zones based on the community that one comes from and also the economic status. CITAM may have attempted to solve one of the challenges by targeting the urban person. For the urban person, English is the language of communication in all CITAM activities: even the materials for Bible study are in English. But as it has been noted in this chapter, the focus on the family and the practice of family values has endeared many to the ministry. As such the church is noted as a magnification of the family.

Theologically, the family language is expected in a church setting. The intentional discipleship with a focus on the basic social unit in the society means that the gospel is translated into people's lives in a more practical way, making it easy for members to identify with CITAM Valley Road. This expression of Christian ministry helps to perpetuate victory that is intergenerational based on the exchange of persons. When the church is family writ large the gates of

---

33. The researcher has been a member of a Safari Group from February 2022 to the present. He does whatever every member of the group is expected to do: leading, contributions, visiting and Bible Study once every week.
34. Kunhiyop, *African Christian Ethics*, 70.
35. Adolwa, *Engaging the City*, 29.

hell will not overcome it, since they have not overcome the family – the oldest social institution and the basic social unit. CITAM attempts to build an African community that is conscious of the urban reality but firmly rooted in Scripture. As the apostle Paul says (Eph 5:32), the mystery of the church is hidden in the marriage and family relationship. It is therefore not an understatement to say that the church is family writ large.

Bibliography

60th Anniversary: CITAM @60 Torch. CITAM Eldoret: CITAM Eldoret TV, 2019.
Adolwa, Linda Ochola. *Engaging the City*. Nairobi: Fearless Influencers, 2010.
Astley, Jeff. *Ordinary Theology: Looking, Listening and Learning Theology*. Explorations in Practical, Pastoral and Empirical Theology. London: Routledge, 2017.
Borruso, Silvano. *The Art of Total Living*. Nairobi: Paulines, 2008.
Castles, Stephen. "Studying Social Transformation." *International Political Science Review* 22.1 (January 2001): 13–32.
Celebrating Milestones: CITAM @ 60. CITAM Online: CITAM Church Online, 2019.
Christ is The Answer Ministries (CITAM) Valley Road. *Transforming God's People to Transform the World: Ministry Booklet*. Nairobi: CITAM Valley Road, n.d.
CITAM. "The Revised Constitution of Christ Is the Answer Ministries 2019." 2019.
Gitau, Wanjiru M. *Megachurch Christianity Reconsidered: Millennials and Social Change in African Perspective*. Downers Grove: InterVarsity Press, 2018.
Henry, Jules. *Culture Against Man*. New York: Random House, n.d.
Janowski, Monica, and Fiona Kerlogue, eds. *Kinship and Food in South East Asia*. Copenhagen: Nordic Institute of Asian Studies, 2007.
Kunhiyop, Samuel Waje. *African Christian Ethics*. Carlisle: HippoBooks, 2008.
Meier, Paul D., Frank B. Minirth, and Frank B. Wichern, eds. *Introduction to Psychology and Counseling: Christian Perspectives and Applications*. Grand Rapids: Baker Book House, 1982.
Mwangi, Paul N. "Religion and Kinship in Social Transformation: Challenges and Opportunities." 2022 International Research Conference. PAC University: PAC University, 2022.
Nairne, James S. *Psychology*. 4th edition. London: Vicki Knight, 2006.
Radcliffe-Brown, Reginald A., and Forde C. Daryll. *Africa Systems of Kinship and Marriage*. London: Oxford University Press, 1950.
Thomas, W. LaVerne. *Sociology: The Study of Human Relationships*. 5th edition. New York: Harcourt Brace & Company, 1995.

14

Paucity of Meditation in Christian Worship

Implications for African Evangelicals

Kelechi Bartram

Baptist College of Theology, Igede-Ekiti, Nigeria

Abstract

The "seemingly noisy" nature of Christian worship in contemporary times has almost eclipsed the significance of the word through meditation. Hence, the worship setting becomes an arena of "joyful noise," without sound spiritual depth in the written word and bereft of inner connectivity with the creator. The absence of meditating on the word of God in Christian worship creates a spiritual vacuum that cannot be filled by mentally constructed numerous diverse church activities such as music and praise in worship with all their wonderful sounds and rhythms. As compelling as they are, they may not substitute for the word of God. Rather, a Christian worship experience should inculcate meditating on the word as written in the Scriptures as part of the worship process. The word of God proclaimed and heard is the bedrock of evangelical ecclesiology and this important element of Christian worship in the contemporary era seems lost in the oblivion of jubilant praise in worship. It is the tangible connection that meditation impacts through contemplation of God's word. Hence, this chapter focuses on one aspect of worship: music as expressed through songs and praises in a worship context. Its unguided use could threaten or eclipse the hearing of God's word and consequently overshadow meditation in worship. Furthermore, it might threaten African evangelical ecclesiology, where the centrality of the word in worship is an enviable heritage. This chapter adopts a historical and theological approach as it attempts to examine experience in worship; an introduction to meditation. Also, the role of music in Christian worship, with a brief historical survey of the use of music in worship. Furthermore, it articulates a theological perspective on meditation, a reflection on ecclesiology and African ecclesiology in particular. Lastly, the paper addresses implications of the study on African ecclesiology. The significance of this study points to the awakening of African evangelical ecclesiology to the importance of meditation on the word of God in the worship context, thereby emphasizing the Scriptures' centrality over every aspect of worship. Meditation on the word of God can transform worshippers' lives and prepare them for ecclesiological mandates and the growth of evangelical churches in Africa.

Key words: meditation, Christian worship, religious experience, ecclesiology, African ecclesiology

Introduction

Claus Westermann stated, "The word's purpose is to reach the listener and cause a response. . . . The word is the content of what God has said . . . and become the subject of reflection. . . . every word of God . . . has a function in what happens between God and humanity."[1] This implies that the actions and reactions of Christians in worship reflect what is contained in the written word. Unfortunately, because the word of God in most Christian worship settings has been eclipsed by sounds of music in praise and songs, the word is hardly heard, and meditating on it is almost forgotten. Therefore, worship activity through music and praise songs that eclipse hearing the word of God could be termed "noisy," as good as it may appear. The word "noisy" is not meant to be derogatory but to indicate that which overshadows the hearing of God's word in a worship setting. The form of Christian worship in contemporary times has almost eclipsed the significance of meditating on the word of the Scriptures, even as the music, songs, and sounds are played.

Hence, one of the cherished heritages of the evangelicals stands threatened; the hearing of the word of God. Sometimes worshippers struggle to hear and

---

1. Claus Westermann, *What Does the Old Testament Say About God?* (Atlanta: John Knox Press, 1979), 17.

understand what is sung in words, such that the worship setting becomes an arena of "joyful noise," without sound spiritual depth and bereft of inner connectivity with the creator, which the scriptural words can effect. The absence of meditation in Christian worship creates a spiritual gulf waiting to be filled – not by mentally constructing numerous diverse church activities but rather by hearing and meditating on the word of God. However, meditation in Christian worship becomes a means to create more depth in spiritual connection with God and enrich Christians' understanding of the creator through his written word, which any aspect of the worship must not eclipse. That is the pursuit of this chapter.

Concept of Experience in Religious Worship

Recently, scholars have described religion as a way of life, a central part of human experience and culture. It has existed at all times and in all societies. James Nelson citing Meissner opined that religion was traditionally used to refer to all aspects of the human relationship to the divine, which is greater than humans are, the "goal of all human life and value."[2] Imasogie conceives of religion as "Man's understanding of his relationship with the Supreme Being."[3] Religion is both transcendent and immanent as it involves a human person, continuous experience, and participation; Leowenthal (citing Ninian Smart) posited that "the immanent nature of religion is perceived as a human activity with some following dimensions; it is practical, ritualistic, and includes prayer, worship, and meditation; experiential, emotional, and materialistic."[4] According to Bolaji Idowu, "Religion has several purposes which belong to the very fabrics of life."[5] Alister Hardy holds that "religion calls for opening up of the self, the letting that which is more than the self, flow through the organism and direct its experience."[6]

---

2. James Nelson, *Psychology, Religion and Spirituality* (New York: Springer Publishers, 2009), 30.

3. O. Imasogie, *African Traditional Religion* (Benin City: Prestige Print Concept, 2008), 33.

4. Kate Loewenthal, *The Psychology of Religion: A Short Introduction* (Oxford: One World, 1995), 2. Citing Smart Ninian, *The World Religion* www.goodreads.com.

5. Bolaji Idowu, *African Traditional Religion: A Definition* (Ibadan: Fountain Publication Press, 1991), 1.

6. Alister Hardy, *The Divine Flame*, Religious Experience Research Unit (RERU) (Oxford: Oxford Press, 1966), 22.

By way of deduction, it could be observed that religion, in its transcendent and immanent aspects, expresses the human-divine relationship in a holistic way as Richard Gehman observed citing John Mbiti: "Religion permeates into all the departments of life."[7] He further posited that "in Africa the people experience religious dimension of life in everything they do."[8]

In addition, it encompasses a sense of awe, sacred, holy, and mysterious yet humanistic in expression, defined by one religious affinity yet somewhat comprehensible even in other traditions. It necessitates feeling, real contact with evidential proofs, religious significance, and mental impulses that give the experiment a concrete stance for better awareness and knowledge of the self and the divine. This buttresses Idowu's assertion that:

> There can be nothing like religion in abstraction or religion considered apart from the person who worships and practices the tenets of their faith, rather the mind and consciousness of man and the consequent ability to apprehend. There can be no religion to speak of, if it has no meaning and significance to the life of its adherents.[9]

The worshipper knows something has happened to him as he engages in worship and meditation.

Furthermore, these experiences are evident in worship. As a religious experience, it exudes the power of the divine, which moves many adherents to worship and acknowledge the greatness of the transcendent power. Also, in prayers: where informal communication holds, some prayers are specific, involving gratitude, repentance, or petition, in silence and listening to the divine.[10] In addition, a solitary attitude opens to what is beyond the everyday busy life of the worshipper to silent reflection on the divine as the worshipper meditates. Lastly is the sense of a divine presence; a sudden awareness of divine presence pervades the mind of adherents who experience the reality of their beliefs in practical and daily life.[11] The fact of this worship experience shows

---

7. Richard Gehman, *African Traditional Religion in Biblical Perspective* (Jos: Oasis International, 2005), 51. Citing John Mbiti, *African Religions and Philosophy* (London: SPCK, 1969), 1.

8. Richard Gehman, *African Traditional Religion in Biblical Perspective*, 51.

9. Idowu, *African Traditional Religion*, 12.

10. Mamanne Rankin, "Introduction to Religious Experience" (Alister Hardy Religious Experience Research Centre, 2005), 13–15.

11. Mamanne, "Introduction to Religious Experience," 17–24.

an encounter has occurred and could be verified in the permanent changes observed in the life and activities of the experiment.

In Nelson's view, certain concrete changes of attitudes that have become permanent could be observed in the lives of worshippers, finding guidance in life, increased awareness of their close connection to the divine, change in profession from unbelief to belief, and a comforting sense of a presence helping a person through life.[12] By implication, in the Christian context, this sought experience occurs in the meditation process, when the adherent, through the written word, encounters the person of God and experiences a positive change in life, expressed in the private life of the worshippers and in their social context.

Meditation

Michael West further observes that meditation is an exercise in which the individual turns attention or awareness to dwell upon a single object, concept, sound, image, or experience, intending to gain greater spiritual insight.[13] In addition, Stephen Ayankeye views meditation "as religious devotion to gain insight into the deep and secret things of God for an improved life of the meditator."[14] Furthermore, some activities experienced by religious adherents are mediated through the mind; meditation is a way of coming to experience life by encountering the mind of the divine directly. Meditation involves keeping human lives in perspective for greater awareness of the mind of the object of worship.

Furthermore, in the Christian context, the questions raised by adherents are: How does meditation as part of the Christian worship experience influence the experiencer's sense of meaning in life concerning beliefs and aspirations? What meaning does it hold for the experiencer? Meditation cannot be practiced in a vacuum. Humans are meaning-seeking, connected to the core sense of their purpose in life, and through it, they can interpret life issues as they understand them.[15] Through meditation, the tangible nature of the spiritual connection is attained. This experience becomes a context for meaning, a

---

12. James, *Psychology, Religion and Spirituality*, 32–33.
13. Michael West, *The Psychology of Meditation: Research and Practice* (New York: Oxford University Press, 1987), 4.
14. Stephen Anayankeye, "Meditation as a Religious Experience in Africa: A Pastoral Psychological Approach," *UMCATC Journal of Theological Studies* 10 (July 2013): 170–77.
15. C. L. Parker, "Religiousness, Spirituality and Health: A Meaning Systems Perspective," *Journal of Behavioral Medicine* 30 (2007): 4–10.

platform fundamental to peoples' understanding of the divinity, their world, and life itself. Therefore, meditation is one way to attain an encounter with God, which in turn creates a positive effect in the worshipper's life, especially through the word in the context of Christian worship as it relates to church music.

Concept of Christian Worship in Relation to Church Music

Worship is the language every culture, race, nationality, and humanity understands. Andrew Teta sees worship as the human response to the divine's perceived presence, which transcends normal human activity and is holy.[16] Worship is not taught to any race; every part of the universe understands what it is. In human society, it is the commemoration of life and community, whether in difficult or happy times, as it makes up the basic incorporated role, which is significant to a communal life in its search for "wholeness" and peaceful co-existence that lie beyond the present experience.[17] In a similar view, transporting the above insight on worship into the Christian domain, worship is fundamental to every Christian community, and one of the ways Christians affirm their commitment to God and one another is expressed through different forms and actions displayed therein.

Furthermore, it is understood that worship could be private and communal in setting, or public and corporate. The fundamental reason for worship is to glorify God through diverse forms faithful to the word of God. One of the aspects of worship that command excitement is music. It is incorporated into the church liturgy and ordinances. It is "both celebration and instruction."[18] In worship through music, the church celebrates all that God is and has done through the word read, taught, sung, or dramatized; the church hears God speak.[19] Millard Erickson observes, "The church centres its attention on whom and what God is, not on self, not on satisfying its feelings."[20] This is not a matter of feeling good; a tangible encounter is needed.

---

16. Andrew Teta, "Sweeter also Than Honey: John Ruskin 'Psalms,'" *Year Book of English Studies* 39.1/2, Literature and Religion (2009), 114–20.

17. AMECA Pastoral Institute, *Living Worship in Africa Today*. Spearhead no. 62, vol. 7 of *An Experimental Source-Book for Religious Education* (Gaba Publications, 1980).

18. Howard Snyder, "A Living Community," in *The Lion Handbook Of Christian Belief*, ed. Robin Keeley (Herts: Lion Publishing, 1982), 382–411.

19. Snyder, "A Living Community," 396.

20. Millard Erickson, *Christian Theology*, 2nd ed. (Grand Rapids: Baker Academic, 1998), 1066.

In addition, when sounds and instruments of hymns, praise, and music evoke feelings that overshadow the content of God's word in the lyrics, in Randy Arnett's position, "the focus moves from God to man. The quality of worship is determined by the efforts from worshipers to manifest . . . as man works worship."[21] Though expression of worship could be done through songs, praises in worship, and dancing, one should understand that music ought to motivate worship on which meditation on the words of the Scripture is exercised. Hence, Charles Hummel reiterates, "The level of noise made during singing, especially regarding the musical instruments, could have to be reduced to enable worshipers to enjoy the music and understand the wordings of the songs. One respondent felt that the noise made by the musical instruments was too much."[22] Corroborating the statement of Hummel is Alain Smith: "the noise made by musical instruments could deafen the ears of worshipers and may put off first-time worshipers."[23] Samson Ayokunle is inclined to the above opinions and highlighted "At times, the worship of diaspora African churches is too noisy."[24] However, Robert Webber applies a more subtle emphasis, expressing that "each of these sounds may be looked on as a means of support for the word . . . the moods and meaning of each part of worship are conveyed in the sound made as well as in words spoken."[25] In as much as the word and sounds of music are authentic to worship, the word of God must not be eclipsed.

Moreover, Conrad Mbewe posits, "Our congregation singing also needs to be more effective in capturing the richness of the full menu of Christian doctrine and experience."[26] George Janvier observed that "music in a worship service makes the audience enjoy the service as they listen to the singing and words of the songs."[27] In all ramifications, as the sounds of music lift the

---

21. Randy Arnett, *Pentecostalization: the Evolution of Baptists in Africa* (Eldon: Randy Arnett, 2017), 137.

22. Charles Hummel, *Fire in the Fireplace: Charismatic Renewal in the Nineties* (Downers Grove: InterVarsity Press, 1993), 243–44.

23. Alain Smith, "Report of our Visit to Teaching-Centred African Baptist Church, Kensington," *Liverpool* (15th March 2006), 1.

24. Samson Ayokunle, *Communities of Faith in Diaspora: Elements and Liturgy of Worship* (Ibadan: Nigerian Baptist Press, 2021), 126.

25. Robert Webber, *Worship Old and New* (Grand Rapids: Zondervan Publishing House, 1982), 177.

26. Conrad Mbewe, "What Should Happen During Worship Service?" Chapter 9 of *God's Design for the Church: A Guide for African Pastors' and Ministry Leaders* (Illinois: Crossway, 2020), 132–39.

27. George Janvier, *Leading the Church in Music and Worship*, 2nd edition (Jos: African Christian Textbooks, 2017), 48.

mind and souls of the worshippers in preparation for an encounter with God, it is the word heard and understood that provides the encounter needed in worship. This view will lead to a brief historical overview of Christian worship in relation to church music.

Brief Historical Overview of Christian Worship in Relation to Church Music

The covenant agreement between God and his people Israel in Exodus 19–24 was the first such gathering, an assembly convened by God. This gathering gave rise to an institution of the covenant consequent upon which worship was predicated. Obedience to the word of the covenant as read to the congregation and their subsequent response to pay allegiance to what was heard meant these words were intelligible, well understood, and made sense to the people. Hence, worship was based on the word of God as written in the Book of the Covenant.

Webber stresses that the ideology that propelled the synagogue institution hinged on the preservation and propagation of the word of God for the Jewish community. Hence, all the activities comprising education, religion, and social/relational teachings were done to encourage understanding of the word of the covenant and to live by it; the *shema* in Deuteronomy 6:4–9, reward and punishment in Deuteronomy 11:13–21, and striving for holiness in Deuteronomy 28:1–11.[28] This meant that the synagogue worship was word-based.

The nature and pattern of the synagogue worship impacted the church of the first century. Worship activities were done within the confines of the synagogue. Merrill Tenney suggests that "the epistle of James 2:1–2 implies that the Christian community to whom it was written was still worshiping there, but because of persistent rejection of the gospel of Christ by Jewish people, the church and the synagogue parted company."[29] He further claims that the "recitation of the *shema* in Deut 6:4–35 was accompanied by a sentence of praise to God . . . and opportunity for silent prayer by the congregation."[30] James White adds that in the apostolic church, "the joy of Christian worship is reflected in singing . . . of Psalms, hymns and making melody unto the Lord. The harp, lyre, and string instruments were used while expressing

---

28. Webber, *Worship Old and New*, 27.
29. Merrill Tenney, *New Testament Survey* (Grand Rapids: Eerdmans, 1961), 94.
30. Tenney, *New Testament Survey*, 94.

the Christological hymns in Phil 2:6–11; Rom 11:33–35; Col 1:15–20."[31] Tenney corroborates the views of James and posits that the apostolic church "witnessed the incorporation of many worship materials; church hymns, baptismal catechetical literature, creedal statements, confession, doxologies, and benedictions."[32] Therein, the songs in worship reflected the words of the Scriptures and did not overshadow them.

In the early church, the spread of Christianity to diverse parts of the world came with the shift in ecclesiastical style of worship as each people, language, or tribe, in their loyalty to Christ, developed peculiar forms of worship congruent with their cultural diversity yet preserved the unity of faith.[33] Bruce Nicholls, observing a church in Ghana, writes: "the worship in this church in Ghana is strongly influenced by the Christian's local and national culture so is the whole way these Christians understand and express their faith."[34] Aside from the liturgy, the paintings, sculptures, and architectural works and the use of the lyrics of Psalms in music stimulated meditation in the worshippers. These ceremonial forms were the means through which worship was conducted; however, the words of the Scripture and sacrament were constant reminders of the death and resurrection of Christ.[35] The tenets of the Christian faith were maintained irrespective of any cultural garb it had; the core of the faith remained.

The Reformation era witnessed the expansion of Christianity to the north and east of Europe; there was an increase in congregational singing. "Roman Catholic and Zwinglian congregations remained largely mute, while Lutherans and Anabaptists burst into singing. The congregation participated fully and vigorously in singing hymns and the rest of liturgy; Calvin insisted that music was welcomed as long as the words were scriptural."[36] This era witnessed the development of various musical instruments, including the pipe organ. The Reformers persisted in prioritizing the word to its ancient and proper place in worship. For the Lutherans,

---

31. James White, *A Brief History of Christian Worship* (Nashville: Abingdon Press, 1993), 36–37.
32. Webber, *Worship Old and New*, 42.
33. White, *A Brief History of Christian Worship*, 40.
34. Bruce Nicholls, "We All Believe Something," in *The Lion Handbook Of Christian Belief*, ed. Robin Keeley (Herts: Lion Publishing, 1982), 30–37.
35. Robert Webber, *Worship Old and New*, 67–70.
36. James, *A Brief History of Christian Worship*, 137.

> the sum of the matter is that everything shall be done so that the word prevails . . . we profit by nothing so much as the word. People must give ear to the word alone; Martin Luther went to the extreme to abolish the use of organ in music, pictures, relics, vestments, and anything that will detract from the centrality of the word.[37]

In connection with the above, John Barber reiterated that Luther "was extremely cautious in protecting the word of God from any admixture, 'I wish to compose sacred hymns so that the word of God may dwell among the people also through songs.'"[38] While the Zwinglians and Calvinists retained to a certain measure the liturgy, which includes words of Scripture, the Puritans comprising the Baptists, Congregationalists, and Quakers in their evangelical faith propagation became anti-liturgical. They emphasized the need for understanding God's word and experiencing God.[39] By way of deduction, loyalty to the word of God superseded form and actions expressed in worship. The insistence by the leading Christian figures of this era that worshippers hear and understand the written word attests to the priority given to the word of God in worship, and any Christian generation must never undermine this.

A Theology of Meditation

The Hebrew word translated "meditation" could imply to mutter, speak, talk, and read Scripture aloud, as was Jewish practice among themselves or to one another in Deuteronomy 6:6–9; Acts 8:26–40.[40] These passages emphasize continuous attention and reflection on the word of God. From the biblical perspective, meditation is a reflection on a subject through muttering, reading, and talking; even if it involves singing, there is something to focus on or contemplate. Several cognates to the term "meditate" appear in the Scriptures, such as "to delight, to remember, to consider, to muse, to search out and to ponder."[41] In Joshua 1:8, the subject of meditation is the word of God in the

---

37. Webber, *Worship Old and New*, 76.
38. John Barber, "Luther and Calvin on Music and Worship," *Reformed Perspectives Magazine* 8, no.2 6 (June 25–July 1, 2006), 2–18.
39. Webber, *Worship Old and New*, 75–77.
40. Warren Wiersbe, "Pentateuch," *Bible Exposition Commentary*, CD-ROM, Version 2.0. 2007.
41. Edward Curtis, "Ancient Psalms and Modern Worship," *Bibliotheca Sacra* 154 (1997), 285–96.

book of the law (the words of the Sinaitic covenant), so also Psalm 1:2. Edward Curtis posits, "Meditation is a central theme in worship reflected in the Psalms and encouraged the focus and meditation on God's truth and deeds that is often called for in Scripture."[42] In the passages in Psalms 77:12, 145:5 and 119:27, the subject to meditate upon is the "works of the Lord" – his action and deeds in the history of personal and national salvation.

Furthermore, in Psalm 119:23 and 48, the statue of the Lord is the subject of meditation. In addition, in passages such as Psalm 119:15 and 7, the focus turns to meditation on the "precepts of the Lord," while in Psalm 63:6, worshippers are urged to meditate on God himself. They also meditate on the word of God in Psalm 119:148 and on the name of God (Mal 3:16). Consequently, the medium through which meditation is done is the heart of the worshipper (Pss 4:4; 77:6). The sovereignty of God, his deeds, his name, his instructions, principles are all inscribed in his written word: the Scriptures. Hence, the worshipper reflects through the word of God on the whole gamut of God's revelation of himself and his relationship with creation and humanity.

Moreover, Jesus Christ said "The words that I speak to you are spirit and they are life" (John 6:63 NKJV). This implies that the worshipper is filled with the life and Spirit of God, who is to be worshipped in spirit and truth, as the Christian meditates on the word of God. This worship could be expressed or embedded in diverse forms such as praise, music, sounds, instruments, chants, liturgical responses, dancing, prayers, and all physical expressions. Yet the main point of focus is on the word of God (what God has revealed as written in Scripture) and must never be subsumed or overshadowed by any of the forms, as mentioned earlier. It is the word, not sound or percussion or dancing, that transforms the heart of worshippers or creates the needed experience with the divine; only the word, which is the power of God unto salvation and can sanctify those who believe in Christ Jesus.

In connection with the above, in Christian meditation, the adherents live in the spiritual presence of the heavenly. They seek to penetrate the mind and heart of God and his holy ones while examining their lives. Adherents communicate their joys or sorrows to God, praise and thank him, sincerely express their failings, and ask for forgiveness. Christians relate to God what and how they intend, to amend their thoughts and act to conform to his will. This they do at times by thinking, imagining, speaking, listening, and expressing emotions, resolving, and ultimately putting their resolve into practice and

---

42. Curtis, "Ancient Psalm and Modern Worship," 285–96.

living in union with God through Christ.⁴³ The word of God in Scripture is the most effective instrument for meditation in worship; by it, he speaks and invites worshippers to fellowship with him. Similarly, meditation on the scripture focuses on contemplation on particular words of the scripture "that enables the mind and heart to be drawn to the mysteries of God" (John 1:14; Heb 4:12).⁴⁴

Meditation here takes the form of prayer to connect with and reflect upon the word of God. There is a great focus on the depth and thoughts of a Bible passage and reflecting on the meaning. Meditation in the Christian religion differs from the other forms of meditation that originated in the East, as it does not utilize repeated mantras to help in enlightenment. Instead, it is believed to deepen the personal relationship with God.⁴⁵

Many modern Christians, who are aware of the need to return to the hidden wisdom of meditation, would not abandon their childhood faith; but are exploring its meaning in depth and practicing meditation along Christian lines. The task of the word is to impact the worshipper and effect a response. This written word is the crux of what God has revealed of himself and, therefore, the subject of reflection.⁴⁶

Ecclesiology

Church, as the English word "ecclesiastical" portrays, has its root in the Greek word *ekklesia*, meaning "called out," formerly used for a call out of citizens for civic meetings or soldiers for battle. It was used mainly in the Old and New Testaments to refer to the people of God.⁴⁷ Olivier Montgomery holds that only people with certain rights could call for the *ekklesia*. He added that it was an assembly of full citizens, which met regularly and afforded each person the right to self-expression on national issues. It had its foundation in political and judicial matters, hence is democratic.⁴⁸ Peter O'Brien, referring

---

43. "Christian Meditation," *Association of Catechumenal Ministry (ACm)*, https://kcgolddome.org/wp-content/uploads/2018/02/christian-meditation.pdf.

44. James Finley, *Christian Meditation: Experience the Presence of God* (New York: Harper Collins Publishers, 2004).

45. Claus Westermann, *What Does the Old Testament Say About God* (Atlanta: John Knox Press, 1979), 17.

46. Olivier Montgomery, *Principles of Church Organization and Administration* (Hagerstown: Review and Herald Publishing Association, 1990), 2.

47. Christopher Wright, *Old Testament Ethics for the People of God* (Leicester: Inter-Varsity Press, 2004), 147.

48. Olivier Montgomery, *Principles of Church Organization and Administration* (Hagerstown: Review and Herald Publishing Association, 1990), 2.

to the LXX, commented that *ekklēsia* was a translation of the Hebrew *qahal* as a congregation of Israel assembled to hear God's word rather than *edah*, which only represents the people as a national unit.[49] The church is conceived as God's people, who have individually accepted Christ as their saviour and lord, with firm faith in his death, burial, resurrection, ascension, and mission, and looking forward to his sure return. They are called out from the world to show forth the light of God to the world through passionate and practical missions, evangelism, and social actions.

The above view shows a transition in meaning and practice, marking the *ekklēsia* as a religious gathering rather than political, which is its original root. Therefore, Israel as a nation was separated and devoted to God,[50] and by the Sinaitic covenant, became God's property. God became their king, and they pledged loyalty and obedience to him.[51] This was God's initiative for worship: "Then the Lord said to Moses, 'Go into Pharaoh and say to him: This is what Yahweh, the God of the Hebrews, says: Let My people go, so that they may worship me'" (Exod 9:1 NKJV).

Therefore, the *ekklēsia* is the worshipping community. Wilbur Donovan explained that "the church is the extended family of God because the members of the church are children of God and God is their Father; it is a worldwide community and the largest extended family in the world."[52] Wayne Grudem described the church as "community of all true believers for all time."[53] Grudem, Millard Erickson, and Norman Geisler believe that the purpose of the church is to glorify God, evangelize, worship, and edify worshipers.[54] Furthermore, Erickson added to this "social work" as another church purpose.[55]

Grudem describes the nature of the church as "visible and invisible," "local and universal" and also speaks of it as a family, with ordinances of the Lord's supper and baptism. He further quotes John Calvin, who opined, "Wherever

---

49. Peter O'Brien, "Church," in *Dictionary of Paul and His Letters*, eds. Gerald F. Hawthorne, Ralph P. Martin, and Daniel G. Reid (Downers Grove: InterVarsity Press, 1993), 124.

50. A. B. Davidson, *The Theology of The Old Testament* (New York: Charles Scribner's Sons, 1904), 258.

51. Davidson, *The Theology of The Old Testament*, 259.

52. Wilbur Donovan, *Biblical Christianity in African Perspective*, 2nd ed. (Carlisle: Paternoster Press), 154.

53. Wayne Grudem, *Systematic Theology: An Introduction to Biblical Doctrine* (Grand Rapids: Zondervan, 2000), 1212.

54. Grudem, *Systematic Theology*, 1230–32; Millard Erickson, *Christian Theology*, 3rd ed. (Grand Rapids: Baker Publishing, 2013), 1053–57; Norman Geisler, *Systematic Theology* (Grand Rapids: Baker Academic, 2013), 1483–84.

55. Millard Erickson, *Christian Theology*, 3rd ed. 1926.

we see the word of God purely preached and heard and the sacraments administered according to Christ's institution, there it is not to be doubted a church of God exists."[56] Ecclesiology refers to teaching about and of the church as explicated in its nature, marks, purposes, purity, power, and unity. This includes church governance, teaching on baptism and the Lord's supper, and her worldwide mission mandate.

African Ecclesiology

In the context of this chapter, African ecclesiology falls within evangelical ecclesiology. Evangelicals hold tenaciously to the proclamation of the gospel, which they uphold alongside the written word of God and the sacraments of the Lord's supper and baptism. Michael Bird observed that the term "evangelical ecclesiology" is almost meaningless in a "strict sense" given the diverse denominations and their ecclesiological perspectives. So:

> ecclesiologies prescribe the confession, order, structure, discipline, governance, and worship in denominations. But there is no prescriptive evangelical equivalent because evangelism is a theological ethos, not a denominational entity. While evangelicals might agree on certain ecclesiological principles, there is in some sense a shared Christian identity and belief in a common mission that connects them across the globe.[57]

In this way, evangelical ecclesiology entails that the word of God draws together diverse denominations such as Presbyterians, Methodists, Baptists, and Pentecostals to create a community of the "word"; a community that belongs to Christ, who propagates his word and deeds, and a community of worshippers.[58] The above is achieved irrespective of place or race; hence, the African ecclesiology comes into being, identifying with the mission and mandate of the Great Commission with the written word of God as its basis for faith and praxis.

African ecclesiology is the communion of saints, a living fellowship of all believers who participate in the world through shared worship, spiritual gifts, graces, material goods, and mutual edification. They engage the word and

---

56. John Calvin, *Institutes of the Christian Religion* IV.1.9; Grudem, *Systematic Theology*, 1227.

57. Michael Bird, *Evangelical Theology: A Biblical and Systematic Introduction* (Grand Rapids: Zondervan Publishing, 2013), 991.

58. Bird, *Evangelical Theology*, 983.

gospel proclamation on the African soil as Africans. It is a fellowship "which sees the local church as God's temple . . . an earthly body of Christ and those in heaven in whom the Spirit of God lives, and combined is the church under the Lordship of Jesus Christ as Saviour and Lord."[59]

Furthermore, Gehman citing John Mbiti writes that "The deep sense of kinship with all it implies, has been one of the strongest forces in traditional life."[60] In addition, Mbiti asserted, "I am because we are, therefore I am. In traditional life, the individual does not exist alone except in corporately [within a group] . . . He is simply part of the whole."[61] African ecclesiology in the light of contextualization will easily adapt to the concept of the church as the "family of Christ Jesus" because Africans hold tenaciously to family closeness and values enshrined in the social-structural kinship bond by the word of God involving both the immediate and extended family.

Hence, African ecclesiology in her practice of brotherhood in Christ must communicate clearly the word of the gospel and ensure it is heard and room given for meditation to stand as a community of the word, where the need of one becomes the need of all. When the church ordained leadership speaks, others listen as Africans have unwavering loyalty to family ties as it defines their life's purpose and pursuit.

In addition, the tenets of the family concept of unity in African life, as Mbiti accounts: "the individual does not exist alone except in corporately [within a group]. . . . He is simply part of the whole"[62] could be adapted in regards to African ecclesiology through which ecclesiological purposes could be expressed. This is reflected as African ecclesiology imbibes worship and praise, evangelism and witness to the word of the gospel, proclaiming salvation, reconciliation, and eternal life; also generosity through social actions, fellowship, and edification through the practice of God's word.[63] This is where the needs of the church family are met by the church family, not soliciting for foreign help.

---

59. Wilbur, *Biblical Christianity in African Perspective*, 154.

60. John Mbiti, *African Religions and Philosophy* (London: SPCK, 1969), 104; cited in Richard Gehman, *African Traditional Religion in the Light of the Bible* (Jos: African Christian Textbook, 2001), 31.

61. John Mbiti, *African Religions and Philosophy*, 104; cited in Gehman, *African Traditional Religion in the Light of the Bible*, 31.

62. John Mbiti, *African Religions and Philosophy*, 108; cited in Gehman, *African Traditional Religion in the Light of the Bible*, 31.

63. Wilbur, *Biblical Christianity in African Perspective*, 157.

In their expression of worship, Africans are naturally musical as they exhibit external bodily forms in diverse cultural forms. J. O. Kayode, while highlighting the importance of African music, wrote that "rhythm, melody and harmony . . . music may be used to announce commencement of festivals, war."[64] Therefore, irrespective of the beauty expressed by sound, music also has an element of information and instruction which must be heard, understood and meditated and acted upon. Hence, no forms of worship through music in African ecclesiology must eclipse the clear hearing of God's word either in liturgy, sacrament or by sound. African ecclesiology must be word-based because it incarnates the life and power of God to change and transform humanity.

Therefore, African ecclesiology, regardless of forms and deeds of worship both then and today, must truly represent God's written word. Webber holds that the worship experience must correspond to the truth.[65] As the community worships, God enables it to care for and feed those in need spiritually and physically, whether in the church or outside.[66] Mutuality in true worship entails generosity, kindness, and virtues often neglected.[67]

Implications for African Ecclesiology

An evangelical heritage, if undermined, will spell doom for the African evangelical ecclesiology in her expression of Christian worship. Whichever form music takes in worship, either through shouts of praise, dancing, or beating of drums, the word of God must be heard, understood, and meditated upon. If not, a gulf has been created between the worship and the true mind of God the people seek. Historically, this heritage has been tenaciously held to in diverse ways from the Old Testament to the present evangelical traditions, although threatened by the quest of this eclectic generation who borrow various forms of worship styles they cannot biblically probe. Hence, the need for evangelical African ecclesiology to address further the centrality of the word and the importance of meditation. Meditation on the word of God becomes the medium through which his power is exerted to transform lives. Meditation

---

64. J. O. Kayode, *Understanding African Traditional Religion* (Ile-Ife: University Press, 1984), 13–14.

65. Robert Webber, "Proclamation and Worship in the 21st Century," *South Western Journal of Theology* 42.3 (Summer, 2000), 14–28, 14.

66. Robert Cornwall, "The Church and Ministry of the Spirit," *Encounter Contemporary Theology* 60.3 (Summer 1999), 466–83.

67. David Crutchly, "Spirituality Out of Africa," *South Western Journal of Theology* 45.2 (Spring, 2003), 65.

is lost when forms in a Christian worship setting eclipse the word, and so also is an encounter with the Lord. Therefore, worship becomes an empty ritual.

Recommendation

In this section, a few recommendations will be proffered:

1. Evangelical church leaders in Africa must ensure that members of their congregation are taught the centrality of the word of God in worship and the importance of meditating on the word.
2. To allow for conscious meditation, no form or aspect of worship must eclipse the clear hearing and understanding of God's word, whether through songs, dancing, clapping, or beating drum sets. As good as these may be, no amount of sound and beats can change a person's heart to Christ; rather, it is the Holy Spirit working through the word.
3. Believers in the place of worship must encounter the word of God and meditate on it as a medium of preparation to contact their world transformationally.
4. African ecclesiology should endeavour to produce a word-based community of Christians in Africa whose faith and practice exhibit the scriptural ecclesiological mandate of worship and praise, mission, evangelism, fellowship, edification, and good works to the glory of God.

Conclusion

Meditation on the word of God is the means through which an encounter between God and his children is attained in the worship setting, which positively affects the worshipers. Church music ushers in an atmosphere which exudes motivation for meditation, however, not in a vacuum but on contemplation on the words of the Scriptures. A reflection on the role of experience in worship shows that worship has the potential to effect positive changes in the lives of worshipers. Although every aspect of worship is very important, the centrality of the African ecclesiology, which is the word of God, must not be eclipsed but rather be allowed to be heard and meditated upon. This has been the stand of God's dealing with his people from the Old to the New Testaments and the very desire of the Reformers to the present-day evangelicals, who must guard against any threat to the African ecclesiological heritage on the centrality of the word of God.

Bibliography

Anayankeye, Stephen. "Meditation as a Religious Experience in Africa: A Pastoral Psychological Approach." *UMCATC Journal of Theological Studies* 10 (July 2013): 168–83.

AMECA Pastoral Institute. *Living Worship in Africa Today*. Spearhead Number 62. Volume 7 of *An Experimental Source-Book for Religious Education*. Gaba Publications, 1980.

Argyle, Michael. *Psychology and Religion: An Introduction*. London: Routledge, 2000.

Arnett, Randy. *Penticostalization: the Evolution of Baptists in Africa*. Eldon: Randy Arnett, 2017.

Ayokunle, Samson. *Communities of Faith in Diaspora: Elements and Liturgy of Worship*. Ibadan: Nigerian Baptist Press, 2021.

Barber, John. "Luther and Calvin on Music and Worship." *Reformed Perspectives Magazine* 8, no. 26 (June 25–July 1, 2006), 2–18.

"Christian Meditation," *Association of Catechumenal Ministry (ACm)*, https://kcgolddome.org/wp-content/uploads/2018/02/christian-meditation.pdf.

Cornwall, Robert. "The Church and Ministry of the Spirit." *Encounter Contemporary Theology* 60.3 (Summer 1999), 466–83.

Crutchly, David. "Spirituality Out of Africa." *South Western Journal of Theology* 45.2 (Spring, 2003): 64–79.

Curtis, Edward. "Ancient Psalms and Modern Worship." *Bibliotheca Sacra* 154 (1997), 285–96.

Davidson, A. B. *The Theology of The Old Testament*. New York: Charles Scribner's Sons, 1904.

Donovan, Wilbur. *Biblical Christianity in African Perspective*. 2nd edition. Carlisle: Paternoster Press, 1996.

Erickson, Millard. *Christian Theology*. 2nd edition. Grand Rapids: Baker Academic, 1998.

Finley, James. *Christian Meditation: Experience the Presence of God*. New York: Harper Collins Publishers, 2004.

Gehman, Richard. *African Traditional Religion in the Light of the Bible*. Jos: African Christian Textbook, 2001.

———. *African Traditional Religion in Biblical Perspective*. Jos: Oasis International, 2005.

Geisler, Norman. *Systematic Theology*. Grand Rapids: Baker Academic, 2013.

Gruden, Wayne. *Systematic Theology: An Introduction to Biblical Doctrine*. Grand Rapids: Zondervan, 2000.

Hardy, Alister. *The Divine Flame*. Religious Experience Research Unit (RERU). Oxford: Oxford University Press, 1966.
Hummel, Charles. *Fire in the Fireplace: Charismatic Renewal in the Nineties*. Downers Grove: InterVarsity Press, 1993.
Idowu, Bolaji. *African Traditional Religion: A Definition*. Ibadan: Fountain Publication Press, 1991.
Imasogie, O. *African Traditional Religion*. Benin City: Prestige Print Concept, 2008.
Janvier, George. *Leading the Church in Music and Worship*. 2nd edition. Jos: African Christian Textbooks, 2017.
Kayode, J. O. *Understanding African Traditional Religion*. Ile-Ife: University Press, 1984.
Keeley, Robin, ed. *Lion Handbook of Christian Beliefs*. London: Lion Publishers, 1982.
Loewenthal, Kate. *The Psychology of Religion: A Short Introduction*. Oxford: One World, 1995.
Mbewe, Conrad. "What Should Happen During Worship Service?" *God's Design for the Church: A Guide for African Pastors and Ministry Leaders*. Wheaton: Crossway, 2020.
Montgomery, Olivier. *Principles of Church Organization and Administration*. Hagerstown: Review and Herald Publishing Association, 1990.
Nelson, James. *Psychology, Religion, and Spirituality*. New York: Springer Publishers, 2009.
Nicholls, Bruce. "We All Believe Something." In *The Lion Handbook of Christian Belief*, edited by Robin Keeley, 30–37. Herts: Lion Publishing, 1982.
O'Brien, Peter. "Church." In *Dictionary of Paul and His Letters*. Edited by Gerald F. Hawthorne, Ralph P. Martin, and Daniel G. Reid. Downers Grove: InterVarsity Press, 1993.
Parker, C. L. "Religiousness, Spirituality and Health: A Meaning Systems Perspective." *Journal of Behavioral Medicine* 30 (2007): 4–19.
Rankin, Mamanne. "Introduction to Religious Experience." Third Series Occasional Paper 2, Religious Experience Research Centre (2005): 13–15.
Smith, Alain. "Report of our Visit to Teaching-Centred African Baptist Church, Kensington." Liverpool (15 March 2006).
Snyder, Howard. "A Living Community." Pages 382–411 in *The Lion Handbook of Christian Belief*. Edited by Robin Keeley. Herts: Lion Publishing, 1982.
Tate, Andrew. "Sweeter also Than Honey: John Ruskin 'Psalms.'" *Year Book of English Studies, Literature and Religion* 39, no. 1/2 (2009), 114–25.
Tenney, Merrill. *New Testament Survey*. Grand Rapids: Eerdmans, 1961.
Webber, Robert. *Worship Old and New*. Grand Rapids: Zondervan Publishing House, 1982.
———. "Proclamation and Worship in the 21st Century." *Southwestern Journal of Theology* 42.3 (Summer, 2000): 14–28.
West, Michael. *The Psychology of Meditation: Research and Practice*. New York: Oxford University Press, 1987.

Westermann, Claus. *What Does the Old Testament Say About God?* Atlanta: John Knox Press, 1979.
White, James. *A Brief History of Christian Worship.* Nashville: Abingdon Press, 1993.
Wiersbe, Warren. "Pentateuch." Bible Exposition Commentary on CD-ROM. Incorporated Version 2.0. 2007.
Wright, Christopher J. H. *Old Testament Ethics for the People of God.* Leicester: Inter-Varsity Press, 2004.

15

Cash, Cleaning and Cooking

The Contribution of the Women's Fellowship in the RCZ

Marike Blok-Sijtsma
VIAA University, Netherlands

Abstract

Women's Fellowships (henceforth WF) or Women's Guilds are relevant stakeholders in the African church of the twenty-first century. However, ecclesiology tends to ignore these organizations that function within the formal, often male-dominated, church structures. Also in African feminist literature, the WF remain invisible: representatives of the Circle of Concerned African Women Theologians are critical of the WF because they affirm patriarchy, propagate stereotypical gender roles and do not speak out against discrimination and exclusion based on gender. Yet, these ecclesiastical women's movements are essential for the sustenance of the church and play an important role in the socio-religious and spiritual lives of their members.

This chapter discusses the role of the WF of the Reformed Church in Zambia. It is based on fieldwork conducted in three local chapters of the WF, the *Chigwirizano cha Azimai*, between 2021–2023 and focuses on the contribution the WF members make to the church in the form of money and time. This article argues that women of the WF of the RCZ exercise their agency in a male-dominated church by mobilizing their resources (money, time) or the withholding thereof. Moreover, it demonstrates that for the members, the act of contributing their resources is meaningful and deeply religious, motivated even within a system that is considered to uphold a patriarchal structure.

Key words: women's fellowship, gender, Reformed Church in Zambia, female leadership, church finances, church resources, agency

Introduction

This chapter focuses on the manner in which the women of the Women's Fellowship (henceforth WF), the *Chigwirizano cha Azimai*, in the Reformed Church in Zambia (henceforth RCZ), contribute to the church through resources and how this gives them agency and dignity in a male-dominated church. The materials presented here are part of ongoing research into the influence of the WF in the RCZ, one of the mainline protestant churches in Zambia.[1]

The RCZ was born out of mission work by the Dutch Reformed Church in South Africa (henceforth DRC), which started its missionary endeavour in eastern Zambia in 1899. In 1966, the RCZ became an independent church; nowadays, it has approximately nine hundred and fifty thousand members.[2] The WF is an organization within the RCZ, structured along the same hierarchical lines as the church at large, at local, regional and national levels. Since the start of mission work by the DRC, there has been a focus on work among women and girls; missionary wives and female missionaries organized prayer meetings and activities for women, such as sewing and literacy classes.[3] Women's work among women acquired a more formal and nationwide structure in 1946, when it became an official fellowship modelled after the *Christelike Sustersbond* (Christian Sisters League) in the DRC.[4] Part of this formalization was the introduction of a uniform: members wear a distinctive black/white uniform that identifies them as members of the WF of the RCZ. Currently, the RCZ WF has about forty-five thousand members. Initially, one of the missionary wives

---

1. This research is part of a broader PhD study on the role and influence of the members of the Women's Fellowship in the RCZ. Supervisor is Prof. Dr. M. T. Frederiks, University of Utrecht, The Netherlands.

2. "The Reformed Church in Zambia (RCZ)," *Reformed Family Forum* (blog), https://rff.christians.co.za/the-reformed-church-in-zambia-rcz/.

3. Gerdien Verstraelen-Gilhuis, *From Dutch Mission Church to Reformed Church in Zambia: The Scope for African Leadership and Initiative in the History of a Zambian Mission Church* (Franeker: Wever, 1982), 186–87.

4. J. M. Cronjé, *Vroue met nardusparfuum: die aandeel van die vrou in die sendingwerk van die Nederduitse Gereformeerde Kerk* (Pretoria: NG Kerkboekhandel Transvaal, 1984), 247–48.

chaired the WF meetings; nowadays, the local chapters of the WF are headed/chaired by pastors' wives. A delegate of the WF represents the women in the formal hierarchy of the church. The church leadership is male-dominated, and while since the early 2000s women can be ordained, the number of female pastors is small; hence women are hardly represented in the formal decision-making structures of the church.

All this may suggest a church in which women – and the WF in particular – have little influence. However, both men and women within the RCZ have repeatedly underscored that the WF is the church's most powerful and influential institution.

Two reasons are given to substantiate this statement: the number of women involved in the WF and the commitment and activities of the women; with its forty-five thousand members, the WF is the largest fellowship of the RCZ. Furthermore, the WF succeeds in mobilizing its members; they raise funds and contribute their time to the benefit of the whole church.[5] Apparently, the influence of the WF members hinges on their sheer numbers and their resources rather than on having a formal position in the decision-making structures. This does not only apply to this particular WF; Deborah Gaitskell and Beverley Haddad, who both studied Women's Fellowships in South Africa, also list fundraising as one of the main characteristics of these ecclesiastical women's movements.[6] However, despite their evident importance, ecclesiology tends to ignore these organizations. African feminist literature acknowledges the value of the WF, but representatives of the Circle of Concerned African Women Theologians are critical of the WF because they affirm patriarchy, propagate stereotypical gender roles and do not speak out against discrimination and gender-based violence.[7]

This chapter proffers a detailed description of the contribution of the WF to the RCZ, thus demonstrating the importance of the WF for the church. The

---

5. William McKinney, "Resources," in *Studying Congregations: A New Handbook*, ed. Nancy Ammerman et al. (Nashville: Abingdon Press, 1998), 132–66.

6. Beverley Haddad, "Church Uniforms as an Indigenous Form of Anglicanism: A South African Case Study," *Journal of Anglican Studies* 14, no. 2 (2016): 156–71; Deborah Lyndall Gaitskell, "Female Mission Initiatives: Black and White Women in Three Witwatersrand Churches, 1903–1939" (Thesis, University of London, 1981), 1.

7. Ifi Amadiume, *Daughters of the Goddess, Daughters of Imperialism: African Women Struggle for Culture, Power, and Democracy*, Black Women Writers Series (London: Zed Books, 2000); Isabel Apawo Phiri, *Women, Presbyterianism and Patriarchy. Religious Experience of Chewa Women in Central Malawi*, Kachere Series (Blantyre: Christian Literature Association in Malawi, 2000), 102, 125; Damaris Parsitau et al., "'Mama I Can't Breathe!': Black/African Women of Faith Groaning for Social Justice and Gender Equality," *Mission Studies* 38 (2021): 448–69, 458.

paper aims to tease out how and why WF members contribute with money and time in a church that accords them little space in decision-making. Therefore, the paper especially focuses on how members perceive these practices and what these practices suggest and imply about the contribution these women (and the WF as an organization) may have in the church. The paper concludes that these practices play an essential role in the spiritual lives of the members, who perceive them as "work done for God"; they believe that the sacrifices they make, not only gives them status and respect in the church but will also be rewarded in the life to come.

The remainder of this chapter comprises four sections. Section 1 focuses on methodology, discussing the positionality of the researcher, the theoretical frame and the research methods used. Section 2 introduces the WF as an organization within the RCZ. Subsequently, section 3 narrates how the WF members contribute their resources and how they perceive this. Section 4 will evaluate the contribution of the WF members, based on an analysis of the findings and in conversation with other scholars: do they exercise influence in the church through their contribution or is compliance to obligations meaningful in a different way?

Methodology
Positionality

Since 4 January 2019, I have been a member of the *Chigwirizano cha Azimai*, the WF of the Reformed Church in Zambia. To become a member, I underwent the so-called "blousing ceremony." During this ritual, a pastor's wife dressed me in the WF uniform, and I was asked to pledge my commitment to the WF by taking the vows; afterwards I was welcomed as a member. But at the same time, I am also a researcher studying the WF. My identity is also defined by other bio-data: I am a Western woman, a (grand)mother, a Christian, a church member and a pastor's wife. So, my positionality is complex and surrounded by epistemological and methodological debates.[8] African feminist scholars (as well as other non-western scholars) criticize the Western hegemony of knowledge construction and the dominance of Western academic discourse and theory

---

8. Jane E. Soothill, *Gender, Social Change and Spiritual Power: Charismatic Christianity in Ghana*, 1st edition (Leiden; Boston: Brill, 2007), 21–22; Bagele Chilisa and Gabo Ntseane, "Resisting Dominant Discourses: Implications of Indigenous, African Feminist Theory and Methods for Gender and Education Research," *Gender and Education* 22, no. 6 (2010): 617; L. J. Joziasse, "Women's Faith Seeking Life: Lived Christologies and the Transformation of Gender Relations in Two Kenyan Churches" (Utrecht University, 2020), 43.

and plead for post-colonial and indigenous feminist research approaches.[9] To deal with my positionality and all the pitfalls in a responsible way, I use the three layers of reflexivity, developed by Ruth Nicholls, as tools to question and evaluate the engagement with myself, with the participants and with the theory during this research; "self-reflexivity," "interpersonal reflexivity," and "collective reflexivity."[10] The first layer, self-reflexivity, means that during the research I was constantly aware of my privileged position of power, the influence of a different cultural background and the need to negotiate this in a constructive way. The second layer, interpersonal reflexivity, calls for an evaluation of interpersonal encounters and the ability to collaborate with others without controlling or imposing my own assumptions or ideas. It requires cultural sensitivity and culturally appropriate strategies in the research process which not only protects the study participants from harm but also improves the quality of data collected.[11] I have done this by explicitly asking for the consent of the informants, anonymizing the data I collected and observing the ethical and privacy regulations of Utrecht University regarding research. The third layer, collective reflexivity, calls for recognition that the researcher, especially one engaged in cross-cultural research, is not all-knowing and all-seeing. Therefore, I have shared and cross-checked my data and discussed my findings and preliminary conclusions with a selected group of participants and with academic peers in the successive stages of the research.

Approach

This research project is an empirical qualitative study in the field of Religious Studies and Theology. As Strausberg and Engler state, qualitative research investigates the meaning individuals and groups ascribe to human or social phenomena.[12] Consequently, it considers the stories and experiences of the

---

9. Chilisa and Gabo Ntseane, "Resisting Dominant Discourses," 617; Cynthia Dillard, "When the Ground Is Black, the Ground Is Fertile: Exploring Endarkened Feminist Epistemology and Healing Methodologies in the Spirit," in *Handbook of Critical and Indigenous Methodologies*, ed. Norman Denzin, Yvonna Lincoln, and Linda Smith (Thousand Oaks: SAGE Publications, Inc., 2008), 276.

10. Ruth Nicholls, "Research and Indigenous Participation: Critical Reflexive Methods," *International Journal of Social Research Methodology* 12, no. 2 (1 April 2009): 117–26.

11. Monique M. Hennink, "Cross-Cultural Focus Group Discussions," in *A New Era in Focus Group Research: Challenges, Innovation and Practice*, ed. Rosaline S. Barbour and David L. Morgan (London: Palgrave Macmillan UK, 2017), 60–61.

12. M. Stausberg and S. Engler, eds., *The Routledge Handbook of Research Methods in the Study of Religion*, 1st ed. (London: Routledge, 2013), 7.

subjects involved in the study to be the primary source of knowledge-finding. To understand the role of religion, Nancy Ammerman, the leading sociologist, introduced the concept of *lived religion*; with it, she foregrounds the religious practices of ordinary people, the non-experts, at the centre of the research rather than formal doctrine or faith statements by theologians, the experts.[13] *Lived religion* is a bottom-up approach, where, according to Annemarie Korte "the aspects of religion that make 'religious worlds' real and present are placed centrally, such as religious rituals that take place in everyday life."[14] When applied to the study of women in patriarchal religions or cultures, this approach aims to overcome the simplistic dichotomy of compliance or resistance. The *lived religion* approach maintains that actions need to be analyzed from the perspective of the one performing the actions.[15] In this contribution, I use the *lived religion* approach in studying how and why women dedicated their time and resources to the WF, thus consciously endeavouring to spotlight the women's meaning-making of their practices rather than my analysis.

Methods

This research is based on fieldwork conducted in the period 2021–2023. Different empirical research techniques were used to collect the data, such as participant observation, focus group discussions and in-depth interviews with members of the WF and church leaders.

The fieldwork was conducted in three local WFs, which are all part of an RCZ congregation. The three congregations, named Shalom, Fountain and Vineyard respectively, belong to the same presbytery of the RCZ.[16] In all three congregations, the women outnumber the men, and the women's fellowship is an active group. However, the location and socio-economic background of the members of the three groups differ. Shalom is a large urban congregation of about one thousand eight hundred communicant church members, of which four hundred and fifty are members of the WF. The congregation is located in

---

13. Nancy T. Ammerman, ed., *Everyday Religion: Observing Modern Religious Lives* (New York: Oxford University Press, 2006), 5.

14. Anne-Marie Korte, "'Feminist Theology,' "Lived Religion" and the Investigation of Women in Conservative Religions as Changing the Agenda of the Study of Religion', *DIVE-IN – An International Journal on Diversity and Inclusion* 2, no. 1 (22 December 2022): 23.

15. Elisabet Le Roux, "Can religious women choose? Holding the tension between complicity and agency," *African Journal of Gender and Religion* 25.1 (2019).

16. To protect the anonymity of the participants these names are not the real names of the three congregations.

a middle-class area. Fountain is a relatively small congregation of about five hundred and twenty members, of which one hundred and fifty-five women are WF members. It is located in a so-called compound, an urban settlement with a high population density, unemployment, and poverty levels are high.[17] Vineyard is a rural congregation, a two-hour drive from Lusaka. Most of its (around) two hundred and sixty communicant members are small-scale farmers and live scattered over a large territory, sometimes at a great distance from the church building. The exact number of WF members is unclear; according to the statistics in the 2021 report of the region, it has about one hundred members, but according to the 2021 presbytery report, it has one hundred and fifty members.[18] All three fellowships have a local board, called the *bungwe six*, chaired by the pastor's or evangelist's wife.

The Women's Fellowship and its Members

Within the structure of the RCZ, all members are supposed to participate in a particular group or fellowship (Sunday School, Youth Fellowship, Men's or Women's Fellowship), depending on their age and sex. Hence, all female communicant members above age thirty-five are eligible to become a member of the WF, should they decide to do so, provided they are not under church discipline.[19] However, looking at the statistics of the three fellowships, it is evident that, especially in Shalom and Fountain, only part of the women are members of the WF and most of the members are over fifty years old.[20] The national and regional leaders confirm that in most congregations, only a few junior members join the WF the moment they reach the age of thirty-five. Women seem hesitant to join because they consider the WF to be for older women, and they shrink back from the financial obligations and the behaviour

---

17. After the Second World War the population of Lusaka experienced a rapid growth resulting in a housing crisis. People started to build houses on agricultural land without authorization. Since then, several programmes have been implemented to upgrade these areas but until today, these areas are over-crowded, and characterized by problems such as insecurity, lack of essential infrastructure, services, and solid waste management. See Chileshe Mulenga, "Urban Slums Report: The Case of Lusaka, Zambia," *Understanding Slums: Case Studies for the Global Report 2003* (2003), https://www.ucl.ac.uk/dpu-projects/Global_Report/pdfs/Lusaka.pdf.

18. Women's Regional Fellowship, "Annual Reports 1st January–31st December 2021," *Annual Report* (Lusaka, 2022); Chelston Presbytery, "Annual General Meeting" (Lusaka, 2022).

19. Reformed Church in Zambia, *Buku La Zinchito Za Chigwirizano Cha Azimai*, 2015, 8.

20. Women's Regional Fellowship, "Annual Reports 1st January–31st December 2021."

expected from WF members.[21] Hence, joining the WF is not an automatic process but a significant step; joining is conceived as coming from the heart, and one must be ready "to work for God."[22]

Formally, being married is not a requirement for membership; single or divorced women are welcome, and some do indeed participate. In practice, the emphasis on marriage, taking care of a family and motherhood seems to be a hurdle for single women to join; as the church secretary of Shalom states: "Some women who are not married think that it is not correct to be a member of the WF; they just feel out of place."[23]

The women who want to join the WF must follow a series of obligatory lessons by the pastor's wife and undergo the blousing ceremony. During this blousing ceremony, the pastor's wife dresses the prospective members in their uniform, which consists of a black headscarf, a white blouse and a long black skirt. After that, the new members take a vow in which they promise to read the Bible and to pray, be a good mother and wife, give faithfully and obey the rules of the WF and the church's leaders. The wearing of the uniform underlines the identity of the bloused members as respectable women of God and is a source of pride and dignity for the members.[24]

The bloused members of the WF are a distinct group within a congregation with access to certain privileges, such as belonging to a local and national network where they receive spiritual and moral support. A WF member is allowed to sing in one of the women's choirs and sit in the front pews during church services and meetings, which is conceived as a place of honour. Once a member dies, she will be buried in her uniform, which is conceived as a great honour for her and the family. Members may take up a leadership position within the WF; leaders experience this as a privilege and an opportunity to learn and grow. One of them states: "We have the chance to be a leader, to attend meetings, even at the highest level, to preach, to lead prayers and to visit the sick. We need to be at the forefront."[25]

---

21. Interview 8, Regional Leader WF 17 October 2021, Focus group 14, National Leaders WF (19 November 2022). For this article, I refer to my data by indicating the type of meeting (individual interview or focus group), the name of the congregation and the date of the interview or focus group discussion. If necessary, I mention the position of the interviewee. Most of the participants were women; if not, I indicate the sex as well.
22. Focus group 2, Shalom (11 June 2021).
23. Interview 2, Shalom, Church Secretary (male) (14 October 2021).
24. Haddad, "Church Uniforms as an Indigenous Form of Anglicanism," 166.
25. Focus group 1, Shalom (21 May 2021).

Membership is not to be taken lightly; therefore, all members renew their vows annually during the renewal ceremony. Members who do not perform according to the rules cannot participate in this ceremony and are no longer permitted to wear the uniform.

Most WFs gather weekly. These meetings follow a prescribed order with prayers, a devotion, choirs and offerings. The pastor's wife represents the WF during church council meetings. Also, at the regional and national level, a WF representative will attend the church's presbytery and synod meetings.

The Women's Fellowship and its Resources

Women contribute to the church with two main forms of resources: money and time. This section first describes the monetary obligations of members of the WF and the way these are perceived. Secondly, it sheds light on the investment of time to keep the church running.

Money

Being a member of the WF implies several prescribed financial obligations. Each member is expected to pay an amount of ZMK 10 weekly and a monthly amount of ZMK 20 (total ZMK 60 per month = c. $3.20).[26] Most women are not formally employed and earn their money at the market or as small-scale farmers. An average salary of a domestic worker is ZMK 840 per month based on forty-eight work hours per week and a primary school teacher receives an average salary of ZMK 4300.[27] Hence, 60 ZMK on a monthly basis is a significant amount of money for women who have a set salary.

---

26. The Zambian Kwacha (ZMK) is the national currency of Zambia. Between January 2021 and August 2022 (the time of the fieldwork), the value of one Zambian Kwacha fluctuated between $0.055 on 1 January 2021 to $0.062 on 30 August 2022. This means that ZMK 100 was the equivalence of $5.52 at the start of 2021 and of $6.62 in August 2022 ("Convert Currency, Zambian Kwacha to U.S. Dollar," https://www.convertworld.com/en/currency/zambia/zmw-to-usd.html). According to the World Bank, 61.4 percent of the Zambian population lives below the international poverty line of $2.15 per person per day (World Bank, "Zambia | Data," https://data.worldbank.org/country/ZM).

27. "Salary Zambia," WageIndicator Foundation, https://wageindicator.org/salary/minimum-wage/zambia; "Primary School Teacher Average Salary in Zambia 2023 – The Complete Guide," http://www.salaryexplorer.com/salary-survey.php?loc=242&loctype=1&job=5886&jobtype=3. Nolipher Moyo points out that the majority of women in Zambian society are economically and socially disadvantaged, in comparison to men; whether this is also the case in the three case-study fellowships is not clear. See N. Moyo, "Revisiting Economic Justice. An Examination of Dignity of Women in a Zambian Context," in *Living with Dignity. African*

The day a woman enters the WF she promises to fulfil all the monetary obligations; one of the vows reads: "Do you promise to give faithfully all that may be needed for the work of God?"[28] At each meeting, the local leaders register all these prescribed payments carefully in the membership card, an activity which takes much time during the meetings. During each meeting, collections are part of the liturgy; on top of their weekly and monthly dues, the women are also invited to put some money in the offering basket. Besides, almost every week, additional contributions are requested for church-related programmes such as the retirement of a pastor, expansion of the church building, a funeral or transport to a meeting.

The women are also expected to pay a fixed amount of 50 ZMK during the annual renewal ceremony, which usually occurs in March. Members who want to renew their vows must ensure that their membership cards with their financial contributions are up to date and that they have paid the renewal contribution. Because many, especially rural, women do not yet have the required cash in March (which is before the harvest), the local board may decide to provide a second occasion to renew vows later in the year.

Moreover, the women, like all members, pay tithes for the general treasury of the congregation and contribute to their choirs. No wonder the board of the WF of Fountain sighs: "Sections need money, money, choirs money, money, congregation, *cigwirizano* requires money. So, we women have how many cards? 3 or 4? For renewal, for WF, for tithes, for offering."[29]

There is a desire to holistically improve the economic situation of women, mainly by introducing skills training or helping women to start a business. In all three WFs, the women have plans to start other income-generating projects, to avoid their dependence on the membership contributions, but so far, this has not been very successful. In the past, Shalom offered sewing courses, but this programme stopped. Fountain introduced a loan system, but because the participants never paid back, the system was terminated. Only the WF of Vineyard participates in a saving system, introduced by the Council of Churches in Zambia, that supports women in case of an emergency.

The constant demand for money gave rise to debate during meetings and Focus Group discussions. Several times participants stated that some women are not able to meet all these financial obligations and have stopped coming

---

Perspectives on Gender Equality, ed. Elna Mouton et al. (Stellenbosch: African Sun Media, 2015), 179–90.

28. Reformed Church in Zambia, *Buku La Zinchito Za Chigwirizano Cha Azimai*, 115.
29. Focus group 9, Fountain (22 April 2022).

to the WF or do not even enter because of it. Senior members in Shalom complained that: "It is very unfair because you cannot be a member when you are not financially stable."[30] In the rural set-up of Vineyard, most women only have cash once a year, after the harvest. Some women refused to join because: "We are farmers and we only find money once a year. Where can we get the money for the monthly meetings?"[31] Most leaders, by contrast, emphasize that they do consider the financial status of their members and allow widows or elderly women to renew their vows even if they have debts.[32]

Another recurring topic of discussion is that participants find it a challenge that the amounts of money they have to pay are imposed on them by the WF leadership. The leaders determine the amount of the allowances for the pastor's wife and the budgets to cover the remittances to the treasury of regional and national WF committees. The members, many of whom are struggling to survive, complain about all the payments they have to make:

> Look at the women in this congregation, they are widows, yeah, they are widows, some sell just small businesses, some tomatoes, vegetables. Now when the budget comes, they need to pay a lot of money which they cannot afford, and that is why they complain a lot.[33]

Ordinary members do not have the feeling that they can influence these budgets because the pastors' wives make these budgets. Even those in leadership positions at a local level "have no teeth to bite."[34] Members respect the church hierarchy and the pastor and his wife, moreover, they pledge to obey the leaders in their vows.[35] So, it is not done to object or to protest, according to senior members in Fountain: "We cannot say this budget is too much or too little because our leaders have already agreed. It is now up to the women how we can divide ourselves to be able to raise that money. So, whatever we are told, we just agree and do."[36] According to the financial reports for 2021,[37] in all three WFs, most of the local budget goes to the support of the pastor's wife, even when the pastor's wife is employed somewhere. This also leads to frustration

---

30. Focus group 1, Shalom (21 May 2021).
31. Focus group 10, Vineyard (26 August 2022).
32. Interview 3, Shalom, Pastor's wife (12 January 2021).
33. Focus group 9, Fountain (22 April 2022).
34. Focus group 5, Shalom (5 November 2021).
35. Reformed Church in Zambia, *Buku La Zinchito Za Chigwirizano Cha Azimai*, 106.
36. FGD6, Fountain, Senior Members.
37. Women's Regional Fellowship, "Annual Reports 1st January–31st December 2021."

among the other members of the board who do their work voluntarily.[38] A second substantial amount of the budget serves to pay the remittances to the regional and national women's committees.[39] As the local leaders in Fountain share: "Whenever they have raised this money, whatever amount is in the card, they end up sending the money for the presbytery."[40] A pastor's wife shared that she feels guilty about the constant demand for money:

> You feel bad even to ask them to give, after giving you get the money there without even telling them, there are some who are struggling, really struggling and they have a heart to give, after giving at your own church, you give it to the higher authorities. So sometimes you feel bad.[41]

Consequently, the WF's budget to support their own members or the community financially is very limited. Support is mainly given in case of bereavement or emergencies. The WF of Shalom helps two women each month: "Though we restrict it to our members, we do identify two women, per month, who receive some groceries."[42] Most members do not benefit from the WF financially, as an older member in Fountain shares: "If you come in church poor, you just stay with your poverty, if you stay without eating, you stay without eating."[43] One of the national leaders acknowledges this problem but says that it is difficult to change:

> A big part of the budget goes to the pastor's wife and you may not even have a component for the support of the vulnerable women within the group which is a miss when they meet to draw the budget . . . How do we empower women? Even giving them start-up capital for small businesses, there is nothing.[44]

Despite all these contestations about money, at the same time, most members emphasize that monetary obligations are part of the vows they made

---

38. The National leadership states that each local WF has the obligation to take care of the pastor's wife and to pay her an allowance, even if she has a paid job elsewhere. The pastor's wife is not employed by the church so formally, the payment is a voluntary token of appreciation, but in praxis, it functions as a salary, because the moment a local WF is not able to pay, it is counted as a debt towards her.
39. Women's Regional Fellowship, "Annual Reports 1st January–31st December 2021."
40. Focus group 9, Fountain (22 April 2022).
41. Interview 7, Fountain, Pastor's wife (9 March 2022).
42. Interview 3, Shalom, Pastor's wife (12 January 2021).
43. Focus group 6, Fountain (4 February 2022).
44. Interview 9, National leader RCZ (male) (6 November 2021).

the day of their blousing and during the renewal: "Everything you agreed on the day that you put on the uniform you need to fulfil."[45] This compliance to financial obligations is considered a sign of the level of commitment to the Christian faith by the women. A senior member commented: "Women at a section, they have many problems, they do not come, they have a lot of credits, and still they say 'I am a Christian', so what kind of Christianity is that? As a Christian, you should show your fruits."[46]

Giving is considered an important part of a Christian lifestyle, and members are encouraged to give joyfully because "you do not pay people, but God."[47] Being able to contribute to certain projects also makes members proud. In Shalom, the WF members showed me a new ablution block and new curtains for the church hall, paid for by the WF members.

Moreover, a strong incentive to fulfil monetary obligations is the conviction that the one who gives will be blessed. Participants in a Focus Group declared:

> And definitely, when you give, God will give back a hundredfold for that matter. So, it is the way we take spirituality, if we understand the Word of God and if we have learnt giving – that if you give to God, God will definitely give back to you . . . and you will find that things will continue moving in your life.[48]

Time and skills

The members of the WF also contribute resources to the WF and the local congregation by giving their time and skills. Women are responsible for cleaning the church, beautifying the church, and making sure that the surroundings and the toilets are clean. Culturally these tasks are female tasks and participants refer to "African culture" explaining their tasks: "We don't expect men to sweep (*laughing*), to prepare beds and things like that, nooo."[49] A gender specialist, teaching at Justo Mwale University,[50] but not a member of the RCZ or the WF, confirms: "We believe this part is for the women. When you go early in

---

45. Focus group 7, Fountain (12 February 2022).
46. Focus group 5, Shalom (5 November 2021).
47. Regional Meeting May 2021.
48. Focus group 4, Shalom (24 September 2021).
49. Focus group 4, Shalom (24 September 2021).
50. Justo Mwale University offers theological training for future pastors within the RCZ. They also offer a special program for the wives of married students to prepare them for their future roles as WF leaders.

the morning you see that women are the ones to clean the church, women are the ones to decorate the church, women are supposed to cook when there is a function."[51]

It is also the task of the women to organize the food and cook for all the visitors during funerals. In the African context, a funeral is a big gathering. Women have the task of cooking for, serving, and looking after the whole welfare of the bereaved family.[52] All these responsibilities are in line with the pledges the WF members make the day they become a member of the WF: to take care of their home, their children and their husband and by extension also of the church family.[53] Just as a woman is responsible for the cleanliness of her house and the well-being of her own family, she, according to the WF theology, is so for the house of the Lord and the church family. As some senior members declare full of pride: "We are playing a mother's role in the church, and we are happy."[54]

The women state that involvement in all these tasks gives joy and satisfaction, based on a solid religious conviction that it is work done for God, work that has a deep religious meaning. As the local leaders in Shalom said: "We are chosen by God to work for him. We can put everything aside and just work for God; it is nice to serve God in the WF."[55] Moreover, God will help and bless the women who serve him, as members of Fountain stated: "It is not only giving money but also using your hands . . . Then God will be able to help us, though sometimes things are difficult, God is happy with someone who gives herself to him."[56]

Evaluation

The WF as an organization provides the structure and the theological rationale to collect and redistribute the monetary resources of its members at both the local and the national level and to mobilize the members to contribute their time to perform particular tasks. Members' experiences are ambiguous and complex. The WF members promise to give faithfully, and most do so, even when they struggle to put food on the table. Women give, according to their

---

51. Interview 14, Gender Specialist (26 October 2022).
52. Interview 3, Shalom, Pastor's wife (12 January 2021).
53. Reformed Church in Zambia, *Buku La Zinchito Za Chigwirizano Cha Azimai*, 115.
54. Focus group 1, Shalom (21 May 2021).
55. Focus group 2, Shalom (11 June 2021).
56. Focus group 7, Fountain (12 February 2022).

own statements, because they are committed to the work of God. Giving, both money and time, means participation in the work of God and obedience to God and his leaders, and is a deeply religious practice. They feel that they are selected by God to work for him, which is conceived to be an honourable position. Moreover, the women are convinced that those who give will be blessed, now and in the hereafter, and hence it is worth the sacrifice. Doing the work of God gives the WF members also status and dignity; they are respected, in and outside the church, as mothers and women of God.

However, in particular, money is also a point of debate for three reasons. First, money – or rather the lack thereof – seems to serve as a mechanism of exclusion. Certain women do not become members of the WF because of its financial obligations; also, there are repercussions for those who do not pay or cannot pay; the leadership defines the criteria by which members who fall short of their financial obligations are allowed to be treated as legitimate members and which privileges they are entitled to.[57] Second, ordinary members do not have a say about the prescribed amount of obligatory contributions nor about the manner in which the money is allocated; the budgets are imposed on them. This is a hierarchical type of leadership, according to a Zambian scholar Jackson Phiri, and is "a common feature in Zambian society, including the church."[58] Third, ordinary members contribute to the economic capital of both the WF and the church but they do not seem to reap any financial benefits from their commitment themselves. In an emergency, occasionally members receive some financial support but first and foremost support takes the form of spiritual and social assistance, such as visits, prayers and practical help offered by their fellow members. Women join the WF not primarily because of the financial benefits, the focus is much more on social and spiritual support and privileges. Members in Fountain shared:

> You cannot have that bad thinking, you cannot develop something bad. Because when you gather here with your friends, here at church, you forget about maybe some problems... At least once, twice a week, we meet at church, at least you know God is there for us, and you can be helped.[59]

---

57. Dominic Abrams, Michael A. Hogg, and José M. Marques, "A Social Psychological Framework for Understanding Social Inclusion and Exclusion," in *Social Psychology of Inclusion and Exclusion* (Hove: Taylor & Francis Group, 2004), 1–24, 18.

58. Jackson Phiri, "Church and Culture: Exploring the Reception of Women's Ministries in the Reformed Church in Zambia in View of 1 Corinthians 14:26-40" (Thesis, Stellenbosch, Stellenbosch University, 2017), 74.

59. Focus group 6, Fountain (4 February 2022).

This is in line with the conclusion of Lyn Holness in her study about the Methodist WF in South Africa. Holness states that membership offers, in particular, marginalized women who do not have a status in society, a place to meet and to pray and most importantly "a sense of identity and a reason to live."[60]

WF members explain the types of tasks assigned to women as part of their Zambian culture. It may also reflect a domesticity ideal as introduced by Western missionaries in the nineteenth and early twentieth centuries.[61] This is a reason that Isabel Phiri, member of the Circle of Concerned African Women, criticizes the existence of WF, because the organizations, according to Phiri, reinforce traditional stereotypical gender roles with a strong emphasis on motherhood and family values, depriving women of their individual freedom.[62]

Lyn Holness, by contrast, states that motherhood for most women in Southern Africa is a central theme in their lives, including all the joy and pain and a respected status. The WF may provide a spiritual resource that relates to their daily experience of being mothers in their families and in the church.[63] Lihle Ngcobozi adds that fulfilling female tasks such as cleaning, cooking and caring for the sick and bereaved, is related to the respected status of motherhood.[64] Being a mother is not perceived as an inferior role within the private sphere but as an acknowledged and respected social identity; hence, motherhood is a central theme in African churches. A mother is someone who takes responsibility not only for her own children but for all children in the community.[65] This role and the acknowledgement of a person as a mother, gives, within the hierarchical and patriarchal structures of power, pride and dignity.[66]

---

60. Lyn Holness, "Women's Piety and Empowerment: An Observer's Understanding of the Methodist Manyano's Movement," *Journal of Theology for Southern Africa* 98 (1998): 21–31.

61. Deborah Gaitskell, "Devout Domesticity? A Century of African Women's Christianity in South Africa," in *Women and Gender in Southern Africa to 1945*, ed. Cherryl Walker (London: James Currey, 1990), 251–72; Cordelia Moyse, *A History of the Mothers' Union: Women, Anglicanism and Globalisation, 1876–2008* (Woodbridge: Boydell & Brewer, 2009), 157.

62. Phiri, *Women, Presbyterianism and Patriarchy*.

63. Lyn Holness, "Motherhood and Spirituality: Faith Reflections from the Inside," *Agenda: Empowering Women for Gender Equity* 61 (2004): 66–71, 68.

64. Lihle Ngcobozi, "[Honour Thy Promise]: The Methodist Church Women's Manyano, the Bifurcated Public Sphere, Divine Strength, Ubufazi and Motherhood in Post-Apartheid South Africa" (Thesis, Rhodes University, 2017), 105.

65. Ngcobozi, "[Honour Thy Promise]," 76.

66. Joan Burke, *These Catholic Sisters Are All Mamas!: Towards the Inculturation of the Sisterhood in Africa, an Ethnographic Study* (Leiden: Brill, 2021).

The question arises if the WF members exercise some kind of influence through their contributions. One of the male leaders at the national level observes that women play a huge informal role by performing tasks "on the ground." Though women have been allowed to become elders and deacons since the beginning of the twenty-first century and the number of female delegates at all levels has increased, it is at a slow pace.[67] If they are present in decision-making meetings, they hardly speak out, according to another leader: "A very few of them can speak during these meetings, yeah very few. Maybe, we are in a culture where when men and women meet to discuss issues, women will say, 'let the men speak.'"[68] However, according to this male church leader, WF members may and do show their content or discontent with certain decisions of the church council by not paying or performing their tasks: "They may not voice out or put it in writing, but they choose by voting not to do something . . . And then you sense the absence of the WF, which is a kind of confusion."[69] Beverley Haddad observed the same and states that the WF may offer women "a space where they can express their opinion in a hidden way that is different from the dominant discourse."[70]

For the women of the WF, performing tasks (or not), and giving money (or not) is asserting performative power, a force that can change plans or decisions.[71] However, during the fieldwork, WF members were not able to give concrete examples of how they influenced decision-making, though I did hear some examples of this in the corridors. And one of the pastor's wives shared that if she does not do her job well (as chair of the WF), her husband (the pastor) and the whole church will suffer because then the contribution of the women would not be great.

> I think you have seen the large membership and the people who are very committed to all the programs of the church are the women. If I handle them well, they are very committed . . . even the whole welfare of the church will be there. If I mishandle them, even my husband starts to suffer.[72]

---

67. Interview 9, National leader RCZ (male) (6 November 2021).
68. Interview 12, National leader RCZ (male) (18 July 2022).
69. Interview 9, National leader RCZ (male) (6 November 2021).
70. Beverley Haddad, "The Manyano Movement in South Africa: Site of Struggle, Survival, and Resistance," *Agenda: Empowering Women for Gender Equity*, 61 (2004): 7.
71. Isaac Ariail Reed, "Power: Relational, Discursive, and Performative Dimensions," *Sociological Theory* 31.3 (1 September 2013): 193–218, 195.
72. Interview 3, Shalom, Pastor's wife (12 January 2021).

Thus, the WF formal influence seems to be limited, but informally the women exercise influence.

Overall, the members of the WF are proud to be part of the WF, because it is "work for God." They deem their practical work in the church to be very important in the eyes of God and people and are proud to contribute to the church's survival. Being a member also generates respect in society, people recognize the members on the bus or in the streets as "women of God."

According to Damaris Parsitau and other members of the Circle, the fact that women, despite their critical role in the maintenance and sustenance of the church, do not have control, is a matter of discrimination and exclusion.[73] By contrast, Le Roux, who follows Saba Mahmood[74] and Orit Avishai,[75] maintains that "[r]eligious women's actions should not automatically be interpreted only in terms of patriarchal resistance or compliance; their religious meaning-making acts should be taken into account."[76] WF members are involved and committed because they choose to do so, and that is, according to Le Roux, in itself an act of agency. Though WF members complain about the financial burden, they do comply with and do not seem to want to challenge the social structure, as this gives meaning to their lives and allows them access to certain privileges.

Conclusion

The members of the WF in the RCZ contribute their resources to the church by dedicating money and time. Their contributions are crucial for the daily affairs of the local congregation as well as the national church. Hence, it is important that ecclesiology reflect on the significance of these women's organizations and the role they have, not merely in the lives of its members, but also in the financial and social viability of the church, both locally and nationally.

WF have been criticized by African Women Theologians because of their acceptance of patriarchy and their propagation of gender stereotypes. This research found that for the women who are members of the WF, the choice to be involved is religiously motivated. WF membership gives meaning to the lives

---

73. Parsitau et al., "'Mama I Can't Breathe!'"458.

74. Saba Mahmood, *Politics of Piety: The Islamic Revival and the Feminist Subject* (Princeton: Princeton University Press, 2005).

75. Orit Avishai, "'Doing Religion' In a Secular World: Women in Conservative Religions and the Question of Agency." *Gender & Society* 22, no. 4 (2008): 409–33.

76. Le Roux, "Can religious women choose?" 15.

of its members because serving through the WF is seen as a way of serving God. While they have a certain performative power, their formal influence seems to be restricted within a hierarchical system of the WF itself and the church at large. The burden of financial obligations, lack of control over funds and a minor role in decision-making is a concern, which requires further thinking about the role of the WF. The reasons for women to be involved in the WF seem to be first and foremost social and spiritual in nature: it gives them dignity and respect and a chance to serve God through serving the church.

Bibliography

Abrams, Dominic, Michael A. Hogg, and José M. Marques. "A Social Psychological Framework for Understanding Social Inclusion and Exclusion." In *Social Psychology of Inclusion and Exclusion*, 1–24. Hove: Taylor & Francis Group, 2004.

Ammerman, Nancy T., ed. *Everyday Religion: Observing Modern Religious Lives*. New York: Oxford University Press, 2006.

Avishai, Orit. "'Doing Religion' In a Secular World: Women in Conservative Religions and the Question of Agency." *Gender & Society* 22, no. 4 (2008): 409–33.

Burke, Joan. *These Catholic Sisters Are All Mamas!: Towards the Inculturation of the Sisterhood in Africa, an Ethnographic Study*. Leiden: Brill, 2021.

Chelston Presbytery. "Annual General Meeting." Lusaka, 2022.

Chilisa, Bagele, and Gabo Ntseane. "Resisting Dominant Discourses: Implications of Indigenous, African Feminist Theory and Methods for Gender and Education Research." *Gender and Education* 22, no. 6 (2010): 617–32.

"Convert Currency, Zambian Kwacha to U.S. Dollar." https://www.convertworld.com/en/currency/zambia/zmw-to-usd.html.

Cronjé, J. M. *Vroue met nardusparfuum: die aandeel van die vrou in die sendingwerk van die Nederduitse Gereformeerde Kerk*. Pretoria: NG Kerkboekhandel Transvaal, 1984.

Dillard, Cynthia. "When the Ground Is Black, the Ground Is Fertile: Exploring Endarkene Feminist Epistemology and Healing Methodologies in the Spirit." In *Handbook of Critical and Indigenous Methodologies*, edited by Norman Denzin, Yvonna Lincoln, and Linda Smith, 277–92. Thousand Oaks: SAGE Publications, Inc., 2008.

Gaitskell, Deborah. "Devout Domesticity? A Century of African Women's Christianity in South Africa." In *Women and Gender in Southern Africa to 1945*, 251–72. London: James Currey, 1990.

Gaitskell, Deborah Lyndall. "Female Mission Initiatives: Black and White Women in Three Witwatersrand Churches, 1903–1939." Thesis, University of London, 1981.

Haddad, Beverley. "Church Uniforms as an Indigenous Form of Anglicanism: A South African Case Study." *Journal of Anglican Studies* 14, no. 2 (2016): 156–71.

———. "The Manyano Movement in South Africa: Site of Struggle, Survival, and Resistance." *Agenda: Empowering Women for Gender Equity* 61 (2004): 4–13.

Hennink, Monique M. "Cross-Cultural Focus Group Discussions." In *A New Era in Focus Group Research: Challenges, Innovation and Practice*, edited by Rosaline S. Barbour and David L. Morgan, 59–82. London: Palgrave Macmillan UK, 2017.

Holness, Lyn. "Motherhood and Spirituality: Faith Reflections from the Inside." *Agenda: Empowering Women for Gender Equity* 61 (2004): 66–71.

———. "Women's Piety and Empowerment: An Observer's Understanding of the Methodist Manyano's Movement." *Journal of Theology for Southern Africa* 98 (1998): 21–31.

Joziasse, L. J. "Women's Faith Seeking Life: Lived Christologies and the Transformation of Gender Relations in Two Kenyan Churches." Utrecht University, 2020.

Korte, Anne-Marie. "'Feminist Theology,' 'Lived Religion' and the Investigation of Women in Conservative Religions as Changing the Agenda of the Study of Religion." *DIVE-IN – An International Journal on Diversity and Inclusion* 2, no. 1 (22 December 2022): 13–32.

Le Roux, Elisabet. "Can Religious Women Choose? Holding the Tension between Complicity and Agency." *African Journal of Gender and Religion* 25, no. 1 (2019).

Mahmood, Saba. *Politics of Piety: The Islamic Revival and the Feminist Subject*. Princeton: Princeton University Press, 2005.

McKinney, William. "Resources." In *Studying Congregations: A New Handbook*, edited by Nancy Ammerman, Jackson Carroll, Carl Dudley, and William McKinney, 132–66. Nashville: Abingdon Press, 1998.

Moyo, N. "Revisiting Economic Justice. An Examination of Dignity of Women in a Zambian Context." In *Living with Dignity. African Perspectives on Gender Equality*, edited by Elna Mouton, Gertrude Kapuma, Len Hansen, and Thomas Thogom, 179–90. Stellenbosch: African Sun Media, 2015.

Moyse, Cordelia. *A History of the Mothers' Union: Women, Anglicanism and Globalisation, 1876–2008*. Woodbridge: Boydell & Brewer, 2009.

Mulenga, Chileshe. "Urban Slums Report: The Case of Lusaka, Zambia." *Understanding Slums: Case Studies for the Global Report 2003* (2003). https://www.ucl.ac.uk/dpu-projects/Global_Report/pdfs/Lusaka.pdf.

Ngcobozi, Lihle. "[Honour Thy Promise]: The Methodist Church Women's Manyano, the Bifurcated Public Sphere, Divine Strength, Ubufazi and Motherhood in Post-Apartheid South Africa." Thesis, Rhodes University, 2017.

Nicholls, Ruth. "Research and Indigenous Participation: Critical Reflexive Methods." *International Journal of Social Research Methodology* 12, no. 2 (1 April 2009): 117–26.

Parsitau, Damaris, Esther Mombo, Ini Dorcas Dah, and Tatiana Wairumi Gitonga. "'Mama I Can't Breathe!': Black/African Women of Faith Groaning for Social Justice and Gender Equality." *Mission Studies* 38 (2021): 448–69.

Phiri, Isabel Apawo. *Women, Presbyterianism and Patriarchy. Religious Experience of Chewa Women in Central Malawi*. Kachere Series. Blantyre: Christian Literature Association in Malawi, 1997.

Phiri, Jackson. "Church and Culture?: Exploring the Reception of Women's Ministries in the Reformed Church in Zambia in View of 1 Corinthians 14:26–40." Thesis, Stellenbosch University, 2017.

"Primary School Teacher Average Salary in Zambia 2023 – The Complete Guide." http://www.salaryexplorer.com/salarysurvey.php?loc=242&loctype=1&job=5886&jobtype=3.

Reed, Isaac Ariail. "Power: Relational, Discursive, and Performative Dimensions." *Sociological Theory* 31, no. 3 (1 September 2013): 193–218.

Reformed Church in Zambia. *Buku La Zinchito Za Chigwirizano Cha Azimai*, 2015.

Reformed Family Forum. "The Reformed Church in Zambia (RCZ)." https://rff.christians.co.za/the-reformed-church-in-zambia-rcz/.

Soothill, Jane E. *Gender, Social Change and Spiritual Power: Charismatic Christianity in Ghana*. 1st edition. Leiden; Boston: Brill, 2007.

Stausberg, M., and S. Engler, eds. *The Routledge Handbook of Research Methods in the Study of Religion*. 1st edition. London: Routledge, 2013.

Verstraelen-Gilhuis, Gerdien. *From Dutch Mission Church to Reformed Church in Zambia: The Scope for African Leadership and Initiative in the History of a Zambian Mission Church*. Franeker: Wever, 1982.

WageIndicator Foundation. "Salary Zambia." https://wageindicator.org/salary/minimum-wage/zambia.

Women's Regional Fellowship. "Annual Reports 1st January–31st December 2021." Annual Report. Lusaka, 2022.

World Bank. "Zambia | Data." https://data.worldbank.org/country/ZM.

16

The Necessity of Balanced Church Growth Strategies in Africa

A Biblical Perspective

Victor Umaru
Baptist College of Theology, Obinze, Owerri, Nigeria

Abstract

Church growth is God's will and a requirement for the church's mission. Church growth is a process that must be painstakingly understood; it does not happen automatically. It requires a systematic approach in order to be accomplished. Church growth results from God's will, not man's. It is a result of God's plan for the church and his final effort to spread the gospel on Earth, not of man's desire for conquest. This chapter aims to appraise biblical church growth strategies for practical and strategic church growth in Africa in the light of the Bible. Therefore, the research employs phenomenological and descriptive methods to achieve the purpose. The study reveals many contemporary church growth strategies for the African church. Some include signs and wonders miracle programmes, powerful preaching, prophetic prayers, children's church, the church building, dynamic leaders, excellent worship services, a conducive atmosphere, and internet outreach. The research also makes some recommendations that leaders of churches should set their priorities right by doing evangelism, church planting, discipleship, and Bible study; that churches should work to increase the bonding of their members; churches should put more effort into developing their members both within and without; churches should pay attention to social ministry; and finally, pastors/leaders of churches should motivate and equip their laity for full participation in the church.

Key words: church growth strategies, Africa, worship, signs and wonders, evangelism, discipleship, social ministry, leadership

Introduction

The state of the church growth in Africa is calling for attention. Church growth is only expanding by tens of hundreds while population growth is increasing by the tens of thousands.[1] Thank God for some localized development, but many churches are stagnating, struggling, and losing ground. Additionally, multitudes of Christians no longer attend church, and the gospel has little to no impact in many towns and cities today. Furthermore, church growth is an essential topic for Christianity. This is because the church of tomorrow depends on the seriousness with which church leaders and their people act today. The church needs to grow in all its aspects as a spiritual entity. This means that for the church to be said to have grown holistically, it must also have increased spiritually, physically, numerically, and financially.

One may observe churches sited throughout several African cities, especially Nigeria, in streets, in almost every nook and cranny. However, as one wanders through these locations, crimes of all kinds – including those committed in churches – are rising. Biblical church growth differs significantly from church growth in modern times. While most churches today are expanding with a sizable portion of unsaved individuals,[2] the first church mentioned in the book of Acts saw a daily increase in the number of saved people (2:47). This chapter suggests that God, who owns the church, is seriously concerned about this.

However, as depicted in several passages of the Bible,[3] growth is necessary to occur for the church in Africa to continue to exist and to impact the lives of current Christians significantly. God anticipates the comprehensive growth

---

1. Jason Mandryk, *Operation World: The Definitive Prayer Guide to Every Nation* (Colorado Springs: Biblica Publishing, 2010). This resource provides detailed information on the state of Christianity in various countries, including growth rates and challenges faced by churches in Africa.

2. Pew Research Center, "Why Americans Go (and Don't Go) to Religious Services," *Pew Forum on Religion & Public Life*, 2018. http://www.pewforum.org/2018/08/01/why-americans-go-to-religious-services. Accessed 11 July 2024.

3. Growth of the Jerusalem church (Acts 1:1–6:7); growth in Palestine and Samaria (Acts 6:8–9:31); growth in Gentile lands (Acts 9:32–12:24); growth through a missionary movement (Acts 12:25–16:5); growth in the urban centres (Acts 16:6–19:20).

of his church, which cannot be accomplished until today's church rises and examines its historical roots in biblical knowledge. The paper aims to investigate this problem of church growth from a biblical perspective, starting with this premise. The historical progression of church growth and its scriptural and theological justification is examined. This chapter makes the case that the African church must follow the biblical model of church growth to flourish and carry out the mission that God has given it, namely, the reconciliation of humanity to God in Christ and one another. The church's enormous and dual responsibility is to unite humanity with God and men with one another. The church cannot be called to be growing if it does not fulfil its obligation to spread the reconciling gospel of Christ and if it does not bring together all men and women of every race, class, and situation in mutual reconciliation. As is evident today, when the church neglects its responsibility for promoting divine and human reconciliation, it neglects the entire purpose of its existence.

The Church Growth Movement's Historical Context

Church growth is no longer a modern phenomenon that is spreading around the globe. It is interesting to note that the church growth movement is a development through missionary effort. The movement, commonly called church growth, began in India, a third-world mission field.[4] Third-generation missionary Donald G. McGavran was looking for better ways to start new churches when he came upon the fundamentals of church growth. C. Peter Wagner, a missionary and teacher, came after him.[5]

McGavran referred to what he considered a mission as "church growth." He defines church growth as "all that is involved in bringing men and women who do not have a personal relationship with Jesus Christ into fellowship with him and responsible church membership."[6] Three significant components are embedded, even if McGavran may not have intended it to be his definition: first, church growth is adult-focused; second, it is Christ-centered; and third, it is church-oriented. At the very least, it may be inferred that the term also emphasizes a church's population expansion.

---

4. D. A. McGavran, *How Churches Grow* (New York: Friendship Press, 1957), 10–17.
5. E. C. Smith, *Balanced Church Growth* (Nashville: Broadman Press, 1984), 10.
6. McGavran, *How Churches Grow*, 17.

Rainer believes that church growth is more than just a pastor's notion or formula and has a missiological foundation.[7] The focus of church growth is on local congregational growth and what has to be done to spur such expansion. This action includes all the resources of people, institutions, and publications dedicated to experiencing the concept and practising church growth principles, beginning with the principle of Donald McGavran. According to mission research, the best and most efficient way to encourage more individuals to make a sincere commitment to trust in Christ is through church growth.[8] Therefore church growth is the overall spiritual development of its members, which manifests itself physically in their standard of living and adherence to the command to make more disciples through soul-winning. Since the early 1970s, various new movements have arisen due to the church growth movement. These movements take the shape of initiatives for church planting, institutes, periodicals, other publications, and degree programmes. These are geared toward the objective of mission, which McGavran first described as an activity devoted to spreading the gospel and convincing people to follow Jesus and be accountable members of his church.[9]

Biblical Basis/Foundation for Church Growth

Church has been described in metaphors, for example, theocentric community,[10] as a mother,[11] clan,[12] political society,[13] mystical body of Christ,[14] communion

---

7. Thom S. Rainer, *The Book on Church Growth: History, Theology, and Principles* (Nashville: Broadman Press, 1993), 167.

8. Southern Baptist/Nigerian Baptist Convention, *The Church Growth Strategies Study/Mission Strategy Conference Report* (Ibadan: SBC/NBC, 1999).

9. Erwin Fahlubusch and William Geoffrey, *The Encyclopedia of Christianity* (Grand Rapids: Eerdmans; Leiden: Brill, 1999), 245.

10. Yusufu A. Obaje, "The Church As a Theocentric Community with Special Reference to Certain Aspects of Traditional African Ideas of God and Man" (PhD Dissertation, University of Edinburgh, 1982), presented the church as a "theocentric community."

11. Israel A. Akanji, "The Church as Mother: an African Christian Perspective" (MTh Thesis, NBTS, Ogbomoso, 1995), utilized the analogy of "mother" to depict the church.

12. John O. Enyinnaya, *God and the Church: Explorations in Contemporary Ecclesiology* (Saarbrücken: Lambert Academic Publishing, 2011), 50–83.

13. Avery Dulles, *Models of Revelation* (Maryknoll: Orbis, 1985), 32.

14. Anders Nygren, *Christ and His Church*, Alan Carlsten, trans. (London: SPCK, 1957), 89.

of saints,[15] people of God,[16] servant,[17] family,[18] etc. The church can be viewed on various levels; the primary level is at home, then the local assembly, which conventionally is referred to as the church, followed by the church universal.[19]

According to Horton, the word "church" and its translated forms *kirche*, *kerk* and *kirk*, were initially used to describe the Lord's house and, later, his people. The word *ekklēsia* is used to refer to a public gathering that a herald calls in the New Testament (Acts 19:32, 39–40); yet, in the Septuagint, it refers to the assembly or congregation of the Israelites, mainly when they are gathered before the Lord for religious purposes.[20] As a result, it alludes to the community that the living God establishes in the New Testament around the Messiah, Jesus. Thus, via three accounts of God's mighty acts in Christ Jesus, the Holy Spirit founded the church, God's spiritual family and the Christian community.[21] The mystery of the church is present everywhere; the spirit links worshipping souls to Christ and one another. More precisely, the one church of God is a supernatural organization growing toward the age to come rather than an institution. She is where the Lord, who has risen and ascended, operates. Her members are all united by a supernatural kinship and are all Christ. Through the power of the Holy Spirit, all of their efforts – which are gifts from Christ and are focused on his final goal – continue the work of Christ. The church will then appear in the upcoming era as the celestial city, and the people of God gathered in one assembly before the throne.[22]

Nevertheless, the biblical treatment of church growth is so thorough that an entire book would be needed to do it right. However, numerous instances of growth are documented in the book of Acts alone, and growth is frequently mentioned in other biblical accounts. Here are a few of these growth perspectives laid out.

---

15. Martin Luther, *A Compend of Luther's Theology*, ed. Hugh Thomson Kerr (Philadelphia: Westminster Press, 1943), 123.

16. Ernst Kasemann, *The Wandering People of God: an Investigation of the Letter to the Hebrews*, Roy A. Harrisville, L. Sandberg, trans. (Minneapolis: Augsburg Publishing House, 1984), 17.

17. Dietrich Bonhoeffer, *Letters and Papers from Prison* (London: SCM Press, 1953), 166.

18. Harry Sawyer, *Creative Evangelism: Towards a New Christian Encounter with Africa* (London: Lutterworth, 1968).

19. Francis Adebayo, *Churching: A Perspective on Church Development* (Lagos: A Roycom Media Publication, 2012), 7.

20. David Horton, ed., *The Portable Seminary: A Master's Level Overview in One Volume* (Grand Rapids: Baker, 2006), 182.

21. Horton, *The Portable Seminary*, 182.

22. Horton, *The Portable Seminary*, 182–3.

Number of church members growing

Statistical accomplishments are carefully documented in the Book of Acts.[23] First is the church's expansion in Jerusalem (Acts 1:1–6:7). Acts 6:7 contains a synopsis of the events in the book of Acts. It suggests that the disciples multiplied considerably, the Gospel spread quickly, and the Jewish priests openly obeyed.[24] The second stage of church growth was essentially a spillage from Jerusalem and the first church there, as seen in Acts 6:8–9:31. The Gospel reached Judea, Galilee, and Samaria as it spread. Two highly significant events introduced a cause-and-effect drive for growth. These incidents included the murder of Stephen and Saul of Tarsus's conversion. The geographical spread of the church is highlighted in Luke's overview of this period (Acts 9:31). Others include expansion through a missionary movement (Acts 12:25–16:5) and growth in Gentile lands (Acts 9:32–12:24).[25] There was also growth in urban centres (Acts 16:6–19:20): great cities such as Philippi, Thessalonica, Berea, Athens, Corinth and Ephesus became the centres of Christian missions.[26] Finally, the gospel reached the centre of the Roman Empire (Acts 19:21–28:31).[27]

Spiritual church growth

The New Testament churches made time for their members' spiritual development while being growth-oriented and appearing to devote their resources to producing disciples. Their dedication to outreach did not prevent them from having quality concerns. There appears to be a direct correlation between the joy of expanding one's spiritual influence and the emergence of a spiritual mindset.

Growth in the strength of the church

Paul frequently discussed the topic of spiritual vigour. He described it as edifying, or the strengthening of the local church, which is the body of Christ. Paul also provided specific guidelines for gauging the church's strength. Paul constantly stressed his desire for a church that was spiritually developed. The

---

23. Thom S. Rainer, "Church Growth and Evangelism in the Book of Acts," *Criswell Theological Review* 5 (Fall, 1990): 64–65.

24. Rainer, "Church Growth," 64–65.

25. Frank R. Tillapaugh, *Unleashing the Church* (Ventura: Regal, 1982), 11.

26. John T. Sisemore, *Church Growth through the Sunday School* (Nashville: Broadman Press, 1983), 23.

27. Sisemore, *Church Growth through the Sunday School*, 23.

entire process of human development was intertwined with church edification. Individual Christians mature as they become more like Christ; the church becomes whole in Christ as they mature. There is, without a doubt, a very significant association between developing churches and growing Christians. The unique spiritual dimension so crucial to a Christian permeates every aspect of the church body. The development of people and the body of Christ are inextricably linked.

Growth in the church's functional capacity

A church is a dynamic, evolving, and active organism. A church must run smoothly and effectively since it is an organism, particularly a living body of Christ. A church needs proper administration and organization in order to function.[28] Like any other creature, a church has the potential to become entirely consumed with the task of sustaining itself. However, this option does not excuse a church from ignoring its practical requirements or disliking structure and administration. Every aspect of a church's growth and ministry depends on meeting its functional demands. An inefficient or laissez-faire manner of running things is inferior to well-organized management. More than a casual attitude toward bodily functions is required for the service of the Lord. Church management demands constant cautious and knowledgeable attention. A church cannot benefit spiritually from an overwhelming need for efficiency or a complete disdain for excellent labour. On the other hand, the spiritual well-being of a church will be significantly impacted by both views.[29]

Biblical Church Growth Strategies

God wants his churches to grow.[30] Biblical teachings firmly support the notion that God wants church growth. The Great Commission is one of the more explicit commands (Matt 28:16–20). The verb "make disciples" contains the direct imperative in the command. Going, baptizing, and teaching are three participles that specify the method or methods by which this discipleship is to be carried out. The goal of the Great Commission is to find, keep, and develop Christ-followers.[31]

---

28. L. E. Schaller, *Survival Tactics in the Parish* (Nashville: Abingdon, 1986), 56.
29. Schaller, *Survival Tactics in the Parish*, 56.
30. Sisemore, *Church Growth through the Sunday School*, 13.
31. Sisemore, *Church Growth through the Sunday School*, 13.

The rapid growth of the New Testament churches is described in the book of Acts, which provides a record of numerical growth. Initially, the Christians were a company of one hundred and twenty people (Acts 1:15). A total of three thousand souls were added on Pentecost (Acts 2:41–42). The author of Acts 4:4 reports that the disciples prayed for courage to proclaim the gospel after facing threats, persecution, and incarceration. As a result, the group grew to five thousand men. In a chapter later in Acts, the focus shifts to many men and women who joined the community (5:14). According to Acts 6:1–7, there were many more disciples than before. Acts 9 starts to document the rise in the number of churches and their membership. It is reported that there were now more congregations in Judea, Samaria, and Galilee (Acts 9:31). The word shift from "church" to "churches" in Acts 16:5 emphasizes the role that organized Christian fellowships (churches) played in the formation of God's missionary strategy. Finally, Paul referred to the expansion of the churches as myriads (countless thousands) (Acts 21:20). Undoubtedly, tens of thousands of people accepted Christ as their saviour and joined his churches.

The Bible has several biblical church growth strategies, but only two of them are covered here:

The first strategy is prayer, the primary driver of the early church's rapid expansion. The small group of believers "joined in unceasing prayer" before Pentecost (Acts 1:14). The persistent waves of the early church's growth were greatly aided by the members' commitment to prayer (Acts 2:42). The church gathered for undivided prayer and reached new heights of missionary audacity when the Sanhedrin threatened the followers with punishment if they continued to speak about the "name" (Acts 4:18). Again, the church remained united in prayer. Development persisted when Herod tried to kill the evangelical zeal by persecution (Acts 12:5).

All of the world's armaments were overcome by the prayer of the "powerless." An angel came to save Peter from jail, and the gospel was spread (Acts 11:11). Herod was killed by the Lord and perished horribly (Acts 11:23). Only shortly afterwards the oppressive behaviour toward the church continued. But because of the effectiveness of prayer, the gospel spread unimpeded.[32]

Satan has always opposed God-favoured church-growth plans throughout history. The final piece of armour for equipping churches is to "pray in the Spirit on all occasions with all kinds of prayers and requests" (Eph 6:18 NIV). The opposition of "the rulers . . . the authorities . . . the powers . . . and the spiritual

---

32. Thom S. Rainer, "Church Growth and Evangelism in Acts," *Criswell Theological Review*, 5 (1990): 57–68.

forces of darkness in the heavenly realms" (Eph 6:12 NIV) is something that every church leader who has witnessed God bless the growth of their church has also experienced. Wagner's empirical study supported the following: "The more deeply I dig beneath the surface of church growth principles, the more thoroughly convinced I become that the real battle is a spiritual battle and that our principal weapon is prayer."[33]

Therefore, the church must stand up and wage unrelenting war against Satan's evil deeds rather than folding its arms and watching as he wrecks the world. The church has not only the power but also the duty to overthrow the kingdom of Satan and free people to worship and serve God. Therefore, the church must mobilize in "offensive prayer and word, and do serious warfare to destroy the works of the devil in the life of men."[34] This was why Jesus came to the world: "The reason the Son of God appeared was to destroy the devil's work" (1 John 3:8 NIV).

Second, according to Rainer, "signs and wonders" or occasionally "power evangelism" are another method for growing churches. Power evangelism was a successful expansion method in the early church and should not be disregarded in modern times. The apostles of the Lord Jesus Christ employed this method of gospel propagation. In their prayer for such a miracle, Peter and John said, "Now, Lord, consider their threats and enable your servants to speak your word with great boldness. Stretch out your hand to heal and perform signs and wonders through the name of your holy servant Jesus" (Acts 4:29–30 NIV). The apostles "performed many signs and wonders among the people" according to Acts 5:12. What is the outcome? "Nevertheless, more and more men and women believed in the Lord and were added to their number" (Acts 5:14 NIV).[35]

Reflection on the Place of Church Growth in Africa

There is no doubt that Christianity and church growth are experiencing growth on African soil, yet facing a significant difficulty. The problem is that holiness and spirituality are neglected in favour of solid numerical development. Some

---

33. C. P. Wagner, *Church Planting for a Greater Harvest* (Ventura: Regal, 1990), 46.

34. Francis Bola Akin-John, *Spiritual Warfare and Church Growth* (Lagos: Church Growth Service INC., 2013), 18–19.

35. Rainer, *The Book of Church Growth: History, Theology, and Principles*, 85–86, cites C. P. Wagner, *Spiritual Power and Church Growth* (Altamonte Springs: Creation House, 1986), 119–20, in which Wagner himself cites an interview with Ausencio Gonzalez, on September 6, 1984.

churches place little emphasis on balanced growth, which, if care is not taken, could lead to a shift in the mission of the church of Jesus Christ, which is to get people ready for his second coming.

A balanced and comprehensive view of church growth includes everything related to the church's expansion, growth, and extension and the accomplishment of the Lord Jesus Christ's Great Commission, as stated in Matthew 28:19–20. Francis Bola Akin-John emphasizes two complementary aspects of church growth, which are numerical and spiritual. These two characteristics serve as the church's two pillars. "The more we have, the more quality we must get from it," the saying goes.[36] According to Akin-John, the church must have more quantity and far higher quality. The church must boost its quality growth in addition to its quantity growth. Both must be held in a permanent state of tension in the church.[37]

Spiritual and numerical growth must coexist in harmony. Neither ought to exist without the other. However, these two vast spectrums are where the church is split. While many support spiritual development, others are steadfastly committed to numerical growth. To be clear, spiritual growth occurs when people genuinely know the Lord, are committed to him, disciple, and mature into strong, active Christians who can serve others. When the church has a procedure to convert sinners to saints, attendees to Christians, Christians to ministers, and leaders to missionaries, it is said to be experiencing quality growth.[38] Such a range of growth may be observed in the holiness, Baptist, Methodist, and evangelical churches. These various denominations of churches uphold God's inerrant and unadulterated word and live with eternity in mind. The conservative outlook on life and opposition to the worldliness, ungodliness, and extravagant living that many Christians today exhibit is still mainly taught to its adherents. These are truly deserving of recognition. Although it is rare to see many of these churches and their leaders in print and electronic media, they are there, unnoticed and occasionally performing tremendous deeds for the Lord. Due to their emphasis on biblical teaching and tough Christian living, scandals and immoral behaviour are relatively low in these churches.[39]

---

36. Francis Bola Akin-John, *Quality and Quantity Growth in Church* (Lagos: Church Growth Service, 2008), 33.

37. Akin-John, *Quality and Quantity Growth in Church*, 33.

38. Akin-John, *Quality and Quantity Growth in Church*, 33.

39. Francis Bola Akin-John, *Church Overseers and Senior Pastors Handbook*, vol. 1 (Lagos: Church Growth Service, 2016), 43–61.

Sadly, many of these churches have little to show for their efforts in terms of membership expansion. Most of them have an internal focus, and some have stagnated. Every year, the same number of people attend. In reality, many of them are losing members to churches with larger congregations. Many of these churches struggle with the development and change occurring around them.[40]

The second group of churches places a greater emphasis on membership expansion. They frequently bring a considerable number of members to the church. The church's events and gatherings are crowded with attendees. The church's festivities draw tens of thousands of participants. However, the story mostly ends there. They are still throngs, showing little to no sign of having encountered Christ. They are nominal Christians who lack the outward manifestations of piety and repentance in their daily conduct. Even though these churches appear to be growing in numbers on the outside, there is interior carnality and a fleshly problem. They mainly concentrate on addressing the people's perceived wants, scarcely addressing their actual requirements. Of course, people adore these places of worship, and one may regularly see them advertised in print and electronic media for various events. These churches' pastors are frequently seen and recognized on television and in the media. They manage their churches as both a business and a private estate. Most people are left unprepared for the Lord – untrained and undisciplined[41]

Most churches in this category do not have any discipleship programme in place, and those that do tend to have teachings that are merely superficial, flimsy, and common sense. Since most of their pastors have never attended a reputable Bible school, it is unsurprising that they understand the Bible incorrectly and only preach when it is convenient. Numerous thousands of people attend these churches' celebration meetings because of the gifts, anointing, and visible manifestations of purported "miracles," yet the spiritual needs of the attendees are neglected. Although they have spent years in the church, the members hardly know the Lord, and even when they do, they still act like immature and carnal baby Christians. Many of their leaders have transformed these churches into cults and sects. They teach, dominate and control their people's eating, drinking, marriage, relationship, and daily living.[42] There are exceptions, whose leaders established a strong foundation for them,

---

40. Gold O. Anie, *Administrative Functions of a Pastor in the Church* (Ibadan: Baptist Press, 2013); Francis Bola Akin-John, *25 Pillars of Church Health* (Lagos: Church Growth Service, 2012), 21–31.

41. Francis Bola Akin-John, *Leading Your Church to Lasting Growth* (Lagos: Church Growth Service, 2017), 37–59.

42. Bola, *Quality and Quantity Growth in Church*, 35.

having recognized the significance of both spiritual and numerical growth. These churches are referred to as "balanced churches" by Akin-John.[43] They plan for numerical and spiritual growth in their churches and implement programmes to transform that growth.

God desires the church to expand. In the church, he desires extraordinary growth. All people must "be saved and to come to a knowledge of the truth," according to God (1 Tim 2:4 NIV). God's desire is for the church to increase the number of souls saved in every country and community. Jesus suffered, died, and rose again for the church to see a significant influx of souls into the kingdom of God. Akin-John says there are two things Jesus is building now: his church here on earth and mansions for his bride in heaven. The mansion in heaven will remain empty if the church is not growing in quality. The Lord has not returned for his bride because many still need to fill those heavenly mansions. The Lord wants as many people as possible to come unto him in true repentance and salvation.[44]

This numerical growth needs to be carefully balanced with spiritual growth. The Lord will not reduce his standards even if he desires for as many people as possible to come to a saving knowledge of Christ. Therefore, the African church is responsible for raising quality people for the Lord as coworkers with God. The church's numerical development must translate into spiritual progress. In the church, spiritual and numerical expansion must coexist in harmony. Holistic church growth must be held in constant tension in any church that sincerely strives to be the true church of Christ in Africa. Every local church's mission and programmes must be focused on preserving this precarious equilibrium. "To have one without the other is a heartbreaking shame."[45] Church leaders who are sincere about going to heaven must actively try to make both happen in their congregation. As is evident in many churches today, numerical expansion without spiritual progress will result in sinful behaviour, carnality, and Christians who are simply a caricature of authentic followers of the Lord. In the same way, the church will stagnate, struggle, become irrelevant, split off, and go into a "downward spiral" if there is no equivalent increase in the number of members.

---

43. Bola, *Quality and Quantity Growth in Church*, 41.
44. Bola, *Quality and Quantity Growth in Church*, 41–42.
45. Bola, *Quality and Quantity Growth in Church*, 42–43.

Contemporary Church Growth Strategies for the African Church

Here are some viable tactics that can help the African church get the required and desired inflow:

Programs about miracles and wonders

The power of the gifts of the Holy Spirit and the presence of God are constant draws for people to the church. This may be due to the numerous issues and demonic oppressions that encourage people to rush and crowd into any church where miracles occur. People will inevitably enter a church where God is at work.

Strong preaching

Intense and energetic preaching is another method of church development that can help the African church expand quickly. Fortunately, this approach has been supported by numerous church growth specialists. They reaffirmed the necessity and significance of preaching to any church's expansion.[46] God has decided to communicate his will, heart, mind, love and strength to people through preaching. Therefore, it is impossible to overstate the importance of preaching in the development of any church.

On the other hand, some African churches are declining every day, perhaps due to the one consistent preaching style.[47] Preaching that is powerful, piercing, penetrating, relevant, vibrant and dynamic – rather than just theoretical – is necessary to increase church attendance. Akin-John says that preaching that tickles the ear but fails to touch the heart will never help the church's growth. Preaching too cold, powerless, and less focused will be valueless.[48]

Today's audience is looking for engaging sermons. Of course, churches with compelling and energetic preachers always experience good and quick growth.[49] Preaching that will promote the expansion of any faith must not be divisive. It must be straightforward, understandable, timely and motivating; it also needs to be alive and capable of providing life-changing decision. Preaching must offer the people comfort, repentance, joy, strength, hope, inspiration, and

---

46. Akin-John, *Quality and Quantity Growth in Church*, 105.
47. Francis Bola Akin-John, *120 Strategies Ways to Increase Church Attendance* (Lagos: Church Growth Service, 2014), 99.
48. Akin-John, *Quality and Quantity Growth in Church*, 105.
49. Akin-John, *120 Strategies Ways to Increase Church Attendance*, 105.

revelation. They must be given direction on continuing their walk with the Lord. It must enable people to overcome obstacles, succeed, develop, advance, and cling to God.[50]

Prophetic prayers

The gift of prophecy is undoubtedly one of God's spiritual gifts reintroduced to the church in these final days. Some churches in Africa seem to support this claim. "The fulfilment of the great commission demands the gifts of prophets."[51] Any church that wants to expand significantly must be open to prophetic prayers.[52] The Lord's revelation and words are given to a person whom the entire church has come to believe as a prophet of God, and prophetic prayers result from those revelations and words.[53] More people visit the church because of the fantastic outcomes and miracles the given prayers bring about.

Children's church

It is disappointing that many churches have not taken this approach seriously. Some churches keep children outside the church or in a rundown old structure. Yet when guided appropriately, the children can genuinely help the church develop. Churches should have a proper children's church with qualified ministers or leaders, not just a class. Parents are searching for churches that genuinely care about their children. A good children's church will, therefore, contribute to the church's growth both now and in the future. Many churches that made wise investments in their children are now experiencing the benefits of their decisions.

---

50. Akin-John, *Quality and Quantity Growth in Church*, 105.
51. Akin-John, *Quality and Quantity Growth in Church*, 107.
52. Prophetic prayers are prayers initiated and guided by the Holy Spirit, aimed at communicating God's will, purposes, and messages. They go beyond personal petitions and intercessions for immediate needs and align with God's broader plans and kingdom purposes. These prayers involve speaking God's words, intercession with insight, edification, encouragement, and comfort, alignment with God's purposes, submission to God's sovereignty, and discernment and testing. They are often used to build up, encourage, and comfort believers, seeking transformation and alignment with God's kingdom values. They are offered in humility and submission to God's wisdom and timing, and should be tested against Scripture and the community of believers (Matt 6:10; 1 Cor 14:3; 1 Thess 5:19–22).
53. Akin-John, *Quality and Quantity Growth in Church*, 107.

The church structure

Despite how depressing it may sound, a church's ability to develop can be aided or hindered by the construction of new facilities.[54] Akin-John describes modern people as "civilized worshippers."[55] They actively seek a quality, appealing, and convenient location for worship. After noticing the structure, they frequently arrive to observe what God is doing within the building. It makes sense that there are enormous churches dotted across the city and frequently packed with worshippers, yet some churches that are narrow-minded about this tactic have empty pews. An inadequately sized, congested and startlingly hot structure will significantly hinder the church's ability to expand. "A small permanent structure usually kills off the evangelism. The force of the gifts of the Holy Spirit and the presence of God are constant draws for people to the church."[56] Increasing church attendance demands that the building be given the serious attention it deserves. "Small buildings or locations will sentence the church to perpetual smallness."[57] When a church building is alluring, appealing, clean and well-decorated inside, people will undoubtedly be drawn to it, and church attendance will undoubtedly rise.

Dynamic leadership

"Until the appropriate leader comes, many churches remain inactive. Leaders define a congregation's destiny more than its physical structures, geographic location, population, history, or traditions."[58] Everybody knows that leadership is what makes things happen. The leader will determine whether the church is alluring and magnetic. Additionally, the leader is the one who will make the church repulsive and repellent. Most of the time, people attend churches because of the clergy. A Pew Research Center survey reveals that people regularly attend religious services to feel closer to God. However, reasons for not attending are more complex. About three-in-ten people who attend only a few times a year are not believers, but a larger share stay away not due to a lack of faith but for other reasons. Some practice their faith in other ways, while others dislike specific congregations or services, such as not finding a church

---

54. Akin-John, *120 Strategies Ways to Increase Church Attendance*, 127.
55. Akin-John, *Quality and Quantity Growth in Church*, 107.
56. Akin-John, *Quality and Quantity Growth in Church*, 127.
57. Akin-John, *Quality and Quantity Growth in Church*, 127.
58. Odunaya Oke, *Leadership for Building a Prevailing Church* (Lagos: Charis Ventures Publication, 2015), 29.

or sermons they like.[59] As a result of the leaders, several of the churches in the city have thousands of members. Many people are quitting some churches just because of their leaders. Akin-John says leaders are the root of 60 percent of the church's growth issues.[60] "It is an unwritten law that the church will become what the minister is."[61]

Planned worship services

Many church growth specialists agree that having a fantastic planned worship service is a solid strategy for expanding the church and increasing attendance.[62] The Sunday worship session must be potent, unique, and extraordinary. Every church must treat its worship sessions seriously if it hopes to expand. A lifeless, ineffective, chilly, stiff and colourless service cannot aid in the church's expansion. A worship session that cannot rejuvenate, recharge, refresh and refire the congregation will not aid in expanding the church. If one were to look around on Sundays in most African cities, one would notice people going from one street to another. While some individuals drive for hours to church, others have churches in their backyards. As a result, an excellent worship service unites people from near and far; distance is not an obstacle. Every worship session must have the potential to grow the church. In the worship session, God must be both heard and seen. When individuals appreciate and encounter God in their worship services meaningfully and personally, they will tell others about it and invite them along the following time.

---

59. Pew Research Center, "Why Americans Go (and Don't Go) to Religious Services," *Pew Forum on Religion & Public Life*, 2018. http://www.pewforum.org/2018/08/01/why-americans-go-to-religious-services. Accessed 11 July 2024. See also, Thom S. Rainer, *Breakout Churches: Discover How to Make the Leap* (Grand Rapids: Zondervan, 2005); Yonggi Cho, *My Church Growth Stories* (Umuahia: Christian Crusaders, n.p); Rick Warren, *The Purpose Driven Church* (Grand Rapids: Zondervan, 2003).

60. Francis Bola Akin-John, *Grow the Pastor Grow the Church* (Lagos: Church Growth Service, 2010), 128.

61. Akin-John, *Grow the Pastor Grow the Church*, 128.

62. L. E. Schaller, *The Local Church Looks to The Future: A Guide to Church Planning* (Abingdon: Abingdon Press, 1968); D. A. McGavran and W. C. Arn, *Ten Steps for Church Growth* (New York: Harper & Row, Publishers, 1977); Waldo J. Werning, *Vision and Strategy for Church Growth* (Chicago: Moody Press, 1977); C. P. Wagner, *Your Church Can Grow: Seven Vital Signs of a Healthy Church* (Ventura: Regal Books, 1985); Peter Falk, *The Growth of the Church in Africa* (Bukuru: ACTS, 1921).

Conducive atmosphere

The atmosphere contributes significantly to attendance. People want to worship God with a minimum of comfort. People will withdraw when the environment is harsh, damp and full of odours. Today's environment must be unhurried, calm, cosy and perfectly suitable for worship. The structure must be sound, roomy, and well-ventilated. The pews and seats should be cosy, with relaxing space for the back. The restrooms and washrooms must be spotless and organized. The conveniences must be helpful and strategically located. While inconsequential to some, these factors help some people choose which church to attend. Some churches that overlooked these items went through a decline and are still declining.

Internet outreach

One of the quickest ways to bring the good news of salvation to millions of people both within and outside of Africa with little to no stress is to preach the gospel or reach out to souls online. Churches inform people about their programmes, church services, seminars, conferences, workshops and summits inside and outside Africa. There are many churches with evangelism-focused websites. Many continue to visit the website because it has several messages about salvation, repentance, the love of God, faith, holiness, hope for the hopeless, and other topics. On YouTube, several recorded messages can be watched and blessed by the public.

Conclusion

The primary purpose of this chapter is to present biblical church growth strategies as a necessity for the African church. To this end, an effort has also been made to give a brief history of the church growth movement. In addition, the church's biblical history and nature were looked upon alongside the biblical examples of church growth strategies. Such strategies are identified factors contributing to expanding churches in the Bible world. The Bible not only encourages but also calls for church development. God wants his churches to expand. Therefore, the African church should aim for expansion because God wants, expects, and promises it. God anticipates growth because it is a characteristic of living things. As healthy bodies grow, so too should healthy churches.

Churches in hostile environments, where the populace is adamantly opposed to the gospel, may see slight expansion. However, churches must not accept these circumstances as a rule or ideal. Many justifications are given for failure to advance, but none are true. Growth rather than stagnation is the usual trend for the Lord's churches. Jesus, the Lord, guarantees development. The power for growth comes from the Holy Spirit. As congregations allow God to instill in them a hope for real church growth, a vision for growth emerges.

The only achievable goal for Christian ministry is balanced church growth, which is what is promoted in this chapter. There is enough power to accomplish the aim. God's people must realize the full significance of balanced church growth. Balanced church growth signifies church planting, making disciples, and ongoing harvest. Only when Christians and churches allow the Holy Spirit to guide them to more efficient means (strategies) of converting people to Christ and incorporating them into vibrant congregations can the aim of reproducing Christians and churches be achieved.

The Holy Spirit is involved in every step of genuine church growth. He encourages growth, directs growth, offers the ability, permits growth and keeps the growth process going.

Recommendations

1. Since some churches are not growing in proper dimensions, and this is due to poor or bad pastoral leadership, the writer recommends that the pastor should set his priorities right. The Great Commission should be vigorously pursued. Aggressive evangelism, church planting, Bible study, and discipleship training should be handled if they need growth in their churches. Churches should be planted where there is none. Churches are advised not to duplicate churches where a church already exists. Practical Bible study and discipleship training will enhance the spiritual growth of church members.

2. The church should work to increase the bonding of its members. This can be done by utilizing small groups, teaching, and informal events such as love feasts and picnics. The goal is to embark on activities and programmes to enhance numerical growth, and the members will be retained.

3. The church's evangelistic effort is also recommended to target those outside and inside. This arises from the discovery that some people in the church are merely strangers and not yet genuinely church members. It is wrong to assume that everybody in the church is a believer. Thus, preaching evangelistic sermons is necessary from

time to time, as well as other efforts geared toward helping strangers become a part of the spiritual community of God.
4. The church needs to pay attention to social ministry. The church has different categories of needy people, including the sick, poor, widows, orphans, unemployed, and retired. The church must minister to its members' spiritual, emotional and physical needs and the community where it is situated. Community service attracts people to the church because people seek a place to feel at home and a sense of belonging.
5. Church leaders must motivate and equip their laity to participate fully in the church. The full involvement of every segment of the church is necessary if the church will not operate below capacity. To this end, more emphasis needs to be placed on spiritual gifts. Spiritual gifts need to be taught, and church life needs to be organized so that duties are distributed based on them.

Bibliography

Adebayo, Francis. *Churching: A Perspective on Church Development*. Lagos: A Roycom Media Publication, 2012.
Akanji, Israel A. "The Church as Mother: an African Christian Perspective." MTh Thesis, NBTS, Ogbomoso, 1995.
Anie, Gold O. *Administrative Functions of a Pastor in the Church*. Ibadan: Baptist Press (Nig.) Limited, 2013.
"Benefits of a Children's Ministry," https://graceplano.church/about/benefits-of-a-childrens-ministry/. Accessed 10 July 2024.
Bola, Francis Akin-John, *120 Strategies Ways to Increase Church Attendance*. Lagos: Church Growth Service, 2014.
———. *25 Pillars of Church Health*. Lagos: Church Growth Service, 2012.
———. *Church Overseers and Senior Pastors Handbook*. Lagos: Church Growth Service, 2016.
———. *Grow the Pastor Grow the Church*. Lagos: Church Growth Service, 2010.
———. *Leading your Church to Lasting Growth*. Lagos: Church Growth Service, 2012.
———. *Quality and Quantity Growth in Church*. Lagos: Church Growth Service, 2008.
———. *Spiritual Warfare and Church Growth*. Lagos: Church Growth Service, 2013.
Bonhoeffer, Dietrich. *Letters and Papers from Prison*. London: SCM Press, 1953.
Callahan, Kennon L. *Twelve Keys to an Effective Church*. San Francisco: Harper & Row, 1983.
Cho, Yonggi. *My Church Growth Stories*. Umuahia: Christian Crusaders, n.p.

Dulles, Avery. *Models of Revelation*. Maryknoll: Orbis, 1985.

Enyinnaya, John O. *God and the Church: Explorations in Contemporary Ecclesiology*. Saarbrücken: Lambert Academic Publishing, 2011.

Fahlubusch, Erwin, and William Geoffrey. *The Encyclopedia of Christianity*. Grand Rapids: Eerdmans; Leiden: Brill, 1999.

Falk, Peter. *The Growth of the Church in Africa*. Bukuru, Jos: ACTS, 1921.

Hadaway, C. Kirk. *Church Growth Principles: Separating Fact from Fictions*. Nashville: Broadman Press, 1991.

Horton, David, ed. *The Portable Seminary: A Master's Level Overview in One Volume*. Grand Rapids: Baker, 2006.

Kasemann, Ernst. *The Wandering People of God: An Investigation of the Letter to the Hebrews*. Translated by Roy A. Harrisville and L. Sandberg. Minneapolis: Augsburg Publishing House, 1984.

Luther, Martin. *A Compend of Luther's Theology*. Edited by Hugh Thomson Kerr. Philadelphia: Westminster Press, 1943.

Mandryk, Jason. *Operation World: The Definitive Prayer Guide to Every Nation*. Colorado Springs: Biblica Publishing, 2010.

McGavran, Donald A., and Winfield C. Arn. *Ten Steps for Church Growth*. New York: Harper & Row Publishers, 1977.

———. *How Churches Grow*. New York: Friendship Press, 1957.

Nygren, Anders. *Christ and His Church*. Translated by Alan Carlsten. London: SPCK, 1957.

Obaje, Yusufu A. "The Church as a Theocentric Community with Special Reference to Certain Aspects of Traditional African Ideas of God and Man." PhD dissertation, University of Edinburgh, 1982.

Oke, Odunaya. *Leadership for Building a Prevailing Church*. Lagos: Charis Ventures Publication, 2015.

Pew Research Center, "Why Americans Go (and Don't Go) to Religious Services," *Pew Forum on Religion & Public Life*, 2018. http://www.pewforum.org/2018/08/01/why-americans-go-to-religious-services. Accessed 11 July 2024.

Rainer, Thom S. "Church Growth and Evangelism in the Book of Acts." *Criswell Theological Review* 5 (Fall, 1990).

———. *The Book on Church Growth: History Theology, and Principles*. Nashville: Broadman Press, 1993.

———. *Breakout Churches: Discover How to Make the Leap*. Grand Rapids: Zondervan, 2005.

Sawyer, Harry. *Creative Evangelism: Towards a New Christian Encounter with Africa*. London: Lutterworth, 1968.

Schaller, Lyle E. *Survival Tactics in the Parish*. Nashville: Abingdon, 1986.

———. *The Local Church Looks to The Future: A Guide to Church Planning*. Nashville: Abingdon, 1968.

Sisemore, John T. *Church Growth Through the Sunday School.* Nashville: Broadman Press, 1983.
Smith, Ebbie C. *Balanced Church Growth.* Nashville: Broadman Press, 1984.
Southern Baptist/Nigerian Baptist Convention. *The Church Growth Strategies Study/Mission Strategy Conference Report.* Ibadan: SBC/NBC, 1999.
Stott, John R.W. *The Spirit, the Church, and the World.* Downers Grove: InterVarsity, 1990.
Tillapaugh, Frank R. *Unleashing the Church.* Ventura: Regal, 1982.
Wagner, C. Peter. *Church Planting for a Greater Harvest.* Ventura: Regal, 1990.
———. *Your Church Can Grow: Seven Vital Signs of a Healthy Church.* Ventura: Regal Books, 1985.
Warren, Rick. *The Purpose Driven Church.* Grand Rapids: Zondervan, 2003.
Werning, Waldo J. *Vision and Strategy for Church Growth.* Chicago: Moody Press, 1977.

17

"A Woman Teaches with Heart"

The Mama Voice in Tanzanian Women's Preaching

Tamie Davis
Angelina Noble Centre

Abstract

This chapter argues for a distinctive female voice in Tanzanian women's preaching: the mama voice. Building on scholars who have noted an expanding role of women in some parts of the African church, and contra to findings that women's preaching style is a replication of male power, it argues that Tanzanian women draw on and deploy their femininity in preaching, gaining authority from it. Using ethnographic interviews with women from a range of denominations and the author's experience in Tanzanian church life over the last decade, it presents evidence for a recognizable cadence, embodiment and content to women's preaching in Tanzania: a mama voice. This mama voice draws on traditional cultural and religious constructions of femininity as enhancers of life at both a societal and familial level and marries them to a theology of the indwelling and transformation of the Holy Spirit. Thus, as a woman preaches, the word of God comes forth from her, inseparable from her femininity and delivered in a feminine way. This chapter argues that this fusion of the word of God and femininity is deeply dignifying for women preachers and for femininity more broadly, and examines how women who preach with a mama voice navigate their authority in their patriarchal society.

Key words: women, preaching, Tanzania, femininity, indwelling of the Holy Spirit, mama voice, women's preaching, embodiment

Introduction

In 2014 I was sitting in a Swahili literature lecture at St John's University of Tanzania in Dodoma, Tanzania. Dismayed at the poor attendance and students walking in late, the lecturer launched into a speech about how she stayed awake at night weeping tears over their tardiness and crying out to God to bring change in these, her children. It struck me as an extraordinarily emotional appeal and one I would never hear from a male lecturer. This lecturer's femininity was not only prominent; it was the vehicle for her appeal to the students. It is one of the first times I recall encountering what I now think of as the "mama voice." I have since heard it many times in women who exercise leadership, including those who preach and teach. In this chapter, I explore what the mama voice is, its cultural background, and its deployment in Christian preaching.

Setting the Scene

In her 2006 article, "World Christianity as a Women's Movement," Dana Robert defended the proposition that a majority of Christians in the world are women. She explored the gender dynamics of conversion based on the fact that "men are typically the formal, ordained religious leaders and theologians."[1] However, there has also been some interest in the ways in which women carve out spaces for themselves, especially in neo-Pentecostal settings.[2] In 2018, four African scholars, Nandera Mhando, Loreen Maseno, Kupakwashe Mtata and Mathew Senga, released a paper looking at the external socio-cultural means of validation used by female independent church leaders in Kenya and Tanzania.[3] Jane Soothill contributed a study of women church leaders in Ghana;

---

1. Dana L. Robert, "World Christianity as a Women's Movement," *International Bulletin of Missionary Research* 30 (2006): 180.

2. See Charlotte Spinks, "Panacea or Painkiller? The Impact of Pentecostal Christianity on Women in Africa," *Critical Half* 1 (2003): 21–25. Two examples of studies of women are, from Nigeria and Mozambique respectively: Samson Fatokun, "Women and Leadership in Nigerian Pentecostal Churches," *Studia Historiae Ecclesiasticae* 32.3 (December 2006): 193–205; and Victor Agadjanian, "Women's Religious Authority in a Sub-Saharan Setting: Dialectics of Empowerment and Dependency," *Gender and Society* 29.6 (2015): 982–1008.

3. Nandera Ernest Mhando, "Modes of Legitimation by Female Pentecostal-Charismatic Preachers in East Africa: A Comparative Study in Kenya and Tanzania," *Journal of Contemporary African Studies* 36.3 (July 2018): 319–33.

Damaris Parsitau and Philomena Mwaura have brought attention to prominent Kenyan women such as Margaret Wanjiru of Jesus is Alive Ministries and Elizabeth Wahome of Single Ladies Interdenominational Ministry (SLIM); and Oyeronke Olademo has profiled Busola Olatu's Daughters of Deborah International Ministry (DODIM) in Nigeria.[4] These scholars have contributed to our understanding of World Christianity and the way that women operate within the church. This chapter seeks to add another country (Tanzania) and another dimension (preaching) to this body of work.

While the above scholars provided valuable insight into the means used by female leaders to legitimize themselves, they did not venture into examining the gender dynamic behind these means. For example, Mhando and her colleagues made no comparison with whether male pastors in neo-Pentecostal churches also employ the methods such as mystery, pomp, charity work, international connections, etc. While we know from their study that women employ such methods, they do not comment on whether these are unique to female leadership or whether there is a relationship between their womanhood and the employment of such methods. It is unclear to what extent their leadership is modelled on other male leaders or to what extent it has feminine characteristics. Two exceptions to this are Jane Soothill's study of Christie Doe Tetteh, and Charity Musvota's work on women in Zimbabwean Pentecostalism. Zimbabwean women declare, "I am not a woman when I stand here, I am a real man," explicitly seeking approval by modelling themselves on men.[5] Meanwhile Soothill found that even Doe Tetteh who exhorts her congregation to, "Be glad your pastor is a woman," ultimately models herself on "the authoritarianism and neo-patrimonialism of 'big man' politics and male charismatic leadership," the "big woman."[6] In both cases, male leadership is the norm and standard. Meanwhile, Olademo who views gender roles in African Christianity as more dynamic than Soothill or Musvota, does not interrogate

---

4. Soothill, *Gender, Social Change and Spiritual Power* (Leiden: Brill, 2007), https://brill.com/view/title/13827; Philomena N. Mwaura and Damaris Seleina Parsitau, "Gendered Charisma: Women in the Mission in the Neo-Pentecostal Churches and Charismatic Movements in Kenya," in *Putting Names with Faces*, eds. Christine Linemann-Perrin, Atola Long Kumer, and Afrie Songco Joye (Nashville: Abingdon Press, 2012), 123–46; Oyeronke Olademo, "New Dimensions in Nigerian Women's Pentecostal Experience: The Case of DODIM, Nigeria," *Journal of World Christianity* 5.1 (2012): 62–74.

5. Charity Musvota, "Rethinking Methods to Curb Gender Discrimination in Church Leadership: The Case of Pentecostal Churches in Zimbabwe," *Studia Historiae Ecclesiasticae* 47.2 (2021): 1–16, 8.

6. Soothill, *Gender, Social Change and Spiritual Power*, 93; Musvota, "Rethinking Methods to Curb Gender Discrimination in Church Leadership," 8.

the gender constructions that enable Olatu's power.[7] There is a need to further examine the relationship of womanhood to female church leadership.

Methodology

This chapter explores a model of femininity deployed in preaching. It is not a theological argument for or justification of such a model: it is an observation and discussion of a model that already exists, the Tanzanian mama voice. Discussions of women's role in the church have tended to take two routes. First, in ecclesiology, there has been a great deal of discussion about what *roles* are permissible or prohibited for women.[8] Many of these prohibitions were passed on to the African church by missionaries though at times they have also been resisted, especially in African Instituted Churches, as Philomena Mwaura has documented.[9] Feminists, including the Circle of Concerned African Women Theologians, have pushed back against the limitation of women's roles.[10] Second, in sociological spaces, the *benefit* of these roles to women has been interrogated.[11] While both of these approaches are important, neither leaves much space for in-depth discussion of the *quality* of women's leadership. The theological discussion has been too preoccupied with what women may or may not do to give much attention to *how* they do it; the sociological discussion is so concerned with outcome that it overlooks or dismisses the lived reality. Additionally advocacy for women's inclusion or empowerment can make male freedoms the standard while failing to examine other models or avenues, especially those available only to women. This chapter seeks to speak into

---

7. Olademo, "New Dimensions in Nigerian Women's Pentecostal Experience," 73.

8. See for example, John Dickson, *Hearing Her Voice, Revised Edition: A Case for Women Giving Sermons*, rev. ed. (Grand Rapids: Zondervan, 2014); Alan F. Johnson (ed.), *How I Changed My Mind about Women in Leadership: Compelling Stories from Prominent Evangelicals* (Grand Rapids: Zondervan Academic, 2010).

9. Philomena N. Mwaura, "Gender and Power in African Christianity: African Instituted Churches and Pentecostal Churches," in Ogbu Kalu (ed.) *African Christianity: An African Story* (Pretoria: University of Pretoria, 2005), 410–45.

10. See Mercy Amba Oduyoye, "Calling the Church to Account: African Women and Liberation," *The Ecumenical Review* 47, no. 4 (October 1995): 479–89; Musimbi Kanyoro, "African Women's Quest for Justice: A Review of African Women's Theology," *The Pacific Journal of Theology* 15 (1996): 77–88; Nyambura J. Njoroge, "The Missing Voice: African Women Doing Theology," *Journal of Theology for Southern Africa* 99 (November 1997): 77–83.

11. Spinks, "Panacea or Painkiller?" 21–25; Gregory Deacon and Damaris Seleina Parsitau, "Empowered to Submit: Pentecostal Women in Nairobi," *Journal of Religion & Society* 19 (2017): 1–17; Mookgo S. Kgatle, "Gender Dimensions in Pentecostal Leadership: The Apostolic Faith Mission of South Africa as a Case Study," *Verbum et Ecclesia* 40, no. 1 (2019): 1–7.

this lacuna, offering a model from Tanzania of women's preaching – the mama voice – and examining its cultural sources and theological underpinnings.[12]

Rather than examining church structures, this chapter explores a parallel role that coexists and interweaves with church structures. It focuses on what a woman is doing in the preaching moment rather than on the role of women in the wider life of the congregation. During my ten years in Tanzania, I have come to know that when a woman gets up to preach or teach in a seminar, it will look and sound different to when a man does, and not just because she is wearing a dress instead of a suit.[13] When I ask Tanzanian Christians about this difference in women's preaching, they immediately know what I am speaking about, with no explanation necessary; they often contrast the female mama voice with the male "prophetic voice."[14] This chapter expounds what the mama voice is, where it comes from and why it is important for the church. I give particular attention to the cultural background of the mama voice before moving on to consider its significance for the nature of preaching, including the female preacher's authority.

I draw on my experiences in the Tanzanian church in this chapter, as well as four ethnographic interviews I conducted in 2021 in which the interviewees commented on the mama voice. These interviews were part of my PhD research about TAFES women's theology of prosperity. The interviewees were women from four different tribes and four different denominations, who live in three different urban centres. The women were from the same class (urban, university educated) of a similar age (all in their forties) and are involved as senior women associates (graduates and supporters) of TAFES. I have given them the pseudonyms Junia, Fibi, Salome and Susannah. All quotes except Junia's were given in Swahili. All translations are mine.

---

12. In offering this model, I am not arguing that it is the only model of women's preaching in Tanzania. There may be others and this could be a fruitful avenue for further research. Additionally, some women may preach in a male style, similar to the cases highlighted by Soothill and Musvota above.

13. My experiences have primarily been in Anglican churches and Tanzania Assemblies of God (TAG) churches, in independent women's seminars, and with the interdenominational university fellowship, Tanzania Fellowship of Evangelical Students (TAFES).

14. The "prophetic voice" is a colloquial term used in Tanzania and does not refer to discussions of prophetic preaching in homiletics or political theology. The male prophetic voice locates authority in its loud, aggressive, male speaker and uses declarative, perlocutionary statements. It is not the only form of male preaching. A study of male preaching styles could be an area for further research.

What is the Mama Voice?

The mama voice is used when women speak in a public forum. It can be heard in university lectures or political speeches as well as when women call into radio shows or participate in panel discussions and social issues. Tanzanian events are highly formalized, so the mama voice can be heard during a speech at a kitchen party or during a community meeting. In Christian circles, such public speeches may include preaching in a Sunday service or teaching at a women's seminar or a leadership conference.

The mama voice in Christian teaching has a distinctive sound. While the male prophetic voice is gravelly, deep and aggressive, the mama voice takes place in a higher register. Even if one doesn't understand the words, the tone and mannerisms are recognizable. These include:

- A maternal tone, perhaps even addressing the congregants as her children
- Use of illustrations from her own life; often things she herself has learned
- Heightened display of emotions and emotional language
- Confident posture
- Forceful but not aggressive speech
- Animated body language e.g. waving of arms, stepping out from behind a lectern
- Decorum e.g. the preacher will rarely become sweaty, or may only lightly dab sweat away
- Formal female dress, in Tanzania, normally a two-piece *kitenge* skirt and blouse.

The tone and mannerisms listed above form an overall impression which is projected to the congregation. This overall impression – what I have called the mama voice – is one of confidence, sharing of wisdom, and loving tone. Thus, human rights lawyer and lay preacher Fibi said, "A woman hugs you with her preaching . . . you feel loved . . . like a chicken cares for her chicks." The preacher walks a delicate line where she is strong, passionate and authoritative, yet never out of control and always seeking the good of those to whom she is preaching.

Some of the above characteristics may be present in men's preaching as well. For example, in the male prophetic voice, the male preacher can become quite emotional. Meanwhile, in other male forms of preaching, decorum is valued. In the mama voice, there is a combination of both of these: heightened emotion and decorum, a dynamic I will explore below. Perhaps there is also a male version of preaching where these two are held in tension. However, this chapter is about the mama voice, not other forms of preaching, and the characteristics listed above are not exclusive to the mama voice but descriptive of it. Furthermore, because a preacher's body is sexed (either female or male), when she or he preaches, she or he does so as a woman or as a man. It is impossible for a preacher to jettison his or her sexed nature.[15] Thus, when a woman preaches, she must be understood as doing so as a woman. It is at this level that I offer the mama voice as a model of women preaching: not to prescribe how women should preach or what role they should inhabit, but as an acknowledgement that this is how these women are preaching in practice. I will go on to explore how they understand this model and its relationship to their gender, including cultural gender roles, but this remains descriptive, not prescriptive.

I refer to this style of preaching as the *mama* voice rather than a female voice because in Tanzania, motherhood is the archetype and ideal for women.[16] Indeed, the late Tanzanian Jesuit Laurenti Magesa declared, "The African woman is supremely mother."[17] The characteristics of this African woman who is mother are illustrated by Okot p'Bitek's poem "Woman Africa":

> Woman of Africa
> Sweeper
> Smearing floors and walls
> With cow dung and black soil
> Cook. Aya, the baby on your back
> Washer of dishes,

---

15. Australian evangelical Andrew Sloane says, "The biblical texts suggest that we are bodies; bodies are not things we inhabit, but the way we inhabit the world as the kind of creatures God has made us . . . Our redemption and final transformation does not erase our embodied nature." Andrew Sloane, "Male and Female He Created Them"? Theological Reflections on Gender, Biology, and Identity" in *The Gender Conversation: Evangelical Perspectives on Gender, Scripture, and the Christian Life*, eds. Edwina Murphy and David Starling (Eugene: Wipf & Stock Publishers, 2016), 347–58.

16. Indeed, in traditional African cultures, a woman's womanhood is practiced and vindicated by her production of children and the more children she produces, the greater her status; failure to do so is shameful and may result in ostracization. See, for example, Judith Westeneng and Ben D'Exelle, "Reproductive Health and Bodily Integrity in Tanzania," *Studies in Family Planning* 48, no. 4 (2017): 323–41, https://www.jstor.org/stable/26384485.

17. Laurenti Magesa, "Christology, African Women And Ministry," *AFER* 38, no. 2 (April 1996): 66–88, 81. There are also conceptions of woman as "foolish, weak, jealous, evil, unfaithful, dependent, frivolous and seductive." However, this woman is not "mama" because mama is wise, strong, others-centered and focused on the good of others. See Jeylan W. Hussein, "The Social and Ethno-Cultural Construction of Masculinity and Femininity in African Proverbs," *African Study Monographs* 26, no. 2 (2005): 59–87.

> Planting, weeding, harvesting
> Store-keeper, builder
> Runner of errands,
> Cart, lorry, donkey . . .
> Woman of Africa
> What are you not?[18]

The strength and omni-competence of this woman of Africa are not an anomaly; they are archetypal of the African woman. This strength may be indicative of the heavy load borne by this woman who is "cart, lorry, donkey," but it also points to her fortitude and the diversity of her experiences. For those who are experiencing challenges in their lives, a woman is therefore a sensible person to listen to: her life experience gives her knowledge which can be of benefit to them.

However, this woman's strength and capability are not divorced from care-giving roles, as evidenced by the way she carries the baby on her back as she goes about her many tasks. Kenyan Catholic Father Patrick Musau says that mothers are known to be "tender and soft hearted and easy to approach so that children find it easier to go through them when they need something which could easily be refused by fathers. Traditional Africa knew the mother to be a place of refuge, an unreachable sacred sanctuary, a source of protection."[19] This is why the mama voice takes on a nurturing tone rather than one of aggression: her knowledge and competence are expressed with compassion.

The Mama Role in Tanzanian Society

As we have seen, the African mama is characterized by competence, knowledge and compassion. These personal qualities have three societal implications.

First, motherhood is of vital importance in Africa because it is inherent in what Magesa sees as the motivating factor in African life: the enhancement of life. In Africa, giving life, protecting life and nurturing life are sacred tasks.[20] These are uniquely feminine tasks. Thus Kenyan Catholic Father Patrick Musau says, "Due to her powers relating to fertility and knowledge of the secret of

---

18. Cited in Magesa, "Christology, African Women And Ministry," 80–81.

19. Patrick Mwania Musau, *The African Woman as an Agent of Evangelization: Her Role and Function in the Mission Activity of the Church in Africa* (Aachen: Shaker Verlag GmbH, 2009), 99.

20. Laurenti Magesa, *African Religion: The Moral Traditions of Abundant Life* (New York: Orbis, 2014), 58, 70.

life, a woman is considered to be more advantaged than men, for she has the monopoly of both human and earthly life."[21] The mama voice, as it teaches in love, is doing something sacred.

Second, this motherhood task spans multiple spheres of life.[22] Magesa argues that womanhood, "incorporates nurturing of life from conception to death as well as acting as go-between and peacemaker in conflict and being central in teaching the children."[23] Here women not only produce, enhance and preserve life through their reproductive capacity, but in their roles as peacemakers and educators. Musau adds to this an economic component because, in addition to "her biological reproductive role, a woman has the potential to grow god-given [sic] food for human sustenance."[24] Traditional roles for women in Africa have also included agriculture, manufacturing and trade. In today's Tanzania, politics can be included as well. While the presidency in Tanzania has been male-dominated since Independence in 1961, Tanzania's current president is a woman, Samia Suluhu Hassan. Colloquially known as "Mama Samia" in political cartoons, her political activity has been depicted in recognizably nurturing or domestic terms, such as tending to prisoners like children who have been unfairly treated, or cleaning house. Mama Samia is seen to exercise the Presidency not as a faux-male but as mama. Indeed, billboards all over Tanzania marked the second anniversary of her Presidency with the slogan *Nani kama Mama* ("Who is like Mama?" or "No one like Mama.").

Third, motherhood is understood to be productive beyond bearing children and can encompass women beyond biological motherhood. When Mama Samia became president, there was a discussion of whether this title was appropriate for her.[25] It was generally agreed that it was a title of respect not necessarily referencing her reproductive history.[26] Musau summarizes:

---

21. Musau, *The African Woman*, 84–85.
22. Musau, *The African Woman*, 84.
23. Musau, *The African Woman*, 81.
24. Musau, *The African Woman*, 84–85.
25. Charles Makakala, "What's in a name? 'Mama Samia' and other misnomers," *The Citizen* (1 April 2021), https://www.thecitizen.co.tz/tanzania/oped/what-s-in-a-name-mama-samia-and-other-misnomers--3344900; see also "Samia Suluhu Hassan: Tanzania's new president," BBC News (19 March 2021), https://www.bbc.com/news/world-africa-56444575.
26. The normal convention in Tanzania is for a woman to be known by her oldest child's name e.g. Mama Neema is effectively shorthand for "Mama of Neema," where her first child is Neema. This is also a term of respect. However, when "Mama" is applied in front a woman's own name, it is particularly clear that the respect is independent of her reproductive history (though it may also be inclusive of it).

> When talking about motherhood in an African sense, we are not referring exclusively to the natural or biological sense of the word but rather to motherhood as a reality which is controlled and overseen by stipulated patterns of behaviour, duties and expectations, values and norms.[27]

Thus, while biological motherhood is intrinsic to African conceptions of womanhood, it is not the sum of it. Whether constructions of motherhood can be assumed without bearing children is contested, but motherhood certainly moves beyond a woman's role with her own children such that societal leadership and domestic care are not seen as separate spheres or roles. They are both expressions of being a mama. This is reminiscent of Deborah's reference to herself in Judges 5:7 as giving courage to Israel and leading it as a "mother in Israel," without reference to her biological motherhood. The mama voice goes beyond one's own reproductive history; it is an assumed role which encompasses the authority of the mama.

The Mama Voice in Preaching

The kind of traditional African womanhood explicated by Musau and Magesa has been disrupted in various ways by colonialism and neo-colonialism but the mama motif nevertheless persists in some form, as illustrated by the language used around Tanzania's female President.[28] My interviewees identified the mama motif in preaching as well, including the three key characteristics of competence, knowledge and compassion.

Regarding *competence*, university lecturer Junia said, "When you go to the church and you say, 'my child' it shows that you go into the role of a mother . . . [which affects] how you perceive issues, how you take care of the things, how you direct issues."[29] For Junia, directing and getting things done competently are part of how women preach. On the issue of *knowledge*,

---

27. Musau, *The African Woman*, 85.
28. Musau, *The African Woman*, 131; Susi Keefe, "Women, Work, and (Re)Marriage: Entrepreneurship among Swahili Women in Coastal Tanzania," *Africa Today* 62 no. 3 (2016): 111–31; Marjorie J. Mbilinyi, "The state of women in Tanzania," *Canadian Journal of African Studies* 6 (1972): 371–77, https://doi.org/10.2307/484210.
29. Addressing someone as "my child" is not exclusive to women. In 1 John the author addresses his readers similarly as "little children" (NRSV) or "dear children" (NIV) six times (1 John 2:12; 1 John 2:28; 1 John 3:18; 1 John 4:4; 1 John 5:21). However, a woman parent is a mother, just as a male parent is a father. (See Robert S. Smith, *How Should We Think About Gender and Identity?* [Bellingham: Lexham, 2022], 34–35.) When these women address the congregation as "my child" they are therefore acting as mamas.

human rights lawyer Fibi pointed to a wealth of life experience as a distinctive of women's preaching. She said that the way a woman "relates and involves her life" shows that a woman "doesn't say things which she doesn't know." Development worker Susannah spoke of a woman as teaching, "a thing which she has lived," in contrast to men who preach in the prophetic voice, mere imitations of other preachers. Women's preaching is not theoretical knowledge but based on lived experience. Finally, *compassion* characterizes Tanzanian women's preaching. Fibi said that many people teach in Tanzania but when, "a woman teaches, she teaches with heart," and that "a woman hugs you with her preaching . . . you feel loved." The women thus identified a distinctively female preaching voice and described it with the characteristics of the Tanzanian mama: competence, knowledge and compassion. While it could be argued that these characteristics should be true of any preacher, the point here is that they are true of Tanzanian womanhood.

Though this mama voice draws on traditional cultural ideas of womanhood, the women also saw these characteristics of competence, knowledge and compassion in Christian terms. For example, development worker and lay preacher Salome spoke of knowledge acquisition as a Christian practice, since God is the source of wisdom, and Susannah added that sharing one's knowledge is a Christian obligation, in order to "not continue the poverty cycle." Furthermore, all interviewees saw these life enhancing roles as consistent with God's heart which is, in Susannah's words, that "he wants us to prosper." Prosperity for these women could not be divorced from having compassion on others and providing for others, with Fibi describing herself as "a bridge to blessing," with her blessings flowing to others. Thus, when a woman preaches in the mama voice, she is not only doing something deeply Tanzanian but deeply Christian as well.

Theologically, the interviewees pointed to the indwelling of the Holy Spirit as enabling the woman preacher. Fibi said, "The word of God lives greatly inside us," and, "Women preach from inside, producing everything which the Holy Spirit has given to her." Susannah concurred that the source of a woman preacher's knowledge is external: "God is the source of wisdom . . . he has put it inside her and she stands on it." When a woman is preaching then, it is not her own wisdom but God's that she brings. However, God's choice of woman as his vehicle means his word becomes fused with her womanhood and comes forth in a feminine way. Fibi described the process this way:

> The word of God lives inside my heart . . . Surely a woman gives it her own voice. You have a performance of ululation and the

mama voice . . . because the word of God has truly entered her . . . we can't separate it out.

The Holy Spirit not only enables a woman to preach; he enables her to preach *as a woman*, that is, in the mama voice. This fusion is exhibited both in the delivery of her preaching and its content.

The feminine may be manifested in *delivery* through ululation but also through a woman's dress, mannerisms and tone. Fibi said, as a woman "I live love . . . so the [mama voice] is me preaching with love from inside me." Preaching in the mama voice is, therefore, a product of an internal state, and for Fibi, displays of feminine or motherly emotion are a sign of a fusion of herself with God's word. She said, "few women are fakes . . . she cries tears not because she is asked to but because the word of God is in her." When a woman preaches then, there is an authenticity to it. It is not a show or a cheap imitation and for this reason, it carries weight. Susannah contrasted this with the prophetic voice. She said that many men think that "in order to be a teacher I must be a preacher with a voice like this. So they become an imitation. This one is despicable, because what is he actually teaching?" Salome was likewise suspicious of the prophetic voice. She considered it to be about making a name for oneself and showing off. For both women, there is an imitation of godliness in the prophetic voice without the substance that the mama voice brings. While the emotion in the prophetic voice testifies to his superficiality, the tears of the mama voice demonstrate how deeply the word of God has affected her and what a great burden she bears for her listeners as she preaches it. In Susannah's view, a woman's depth of reflection and confidence in what God has given her to say mean she delivers her sermon with kindness and a sense of peace.

Just as feminine attributes affect the delivery of a sermon, female experiences shape the *content* of a woman's sermon. Fibi said her preaching is not only based on "what I have read but it is Scripture that I have taken and worn." For Susannah, part of women's experiences is the hardships they experience and tolerate. These difficult experiences engender a capacity for patience which means a woman does not rush through preparing a sermon, instead allowing God's word to take root in her heart. This "tolerance and patience in which she has sat," results in a deeper reflection on God's word. This is not to justify those difficult experiences or suggest that women should simply put up with them, but to see God use for good what men meant for evil. Indeed, a woman need not cordon off these hardships: her preaching is enriched by the interaction of all her womanly experiences with the word of God. When she preaches then, the fusion of the word of God with her experiences produces preaching which is highly useful to the listeners. Her preaching is not theoretical: the message from the Bible which she brings has been tested in her own life and grown out of it. Susannah contrasted listening to a woman, where the congregants "are able to use [her teaching] straight away," with needing to wait to see if the blessings promised by a male prophet will materialize. In the mama voice, the word of God is made immediately applicable to the Christian life because the content of the sermon flows out of the impact the word of God has had on the woman preacher's life.

This fusion of the word of God with womanhood is deeply dignifying of female preachers and femininity more broadly. In the mama voice the female mouth, body and heart are worthy vehicles of God's word; so too are their experiences useful in bringing God's word to bear on the congregants. For Fibi, when women preach, their femininity is a tool, "which we can use to do things for God's heart." With her whole self at God's service, including her gender, a preaching women can stand, in Fibi's words, "as herself even as she carries the word of God." When women enact their motherly role in preaching, bringing life in the fusion of the word of God and their own experiences, they are doing God's work.

The Authority of the Mama Voice in Preaching

As women go about doing God's work, using their mama voices in preaching, they navigate complex cultural gender dynamics. British anthropologist Naomi Haynes argues in her study of Zambian Pentecostal leaders that women whose preaching consists of sharing their experiences cannot compete with men, because while a woman preacher can only point to how God has changed her life, the men offer themselves as mediators of that dispensation.[30] When a woman preaches, you hear about blessing; when a man preaches, you can receive it. However, we have already seen that it is not as simple as that, because what one hears from women is useful in one's life and the promises of blessing made by the "big men" often have little authenticity. Nevertheless, the mama voice does play out in a patriarchal context: Junia casually pointed out that, "you know, in Tanzania we are patriarchal." Susannah said that men view their authority "as automatic" irrespective of competence, while Junia said that

---

30. Naomi Haynes, *Moving by the Spirit: Pentecostal Social Life on the Zambian Copperbelt* (Oakland: University of California Press, 2017), 92–109. Haynes work is in a Pentecostal setting but a similar argument could be advanced in other denominations, such as liturgical settings where a male priest pronounces absolution or administers the sacraments.

competence does not necessarily lead to seniority for women. This may also mirror a Tanzanian patriarchal home, where the woman is omni-competent yet her husband has the authority as head. Indeed, Junia referenced wifely submission as both a cultural and a biblical value. When women preach with the mama voice, these factors are also at play.

Power is exercised in intricate ways in African contexts. Niara Sudarkasa's work from the 1980s on women in African indigenous societies found that comparing "the placement of females relative to males in a two-leveled hierarchy" was inadequate.[31] She found that women are only required to be deferential within their conjugal relationships, that is, with their husbands. Meanwhile in other aspects of society, "seniority and personal attributes (especially accumulated resources) rather than gender serve as the primary basis of status in the hierarchical sense."[32] In other words, submission in one relationship need not indicate submission in others. Such a background is relevant when discussing the mama voice because even while Junia argued for the prevalence of patriarchy in Tanzania, she also insisted that the mama voice compels its listeners to, "be submissive to the voice because you are a child and you follow what the mother is doing." Whether listeners are male or female, then, they are placed in a subordinate role to the woman preaching, at least for that time.

As in Sudarkasa's findings, the authoritative role of the mama voice is not necessarily curated by the preacher's husband, but neither is the nature of their relationship absent. Wifely submission is often prominent at the start of a woman's preaching. She will rise to preach and begin by thanking her husband for his permission or acknowledging his encouragement of her to speak. Deacon and Parsitau observed a similar dynamic in Dr Gladys Mwiti, a leading Kenyan clinical psychologist and PhD holder, who, when speaking at *Mavuno* Church, thanked God for making her a woman while also insisting that she is a submissive wife.[33] While Deacon and Parsitau read this as an inconsistency, this declaration of deference to one's husband can function as an authentication of a woman preacher's authority, not an undermining of it. It deals with the question of whether she has some kind of agenda of social upheaval: by claiming to be a submissive wife, suspicion is put to rest and the woman is free to bring the word of God to the congregants. This ritual of wifely submission, therefore, *elevates* the status of the woman preacher in the eyes

---

31. Niara Sudarkasa, "'The Status of Women' in Indigenous African Societies," *Feminist Studies* 12 no. 1 (1986): 91–103, 92, https://doi.org/10.2307/3177985.
32. Sudarkasa, "'The Status of Women,'" 98.
33. Deacon and Parsitau, "Empowered to Submit," 5.

of the congregants by making her intentions clear: her focus is only bringing the word of God to the congregants. The woman's authority here is grounded in her own behaviour, not in who her husband is.

Similarly, cultural expectations of women's behaviour serve to both limit and empower women preachers. Salome said, "A woman must do things the right way," and that, "women get in trouble if they talk with the voice of a man." Women must therefore be careful not to transgress these boundaries, lest they themselves be silenced. However, a woman's conformity to these gender norms also identifies her as mama, giving her an understood role which does not threaten the status quo, yet has its own authority. It thus carves out female space and authority even in a patriarchal context.[34] Drawing on traditional African values, the mama voice is both authoritative and non-threatening; it maintains the broader social fabric while bringing challenge to individuals in the congregation, including men. While scholars such as British African studies professor Paul Gifford are pessimistic about what can be achieved in such an approach, Zimbabwean Lovemore Togarasei and political scientist Ruth Marshall have both observed that changes in individual men's lives greatly benefit the women associated with them by reduction of substance abuse, promotion of wise management of money, and greater engagement in the domestic sphere.[35] Similarly, while the mama voice does not seek direct confrontation with patriarchy, and may even appear to uphold the status quo, it can challenge some patriarchal norms.

Conclusion

The mama voice in preaching in Tanzania gives women access to congregants and authority over them. However, it is not a mere tool or strategy, because it is grounded in a deep encounter with the word of God. In that process, a woman preacher has been transformed by the indwelling of the Holy Spirit and the word of God has become fused with her femininity such that it is brought to the

---

34. Charlotte Spinks and Deacon and Parsitau have observed a similar phenomenon in their studies of women in Pentecostal churches. Spinks, "Panacea or Painkiller?" 24; Deacon and Parsitau, "Empowered to Submit," 8, 11.

35. Paul Gifford, "The Development and Political Role of Africa's Pentecostal Churches," in *"Small" States in International Politics*, ed. Gerhard Wahlers (Konrad Adenauer Stiftung, 2015), 81–94, www.jstor.org/stable/resrep10119.8; Lovemore Togarasei, "The Pentecostal Gospel of Prosperity in African Contexts of Poverty: An Appraisal," *Exchange* 40 no. 4 (October 2011): 336–50, https://doi.org/10.1163/157254311X600744; Ruth Marshall, "Power in the Name of Jesus," *Review of African Political Economy*, 52 (1991): 21–37, https://www.jstor.org/stable/4005954.

congregation in a feminine way. This feminine mode both protects the woman from accusation and gives her a way to be heard. However, these functional aspects of the mama voice ought not to overshadow its sacred role: it is not a ploy for women to be heard but a means by which *the word of God* can be heard. The word of God can be heard even more deeply when it comes in this feminine form because the life experiences of the woman enrich reflection on the word of God. Thus, the mama voice in preaching is a demonstration of the word of God in feminine garb. Such a demonstration is beneficial not only to women but also to men, who need mama's wisdom.

Bibliography

Agadjanian, Victor. "Women's Religious Authority in a Sub-Saharan Setting: Dialectics of Empowerment and Dependency." *Gender and Society* 29, no. 6 (2015): 982–1008.

Deacon, Gregory, and Damaris Seleina Parsitau. "Empowered to Submit: Pentecostal Women in Nairobi." *Journal of Religion & Society* 19 (2017): 1–17.

Dickson, John. *Hearing Her Voice, Revised Edition: A Case for Women Giving Sermons*. Revised ed. Grand Rapids: Zondervan, 2014.

Fatokun, Samson. "Women and Leadership in Nigerian Pentecostal Churches." *Studia Historiae Ecclesiasticae* 32, no. 3 (December 2006): 193–205.

Gifford, Paul. "The Development and Political Role of Africa's Pentecostal Churches." Pages 81–94 in *"Small" States in International Politics*. Edited by Gerhard Wahlers. Konrad Adenauer Stiftung, 2015. www.jstor.org/stable/resrep10119.8.

Haynes, Naomi. "Prosperity, Charisma, and the Problem of Gender." Pages 92–109 in *Moving by the Spirit*. 1st ed. Pentecostal Social Life on the Zambian Copperbelt. University of California Press, 2017. https://www.jstor.org/stable/10.1525/j.ctt1mf6xx5.13.

Johnson, Alan F. (ed). *How I Changed My Mind about Women in Leadership: Compelling Stories from Prominent Evangelicals*. Edited by Alan F. Johnson. Grand Rapids: Zondervan Academic, 2010.

Kanyoro, Musimbi. "African Women's Quest for Justice: A Review of African Women's Theology." *The Pacific Journal of Theology* 15 (1996): 77–88.

Keefe, Susi. "Women, Work, and (Re)Marriage: Entrepreneurship among Swahili Women in Coastal Tanzania." *Africa Today* 62, no. 3 (2016): 111–31. https://doi.org/10.2979/africatoday.62.3.111.

Kgatle, Mookgo S. "Gender Dimensions in Pentecostal Leadership: The Apostolic Faith Mission of South Africa as a Case Study." *Verbum et Ecclesia* 40, no. 1.

Magesa, Laurenti. "Christology, African Women And Ministry." *AFER* 38, no. 2 (April 1996): 66–88.

Marshall, Ruth. "Power in the Name of Jesus." *Review of African Political Economy*, 52 (1991): 21–37. https://www.jstor.org/stable/4005954.

Mhando, Nandera Ernest. "Modes of Legitimation by Female Pentecostal-Charismatic Preachers in East Africa: A Comparative Study in Kenya and Tanzania." *Journal of Contemporary African Studies* 36, no. 3 (July 2018): 319–33.

Musau, Patrick Mwania. *The African Woman as an Agent of Evangelization: Her Role and Function in the Mission Activity of the Church in Africa*. Aachen: Shaker Verlag GmbH, 2009.

Musvota, Charity. "Rethinking Methods to Curb Gender Discrimination in Church Leadership: The Case of Pentecostal Churches in Zimbabwe." *Studia Historiae Ecclesiasticae* 47, no. 2 (2021): 1–16.

Mwaura, Philomena N. "Gender and Power in African Christianity: African Instituted Churches and Pentecostal Churches." Pages 410–45 in *African Christianity: An African Story*. Edited by Ogbu Kalu. Pretoria: Dept. of Church History, University of Pretoria, 2005.

Mwaura, Philomena N., and Damaris Seleina Parsitau. "Gendered Charisma: Women in the Mission in the Neo-Pentecostal Churches and Charismatic Movements in Kenya." Pages 123–46 in *Putting Names with Faces*. Edited by Christine Lienemann-Perrin, Atola Long Kumer, and Afrie Songco Joye. Nashville: Abingdon Press, 2012.

Njoroge, Nyambura J. "The Missing Voice: African Women Doing Theology." *Journal of Theology for Southern Africa* 99 (November 1997): 77–83.

Oduyoye, Mercy Amba. "Calling the Church to Account: African Women and Liberation." *The Ecumenical Review* 47, no. 4 (October 1995): 479–89.

Olademo, Oyeronke. "New Dimensions in Nigerian Women's Pentecostal Experience: The Case of DODIM, Nigeria." *Journal of World Christianity* 5, no. 1 (2012): 62–74. https://doi.org/10.5325/jworlchri.5.1.0062.

Sloane, Andrew. "Male and Female He Created Them"? Theological Reflections on Gender, Biology, and Identity." Pages 347–58 in *The Gender Conversation: Evangelical Perspectives on Gender, Scripture, and the Christian Life*. Edited by Edwina Murphy and David Starling. Eugene: Wipf & Stock Publishers, 2016.

Smith, Robert S. *How Should We Think about Gender and Identity?* Bellingham: Lexham, 2022.

Soothill, Jane E. *Gender, Social Change and Spiritual Power*. Leiden: Brill, 2007. https://brill.com/view/title/13827.

Spinks, Charlotte. "Panacea or Painkiller? The Impact of Pentecostal Christianity on Women in Africa." *Critical Half* 1, no. 1 (2003): 21–25.

Sudarkasa, Niara. "'The Status of Women' in Indigenous African Societies." *Feminist Studies* 12, no. 1 (1986): 91–103. https://doi.org/10.2307/3177985.

Togarasei, Lovemore. "The Pentecostal Gospel of Prosperity in African Contexts of Poverty: An Appraisal." *Exchange* 40, no. 4 (October 2011): 336–50. https://doi.org/10.1163/157254311X600744.

Westeneng, Judith, and Ben D'Exelle. "Reproductive Health and Bodily Integrity in Tanzania." *Studies in Family Planning* 48, no. 4 (2017): 323–41. https://www.jstor.org/stable/26384485.

18

The Camel Has Four Legs

A Contextual African Practical Ecclesiology

Joshua Robert Barron
Association for Christian Theological Education in Africa (ACTEA)

Abstract

Andrew F. Walls, in his "visitor from Mars" thought experiment, has famously observed that what the church looks like has varied throughout the centuries and across geographies, languages, and cultures.[1] It is increasingly recognized that all articulations of Christian theology are culturally contingent. Likewise expressions of ecclesiology, including ecclesial polity, are culturally contingent, though this observation is contested in some quarters. For example, Roman Catholic and Orthodox ecclesial polity are reflections of the imperial political polities of the Roman Empire. AICs ("African Initiated Churches," "African Independent Churches," and/or "African Indigenous Churches") which have arisen during the modern era in Africa have ecclesiologies which reflect their cultural contexts. Regardless of differences in ecclesiology and in ecclesial polity, four key shared elements can be recognized across different ecclesial bodies that are signs of ecclesial health. In African contexts, these can be

---

1. Andrew F. Walls, "The Gospel as Prisoner and Liberator of Culture," in *The Missionary Movement in Christian History: Studies in the Transmission of the Faith* (Maryknoll: Orbis Books, 1996), 3–15, 3–7. Walls imagines "a long-living scholarly space visitor"; this was a deliberate allusion to "a visitor from Mars" observing the then-current state of world Christianity in Henry P. Van Dusen, *World Christianity: Yesterday, Today, Tomorrow* (New York: Abingdon-Cokesbury, 1947), 46–56, 80–81, 235–36.

discussed as a parable of the four legs – local leadership, vision for participation in God's mission, use of vernacular Scripture, and prayer. If a camel in the bush or desert has injured or lost a leg, apart from intensive medical care it will not be long for the world but will soon die. Likewise when any of these four elements in a particular church are missing or weak, the church is at risk of failing to fulfil its purpose and perhaps of dying. This will be shown through a review of several examples from the history of world Christianity within Africa (though similar examples abound from Asia and Europe as well). This chapter will then introduce an ecclesial polity practiced by Turkana Christians in Kenya and Maasai Christians in Kenya and Tanzania and examine whether it has four healthy "legs."

Key words: contextual ecclesiology, ecclesial polity, local leadership, mission, vernacular Scripture, prayer, Turkana, Maasai

"all churches are culture churches – including our own."[2]

Introduction

Too often parts of the church are, or have been, off-balance because their ecclesiologies, whether implicit or explicit, are inadequate: they have failed to build their ministries on a solid fourfold foundation of a culture of prayer, accessible vernacular Scripture, a vision for participation in the *missio Dei*, and local ecclesial leadership. When a church fails to recognize the importance of any of these four "legs," it will take what seem to be shortcuts in its ecclesial life and praxis. But just as a house built upon the sand will be easily washed away by the torrents of a flood (Matt 7:24–27; Luke 6:46–49), so a church that is not built upon all four of these "legs" will easily falter. I have observed this across cultures, times, and geographies – both through historical study and with my own eyes.

---

2. Walls, "The Gospel as Prisoner and Liberator of Culture," 8.

All theology is contextual. All theology is culturally contingent:[3] "historically speaking, there has never been a 'universal theology,' but always particular theologies, although these are later universalized."[4] This is widely recognized by missiologists and scholars who work from world Christianity perspectives,[5] though it is still denied by the culturally myopic and by fundamentalists. This is also true of ecclesiology, which is contingent upon the culture and society in which it developed.[6] All ecclesiology is culturally contingent and contextual – it either arises from its context or it arose in the context of the ancestors who passed down to us their ecclesiology. A careful examination of the development of early Christian polity in the Roman and Parthian Empires shows that Christians modelled their organizational structures after local imperial polities. Even today, the ecclesial polities of the Roman Catholic Church and the various Orthodox churches continue to mirror those ancient imperial polities. Beyond the borders of Roman authority, the Gothic Arian church of Christian Goths had its "own native clergy, was separate in language and organization, and was independent of the structures and religion of the empire."[7] In Central Asia during the Middle Ages, roving missionary-bishops of the church of the East were assigned to migrating tribal clans of Mongolian and Turkic tribes. Their congregations regularly moved,

---

3. I have discussed the inherent contingency of all Christian theology on both language and culture elsewhere. E.g., my "Andrew F. Walls: Apostle of World Christianity," *Missio Dei: A Journal of Missional Theology and Praxis* 12, no. 2 (Summer–Fall 2021): np, https://missiodeijournal.com/issues/md-12-2/authors/md-12-2-barron/.

4. Michel Willy Libambu, "La contribution des études patristiques à la théologie africaine [The contribution of patristic studies to African theology: The study of the Fathers of the Church at the theological school of Kinshasa] (1957–2013)," in *Patristic Studies in the Twenty-First Century: Proceedings of an International Conference to Mark the 50th Anniversary of the International Association of Patristic Studies*, eds. Carol Harrison, Brouria Bitton-Ashkelony, and Théodore De Bruyn (Turnhout: Brepols, 2015), 163–19, 172; my translation.

5. E.g., A. Ngindu Mushete correctly asserts that "all theology is culturally and socially situated . . . and we would do much better to be aware of this rather than to pretend not to know it." "An Overview of African Theology," in *Paths of African Theology*, ed. Rosino Gibellini (Maryknoll: Orbis Books, 1994), 9–26, 19.

6. Harvey Kwiyani agrees with this thesis, writing that "Though we may not admit it, our theologies, ecclesiologies and even missiologies are all shaped by a large extent by our circumstances . . . all theologies are contextual . . . There is no theology that is culture-free . . . Our understanding of God is shaped by how our culture perceives and talks about God. In addition, our ecclesiologies are shaped by the culture in which we are located." Harvey Kwiyani, *Multicultural Kingdom: Ethnic Diversity, Mission and the Church* (London: SCM Press, 2020), 109.

7. Jehu J. Hanciles, *Migration and the Making of Global Christianity* (Grand Rapids: Eerdmans, 2021), 212.

so the bishops moved with them. Frequently their episcopal "cathedrals" were probably no more than "tent chapels mounted on wagons."[8]

The growth of national identities led to national churches – first in ancient Ethiopia in Africa and in Armenia and Georgia in Asia, then in Nubia (modern Sudan and South Sudan), and eventually in the national Protestant churches of Western Europe. Denominations which arose from revitalization movements in the early American Republic tend to be democratic in polity and ecclesiology.[9] Likewise many AICs ("African Initiated Churches," "African Independent Churches," and/or "African Indigenous Churches") have patterned their ecclesiology after various local "cultural communal models."[10] Notably, "the phenomenon of church independency in Africa in the twentieth-century is analogous to the phenomenon of the Reformation in Europe."[11] In both cases, their ecclesiologies reflect their cultural contexts. When the Church of England expanded into what is now Uganda, Bishop Alfred Tucker (1849–1914) deliberately "adapted the administration of the Church ... to correspond very closely" with traditional Buganda political systems."[12] Within the ecclesiologies of African megachurches, "the particularities of church polity and practices, worship and liturgy, education and community formation, prophetic witness, and missionary work are cultural matters left up to the leadership."[13] The same is true for many church groups in Africa, and perhaps especially those influenced by the traditions of free church catholicity.[14]

Recognizing that "church polity could even be regarded as a 'practical ecclesiology,'" Dreyer notes that a given ecclesial structure "should not be

---

8. Samuel Hugh Moffett, *A History of Christianity in Asia, vol. I: Beginnings to 1500* (Maryknoll: Orbis Books, 1998), 449.

9. These notably include the descendant denominations of the Restoration Movement or Stone-Campbell Movement. For the democratic character of American ecclesiology generally, see Nathan O. Hatch, *The Democratization of American Christianity* (New Haven: Yale University Press, 1989). For a Roman Catholic perspective on democratization in the Church, see Peter C. Phan's discussion in "A North American Ecclesiology: The Achievement of Patrick Granfield," in *The Gift of the Church: A Textbook on Ecclesiology in Honor of Patrick Granfield*, O.S.B., ed. Peter C. Phan (Collegeville: Liturgical Press, 2000), 469–502, 481–84.

10. Stephanie Lowery, "Ecclesiology in Africa: Apprentices on a Mission," *Africa Journal of Evangelical Theology* 37, no. 1 (2018): 3–17, 7.

11. J. N. K. Mugambi, *Christianity and African Culture*, Christian Theology in African Scholarship (Nairobi: Acton Publishers, 2002), 9.

12. Bengt Sundkler, *The Christian Ministry in Africa* (London: SCM Press, 1962), 52–53.

13. Wanjiru M. Gitau, *Megachurch Christianity Reconsidered: Millennials and Social Change in African Perspective, Missiological Engagements* (Downers Grove: IVP Academic, 2018), 179.

14. For example, as articulated by William Robinson, *The Biblical Doctrine of the Church*, rev. ed. (St. Louis: Bethany Press, 1955).

regarded as an immutable historical document with everlasting authority, but rather as an instrument that could facilitate change and ecclesial praxis in the spirit of *ecclesia semper reformanda*."[15] Along these lines, Andrew F. Walls reminds us that "Eurocentric historical thinking and Eurocentric Christian terminology will become less useful as Christianity increasingly becomes a non-Western religion again."[16] African Pentecostal and AIC churches have challenged the revered polities which had been inherited, and then passed on, by the envoys of the modern missionary movement.[17] While some have asserted that "one cause of the formation of" AICs was a deficient ecclesiology,[18] it should be noted that "the dominate motive in [the early twentieth century] secessions [of AICs] was the desire for spiritual independence, rather than any quarrel with the orthodox practices or opinions of the older churches."[19]

Contrary to popular conceptions, when Jesus declared "I will build my *ekklēsia*" (Matt 16:18), "it was never clear what form or structure that Ecclesia would take"[20] – not least because the pages of the New Testament contain many different ecclesiologies.[21] Jesse Mugambi locates a fluid and "open-minded ecclesiology" in Paul's epistles.[22] Because "ecclesiology must account for context,"[23] we should expect different ecclesiologies to arise from African contexts. Western ecclesiological models simply do "not always comfortably

---

15. Wim A. Dreyer, "The priesthood of believers: The forgotten legacy of the reformation," *HTS Teologiese Studies / Theological Studies* 76, no. 4, a6021 (2020): 1–7, 1. *Ecclesia semper reformanda* is a Latin phrase meaning "the church always reforming."

16. Andrew F. Walls, "Documentation and ecclesial Deficit: A personal plea to Churches," in *Christian Movements in Southeast Asia: A Theological Exploration*, ed. Michael Nai-Chiu Poon, CSCA Christianity in Southeast Asia Series (Singapore: Genesis Books, 2010), 121–132, 123.

17. Babatomiwa M. Owojaiye, *Evangelical Response to the Coronavirus Lock Down* (Insights from the Evangelical Church Winning All) (Bloomington: WestBow Press, 2020), 58.

18. As F. B. Welbourn and B. A. Ogot report in *A Place to Feel at Home: A Study of Two Independent Churches in Western Kenya* (Nairobi: Oxford University Press, 1966), 137.

19. H. W. Turner, *History of an African Independent Church*, vol. 1, *The Church of the Lord (Aladura)* (Oxford: Clarendon Press, 1967), 10.

20. Douglas W. Waruta, "Towards an African Church," in *The Church in African Christianity: Innovative Essays in Ecclesiology*, eds. J. N. K. Mugambi and Laurenti Magesa, African Challenge Series 1 (Nairobi: Initiatives, 1990), 29–42, 31.

21. Frank J. Matera, "Theologies of the Church in the New Testament," in *The Gift of the Church: A Textbook on Ecclesiology in Honor of Patrick Granfield, O.S.B*, ed. Peter C. Phan (Collegeville: Liturgical Press, 2000), 3–21, 3.

22. Jesse N. K. Mugambi, "Theology of reconstruction," in *African Theology on the Way*, ed. Diane B. Stinton (International Study Guides. Minneapolis: Fortress Press, 2015), 139–49, 148.

23. Stephanie A. Lowery, *Identity and Ecclesiology: Their Relationship among Select African Theologians* (Eugene: Pickwick Publications, 2017), 142.

fit a non-western society."[24] Frequently missionary ecclesiologies have been "incompatible with African expectations and their simple biblical understanding of the church."[25] After Vatican II (1962–1965), even Roman Catholic African theologians recognized the mutability of ecclesiology, discerning between primitive, patristic, medieval, Enlightenment, and Romantic ecclesiologies.[26] The search for an appropriate and culturally relevant African ecclesiology, Engelbert Mveng insists, is a "necessity imposed by fidelity to Jesus Christ," something that is a matter of our being honest before God.[27] Likewise John Mary Waliggo insists that it is strictly necessary for African theologians to develop their own *African* models of ecclesiology.[28] Just as the theologizing of African Christianity is "a gift to World Christianity,"[29] so ecclesiologically "the local churches in sub-Saharan Africa have something distinctive to share with the . . . churches of the world, concerning the way the kingdom community takes shape in the daily lives of the people of God."[30] As Andrew Walls reminds us, "Christ takes all the cultures in the world to build his church."[31]

Sociologically, *igbo enweghi eze* ([the Igbo people] have no king) – their traditional polity is composed of autonomous communities of village groups,

---

24. Warren B. Newberry, "Contextualizing Indigenous Church Principles: An African Model," *Asian Journal of Pentecostal Studies* 8, no. 1 (2005): 95–115, 106.

25. Yusufu Turaki, "Evangelical missiology from Africa: strengths and weaknesses," in *Global Missiology from the 21st Century: The Iguassu Dialogue*, ed. William D. Taylor (Grand Rapids: Baker Academic, 2000), 271–83, 278.

26. E.g., see Robert Rweyemamu, *People of God in the Missionary Nature of the Church: A Study of Concilian Ecclesiology Applied to the Missionary Pastoral in Africa*, Neue Zeitschrift für Missionswissenschaft (Rome: Schöneck/Beckenried, 1968), 1.

27. The Spanish text reads "La búsqueda de una «eclesiología africana» es una necesidad que impone la fidelidad a Jesucristo. Las leyes que rigen la vida de las comunidades cristianas deben ser pertinentes en relación con esas comunidades. Las investigaciones sobre el *derecho eclesiástico de las Iglesias de África* no son un asunto de demagogia, sino de honestidad ante Dios." Englebert Mveng, *Identidad Africana y Christianismo: Palabras de un creyente* [African Identity and Christianity: Words from a Believer], traducido por Miguel Montes (Estella: Editorial Verbo Divino, 1999), 282.

28. John Mary Waliggo, "The African Clan as the True Model of the African Church," in *The Church in African Christianity: Innovative Essays in Ecclesiology*, eds. J. N. K. Mugambi and Laurenti Magesa, African Challenge Series 1 (Nairobi: Initiatives, 1990), 111–28, 117.

29. Joshua Robert Barron, "My God is enkAi: a reflection of vernacular theology," *Journal of Language, Culture, and Religion* 2, no. 1 (2021): 1–20, 2.

30. Jean-Marie Hyacinth Quenum, "Toward a Prophetic and Life-Oriented Ecclesiology for sub-Saharan Africa," *African Christian Studies* 26, no. 3 (2010): 5–31, 6.

31. Andrew F. Walls, "Rethinking Mission: New Direction for a New Century," in *World Mission in the 21st Century: Rethinking Mission: New Direction for a New Century*, ed. Kwang Soon Lee (Seoul, South Korea: Center for World Mission, Presbyterian College and Theological Seminary, 2005), 69–80, 77.

federations of clans.³² Why should Igbo ecclesial polity be modeled after ancient Mediterranean forms of polity? Prior to colonization by European powers, but after colonization of coastal areas by Muslim Arabs, the majority of communities across East Africa developed polities that were less centralized.³³ Uzukwu also observes that "many African traditional societies are democratically organized," although "democratic life as experienced in African communitarianism" may well look quite different from Western democracies.³⁴ Naturally, democratic forms of African ecclesial polity will also look different from Western models. Why should Turkana or Maasai ecclesial polity be monarchical?

The Camel Has Four Legs

"The camel has four legs." That sounds obvious. But imagine that you are a pastoralist in the deserts of Turkana Land in northwest Kenya. What do you know? What is familiar? Hot. Hot is familiar. Dusty is familiar. Sand. Thorns. Thorns are very familiar. Water? It depends on where you live. You might have to walk a long way and dig in a dry riverbed to find some. Goats are the basis of your livelihood. Goats and, if you're more well off, camels. Camels are the quintessential livestock for the Turkana people. Camels are familiar. The knowledge of how to care for your camels is the knowledge of how to keep your family alive.

Imagine with me, if you will, a camel that has only three legs. Or maybe just two. It won't be able to keep up with the herd. Ultimately, it is only going to be eaten. Either the family will sell it to be butchered, butcher it themselves, or the hyenas will eat it. Perhaps in your context, camels are not familiar. For other pastoralist contexts, such as those of the Maasai and Samburu, consider the cow. For an urban context, imagine a car. Just as camels and cows have four legs, cars have four wheels. Suppose you're driving on a flat tire, or on two flat tires. Your forward progress, and possibly your direction, will be impeded. We were once driving from Kenya to Tanzania when our front passenger wheel – the whole wheel, not just the tire – suddenly came off our Land Cruiser when we were at a speed of about 80 kph (50 mph). It went bouncing across the plain

---

32. Elochukwu Eugene Uzukwu, *A Listening Church: Autonomy and Communion in African Churches* (Eugene: Wipf & Stock, 2006), 15.

33. Paul Kollman and Cynthia Toms Smedley, *Understanding World Christianity: Eastern Africa* (Minneapolis: Fortress Press, 2018), 11.

34. Uzukwu, *A Listening Church*, 12.

leaping over fences. Our forward progress was immediately impeded and our journey was substantially delayed.

I was in the midst of teaching my church history course to a group of Turkana church leaders when I realized that the church is like a camel, having "four legs." An examination of the history of the church across cultures, languages, geographies, and centuries demonstrates that just as a healthy camel or cow has four legs, or a car in good working order has four wheels, a healthy church always has "four legs." North American missiologist Susan Higgins has asked, "What patterns of *ekklesia* will best serve North American churches in the future?" Here in Africa we need to ask ourselves "what patterns of *ekklēsia* will best serve African churches in the future?" and to consider constructing ecclesiologies which are "capable of empowering the [African] church for fuller participation in the divine life and mission."[35] Toward that end, after reviewing existing discussions on the "marks of the church," I will propose a contextual ecclesiology of "the four legs."

Marks of the Church

Throughout the history of Christianity, there have been many proposed lists of essential characteristics, or marks, of the church. The Jerusalem Council laid out the "Jerusalem Quadrilateral" marks of the church: "continuing in apostolic doctrine/teaching, fellowship [*koinonia*], the breaking of bread, and prayer" (Acts 2:42). John Samuel Pobee identifies the basic ecclesiology of "the earliest Christian community's self-understanding as consisting of" a fivefold "koinonia – communion/community/fellowship/solidarity/sharing (Acts 2:42–47)."[36] For traditional Roman Catholic ecclesiology, the four marks of the church's identity are "unity, holiness, catholicity, apostolicity"; all of these, of course, are ontological in nature and do not speak to the function or actual life of the church or of its members.[37] The three marks of the church in the Reformed traditions of Protestantism are "preaching of the word, the

---

35. Susan Higgins, "An Elephant in the Household," *Leaven* 15, no. 1 (2011): 40–45, 41.
36. John Samuel Pobee, *Giving Account of Faith and Hope in Africa* (Eugene: Wipf & Stock, 2017), 51.
37. Solomon Andria and Willem Saayman, "Missiology and Ecclesiology: A Perspective from Africa," *Missionalia* 31, no. 3 (2003): 503–17, 503, 507. Philip Chika Omenukwa devotes two chapters to these four marks in *An Ecclesiological Exploration of the Four Marks of the Church: An Ecumenical Option for the Church in Nigeria*, African Theological Studies / Études Théologiques Africaines 5 (Frankfurt am Main: Peter Lang, 2014).

administration of the sacraments, and the exercise of discipline";[38] of these two, word and sacrament are ultimate. Martin Luther identified seven "marks (*notae*) in the visible church: the word of God, baptism, the Lord's Supper, the keys, a properly functioning ministry, prayer and public worship, and suffering."[39] Building on the classic "pentecostal fivefold gospel of Jesus as savior, sanctifier, Spirit Baptizer, healer, and coming king," some Pentecostals have developed a "'fivefold' ecclesiology [in which] the church is understood as a redeemed, sanctified, empowered, healing, and eschatological community."[40] In his examination of the *Aladura* "Church of the Lord" and other AICs in West Africa, Harold Turner identifies three minimal marks of a true Christian church: open acceptance of the Scriptures, interpretation of biblical texts which "is manifested by sharing in the mission and service of Christ to men," and "nothing in its teaching or action . . . openly denies [the] person or work" of Christ.[41] Andrew Walls, Cathy Ross, and their colleagues have developed "five marks of mission" which apply equally to ecclesiology as to missiology:[42]

1. To proclaim the good news of the Kingdom
2. To teach, baptize, and nurture new believers
3. To respond to human need by loving service
4. To seek to transform unjust structures of society
5. To strive to safeguard the integrity of creation and sustain and renew the life of the earth.

Fabrice Katembo emphasizes simply that "one of the great marks of the body of Christ" is love.[43] The possibilities of identifying "marks" of the church seem endless! – but just as no one language can fully conceptualize the mystery of the incarnation, so no single culture can embody the fulness of the nature

---

38. H. W. Turner, *History of an African Independent Church*, vol. 2, *The Life and Faith of the Church of the Lord (Aladura)*, 328.

39. Mark A. Noll, "Martin Luther and the Concept of a 'True' Church," *The Evangelical Quarterly* 50, no. 2 (1978): 79–85, 83.

40. Amos Yong, *Renewing Christian Theology: Systematics for a Global Christianity* (Waco: Baylor University Press, 2014), 165.

41. H. W. Turner, *History of an African Independent Church*, vol. 2, 332. Aladura is a Yorùbá word meaning "praying person." Currently there are approximately fifty million native speakers of Yorùbá, primarily in Nigeria.

42. Andrew Walls and Cathy Ross, eds., *Mission in the 21st Century: Exploring the Five Marks of Global Mission* (Maryknoll: Orbis Books, 2008).

43. Fabrice S. Katembo, *The Mystery of the Church: Applying Paul's Ecclesiology in Africa* (Carlisle: HippoBooks, 2020), 71; see also 33.

of the church.[44] Thus I offer yet another model not to compete with existing ones, but to supplement them.

The Four Legs of the Camel

Like the camel, the church has four legs. Or imagine a typical four-legged African stool[45] – cut off one of the legs and sit down and you are sure to topple! These legs are

    4. Local Leadership

    3. Vision for Mission

    2. Accessible Vernacular Scripture

    1. Culture of Prayer

I present these in an inverse order because the second through fourth, in my numeration, are arguably sociological and, as such, are much easier to see and to assess. Prayer, of course, is more explicitly spiritual and as such, is more difficult to access. So I start with the easier and progress to the more difficult. Historically, when the "leg" of a culture of prayer is in place, the other legs are much more likely to be discovered and practiced. When the culture of prayer and vernacular Bible intake are both in place, Christians are more likely to discover a vision for mission and discipleship and to insist upon local

---

44. Referring to the ecclesiological model of the "integral family" ("*famille intégrale*") in parts of Roman Catholicism in Sub-Saharan Africa, Sylvain Kalamba Nsapo speaks of the expression of the ecclesial mystery which cannot be exhausted by a single culture (*du mystère ecclésial dont l'expression ne saurait être épuisée par une seule culture*); "Une Théologie de «l'Église-Famille» En Afrique Sub-Saharienne," *Ephemerides Theologicae Lovanienses* 75.1 (April 1999): 157–74, 157.

45. I first developed this ecclesiological parable with a stool in a drama I performed for one of my church history cohorts in Turkana land in 2010 or 2011. Later that day I changed the analogy to "the four legs of the camel" (which was more appropriate as traditional Turkana stools, atypically, have a single leg). More recently, Elizabeth Mburu has skillfully applied the common cultural image of the four-legged African stool to biblical hermeneutics. See "An African Hermeneutic: A Four-Legged Stool," chapter 4 in her *African Hermeneutics* (Carlisle: HippoBooks, 2019).

leadership.[46] So these are like rungs of a ladder up which churches must ascend.[47] When any of these four "legs" are missing, or even just weak and neglected, in a regional church or local congregation, the growth and direction of the church are impeded. Sometimes, the church may disappear completely from an area.

Local leadership

It is essential that a local church is not dependent upon outside sources or places for leadership. Even though Jerusalem can be rightfully considered "the mother church" in the first decades of Christian history, it

> should not be understood as an institutionalized center of the numerous Christian communities born during these years: the churches in Syria and Cilicia, in Galatia and in the province of Asia, in Macedonia and in Achaia, in Rome and in North Africa were established and developed independently of a "center" that exercised control.[48]

Instead, Christianity has always been polycentric, with Syrian Antioch, Corinth, Ephesus, Rome, and Alexandria quickly becoming centres as important as Jerusalem[49] and having their own local leadership from the days of the apostles. The great missionary statesman Henry Venn (1796–1873) recognized three primary and "elementary principles" of sound ecclesiology:

---

46. Of course exceptions to this pattern can be found, but this is my conclusion from over thirty years of studying Christian history and over forty years as a baptized follower of Jesus.

47. Such ladder imagery is ancient within the Christian tradition, building on the narrative of Jacob's Ladder in Genesis 28:10–19. Notable works include the late fourth or early fifth century Syriac text *Book of Steps* (often known by its Latin title, *Liber Graduum*) and the early seventh century Greek text *The Ladder of Divine Ascent* written by John Climacus (c. 579 – 649). For those texts in English translation, see Robert R. Kitchen and Maartien F. G. Parmentier, trans., *The Book of Steps: The Syriac Liber Graduum*, Cistercian Studies Series 196 (Kalamazoo: Cistercian Publications, 2004) and John Climacus, *The Ladder of Divine Ascent*, trans. Colm Luibheid and Normal Russell, Classics of Western Spirituality (Mahwah: Paulist Press, 1982).

48. Eckhard J. Schnabel, *Early Christian Mission*, vol. 2, *Paul & the Early Church* (Downers Grove: InterVarsity Press 2004), 1490.

49. Schnabel, *Early Christian Mission*, 1489–1493. See also Klaus Koschorke, "Transcontinental Links, Enlarged Maps, and Polycentric Structures in the History of World Christianity," *World Christianity* 6.1 (2016): 28–56, 34–42; and Tite Tiénou, "Forming Indigenous Theologies," in *Toward the Twenty-first Century in Christian Mission: Essays in honor of Gerald H. Anderson*, ed. James M. Phillips and Robert T. Coote (Grand Rapids: Eerdmans, 1993), 248–49.

"self-support and self-government and self-extension."⁵⁰ These principles were also independently developed by Rufus Anderson (1796–1880) and John L. Nevius (1829–1893) and are usually listed as *self-governing, self-supporting,* and *self-propagation*. By the mid-nineteenth century, the concept of the "Three Selves" had become "key elements of an accepted missionary strategy."⁵¹ This ideal was frequently embraced by local church leaders. Thus in "1974, the Kenyan bishops . . . stated categorically their 'aim to form a community that is self-supporting, self-ministering and self-propagating.'"⁵² More recently, Paul Hiebert (1932–2007) and David Bosch (1929–1992) recognized that a "fourth self," *self-theologizing*, is a necessary characteristic of ecclesial maturity,⁵³ as Christian "theologizing must be a living, growing experience" that turns to Scripture to answer the questions actually arising in new cultures.⁵⁴ A failure for a church to be self-theologizing is like a camel trying to walk with one elephant leg, one lion leg, one giraffe leg, and one whale flipper.⁵⁵

But frequently foreign missionaries and local church planters have not heeded this wisdom regarding these aspects of local church leadership and ecclesial life. Iheanacho, a Nigerian Roman Catholic historian of Christianity, attributes the disappearance of the earliest Roman Catholic communities in

---

50. Henry Venn, "The Organization of Native Churches" (1861), quoted in *Classic Texts in Mission & World Christianity*, ed. with introductions by Norman E. Thomas (Maryknoll: Orbis Books, 1995), 208–209. See also Andrew F. Walls's excellent discussion on the three self principles in *The Missionary Movement from the West: A Biography from Birth to Old Age*, ed. Brian Stanley, Studies in Christian Mission (Grand Rapids: Eerdmans, 2023), 105–108.

51. Klaus Koschorke, "'Dialectics of the Three Selves': The ideal of a 'self-governing native church,'" in *Internationalising Higher Education: From South Africa to England via New Zealand: Essays in Honour of Professor Gerald Pillay*, eds. Hoffie (J. W.) Hofmeyr and John Stenhouse, (Centurion: Mediakor, 2018), 127–42 , 129. Similarly, Nigerian theologian Yusuf Turaki warns the African church to avoid what could be called the three anti-self characteristics: "paternalism, dependency and dominance"; "Evangelical missiology from Africa," 279.

52. Valentine Ugochukwu Iheanacho, *Historical Trajectories of Catholicism in Africa* (Eugene: Resource Publications, 2021), 136; citing James D. Sangu, *Report on the Experiences of the Church in the Work of Evangelisation in Africa* (1974), 13.

53. E.g., Paul G. Hiebert, "The Fourth Self," chapter 8 in his *Anthropological Insights for Missionaries* (Grand Rapids: Baker Book House, 1985), 193–224; David J. Bosch, *Transforming Mission: Paradigm Shifts in Theology of Mission* (Maryknoll: Orbis Books, 1991), 451–52; see also Richard E. Trull Jr., *The Fourth Self: Theological Education to Facilitate Self-Theologizing for Local Church Leaders in Kenya*, Bible and Theology in Africa 14, ed. Knut Holter (New York: Peter Lang, 2013). For a helpful discussion of the development of Hiebert's thought on this point, see esp. Rochelle Cathcart and Mike Nicholls, "Self-Theology, Global Theology, and Missional Theology," *Trinity Journal* 30, no. 2 (2009): 209–21.

54. Paul G. Hiebert, "Critical Contextualization," *Missiology* 12, no. 3 (1984): 287–96, 295.

55. Ruth Barron suggested to me that only using imported theologies from other contexts is like the childhood plastic toy that allows one to create monstrosities from mismatched parts of different animals.

China and Japan to "the absence of indigenous priests."[56] After a promising beginning with the appointment of Samuel Ajayi Crowther (1809–1891) as a bishop in 1864, the next generation of British missionaries reasserted control over churches in West Africa. This proved untenable and was a key issue in the eventual secession of the *Aladura* and other AICs from the mission churches. To this day, many AICs "emphasize the Africanness of the church" precisely in order to stress "the autonomy or independence of the church from external ecclesiastical control and its indigenization in Africa."[57] Even Roman Catholic theologians, with their commitment to a polity of the episcopal primacy of the bishop of Rome, increasingly recognize the necessity of autonomy for the church in a given region.[58] Small Christian Communities (SCCs; known as *Communautés Ecclésiales Vivantes de Base* – "Basic Living Church Communities" – or CEVBs in Francophone Africa) embody a move within African Roman Catholicism away from its top-down traditional ecclesiology and encouraging local grassroots lay leadership.[59]

When a local church depends upon outside sources for leadership, the leadership is at risk of being out-of-touch with the local culture, language, and worldview of local Christians. In addition to this, local churches can be prevented from growing into maturity precisely because their members remain dependents underneath the rule of foreign "parents." Finally, the vicissitudes of history and of geopolitics can cut a dependent regional church from its mother church, which can have devastating effect, as we shall see below. This local autonomy is essential even though it is not absolute; regional churches should be interdependent and in communion with each other. But the young churches of Africa "must be 'localized' by being able to live on their own resources" – including the resource of church leaders – and must "be able to stand on their

---

56. Iheanacho, *Historical Trajectories of Catholicism in Africa*, 89.

57. James N. Amanze, *African Christianity in Botswana: The Case of African Independent Churches* (Gweru: Mambo Press, 1998), 128. Likewise Nthamburi observes that most AICs, "particularly those that were founded in the early period, arose out of the protest against white domination within the mission-founded churches." Zablon J. Nthamburi, "Ecclesiology of African Independent Churches," in *The Church in African Christianity: Innovative Essays in Ecclesiology*, eds. by J. N. K. Mugambi and Laurenti Magesa, African Challenge Series 1 (Nairobi: Initiatives, 1990), 43–56, 44.

58. E.g., see Uzukwu, *A Listening Church*, 12–13, 48.

59. J. J. Carney, "The People Bonded Together by Love: Eucharistic Ecclesiology and Small Christian Communities in Africa," *Modern Theology* 30, no. 2 (2014): 300–18, 302–4. These SCCs are similar to the Base Ecclesial Communities in Latin America. Of course, this movement is taking place within the context of episcopacy and with the retention of the claim of primacy for the Roman Catholic bishop of Rome.

own feet."[60] Iheanacho notes that "a local church that continuously relies on foreign aid and charity for its existence and essential services will always remain an unhealthy church that has not been fully established as a truly local and viable church."[61] It is precisely autonomous (or semi-autonomous) local churches which "are self-governing, independent of any central control, [that] can give to [people] a sense of being a home."[62]

Vision for mission

It is clear throughout church history that an outward vision for missions and discipleship is essential to the health of the sending church. When the *Balokole* of the East African Revival[63] turned inward, developing a focus on internal and personal spiritual self-improvement and failing to maintain an outward vision for missions and discipleship,[64] this ultimately led to the fizzling out of the movement. Missiology and ecclesiology are necessarily entwined[65] and sound ecclesiologies recognize that the church is ontologically "the People of Mission."[66] There is thus an "instinctive conjunction between ecclesiology and missiology" and "our ecclesiology must be rooted in missiology."[67] Mission is not merely "one aspect of what the church does . . . but who and what the church

---

60. Jean-Marc Éla, "Ecclesial Ministry and the Problems of the Young Churches," in *The Churches of Africa: Future Prospects*, eds. Claude Geffré and Bertrand Luneau. Concilium: Religion in the Seventies (New York: Seabury Press, 1977), 45–52, 51.

61. Ineanacho, *Historical Trajectories*, 57; see also 138–39; citing Adrian Hastings, "In the Field," in *The Church is Mission*, ed. Edna McDonagh (London: Geoffrey Chapman, 1969), 80–98, 94.

62. Welbourn and Ogot, *A Place to Feel at Home*, 145.

63. *Balokole* means "the saved people" in the Luganda language and refers to members of the East African Revival movement.

64. See Stephanie A. Lowery's discussion of David Gitari's critique of this "deficient ecclesiology" – that is, an isolationist ecclesiology that lacks a vision for mission – in "A 'Radical', Prophetic Ecclesiology? Recovering Ecclesiological Insights from Archbishop David Gitari," *African Christian Theology* 1, no. 1 (2024): 121–37, 124–32.

65. Mercy Amba Oduyoye notes that "ecclesiology goes together with missiology"; *Introducing African Women's Theology*, Introductions in Feminist Theology (Sheffield, England: Sheffield Academic Press, 2001), 87. Kalemba Mwambazambi asserts that "ecclesiology grows out of missiology and at the same time, forms a dimension of missiology"; "A missiological reflection on African ecclesiology," *Verbum et Ecclesia* 32.1 (2011): a482, 1–8, 1.

66. This is the subtitle of Part III of Christopher J. H. Wright's magisterial *The Mission of God: Unlocking the Bible's Grand Narrative* (Nottingham: Inter-Varsity Press, 2006), 188–392.

67. Wright, *The Mission of God*, 189, 322.

is."⁶⁸ The "tremendous missionary zeal" of some AICs has not been "based on professional training as such but on personal conviction that members of the church were each empowered to be a missionary."⁶⁹ As Mwambazambi reminds us, "church and mission have to work together, because it is difficult for any group of Christians to survive without forming ecclesia [community] and ecclesia cannot survive without mission."⁷⁰ Thus Mugambi recognizes that mission is the very "core of ecclesiastical vocation."⁷¹ Because "God entrusts this mission of his to communities of love which make up the Church," our participation in mission is the "very way to salvation."⁷²

Accessible vernacular Scripture

As we consider the pattern of church history, the rise and fall of the church through time and place, it is very clear that hearing the word of God in the local language is essential; Pentecost demonstrates that clearly. As it is essential for missionaries and evangelists to "tell the story and work of Christ in the language of those to whom he calls us,"⁷³ so it is also essential for Christians to "eat the Word of God"⁷⁴ in their own heart language. The incisive work on the translatability principle of Christianity by Lamin Sanneh, Kwame Bediako, and Andrew F. Walls is conclusive.⁷⁵ A Bible translation in the local language

---

68. Susann Liubinskas, "The Body of Christ in Mission: Paul's Ecclesiology and the Role of the Church in Mission," *Missiology: An International Review* 41, no. 4 (2013): 402–15, 411.

69. Amanze, *African Christianity in Botswana*, 131.

70. Mwambazambi, "A missiological reflection," 7.

71. Jesse N. K. Mugambi, *The Biblical Basis for Evangelization: Theological Reflections Based on an African Experience* (Nairobi: Oxford University Press, 1989), 61.

72. Kä Mana, *Christians and Churches of Africa: Salvation in Christ and Building a New African Society*, Theology in Africa Series (Maryknoll: Orbis Books, 2004), 55.

73. David Zac Niringiye, *The Church: God's Pilgrim People* (Carlisle: Langham Global Library, 2014), 144.

74. "Eating the Word of God" is the translation of the title of the textbook on congregational hermeneutics used by CCBTI (see the next section on church clusters, below). Joshua Barron and Ruth Barron, *Enkinosata Ororei Le Nkai*, eds. Francis ole Yenko and Cosmas ole Lemein (Nairobi: Community Christian Church, 2008).This Maa language text has also been published in Kiswahili as *Kujilisha kwa Neno la Mungu* (2015) and in NgaTurkana as *Akiyen Akiroit A Akuj* (2017).

75. E.g., Lamin Sanneh, *Translating the Message: The Missionary Impact on Culture* (Maryknoll: Orbis Books, 1989) and its second, revised edition (2009); Lamin Sanneh, "Gospel and Culture: Ramifying Effects of Scriptural Translation," 1–23 in *Bible Translation and the Spread of the Church*, ed. Philip C. Stine (Leiden: Brill, 1990); Kwame Bediako, "Biblical Exegesis in Africa: The Significance of the Translated Scripture," in *African Theology on the Way: Current Conversations*, ed. Diane B. Stinton (London: SPCK, 2010), 12–20; Andrew F. Walls, "The

is essential to the life and future of every church. Without this, a church may grow for a few seasons or centuries. But unless this lack is supplied, statistics are against its survival.

A culture of prayer

Throughout the biblical narratives, we see that God acts in response to God's people praying. Niringiye reminds us that "through teaching and prayer the apostles led the growing church in understanding the will and purpose of God."[76] This has continued throughout Christian history. Committed prayer by Christians in monasteries across Europe, Asia, and Northeast Africa have repeatedly led to reformation, renewal, and new Christian growth. Calls for prayer and renewed eucharistic devotion led to the Great Awakenings and the evangelical movement. Revivals across Africa in the early 1900s were characterized by a renewal of prayer.[77] The *Aladura* movement was named for its commitment to prayer. The *Balokole* of the East African Revival were known, among other things, for their "all night prayer vigils."[78] Paul teaches us that we should "pray without ceasing" (1 Thess 5:17). Whenever Christians have been powerfully committed to prayer, the church's heart is heard to be beating.

When Legs Go Missing (or Are Re-attached)

A close reading of Christian history demonstrates that when any of these four "legs" are missing or simply weak, the health of the church suffers. If one or more legs are missing altogether for a prolonged period, it is even possible for the church in that area to completely disappear. For reasons of scope, I will limit the few examples I have space to share to ones from Africa; with more space and time similar examples could be shared from other regions.

Translation Principle in Christian History," in *Bible Translation and the Spread of the Church*, ed. Philip C. Stine (Leiden: Brill, 1990), 24–39.

76. Niringiye, *The Church*, 144.

77. E.g., see J. Edwin Orr, "The African Awakenings," chapter 16 in *Evangelical Awakenings in Africa*, 134–46 (Minneapolis: Bethany Fellowship, 1975).

78. Graham Duncan and Ogbu U. Kalu, "Bakuzufu: Revival Movements and Indigenous Appropriation in African Christianity," in *African Christianity: An African Story*, ed. Ogbu U. Kalu (Trenton: Africa World Press, 2007), 245–69, 255.

North Africa: the camel is eaten

Latin became a truly Christian language in North Africa before it was adopted for Christian use even in Italy, and the first Latin translations of Scripture were prepared in Africa for Africans. But while thoroughly African – Augustine of Hippo emphasizes his self-identity as an African when he refers to himself and his compatriots as "us Africans"[79] – the Latin-speaking church failed to provide Bible translation into the native Berber and Punic dialects. While a Bible translation was lacking, there is abundant evidence that the Donatist church of North Africa was deeply tied to Berber culture and represented an authentically African church – before the Latin / Roman Catholic church of Augustine enlisted imperial might to crush it.[80] Moreover, Arab Christians who lived before the time of Mohammed had failed to translate the Scripture into Arabic, depending on either Greek or Syriac language Bibles. After the Vandal conquest of the area (429–435), Arian kings prevented both Catholic and Donatist churches from electing bishops.[81] Thus prior to the Islamic conquest (647–709), the North African church had lost two of its legs – local leadership and accessible Scriptures in local vernacular languages. But its other two legs were only ever strong in Latin-speaking areas. While small monastic foundations, always important centres of prayer, existed, "North Africa failed to develop a popular monastic tradition which could have preserved Christianity in the rural [Berber- and Punic-speaking] areas after church structures in the towns collapsed."[82] Importantly, North African Christianity never seemed to be a missionary faith; there is no evidence of its ever extending beyond the borders of the Roman Empire. Certainly there is no record of any North African bishoprics outside of Roman jurisdictions,[83] an important point given that the North African church was preeminently a "church of bishops."[84] After

---

79. Augustine, *Letters of St. Augustin* 138.4.19 (*NPNF1* 1:697).

80. J. F. Ade Ajayi and E. A. Ayandele. "Writing African Church History," in *The Church Crossing Frontiers: Essays on the nature of mission: In honour of Bengt Sundkler*, eds. Peter Beyerhaus and Carl F. Hallencreutz, Studia Missionalia Upsaliensia 11 (Lund: Gleerup, 1969), 90–108, 104–105.

81. Maureen A. Tilley, "The Collapse of a Collegial Church: North African Christianity on the Eve of Islam," *Theological Studies* 62, no. 1 (2001): 3–22, 10.

82. Calvin E. Shenk, "The Demise of the Church in North Africa and Nubia and Its Survival in Egypt and Ethiopia: A Question of Contextualization?" *Missiology: An International Review* 21.2 (April 1993): 131–54, 133.

83. Shenk, "The Demise of the Church in North Africa," 132.

84. Stephen Neill popularized the characterization that "the Church of North Africa was a Church of bishops" in *A History of Christian Missions* (1964). In the 1990 Penguin Books reprint of the 1986 second edition, revised by Owen Chadwick, this quote appears on p. 34.

the Islamic conquest, and contrary to other areas where the church survived under Islam, even if in a state of dhimmitude, North African Christianity gradually disappeared from view.

Egypt: the camel survives and sometimes thrives

Whereas the African Latin church failed to provide translations into African vernaculars, the Coptic Christians of Egypt took matters in their own hands and quickly produced Bible translations into at least three dialects of their language. Christianity entered the Egyptian culture so deeply that "Coptic" and "Christian" came to be synonymous. This was aided by the monastic movement began by native Copts Anthony and Pakhom, in which "Coptic speakers [were] caught up in a wave of mass conversion in the African countryside."[85] Christianity was so deeply indigenized into Coptic language and culture that when some Egyptian Christians later proselytized away from their indigenous Christian faith into Islam, they were no longer counted as Copts but were considered Arabs. In addition to this, "throughout Egypt, Ethiopia, and Nubia, monasteries [provided] leadership for the African Church."[86] The monasteries were centres of prayer as well as missionary training centers.

At the time of the Islamic conquest of Egypt, the church of Egypt was standing strongly on four legs. The survival of the Coptic church under centuries of oppression "can be greatly attributed to the monastic communities within the church"; these communities not only preserved a culture of prayer and the uniquely African spirituality of Coptic Christianity but also enabled the Coptic church "to carry out missions both within and outside of Egypt for the length of time it did."[87] After centuries of oppression during which it was pushed into survival mode, Coptic Christianity's leg of mission was largely hobbled, but with three well-established legs it has survived to this day. Then in the 1950s, the contemporary Coptic missionary movement emerged, renewing the mission focus of the Coptic church[88] and arguably leading to a

---

85. Adrian Hastings, *The Church in Africa 1450–1950* (Oxford: Clarendon Press, 1994), 7. Note that Anthony is also known as Antony and Pakhom as Pachom and Pachomius.

86. Joshua Robert Barron, "Connections and Collaborations among the Nubian, Coptic, and Ethiopian Churches," in *Globalizing Linkages: The Intermingling Story of Christianity in Africa*, eds. Wanjiru M. Gitau and Mark A. Lamport (Eugene: Cascade Books, 2024), 93–107, 97.

87. Francis Omondi, "Coptic community, spirituality, and mission," in *Global Missiology from the 21st Century: The Iguassu Dialogue*, ed. William D. Taylor (Grand Rapids: Baker Academic, 2000), 511–14, 511.

88. Omondi, "Coptic community, spirituality, and mission," 512.

general renewal of Coptic Christianity. There continues to be a "monastic-centered approach to mission" in these churches, which focuses on training and spiritual formation of local believers in areas throughout sub-Saharan Africa where new churches are planted.[89] Walking again on four legs, in spite of Islamic persecution the future of the Coptic church looks hopeful.

Nubia: the camel thrives but is eventually hobbled and then eaten

Nubian Christianity has a glorious, though often overlooked, history of a thousand years.[90] It represented an expression of faith that was both authentically African and authentically Christian. But eventually its history came to an end. While the depredations of Islamic military advance,[91] economic pressure due to treaty obligations with Islamic Egypt,[92] and environmental

---

89. Omondi, "Coptic community, spirituality, and mission," 514.

90. For an overview, see my "Connections and Collaborations"; also see Mark Shaw and Wanjiru M. Gitau, *The Kingdom of God in Africa: A History of African Christianity*, rev. ed. (Carlisle: Langham Global Library, 2020), 71–79 and 105–11; Bengt Sundkler and Christopher Steed, *A History of the Church in Africa*, Studia Missionalia Upsaliensia 74 (Cambridge: Cambridge University Press, 2000), 30–34; and Hastings, *The Church in Africa*, 67–70. For a detailed yet summary narrative, see the first five chapters in Roland Werner, William Anderson, and Andrew Wheeler, *Day of Devastation, Day of Contentment* (Nairobi: Paulines Publications Africa, 2010). The literature on Christian Nubia is vast and growing, but often remains known only to specialists. E.g., William Y. Adams, *Nubia: Corridor to Africa* (Princeton: Princeton University Press, 1977); William B. Anderson and Ogbu U. Kalu, "Christianity in Sudan and Ethiopia" in *African Christianity: An African Story*, ed. Ogbu U. Kalu (Trenton: Africa World Press, 2007), 67–101; Paul Bowers, "Nubian Christianity: The Neglected Heritage," *East African Journal of Evangelical Theology* 4, no. 1 (1985): 3–23; Salim Faraji, *Roots of Nubian Christianity Uncovered: The Triumph of the Last Pharaoh* (Trenton: Africa World Press, 2012); Richard A. Lobban Jr, *Historical Dictionary of Medieval Christian Nubia*, Historical Dictionaries of Ancient Civilizations and Historical Eras (London: Rowman and Littlefield, 2020); Artur Obłuski, *The Rise of Nobadia: Social Changes in Northern Nubia in Late Antiquity*, trans. Iwona Zych, The Journal of Juristic Papyrology Supplements 20 (Warsaw: Faculty of Law and Administration of the University of Warsaw, the Institute of Archaeology of the University of Warsaw, and the Raphael Taubenschlag Foundation, 2014); and Derek A. Welsby, *The Medieval Kingdoms of Nubia: Pagans, Christians and Muslims along the Middle Nile* (London: The British Museum Press, 2002).

91. After conquering Roman (and largely Christian) Egypt, in 642 a Muslim army invaded Christian Nubia in an unsuccessful attempt to conquer it. This was repeated in 1172. The intervening years would see occasional military conflict between Muslim Egypt and Christian Nubia. Continuous assaults from Egypt eventually contributed to the fall of the Nubian kingdoms.

92. For an alternative interpretation of this treaty, see Jay Spaulding, "Medieval Christian Nubia and the Islamic World: A Reconsideration of the *Baqt* Treaty," *International Journal of African Historical Studies* 28.3 (1995): 577–94.

change[93] played roles in the collapse of Christian Nubia, ultimately each of its four legs were hobbled. The terms of Nubia's trade agreement with Egypt required them to provide an annual tribute of slaves[94] – how effective can you be at evangelizing your neighbours when you are periodically enslaving some of them? Throughout its history, Nubian Christianity was dependent upon the Egyptian church for ordination of its bishops. When the Islamic rulers of Egypt eventually cut off communication between Christians in the two countries, the Nubian church lost its source of local church leadership,[95] because only bishops could ordain presbyters/priests. Throughout Northeast Africa, monasteries were a place where a culture of prayer was nourished as well as an incubator for church leaders. Nubia had never had as many monasteries as Egypt and Ethiopia, and as Nubian Christians entered a survival mode in the face of Islam – albeit after centuries of resistance – these were gradually abandoned.

By 1520, Nubian Christians sent an envoy to Ethiopia to ask for a bishop, priests, and monks to be sent to Nubia, as they had not had a living bishop for years and thus no source for ordained local leadership.[96] The Ethiopian king declined, as the Ethiopian church was also dependent upon the patriarch of Alexandria in Egypt for their *Abuna*.[97] As ordained clergy were responsible for maintaining copies of Scripture, eventually Nubians lost access to the Bible in their language. While there is archaeological evidence of Nubian Christian presence as far inland as the northern shores of Lake Chad,[98] there currently is not evidence of Nubian Christian missionary outreach to neighbouring ethnic groups.[99] By the early 1700s, there were only scattered remnants of Christians

---

93. On the impact of the encroaching sands of the Sahara, for example, see Adam Łajtar, "Late Christian Nubia through Visitors' inscriptions from the Upper Church at Banga-narti," in *Between the Cataracts: Proceedings of the 11th Conference of Nubian Studies: Warsaw University, 27 August – 2 September 2006*, Part 1: Main Papers (PAM Supplement Series 2.1), eds. Włodzimierz Godlewski and Adam Łajtar (Warsaw: Warsaw University Press, 2008), 321–31, 323.

94. Sundkler and Steed, *A History of the Church in Africa*, 32.

95. Werner et al., *Day of Devastation*, 100.

96. Werner et al., *Day of Devastation*, 93; Welsby, *The Medieval Kingdoms of Nubia*, 256.

97. *Abuna* means "our father" in Geʿez (Old Ethiopic) and in derivative languages such as Amharic and Tigrinya. Historically, the *Abuna* was the bishop appointed by the Coptic Patriarch of Alexandria to serve as Ethiopia's metropolitan bishop, functioning as the equivalent of the Archbishop of Canterbury in English Christianity. Today *Abuna* is primarily used as the title of the patriarch of Ethiopia, but can be used as an honorific for any bishop in the Ethiopian and Eritrean Orthodox Tewahedo Churches.

98. Viera Pawliková-Vilhanová, "The Archaeology of Ancient Christianity in Nubia and its Encounter with Islam," in *Eastern Christianity, Judaism and Islam between the Death of Muhammad and Tamerlane (632–1405)*, eds. Jozef Marián Gálik and Martin Slobodník, 2nd ed. (Bratislav: Institute of Oriental Studies, Slovak Academy of Sciences, 2014), 93–114, 107.

99. Shenk, "The Demise of the Church," 100.

in Nubia, although many Nubians still recalled that they used to be Christian. With no indigenous local leadership, Nubian Christianity's dependence upon foreign resources ultimately resulted in its "being 'starved' to death" when it was separated from its mother church of Egypt.[100]

Ethiopia/Eritrea: the camel survives and sometimes thrives

The story of Christianity in Ethiopia and Eritrea begins in the ancient kingdom of Aksum in a cosmopolitan context. The Aksumite court and those involved in trade were fluent in Greek, and so Greek Scriptures were immediately available. As the Christian faith spread into rural areas, biblical texts were soon translated into the local vernacular, Geʿez. This process was completed by the *Nine Saints*, a multi-ethnic missionary band that arrived in Ethiopia in 494. These missionaries "revived existing churches, took the Christian faith to new lands, catalyzed the flourishing of Geʿez literature, and strengthened collaborative networks between Ethiopian and Coptic Christianity."[101] A key part of their methodology was the establishment of monasteries which, as was usually the case in patristic and medieval Christianity, became centres of both prayer and of mission.

However, the Ethiopian church was dependent upon the Egyptian church for its ordained church leadership. More than once, this led to existential crises for the Ethiopian church.[102] At other times, Ethiopian Christianity took ethnocentric turns – to be Christian and to be Ethiopian were conflated, as was typically the case within European Christendom. This resulted in a loss of an outward-looking vision for mission. Overtime, Geʿez came to be an ecclesiastical language known only to scholars, as was the case with Latin in Europe, and ordinary Ethiopian Christians lacked access to the Scriptures in

---

100. Mercy Amba Oduyoye, *Hearing and Knowing: Theological Reflections on Christianity in Africa* (Maryknoll: Orbis Books, 1986), 27; Shenk, "The Demise of the Church," 140.

101. Barron, "Connections and Collaborations," 100.

102. For example, during the 900s for many years "the patriarchate of Alexandria refused to appoint [metropolitan bishops] to Ethiopia, and thus new priests could not be ordained." Alarmed at the effects of this on the churches of Ethiopia, Ethiopia's king sent an urgent appeal to the patriarch begging for assistance and renewed relationship. Marie-Laure Derat, "Before the Solomonids: Crisis, Renaissance and the Emergence of the Zagʷe Dynasty (Seventh–Eleventh Centuries)," in *A Companion to Medieval Ethiopia and Eritrea*, ed. Samantha Kelly (Leiden: Brill, 2020), 31–56, 39.

their own language.[103] Periodic Christian revitalization movements served to revive Ethiopian Christianity after times of beleaguerment. Like Egyptian Christianity and unlike North African and Nubian Christianity, Ethiopian Christianity was sometimes hobbled and unhealthy but ultimately survived.

The process which granted the Ethiopian Orthodox *Täwaḥədo* Church (EOTC) autocephaly did not begin until 1948. It was 1959 before the *Abuna* was granted patriarchal status. This finally, after some 1600 years, allowed this church to truly have local leadership. This push for local autonomy led to the autocephaly of the Eritrean Orthodox *Täwaḥədo* Church in 1993, with Eritrea having then gained independence from Ethiopia. Recent schismatic moves by Tigrayan and Oromo members and clergy within the EOTC may be attributable in part to the natural human drive for autonomy. Today the Ethiopian Orthodox church has planted congregations in countries in the West / Global North, but this is not necessarily attributable to a renewed vision for mission as "the intention is usually less self-expansion than self-preservation."[104]

Church Clusters: a Non-Hierarchical Diocesan Polity in East Africa

While Africans may be "notoriously religious,"[105] the Maasai of Kenya and Tanzania have been notoriously resistant not only to Westernization but also to the influence of Christianity;[106] the same largely has been true of the Turkana of northwestern Kenya. The first missionaries to witness major accessions to Christianity among the Kenyan Maasai came from a free church catholic tradition, arriving in Maasai Land in the 1970s. From the beginning, the missionaries worked to raise up local evangelists and church elders, fostering local agency and local leadership. At first the churches they planted joined Africa Inland Church–Kenya; later such congregations affiliated with the Kenya Church of Christ. For reasons beyond the scope of this chapter, they eventually

---

103. An Amharic translation of the Bible did not exist until Abu Rumi (c. 1750–1819) began a translation from an Arabic Bible (not, interestingly enough, from Geʻez); portions of Scripture in Tigrayan are not known to have existed before the 1840s. Edward Ullendorff, *Ethiopia and the Bible*, The Schweich Lectures of the British Academy 1967 (London: Oxford University Press, 1968), 62–69.

104. Jehu J. Hanciles, "Beyond Christendom: African Migration and Transformations in Global Christianity," *Studies in World Christianity* 10, no. 1 (2004): 93–113, 106.

105. "Africans are notoriously religious" is the famous (or infamous) opening line of Kenyan theologian John S. Mbiti's *African Religious and Philosophy* (London: Heinemann, 1969), 1.

106. See Valeer Neckebrouck, *Le Maasai et le Christianism: Le Temps du Grand Refus*, Annua Nuntia Lovaniensia XLI (Leuven: Peeters, 2002).

formed their own AIC, registered as Community Christian Church (CCC).[107] The CCC has its strongest presence in Turkana County, among the Maasai in Narok and Kajiado Counties, and among the Maasai in Tanzania. In 1991, The Bible Society of Kenya published a Maa translation of the Bible; the NgaTurkana Bible followed in 2001.[108] Literacy programmes, first run by missionaries and later run by Kenyan members of the CCC, equipped the first generations of Maasai and Turkana church leaders to be able to access the Scripture in their own languages. Instruction in Community Christian Bible Training Institute (CCBTI) is given in the local vernaculars of Maa and NgaTurkana.

A polity of clusters

Instead of adopting an inherited polity from missionaries, the CCC has, like many other AICs, devised its own polity. According to the CCC's constitution (an instrument required by the Government of Kenya's Registrar of Societies), expatriate missionaries can participate as partners in ministry but are limited as to leadership roles.[109] The leadership is robustly local. Congregations are semi-autonomous and arranged into geographic clusters. The elders and pastors of all of the congregations in a given cluster will cooperate on matters of church discipine, ministry outreach, and development of infrastructure (e.g., building of church buildings or raising funds for scholarships for school fees).

The cluster organization allows a degree of cooperation and mutuality unheard of in many Western ecclesial contexts. In 2008, for example, the pastor of the CCC congregation in Mararianta had a seemingly intractable disagreement with the other congregational elders. So the pastor of the CCC congregation in Endoinyo Erinka, who was currently serving as the cluster chair, organized for as many of the other pastors and elders in the Mara North cluster who were able to go to Mararianta and sit together until consensus and reconciliation was obtained. This type of event is typical for the CCC – it is also reflective of the conciliar democracy of traditional Maasai culture. This

---

107. I have been an active partner with CCC ministries since 2007.

108. Unfortunately these were not prepared from biblical languages and I have found that parts of the 1991 Maa Bible are incomprehensible to monolingual Maa speakers.

109. Under certain conditions, an expatriate missionary can serve as a pastor of a CCC congregation, but only at the invitation and pleasure, and under the authority, of the cluster of that congregation (*Constitution of the Community Christian Church* (Nairobi: Community Christian Church, 2010), V. A–B). To the best of my knowledge, however, the CCC has not actually had any expatriate pastors since before it organized as an AIC and was recognized by the Government of Kenya's Registrar of Societies.

ecclesiology works well as "a pattern of living Christian community in Africa that pays close attention to African sociopolitical and religious resources as well as to the Christian tradition."[110] Importantly, similar to an increasing number of African Roman Catholic theologians, the Maasai and Turkana in the CCC do not "define the church in terms of the clergy" but instead recognize that the church is "a people of God in which every member has both rights and duties and is entitled to full respect and involvement in what goes on in the church."[111]

The other two "legs" seem to be in place as well, albeit with varying degrees of health. Some of the clusters have large numbers of believers who are devoted to prayer and all-night prayer vigils are frequent; these experience successive revivals and have seen an explosion of new church plants. A few of the clusters lack this commitment to prayer and, not unsurprisingly, seem to be suffering from a general malaise. But the presence of both prayer and revival is more typical.

The story of ole Kijabe in Olepishet

In 1987, according to local oral traditions, missionaries first came to proclaim the word of God in the valley of Olepishet and the surrounding area, west of Naroosura in what is now Narok County. According to the oral history of the CCC in the Naroosura cluster,[112] the missionaries planted eight small congregations.[113] But after the missionaries left for other pastures, in 1998 or 1999, seven of those young churches simply withered on the vine, leaving only a remnant in Olepishet itself – *meisisi olAitoriaini* ("May the Lord be praised") is the liturgical interjection heard at this point of the recitation. When my wife Ruth and I collected this oral history in 2008, there was a venerable old elder

---

110. Uzukwu, *A Listening Church*, 7.

111. John Mary Waliggo, "'The Synod of Hope' at a time of crisis in Africa," in *African Theology on the Way*, ed. Diane B. Stinton, International Study Guides (Minneapolis: Fortress Press, 2015), 35–45, 36–37. What Waliggo prescribes as a necessary change in his Roman Catholic context, the CCC has realized.

112. What follows is a paraphrase of a Maa language text, recorded by Patrick ole Sayialel at our request, which is included in Barron and Barron, *Enkinosata Ororei Le Nkai*, 37, with some additional material added from other informants. At this writing, ole Sayialel is serving as the national overseer, or presiding bishop, of CCC-Kenya.

113. Francis ole Yenko, an elder of the CCC congregation in Olepishet and Director of the Maasai Discipleship Training Institute, counts congregations in five communities – Oltulelei, Oloirowua, Olmanguai, Olodukulupuoni, and Olepishet – perhaps the remaining three included by ole Sayialel included "preaching points" rather than congregations? But according to Olepishet CCC church records, Olepishet services in 1996 had only 4–5 attendees. Private correspondence, 9 February 2023.

in the Olepishet congregation called Shinana Ololmunyei ole Kijabe, who was well known for his exceptional piety and "fear of the Lord." When we met him in 2007, most of the community addressed him respectfully (and affectionately) as *Papaai* ("my father"). When the missionaries departed from Olepishet, all of the believers fell away except for ole Kijabe and his believing wife.[114] Although ole Kijabe could neither read nor write and had not had an opportunity to learn the stories of Scripture nor even songs of the Christian faith, he did know Jesus, and he knew that life with Jesus was better than what he had had before Jesus. And he knew how to pray. For years he and his believing wife prayed for the people of Olepishet. Eventually that congregation was re-established under his leadership. He used to pray for the church so that the church would get young people, young men and young women. God answered his prayer so that by the time we collected his story, the church in Olepishet had ordained five elders and Sunday attendance could be two hundred. At that time, ole Kijabe was one of those elders, still committed to a vision for prayer. The other four church elders were younger men – then in their thirties, married and with children – whom ole Kijabe had discipled. Ole Kijabe completed his race several years ago, but his legacy lives within the ecclesial culture of prayer which he established – and CCC leaders who are from Olepishet have planted large numbers of new congregations and witnessed too many baptisms to count, including in a neighbouring village long dominated by one of the regional *laibons*.[115] According to one of the current elders of the Olepishet CCC, "Olepishet survived because of Papaai Ole Kijape."[116] Through a life of prayer, he became a father of a multitude.

Enkiriwaroto:[117] *the CCC on mission*

In TransMara, Maasai CCC church leaders frequently discuss how they might reach the neighbouring Kalenjin for *Yesu Kristo*; this is remarkable given that

---

114. Ole Kijabe had married two wives before he ever heard the gospel; at this point only one of his wives had become a Christian with him – but that's another story for another time.

115. *Laibon* is the anglicization of *olaiboni*; the plural is *ilaibok*. The laibons are the ritual experts of traditional Maasai religion and are understood to have special access to spiritual forces and to the ability to curse or to bless. English-speaking Maasai Christians sometimes call them "witch doctors," though sociologically that may be somewhat unfair. Nonetheless, laibons are seen within Maasai Christian cosmology as foci for malevolent power and spiritual darkness.

116. "Papaai" is a vocative form of address in Maa meaning "my father" Francis ole Yenko, private correspondence, 9 February 2023.

117. *Enkiriwaroto* is the preferred Maa language word for "mission"; it derives from a verb meaning "to send."

the Maasai and Kalenjin have been traditional rivals and sometimes enemies. In Kajiado County, Maasai CCC church leaders are asking how they can evangelize the Muslim traders and migrants who are moving into their area. Church leaders in the vicinity of Narok have cast an evangelistic eye toward the Rendille in northeast Kenya. Turkana students at the Lodwar campus of CCBTI are serving as missionary-evangelists in remote and unreached areas of Turkana Land, far from their homes. CCC leaders have founded their own missions society, though so far it has struggled to gain traction. Toroyian ole Sinkua, a Maasai church leader and the national bishop emeritus of CCC-Kenya, is now serving as a missionary in North Africa. Anthropologists can speak about the resistance of these groups to outside influence, and theologians can mourn their resistance to the gospel, but on the ground the CCC has experienced rapid growth. Moreover, a large number of Maasai church leaders in other denominations that have more recently entered Maasai Land were discipled in CCC contexts.

Conclusion

Local leadership, local language Scripture, vision for mission, and prayer: these are four legs upon which any church can not only stand but can move forward. Likewise, when any of these are missing from or weak within the life of the church, that is symptomatic of a lack of ecclesial health. When a church is dependent upon outside sources of leadership, its dependence will prevent it from attaining full maturity. Only when a church raises up its own leaders and trains them for service can the church "pass on both the vision and the burden of mission."[118] Missiology is essentially ecclesiology, because "talking about mission really means nothing more or less than talking about what the church is, what it should look like, and how it relates to our human identities and practices."[119] Thus when there is no mission, arguably there is no church. This is a particular danger for when a church in a given region takes a "national shape,"[120] conflating an ethnocultural identity (e.g., Egyptian, English, Ethiopian, German, Nubian, etc.) with being Christian; when this has happened historically, such churches often either lose a vision for mission or embrace the path of proselytization rather than true conversion and discipleship. The

---

118. Turaki, "Evangelical missiology," 273.

119. Anika Fast, "Reclaiming Mission: Reflections on Mission as Global Interconnectedness and Spirit-Empowered Evangelism," *Anabaptist Witness* 5, no. 2 (October 2018): 51–61, 52.

120. Robinson, *Biblical Doctrine of the Church*, 132.

translatability both of Scripture and of the Christian faith confers upon all vernacular languages "an autonomous, consecrated status as the medium of God's word,"[121] and makes actual Christian conversion possible – we are called to make disciples who turn to Christ "within the context of [their] culture[s],"[122] not to make proselytes.[123] Only thus can we fulfill the vision of Revelation 7:9, with the bride of Christ being composed of people "from every nation, people, tribe, and language." Thus the vernacular principle leads us to a place of broad vision for missions and evangelism. As Andria and Saayman remind us, "ecclesiology should be based on missiology . . . mission should be an integral dimension of ecclesiology."[124] Finally, Charles Nyamiti observes that "*the life of African Christians, and of any other Christian, should be marked by regular or frequent prayer and ritual worship.*"[125] When this is lacking, the Christian and the church suffer. When we return and renew a commitment to prayer, we can return to health.

Ecclesiology has always been "shaped by historical and cultural circumstances" and changes to the church's "self-understanding" will "continue for each historical period and culture"[126] in which Christians exist until Christ returns. As Walls has observed,

> one of the most noticed features of modern Christian history in Africa has been the emergence of churches that owe little to Western models of how a church should operate, and much to African readings of Scripture, for which the conditions of African life often provide a hall of echoes.[127]

One example of this is the cluster ecclesiology of the CCC churches in Kenya and Tanzania, which are a synthesis of indigenous Maasai and Turkana,

---

121. Sanneh, *Translating the Message*, 2nd edition, 251.

122. Joshua Robert Barron, "Conversion or Proselytization? Being Maasai, Becoming Christian," *Global Missiology* 18, no. 2 (April 2021): 1–12, 1.

123. Andrew F. Walls, "Converts or Proselytes? The Crisis over Conversion in the Early Church," *International Bulletin of Missionary Research* 28, no. 1 (2004): 2–6.

124. Andria and Saayman, "Missiology and Ecclesiology," 506.

125. Charles Nyamiti, "The Church as Christ's Ancestral Mediation," in *The Church in African Christianity: Innovative Essays in Ecclesiology*, eds. J. N. K. Mugambi and Laurenti Magesa, African Challenge Series 1 (Nairobi: Initiatives, 1990), 129–78, 139; emphasis is Nyamiti's.

126. Harvey J. Sindima, *Drums of Redemption: An Introduction to African Christianity*, Contributions to the Study of Religion 55 (London: Greenwood Press, 1994), 148.

127. Andrew F. Walls, *The Cross-Cultural Process in Christian History* (Maryknoll: Orbis Books, 2002), 17.

which is to say, African, models of how a church should operate – a model which can nurture all "four legs of the camel."

Bibliography

Adams, William Y. *Nubia: Corridor to Africa*. Princeton: Princeton University Press, 1977.
Ajayi, J. F. Ade, and E. A. Ayandele. "Writing African Church History." In *The Church Crossing Frontiers: Essays on the Nature of Mission: In Honour of Bengt Sundkler*, edited by Peter Beyerhaus and Carl F. Hallencreutz, 90–108. Studia Missionalia Upsaliensia 11. Lund: Gleerup, 1969.
Amanze, James N. *African Christianity in Botswana: The Case of African Independent Churches*. Gweru: Mambo Press, 1998.
Anderson, William B., and Ogbu U. Kalu. "Christianity in Sudan and Ethiopia." In *African Christianity: An African Story*, edited by Ogbu U. Kalu, 67–101. Trenton: Africa World Press, 2007.
Andria, Solomon, and Willem Saayman. "Missiology and Ecclesiology: A Perspective from Africa." *Missionalia* 31, no. 3 (2003): 503–17.
Augustine. *The Letters of St. Augustin*. In volume 1 of *The Nicene and Post-Nicene Fathers*, Series 1, edited by Philip Schaff, 1886–89. 14 volumes. Repr., Peabody: Hendrickson, 1994.
Barron, Joshua Robert. "Andrew F. Walls: Apostle of World Christianity." *Missio Dei: A Journal of Missional Theology and Praxis* 12, no. 2 (Summer–Fall 2021): np. https://missiodeijournal.com/issues/md-12-2/authors/md-12-2-barron/.
———. "Connections and Collaborations among the Nubian, Coptic, and Ethiopian Churches." Chapter 6 in *Globalizing Linkages: The Intermingling Story of Christianity in Africa*, edited by Wanjiru M. Gitau and Mark A. Lamport, 93–107. Introduction by Mark R. Shaw. *The Global Story of Christianity: History, Context, and Communities* 3. Edited by Emma Wild-Wood and Mark A. Lamport. Series Introduction by Dana L. Robert. Eugene: Cascade Books, 2024.
———. "Conversion or Proselytization? Being Maasai, Becoming Christian." *Global Missiology* 18, no. 2 (April 2021): 1–12.
———. "My God is enkAi: a reflection of vernacular theology." *Journal of Language, Culture, and Religion* 2, no. 1 (2021): 1–20.

Barron, Joshua, and Ruth Barron. *Enkinosata Ororei Le Nkai: Enkibungʼata Bibilia Sinyati* [Eating the Word of God: Understanding the Bible]. Edited by Francis ole Yenko and Cosmas ole Lemein. Nairobi: Community Christian Church, 2008.

Bediako, Kwame. "Biblical Exegesis in Africa: The Significance of the Translated Scripture." In *African Theology on the Way: Current Conversations*, edited by Diane B. Stinton, 12–20. London: SPCK, 2010.

Bosch, David J. *Transforming Mission: Paradigm Shifts in Theology of Mission*. American Society of Missiology Series 16. Maryknoll: Orbis Books, 1991.

Bowers, Paul. "Nubian Christianity: The Neglected Heritage." *East African Journal of Evangelical Theology* 4, no. 1 (1985): 3–23.

Carney, J. J. "The People Bonded Together by Love: Eucharistic Ecclesiology and Small Christian Communities in Africa." *Modern Theology* 30, no. 2 (2014): 300–18.

Cathcart, Rochelle, and Mike Nicholls. "Self-Theology, Global Theology, and Missional Theology in the Writings of Paul Hiebert." *Trinity Journal* 30, no. 2 (2009): 209–21.

Climacus, John. *The Ladder of Divine Ascent*. Translated by Colm Luibheid and Normal Russell. Notes on Translation by Norman Russell. Introduction by Kallistos Ware. Preface by Colm Luibheid. Classics of Western Spirituality. Mahwah: Paulist Press, 1982.

Constitution of the Community Christian Church.[128] Nairobi: Community Christian Church, 2010.

Derat, Marie-Laure. "Before the Solomonids: Crisis, Renaissance and the Emergence of the Zagʷe Dynasty (Seventh–Eleventh Centuries)." Chapter 2 in *A Companion to Medieval Ethiopia and Eritrea*, edited by Samantha Kelly, 31–56. Leiden: Brill, 2020. Dreyer, Wim A. "The priesthood of believers: The forgotten legacy of the reformation."*HTS Teologiese Studies / Theological Studies* 76, no. 4 a6021 (2020): 1–7, https://doi. org/10.4102/hts.v76i4.6021.

Duncan, Graham, and Ogbu U. Kalu. "*Bakuzufu*: Revival Movements and Indigenous Appropriation in African Christianity." In *African Christianity: An African Story*, edited by Ogbu U. Kalu, 245–69. Trenton: Africa World Press, 2007.

Éla, Jean-Marc. "Ecclesial Ministry and the Problems of the Young Churches." In *The Churches of Africa: Future Prospects*, edited by Claude Geffré and Bertrand Luneau, 45–52. Concilium: Religion in the Seventies. New York: Seabury Press, 1977.

Faraji, Salim. *Roots of Nubian Christianity Uncovered: The Triumph of the Last Pharaoh*. Trenton: Africa World Press, 2012.

Fast, Anika. "Reclaiming Mission: Reflections on Mission as Global Interconnectedness and Spirit-Empowered Evangelism." *Anabaptist Witness* 5, no. 2 (October 2018): 51–61.

---

128. This is the constitution of CCC-Kenya; CCC-Tanzania has its own (though similar) constitution.

Gitau, Wanjiru M. *Megachurch Christianity Reconsidered: Millennials and Social Change in African Perspective*. Missiological Engagements. Foreword by Mark R. Shaw. Downers Grove: IVP Academic, 2018.

Hanciles, Jehu J. "Beyond Christendom: African Migration and Transformations in Global Christianity." *Studies in World Christianity* 10, no. 1 (2004): 93–113.

———. *Migration and the Making of Global Christianity*. Foreword by Philip Jenkins. Grand Rapids: Eerdmans, 2021.

Hastings, Adrian. "In the Field." In *The Church is Mission*, edited by Edna McDonagh, 80–98. London: Geoffrey Chapman, 1969.

———. *The Church in Africa 1450–1950*. Oxford: Clarendon Press, 1994.

Hatch, Nathan O. *The Democratization of American Christianity*. New Haven: Yale University Press, 1989.

Hiebert, Paul G. "Critical Contextualization." *Missiology* 12, no. 3 (1984): 287–96.

———. *Anthropological Insights for Missionaries*. Grand Rapids: Baker Book House, 1985.

Higgins, Susan. "An Elephant in the Household." *Leaven* 15, no. 1 (2011): 40–45.

Iheanacho, Valentine Ugochukwu. *Historical Trajectories of Catholicism in Africa: From Catholicae Ecclesiae to Ecclesia in Africa*. Foreword by Paul Steffen. Eugene: Resource Publications, 2021.

Kalamba Nsapo, Sylvain. "Une Théologie de «l'Église-Famille» En Afrique Sub-Saharienne [A Theology of 'the Church-Family' in Sub-Saharan Africa']." *Ephemerides Theologicae Lovanienses* 75, no. 1 (April 1999): 157–74.

Katembo, Fabrice S. *The Mystery of the Church: Applying Paul's Ecclesiology in Africa*. Carlisle: HippoBooks, 2020.

Kitchen, Robert R., and Maartien F. G. Parmentier, trans. *The Book of Steps: The Syriac Liber Graduum*. Cistercian Studies Series 196. With Introduction and Notes by Robert R. Kitchen and Maartien F. G. Parmentier. Kalamazoo: Cistercian Publications, 2004.

Kollman, Paul, and Cynthia Toms Smedley. *Understanding World Christianity: Eastern Africa*. Minneapolis: Fortress Press, 2018.

Koschorke, Klaus. "'Dialectics of the Three Selves': The ideal of a 'self-governing' native church – from a missionary concept to an emancipatory slogan of Asian and African Christians in the 19th and early 20th centuries." In *Internationalising Higher Education: From South Africa to England via New Zealand: Essays in Honour of Professor Gerald Pillay*, edited by Hoffie (J. W.) Hofmeyr and John Stenhouse, 127–42. Centurion, South Africa: Mediakor, 2018.

———. "Transcontinental Links, Enlarged Maps, and Polycentric Structures in the History of World Christianity." *World Christianity* 6, no. 1 (2016): 28–56.

Kwiyani, Harvey. *Multicultural Kingdom: Ethnic Diversity, Mission and the Church*. London: SCM Press, 2020.

Łajtar, Adam, "Late Christian Nubia through Visitors' inscriptions from the Upper Church at Banga-narti." In *Between the Cataracts: Proceedings of the 11th Conference of Nubian Studies: Warsaw University, 27 August – 2 September 2006*, Part 1: Main Papers (PAM Supplement Series 2.1), edited by Włodzimierz Godlewski and Adam Łajtar, 321–31. Warsaw: Warsaw University Press, 2008.

Libambu, Michel Willy. "La contribution des études patristiques à la théologie africaine: L'étude des Pères de l'Église à l'école théologique de Kinshasa [The Contribution of patristic studies to African theology: The study of the Fathers of the Church at the theological school of Kinshasa] (1957–2013)." In *Patristic Studies in the Twenty-First Century: Proceedings of an International Conference to Mark the 50th Anniversary of the International Association of Patristic Studies*, edited by Carol Harrison, Brouria Bitton-Ashkelony, and Théodore De Bruyn, 163–93. Turnhout: Brepols, 2015.

Liubinskas, Susann. "The Body of Christ in Mission: Paul's Ecclesiology and the Role of the Church in Mission." *Missiology: An International Review* 41, 4 (2013): 402–15.

Lobban, Richard A., Jr. *Historical Dictionary of Medieval Christian Nubia*. Historical Dictionaries of Ancient Civilizations and Historical Eras. London: Rowman and Littlefield, 2020.

Lowery, Stephanie. "Ecclesiology in Africa: Apprentices on a Mission." *Africa Journal of Evangelical Theology* 37, no. 1 (2018): 3–17.

———. *Identity and Ecclesiology: Their Relationship among Select African Theologians*. Foreword by Daniel J. Treier. Eugene: Pickwick Publications, 2017.

———. "A 'Radical', Prophetic Ecclesiology? Recovering Ecclesiological Insights from Archbishop David Gitari." *African Christian Theology* 1, no. 1 (2024): 121–37.

Mana, Kä. *Christians and Churches of Africa: Salvation in Christ and Building a New African Society*. Theology in Africa Series. Maryknoll: Orbis Books, 2004.

Matera, Frank J. "Theologies of the Church in the New Testament." In *The Gift of the Church: A Textbook on Ecclesiology in Honor of Patrick Granfield, O.S.B.*, edited by Peter C. Phan, 3–21. Collegeville: Liturgical Press, 2000.

Mbiti, John S. *African Religious and Philosophy*. London: Heinemann, 1969.

Mburu, Elizabeth. *African Hermeneutics*. Carlisle: HippoBooks, 2019.

Moffett, Samuel Hugh. *A History of Christianity in Asia*, vol. I: *Beginnings to 1500*. Maryknoll: Orbis Books, 1998.

Mugambi, Jesse N. K. *The Biblical Basis for Evangelization: Theological Reflections based on an African Experience*. Nairobi: Oxford University Press, 1989.

———. *Christianity and African Culture*. Christian Theology in African Scholarship. Nairobi: Acton Publishers, 2002.

———. "Theology of reconstruction." In *African Theology on the Way*, edited by Diane B. Stinton, 139–49. International Study Guides. Minneapolis: Fortress Press, 2015.

Mushete, A. [Alphonse] Ngindu. "An Overview of African Theology." In *Paths of African Theology*, edited by Rosino Gibellini, 9–26. Maryknoll: Orbis Books, 1994.

Mveng, Engelbert. *Identidad Africana y Christianismo: Palabras de un creyente* [African Identity and Christianity: Words from a Believer]. Traducido por Miguel Montes.

Estella: Editorial Verbo Divino, 1999. [Translated from *L'Afrique dans l'Église: Paroles d'un croyant*. Paris: Éditions l'Harmattan, 1985.]

Mwambazambi, Kalemba. "A missiological reflection on African ecclesiology." *Verbum et Ecclesia* 32, no. 1 (2011): a482, 1–8.

Neckebrouck, Valeer. *Le Maasai et le Christianism: Le temps du grand refus*. Annua Nuntia Lovaniensia XLI. Leuven: Peeters, 2002.

Neill, Stephen. *A History of Christian Missions*. 2nd ed. Revised by Owen Chadwick. The Penguin History of the Church. London: Penguin Books, 1990.

Newberry, Warren B. "Contextualizing Indigenous Church Principles: An African Model." *Asian Journal of Pentecostal Studies* 8, no. 1 (2005): 95–115.

Niringiye, David Zac. *The Church: God's Pilgrim People*. Carlisle: Langham Global Library, 2014. [North American edition published by IVP Academic, 2015.]

Noll, Mark A. "Martin Luther and the Concept of a 'True' Church." *The Evangelical Quarterly* 50, no. 2 (1978): 79–85.

Nthamburi, Zablon J. "Ecclesiology of African Independent Churches." In *The Church in African Christianity: Innovative Essays in Ecclesiology*, edited by J. N. K. Mugambi and Laurenti Magesa, 43–56. African Challenge Series 1. Nairobi: Initiatives, 1990.

Nyamiti, Charles. "The Church as Christ's Ancestral Mediation." In *The Church in African Christianity: Innovative Essays in Ecclesiology*, edited by J. N. K. Mugambi and Laurenti Magesa, 129–78. African Challenge Series 1. Nairobi: Initiatives, 1990.

Obłuski, Artur. *The Rise of Nobadia: Social Changes in Northern Nubia in Late Antiquity*. Translated by Iwona Zych. *The Journal of Juristic Papyrology* Supplements 20. Warsaw: Faculty of Law and Administration of the University of Warsaw, the Institute of Archaeology of the University of Warsaw, and the Raphael Taubenschlag Foundation, 2014.

Oduyoye, Mercy Amba. *Hearing and Knowing: Theological Reflections on Christianity in Africa*. Maryknoll: Orbis Books, 1986.

———. *Introducing African Women's Theology*. Introductions in Feminist Theology. Sheffield: Sheffield Academic Press, 2001.

Omenukwa, Philip Chika. *An Ecclesiological Exploration of the Four Marks of the Church: An Ecumenical Option for the Church in Nigeria*. African Theological Studies / Études Théologiques Africaines 5. Frankfurt am Main: Peter Lang, 2014.

Omondi, Francis. "Coptic community, spirituality, and mission." In *Global Missiology from the 21st Century: The Iguassu Dialogue*, edited by William D. Taylor, 511–14. Grand Rapids: Baker Academic, 2000.

Orr, J. Edwin. *Evangelical Awakenings in Africa*. Minneapolis: Bethany Fellowship, 1975.

Owojaiye, Babatomiwa M. *Evangelical Response to the Coronavirus Lock Down (Insights from the Evangelical Church Winning All)*. Foreword by Wanjiru M. Gitau. Bloomington: WestBow Press, 2020.

Pawliková-Vilhanová, Viera. "The Archaeology of Ancient Christianity in Nubia and its Encounter with Islam." In *Eastern Christianity, Judaism and Islam between the Death of Muhammad and Tamerlane (632–1405)*, edited by Jozef Marián Gálik and Martin Slobodník, 93–114. 2nd ed. Bratislava: Institute of Oriental Studies, Slovak Academy of Sciences, 2014. [Pp. 99–119 in first edition, 2011.]

Phan, Peter C. "A North American Ecclesiology: The Achievement of Patrick Granfield." In *The Gift of the Church: A Textbook on Ecclesiology in Honor of Patrick Granfield, O.S.B.*, edited by Peter C. Phan, 469–502. Collegeville: Liturgical Press, 2000.

Pobee, John Samuel. *Giving Account of Faith and Hope in Africa*. Eugene: Wipf & Stock, 2017.

Quenum, Jean-Marie Hyacinth. "Toward a Prophetic and Life-Oriented Ecclesiology for sub-Saharan Africa." *African Christian Studies* 26, no. 3 (2010): 5–31.

Robinson, William. *The Biblical Doctrine of the Church*. Revised ed. St. Louis: Bethany Press, 1955.

Rweyemamu, Robert. *People of God in the Missionary Nature of the Church: A Study of Concilian Ecclesiology Applied to the Missionary Pastoral in Africa*. Neue Zeitschrift für Missionswissenschaft. Rome: Schöneck/Beckenried, 1968.

Sanneh, Lamin. "Gospel and Culture: Ramifying Effects of Scriptural Translation." In *Bible Translation and the Spread of the Church*, edited by Philip C. Stine, 1–23. Leiden: Brill, 1990.

———. *Translating the Message: The Missionary Impact on Culture*. The American Society of Missiology Series 13. Maryknoll: Orbis Books, 1989; 2nd edition, revised and expanded, 2009.

Schnabel, Eckhard J. *Early Christian Mission, vol. 2, Paul & the Early Church*. Downers Grove: InterVarsity Press, 2004.

Shaw, Mark, and Wanjiru M. Gitau. *The Kingdom of God in Africa: A History of African Christianity*. Revised and updated edition. Carlisle: Langham Global Library, 2020.

Shenk, Calvin E. "The Demise of the Church in North Africa and Nubia and Its Survival in Egypt and Ethiopia: A Question of Contextualization?" *Missiology: An International Review* 21, no. 2 (April 1993): 131–54.

Sindima, Harvey J. *Drums of Redemption: An Introduction to African Christianity*. Contributions to the Study of Religion 55. London: Greenwood Press, 1994.

Spaulding, Jay. "Medieval Christian Nubia and the Islam World: A Reconsideration of the *Baqt* Treaty." *International Journal of African Historical Studies* 28, no. 3 (1995): 577–94.

Sundkler, Bengt. *The Christian Ministry in Africa*. London: SCM Press, 1962.

Sundkler, Bengt and Christopher Steed. *A History of the Church in Africa*. Studia Missionalia Upsaliensia 74. Cambridge: Cambridge University Press, 2000.

Thomas, Norman E., ed. *Classic Texts in Mission & World Christianity*. Introductions by Norman E. Thomas. American Society of Missiology Series 20. Maryknoll : Orbis Books, 1995.

Tiénou, Tite. "Forming Indigenous Theologies." In *Toward the Twenty-first Century in Christian Mission: Essays in honor of Gerald H. Anderson*, edited by James M. Phillips and Robert T. Coote, 245–52. Grand Rapids: Eerdmans, 1993.

Tilley, Maureen A. "The Collapse of a Collegial Church: North African Christianity on the Eve of Islam." *Theological Studies* 62, no. 1 (2001): 3–22.

Trull, Richard E., Jr. *The Fourth Self: Theological Education to Facilitate Self-Theologizing for Local Church Leaders in Kenya*. Bible and Theology in Africa 14. Edited by Knut Holter. New York: Peter Lang, 2013.

Turaki, Yusufu. "Evangelical missiology from Africa: strengths and weaknesses." In *Global Missiology from the 21st Century: The Iguassu Dialogue*, edited by William D. Taylor, 271–283. Grand Rapids: Baker Academic, 2000.

Turner, H. W. *History of an African Independent Church*. Volume 1, *The Church of the Lord (Aladura)*. Oxford: Clarendon Press, 1967.

———. *History of an African Independent Church*. Volume 2, *The Life and Faith of the Church of the Lord (Aladura)*. Oxford: Clarendon Press, 1967.

Ullendorff, Edward. *Ethiopia and the Bible*. The Schweich Lectures of the British Academy 1967. London: Oxford University Press, 1968.

Uzukwu, Elochukwu Eugene. *A Listening Church: Autonomy and Communion in African Churches*. Eugene: Wipf & Stock, 2006. [first edition: Orbis Books, 1996]

Van Dusen, Henry P. *World Christianity: Yesterday, Today, Tomorrow*. New York: Abingdon-Cokesbury, 1947.

Waliggo, John Mary. "The African Clan as the True Model of the African Church." In *The Church in African Christianity: Innovative Essays in Ecclesiology*, edited by J. N. K. Mugambi and Laurenti Magesa, 111–28. African Challenge Series 1. Nairobi: Initiatives, 1990.

———. "'The Synod of Hope' at a time of crisis in Africa." In *African Theology on the Way*, edited by Diane B. Stinton, 35–45. International Study Guides. Fortress Press, 2015.

Walls, Andrew F. "Converts or Proselytes? The Crisis over Conversion in the Early Church." *International Bulletin of Missionary Research* 28, no. 1 (2004): 2–6.

———. *The Cross-Cultural Process in Christian History*. Maryknoll: Orbis Books, 2002.

———. "Documentation and ecclesial Deficit: A personal plea to Churches." In *Christian Movements in Southeast Asia: A Theological Exploration*, edited by Michael Nai-Chiu Poon, 121–32. CSCA Christianity in Southeast Asia Series. Singapore: Genesis Books, 2010.

———. "The Gospel as Prisoner and Liberator of Culture." In *The Missionary Movement in Christian History: Studies in the Transmission of the Faith*. Maryknoll: Orbis Books, 1996.

———. *The Missionary Movement from the West: A Biography from Birth to Old Age*. Edited by Brian Stanley. Foreword by Gillian Mary Bediako. Studies in Christian Mission. Grand Rapids: Eerdmans, 2023.

———. "Rethinking Mission: New Direction for a New Century." In *World Mission in the 21st Century: Rethinking Mission: New Direction for a New Century*. Edited by Kwang Soon Lee, 69–80. Seoul: Center for World Mission, Presbyterian College and Theological Seminary, 2005.

———. "The Translation Principle in Christian History." In *Bible Translation and the Spread of the Church*, edited by Philip C. Stine, 24–39. Leiden: Brill, 1990.

Walls, Andrew, and Cathy Ross, eds. *Mission in the 21st Century: Exploring the Five Marks of Global Mission*. Maryknoll: Orbis Books, 2008.

Waruta, Douglas W. "Towards an African Church." In *The Church in African Christianity: Innovative Essays in Ecclesiology*, edited by J. N. K. Mugambi and Laurenti Magesa, 29–42. African Challenge Series 1. Nairobi: Initiatives, 1990.

Welbourn, Frederick B., and Bethwell A. Ogot. *A Place to Feel at Home: A Study of Two Independent Churches in Western Kenya*. Nairobi: Oxford University Press, 1966.

Welsby, Derek A. *The Medieval Kingdoms of Nubia: Pagans, Christians and Muslims along the Middle Nile*. London: The British Museum Press, 2002.

Werner, Roland, William Anderson, and Andrew Wheeler. *Day of Devastation, Day of Contentment: The History of the Sudanese Church across 2000 years*. 2nd ed. Nairobi: Paulines Publications Africa, 2010.

Wright, Christopher J. H. *The Mission of God: Unlocking the Bible's Grand Narrative*. Nottingham: Inter-Varsity Press, 2006.

Yong, Amos. *Renewing Christian Theology: Systematics for a Global Christianity*. With artistic images and commentary by Jonathan A. Anderson. Waco: Baylor University Press, 2014.

Contributors

Benjamin Akano holds a PhD in intercultural studies from the Nigerian Baptist Theological Seminary, Ogbomoso, where he lectures and serves as director of partnership and networking.

Isaac Ampong is a pastor for youth and families at St. Paul's Anglican Church in Belgium.

Joshua Robert Barron is a theological educator and curriculum developer in Kenya. He is series co-editor for the African Christian Studies Series, series editor for *Rethinking Church in the 21st Century* (Langham Global Library), and a managing editor of the African Christian Theology journal.

Kelechi Bartram, PhD, serves as a lecturer in Old Testament theology and literature at Baptist College of Theology, Igede-Ekiti, Nigeria.

Edwin Buertey is a PhD candidate in the department for the study of religions at the University of Ghana, Legon.

Catherine W. Chege is an adjunct lecturer of New Testament and Greek at Pan Africa Christian University, Nairobi Kenya.

Tamie Davis has a PhD from Sydney Missionary Bible College, Australia, about the theology of prosperity held by women of the Tanzania Fellowship of Evangelical Students (TAFES) and is an associate researcher at the Angelina Noble Centre.

Cornelia van Deventer is the academic dean of the South African Theological Seminary. She has a PhD in New Testament from Stellenbosch University and specialises in Johannine Literature.

Rowland D. Van Es, Jr is a lecturer at St. Paul's University, Limuru, Kenya. He is a missionary of the Reformed Church in America (RCA), who has lived in Africa for over thirty-three years, the last twenty in Kenya.

Robert Falconer holds degrees in architecture and theology. He works as the Head of Research and Publishing at the South African Theological Seminary (SATS).

Alberto Cotelo Gomes serves in the Evangelical Congregational Church of Angola. He is a parish minister and teacher at Seminário Emanuel do Dondi.

Florah M. Kidula is a doctoral candidate at Africa International University, Nairobi, Kenya,. She is the team leader and project manager at Transformational Leadership in Africa (TLAfrica) in Kenya.

Jesse Fungwa Kipimo has a PhD in theology with specialization in Pentecostal missiology. He serves as the head of the teaching and learning department at South African Theological Seminary, where he is also a lecturer.

Abraham Nana Opare Kwakye is a senior lecturer in church history and Christian missions at the University of Ghana, Legon.

Paul N. Mwangi is a theologian and a church historian. He holds a PhD in Religious Studies from the University of Nairobi, and is a lecturer at South Eastern Kenya University.

David K. Ngaruiya is an associate professor, former acting deputy vice chancellor for academic affairs, and director of the PhD in theological studies program at International Leadership University, Kenya. He has a PhD in intercultural studies from Trinity Evangelical Divinity School, Illinois, USA and previously served as chair of the Africa Society of Evangelical Theology.

Dieudonne Komla Nuekpe has a PhD in intercultural studies from Torch Trinity Graduate University, South Korea. As an ordained minister, he serves in various capacities, including as executive council member of the Church of Pentecost, Ghana, and as a board member of the Sanneh Institute.

E. Okelloh Ogera serves as the principal of Bishop Okullu School of Theology at the Great Lakes University of Kisumu, Kenya.

Rodney L. Reed is a missionary educator who has been serving at Africa Nazarene University in Nairobi, Kenya, since 2001. He is the former deputy vice-chancellor of academic affairs, and prior to that, was the chair of the department of religion. He has a PhD in theological ethics from Drew University, New Jersey, USA, and is an ordained minister in the Church of the Nazarene.

Calum Samuelson works with the Oxford Centre for Mission Studies on the Ethiopian Orthodox Project (funded by the Templeton Trust) in partnership with Sankt Ignatios College, Stockholm, Sweden. He is also a leader in the Lausanne-Orthodox Initiative.

Marike Blok-Sijtsma is a lecturer in practical theology at Viaa Christian University of Applied Sciences, Netherlands. She is pursuing a PhD at Utrecht University, Netherlands, researching the women's fellowship in the Reformed Church in Zambia.

Victor Umaru is a lecturer at the Baptist College of Theology, Obinze-Owerri, Nigeria. His research interests include ecclesiology, ecological care, leadership and missiology as related to the Bible. He also serves as the editor of *BETFA: Journal of the Baptist College of Theology, Obinze*.

Judy Wanjiru Wang'ombe, PhD, is a faculty member at Africa International University (AIU), Nairobi, Kenya, where she teaches in the Mission department. She is also the coordinator of the PhD Interreligious Studies program at AIU.

Subject Index

A
African Christianity 78, 124–25, 173, 194, 203, 205, 370
African Christians 45, 52, 58, 124–25, 172–73, 175, 178, 181, 193–94, 199, 200–2, 206, 209, 211–13, 223, 234–35, 241, 261, 391
African churches 80, 93, 103, 178, 180, 194, 202, 205, 210, 252, 282, 318, 337, 372
African culture 53–54, 175, 184, 200, 212, 241, 253, 280, 315
African Instituted Church *See* AIC
African missional hermeneutic 182-83, 189
African Public Theology 255
African traditional culture 51
African vernacular architecture 62-64, 66, 84–85
African vernacular churches 69, 79, 83
AIC 69, 110–11, 119–21, 202, 213, 369, 377, 387
Ancient Near East 27, 29
Anim, Emmanuel Nyantakyi 112
apostle 57, 153–69, 219–20, 333, 375, 380
apostolos 156–58, 167–68

B
Bediako, Kwame 109–10, 117, 200, 379
Bible Study and Prayer Group *See* BSPG
BSPG 111, 119-21, 126
Bible translation 379, 381
Bosch, David 159, 178

C
Catholics 11, 221
CCC 387–91

cessationist 154-55, 163
challenge-riposte 48, 55
charismata 161, 166
church
    African 45–46, 58, 78, 147, 172–80, 183–87, 189–90, 203, 226, 252, 327, 336–37, 341, 350, 372
    architecture 63, 68, 85
    as family 138, 140–41
    as the household of God 131–51
    attendance 337, 339
    buildings 63, 76, 79, 85
    children's 338
    community 142, 144–47
    contemporary African 187, 239
    Ethiopian 384–85
    growth 271–72, 325–46
    images of the 133
    in Nigeria 93
    in Africa 103
    metaphors 239
    North African 381-82
    numerical expansion 386
    numerical growth 334
    Pentecostal and charismatic 119, 155
    planting 236, 242, 253, 325, 328, 342
    youth 145
Circle of Concerned African Women Theologians 305, 318, 350
CITAM 267–82
Congregationalists 17, 292
contemporary Africa 234
COVID-19 2, 15–17, 19, 187, 234, 244–46, 248, 250, 252, 259, 279, 281

D
Dalby, Keith 11
DBS 253

Docetism 50, 57
Doyle, Robert 11
DRC 304
dyadism 47–48

E
ecclesial groupings 224
ecclesiology 134, 138, 179, 202, 209, 212, 224, 235–36, 244, 247, 249, 255–58, 320, 350, 367–70, 372, 378, 388, 390–91
   African 52, 171, 176–78, 180–82, 184, 189, 218, 226, 229, 260–61, 284, 296–99
   consumer 238
   defective 176
   evangelical 283–84, 296, 298
   familial 252–53
   in Africa 175, 235, 261
   missional 172–74, 177, 182, 187, 189, 248
   Pentecostal 373
   re-imagining African 181, 184
   Roman Catholic 372
ekklēsia 174, 177, 184, 190, 294–95, 329, 369, 372
   New Testament 44–45, 173–74, 252
EOTC 195–98, 202–13, 386
Ethiopian Christians 196, 204, 206–7, 209–10, 385
Ethiopian Orthodox Christians 196
Ethiopian Orthodox *Täwaḥǝdo* Church *See* EOTC
Eucharist 3, 10–15, 17, 209–10,
evangelicals 163, 195, 284, 296, 300

F
false prophet 28, 33, 35, 38–39
false prosperity prophets 37
FEM 221
feminine 349, 354, 357–58, 362
femininity 359, 361

G
Gaffin, Richard 154, 160

globalization 65–67, 201, 220
Gnosticism 50–51
Greco-Roman religion 49
Grudem, Wayne 164

H
household 6, 136, 142, 147, 234, 240–41, 251, 253, 259
   of God 133–40, 239

I
IECA 3, 14, 16, 19
incarnational 186
indigenous Pentecostalism 248
individual Christians 203

J
JCC 218, 221-22, 225, 277
John Calvin 10, 14, 296

K
Kéré, Diébédo Francis 63

L
lived religion 308

M
mama voice 352, 356
Martin Luther 10, 206, 292, 373
Mbiti, John S. 46, 51, 92, 198, 243, 259, 286, 297
Mburu, Elizabeth 52–53, 182–83
meditation 285–89, 291–94, 297, 299
Michael, Matthew 139
missio Dei 180–83, 189, 236–38, 242, 250, 256, 258, 261, 366
missiology 177, 180, 236, 373, 378, 390–91
   African 178
   public 184–85, 187, 190
missionary 158
   Western 108
monastics 194
Musau, Patrick 354

N

New Testament synagogue 70
North African Christianity 381–82, 386
Nubian Christianity 383–86

O

Ogden, Greg 12

P

para-churches 176
patriarchal perspective 225
PCG 109–17, 119–28
Pentecostal power manifestation 235, 249, 251, 260–61
pneumatic apostolicity 164
power evangelism 333
preaching 10, 14-15, 39, 51, 55, 80, 118, 127, 159, 165, 260, 337, 342, 348, 350–53, 356–62, 372
priesthood of all believers 2–3, 10, 16–17, 19
  in the New Testament 5
  in the Old Testament 4-5
priests 2-5, 8-12, 16, 19, 126, 207, 221, 330
prosperity theology 36
Protestants 165, 195–96, 212
Puritans 292

R

RCZ 304-6, 308-9, 315, 320
Reformed Church of Zimbabwe 93
Reformed Church in Zambia *See* RCZ
Reformers 2–3, 11, 163, 291, 300
Rwandan genocide 197

S

shalom 234, 242, 254, 269
Shona culture 91
singleness 90-93, 98, 103
single parenthood 220
social scientific criticism 46–47

Solomon's temple 63, 69-71, 73, 75, 76, 77, 80, 136
spiritual growth 195, 199, 201, 334, 336
spiritual parenthood 219–20, 223–24, 227–28
spiritual sacrifices 7–10
spiritual warfare 210, 249

T

tekna 142–43
theology of deliverance 125
theosis 196, 205, 207, 209, 211
Turaki, Yusufu 46, 54

U

ubuntu 117, 203, 218, 223–25, 227, 229

V

veneration 139. 196, 204–6, 212
vernacular architecture 65

W

Wesleyan tradition 203, 209
Western ecclesiological models 369
Western missionaries 108, 175, 179, 318
WF 304–21
word of God 6, 10. 15, 284, 285, 288–90, 292–94, 296–99, 357–62, 373, 379, 388
worship 81, 132, 144, 209, 243–44, 288, 299, 340

Y

Yahweh 24–35, 37–39, 239, 295

Scripture Index

OLD TESTAMENT

Genesis
2:18 92–93
8:20 4
14:18 4
24 97
41:8 155
45:5 155

Exodus
3:13–5 155
9:1 295
12:1–11 .... 6, 16
13:21–22 136
18:1 4
19:5–6 8
19:6 2

Leviticus
4:3–21 5
9:1–24 5
21:6–8 5

Numbers
10:29 30
10:35 32
18:1–7 4
21:21–24 25
23:19 34
27:21 .... 5, 27

Deuteronomy
4:10 174
6:4–9 290
6:4–35 290
6:6–9 292
11:13–21 290
13:1–11 31

18:14–22 31
18:18–20 35
18:21–22 .... 35, 38
33:17 30

Joshua
1:8 292
9:2 30

Judges
3:26–30 25
5:7 356
6:14 155
14:5 33
16:5 33
20:27–28 27

1 Samuel
11:11 32
15:29 33
23:9 27
30:7 27
30:7–8 27

2 Samuel
5:2 32

1 Kings
5:3 70
5:5 70
5:6–9 70
5–8 .... 69, 76
5:13–18 71
5:15–18 71
5:17 73
6:7 71
6:15–18 71

6:20–28 71
6:23 71
6:29 72
6:31–33 71
6:31–35 73
6:32 72
6:34 73
6:35 73
6:37 73
6:37–38 75
7:15–22 74
7:17–18 72
7:19–20 72
7:23–26 74
7:25–26 74
7:28–30 74
7:32–33 74
7:36 74
7:38–40 75
7:48–50 75
8:10–11 136
8:13 136
8:15–16 75
8:62–66 5
12:6 145
12:6–24 145
13 27
14:6 155
16:29 25
16:32 25
18 27
19:14 27
20 25
20:32–34 25
21 25
22 .... 33, 37
22:1–28 .... xiv, 24–25, 39

22:1–40 25
22:6 .... 28, 35, 37
22:7 37
22:11–12 37
22:13 37
22:17 32
22:17–23 32
22:19 34
22:20 32
22:20–23 37
22:22 33
22:22–23 .... 34, 37
22:23 34
22:24 38
22:26 35
22:28 35
22:29–40 25
22:33–36 38

2 Kings
1–10 25
2:12 219
2:19–22 .... 112, 119
7:1–10 177
7:9 177
9:1–3 30
9:4–10 30
9:11–13 30
13 25

1 Chronicles
16:13 8

2 Chronicles
17:3–4 27
18:1–27 25
18:2 27
19:2 39
19:11 5
28:16 155

Esther
7:9 30

Job
12:12 145
16:10 35

Psalms
1:2 293
3:8 35
4:4 293
45:2 30
63:6 293
68:2 32
77:6 293
77:12 293
88:4 8
89:3 8
103:21 34
104:6 8
118:22 7
119:15 293
119:23 293
119:27 293
119:48 293
119:148 293
145:5 293

Proverbs
1:10 33
16:29 33
20:29 145

Ecclesiastes
11:9–12:1 145

Isaiah
9:14 38
30:20 35

56 5
61:1–3 187
61:6 2
65:9 8
65:15 8
65:23 8
66:18–21 5

Jeremiah
20:7 33
25:34 32
48:25 30

Lamentations
3:10 35

Ezekiel
13:7 38
13:9 38
14:6–11 38
14:9 33
34:4 32
34:5 32
34:5–6 32
34:6 32

Hosea
2:16 33

Malachi
3:16 293
4:5–6 271

Micah
4:14 35

Zechariah
2:1 30
13:7 32

NEW TESTAMENT

Matthew
1:19 95

3:9 143
5:48 198

7:21–23 38
10:5–14 157

Scripture Index

10:6 157
10:21 142
10:40–42 156
15:24 157
16:16 108
16:16–18 162
16:18 .... xiii, 108, 172, 174, 180–81, 189–90, 241, 369
19:13–15 144
19:28 156
21:28 142
23:9 221
23:37 143
28:16–20 331
28:18–19 6
28:18–20 183
28:19–20 .... 236, 334

Mark
2:5 142
3:14–15 156
6:7–11 157
6:30 156
7:27 143
8:29 99
8:32 99
10:13–16 144

Luke
2:5 95
2:13 34
4:18 157
4:43 157
6:43–45 38
7:24 156
7:35 143
8:2 100
9:1–5 157
9:52 156
15:31 142
18:15–17 144
22:7–14 6
24:35 6

John
1:4 7
1:9 99
1:12 96
1:14 .... 185, 294
2 95
2:1 94
2:2 95
2:3 .... 95, 98
2:5 95
2:11 95
3 97
4 .... 94, 97
4:11 97
4:12 97
4:15 97
4:26 97
4:28–29 97
4:38 98
4:41 98
4:42 98
4:46–54 95
6:25–58 97
6:63 293
10:10 108
10:24 99
10:33 99
11 98
11:3 98
11:27 98
11:39 99
12:5 100
12:7–8 .... 100, 102
13:1–30 102
13:16 156
17:18 220
19:25 100
19:26 94
19:27 96
19:38–42 100
20:11–18 100
20:16 101
20:17 101
20:17–18 101
20:19–23 183
20:22 187
20:29 102
20:31 .... 99, 102

Acts
1:1–6:7 330
1:2 160
1:8 160
1:14 332
1:15 332
1:21–22 163
1:21–22 156
2:39 161
2:41–42 332
2:42 332
4:4 332
4:18 332
4:29–30 333
4:36 168
5:1–11 167
5:12 .... 157, 333
5:14 332–33
6:1–7 332
6:2 156
6:7 330
6:8–9:31 330
8:14 167
8:15–17 167
8:26–40 292
9 332
9:27 168
9:31 .... 330, 332
9:32 167
9:32–12:24 330
11:11 332
11:23 332
12:5 332
12:25–16:5 330
13:1–3 .... 161, 166–67
14:4 .... 157, 168
14:14 .... 157, 168
14:27 168
15:6 167
16:3–5 6
16:5 332

16:6–19:20 330	12 161	**Ephesians**
16:13–15 6	12:1–11 166	1:1 167
19:1–7 162	12:12 133	1:1–3:21 239
19:17 239	12:27 133	1:18–22 162
19:21–28:31 330	12:28 168	1:22–23 239
19:32 329	12:28–29 166	1:23 239
19:39–40 329	13:8–12 161	2:10 237
20:17 242	14:26 6	2:15 239
21:20 332	15:1–10 167	2:19 239
	15:3–10 167	2:19–22 8
Romans	15:5–8 157	2:20 .... 154, 156, 158,
1:1 167	15:8 163	160–61, 167
1:5–7 167	15:10 167	2:20–22 239
1:13–15 167		2:21–22 8
5:5 238	**2 Corinthians**	2:22 133
5:8 238	1:1 167	3:5 160
11:13 167	1:14 168	3:6–7 241
11:33–35 291	2:14–5:21 167	4:1–6:24 239
12:1 9	3:17 162	4:7 166
12:3–8 .... 161, 166	5:16 .... 162, 167	4:8 166
12:4–5 133	6:4–10 167	4:11 .... 154–55, 158–62,
15:19 157	6:16 .... 8, 133	166–68
16:1–2 6	8:23 157	4:11–12 .... 5, 159
	11:2 168	4:12 .... 133, 239
1 Corinthians	12:7–10 167	5:1–2 9
1:1 167	12:12 157	5:21–6:9 142
1:8 168	13:3–4 167	5:22–23 239
1:11 6		5:22–24 142
1:18 160	**Galatians**	5:23–24 239
1:23 160	1:1 167	5:25–28 142
2:7 167	1:9 157	5:27 168
3:10 161	1:10 37	5:28–32 239
3:11 160	1:11–12 160	5:30 133
3:16 136	1:12 167	5:32 282
3:16–4:19 8	1:15–16 167	6:1 142–43
3:16–17 .... 7, 133	1:16 167	6:1–2 142
4:15 219	2:8 167	6:4 142–43
5:7 18	2:11–14 167	6:5–8 142
7:32–35 103	4:14 156	6:9 142
9:1 .... 101, 160	5:22–23 224	6:12 333
9:1–5 167	6:2 10	6:18 332
10:17 133	6:14 167	
11 19	6:17 167	**Philippians**
11:1 198		1:1 167
11:17–34 3		2:5–8 185

2:6–11 291	3:14 135	2:4–9 2
2:15 168	3:14–15 134–35	2:4–10 7
2:17 9	3:14–16 133	2:5 .... 5, 7, 9, 133, 136
2:20–22 160	3:15 136	2:9 5–6
2:25 .... 157, 167	5:1–2 141	
3:10 167		**2 Peter**
3:12–21 198	**2 Timothy**	1:4 211
3:14 208	1:1 167	
3:17 167	1:11 156	**1 John**
	1:14 160	1:18–25 47
Colossians	2:8 160	2:14 145
1:1 .... 158, 167	3:10–11 221	2:18 55
1:15–20 291	4:3 39	2:18–25 46–47
1:18 133		2:19 56
1:24–2:5 158	**Titus**	2:22–23 57–58
3:18 142	1:5–9 5	3:8 333
3:18–4:1 142	1:7 137	4:1–6 46–47
3:19 142	2:1–10 141	4:2 58
3:20 142	2:2 142	4:2–3 57
3:21 142	2:3–5 142	
3:22 142		
4:1 142	**Philemon**	
4:15 6	1 167	
1 Thessalonians	**Hebrews**	
1:6 167	3:1 157	
2:4 158	4:12 294	
2:7 157	7 5	
2:10–12 168	8:6 6	
2:13 160	8:13 9	
3:2 160	9:25–28 5	
5:23 168	10:18 5	
	12:1 208	
2 Thessalonian	13:9 9	
2:3–11 38	13:15 9	
	13:15–16 9	
1 Timothy		
1:1 167	**James**	
1:4 137	2:1–2 290	
1:18 135	5:16 6	
2:7 156		
3:1–12 5	**1 Peter**	
3:4 136	1:3 7	
3:5 136	2:4 7	
3:12 136	2:4–5 .... 6, 10, 18	

Langham Literature and its imprints are a ministry of Langham Partnership.

Langham Partnership is a global fellowship working in pursuit of the vision God entrusted to its founder John Stott –

> *to facilitate the growth of the church in maturity and Christ-likeness through raising the standards of biblical preaching and teaching.*

Our vision is to see churches in the Majority World equipped for mission and growing to maturity in Christ through the ministry of pastors and leaders who believe, teach and live by the word of God.

Our mission is to strengthen the ministry of the word of God through:
- nurturing national movements for biblical preaching
- fostering the creation and distribution of evangelical literature
- enhancing evangelical theological education

especially in countries where churches are under-resourced.

Our ministry

Langham Preaching partners with national leaders to nurture indigenous biblical preaching movements for pastors and lay preachers all around the world. With the support of a team of trainers from many countries, a multi-level programme of seminars provides practical training, and is followed by a programme for training local facilitators. Local preachers' groups and national and regional networks ensure continuity and ongoing development, seeking to build vigorous movements committed to Bible exposition.

Langham Literature provides Majority World preachers, scholars and seminary libraries with evangelical books and electronic resources through publishing and distribution, grants and discounts. The programme also fosters the creation of indigenous evangelical books in many languages, through writer's grants, strengthening local evangelical publishing houses, and investment in major regional literature projects, such as one volume Bible commentaries like *The Africa Bible Commentary* and *The South Asia Bible Commentary*.

Langham Scholars provides financial support for evangelical doctoral students from the Majority World so that, when they return home, they may train pastors and other Christian leaders with sound, biblical and theological teaching. This programme equips those who equip others. Langham Scholars also works in partnership with Majority World seminaries in strengthening evangelical theological education. A growing number of Langham Scholars study in high quality doctoral programmes in the Majority World itself. As well as teaching the next generation of pastors, graduated Langham Scholars exercise significant influence through their writing and leadership.

To learn more about Langham Partnership and the work we do visit **langham.org**

www.ingramcontent.com/pod-product-compliance
Lightning Source LLC
Chambersburg PA
CBHW071223230426
43668CB00011B/1285